NATIONAL GEOGRAPHIC
TRAVELER

india

india

by Louise Nicholson

National Geographic
Washington, D.C.

CONTENTS

Pages 2–3: Brahmans and pilgrims at Dashashwamedha Ghat, Varanasi
Opposite: A gaily painted elephant, proceeding at a Mumbai festival

TRAVELING WITH EYES OPEN

Alert travelers go with a purpose and leave with a benefit. If you travel responsibly, you can help support wildlife conservation, historic preservation, and cultural enrichment in the places you visit. You can enrich your own travel experience as well.

To be a geo-savvy traveler:

- Recognize that your presence has an impact on the places you visit.

- Spend your time and money in ways that sustain local character. (Besides, it's more interesting that way.)

- Value the destination's natural and cultural heritage.

- Respect the local customs and traditions.

- Express appreciation to local people about things you find interesting and unique to the place: its nature and scenery, music and food, historic villages and buildings.

- Vote with your wallet: Support the people who support the place, patronizing businesses that make an effort to celebrate and protect what's special there. Seek out shops, local restaurants, inns, and tour operators who love their home—who love taking care of it and showing it off. Avoid businesses that detract from the character of the place.

- Enrich yourself, taking home memories and stories to tell, knowing that you have contributed to the preservation and enhancement of the destination.

That is the type of travel now called geotourism, defined as "tourism that sustains or enhances the geographical character of a place—its environment, culture, aesthetics, heritage, and the well-being of its residents." To learn more, visit National Geographic's Center for Sustainable Destinations at *nationalgeographic.com/travel/sustainable.*

india

ABOUT THE AUTHORS

Louise Nicholson, a British art historian living in New York, catalogued Indian art at the London auctioneers Christie's before spending her honeymoon in India in 1980. Since then she has returned more than 200 times.

Nicholson finds all aspects of the country endlessly fascinating, from the buildings, traditions, and colorful festivals to the exotic birdlife, weaving traditions, and contemporary culture. She has traveled to all parts accompanying travelers and doing research for books and journalism articles—most of her 27 books are about India or London. She was associate director for the acclaimed six-part TV series *The Great Mughals.* Nicholson shares her considerable knowledge and practical experience of India by leading lecture tours, advising private travelers, and taking her family on exciting Indian adventures. In 1985, Nicholson founded Save a Child *(saveachild.org.uk),* a charity that gives deprived Indian children a second and better chance at life through sponsorship.

Her website is *louisesindia.com.*

Amit Kapil grew up in the forests of Madhya Pradesh, thanks to his father, who was in the Indian Forest Service. Besides keeping two panthers as pets for two years, he explored the jungles in his childhood, which contributed to his passion for adventure, travel, and wildlife.

After completing his MBA at the George Washington University, he returned to India to start his own business. Itchy feet got him traveling around this vast country, and he proudly claims to have driven to all four corners of India. The Himalayan state of Uttarakhand is his favorite region—it's also where his beloved dog was born. Besides traveling on his own, he also advises private travelers and plans trips for family and friends. Kapil blogs about his travels on *travelinglightindia.blogspot.com.*

Charting Your Trip

The great thing about visiting India is that there are no rules on where to go or what to do first. Its geography caters to demands for warmth or coolness, for dramatic desert scenery or lush mountains; its culture in every corner is staggeringly rich, diverse, and sophisticated.

Make of India what you choose. The country is far too big to absorb on one trip—or even ten. The ideal first visit might take in a week in the south, then a week in the north. Seeing the pure and earlier Hindu culture of southern India first makes a good base for an encounter with northern India's cocktail of cultures resulting from waves of invasion, internal power struggles, and foreign traders. You can build a trip to suit any interest, be it history, birdlife, philosophy, architecture, trekking, music, cooking, staying in palace hotels, or a potpourri of these.

It does not follow that the more time you have in India, the more areas you should visit; instead, consider investing more nights in each place; that way you can learn about the local cuisine, visit local craftsmen, go on outings to isolated spots, and wander the backstreets to see how people live. Indian people are friendly, keen to converse, and often speak beautiful English. They are also very inclusive in their celebrations.

Air travel is useful for big leaps across the country, but planes can be delayed and are best avoided for short trips. While domestic airlines come and go, at press time the three domestic airlines are Indigo (*goindigo.in*), GoAir (*goair .in*), and Jet Airways (*jetairways.com*). To compare prices and schedules, check *cleartrip.com* and *kayak .co.in*. For many visitors, a train journey is essential—and the ideal option for shorter trips. Rail schedules and tickets are available at *irctc.co.in*. You can also hire a car (with a driver), the most luxurious (and expensive) way to travel around India. Joining a tour group (see Travelwise pp. 335–336) is also a good option.

Due to India's size, consider flying into a city near the area you're visiting; Chennai (Madras), Mumbai (Bombay), and Delhi are popular starting points.

Chennai: Gateway to India's Southeast

Having explored congenial Chennai, capital of Tamil Nadu state at India's southern tip, you can tour the area to the south by bus, car, or train: **Mahabalipuram's** monumental sculptures cut into sandstone cliffs (50 miles/30 km south of Chennai); formerly French-ruled **Puducherry** (Pondicherry; 85 miles/137 km south of Chennai), with its lingering French atmosphere; and

Visitor Information

When planning your trip, the starting point for information, maps, brochures, and advice is one of the Government of India Tourist Offices. For a full list, visit *incredible india.org* (see also *india-tourism .com*). India can be overwhelming, so use a travel agent with experience of booking vacations there. They can make reservations, using reliable agents in India, saving you time. Local agents will ensure that reservations for hotels, cars, and guides meet your expectations.

In the side columns of this guidebook, look for addresses and contact details of local, state, and Government of India tourist offices under Visitor Information (see also Travelwlse pp. 334-341).

beyond to the great temple cities of **Thanjavur, Tiruchchirappalli,** and **Madurai,** with their resident elephants, markets, and pilgrims. This sampling provides a great introduction to India's predominantly Hindu culture.

Mumbai & the Southwest Coast

The dynamic business capital of Mumbai contains plenty to see and do, especially shopping, nightclubs, and restaurants, plus many options for off-beat trips, including **Bassein's** romantically overgrown Portuguese fort.

From Mumbai, take a one-hour flight northeast to Aurangabad and visit **Ajanta's** miraculously preserved early Buddhist cave paintings and **Ellora's** Kailasha temple chiseled out of the rocky outcrop. From here, it is a long day's drive north for the reward of staying at Maheshwar's **Ahilya Fort.** Or you could fly an hour and a half east from Mumbai to **Hubli** and enjoy two or three days visiting the huge ruined city of **Vijayanagar;** it is a short drive to the early, quality monuments of **Badami, Aihole,** and **Pattadakal.**

South down the coast from Mumbai lie first tiny **Goa** state (120 miles/195 km from Badami) and **Kochi** (Cochin; 410 miles/660 km), portal to Kerala state's spice plantations, backwaters, and distinct Hindu and Christian traditions.

Delhi & the North

India's capital is a huge historic city sprawling over the northern plains. Plan your days carefully to see the widely scattered monuments dating from the 12th to 20th centuries. Highlights include the Qutub Minar, Humayun's Tomb, and Sir Edwin Lutyens's New Delhi.

From here you can go in any direction. A two-hour train journey south (easier and faster than going by car or plane) brings you

A Chola-period bronze of Shiva Nataraja

Namaste

Namaste is the common salutation when you meet someone, socially or when doing business. Simultaneously, you bow slightly and bring your hands together at chest level, fingers pointing upward—be sure not to put your hands higher as that has a different meaning and is for worshipping a deity. The word "namaste" derives from Sanskrit and may be roughly translated as "I bow to the divinity that is inherent in you."

to **Agra,** whose **Taj Mahal** and other Mughal monuments deserve at least a two-day stay.

Immediately west of Delhi lie the fairy-tale cities of mostly flat and dry Rajasthan state. **Jaipur** is a five-hour drive away; beyond lie **Udaipur, Jodhpur,** and many smaller former Rajput capitals, all brimming with luxurious hotels, romantic forts, and colorful bazaars. Rajasthan is India's most touristed area, with prices to match, yet even here it is easy to slip off the beaten path; **Bikaner** (145 miles/231 km north of Jodhpur), a palace-filled town built on trade route richesse, for example, has surprisingly few visitors.

North of Delhi tower the **Himalaya,** where, depending on the month, you can trek to see flowers and birds, visit the source of the Ganga River, explore British-built **Shimla** (Simla) and its forested hills (215 miles/350 km from Delhi), or even heli-ski in **Manali** (80 miles/130 km north of Shimla). On your way back down the mountains, a two-hour deviation west takes you to Le Corbusier's urban showpiece of **Chandigarh** and, beyond that, the Sikh people's holy city of **Amritsar.**

Some 420 miles (680 km) east of Delhi lies **Varanasi,** the Hindus' most sacred city. From here, fly to **Khajuraho** to enjoy sculpture-coated temples, then drive on to **Orchha** and **Datia** to clamber around peaceful Rajput forts. From here, take the efficient *Shatabdi Express* train (the closest train station is at nearby Jhansi) either north back to Delhi via **Gwalior** and **Agra** (4 hours, 35 minutes), or south to **Bhopal** (3 hours, 10 minutes) to see **Sanchi's** remarkable Buddhist remains and **Bhimbetka's** prehistoric paintings. With a few more days in this region, you could include a visit to some of India's best wildlife parks with excellent lodges.

More Gateway Possibilities

Other cities have international airports, too. Flying directly into **Kochi,** along India's southeast tip, brings you into Kerala's laid-back lushness, backwaters cruising, and serious ayurvedic retreats, with options to continue east over the hills to **Tamil Nadu,** north to explore simple coastal towns, or west out of India to the

Travel Safety in India

Recent well-publicized crimes have raised concerns about the safety of women traveling in India. India can be a culture shock, but some basic precautions should keep you safe. Avoid traveling alone at night. Ask your hotel to book a cab for transfers to bus and rail stations, and use the pre-paid taxi counters wherever possible. Don't accept a hotel room that doesn't lock properly from the inside. Ignore men who approach you at tourist sights or over-friendly hotel staff, and never accept alcoholic drinks from strangers. Stay off the streets after dark and never walk alone in the countryside. Men will stare—ignore them and walk away. Always carry a cell phone and call for help if you feel uncomfortable.

Although their profession appears to be waning in India, snake charmers still perform in many cities.

Maldive Islands for snorkeling, diving, and total relaxation. Along the coast north of Kerala and beyond Karnataka is **Goa** state, whose airport is located at the mid-point of its beach-lined coast.

Arriving direct into **Kolkata** (Calcutta) in eastern India, you find a most fascinating and challenging city, where a local Bengali guide is essential. You might then go north into the mountains to stay in a tea garden or trek among springtime orchids in **Sikkim** state (285 miles/458 km north of Kolkata), adjacent to Nepal. Hardened travelers can fly 1.5 hours east over Bangladesh to see India's less visited northeastern states, such as **Assam.** Northwest of Kolkata, about 90 minutes by air, lies **Patna,** the springboard for visiting **Bodh Gaya** and other Buddhist sites, and, in November, for attending Asia's largest agricultural fair, **Sonepur.**

Flying into **Hyderabad,** in the Deccan area of the south, puts you on the doorstep of the great sultanate kingdoms. This little-explored rural region has only modest accommodations, but you reap rich rewards in architecture and its mystical mixture of local, northern, southern, and Iranian cultures.

The area north of **Bangalore** offers similar rich history, with **Vijayanagar's** and **Badami's** splendors along the way. The cool hills to the west of this information technology city offer quiet stays on coffee estates. From there, you can visit laid-back **Mysore** and perhaps **Nagarhole National Park,** a wildlife park with herds of elephants.

Currency & Counting

India's currency is the Indian rupee (INR) which is now written as, for example, ₹500. The ₹ sign was introduced in 2010. The word "rupee" comes from the Sanskrit *rupyakam,* meaning "silver coin." One rupee has 100 paise. Travelers should carry plenty of ₹10 and ₹50 notes for tips. Counting rupees—and counting in general in India—is more complex: 100,000 is called a lakh, and 10 million is a crore. Thus, a crowd of 200,000 attending a *puja* (worship) would be referred to as 2 lakhs, and the population of Rajasthan not as 56 million but as 5.6 crores.

History & Culture

A red-powdered boy celebrates the Ganpati festival in Mumbai.
Opposite: The Taj Mahal is the tomb of Shah Jahan's wife, Mumtaz Mahal.

India Today

India has always intrigued foreigners. Alexander the Great's men were amazed by the elephants. William Shakespeare, who never visited India, alluded to its exotic trading wealth in *A Midsummer Night's Dream*. Mark Twain called India "the one land that all men desire to see." Today, India continues to fascinate with equal force as it mixes tradition and religion with thrusting global enterprise.

Land of Contrasts

India is a land of sharp contrasts where history and tradition go hand in hand with the dynamic present. It is second only to the United States in information technology, yet home life remains traditional and families eat together, enjoying laboriously prepared fresh dishes rather than convenience fast foods. Examples of this contrast abound throughout the whole of this vast country: A highly skilled silk-weaver from a village near Chennai will confirm his orders by cell phone, while young students of international law at Delhi University volunteer to have their marriages arranged by their families; in a Rajasthan village a group of women swathed in magenta and saffron saris sits on the ground selling their vegetables next to an Internet café.

When you first visit India, it assaults the senses, stretching them further than you may have thought possible.

Contrasts are obvious from the moment you arrive. On a busy stretch of road outside the capital, New Delhi, you could see a camel, a bullock cart, a bicycle, a herd of goats, a Harley-Davidson motorcycle, an elaborately hand-painted truck, the latest model Mercedes car, a wandering cow, a streamlined, air-conditioned bus, and even an elephant—all somehow getting along together with remarkably few accidents.

And the contrasts extend to huge differences in material wealth. The appalling poverty that was so vividly publicized by Mother Teresa and continues to be a living horror exists alongside India's less well-known vast wealth in natural resources, wildlife, culture, crafts and skills, and personal affluence. India has the globe's fastest growing number of millionaires, and real estate prices are among the world's highest. And there are regular displays of outrageous extravagance. At some Hindu festivals, intricate images of the gods that take a full year to make are paraded once and then cast into the sea, where they disintegrate in moments. During the wedding season, thousands of families fall into debt in their efforts to put on an impressive show.

When you first visit India, it assaults the senses, stretching them further than you may have thought possible. You may hear calming religious music, see women dressed in vivid colors, and taste new flavors—not all of them spicy. You will smell fresh coconut milk and jasmine blossoms, and feel the smooth stones of temple floors beneath your bare feet.

Stretching along palm-lined Back Bay, a natural inlet of the Arabian Sea, Marine Drive is a vital transportation corridor for Mumbai's more than 18 million inhabitants.

India can make you laugh for joy and catch your breath in wonder; it can turn your ideas upside-down and introduce whole new subjects to think about—and, occasionally, it may well make you lose your patience.

People talk of seeing "the real India," when they have taken a local bus or spent time living in a village. This is indeed India, but there is much, much more to it than that. To get anywhere near the real India, you should take advantage of every opportunity available to experience as many different sides as possible of this immensely rich, varied, and stimulating land.

India's Democracy: Coherence & Diversity

The government of India is, in many ways, a daily miracle in the way that it administers a vast area inhabited by an enormous population. This huge land is home to more than a billion people (only China has a larger population), making India the world's largest democracy. It has a president as head of state, a prime minister as head of government, and a two-house parliament elected by universal suffrage—Lok Sabha (House of the People, up to 552 seats) and Rajya Sabha (Council of States, up to 250 seats). Based on the British Parliament, the political structure also draws on the United States' system and incorporates a bill of rights.

The country is divided into 28 states and seven union territories; the northern city of Delhi, the capital since 1911, is the National Capital Territory due to its large population. Because the states have been created since independence (see pp. 46–47) on broadly historical and linguistic criteria, each has its own distinct character, culture, achievements, and disadvantages, and many have their own language. Looking at a political map of India, you can see how the states vary in size, from huge Rajasthan to tiny Goa. Their populations vary too: Uttar Pradesh contains more than 199 million people, while remote Sikkim has only about 607,690 residents.

EXPERIENCE: Helping India's Disadvantaged

India does not hide its problems. Visitors can see both its wealth and its poverty in a single glance: beggars outside Agra's Taj Mahal, a lame child by Kolkata's upscale Oberoi Grand Hotel. Despite India's economic surge, acute poverty, malnutrition, and health problems persist. Mother Teresa (1910–1997) shined a spotlight on Kolkata, which then widened across India. Born in Albania, she joined the Sisters of Loreto and took her vows in Darjeeling in 1931 before founding the Missionaries of Charity, which focus on helping the dying. She was an outspoken campaigner, a brave critic of the rich and powerful, and was awarded the Nobel Peace Prize in 1979. Like her, visitors today often want to help the disadvantaged. With the increased professionalism and accountability of the huge numbers of Indian and international charities working at all levels and sectors—health, education, children, women, the environment, and many more—it is easy to find one to suit your interest and comfort level, and perhaps one with a project on your travel itinerary. The Web is an invaluable tool when looking for a volunteering opportunity in India. **NGOs India** (*ngosindia.com*) is a good place to begin your search.

As each state sends its members of parliament to Delhi, so Delhi sends a governor to each state. Each state also has its own administration, called the Legislative Assembly, and elects its own representatives, who can keep in touch with local needs—Delhi can be far away, in thought and culture as well as miles.

Government at all levels is cumbersome. Although India has two national languages, Hindi (written in Devanagari script) and English, there are 22 officially recognized languages, many with their own script. As you travel, you hear Bengali in West Bengal, Malayalam in Kerala, and Marathi in Maharashtra. Imagine the complexities of a Lok Sabha debate between MPs from several states.

More Than a Billion People

With such a huge population, it's no wonder that the government struggles. The statistics reflect the extent of some of the country's complexities. With 1.2 billion people, India has 16 percent of the world's population living on 2.42 percent of the world's total area. The population explosion after independence, when it stood at 350 million, was mainly caused by increased longevity thanks to a better diet, control of famines, and treatment of diseases such as malaria, smallpox, and cholera. The average life expectancy has risen from less than 40 years to about 65 years. Population growth is now being curbed by successful family planning programs: India's growth rate has been reduced from 2.5 percent in the 1960s to a current rate of 1.5 percent.

Women are playing a leading role in this effort and in India's impressive literacy campaign, especially in the south. Kerala's literacy is around 93 percent, Tamil Nadu's 80 percent. In the north, tourist-popular Rajasthan's literacy has leapt recently from 38.5 percent to an estimated 67 percent; seen another way, 76 percent of Rajasthan's males are literate but only 44 percent of females. In all, India's literacy rate has risen from 18 percent at independence in 1947 to an estimated 73 percent today.

Other major changes have come about since independence: Until the 1970s, India's people lived in a mainly rural land; fewer than 20 percent lived in cities. Today, migration and population growth have increased this number to more than 30 percent, straining cities to their limits—18.4 million live in Mumbai (formerly Bombay), 14.11 million in Kolkata (Calcutta), and 16.75 million in the capital of Delhi. The population density of Mumbai is about 30,000 per .38 square mile (1 sq km), that of Hyderabad is 18,480; in the United States, for example, New York's is 10,032 per .38 square mile (1 sq km).

The liberalization of the economy since 1991 has turned India from an inward-looking, highly regulated country into one taking part in the global economy. It sustains 22 stock exchanges, from Mumbai to Bhubaneshwar, from Delhi to Chennai (Madras).

A Cell Phone Revolution

Here are facts that tell a tale: 221.6 million cell phones were sold in India in 2012 alone; the current estimated subscriber base is 929.37 million; Nokia has a 21.8 percent share in handsets, while Samsung has 13.7 percent. The cell phone has done more to lift India's population than the computer. With coverage in almost every village and field, most people have access to a cell phone. Farmers, weavers, and small producers can be in direct contact with market prices, suppliers, and retailers, responding to orders immediately and preventing middlemen from ripping them off. For them, the cell phone is the fifth most important household factor after food, clothing, shelter, and education.

Many festivals and political rallies draw huge crowds in India.

While India has made huge strides in many areas in recent years—the "green revolution" helped make the country self-sufficient in food with some produce left over to export—some problems persist. Officials calculate that at least 30 percent of India's population still lives below the poverty line (a reduction from 54 percent in the 1970s). This is most acute in the states of Bihar, Madhya Pradesh, and Orissa. Health problems persist, too. The government, in partnership with thousands of nongovernmental organizations, is focusing on providing clean water and sanitation to more rural areas and on tackling the persistent presence of malaria, leprosy, and—the most acute problems—AIDS and tuberculosis.

Visitors in India

It is important for visitors to be aware that India plays a minor role in world tourism, even though, from the opposite point of view, tourism is India's third largest export industry (after gems and jewelry, and ready-made garments). Tourist activity (and therefore spending) in India is concentrated in the Golden Triangle formed by Delhi, Agra, and Jaipur, and in the increasingly popular state of Rajasthan. Elsewhere, with exceptions such as Ajanta's caves and Varanasi, the more adventurous traveler will find most of India refreshingly quiet.

Traveling around the country is easy. There are good road, railroad, and air networks, and the Indian people are particularly helpful and friendly. It is easy to observe and take part in local life. A host of major festivals is augmented by thousands of smaller, equally charming ones. You can stop to join in the celebrations of a village deity, inspect the goats at an agricultural fair, and watch the lively wedding processions that dance their way through the streets.

In villages you can find craftsmen practicing ancient skills—making gold jewelry, weaving silk saris, or casting in bronze. The village elementary school usually welcomes a spontaneous visit and an exchange of songs. In the fields you can see the traditional irrigation methods, the planting of wheat and paddy, the gathering in of harvests of cotton, chilies, oil seeds, tea, rubber, lentils, and more—about 62 percent of Indians depend on agriculture for their livelihood. You will be welcomed into temples, *gurudwaras* (Sikh temples), and mosques to observe the faithful and their rituals.

Cities are places for finding top-quality cultural performances, seeing one of India's "Bollywood" movies (the name is a pun on the idea of Hollywood in Bombay), visiting the large markets and high-quality stores, and obtaining information on the surrounding area from the visitor information office.

To find out what is important to Indians now, pick up a copy of the periodical *India Today* or one of the other many English-language newspapers; or explore the many English-language television channels. For a glimpse into sophisticated high society, take a look at India's edition of *Hello!* magazine or *Vogue*.

Gone are the days when travelers in India had to compromise on their accustomed comforts. The country's burgeoning affluence means that in most metropolitan areas cars are comfortable, hotels efficient, communications streamlined, and stores now stocked with a wide range of international goods. ∎

Cultural Etiquette

Indian people are so polite and so anxious to put visitors at ease that it is easy to be unaware of causing them offense, especially in the more traditional, rural areas. To help show your respect for different customs, here are some tips.

When you visit a place of worship—a temple, *gurudwara*, or mosque—remove your shoes. In a mosque, you should cover your head, arms, and legs. Be sure not to interfere with any ritual taking place; for instance, at a *puja* ceremony in a temple never stand between the deity and the worshipper. Also, respect the sanctity of the building and any requests for no photography, no cameras inside, and no leather objects; such things can be left in lockers or with a guardian.

The left hand and foot are considered unclean. Focus carefully on using only your right hand to touch a holy object, point to anything, and, of course, to eat food—this may take a bit of practice, but it is worth the effort.

When you meet someone, shaking hands is not obligatory, and in more traditional situations such touching is not expected. Instead, put your hands together at chest level, bow slightly, and say *namaste* (see sidebar p. 10) on arrival and departure.

When shopping in markets and tourist stores, you are expected to bargain. It is part of the fun of making the deal, but it is not nearly as aggressive as in the Far East. Elsewhere, prices are usually fixed.

Local transportation now has mostly fixed pricing for short journeys using auto-rickshaws or taxis. But for longer ones—a half day, say—it is open. Discuss your route, agree on a fare before you set off (if in doubt, check with your hotel that it is reasonable), and pay at the end, adding a tip for good service—and accept that a foreigner will pay more than a local.

You will certainly encounter beggars. The solution is not necessarily to give alms, which may not be kept by the beggar and which also perpetuates the culture, especially with children. Consider instead asking children to show their schoolbooks, thus giving their studies status; or give out postcards from your home city and explain where in the world you live. You can also get involved in a reliable charity (see sidebar p. 16). If you feel you must give to a beggar, then do so as you leave the site to avoid being mobbed.

A Good Book

Indian literature—written by Indians and non-Indians—is a rich and unending feast of intimate diaries, romantic fiction, matter-of-fact reports, and golden prose. And it keeps on coming: Unknown texts are continually being rediscovered and newly published; familiar favorites such as Rudyard Kipling's *Kim* are reprinted; and new writing on India is as fresh as ever.

Indians are voracious readers of books and newspapers in English and in their own local languages.

In India it's easy to find good reading material to suit every taste. Moreover, the bigger cities have well-stocked bookstores with much lower prices than in the West.

India's literature may be daunting. However, a child's edition, or the children's cartoon strip magazines that recount the main epics episodically, are easy ways of grasping the background stories and a knowledge of these can help you enjoy India's paintings, dance-drama, and sculpture. The *Mahabharata* is an epic poem recounting the civil war between the Pandavas, led by Arjuna, and the Kurus. In a later addition, the *Bhagavad Gita,* Krishna discusses with Arjuna the human struggle for love, light, and redemption. The other great epic is the *Ramayana,* in which good king Rama, helped by monkey and bear allies, rescues his wife, Sita, from Ravana, the multiheaded demon king of Sri Lanka. The ancient *Puranas,* meanwhile, include the popular stories of Vishnu's incarnation as the vivacious human, Krishna.

Early and classical devotional poetry can be read in sensitive full translations. Try the Penguin editions of *The Kural* by the Tamil writer Tiruvalluvar, or the Sanskrit lyrical poems of Bhartrihari and Bilhana.

Early Writings

The West first learned about India through written accounts. The diaries, travel writing, and letters of early travelers formed the basis of Western knowledge of India until relatively recently. Images of India only became common when the uncle-nephew team of Thomas and William Daniells published prints of India in London in the 1790s.

Jawaharlal Nehru wrote *An Autobiography* and *Glimpses of World History*. His contemporaries, equally aware of India's changing state, included Mulk Raj Anand (*Untouchable, Coolie*), Nirad Chaudhuri (*The Autobiography of an Unknown Indian*), and S. H. Manto, whose short stories include "Toba Tek Singh."

Recent Generations

Among recent generations of Indian writers, some of whom live outside the country, are Vikram Seth, whose epic novel *A Suitable Boy* explores post-independent northern India; Anita Desai, whose novels (for example *Clear Light of Day*) keep mainly to her home city of Delhi, and R. K. Narayan, whose novels are set in the south. Salman Rushdie, best known for *Midnight's Children*, explores Kerala and Mumbai in *The Moor's Last Sigh,* while Rohinton Mistry's *Such a Long Journey* and *A Fine Balance* have a broader base. Although he grew up in the Caribbean, amost all of V. S. Naipaul's candid observations about Indian life and his predictions ring true, beginning with *An Area of Darkness.*

Among younger writers, Kiran Desai, the daughter of Anita Desai, is a standout: Her *Hullabaloo in the Guava Orchard* was followed by *The Inheritance of Loss,* which won the British Man Booker Prize in 2006. Following in her

footsteps, Aravind Adiga won the same prize in 2008 for his novel *The White Tiger.*

A good way to enjoy a range of historic writing is to read an anthology. Bruce Palling's *A Literary Companion: India* includes the reactions to India of 4th-century Chinese Buddhist traveler Fa Hsien, 19th-century Bishop Heber of Calcutta, and 20th-century English novelist Evelyn Waugh. It is surprising just how many outsiders have written about India—American novelist Mark Twain (1835–1910), humorist Edward Lear (1812–1888), poet W. H. Auden (1907–1973), photographer Sir Cecil Beaton (1904–1980), explorer Sir Richard Burton (1821–1890), novelist E. M. Forster (1879–1970), and many more.

Aravind Adiga, whose *The White Tiger* won the 2008 British Man Booker Prize for fiction, exemplifies the literary talent in India today.

History & Culture

India's history stretches back several millennia, through warring states and empires, invasions and conquests. Foreign rulers have pillaged, destroyed, rebuilt, and made cultural contributions, while rival religions, imported and homegrown, have clashed and merged. Traders from near and far away have brought their own languages and cultures. India absorbs all this, even today.

Prehistory to the Classical Age

The subcontinent abounds in uncharted archaeological remains and, therefore, much archaeological activity. Scholars are still reassessing India's early history: Recent theories have early man arriving along the west coast from Africa, reaching down to Kerala. Discovered only in 1957, the most spectacular group of inhabited rock shelters are the thousand or so strung along a ridge at Bhimbetka, near Bhopal. Half of them are decorated with paintings; estimates of the paintings' age range from 10,000 to 40,000 years. Vestiges of human life on the subcontinent go back some 400,000 years. Crudely sharpened stones dating from the period of the Himalayan glaciations (Pleistocene) have been found in India. Stone hammers from the Upper Paleolithic (up to 30,000 years ago) have been found at Pushkar, in Rajasthan, where quartz, agate, and carnelian have been used and arrowheads carved to a beauty and precision far beyond their practical demands.

During these early times, the Upper Paleolithic and Mesolithic periods, early settlements displayed evidence of various lifestyles—fishing, hunting, gathering, simple agriculture and husbandry, and organized trading. Paintings from this era show foreign visitors, and activities such as dancing, hunting, and ambushing. In the Indus Valley, barley and wheat were cultivated; sheep and goats were domesticated; and by 5000 B.C. the familiar humped Indian cattle were the most common domesticated animals.

Where the Indus Is Very Young

Archaeologists are slowly unraveling the early chapters of India's history. In the Himalaya region of India and Pakistan, signs of Paleolithic and Neolithic man's activities abound, such as hunting scenes carved into rocks beside the Indus. For instance, in Ladakh a mysterious shroud is carved into a rock near Dha, probably made by the Indo-Aryan Dard people who still live there today. If you are trekking in this area, keep an eye out for scratched images, especially on riverside rocks.

The potter's wheel appeared around 3500 B.C., ushering in mass production, as did grain storehouses built of mud bricks, which are evidence of large, organized communities. Major excavation sites include Banavali and Mitathal (Haryana) and Surkotada (Kachchh). Meanwhile, the Ganga plains reveal evidence of similar but independent developments.

Indus Valley Civilization: Within this widespread cultural network, with its increased use of the floodplains for more productive farming, arose the urbanized Indus Valley Civilization, also known as the Mature Harappan culture, which peaked

Hindu temples feature riotous carvings on the soaring roofs and gateways.

around 2500 B.C. Its best known cities, Mohenjodaro and Harappa, are in Pakistan, but India's sites include fascinating Lothal port and the spectacular fortress city of Dholavira, both in Gujarat, and Kalibangan in Rajasthan.

These and other cities of this sophisticated civilization were much advanced in comparison with earlier ones. They usually had a clear city plan focused on a high mound, probably a religious-political center. There were special areas for craftspeople, housing for the wealthy, and workers' accommodations. There were large granaries, efficient water and drainage systems, and evidence of international trading.

This intriguing, unified social and political organization extended over present-day Pakistan and much of northern India. Yet two mysteries about the culture remain. Its tantalizing stone seals have not yet been deciphered, and the cause of its final decline around 1700 B.C. is in question. Was it invasion, famine, overfarming, or something else? Whatever the answer, much of the culture was passed down to later Indian society.

A group of men sing and dance to celebrate Holi, the arrival of spring, in Jodhpur, western Rajasthan.

Vedic Age: 1500–1000 B.C.: Between 1500 and 1300 B.C., seminomadic Aryan tribes from the Iranian plateau began to migrate over the mountains into northern India. These pastoralists formed farming village communities different from the sophisticated Harappan cities. Each had a warrior chief—raja—who received tribute in return for being the villagers' protector. Cattle were the main form of wealth, and thus a main reason for war.

The raja's status was confirmed by his priests—brahmans—who compiled the great hymns and verses in Vedic Sanskrit, at first handed down orally but later written down; the *Rig Veda* is the best known. These and other texts, such as the *Upanishads,* the epic *Mahabharata,* and the *Puranas,* tell us about Vedic history, life, and thought; the abstract doctrine of karma has its roots in Vedic philosophy. The Vedic rituals centered on the worship of personified forces of nature and abstract divinities.

> **The Vedic rituals centered on the worship of personified forces of nature and abstract divinities. This became the basis of Hinduism.**

ties. This became the basis of Hinduism (see pp. 56–59). The religion emphasized sacrifice, chanting of hymns, and the importance of the priest as mediator.

As tribal identity became territorial, so royal power was symbolized with coronation and sacrifice, the old tribute became a tax, and trade and agriculture flourished.

Most important of all, a new social order of caste hierarchy emerged, the *varna;* this powerful cohesive force would endure as empires rose and fell over the next 3,000 years. Varna means color, and at first the distinction was between the pale Aryan immigrants and darker non-Aryan people of India. The Aryans were divided into priests and teachers (brahmans), warriors and rulers *(kshatriyas),* and merchants and cultivators *(vaishyas),* while the non-Aryans and other economically low groups formed the *shudras,* whose purpose was to serve the three superior castes. Ritual status and subcastes called *jatis* soon evolved, as did the idea of purity of caste and its opposing pollution. This brought two results: strict caste rules pervading social life, and a fifth caste, the untouchables, whose occupations were considered impure. Mahatma Gandhi later attempted to give these people status by renaming them *harijans* (children of God).

Gradually, Aryan and non-Aryan cultures fused in northern India, creating an Indo-Aryan society whose language groups are the roots of 74 percent of the Indian population today; they include Hindi, Punjabi, Rajasthani, and Bengali. Meanwhile, in southern India, the Dravidian culture remained isolated from Aryan culture, as reflected in its main languages, which predate Indo-Aryan ones: Telegu, Tamil, Kannada, and Malayalam. India never had a common language, but Sanskrit, the most highly developed Indo-Aryan language, remained the language of the educated people until English usurped it during the Raj and became the lingua franca, still used.

Early Empires, New Faiths: In all, India was unified by its trade routes and by its traders, who enjoyed unprecedented status, patronized the arts, and encouraged the growth of towns. By about 600 B.C., trading had stimulated the rise of port towns (called *puras*) along the rivers, such as Varanasi and Vaishali, marking the start of India's second widespread urbanization, this time in the Ganga Valley.

Economic developments followed, including a common script, coinage, and banking. Meanwhile, invasions from the northwest by the Persian Achaemenid emperor Cyrus in 530 B.C. created a Persian cultural and trading bridge. In this post-Vedic world of republics, monarchies, and powerful traders, the strictures of Vedic Hinduism came into question, and two princes of northern India founded Buddhism and Jainism, instantly successful back-to-basics religions whose practicality and equality appealed especially to the increasingly powerful trading castes.

The Magadha kingdom eventually emerged preeminent; its rulers Bimbisara (543–491 B.C.) and Ajatashatru (491–461 B.C.) founded Rajagriha (Rajgir, near Patna), then Pataliputra (Patna). By the late fourth century B.C., however, the kingdom was embroiled in a dispute over succession. The decline of the Magadhan kingdom coincided with the arrival of Alexander the Great, who invaded the Punjab in 327 B.C. He left garrisons and governors behind when he departed two years later, but his death in 323 B.C. rendered the fledgling Greek province dangerously unstable.

Chandragupta Maurya, who had taken over the weakened Magadhan throne in 321 B.C., threw the Greeks out in 305 B.C.: The powerful Mauryan empire (321–185 B.C.) was born. The first of India's many great empires, it stretched from Assam to Afghanistan, from Kashmir to Mysore. Its legendary capital was at Pataliputra (Patna). Chandragupta, abdicated to join a Jain community and died by *sallekhana* (death by fasting and meditation). His grandson was the greatest Mauryan ruler, Ashoka (r. ca 269–232 B.C.). He converted to Buddhism and promoted its concept of dharma—social responsibility to maintain human dignity and socioreligious harmony. Buddhist edicts on social values and behavior were engraved onto rocks and columns across his empire, usually using Brahmi script and the Pankrit language.

India's Lion Emblem

The lion head that graces government buildings, government letterheads, and anything else to do with the government is India's carefully chosen emblem, adopted on January 26, 1950. Neither Hindu nor Muslim, it is a detail from a large, beautifully carved and polished sandstone capital dating from the Buddhist emperor Ashoka's rule (269–232 B.C.). The Lion Capital has four lions mounted on a circular abacus. The profile of the Lion Capital shows three lions with a Buddhist Wheel of Law (Dharma Chakra) in the center, a bull on the right, and a galloping horse on the left. The wheel was discovered at Sarnath, and you can see it in the lobby of the museum there.

The Shungas and Kanvas succeeded the Mauryas before the focus moved to the northwest. Here the Bactrian Greeks invaded from Afghanistan in 190 B.C. and ruled Gandhara (in modern Pakistan); at its peak their kingdom stretched to Mathura, south of Delhi, only to be supplanted by the Scythians in the first century B.C. and then the Parthians, both Central Asian tribes.

K. Ramaswamy was born an untouchable, yet he became a justice of India's Supreme Court.

India's second important kingdom, the Kushana, flourished from the first century B.C. to the third century A.D. Its borders encompassed Central Asia and northern India, stretching to Varanasi and Vaishali (near Bhopal); its capitals were at Peshawar (now in Pakistan) and Mathura. Under its greatest ruler, the Buddhist convert Kanishka (r. ca A.D. 100–120), sculpture and other arts flourished, influenced by the Hellenistic art of the Roman Empire. At this time the impressive Buddhist monastery and stupas at Sanchi were built, financed by the traders of nearby Vaishali. Meanwhile, among the kingdoms of the Deccan (now made up of the states of Karnataka and Andhra Pradesh), the Satavahanas rose in the first century B.C. to enjoy four centuries of preeminence. They maintained a careful mix of Vedic principles, Mauryan political philosophy, and tolerance toward the powerful Buddhist traders. Their patronage is evident in the rock-cut temples of Karla and Kanheri, both on trade routes to the Konkan ports.

Farther south, the Chola, Chera, and Pandya chiefs were supreme. Their body of literature, called the *Sangam,* reveals a mainly non-Aryan society whose peasant communities developed ports that thrived. Until the fall of the Roman Empire, trade was brisk in jewels, ivory, fragrant woods, perfumes, and spices, the last an essential part of European culture. When the Visigoth Alaric sacked Rome in A.D. 410, his ransom was 3,000 pounds of Indian pepper, not gold. A Roman cohort was maintained at Calicut on the Malabar coast, and coins, pottery, and other objects testify to foreign trading communities in the coastal ports and at the commercial city of Madurai.

(continued on p. 30)

India Time Line

With India's history being so long, complex, and varied, here is a skeleton of dates to help make sense of it all.

ca 2500 B.C. Peak of Indus Valley Civilization.

327 B.C. Alexander the Great invades.

ca 269–232 B.C. Ashoka rules Mauryan empire.

190 B.C. Greeks from Bactria invade.

ca A.D. 100–120 Kanishka rules Kushana empire.

A first-century seated Bodhisattva found at Mathura, now in the National Museum of India

ca A.D. 335–415 Chandragupta II rules Gupta empire.

ca 600–630 Mahendravarman I rules Pallava empire in southern India.

8th century on Rajputs rise to power in northern India.

805–1278 Chola empire dominates Tamil Nadu.

1192 Qutb-ud-din-Aibak takes Delhi; in 1206 establishes Slave Sultanate, India's first Muslim kingdom.

1206–1596 The Delhi sultanates: Slave, Khilji, Tughlaq, Sayyid, and Lodi

1336–1565 Vijayanagara empire unites southern India.

1398 Timur (Tamburlaine) sacks Delhi.

1509 Alfonso de Alburquerque takes Goa, makes it capital of Portugal's maritime empire.

1526 Babur invades, takes Agra, initiates Mughal empire, and crushes Rajput confederacy the next year.

1527–1707 Height of Mughal empire under Emperors Babur, Humayun, Akbar, Jahangir, Shah Jahan, and Aurangzeb.

1562 Akbar's first Rajput alliance, with Amer (Jaipur).

1565 The combined forces of the Deccan sultanates defeat Vijayanagara's army at the Battle of Talikota.

1616 on Sir Thomas Roe wins trading rights from Jahangir; Portuguese power begins to wane and English power to rise under the East India Company.

1631 Mumtaz Mahal dies and Shah Jahan will build the Taj Mahal as her mausoleum.

1639 Madras founded as English trading headquarters.

1648 Shah Jahan returns the Mughal capital to Delhi.

1772 British administrative capital moves from Madras to Calcutta.

1799 Arthur Wellesley defeats Tipu Sultan of Mysore; Ranjit Singh takes Lahore and establishes the first Sikh kingdom.

1840–1914 India becomes Britain's most important trading partner.

1857–1858 Rebellion against the British at Delhi, Lucknow, and Kanpur. Delhi retaken; Bahadur Shah II deposed, ending Mogul empire. British power, known as the Raj, is now direct from Westminster.

1864–1939 For six months a year, Shimla is the British government's summer capital.

1869 Suez Canal opens.

1885 National Congress founded to fight for India's freedom.

1906 All India Muslim League founded to safeguard Indian Muslims' interests.

1911 King-Emperor George V announces British capital to move to Delhi.

1915 Gandhi returns from South Africa to fight for India's freedom.

1930 Gandhi leads the Salt March protesting against the British salt tax.

1931 Garden city of New Delhi is inaugurated.

1947 Independence for India; East and West Pakistan created. Jawaharlal Nehru is India's first prime minister.

1950 Republic of India inaugurated and constitution effective on January 26.

1966–1977, 1980–1984 Indira Gandhi is prime minister.

1971 East Pakistan becomes Bangladesh.

1991–1996 Narasimha Rao prime minister; India opens to global markets.

1998 India conducts nuclear tests.

Simple in his lifestyle, Mahatma Gandhi sits cross-legged, wrapped in a shawl, to write.

2001 India's population hits one billion.

2004 Dr. Manmohan Singh becomes prime minister, reelected in 2009; India's economic upsurge continues; tsunami hits Tamil Nadu.

2008 India launches spacecraft on lunar exploration mission.

2012 A total of 221.6 million cell phones are sold in India in this year.

Indian Lunar Calendars

India observes two lunar calendars in addition to the Gregorian; they both start with the month Chaitra. Saka, adopted after independence, has 365 days and always starts on March 22 (Chaitra 1 Saka 1879 = March 22, 1957). The Saka is a tidied-up version of the traditional Hindu Vikram Samvat, whose 12 shorter lunar months total just over 354 days, requiring an extra month added every 30 months. Thus, each year the months shift and the festival dates change. For instance, the festival of Diwali is on November 3 in 2013 and on October 23 in 2014.

Seated Buddhas, painted in the fifth century with tremendous virtuosity, are just a fragment of the many vibrant, naturalistic frescoes that coat several caves at Ajanta.

Classical Age: 300–650

India's classical age was dominated by the Gupta dynasty (ca 319–ca 467) in northern India, while the Gangas were powerful in Orissa, the Kadambas in the Deccan, and the Pallavas (fourth to seventh centuries) in the deep south.

Chandragupta I (r. 319–335) brought the Guptas to power, widening his empire to the Indus in the west and the Bay of Bengal in the east. His principal cities were on the Ganga at Ayodhya and Allahabad. Their influence stretched southward to the Pallavas' territory around Kanchipuram. They dominated trade from coast to coast as well as to central Asia and to the old Silk Route between China and Bactria (Afghanistan).

Gupta rulers performed Vedic sacrifices (which sometimes involved animals) to legitimize their rule. They patronized the brahmans and senior courtiers by giving them land grants and privileges, and they supported Buddhism. During this period, essential elements of Hinduism emerged, such as bhakti (see p. 58) and image worship. So, too, did the importance of the Mother Goddess, the temple as the center of social and religious life, and Vishnu and Shiva, whose complex myths and legends were written in the *Purana* texts.

Under the Gupta patronage of art and literature, especially under Chandragupta II (r. ca 335–415), a new classical style emerged that became the aesthetic yardstick for subsequent artists and craftsmen. Sanskrit poetry reached its apogee in the works of Kalidasa, which include *Raghuvamsa* and *Kumarasambhava*. Sculpture reached new heights of technique, spirituality, and three-dimensional expression. Architecture witnessed the formative phases of the Nagara and Dravida temple styles. Coins had fine designs, and the paintings of Ajanta and Bhaja influenced Buddhist art across Asia. Formal principles that were followed for centuries were laid down in treatises: Vastu for architecture, Shilpa for sculpture, and Chitra for painting.

India was already at the forefront of studies in subjects such as astronomy and medicine. Now, Aryabhata and Varahamihira pushed the study of astronomy further. Under the Guptas, new ideas in mathematics, the cipher, and numerals were exported via the Arabs to Europe. Legal texts abounded, and covered every subject, from social problems to property rights. An almost humanist interest in the ideal citizen preoccupied the philosopher-writers of the time, and Vatsyayana wrote the sophisticated treatise on the art of love, the *Kamasutra*. Only when waves of Huns, then Gurjara, had succeeded in disrupting trade, did Gupta power wane. Some of these invaders were ancestors of the Rajput clans of Rajasthan.

In southern India, most kingdoms of this period followed the Vedic rituals. Kingdoms usually worshipped either Shiva or Vishnu, and promoted royal-religious power in the Gupta style by giving land grants to both priests and temples. The temple became the central element in the government of what was an agrarian community, where rice was both the main crop and the standard bartering unit.

Under the Guptas, new ideas in mathematics, the cipher, and numerals were exported via the Arabs to Europe.

Temple architecture blossomed under the early Pallava rulers, who believed they were descended from Brahma. Much of their work survives at their capital, Kanchipuram, and at their port, Mahabalipuram (Mamallapuram). Mahendravarman I (r. ca 600–630) was a dramatist and poet who converted from Jainism to Shaivism (the worship of Shiva), and under his patronage architecture, literature, and the applied arts began to acquire their distinct Dravidian character.

The Pallavas' arch enemies were the Chalukyas, who ruled in the Deccan, first from Aihole and later from Badami. During the post-Gupta disruptions in the north, Harsha Vadhana eventually lost his kingdom to the Chalukya king Pulakeshin II.

A classical Indian culture developed from the collective achievement of the remarkable individuals of this period. Its wide scope of learning pushed knowledge forward in a range of subjects, from the development of Sanskrit to the concept of a god-king, from Buddhist philosophy to the *Ramayana* stories. Traders carried this sophisticated culture into the east, where it profoundly influenced other cultures.

From the Classical Age to Islam's Arrival: 650–1206

Post-Gupta northern India saw the growth of regional states, while southern India rose to a new prominence. Here, artistic innovation flourished, as seen in the vigorous sculptures of Elephanta and Ajanta and in the creation of monumental stone temples such as those at Thanjavur, Chidambaram, and Gangakondacholapuram. These temples became a focus for all the arts, especially sculpture, bronze-casting, dance, music, and painting. Patronized by rulers, they played a vital role in endorsing royal power.

During these centuries, autonomous village government was established; it is still strong today. Indian merchants' guilds specializing in textiles, gems, and spices expanded to trade with the Jewish, Arab, and Chinese peoples. Sanskrit was the language of officials and high literature. As Buddhism and Jainism waned, Hinduism absorbed local cults to acquire regional characteristics.

In the north, the Ganga Valley and its main city, Kanauj, were under the control of first, the Pratiharas; then, the Palas; and finally the Rashtrakutas, the first Deccan dynasty to reach this area. To the east, the Somavamshis established their capital at Bhubaneshwar, whose fine temples survive.

In the Deccan and far south, wars were fought over the fertile valleys and lucrative trade routes, but in peacetime fine temples were built. The Chalukyas built theirs at Aihole, Pattadakal, and Badami, while the later Hoysalas left intricately carved temples in and around their capital, Halebid.

Farther south, the Pallava rulers, still at loggerheads with the Chalukyas, continued to build temples at their port of Mahabalipuram and their capital, Kanchipuram, one of the seven sacred cities for Hindus, and southern India's largest international textile center. They enjoyed lucrative maritime trade with Sri Lanka, Arabia, and southeast Asia.

A sixth-century, three-headed carving of Shiva, in the Elephanta Island cave temple, Mumbai

In the mid ninth century, the Cholas (805–1278), longtime chieftains in the area, created the most powerful southern state. Their greatest rulers—Rajaraja I (r. 984–1014), Rajendra (r. 1014–1044), and Kulottunga I (r. 1070–1118)—expanded their territories to cover Tamil Nadu, southern Karnataka, southern Kerala, and northern Sri Lanka. From their principal port, Nagappattinam, at the mouth of the Kaveri River, Chola trading extended to China.

Back in the north, Rajput clans were rising to power. These immigrant clans acquired kshatriya (see p. 25) status in the caste system and traced their lineage to the sun and moon. Some called themselves Agni-kul (Fire Family) and claimed descent from a mythical figure that arose out of a vast sacrificial pit near Mount Abu. These clans included the Kachwahas (Jaipur) and Sisodias (Udaipur) of Rajasthan, as well as the Chandellas (Khajuraho) and the Tomars who founded Delhi around 736. They warred constantly. It was the great Chauhan hero Prithviraj III who took the Tomars'

> **Islam, not Hinduism, would now be the dominant political, social, and cultural force in northern India for six centuries.**

Delhi and managed to fight off an early Islamic invader, Mohammad of Ghor, in 1191.

But even Prithviraj could not stop Islam from taking hold. Arab Muhammad bin Qasim arrived in 711, by sea from Baghdad at a point east of Karachi. Mahmud of Ghazni, a Turk, made repeated raids between 1000 and 1026, his men crossing the Hindu Kush to plunder the northern plains and their rich temples. Then, in 1192, the Turkish invader Mohammad of Ghor's slave general, Qutb-ud-din-Aibak, defeated Prithviraj III and took Delhi. When Mohammad of Ghor was assassinated in Lahore in 1206, Aibak assumed control, made Delhi the capital of India's first, if unstable, Muslim kingdom, and initiated the Delhi Sultanate that would be succeeded by the Mughals. Islam, not Hinduism, would now be the dominant political, social, and cultural force in northern India for six centuries. The capitals, Delhi and for a while Agra, saw the creation of a rich Indo-Islamic culture, much of which survives today in palaces, tombs, cuisine, inlaid marble, and in music and other arts.

The Delhi Sultanate: 1206–1526

Aibak's own lieutenant, Iltutmish, seized power in 1211, ruling for the next 25 years. Iltutmish consolidated his empire, and his Slave dynasty (1206–1290) was the first of five successive sultanates to rule Delhi. Iltutmish was himself a Mamluk, a Turkish "slave." There followed the Khiljis (1290–1320), Tughlaqs (1320–1413), Sayyids (1414–1451), and Lodis (1451–1526).

Iltutmish benefited from dramatic events in Central Asia: Ghengis Khan and the Mongols swept through between 1219 and 1222, removing threats to India and ensuring that Muslim India would carve its own history. The Slave usurper was able to annex Sind and Bengal, and his men provided the military leadership, provincial governors, and officers of court—a pattern that would be repeated in subsequent dynasties. His richly carved but modest-size tomb stands behind the mosque at Lal Kot.

The Mongols made repeated raids into northern India in the 13th and 14th centuries. Meanwhile, Delhi became the chosen refuge from the Central Asian hotbed for many immigrant nobles, bureaucrats, and adventurers. One of these groups, the Turkish Khiljis, succeeded the Slave sultans. Their popular and capable ruler Ala-ud-din Khilji (r. 1296–1315) survived a Mongol siege in 1303, conquered wealthy Gujarat, took the great

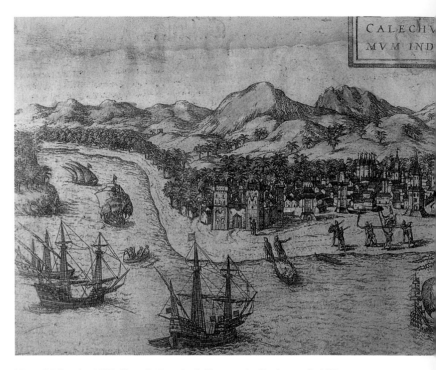

CALECHV
MVM IND

View of Calicut (ca 1600). Vasco da Gama landed here on the Kerala coast in 1498.

Rajput forts of Ranthambore and Chittaurgarh, and pushed his empire far southward to Daulatabad, near Aurangabad. His Delhi city, known as Siri, had a great reservoir and a fine university.

Having overstretched themselves, the Khiljis lost out to Ghiyath-ud-din Tughlaq, a Turko-Mongol. His successor, Muhammad (r. 1324–1351), was the most colorful and controversial sultan of all, a mixture of extreme generosity and brutality. He strengthened the Muslim administration by inviting Muslim immigrants to Delhi. One was a Moroccan, Ibn Battuta, who wrote a detailed account of 14th-century India. Muhammad then moved the capital from Delhi to Daulatabad in 1327 to encourage Muslim colonization of the south, only to relocate back to Delhi (ca 1330) to maintain power in the north.

Muhammad's huge empire began to crack. Bengal became an independent sultanate (1335), as did Kashmir (1346) and the Deccan (1347), which went to the Bahmani sultans. Muhammad's successor was the enlightened Feroz Shah Tughlaq (r. 1351–1388), whose Delhi was renowned for its beauty, refinement, and intellectual life. Feroz Shah chose to be buried in a fortlike tomb beside Ala-ud-din Khilji's reservoir. After his death, the empire's disintegration sped up. The Asian conqueror Timur (Tamburlaine) sacked Delhi in 1398. In northern and central India, Jaunpur (1400), Malwa (1406), and Gujarat (1407) went independent, while the Rajput states of Marwar and Mewar emerged.

In the Deccan, the Bahmani state gradually broke up to form five competing sultanates: Gulbarga (later Bidar), Ahmednagar, Berar, Bijapur, and finally Golconda. South of

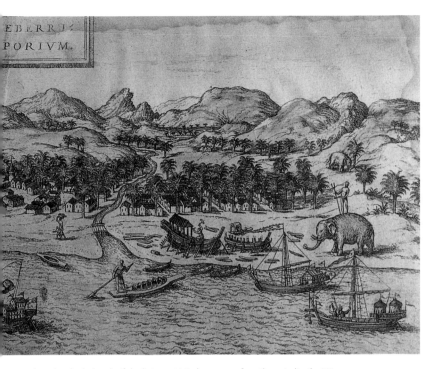

them lay the bulwark of the last great Hindu power of southern India, the Vijayanagara, which peaked under the rule of Krishnadevaraya (r. 1509–1530). By uniting all smaller southern Hindu states, the Vijayanagara empire (1336–1565) could remain powerful until four of the five sultanates, usually competing against each other, united. At the Battle of Talikota in 1565, the Vijayanagara forces were roundly defeated.

Thus, the territory ruled by Delhi's last two sultanates, the Sayyids and the Lodis, was reduced to just one of many Muslim states in India. In each, power lay with a minority of Muslims and was dependent upon raising land taxes and controlling trade routes and ports. There was relatively little conversion of the local, mostly Hindu, people. At the various courts, with their cosmopolitan mixtures of Muslims and Hindus, the rich Indo-Muslim cultures evolved. You can trace these in surviving buildings, sculptures, and metalwork in the Islamic remains of Delhi, Ahmedabad, Bijapur, Bidar, and a number of other medieval Muslim cities.

At the various courts, with their cosmopolitan mixtures of Muslims and Hindus, the rich Indo-Muslim cultures evolved.

In 1502 Sikander Lodi left Delhi, moving his power base 122 miles (196 km) south to Agra. The once legendary capital became nothing but a necropolis surrounding the village of Nizamuddin, where the *dargah* (shrine) of the Sufi saint Shaikh Nizam-ud-din Auliya (1238–1325) was maintained by the faithful. His royal devotees had included Muhammad and Feroz Shah Tughlaq, and would number several Mughal emperors.

Mughal Empire's Great Age: 1526–1707

Into this fragmented India, Babur, a Barlas Turk, arrived in 1526, enticed by India's wealth and encouraged by the invitation of disgruntled Afghan chiefs governing Ibrahim Lodi's Punjab territories. Victory over Ibrahim Lodi at Panipat was easy. But when the quarrelsome Rajput clans united under one flag for the first time, under the Sisodia ruler Rana Sanga of Mewar, Babur faced a far greater test. To encourage his men, Babur promised unconquered lands to his own nobles, declared jihad (holy war in the name of sacred duty) on the Rajputs, renounced wine, and took a vow to fight to the death. Then, mustering his immense leadership skills and the superior war tactics of Central Asia, Babur crushed the Rajputs in March 1527.

The Mughals had arrived: They would become the greatest and the last of India's Islamic empires (1526–1858). The first six emperors, known as the Great Mughals (1526–1707), ruled from father to son: Babur, Humayun, Akbar, Jahangir, Shah Jahan, and Aurangzeb. All were great leaders, politicians, and soldiers; all were scholars and highly cultured; all were prone to weaknesses, such as alcohol, opium, or plain superstition; and all oscillated between religious tolerance and orthodoxy. Their frank diaries reveal their relationship with India (Babur praised peacock meat but missed Persian gardens), their weaknesses (Jahangir had his drinking problem noted glass by glass), and the later stultifying court life (seen in Shah Jahan's opulent Padshahnamah manuscript).

Babur (r. 1526–1530) celebrated his triumph with an international gathering and huge feast at Agra. But it was short-lived. After he had defeated a joint force of Afghans

The Exquisite Art of Miniature Painting

The ebullient, jewel-bright images in miniature paintings bring alive the now silent and empty forts and palaces of India. It was at the increasingly wealthy Rajput courts of the 16th century that the tradition of commissioning small paintings on paper took off: Paintings of kings in court, battles being won, lovers parting or uniting, and scenes from the great Hindu epics were depicted in bold patterns, with little perspective and using flat areas of nonrealistic color.

The arrival of the Mughals introduced a complete antithesis: a Persian delicacy, subtleness, and the depiction of nature and space, often recording historical events in specific buildings, a fascination with nature, a precise portrait, a given moment at court. As the Mughal presence strengthened, the emperors' lavishly funded court ateliers drew the best artists from the Central Asian courts

and the Rajput ones. A mingling began that in turn influenced the Rajput courts, producing distinctive hybrid styles. The golden period was from the late 16th through the 18th centuries; in the 19th century, many courts turned to photography. The palaces of Udaipur, Jodhpur, and Jaipur, as well as Delhi's National Museum, display some miniature paintings made at the different courts.

Despite the lack of court patrons, the art of miniature painting continues today, both in the traditional style and with a contemporary twist. In Jaipur's City Palace, artists work in the traditional way: preparing a sketch, mixing the earth colors in individual shells, applying them with a fine brush, then adding gold highlights before burnishing the whole painting. Artists must undergo a full apprenticeship in an atelier, requiring several years of strict discipline.

and Bengalis near Varanasi in 1529, his health failed. He returned to Agra, and then to Lahore, where he died in December 1530.

Humayun (r. 1530–1540, 1555–1556) inherited an as yet unstable empire and made the decision to move the capital back to Delhi. This gifted soldier matched his great victories with equally great parties and indulgences, a combination that allowed the already superior military and political skills of Sher Shah Suri, the Afghan leader in eastern India, to flourish. Lacking his father's charisma, Humayun lost his supporters, was deposed in 1540, and fled westward across Rajasthan and up to Shah Tahmasp's Persian court.

The brief rule of Sher Shah Suri (r. 1540–1545), whose handsome tomb lies east of Varanasi, was important for the future of the Mughals. Not only did he develop a strong central army but he also built roads and large travelers' lodgings, including the Grand Trunk Road that stretched from Kabul through Lahore and Delhi eventually to Kolkata. Sher Shah Suri also standardized weights and measures, regularized trade tariffs, and, maybe most important of all, created a tax revenue system that would be the blueprint for the next Mughal emperor, Akbar.

In the chaos that followed the death of Sher Shah Suri's son, Islam Shah (r. 1545–1553), Humayun retook his throne in 1555, only to die in Delhi the following year. His teenage son, quickly brought to Delhi from the Punjab, would prove to be the successor to Sher Shah Suri's legacy.

Emperor Akbar passes the crown from his son Jahangir to his grandson Shah Jahan.

The 14-year-old Akbar (r. 1556–1605) first reconquered the Mughal empire, then expanded and consolidated it. Under the guidance of his regent, Bairam Khan, he retook most of central India and the Rajput states, including the great forts of Chittorgarh and Ranthambore in 1567–1568. These conquests he cemented with marriage alliances and employment in the Mughal army for the conquered people. In 1562, on his way to Ajmer, Akbar met with Raja Bihar Mal of Amer (Jaipur's old capital). Akbar agreed to marry Bihar Mal's daughter and take his adopted grandson Man Singh into Mughal service—providing the basis of Jaipur's wealth. Only Mewar, under Rana Pratap and Amar Singh, refused to bow down to Mughal power.

With this stability and his new fort (1567–1575) underway, in 1571 Akbar began to create Fatehpur Sikri, a palace-city emulating the Timurid courts. It was from here that, in 1573, he left to conquer Gujarat, a rich land on the Muslim pilgrimage route to Mecca. To celebrate his victory, he built the Buland Darwaza, the great gate of Fatehpur

Maharaja Jai Singh blended Hindu and Muslim styles in his 17th-century additions to Amer Fort.

Sikri's mosque. By 1576 Akbar had completed his victories in eastern India, and in the 1580s and 1590s he extended his empire to the trading cities of Kabul and Qandahar, and to the provinces of Ghazni, Kashmir, Orissa, and Bengal, and to all the land down to the Godavari River.

Akbar now ruled over a large, centralized state defended by nobles of various ethnic and religious groups—Rajputs, Persians, Indians, Muslims, and others. He was a strong, nonsectarian ruler, a soldier and statesman, an art patron, and a liberal philosopher, all of which he used to strengthen his position as emperor.

The administrative framework created during Akbar's rule sustained the empire until the 18th century. It kept the peasantry and nobility happy while filling the state coffers. Akbar stayed close to the ruling Rajput clans and displayed religious tolerance. He had Hindu advisers and discoursed with the resentful but powerful Muslim orthodoxy in the form of the ulema (learned men). Akbar's liberal views led him to lift the *jizya* (poll tax) on non-Muslims and to welcome the Portuguese missionary Father Monserrat for discussions at Fatehpur Sikri. His ideas on kingship, though, led him to initiate the Mughal tradition of the emperor showing himself to his people at sunrise, identifying himself with the ultimate source of energy and endowing himself with supernatural divinity.

> **From the prevailing atmosphere of tolerance during Akbar's rule, India's last great new religion began to emerge: Sikhism.**

From the prevailing atmosphere of tolerance during Akbar's rule, India's last great new religion began to emerge: Sikhism (see pp. 60–61). The faith's ten Gurus (teachers) span the 16th and 17th centuries and their ideas were eventually formalized in 1699.

Akbar's son Salim, born to his Hindu wife from Amer, ascended the throne as Jahangir, or Conqueror of the World (r. 1605–1627). He was 36 years old. His intense interest in painting, science, and coins lifted the Mughal court to new cultural heights, but it was matched by a lifelong addiction to alcohol and opium. At a political and military level, he ended Mughal–Mewar conflict, expanded the empire into the Himalaya and Kachchh, consolidated control of Bengal and Orissa, and campaigned down in the Deccan.

Ghiyas Beg, a Persian adventurer who had entered Akbar's court, became chief minister, or Itimad-ud-Daulah (Pillar of Government) on Jahangir's accession. His clever, ambitious daughter married Jahangir in 1611 and was soon given the title Nur Jahan (Light of the World). She effectively ruled from behind the veil. Her daughter by an earlier marriage married Jahangir's eldest son and heir, Khusrau. Meanwhile, Ghiyas Beg's equally clever and ambitious son, Asaf Khan, had become deputy prime minister and in 1612 gave his daughter, Arjumand Banu, in marriage to Jahangir's third son, Khurram. The couple later rebelled against the emperor and sought refuge at the stoically anti-Mughal Mewar court at Udaipur. When Jahangir's cocktail of drink, drugs, and asthma finally killed him, Asaf Khan triumphed over his sister in the political fallout: Khurram became the next emperor, under the name Shah Jahan (Ruler of the World), and his wife took the title Mumtaz Mahal (Chosen One of the Palace).

For most of Shah Jahan's rule (1627–1658), political and economic stability were sustained throughout the ever expanding empire. The emperor and his vast army, which grew fourfold during his reign, secured Muslim territories in the Deccan, southern Hindu kingdoms, the eastern Assam border, and the northwest frontier to Kabul.

Large, cosmopolitan cities appeared—Lahore, Agra, Ahmedabad—whose citizens traded with Asians and newcomer Europeans and were the patrons of sophisticated crafts and grand architecture. Land revenue from the now enormous empire sustained the parasite Mughal nobles and the army; dependence on this income would eventually cause the breakup of the empire. Shah Jahan's increasingly rich, ostentatious, and unwieldy Mughal court, weighed down with ritual and sheer size, no longer moved from place to place. At Lahore and Agra he and Mumtaz rebuilt the sandstone royal rooms and state audience halls in marble, showing a new refinement in their proportions and decorating them with floral patterns of semiprecious stone inlay, called *pietra dura* (meaning "hard stone" in Italian).

> **Shah Jahan commissioned the Taj Mahal as the mausoleum for his beloved Mumtaz and the magnificent marble Pearl Mosque in Agra Fort.**

In June 1631 Mumtaz died giving birth to their 14th child at Burhanpur while on campaign with her husband. It was a watershed for Shah Jahan and his empire. With his rock gone, he first mourned for two years, giving up music, fine clothes, and celebrations. Then, ill-advisedly putting his campaigns into the hands of his four sons, he threw himself into ambitious building projects. At a personal level, he mixed rigorous orthodoxy with unashamed debauchery. The jizya tax was reinstated on non-Muslims, conversion was encouraged, and building of Hindu temples discouraged.

Shah Jahan commissioned the Taj Mahal as the mausoleum for his beloved Mumtaz and the magnificent marble Pearl Mosque in Agra Fort. He also promoted the building of mosques across his empire. He laid out an entire new city at the traditional capital, Delhi, calling it Shahjahanabad, today's Old Delhi. The emperor and his court moved there in 1648. Today, the palace is forgotten but the walled city outside it buzzes with life, and the great Jama Masjid is the most important mosque for India's Muslims.

Shah Jahan's sons, meanwhile, watched for their chance. It came in 1657, when the emperor became ill. In Mughal tradition, the sons plotted and competed for the throne. After a series of false alliances, tricks, and murders, the third son, Aurangzeb, won power.

The long rule of Aurangzeb (r. 1658–1707) saw the empire stretch to its farthest limit and begin its collapse. Campaigns to keep the northwest and the Rajput princes in line led Aurangzeb unwisely to take control of Jodhpur and later demolish its temples. As a result, not one Rajput chief fought for the Mughals in the later Sikh war.

Aurangzeb then turned his attention south. In 1681 he left Delhi for good. His ambition was to control all of peninsular India and to convert its people to Islam. He had already faced the newly strong Marathas of the Deccan, under their hero leader Shivaji (see pp. 178–179). Jai Singh II, the Jaipur ruler who commanded a large Mughal force, captured Shivaji in 1666, but he escaped from Agra and later became king (1674–1680) of his followers. The Marathas would continue to wield their power and, in the 18th century, expand from their base in Pune across southern India.

Aurangzeb's relentless campaigns, which in some years he continued through the monsoon, brought depression and illness to his soldiers. Eventually he nominally won almost the whole peninsula, but few of his gains were consolidated. Aurangzeb further weakened his position by doggedly reinforcing his orthodoxy. He called his campaigns jihad, enforced the jizya tax, and replaced Hindu administrators with Muslims.

Aurangzeb, the last of the six Great Mughals died devoutly and quietly in the Deccan. Unlike his predecessors, with their lavish and magnificent tombs at Delhi, Agra, and Lahore, Aurangzeb followed the Koran's demand for simplicity. His unadorned white stone slab lies in the precincts of a modest mosque at Khuldabad, near Aurangabad.

European Traders Arrive: 1498–1858

While Delhi lost its control and whole tracts of the Mughal Empire became independent, from Bengal and Avadh in the north to Bijapur and Golconda in the south, Hindu rulers and landowners asserted their power. The Jats were able to raid Agra for some of its marble inlay to decorate their palace at Deeg; the Marathas took the wealthy central kingdom of Malwa and started menacing the Rajputs. The Persian despot Nadir Shah had little trouble sacking Delhi of her wealth in 1739. The Afghans sacked Delhi again in 1757. In the power vacuum, new centers of Mughal power emerged: Murshidabad in Bengal, Lucknow in Avadh, east of Delhi, and Hyderabad in the Deccan.

Into this complex readjusting of boundaries and centers of power, with its attendant conflicts, came the European traders. Trade with the West was not new, but it dramatically increased in the 16th century, stimulated by the desire of European powers to break the monopoly of the eastern trade held by Venice and the Levantine. The solution was to bypass Venice, using sea routes around Africa. The Portuguese led the way, spurred on by Prince Henry the Navigator and the Catholic Church's missionary zeal. In 1498 Vasco da Gama (1469–1524) rounded the Cape of Good Hope and sailed across the Indian Ocean to land at Calicut, in Kerala, where Christianity had been flourishing since St. Thomas the Apostle's arrival in A.D. 52.

The second Portuguese expedition arrived in 1503, led by Alfonso de Albuquerque, who built a church and fort at Cochin. In 1509 he came again and took thriving Goa city from the Bijapur rulers. Goa *dourada* ("golden Goa") was soon a wealthy entrepôt and capital of Europe's largest maritime empire, one that stretched along the coasts of Africa up to Hormuz and included Diu, Daman, Goa, and Cochin on the west coast of India and, on the east coast, Hooghly near modern Kolkata, and on to Malacca in Malaysia. By 1580 Goa's population was 60,000 (Lisbon's was then 110,000), excluding the vast numbers of clergy and slaves. Each year a flotilla of 300 ships laden with spices, gold, and other luxuries would leave Goa for Lisbon. At a social level, while intermarriage between the Portuguese and the Indians was encouraged, European intolerance revealed itself in the wanton destruction of Hindu temples.

The Law in India: A Blend of East & West

India has one of the world's oldest legal systems. After 1947, independent India continued to base its legal system on English common and statutory law, first established in India with King George I's 1726 charter for administering Bombay, Madras, and Calcutta. India has no official religion; its constitution guarantees freedom for every recognized religious denomination or sect to manage its religious affairs. This presents challenges in a country with centuries-old sophisticated Hindu and Muslim legal traditions. What has been very successful is the revival of the Panchayat system, traditional village administration for local social and economic decision-making. Today there are two million representatives sitting on 238,054 Panchayat boards.

The Portuguese had missionary ambitions, and in 1540 the ideology of the Counter-Reformation arrived in Goa, followed by Francis Xavier (1506–1552) and the Jesuits two years later. Mass conversions began. When Xavier died in China, his body was brought to Goa for burial; in 1560 the Inquisition arrived and not surprisingly banned all non-Christian teaching and ritual. Despite Portugal's position as suppliers of horses to the Vijayanagara empire and as naval auxiliaries of the Mughals, the Portuguese were regarded as cruel, untrustworthy, and intolerant by the Indians.

Eventually, the Dutch, Danes, French, and finally the English set sail for India, each competing to establish trading stations. The English successfully expanded, but the Dutch were reduced to Chinsura near Kolkata, and the Danes to nearby Serampore and on the Tamil Nadu coast at Tranquebar (Tharangambadi). The French kept their main base at Pondicherry, with smaller stations at Mahe in Kerala and Chandernagore in West Bengal.

The extensive lands of the Khan of Kelat (seated center) became British territory in 1887. They included the strategically important Bolan Pass, which then linked British India with Afghanistan.

The British came to India looking for trading opportunities after they failed to break the Dutch trading monopoly in the East Indies. On December 31, 1600, Queen Elizabeth I (r. 1558–1603) granted the East India Company its charter "... as much for the honour of this our realm of England as for the increase of our navigation and advancement of trade." A few years later English trade moved forward when Sir Thomas Roe, a senior diplomat, arrived in India from the court of James I (r. 1603–1625). In January 1616 Roe finally met the Mughal emperor Jahangir when his itinerant court was at

Ajmer. Roe soon sealed the relationship between England and India that would grow into the greatest trading partnership and cultural exchange the world has known.

Using diplomacy rather than force, the English had established 23 trading factories by 1647, of which Surat (1613) on the west coast and Madras, today's Chennai, (1639) on the east coast were the most important. However, in 1661 the company acquired the marshy, malarial islands of Bombay (Mumbai) as part of Portuguese princess Catherine of Braganza's dowry on her marriage to Charles II (r. 1660–1685). A great trading city was born under Governor Gerald Aungier (1672–1677). Already, forays north had led to Calcutta's (now Kolkata) founding by Job Charnock in 1690. But it was farther south on the east coast, where the climate was healthier, that English trading really flourished. Francis Day founded Madras (now Chennai) in 1639, well placed for trading cotton. By 1700 its population was 300,000; by 1740 trade with India represented 10 percent of British revenue and much of it passed through Madras.

> **Roe soon sealed the relationship between England and India that would grow into the greatest trading partnership and cultural exchange the world has known.**

East India Company Expands

British initiatives were gradually transformed into political power. Rivalry between the southern states enabled the British and the French to play out their rivalry too, but supporting different sides. The young British soldier (later governor of Bengal) Robert Clive (1725–1774), supporting the Nawab of Arcot, defeated the French under the Marquis de Dupleix in 1751, and British supremacy in the south was confirmed nine years later at the Battle of Wandiwash. In the north, Clive's triumph at Plassey in 1757 was confirmed by Hector Munro's decisive victory at the Battle of Buxar in 1764 against the kings of Delhi and Oudh.

The result was a trade boom throughout eastern India. Madras expanded, Calcutta was established as the headquarters of the East India Company, and from 1774 a string of governors-general, later called viceroys, began with Warren Hastings (1732–1818). European and Indian traders made fortunes from gifts, monopolies, and looting. In the 1780s, with Calcutta's population at 250,000, land revenues and the system of district collectors were fixed, so that, despite famines, the company amassed four million dollars annually.

The company's influence soon expanded across India. From small Benares (Varanasi) kingdom to vast Hyderabad state, the majority of Indian rulers found themselves in debt to the company as a result of trade agreements. There were exceptions. The clever Mysore ruler Haider Ali brought prosperity to the Deccan and wanted, like the British, to benefit from sea trade along their coast. But his son, Tipu Sultan, was finally defeated at Srirangapatnam (1799). In the northwest, the British made a pact with the Sikhs, whose hero king, Ranjit Singh, took Lahore (1799) and established the first Sikh state, which included all of verdant Punjab. The Maratha confederacy, supported by the French and including the Scindias of Gwalior, the Holkars of Indore, and the Gaekwads of Baroda, stretched from Agra down to Karnataka. But their raids on Rajput territories such as Jaipur (1803) and Udaipur (1803) only helped the British win control of major princely states, and during 1816–1818 the British finally defeated the Marathas. In the mountains, the Gurkhas were defeated (1818) and the rulers of potentially threatening Persia and Afghanistan were dissuaded from allying with the French or Russians.

Gujarat Vidyapith, a school founded in Ahmedabad by Gandhi in 1920 to produce *khadi,* **homespun cloth**

The British expanded out of their forts and beyond the open space of the *maidan,* building grand stucco mansions and public buildings, keeping rigidly to classical designs to satisfy their own aspirations and confirm symbolic order and government over their surroundings. Modifications were made for deeper verandas, or to create cross-drafts. New kinds of buildings appeared: churches, cemeteries, cantonments (military stations), bungalows (which originated in Bengal), and social clubs. This westernization was most evident in Calcutta and Madras, which became elegant neoclassical cities. Soon both Indian rulers and merchants were building hybrid houses, mixing Hindu or Muslim traditions with European elements, initiating a new cross-fertilization of styles.

To escape the searing summer sun entirely, the British fled to India's hills. Between 1815 and 1947 the British built more than 80 hill stations. Each was a nostalgic

re-creation of British feudal society, whose informal buildings belied a strict social structure. From 1864 to 1939 the entire government moved from Calcutta to Shimla annually, governing one-fifth of the world's population from a quaint, isolated, hillside town for half the year.

Problems began in the 1830s when, among other calamities, sales of cotton and opium to China and indigo to Europe dropped, British-made cloth put Indian weavers out of jobs, and famines swept the countryside. Despite social reforms implemented by William Bentinck and William Macaulay, India was becoming dissatisfied with company rule. Furthermore, the British modernizing projects of the railroads (1853) and telegraph (1865), and the building of irrigation canals and roads, at first disturbed the conservative basis of Indian society. Small, uncoordinated revolts took place all over India, including grain riots in defiance of revenue payments.

Against this background, the Rebellion of 1857—also known as the Mutiny—is not such a surprise. It was sparked by the Bengal army's irritation at the loss of privileges, the introduction of lower castes, the high local land revenues demanded by the British, and the possible pollution from the pork and beef grease on the new Lee Enfield rifles' cartridges, which the soldiers had to break between their teeth. Starting with the mutiny of the garrison at Meerut on May 10, 1857, uprisings in Delhi, Lucknow, and Kanpur (Cawnpore) spread across Bengal. Although Delhi was retaken in November 1857, the British government was badly shaken. The East India Company was abolished in 1858, and the last Mughal king, Bahadur Shah Zafar II, who had encouraged the rebels, was deposed. From 1858 onward, the British crown, using mainly British law, administered India directly. The Raj had begun.

> **From 1858 onward, the British crown, using mainly British law, administered India directly. The Raj had begun.**

British Imperialism to Indian Independence: 1858–1947

India was now part of the British Empire, with a viceroy as chief executive. Indians were subjects of Queen Victoria. From 1840 to 1914 India was Britain's most important trading partner. In Bombay, the economic boom was further boosted when, during the American Civil War, the Confederacy ports were blocked, temporarily diverting more cotton trade to India. It was during this time that Bombay's Parsee community rose in importance, including the Sassoon, Wadia, Readymoney, Jeejeebhoy, and Tata families, and Bombay acquired the world's grandest set of Victorian Gothic public buildings.

In making Queen Victoria the Empress of India in 1877, Britain saw itself as a grand feudal power controlling the vassals of India. In 1911, King-Emperor George V visited, announcing on December 12 to 562 maharajas that the capital would move from Calcutta to its traditional and strategic site, Delhi, where an entirely new city would be built. Designed by Edwin Lutyens, assisted by Herbert Baker, it reflected the size and power of the British Empire. At the city's inauguration on February 9, 1931, few people recognized the gathering storm clouds that would bring independence to India in just 16 years.

Growing Indian political awareness percolated down to the masses from the intelligentsia, who had benefited from the education opportunities.

The British administrators recognized an awkward link between empire and unequal trade. Their policies to bridge the gap included Indianizing government building styles, promoting English education, building universities and high courts, and including more Indians in government. But only after World War II did the British fully accept that independence was unavoidable and that foreign enterprise could not answer India's problems.

Growing Indian political awareness percolated down to the masses from the intelligentsia, who had benefited from the education opportunities. Agitation began in the 1870s, seeking a national culture and interests. The Indian National Congress party was founded in 1885, and in 1905 British attempts to weaken the unified National Movement were answered by a countryside boycott of British goods. The next year, Muslims who felt that Congress did not represent them formed the All India Muslim League. While Hindus demanded the recognition of the Hindi language written in Devanagari script, Muslims wanted Urdu in Perso-Arabic script.

India's struggle for freedom entered a new phase in 1915, when Mohandas Karamchand Gandhi (1869–1948)—later known as the Mahatma, or Great Soul—returned from South Africa, where he had experienced racial prejudice. He led a moral protest against oppression (the British presence). Known as civil disobedience, it involved defying laws peacefully and taking punishment willingly. In noncooperation, India had a truly national and popular political campaign for the first time, promoted by nationalist leaders including Bal Gangadhar Tilak, Sir Sayyid Ahmad Khan, C. Rajagopalachari, Sardar Vallabhbhai Patel, A. K. Azad, and M. A. Jinnah.

In 1930, Gandhi led the Salt March, which protested the British monopoly on salt production. In the same year Congress, with the young Jawaharlal Nehru as president, adopted the resolution for complete independence for India. The 1935 Government of India Act gave Indians who met stringent educational and property-owning requirements (about 14 percent of the population) the right to vote to elect representatives. Congress swept the polls. Agitation continued, and in 1942 Congress called for the British to "Quit India." Meanwhile, the Muslim League demanded a separate state for Muslims, to be called Pakistan. Back in Britain, Prime Minister Clement Atlee (1883–1967) and the postwar Labour government encouraged independence.

In 1947 independence and partition came simultaneously. On August 14 the last viceroy, Lord Louis Mountbatten, witnessed the creation of Pakistan—in two parts, 1,200 miles (1,931 km) apart, to be called West and East Pakistan. East Pakistan became the independent country of Bangladesh in 1971. At midnight on August 14–15, 1947, in front of the Red Fort in Old Delhi, Mountbatten formally transferred British power to India's first Prime Minister, Pandit Jawaharlal Nehru (1889–1964), and India's saffron, white, and green flag was flown for the first time. Later, the two leaders toasted each other in Viceroy's House, soon to be renamed Rashtrapati Bhavan. Meanwhile, hundreds of thousands of people fled their homelands: Hindus from Pakistan, now a Muslim state, into India; Muslims from what they believed would be a Hindu state, into Pakistan. It is estimated that up to two million people died in communal massacres during this mass cross-migration. Gandhi wept over the violence, the loss of a single India, and the new hatred. On January 30, 1948, he was assassinated by a fundamentalist Hindu.

A Young Nation Steeped in History: 1947–Present

At independence about two-fifths of India, belonged not to the Indian government but to the Indian princes. These states—representing Jat, Rajput, Maratha, Hindu, Sikh, and Muslim people—were scattered across the country and ranged in size from Hyderabad's 82,000 square miles (212,380 sq km) and 14 million population to tiny Kathiawar's less than half a square mile (1 sq km) and 200 inhabitants. But the autocratic rule and preference for traditional lifestyles displayed by most princes were at odds with those building a new, modern country. Gradually, the princes were absorbed into the new states—which loosely followed geographical, cultural, and linguistic boundaries—and the majority of their lands, palaces, villages, personal wealth, titles, and honors were officially removed. The state of Rajasthan was not completely formed until 1956, nor was Andhra Pradesh, which contains much of former Hyderabad. Today, only a handful of the former rulers and their families maintain their feudal customs and they take their consequent responsibilities seriously.

This is just one example of the massive reorganization that faced the government of Asia's new and huge democracy in 1947. For this, the guiding principle was to maintain national unity and integrity against all potential internal and external threats.

India & Pakistan: Separate Ways

Salman Rushdie's Man Booker Prize-winning novel *Midnight's Children* (1981) tells the tale of Indian children born at midnight on August 15, 1947, whose fates are forever twinned with their newly independent homeland.

In reality, many children born into the new India would soon become refugees. The new state was midwifed through the partition of British India along religious lines. An estimated 25 million Hindus, Muslims, and Sikhs have since crossed the borders drawn under the Mountbatten Plan, with Hindus and Sikhs fleeing into India, and Muslims into Pakistan. In 1947 alone, the refugee count was approximately 10 million. The new states were hopelessly unprepared for what quickly became one of the largest migrations in history. Sectarian violence followed, leaving hundreds of thousands dead. A lingering air of mutual suspicion and aggression has poisoned relations between the neighboring states ever since.

The hotly disputed terrain of Kashmir has spawned three wars and multiple incidents: The Indo-Pakistan War of 1971 led to further partition and the creation of the state of Bangladesh. In 1999, the Kargil Conflict sparked new tensions, ratcheted dramatically higher by the rivals' recently acquired nuclear arsenals.

Despite this air of mutual mistrust, India remains home to about 143 million Muslims, while Pakistan is still home to more than three million Hindus and Sikhs.

Multinational signs along National Highway 8 in Gurgaon exemplify India's globalized economy.

Gandhi's leadership was the model; India's people who had struggled for freedom were its motivation. There was a need to balance modernization with India's strong traditions. Thus, political and judicial equality, a secular state, and improved farming methods were matched with tolerance for all religious practices and some religious law, and recognition of the existing social order, including caste. The ancient custom of Indian rulers holding morning and evening audiences with the people was adopted by the democratically elected politicians. At the same time, the new country benefited from some of the practical legacies of British rule—the system of law and administration, the civil service, the railroads, roads and irrigation systems, a nonpolitical army, a free press, and a ready-made capital city. There was also the concept of India as a single country with, most important, a unifying language: English.

On January 26, 1950, the Republic of India was inaugurated and the constitution implemented, an event now celebrated annually with a public holiday and grand parades through Delhi. In the face of major north–south controversies and independence bids from the Punjab, Kashmir, Assam, and other areas, there were two distinct visions of a unified India: Gandhi's decentralized village system and the new leaders' centralized, state-controlled system. The second vision prevailed, modified by the first.

Pandit Jawaharlal Nehru was prime minister from 1947 until his death in 1964, during which time his National Congress Party remained unchallenged. His ideology and ambitions for India were practical and realistic, and they set the tone for the next 50 years. They incorporated a gentle socialism, a secular state (India has no state religion), state-directed economic progress, and nonalignment in foreign affairs.

To these ends, India operated a closed economy until the 1990s, promoting its own industries and products. At the same time, India's high-quality hand loom–weaving and other handicrafts were revived and encouraged, with prestigious national awards and government-run stores to control quality. In food production, India achieved self-sufficiency with some to spare for export. Today, India's principal crops are rice, wheat, other cereals, pulses, oil seeds, cotton, and sugarcane. In foreign affairs, India's sheer size and strategic position have forced it to play a sensitive role with its smaller neighbors; internationally, it has maintained its nonaligned position and keeps a careful balance of friendship with China, Russia, and the West.

Nehru can be seen as the head of what has been virtually a dynastic rule over independent India, albeit a democratically elected one. Indira Gandhi, his daughter and no relation to the Mahatma, was prime minister for 15 years, 1966–1977 and 1980–1984. She governed in a highly personalized and centralized way, which became dictatorial during the Emergency (1975–1977); yet, after a spell out of office, she was reelected. On her assassination, her son, Rajiv, was reluctantly hurled into the job and began to open up India economically before he, too, was assassinated by a suicide bomber in 1991. His widow, Sonia—head of the Congress Party since 1998—and his children, Rahul and Priyanka, are all now on the political scene.

Recent prime ministers, from Narasimha Rao (1991 1996) to Dr. Manmohan Singh (2004–), have encouraged India's modernization and the increased determination by individual states to choose their own destinies. This drive for self-improvement is especially true of the southern states (Maharashtra, Karnataka, Andhra Pradesh, Tamil Nadu, and Kerala), where progress and prosperity are evident in the cities and villages, in manufacturing and transportation, in education and health.

India's Place in the Global Economy

It was Rajiv Gandhi who in the mid-1980s had the vision of technology-driven India leapfrogging into the 21st century. Real changes soon followed. In the 1990s, India's closed economy opened to the world, most famously in information technology software and services. India's IT services account for 40 percent of its GDP and 30 percent of expat earnings. Expanding at an annual rate of 30 percent, the revenues of India's IT services combined with its business process outsourcing was estimated at an aggregated $100 billion in 2012. India is now the world leader in outsourcing; it has the world's fastest cell phone growth; and the benefits now reach into rural areas.

> In the 1990s, India's closed economy opened to the world, most famously in information technology software and services.

India's rapid growth has touched almost every village. Farmers check market prices using cell phones; the Internet reaches into the countryside; there are more than 50 TV news channels; and the micro-loan system enables bicycles to be exchanged for motorbikes. Goldman Sachs has predicted India's economy will be greater than the United States' by 2020. Yet clean water, basic sewerage, food distribution, and basic health and education remain deplorably unresolved.

With this intense but patchy advancement, India now stands at a fork in the road. Recent governments of the world's most populous democracy seem to be ambivalent about choosing between the path of measured advancement that concurrently addresses the fundamental problems of the masses, and the path that surges forward to benefit the few until the bubble bursts. ■

Land & Landscape

India is the world's seventh largest country. It stretches from 8° to 36° north latitude and from 68° to 97° east longitude. A landscape of rivers, fields, forests, mountains, and deserts, India is diamond-shaped. To the north, it is cut off from the rest of Asia by the Himalaya. To the south, a 2,000-mile (3,218 km) coastline is washed by the Arabian Sea, the Indian Ocean, and the Bay of Bengal.

These mountains and seas separate India from surrounding countries. Pakistan and Bangladesh, which shared India's history until 1947, are the exceptions. Historically, the mountains have been a natural defense, and only the most determined

Barren, beautiful Ladakh is believed to have been inhabited first by herdsmen from Tibet.

invaders penetrated them. The coast, on the other hand, benefited from the east–west sea trade routes and is dotted with ancient trading posts, especially on the Konkani, Malabar, and Coromandel stretches.

Modern India occupies a strategic position in Asia, looking westward to the Middle East and eastward to Malaysia, Indonesia, and China. Its borders meet, from west to east, Pakistan, Afghanistan, China's Sinkiang Province, Tibet, Nepal, Bhutan, Myanmar (Burma), and Bangladesh. The long strip of the Andaman and Nicobar Islands in the Bay of Bengal and the Lakshadweep Islands in the Arabian Sea are part of the Republic of India.

Mountains

India claims part of the great Himalayan range, the world's highest mountain system and one of its youngest, created when the drifting Indian plate collided with the Tibetan plate of south Asia about 50 million years ago. Mountains, including Everest and 95 other peaks rising above 24,600 feet (7,500 m), were formed well after that, by movement of the continental plates. Today much of India's forest, which covers 20 percent of the land, is in this region.

India's lesser ranges include the Aravallis, one of the world's oldest mountain systems, in southern Rajasthan, west of which lies the Thar Desert. Here lies some of India's mineral wealth—copper ore, lead-zinc complexes, and rock phosphate. The Vindhya and Satpura Mountains, a barrier to invaders' southern progress, cross central India. They rise to the Deccan and Mysore Plateaus, from which the Sahyadris (Western Ghats) drop sharply to the west coast and the gentler Eastern Ghats to the east coast. Iron ore mined here makes India the world's largest producer of that metal. Gold and diamonds are mined farther south, and rubies and other gems are mined in Kerala.

All of India's mountains help gather the country's precious waters from its two monsoons. The great southwest monsoon begins in Kerala in June and sweeps up north across India through July, August, and September, dumping its final gallons in the Himalayan mountains. The smaller southeast monsoon drenches the east coast intermittently in October and November, enabling Tamil Nadu farmers to harvest three rice crops annually, but sometimes bringing cyclones and destruction, as in Bangladesh and west Bengal in 2009. After this, the weather is at its best throughout most of India until April, when the heat arrives and the mountains become cool retreats.

> **All of India's mountains help gather the country's precious waters from its two monsoons.**

EXPERIENCE: Hooking a *Mahseer*

India's abundant rivers provide anglers with ample options for days of relaxing fishing and solitude in splendid scenery.

Most anglers dream of hooking a wild *mahseer* (carp). Your chances are good in Uttarakhand's remote Garhwal and Kumaun Hills, with their spectacular mountain valleys and fast-flowing rivers; if the mahseer eludes your hook, *goonch* (catfish) is a good catch. In Arunachal Pradesh state (which requires a special tourist permit), make Pasighat your base for mahseer fishing and, in the colder waters, angling for golden and rainbow trout. Alternatively, head south to the Cauvery River, which flows through Nagarhole, Bandipur, and Mudumalai National Parks in Karnataka state (see pp. 228–232)—there is a fishing camp at Bheemeshwari.

For general angling in the Uttarakhand hills, consider the Nayar River at Vyas Ghat, the Sarju at Pancheshwar, and the Sarju and Eastern Ramganga. In Assam, the Jia Bhoroli, a tributary of the Brahmaputra, can be a delight. There is a seasonal fishing camp at Potasah, near Tezpur.

In Himachal Pradesh, the rivers of the Pabbar Valley are rich in brown and rainbow trout—good sites include Chirgaon, Seema, Mandil, Sandasu, Tikri, and Dhamvari. The tributaries of the Beas River, which runs through the beautiful Kullu Valley, have good spots, too.

Visit *travel-himalayas.com, otterreserves.com*, and *himalyanoutback.com* to find a variety of fishing trips and information. Bring your own fishing equipment: It can be hard to find quality gear in India.

Rivers

Rivers originating from these mountain watersheds nourish India's soil. From the Himalayan mountains you can trace the path of the great Indus, the Ganga (Ganges), and, in the east, the Brahmaputra. The Indus waters the Punjab, India's wheat bowl. The Ganga, Hindus' holiest river, rises near the Gangotri Glacier, and, with its tributaries, flows through the heartland of rice-growing ancient India to the Bay of Bengal, creating India's largest river basin, which covers 25 percent of the country.

Most of the great rivers of the peninsula meander through flat valleys to the Bay of Bengal. The Brahmani and Mahanadi irrigate Orissa; the Godavari and Krishna flow off the Deccan Plateau, and the Penner and the Kaveri (Cauvery) flow from the Mysore Plateau. The great Kaveri benefits from two monsoons and is southern India's holiest river, but siphoning off its waters for irrigation is a contentious issue between Karnataka and Tamil Nadu states. The Narmada—with its controversial dam—and Tapti Rivers flow down from the Vindhya and Satpura ranges to the Arabian Sea.

Natural Disasters

The rhythm of life can, however, go wrong. India, surrounded by warm oceans, straddles the Tropic of Cancer and is at one of Earth's major plate junctions. This means that periodically it suffers from violent natural events that may leave disaster in their wake. Tropical cyclones are frequent in the Bay of Bengal, while the relative youth of the region's geology generates earthquakes, such as the 2004 Indian Ocean quake that caused a tsunami, and the Himalayan earthquake of 2005.

The country's monsoons are relied upon to provide water for growing crops. Heavy monsoons, however, can bring floods and a high death toll. These floods have been exacerbated by industrial and agricultural deforestation. It is a fine balance between having plenty of water to flood the rice fields and having too much so that crops, homes, and even lives are lost. The alternative to the floods may be famines. However, India's infrastructure can now deal successfully with these: When the monsoon fails in one area, the army is able to move supplies to the drought-stricken area. As a result of this organization, few lives were lost in the Maharashtra famines of 1965–1966 and 1974–1975, while more than two million people died in the Bengal famine of 1943. ∎

A young Kashmiri boy collects grass from a lake bed, for use as a crop fertilizer.

Food & Drink

Climate, geography, religion, and tradition have shaped the many cuisines of India. There is a huge variety of foods to eat, from the simple to the extravagantly rich. Even the staple southern Indian meal of rice and *dhal* (pulse—peas, beans, and lentils) varies subtly from town to town; indeed, so many kinds of pulse are grown in India that the financial papers give the pulses stock exchange prices a special section of their own.

Dried chilies, powdered turmeric, and other aromatic products for sale in Old Delhi's spice market

Curry

India is traditionally associated with spicy food such as curries. The word "curry" itself has confusing connotations. For many it implies a highly spiced and rich meat casserole that may be difficult to digest. In fact, the word comes from Tamil, a southern Indian language: *Kari* simply means "to eat by biting." But for centuries it has referred to a savory sauce of meat, fish, fruit, or vegetables cooked with a *masala,* a blend of locally available bruised or ground spices. This was traditionally added to the rather bland staple food of grain, either flour, baked into unleavened bread (in the north), or boiled rice (in the east and south). Thus, karis gave interest and variety—one fifth-century text describes the hero taking "rice dressed in butter, with its full accompaniment of curries." Today, India's array of curries fulfills the same function.

Cuisine Crossroads

India's sheer size and diversity mean that most foods are produced somewhere in the country. To visit the vast wholesale market outside Delhi is to be at the crossroads of a countrywide food-trading network. Here you see up to 20 kinds of bananas from the south, oranges from the Lower Himalaya, rice from Bengal and Tamil Nadu, and sackfuls of spices.

In the north, try the breads—naan, chappati, roti, *paratha*, and the paper-thin *romali roti* (handkerchief bread). They go well with mildly spiced lamb or chicken barbecued on skewers in a tandoor (clay oven). In Rajasthan the food is quite gentle, but watch out for the chili peppers. Meat, dhal, and *sabzi* (vegetables) are scooped up with pieces of nutty-textured breads made from maize, millet, or gram. A spoonful of spice-hot *brinjal* (eggplant) or *nimbu* (lime) pickle completes the meal.

In contrast, the dishes inspired by the Islamic courts of Agra, Delhi, Lucknow, and Hyderabad are rich and complicated. Meat is cooked slowly with cream, almonds, and dried fruits until it is very soft. Vegetables are just as rich, be they okra, *saag* (spinach), *mattar* (peas), or *aloo* (potato).

Even the essential dhal has added cream, and breads are sometimes stuffed. So it is essential to have plenty of rice to balance the meal—and to wait until your body is acclimatized before enjoying this kind of feast. Should you wish for some wine, India now has vineyards on the Deccan Plateau. Or, do as the Indians do: Stick to the light local beers and bottled water.

Along the coast, you can relax in the shade over grilled giant shrimp or a pomfret fish cooked with plenty of coconut, which helps to balance the fire-hot spices. As the sun sets in Goa, you might like a glass of *feni*—or a fruit juice, such as mango, papaya, or watermelon. Other thirst-quenching drinks found all over India are *lassi* (thin yogurt drink) and fresh lime juice with either sparkling or still water. The ubiquitous chai (tea) is drunk strong with milk and sugar, a delicious, reviving drink.

Vegetables

Vegetables are popular countrywide, but it is in the mostly vegetarian south that they are the star. The best way to sample the variety is to order a *thali* (platter). This plate has six or more *katoris* (little dishes) around the edge, each containing a different vegetable or pulse. There will also be *dahi* (yogurt), chutney, and *mithai* (sweet pudding). Start with the *rasam* (clear soup) and work round, mixing boiled rice from the center into each dish. A thali is utterly delicious, healthy, and always a little bit different to the last one.

EXPERIENCE: Cooking—Demystifying the Spices

An integral part of any visit to India is sampling the cuisines of the different areas—Persian-influenced Mughal food in Agra, sweet vegetarian dishes in Ahmedabad, Indo-Portuguese fusions in Goa, rice-flour *dosas* in Tamil Nadu. But how to cook them yourself when you get home? Some hotels run short pre-dinner demonstrations, making a few dishes and then supplying the recipes; the **Casino Group** (*casinogroupkerala.com*) does this well. Others invite guests into the kitchens, such as **Chhatra Sagar** (*chhatrasagar.com*) in Rajasthan and other family-run hotels. Just ask; soon you will be going to the market, chopping onions, and even helping prepare the housewife's pride, raw mango pickle.

Land of Many Faiths

Religion is a vital element in today's India, and it is integral to its history, arts, and monuments. Hinduism is practiced by the majority of Indians. Out of it were born Buddhism, Jainism, and Sikhism. Indians also observe outside faiths, giving each a regional distinctiveness; modern movements, including hedonistic ashrams; and nature worship and other ancient practices.

These faiths generally thrive peacefully side by side. A typical fishing village has room for a temple, mosque, and church. Travelers pausing to observe the rituals in urban and rural places of worship, or to talk to local people about their faith, are almost always welcome provided customs such as removing shoes are observed.

Faiths that Evolved in India

Hinduism: Some 820 million people in India are Hindu—about 82 percent. Yet for all its popularity Hinduism is an elusive religion, and difficult for non-Hindus to understand. Hinduism has no single sacred text, no dogma, no single prophet, and it demands no formal congregational worship. Nor are the faithful obliged to go to the temple, tackle its abstract philosophy, follow specific rituals, or know its sacred language, Sanskrit. Ideas of rebirth and a plethora of deities add to the confusion.

The beginnings of worship on the subcontinent predate the Indus Valley Civilization and suggest a reverence for natural elements. These were given definition by the pastoral Aryans (see p. 25) who worshipped the sun as "Surya," and introduced ideas of a distinct religion that included precise rituals, sacrifice, and priests (brahmans) to mediate between the people and their gods. These ideas were set out in the four Vedic texts, composed in early Sanskrit, sung by heart, and passed down through generations orally; writing seems to have begun only about 500 B.C.

> **Hinduism has no single sacred text, no dogma, no single prophet, and it demands no formal congregational worship.**

Later texts such as the *Upanishads* (philosophical treatises on the soul) and the *Brahmanas* (on ritual) reflect important new ideas: spiritual karma and increased temporal brahman power. Karma may be understood to be the power of each person's good or bad thoughts and actions to affect the spirit's movement across generations. The spirit thus endures a series of rebirths with varying degrees of suffering and desire, as the soul progresses or regresses in response to past deeds. The soul makes its final escape either through nirvana, when personal identity is extinguished, or through *moksha,* the final release from the cycle of rebirth. Meanwhile, as these ideas became more abstract, ritual more convoluted, and Sanskrit more refined and unintelligible, so brahman power increased. Ordinary people felt excluded and were attracted to new, back-to-basics religions; of these, Buddhism (see pp. 59–60) and Jainism (see p. 60) were the longest lasting and won merchant and royal patronage.

A Hindu sadhu (holy man) who follows Shiva performs *puja* (worship) at Varanasi.

Children sell flowers and tiny oil lamps for pilgrims to float as tributes on the Ganga at Varanasi.

During and after the classical Gupta period (see pp. 30–31) local spirits, gods, and heroes were absorbed into the central pantheon of gods. Gradually, Hindus began to focus their worship on one of these, with a passionate devotion known as bhakti. This encouraged elaborate ritual and the final, very long forms of the great epics (see p. 20): the *Ramayana* and the *Mahabharata.* This last includes the *Bhagavad Gita,* a discussion between Krishna and Arjuna on the essence of Hindu philosophy: the theory of karma and the human struggle for love, light, and redemption.

Over the centuries, Hindu philosophy, ritual, and myth have permeated almost every aspect of the believer's life. Hindus live, for the most part, in the grip of the caste system (see p. 25), even if modern social and business life seems to deny this. Marriage is usually arranged within the same caste, and dowries require ever spiraling debt as motorcycles and freezers are added to silks and jewelry.

Pilgrimages are the most popular form of Indian tourism, often undertaken in busloads, with much singing and souvenir shopping. The destination may be one of the Seven Sacred Cities or the temple of the believers' chosen deity. This deity is likely to be one form, or aspect, of what may be seen as the extended family of Hindu gods, whose presiding trinity are Brahma (the Creator), Shiva (the Energy, the Destroyer), and Vishnu (the Preserver). The faithful may do *puja* (worship) to this chosen deity in a corner at home or at the local temple, whose plan follows the ancient *shastras* (treatises). The priest, who receives the worshipper's offering, holds his position by inheritance and ensures the temple receives a steady flow of donations.

For all its vagueness in definition, Hinduism provides a clear pattern for life. There are four stages: childhood and learning, marriage and rearing a family, celibacy and meditation, and finally a renunciation of all worldly possessions in the hope of achieving nirvana or moksha. Throughout, the Hindu has four supreme aims: dharma (virtue, living the right way), *artha* (wealth achieved in the right way), karma (giving and receiving love and friendship), and, if these three are correctly followed, moksha.

Buddhism: India has just eight million Buddhists, yet this is the birthplace of Buddha (Awakened One). The conventional dates for Buddha's life are 563–483 B.C., but recent research suggests about 450–350 B.C. or even later. A prince of the *kshatriya* caste (see p. 25), Buddha lived at Lumbini, now in Nepal. At the age of about 30, he questioned the point of Hindu austerity and asceticism, renounced his privileged life, and left home. Five years later Buddha attained *bodhi* (enlightenment) after meditating under a pipal (bodhi) tree at Bodh Gaya.

Offering insight rather than divine revelation, Buddha began his lifelong missionary work with his "Setting in Motion the Wheel of Righteousness" sermon preached at Sarnath. It presented life's overwhelming problem—desire—and its solution, The Middle Path (moderation) and dharma (faith as seen in the true nature of the world, human nature, and spiritual attainment). These, with *sangha* (monasticism for men and women), could lead to the goal, nirvana.

Reacting to Hinduism's inaccessibility, Buddha preached a rational, simple philosophy in the vernacular. His dogma was popular, especially among the merchants who, together with rulers from Ashoka Maurya to the Guptas, patronized India's first substantial stone

India's Benign Trees

Trees in India are revered—they give shade, they produce medicines, and they provide housing and firewood. And in this land redolent with myth they are sometimes the abodes of gods, ancient animist beliefs absorbed into India's religions. A seal dating from the Indus Valley Civilization depicts a horned goddess in a pipal tree. Today you can see images of gods and sacred animals such as snakes carved into trees or propped up against revered ones: Locals come to worship a complete *navratra* (the nine forms of Devi) outside Chennai's fort.

Revered since Vedic times, the pipal, with its distinctive elegant glossy leaves that taper at the tip, is sacred to Buddhists because Prince Siddhartha attained enlightenment while sitting beneath it, becoming the Buddha. And Hindus consider it a manifestation of Vishnu, who was born under a pipal; Brahmin Hindus believe the pipal is a Brahmin and may wrap the sacred triple cord around it.

Other easy-to-recognize trees include the barna with its pale yellow spring flowers, which Muslims often plant near tombs; the spreading, shade-giving banyan with its lateral roots; and the neem with its rows of useful, mildly antiseptic elongated leaves with serrated edges. The gulmohur has lacelike leaves and fire red blooms, the hardwood teak has big coarse leaves, and the umbrella-shaped rain tree of South India is coated with pink blossoms. Tamarind trees, often found lining roads in South India, provide hard insect-resistant wood and Kerala cuisine's most essential ingredient, the fruit pulp that is used as a souring agent.

buildings (stupas) and sculpture, mostly sited along trade routes. Followers formed monasteries (sanghas), some with adjoining universities such as at Nalanda.

After Buddha's death, the sanghas continued his teachings. Then came the schism. The Hinayana (Lesser Vehicle) sect saw Buddha as the Great Master and spread his ideas to Ceylon, Burma, and Siam. The Mahayana (Great Vehicle) sect considered Buddha to be God and spread his ideas to China, Japan, Tibet, and Mongolia. Buddhism was India's dominant religion for several centuries, but lost out to reformed Hinduism in the seventh century. Thereafter it continued on a long decline.

Today, India has a growing group of neo-Buddhists, mostly farmers from Maharashtra inspired by the Buddhist convert Dr. Bhim Rao Ambedkar. Dharamsala is home to the Dalai Lama, the head of Tibetan Buddhism and leader of the exiled Tibetan people.

Buddhism was India's dominant religion for several centuries, but lost out to reformed Hinduism in the seventh century.

Jainism: India's four million Jains tend to live in the west, near their sacred hills, to which regular pilgrimage is required. Their founder, Mahavira (Great Hero), is thought to have lived in the sixth century B.C. A religious reformer, like Buddha, he left his birthplace, Patna, to live as a naked ascetic until he achieved spiritual knowledge. He became a *jina* (conqueror), and his followers were known as Jains.

Mahavira taught his followers that the universe is infinite, not created, and that *jivas* (souls) are present in everything. Hence, Jains believe in *ahimsa* (reverence for all life), which demands strict vegetarianism. Adherence to ahimsa, together with the practice of a strict code of behavior can lead to moksha—like Hindus and Buddhists, Jains believe in both reincarnation and salvation. They also reject sacrifice and oppose the caste system, but they do permit *sallekhana* (death by fasting and meditation).

There are two Jain sects. The rigorous "sky-clad" sect, or Digambaras, have no possessions and believe that only men are able to achieve moksha. The white-clad sect, Shvetambaras, are less strict. In today's India Jains are mostly Shvetambaras, who are often commercially successful and may be substantial donors to hospitals, schools, and libraries.

Sikhism: Most of India's 20 million Sikhs live in the Punjab and Delhi area and are distinguished by their smoothly wrapped turbans. Sikhs follow a philosophy founded by Guru Nanak (1469–1539), who was born near Lahore in today's Pakistan. One of several Hindu Sants (poet-philosophers) who introduced Islamic elements into Hinduism, he advocated a single God who is *sat* (truth) and reveals himself through his gurus (teachers). He promoted meditation and equality and he opposed caste, ritual, superstition, astrology, and sex discrimination.

Nine more gurus consolidated Nanak's teachings. The tenth, Gobind Singh (1666–1708), formalized the new religion in 1699. He began the *gurpurb* (baptism) ceremony, which removed Hindu caste names, and he insisted men adopt the five *kakars: kesh* (uncut hair), *kangha* (comb), *kachha* (shorts), *kara* (steel bracelet), and *kirpan* (sword). He also encouraged military prowess, forbade tobacco smoking, and declared that henceforth guruship would rest in the *Guru Granth Sahib* (Sikhs' sacred texts). The most revered copy is kept in the *gurudwara* (temple) at Amritsar.

Faiths Brought to India

Islam: India's 120 million Muslims form the country's second largest religious community and the world's second largest Muslim community, after Indonesia's. The Prophet Muhammad (ca 570–632) preached Islam (submission to God): one God and one community whose jihad (sacred duty) is to spread the word of Allah, if necessary by war. He proclaimed Mecca to be Islam's pilgrimage center and Ka'ba (a cube-shaped building housing a stone believed to have been given by Gabriel to Abraham) its most sacred shrine. Just 80 years later, Islam reached India, the first of many Islamic incursions that would end with that of the Mughals.

An early doctrinal split over the Prophet's successor created two sects, Sunni and Shia. Most Indian Muslims are Sunni. Many also follow the Sufi path, a mystical thread in Islamic thought that arose in the tenth century in opposition to the militaristic and orthodox mainstream, and whose spiritualism, asceticism, and indulgence of festivals and singing suited Hindu converts.

Muslims believe fatalistically in total surrender to the will of Allah (God) and in equality in life and death—reasons for Islam's early popularity with lower social

Hari Mandir—the Sikhs' most holy *gurudwara*, temple—rises from the Amrit Sarovar at Amritsar.

groups. The Koran, Islam's sacred book, records the Prophet's revelations, much of it similar to the Old Testament. A Muslim has five duties: belief in one God with Muhammad as his Prophet; showing humility by praying five times daily; fasting from dawn to dusk during Ramadan, the month Muhammad received his revelation; doing charitable work; and going on hajj (pilgrimage) to Mecca at least once. To avoid idolatry, no images of Allah are permitted, so *masjids* (places of prostration, mosques) have no figural decoration.

Christianity: India's 25 million Christians belong to a variety of denominations introduced down the centuries. The Syrian Christians of Kerala, still a powerful force locally, trace their conversion to St. Thomas the Apostle, who landed at Kodungallur (Cranganore) in A.D. 52 and later died at Chennai (Madras).

The Portuguese traders of the 16th century brought Roman Catholicism to India, in particular to the western region of Goa. Locals underwent mass conversion and, from 1542, received the zeal of St. Francis Xavier (see sidebar p. 191), whose Jesuits brought the first printing press to India. Conversion from Hinduism, although often nominal, brought with it the attractive promises of one life and equality in death.

By the 18th century India had congregations of most denominations, from Anglicans and Methodists to Baptists, and these still thrive today.

Judaism: Jewish people have played a significant role in India's past. Refugees possibly arrived in Kerala after the fall of Jerusalem in 587 B.C. Jewish and Arab traders later carried shiploads of spices and luxury goods from India's western ports to the Roman Empire. A Jewish community lived for centuries at Cranganore (Kodungallur), then Cochin, where three synagogues still stand, although only one is used. "White Jews," who did not intermarry with locals, enjoyed high status; "Black Jews," who did, had less status.

During the British period, Jews arrived from Baghdad and were important bankers, businessmen, and philanthropists such as the Sassoons of Bombay. Most of India's Jews have emigrated to Israel; fewer than 5,000, mostly elderly people, remain.

> The Portuguese traders of the 16th century brought Roman Catholicism to India, in particular to the western region of Goa.

Zoroastrianism: India's Zoroastrians are better known as Parsees, an elite community that played a key role in building up Bombay (Mumbai).

Zoroastrianism was founded in Iran by the Persian philosopher Zarathustra (Golden Light) sometime between 6000 B.C. and 1500 B.C. Its dual philosophy focuses on the opposing powers of good and evil—the good found in the sacred elements (earth, water, sky, and fire), animals, and plants; the bad in decaying and dead matter. Bodies of the dead are left for the flesh to be eaten by vultures and the bones to be cleansed by the sun and wind, rather than allowed to pollute sacred fire or earth.

Fleeing the Arab Islamic conquests, some Parsees arrived in Gujarat in A.D. 936. Later, in 19th-century Bombay, they shared in the phenomenal business and trading success of the British, whose lifestyles they mimicked. ■

A sprawling metropolis replete with ancient monuments that testify to the attraction of this site for Hindu, Muslim, and British rulers

Delhi

Raj Ghat marks the spot where Mahatma Gandhi was cremated.

Delhi

The city of Delhi is the political nerve center of all India and the largest commercial hub in northern India. Most of its 16 million-plus inhabitants live in the sprawling 580 square miles (1,500 sq km) that surround the historic seven successive cities. Delhi is its own political unit, whose administration has to cope with an alarming recent growth rate and a dry climate with intensely hot summers and cold winters.

If you had the time, you'd find more than a thousand historic buildings in Delhi, down backstreets, in people's backyards, on golf courses. The flat river plain enabled successive conquerors simply to abandon one city and build a fresh one. In theory all monuments are protected, but most are left to take their chances amid Delhi's burden of humanity.

By studying the map opposite you can trace an instant history of Delhi. Begin in the south, at Lal Kot, where tantalizing remains of the Tomar and Chauhan Rajputs' 11th- and 12th-century temples were used by Delhi's first Muslim conqueror, Qutb-ud-din-Aibak, to build his great mosque, begun in 1193. Here, too, is the Qutab Minar, Delhi's landmark tower. Scant remains of Siri, Delhi's second major city, lie to the north.

Next come the three Tughlaq cities. Tughlaqabad's rarely visited fort is 5 miles (8 km) east of Lal Kot, while the remains of Sultan Muhammad's never completed Jahapanah are near Siri. The citadel of the last and grandest of the Tughlaq cities, Feroz Shah Kotla, stands east of Connaught Place and once overlooked the Yamuna, Delhi's almost forgotten river, which flows down to Agra and joins the Ganga above Varanasi.

Delhi's sixth city, Purana Qila (the Old Fort) and its environs, was founded by the Mughal emperor Humayun in 1533 and enlarged by his usurper Sher Shah Suri; today it is the focus of New Delhi's processional route, Raj Path. Farther upstream, Humayun's great-grandson Shah Jahan entered his vibrant Shahjahanabad (Old Delhi) in 1648.

Finally, after Delhi had languished as a backwater for a century or so, the British moved their headquarters here from Calcutta. On February 9, 1931, the British viceroy inaugurated New Delhi, designed by Sir Edwin Lutyens and Herbert Baker to allow for infinite expansion and to encompass all previous Delhi remains without destruction.

Delhi has spilled into neighboring Haiyana state for its newest city, Gurgaon—now one of north India's major service industry and manufacturing centers. Crossing Delhi takes time. Traffic congestion during the rush hours and at midday slows down all movement. You might want to cut through it by subway. ∎

NOT TO BE MISSED:

A rickshaw ride through Old Delhi's Kinari Bazar **69**

The Sufi village of Nizamuddin, Delhi's oldest living area **70–71**

Humayun's restored garden tomb, precursor to the Taj Mahal **71**

Mahatma Gandhi's tranquil garden memorial **74–75**

Riding the Metro **77**

Early morning walking, jogging, or yoga in Lodi Gardens **78–79**

Walking up Raisina Hill to Rashtrapati Bhavan at sunset **84**

Indira Gandhi's museum home **85**

Contemporary art at the Devi Art Foundation **88**

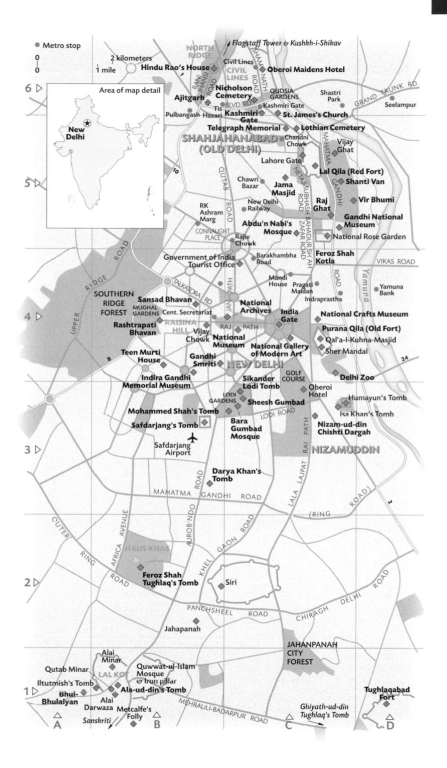

- Metro stop

2 kilometers

1 mile

Area of map detail

New
Delhi

Flagstaff Tower & Kushkh-i-Shikav

NORTH
RIDGE

Civil Lines

Hindu Rao's House

CIVIL
LINES

Oberoi Maidens Hotel

**Nicholson
Cemetery**

QUDSIA
GARDENS

Shastri
Park

Ajitgarh

GRAND TRUNK RD.

Tis
Hazari

Kashmiri Gate

Seelampur

Pulbangash

**Kashmiri
Gate**

St. James's Church

Telegraph Memorial

Lothian Cemetery

**SHAHJAHANABAD
(OLD DELHI)**

Chandni
Chowk

Vijay
Ghat

Lahore Gate

Lal Qila (Red Fort)

Chawri
Bazar

**Jama
Masjid**

Shanti Van

New
Delhi
Railway

**Raj
Ghat**

Vir Bhumi

RK
Ashram
Marg

**Abdu'n Nabi's
Mosque**

**Gandhi National
Museum**

CONNAUGHT
PLACE

Rajiv
Chowk

National Rose Garden

**Government of India
Tourist Office**

Barakhambha
Road

**Feroz Shah
Kotla**

VIKAS ROAD

Mandi
House

Pragati
Maidan

Yamuna
Bank

TALKATORA RD.

Indraprastha

**SOUTHERN
RIDGE
FOREST**

MUGHAL
GARDENS

Sansad Bhavan

Cent. Secretariat

**National
Archives**

**India
Gate**

National Crafts Museum

**Rashtrapati
Bhavan**

RAISINA
HILL

Vijay
Chowk

**National
Museum**

Purana Qila (Old Fort)

Qal'a-I-Kuhna-Masjid

**Teen Murti
House**

**Gandhi
Smriti**

**National Gallery
of Modern Art**

Sher Mandal

NEW DELHI

**Indira Gandhi
Memorial Museum**

**Sikander
Lodi Tomb**

GOLF
COURSE

Delhi Zoo

LODI
GARDENS

Oberoi
Hotel

Humayun's Tomb

Mohammed Shah's Tomb

Sheesh Gumbad

Safdarjang's Tomb

**Bara
Gumbad
Mosque**

Isa Khan's Tomb

**Nizam-ud-din
Chishti Dargah**

**Safdarjang
Airport**

NIZAMUDDIN

**Darya Khan's
Tomb**

MAHATMA

GANDHI ROAD

(RING

HAUS KHAS

**Feroz Shah
Tughlaq's Tomb**

Siri

PANCHSHEEL

ROAD

CHIRAGH

DELHI

Jahapanah

**JAHANPANAH
CITY
FOREST**

Alai
Minar

Qutab Minar

**Quwwat-ul-Islam
Mosque
& Iron pillar**

Iltutmish's Tomb

LAL KOT

Ala-ud-din's Tomb

**Bhul-
Bhulaiyan**

Alai
Darwaza

Metcalfe's
Folly

**Tughlaqabad
Fort**

Sanskriti

MEHRAULI-BADARPUR ROAD

*Ghiyath-ud-din
Tughlaq's Tomb*

A   B   C   D

6

5

4

3

2

1

Shahjahanabad

Wandering through the back lanes of bustling Old Delhi, it is easy to imagine the great Muslim city built by the powerful Mughal emperor Shah Jahan to be the new capital of his secure, vast, and extremely wealthy empire. The lifeless, languishing Lal Qila, or Red Fort, once its centerpiece, is less convincing.

Jama Masjid, completed in 1659, is the most important mosque for India's 120 million Muslims.

Shahjahanabad
🅰 65 C5
Visitor Information
✉ India Tourist
Office,
88 Janpath,
New Delhi
☎ 011/332-0005
delhitourism.nic.in

In 1638, Shah Jahan's fort at Agra, in need of maintenance and unsuitable for the now extensive court ritual, was spilling over with courtiers. The court was no longer itinerant and it needed more space. So with the Taj Mahal (see pp. 98–101) well under way, the now more orthodox widower was drawn back to Delhi. This was the traditional power base in northern India; it was also the burial place of Shaikh Nizam-uddin Auliya (see

pp. 70–71), a Sufi saint revered by the Mughals. Shah Jahan intended to associate himself with previous rulers and holy men, while totally outshining them with his new city, Shahjahanabad. If the Taj Mahal was to be one symbol of imperial Mughal power, this specially built city was to be another, more impressive one.

To enjoy Shah Jahan's masterpiece, it is best first to visit the old city and its impressive mosque opposite the fort, the

Jama Masjid (see pp. 68–69). This is India's largest mosque and was finished in 1656. You can see thousands of Muslims offering prayers there today, just as they did in Shah Jahan's time. Nearby are stores and restaurants, good for souvenirs and exotic food.

Lal Qila

Using his administrative skills, wealth, aesthetic sense, and knowledge of architecture, Shah Jahan laid out a new fort, Lal Qila, or Red Fort, to suit his needs. Its Lahore Gate opened into the main street of a carefully planned adjoining city that thrives almost unchanged four centuries later, and which contains the Jama Masjid.

The site was north of previous cities and beside the Yamuna River, which has since changed its course. In 1639 the foundation stone was laid for the great sandstone walls. Fort and city were divided only after the British created an open space that is now a roaring highway.

The fort's great bastion is an addition by Emperor Aurangzeb. Here, Jawaharlal Nehru addressed the people on India's independence day—August 15, 1947—and here the Indian flag was first raised.

Shah Jahan's building begins with **Chatta Chowk,** a covered market that still thrives today and has some interesting art stores at one end. Beyond it, you must use your imagination, as the British destroyed most of the buildings in 1858 (see p. 72).

The **Naqqar-khana** ("royal drum house") stands straight

ahead, where musicians heralded important arrivals through this official entrance into the **Diwan-i-Am** ("public audience hall"). The emperor would sit on the magnificent inlaid marble throne for the crowded daily *durbar* (audience), an event consisting of music, displays of gifts, dancing, news from the empire, and the meting out of justice.

Only the most favored reached the inner palaces, beyond high-walled courtyards and gardens that are today just empty lawns. Start at the right end with **Mumtaz Mahal** (Mumtaz Palace), now the fort's museum. Next comes **Rang Mahal,** the queens' palace, where the cooling Nahar-I-Bahisht (Stream of Paradise) flowing

INSIDER TIP:

In India, local or regional political events can stall a whole city. They are usually announced beforehand in the news-papers or on television.

—ADITI SENSHARMA
National Geographic contributor

through the palaces broadened out into a marble pool. **Khas Mahal** ("private palace") follows: Its modest rooms were where Shah Jahan slept, worshipped, ate, and at sunrise appeared to his people on the balcony.

The **Diwan-i-Khas** ("private audience hall") was where favored diplomats and merchants were called before the emperor. ∎

Jama Masjid

- 65 C5
- ⊠ Off Netaji Subhash Rd.
- ⏰ Closed to non-Muslims during prayer

Lal Qila
- 65 C5
- ⊠ Chandni Chowk
- ⏰ Closed Mon.; son-et-lumière times vary.

A Rickshaw Ride Around Old Delhi

The best days to enjoy the fun of a rickshaw ride are Monday to Thursday; Jama Masjid (the mosque) is very crowded on Friday. Agree on a price before you start, pay only on completion, and add a tip if appropriate. The driver will wait while you make visits.

A bicycle rickshaw ferries a passenger to his destination in Old Delhi.

Leaving **Lal Qila** ❶ (see p. 67) behind you, cross the very busy Netaji Subhash Road into Chandni Chowk, Old Delhi's main street, which used to run right up to the fort. There are three landmarks on the left. First is the **Digamber Jain Temple and Bird Hospital** ❷ *(donation)*. The Bird Hospital, located within the precincts of the temple, is where injured birds can be brought for free treatment. Next, behind the busy flower stalls, is **Sisganj Gurdwara** ❸, a Sikh temple dedicated to the ninth guru, Tegh Bahadur. Finally, you come to **Sonehri Masjid** (Golden Mosque) where in 1739 Nadir Shah stood watching the destruction of Delhi and thousands of its inhabitants.

NOT TO BE MISSED:

Jama Masjid • Kinari Bazar • Gadodia Bazar

Turn left on **Dariba Kalan,** a narrow street lined with silver and gold shops that locals use as a kind of savings bank. At the intersection, turn right and follow the road around to the left, past art stores and fireworks suppliers, to the 1656 **Jama Masjid** ❹, well worth visiting. Leave your shoes at the top of the great steps, and borrow a cotton overcoat to cover you if your arms or legs are exposed *(give a modest tip afterward)*. Shah Jahan's last building proclaims

INSIDER TIP:

For a more local experience, see New Delhi by auto-rickshaw; the best way to see the busy pedestrian-filled streets of Old Delhi is by bicycle rickshaw.

—KEN ROSE
National Geographic grantee

Islam's power and is still India's principal mosque. Designed by Ustad Khalil on Delhi's only mound, it uses glowing red sandstone inlaid with marble and brass, and it has excellent views of the Red Fort from the courtyard. The mosque design, inspired by the Prophet's house at Medina, is simple: a large courtyard with a vaulted hall at one end. The faithful wash ritually in the courtyard's pool, then pray facing the central mihrab (niche) of the hall, which indicates the direction of Mecca. The *mimbar* (pulpit) is for the sermon at midday communal prayers on Friday, the Muslims' holy day; the minaret (slender tower) is where the muezzin summons the faithful to prayer.

Ride back into Dariba Kalan and turn left for **Kinari Bazar,** Old Delhi's wedding equipment street. Tiny, boxlike stores are filled from floor to ceiling with glittering braids, gold lamé grooms' turbans, currency note garlands, plumes, and tinsel. In October, they also stock the papier-mâché masks for the Ram Lila festival. Almost at the end, bear left along Paratha Walan and Nai Sarak. Turn right, passing stores piled with stationery.

Turn left onto Chandni Chowk. At the end, turn right, then left on Khari Baoli. Here is **Naya Bazar** ❺, the market selling spices, dried fruit, and nuts from Kashmir and Afghanistan. You can taste before buying. The wholesale spice market, **Gadodia Bazar** ❻, is farther along Khari Baoli, through an arch on the left. Sackfuls of tamarind, ginger, turmeric, and chilies are weighed out on huge iron scales, then humped around by workers who shout loudly if you are in their way.

Return along Chandni Chowk; the statue in front of **Old Delhi Town Hall** (1860) ❼ is of the liberal nationalist hero, Swami Shraddhanand, who was murdered by a fanatic.

⊠	See also area map p. 65
➤	Outside the Red Fort
↔	About 2 miles (3.5 km)
⊕	1–2 hours
➤	Old Delhi Town Hall

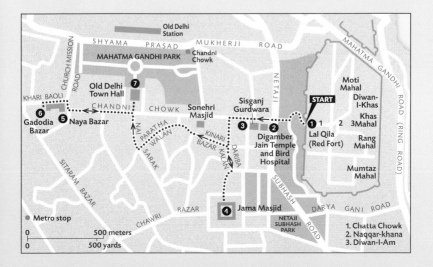

East & North Delhi

Down the centuries, the Yamuna River has been Delhi's highway and local water source. Its western banks are thus the sites of major ancient monuments and, happily, are being rediscovered. A day spent moving northward along the river takes in a variety of top sights. There should be something to suit every interest: Simply skip the ones that do not appeal.

The *dargah* of Shaikh Nizamuddin Chishti is the focus of a Muslim burial ground for nobility.

Nizamuddin

🅰 65 C3

✉ W of Mathura Rd.

Nizamuddin to Purana Qila

The streets behind the deluxe Oberoi Hotel have a medieval air about them. They form the village of **Nizamuddin,** whose heart is the *dargah* (shrine) of the Sufi saint Shaikh Nizamuddin Chishti (1238–1325). One of the great mystic orders,

Sufism was brought to India by Khwaja Muin-ud-din Chishti, who settled in Ajmer (see p. 131). It has been said that the Sufis, whose devotion, piety, asceticism, and tolerance were so attractive to Hindus, were the true missionaries of Islam to India. The Chishti order's influential followers included many of the Sultanate rulers and Mughal royal families.

To visit the **dargah,** follow the streets past stores and stalls selling everything from the Koran to cassettes of devotional songs. The shrine itself is surrounded by royal tombs, including those of two Tughlaq rulers and Shah Jahan's daughter, Jahanara (see p. 95) Here, too, lies Amir Khusrau (died 1325), whose poetry includes this couplet: "If there is a paradise on Earth, it is this, it is this, it is this"—possibly referring to Shah Jahan's Diwan-i-Am building in the Red Fort (see p. 67). He also wrote qawwalis that you might hear in the daily singing there. All these tombs benefit from the spiritual strength of the saint's presence.

This is why the Mughal emperor Humayun is buried nearby in the finest of Delhi's tombs. It is an essential stop if you are intending to visit the Taj Mahal later, for this is its forerunner. **Humayun's tomb** was built in 1565 by his wife, Bega Begum. She employed the Persian architect Mirak Mirza Ghiyas to design the first great Mughal garden tomb. With his knowledge of monumental Timurid tombs, he created something new using local sandstone and marble, and employing local stonemasons.

Inside the Dargah: Once inside, move along through a series of walls pierced by gateways. Inside the first, turn right to Isa Khan's sturdy tomb (1547), already adopting Hindu details such as projecting eaves and domed kiosks. The final wall surrounds a formal *char bagh* (four gardens) that reflects the Koran's description of paradise. Look at the great tomb from here, the double dome making possible a soaring exterior and well-proportioned interior. Through the restored gardens, steep steps lead to the platform to see the emperor's cenotaph (monument) in the mausoleum, and those of his son Dara Shikoh and other Mughal royals. In accordance with Islamic custom, their bodies lie buried at ground level. Before leaving, see if you can spot Purana Qila fort, the next stop.

Humayun's Tomb

▲ 65 C3

✉ Off Mathura Rd.

$ $

EXPERIENCE: Interact with the Bharany Family, Connoisseurs of Jewelry & Textiles

Visiting the Bharany family-owned store (*14 Sunder Nagar market, tel 011/2435-8528, or 011/2435-3957, closed Sun., bharanys.com*), near Humayun's Tomb, is a feast for the eyes and mind. The little store is lined from floor to ceiling with exquisite old Indian textiles and glass cases displaying tradition-inspired jewelry of the finest gems and craftsmanship. In a back room, Chhote Bharany shares his consummate textile knowledge with interested visitors. Meanwhile his sons Ramji, a trained gemologist, and Mahesh enthusiastically explain the skills required to realize their jewelry designs, which are often backed with *meenakari* inlay work. Discerning locals and repeat-visit foreigners drop by all the time, each warmly welcomed with gossip and a good cup of tea.

The Rediscovery of India

The British relationship with India's ancient sites and monuments was complicated. Progress in archaeology was pioneered by a few, such as Sir William Jones, who, with a group of fellow enthusiasts, founded the Asiatic Society in 1784. Discoveries were often by-products of military measures. This was true of the Survey of India, begun in 1800, which aimed to map the whole subcontinent from south to north.

The well-preserved Taj Mahal, symbol of India

On this project and others, rediscoveries of overgrown, forgotten monuments abounded—the Chalukyan caves of Badami, the Buddhist stupas of Sanchi, the temples of Khajuraho, Ajanta's painted caves.

Ideas of restoration and conservation began in the mid-19th century. But many British administrators still did not appreciate the significance of India's wealth of historical monuments. After Delhi was retaken, the British spent 1858 ransacking the city. They looted the imperial palaces and desecrated the mosques. Two-thirds of the Red Fort buildings were pulled down. The remaining became the military garrison, and the area in front was cleared for security reasons. Suggestions for the fate of the Jama Masjid were that it be blown up, sold, turned into barracks or, worse, into a Hall of Remembrance to British victims of the war. This provoked an outcry among the

enlightened. As the pioneering architectural historian James Fergusson argued, the military excuse for this destruction did not hold up.

Saving the Monuments

In 1861 Sir Alexander Cunningham was appointed archaeological surveyor of India. Projects such as the restoration of Sanchi and Gwalior, and the publication of copies of the Ajanta frescoes, followed. When Lord Curzon arrived as viceroy in 1899, he recognized that India had "the most glorious galaxy of monuments in the world," whose maintenance was an imperial responsibility. He reorganized the Archaeological Survey, arranged funds for it, and in 1902 appointed Sir John Marshall as its first director-general. Indian scholars were employed, excavations and drawings made, laws for the protection of ancient monuments passed. While the public's attention was closely focused on Agra's Mughal buildings, the temples of Kanchipuram, mosques of Bijapur, and other monuments were also restored. Since independence, this vast body of knowledge has continued to grow under the aegis of the Archaeological Survey of India (asi.nic.in), headquartered in Delhi.

The nongovernmental organization Indian National Trust for Art and Cultural Heritage (INTACH; tel 011/2469-2774 or 011/2463-1818, intach.org) was founded in 1984. This conservation group's enthusiastic, dedicated, and knowledgeable members have already achieved impressive results, including the restoration of Elephanta's cave, work on Jodhpur Fort, fixing some of Varanasi's ghats, and creating a heritage plan for Kochi (Cochin) and Mattancherry.

Established in 1959, **Delhi Zoo** is India's biggest and most important zoo and lies between Humayun's tomb and Purana Qila. Due to poor management the potentially fascinating collection, which includes the one-horned rhinoceros from Assam, the Asiatic lion from Gujarat, and other examples of India's rich wildlife, is not always a joy to visit. Better conditions for the animals would greatly enhance this zoo.

Purana Qila (Old Fort) rises above it. Archaeologists say this spot may have been where Arjuna, one of the five Pandava hero brothers, founded the sacred site of Indraprastha (City of Indra) as recounted in the epic *Mahabharata* (see p. 20). More certainly, the second Mughal emperor, Humayun, brought the capital back here from Agra and in 1533 founded Dinpanah (Shelter of the Faith). The soaring walls and their three gates are his, but his usurper, Sher Shah Suri (see p. 37), erected the two buildings inside: the **Qala-I-Kuhna-Masjid**, with its five great arches and proto-Mughal decoration, and the **Sher Mandal.** It was from the roof of this building that Humayun, having regained his throne in 1555, fell down the stairs and died in 1556.

National Crafts Museum

Sited in the shadow of the Purana Qila, this is arguably one of the finest museums of its kind and a must for anyone interested in the huge range of fine craftsmanship to be seen all over India. The

museum constantly commissions pieces and adds to the several thousand quality examples already displayed in a congenial, unstuffy atmosphere. U.S. First Lady, Michelle Obama, visited the museum in 2010.

This is a museum that is guaranteed to bring smiles. A warren of courtyards and rooms designed by Charles Correa houses the primary collection. Do not miss the life-size carved wooden cows and horses, a model of a whole village, tribal metalwork animals of all shapes, and rooms covered with folk paintings. Giant storage pots, plastered walls, a temple chariot, and a carved wooden dovecote lead to the dazzling fabric collection upstairs.

INSIDER TIP:

If you're in Delhi in October, try to see the Ananya Dance festival, which uses the south gate of the Purana Qila as its dramatic backdrop.

—BILL WEIR
National Geographic author

Outside, there are sacred terra-cotta horses, a group of vernacular painted huts, a good gift shop, and a café. A highlight is watching craftsmen from all over India brought here to spend a three-month period making their own goods. You may find a weaver from Assam, a painter of miniatures from Jodhpur, or a

Delhi Zoo
🗺 65 C4
✉ Mathura Rd.
🕐 Closed Fri.

Purana Qila
🗺 65 C4
✉ Mathura Rd.
🕐 Son-et-lumière times vary.

National Crafts Museum
🗺 65 C4
✉ Pragati Maidan (enter on Bhairion)
🕐 Exhibition galleries closed Mon. & July–Sept.
 nationalcrafts museum.nic.in

Feroz Shah Kotla
 65 C4
 Bahadur Shah
Zafar Marg

Raj Ghat
 65 C5
 Mahatma
Gandhi Rd.

potter from Tamil Nadu. You can buy direct from them.

Feroz Shah Kotla & Surroundings

The centerpiece of this group of sites north of Purana Qila is Feroz Shah Kotla, entered from Bahadur Shah Zafar Road. It is the ruined citadel of a vast city that, in its heyday under Feroz Shah Tughlaq (r. 1351–1388), stretched from North Ridge down to Lal Kot and was famed for its palaces, reservoirs, hunting lodges, mosques, and intellectual life. Then, in 1398, Timur (Tamburlaine) sacked it and carried off its treasures. His

A Gujarat basketmaker at the National Crafts Museum

descendant, Babur, later invaded India and founded the Mughal dynasty (see pp. 36–37). Imagine this as you wander the lawns around a ruined mosque, palace, and *baoli* (step well).

Feroz Shah, a weak ruler but a great builder, intellectual, and antique collector, brought the mysterious carved pillar here from Meerut (and brought another to North Ridge), believing the inscriptions to be a magic charm. In fact, when the scholar James Princep unraveled the pillar's Brahmi script in 1837, it was discovered that the inscriptions were Ashoka's edicts (see p. 26) promoting dharma.

Within the complex lies the **National Rose Garden,** usually glorious in February and March. Across the main road you can see **Abdu'n Nabi's Mosque** (1575–1576), built by Akbar's ecclesiastical registrar, who, failing to account for money that he had supposedly taken to the poor in Mecca, was summarily murdered.

Memorials to Mahatma & Others

The land left behind by the Yamuna when its course altered is now an undulating park devoted to the memory of India's modern heroes. Planted with fine trees and well kept, this is a tranquil and pleasant place for a walk in winter or during cool summer hours.

The first and most visited memorial is **Raj Ghat.** A platform marks the spot where Mahatma Gandhi (see pp. 148–149) was cremated after his assassination on January 30, 1948. It was then made into an oasis of peace using Vanu G. Bhuta's design of a walled, square garden entered through a simple arch. For Indians, this is a place of pilgrimage. If you wish to know more, you can visit the modest but informative **Gandhi National Museum** across the main road, where photographs, quotes, descriptions, and sometimes documentaries pay tribute to the Mahatma; literature is on sale at the gift shop.

Tragedy was to strike other Indian leaders after 1948. Just north of here, in a less formal setting, a string of memorials begins with **Vir Bhumi,** where Rajiv Gandhi (assassinated May 21, 1991) was cremated. The memorial to his brother Sanjay Gandhi (died in a plane accident, June 1980) is nearby. Their mother, Indira (assassinated October 31, 1984), was cremated at **Shakti Sthal** (Place of Strength and Power). Her father, India's first prime minister, Jawaharlal Nehru (died May 27, 1964), was cremated at **Shanti Van** (Forest of Peace). Finally, **Vijay Ghat** remembers Lal Bahadur Shashtri, India's second prime minister (died January 11, 1966). If you get this far, you can enjoy views of Shah Jahan's riverside palaces.

Civil Lines & North Ridge

For those interested in learning more about the British period in India's history, a short trip into the rarely visited area that was British Delhi from the 18th century until New Delhi was built brings fascinating

rewards. (See also Lucknow, pp. 308–311.)

Up on Mahatma Gandhi Road and into Lothian Road, the tumbledown **Lothian Cemetery** is just before an arched ruin mid-road. The ruin is the remains of the British Magazine, a huge ammunition storehouse. It was

INSIDER TIP:

After a long flight, visit an ayurvedic center for a taste of India's ancient healing system. You can get a *dosha* consultation and a hot oil massage for quite the bargain!

—DANIELLE WILLIAMS
National Geographic contributor

deliberately blown up by the British on May 11, 1857, to prevent the freedom fighters—Indian soldiers in the British Army who had mutinied in Meerut the previous day—from seizing it. The bang was said to have been heard in Meerut, 31 miles (50 km) away. Just beyond, the gray obelisk is the **Telegraph Memorial,** from which the Anglo-Indian operator warned the British Army of the mutineers' approach. On the right, the dilapidated, columned building dates from an earlier time: In 1803 it became Delhi's first **British Residency.**

The distinctive yellow-plastered and domed **St. James's** (consecrated 1836) was Delhi's

Gandhi National Museum
 65 C5
✉ Opposite Raj Ghat, Mahatma Gandhi Rd.
☎ 011/2331-1793
🕐 Closed Mon.
gandhimuseum.org

Vir Bhumi
 65 C5
✉ Mahatma Gandhi Rd.

Shanti Van
 65 C5
✉ Mahatma Gandhi Rd.

Vijay Ghat
 65 C5
✉ Mahatma Gandhi Rd.

Lothian Cemetery
 65 C5
✉ Lothian Rd.

St. James's Church
 65 C6
✉ Lothian Rd.

Nicholson Cemetery

🄰 65 C6

✉ Qudsia Rd.

Kushkh-i-shikav

🄰 65 C6

Hindu Rao's House

🄰 65 B6

Ajitgarh

🄰 65 B6

first church, and it merits a stop. This was built by Col. James Skinner (ca 1778–1841), the son of a Scotsman and a Rajput, who founded Skinner's Horse, crack cavalry regiments distinguished by their yellow uniforms. Skinner family tombs stand in the church-yard. Inside the church, the family pew is at the front, and Skinner's tomb is by the altar.

Lothian Road now passes a lone survivor of Shah Jahan's many-gated city (see p. 66): **Kashmiri Gate,** so called because the Mughal emperors and their

INSIDER TIP:

Never forgo an oppor-tunity for spicy *dal makhani* served with a dollop of yogurt over rice. By far, it ranks as north India's best nutritious pulse dish.

—DONOVAN WEBSTER
National Geographic Traveler
magazine writer

court would leave Delhi's searing summer heat through this gate on their way to the cool Kashmir hills. In September 1857, 5,000 British troops swarmed down from the ridge, breached the walls, confronted up to 20,000 rebelling Indians and, after six days of fighting, retook Delhi. Brig. Gen. John Nicholson, who died at the gate, is buried in **Nicholson Cemetery** up the road on the left, across from Qudsia Gardens.

Here Lothian Road is called Sham Nath Marg. On the right, the delightful **Oberoi Maidens Hotel** (see Travelwise p. 344), built in 1900, may be just the place for some refreshment; Sir Edwin Lutyens lived here while his New Delhi was being built.

From here follow Underhill Road, which passes forgotten grand colonial houses set on large, leafy grounds. At the end turn left on Rajpur Road, then left again at the top on Rani Jhansi Marg. This takes you to North Ridge, from which British troops poured down to retake Delhi. **Flagstaff Tower,** on its crest, is where the British women and children gathered five months earlier, before fleeing to Karnal as the mutineers approached.

Near here you can find odds and ends from Delhi's history: first, the remains of one of Feroz Shah Tughlaq's hunting palaces, **Kushkh-i-shikav** (1356), on the right; then, William Fraser's country retreat, on the same side, called **Hindu Rao's House** (1830). Fraser, who had six or seven wives, fathered uncounted children, and knew India bet-ter than most Europeans, was Resident of Delhi until his murder in 1835.

On the way down from the ridge you can see the small, tapering Gothic tower of the Mutiny Memorial. Built to remember the British dead, it is now renamed **Ajitgarh** and remembers Indian martyrs who died fighting colonial rule. A left turn on Boulevard Road takes you back to Kashmiri Gate. ∎

EXPERIENCE: Riding Delhi's Shining Metro System

The construction of Delhi's Metro has been symbolic of the new India. In contrast to Kolkata's subway system—the first in India—where the project was hampered by countless delays, Delhi's opened on time and within budget on December 25, 2002. It is more extensive, carries more passengers, and is the largest urban transportation project since independence. And it already has its own Metro Museum (closed Mon.) at Patel Chowk Station.

Built in one of the world's most congested and densely inhabited cities, the Metro—officially Delhi Metro Rail Corporation (DMRC)—aims to provide commuting workers with, as they put it themselves, "a fast, reliable, safe, and comfortable means of transport in the city characterized by rickety vehicles and unreliable operators."

With much of the construction funded by a loan from the Japan Bank for International Cooperation, work began in 1995, using an international team of experts and cutting-edge technology from Germany, France, Korea, and Japan. This expertise helped achieve Chawri Bazaar Station, the world's second deepest underground train station. Local design details include a sari guard on escalators to prevent loose fabric from getting caught in the mechanism.

Impressively, all ticketing is automatic and the managers claim to have fiscally operated in the black from the start. Certainly, it is popular: 1.2 million people used it on the first day when the first six stations opened. Today, there are six lines with a total of 135 stations (see map inside back cover). In May 2009, Yamuna Bank

Metro riders wait for a train at one of Delhi's 67 subway stations.

station opened five months ahead of schedule. In such a demanding service industry, employees are trained both in their practical jobs and in the importance of spiritualism as set out in the *Bhagavad Gita*.

Getting Onboard

For visitors to Delhi, the Metro is easy to use. It runs from 6 a.m. until 11 p.m., but it is best used during the day; trains come every 8 to 12 minutes. A suggested short trip is the ride from Rajiv Chowk, the Connaught Place station, up to Chandni Chowk to visit Old Delhi. For a longer, more adventurous traffic-free sightseeing route, travel from Central Secretariat to Haus Khas, Qutab Minar, and on to Devi Art Foundation at the HUDA City Centre Station at Gurgaon. For more information, see *delhimetrorail.com*.

South Delhi

Interesting remnants of Delhi's pre-Mughal cities are scattered over the large area of fashionable and increasingly built-up south Delhi. To use your time well, it is best to take a taxi or hire a car and driver for a long morning or, better still, a whole day. The following route works well; remember to take drinks and snacks.

Lodi Gardens

🗺 65 C3

✉ Lodi Rd.

Lodi Gardens

A stroll through Lodi Gardens in the morning is a good start to the day; your driver will deliver you to one entrance and collect you from the other.

Feroz Shah Tughlaq's tomb looks to Afghan fort architecture for inspiration.

Lady Willingdon, whose husband was viceroy from 1931 to 1936, saved this group of majestic domed tombs from New Delhi developers in the 1930s, laying out lawns, shrubs, and shady trees around them. The tombs were built during the weak Sayyid and Lodi sultanates (see p. 35), whose rulers allowed noble power to grow. Neither dynasty built a great city, but both added more tombs and mosques to Delhi. After Sikander Lodi (r. 1489–1517) moved to Agra in 1502, the forlorn former capital that was left behind was nothing but a great necropolis.

If you enter from Lodi Road, you come first to the **tomb of Mohammad Shah,** the third Sayyid ruler. Built in 1450, its octagonal plan has sloping buttresses that contrast with the soft lotus patterns on the ceiling. Next comes the **Bara Gumbad Mosque** (1494), built during the reign of Sikander Lodi. In addition to the fine domed gateway, some of the best plaster decoration in India survives here; see the delicate filigree work and elaborate facade. The contemporary **Sheesh Gumbad** (glass dome), so-called because its dome used to have glazed blue tiles that glittered in the sun, stands on the hillock; the double-story room inside has wonderful stucco and painted decoration. The **tomb of Sikander Lodi** preserves its walled enclosure and adjoining mosque. Nearby is the **Athpula,** a seven-arched Mughal bridge built in the 16th century.

Southward to Haus Khas

South along Sri Aurobindo Road toward Lal Kot, the first landmark building is the **tomb of Safdarjang,** the Nawab of Oudh (Avadh), a powerful minister to the dissipated, unpopular late Mughal ruler Ahmad Shah. Built in 1754, this is the last of the great Mughal garden tombs, keeping the formal layout of Humayun's (see p. 71), but lacking its grace or style. Half a mile (1 km) farther down Sri Aurobindo Road, a left turn to Kidwai Nagar reaches

the grand tomb of **Darya Khan,** who served all the Lodi sultans.

The city of Siri, begun in 1304 by the popular and capable ruler Ala-ud-din Khilji (r. 1296–1316), lay beyond here, but little now remains. To get an idea of this former city, continue down Sri Aurobindo Road and turn right into **Haus Khas village,** where many old houses have been renovated into upscale boutiques and restaurants. At the other end of the village street is a walled garden opening onto a huge sunken space. This was the *haus* (reservoir) that provided water for Siri's citizens. To the left are the steps, pavilions, and university buildings added by Feroz Shah Tughlaq in 1354. His austere **tomb** (1390) stands at the corner; its interior has fine plasterwork.

Safdarjang's Tomb

🔺 65 B3

✉ Junction of Lodi Rd. & Sri Aurobindo Rd.

Haus Khas village

🔺 65 B2

✉ W off Sri Aurobindo Rd.

Handicrafts Bazaars in Delhi

Dilli Haat is a hugely popular open-air craft and food plaza in Delhi. *Haat* means a rural market, and Dilli Haat brings rural India to the visitor. Here, you'll find everything from handwoven silks and finely crafted embroideries to intricate miniature paintings, from silver and semi-precious jewelry to spicy pickles and *poppadoms* (round, crisp bread). The stalls are allotted on a rotational basis to craftspeople from all corners of India to sell their wares. Occasionally, you might also find stalls from countries such as Sri Lanka or Pakistan. Besides shopping, Dilli Haat also has permanent food stalls representing the different Indian states and an open stage for cultural programs.

Another arts and crafts success story is Dastkar (Artisan; *dastkar.org*),

a cooperative society of traditional craftspeople. This organization aims to improve the economic conditions of India's craftsmen, most of whom practice a skill handed down within their families for generations, and who live in far-flung villages, distant from large markets. Dastkar was founded in 1981, and its shops, exhibitions, and bazaars in India's larger cities now connect the craftspeople with an ever-expanding urban clientele. Artisans sell their products to consumers directly, which has provided them with new knowledge about market trends and taste, resulting in fine quality products, including silk bags, organic cotton materials, handwoven, delicately embroidered cashmere sweaters, and jewelry. For more information visit *delhitourism.gov.in*.

Lal Kot

65 B1

Junction of Sri
Aurobindo Rd.
& Mehrauli–
Badarpur Rd.

Lal Kot

About 7 miles (11 km) south
of Lodi Gardens down Sri
Aurobindo Road is the spot
where historical Delhi began. Lal
Kot was the Rajput citadel built
by the Tomar king Anangpal in
about 1060. Enlarged, fortified,
and given 13 gates by the Chauhan king Prithviraj III in 1080,
this thriving city was captured
by Qutb-ud-din-Aibak in 1192,
marking the arrival of Islam in
today's India (see p. 33). The
next year Aibak began building
a mosque, and six years later he
began the Qutab Minar.

INSIDER TIP:

**India can be a mentally
exhausting country
to visit. Prepare to be
bombarded daily with
both stimulation and
annoyances. Stay sharp
and well informed.**

—TALA KATNER
National Geographic contributor

There is a lot to see in the
complex. Through the arched
entrance, remains of Ala-ud-din's
southernmost Siri buildings survive
on the right. Farther ahead, you
find the base of **Alai Minar,** an
unfinished tower he intended to
be twice the size of the Qutab
Minar (he died before much
was built).

Aibak's mosque lies ahead:
the **Quwwat-ul-Islam** (Might
of Islam) mosque (1193–1197),
given additions by Iltutmish (1230)
and Ala-ud-din (1315). Delicate
stones taken from Hindu and
Jain temples were used in the
construction—you can see the
ropes, bells, cows, and defaced
figures on some. Cloisters lead to
a courtyard and the monumental
screen of the now vanished prayer
hall, built by local Hindu masons.
You can see how later parts of the
magnificent, bold screen carving
exchange floral and leaf motifs for
more rigorously abstract Islamic
arabesques and surahs (chapters)
from the Koran. The Gupta **iron
pillar** (fourth to fifth century), with
its Sanskrit inscription, is a mystery
in origins and casting, but legend
says that those who encircle it with
their arms behind their back will
have their wish granted. Alas, so
many visitors did this that authori-
ties were forced to erect a fence
around the ancient pillar.

To the left of the screen,
cross the ditch and turn right
to find, at the end of the path,
the modest **tomb of Iltutmish**
(r. 1210–1236), Aibak's son-in-law
and successor. This is the earliest
tomb of an Indian Islamic ruler,
with beautifully carved walls. Back
along the path, the ruins on the
mound ahead are of Ala-ud-din's
unfinished **tomb** and his **college.**
Leaving them through an opening
on the left, there are views over
the whole complex, including
Aibak's intricately carved, five-
story **Qutab Minar** (the top two
stories were rebuilt in marble by
Feroz Shah), which served as a
tower of victory and a minaret for
calling the faithful to prayer. The
stocky, square building to the right

of it is **Alai Darwaza** (1311), the impressive entrance to Ala-ud-din's now-lost mosque extension. Its restrained bulk and large panels of low-relief carving make it the most Islamic building here. Beyond, the Gothic-style cupola added to the Qutab Minar by the British was so ridiculed that it now stands in a corner of the lawn.

Other South Delhi Sites

These real treats require a strong pair of walking shoes, curiosity, and determination to seek them out.

Take the street at the back of the Lal Kot parking lot onto the open plains dotted with Islamic monuments. Right ahead is **Metcalfe's Folly,** two ruined tombs bought by Sir Thomas Metcalfe, Delhi's British Resident from 1835 to 1853, and turned into a country retreat to which he would ride on horseback from Civil Lines (see p. 75). **Jamali-Kamali** (1528), the mosque and tombs of a poet-saint and his brother, lie beyond; you can walk or drive to them.

Next, head for Mehrauli village, half a mile (1 km) west of Lal Kot, where you'll find **Bhul-Bhulaiyan** (1562), the double tomb of Adham Khan and his powerful mother, Maham Anga, wet nurse to the Mughal emperor Akbar. Just beyond it, a street on the left leads to a cluster of mosques, a *baoli* (step well), and tombs of three late Mughal emperors.

If you enjoyed the National Crafts Museum (see pp. 73–74), then it is worth making reservations to visit **Sanskriti,** which lies

At Lal Kot, skilled craftsmen were employed to create the intricate carving adorning the tomb of Iltutmish.

south of Lal Kot. Here O. P. Jain, a collector of Indian crafts, exhibits his collection of everyday objects, terra-cotta, and textiles in a garden bordered by artists' houses.

Finally, head eastward to **Tughlaqabad Fort** to find the massive ruins of the city built by Ghiyath-ud-din Tughlaq from 1321 to 1325. Here you can ramble over the fortifications, the palace precincts, and the citadel. Across the road stands Ghiyath-ud-din's fortified tomb (ca 1325), once surrounded by a lake. ■

Sanskriti

  65 B1

✉ Anadgram, Mehrauli– Gurgaon Rd.

☎ 011/2652-7707 or 011/2650-1796

🕐 Closed Mon.

sanskritifoundation .org

Tughlaqabad Fort

  65 D1

✉ Off Mehrauli– Gurgaon Rd.

New Delhi

The British had their headquarters first at Chennai (Madras), then at Kolkata (Calcutta). Delhi, strategic as it had been for past rulers, was a backwater. Agra, not Delhi, was capital of the Northwest Provinces that stretched up to the Hindu Kush.

The sun sets behind the Rashtrapati Bhavan's Sanchi-inspired dome, while egrets sport on the lake.

New Delhi
🗺 65 C4

Then, to everyone's surprise, during his royal visit to India in 1911, King-Emperor George V announced that the capital of British India was to move from Calcutta to Delhi. Delhi was to rise, phoenixlike, to be the specially built imperial capital of the subcontinent. The King-Emperor and Queen-Empress Mary then laid a foundation stone north of Old Delhi and went home.

In 1913 British architect Edwin Lutyens sailed for India. He and

his Planning Commission—Sir Herbert Baker, J. A. Brodie, G. S. C. Swinton, and others—disliked the original site, so they rode around Delhi's scrubland on elephants and settled on another. One night they quietly dug up the foundation stone, put it on a bullock cart, and relaid it on Raisina Hill.

This uncompromising approach was characteristic of Lutyens, who was responsible for the overall design of the new capital, called New Delhi, Viceroy's

House (Rashtrapati Bhavan), and some designs along Raj Path. His team designed the rest— quantities of public buildings plus more than 4,000 flat-roofed, stuccoed brick bungalows.

To prepare, Lutyens toured northern India. Unimpressed by Mughal buildings (he thought Fatehpur Sikri "the work of monkeys"), he found Sanchi's Buddhist stupas inspiration for his domes. Then he got to work on his plan: classical buildings with Indian details, such as deep shading eaves, set in a gracious garden city capable of endless expansion. He described it as "an Englishman dressed for the climate."

More than 30,000 laborers were hired to transform the hilly, dry site. Glorious red sandstone was brought from Dholpur. William Robertson Mustoe, trained at London's Kew Gardens, advised on the planting of 10,000 trees.

Costs soared: The budget passed £15 billion ($21 billion). Lutyens fought hard but plans were occasionally modified.

On February 15, 1931, New Delhi was inaugurated by the viceroy, Lord Irwin. Two weeks of festivities included a performance of *Madame Butterfly* in the Red Fort, Scottish dancing, a pageant of painted elephants, and a 21-gun salute to herald the unveiling of Baker's Ashokan columns.

Sixteen years later, New Delhi was one of the most useful, if unintended, legacies the British left to the newly independent India: a ready-made capital.

Raisina Hill

This is the heart of New Delhi, and India's political center. A good way to see it is to walk from Vijay Chowk to Raisina Hill's controversial gradient: Lutyens accused Baker of

---

EXPERIENCE: See Parliament in Action

If the workings of the world's largest democracy intrigue you, go and watch it in action. Foreigners are welcome to attend sessions of India's Parliament. All you need is a letter of introduction from your foreign office before you leave home, or your embassy in Delhi. Indian nationals, of course, do not need to do this. Visitors must first stop at the reception desk at the Raisina Road entrance of the Herbert Baker–designed Sansad Bhavan (Parliament House). Originally called Circular Building, it was built in the 1920s during British rule as a result of the Montague-Chelmsford Reforms of 1919. It sits at the bottom of Raisina Hill,

a later addition to the grand centerpiece of Lutyens's New Delhi, where the British Empire had its government headquarters, Viceroy's House (now Rashtrapati Bhavan).

You may wander the spacious outer hall—notice the India-inspired stone *jali* (cutwork) screens—before visiting the Lok Sabha (Lower House), Rajya Sabha (Upper House), and the library.

If you are lucky you may witness a bill being debated, or a foreign policy being outlined; when the repartee gets lively, official Hindi and English can be peppered with a spattering of India's 22 official regional languages.

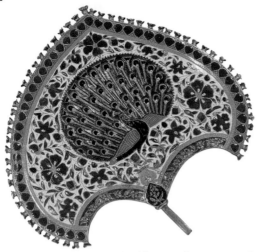

An elaborate 19th-century *sarpesh* (turban ornament) made in Jaipur

National Gallery of Modern Art

🅰 65 C4

✉ Jaipur House, India Gate

🕐 Closed Mon.

💲 $

ngmaindia.gov.in

National Archives

🅰 65 C4

✉ Jan Path

🕐 Closed Mon.

nationalarchives.gov.in

making it too steep and blocking the view of his masterpiece, Viceroy's House.

Vijay Chowk is where the military parade known as Beating Retreat is held each January, at sunset; to the north, the circular building is **Sansad Bhavan** (Parliament House). Moving up the hill, the first pavilion provides breathtaking views. Raj Path sweeps down from this citadel of power, crossing Jan Path, past India Gate and into the far distance. The grand parade on Republic Day, January 26, moves along here. The area on the right is a vast triangle of once residential buildings; that to the left leads north to Connaught Place, now just one of Delhi's shopping centers.

The brow of Raisina Hill is unashamedly imperial. A wide avenue runs between Baker's **Secretariats,** their design a mixture of English baroque, Mughal doorways, and lotus-decorated domes, and leads to an ornate entrance screen. Beyond lies

Rashtrapati Bhavan (President's Palace, formerly Viceroy's House; *private*). Peer through the gates to see **Jaipur Column,** given by the Maharaja of Jaipur, a close British ally, standing in the courtyard. Behind, Lutyens's masterpiece has a facade 630 feet (192 m) wide and a plan covering 200,000 square feet (18,580 sq m), making it larger than Versailles. It was here that Britain's last viceroy, Lord Mountbatten, stood in the Durbar Hall to hand power over to India's first prime minister, Jawaharlal Nehru. Behind the house, President's Estate includes the spectacular **Mughal Gardens.** Inspired by the Mughal Gardens of Kashmir and Gertrude Jekyll's

INSIDER TIP:

In Delhi, stop by Gulab Singh Johrimal [est. 1816] in Chandni Chowk to stock up on high-quality essential oils, such as cardamom and sandalwood. You'll smell intoxicating for months to come.

—SARAH WHITE
National Geographic grantee

work in England, they are kept in shape by 150 gardeners and are open to the public each spring.

Civic New Delhi

To get a flavor of the city as it was, drive along Raj Path to **India Gate,** which remembers the 90,000 Indian soldiers who died in World War I and the Afghan War (1919). An eternal flame honors the Unknown Soldier. The graceful sandstone pavilion farther along once held a statue of George V but now stands empty. A clutch of very grand former palaces surrounds it: Hyderabad, Baroda, Bikaner, and Jaipur Houses. The last is now the **National Gallery of Modern Art,** which documents the 20th-century emergence of Indian contemporary art and hosts art shows.

of India's most glorious artistic achievements. Upstairs are fine miniature paintings, musical instruments, and glittering jewelry.

Three New Delhi Houses

Here is a fascinating insider's view of New Delhi. The palatial **Teen Murti House** (1930) and its flower-filled garden were built for the commander-in-chief. Nehru lived here from 1948 until his death in 1964, and his desk, library, and bedroom are as he left them. Next is the contrasting **Indira Gandhi**

National Museum
- 65 C4
- ✉ Jan Path
- 🕐 Closed Mon.
- 💲 $
- nationalmuseum india.gov.in

Teen Murti House
- 65 B4
- ✉ Teen Murti Rd.
- 🕐 Closed Mon.

The Gandhi Factor

Politics can turn on a surname. When Indira Nehru, daughter of Prime Minister Jawaharlal Nehru, a Kashmiri of the Brahman caste, married a Parsee man named Feroz Gandhi, she arguably acquired her most useful political tool.

The very name of Gandhi contained echoes of the greatness of the revered Mahatma, Mohandas Kamarchand Gandhi, although there was no blood connection. Even some Indians would

be confused, and no Congress Party campaigners would risk losing votes by putting them right. The hero of the struggle for freedom would be allowed to radiate his influence to the benefit of all, even into the murky waters of politics. Rajiv Gandhi benefited, too, and today, as his son rises in the political theater, people throughout India continue to speak not of the Nehru inheritance but of the Gandhi dynasty.

Back along Raj Path, the intersection with Jan Path boasts two public buildings. The **National Archives** exhibits items from its collection of books and manuscripts on political, social, and economic history. The **National Museum**'s impressive collection makes a good introduction to Indian art. The stone and bronze sculptures from Mathura, Bharhut, Sarnath, and Kausambi and southern India, exhibited in the entrance hall, corridors, and first-floor rooms, are some

Memorial Museum, a small bungalow in lush surroundings where Nehru's daughter lived. Photographs lining the walls recount the story of her leadership and the fates of her sons. On the grounds a sculpted river of glass marks the spot where, on October 31, 1984, she was assassinated. **Gandhi Smriti** (Birla House) is where, on January 30, 1948, Mahatma Gandhi was shot by a Hindu fanatic who believed he was too tolerant toward Muslims. ∎

Indira Gandhi Memorial Museum
- 65 B4
- ✉ 1 Safdar Jang Rd.
- 🕐 Closed Mon.

Gandhi Smriti
- 65 B4
- ✉ Hall of Nations Bldg., 5 Tees January Rd.
- 🕐 Closed Mon.

Creating a Modern Architecture

When the French architect Le Corbusier (1887–1965) came to India in 1951, he was already 64 years old with a reputation as a brilliant, if controversial, architect and a semiabstract painter, sculptor, and writer. He turned Indian architecture upside down, and it is only now beginning to find itself again.

Le Corbusier's 1958 Secretariat building in Chandigarh shows his love of geometric shapes and scale.

Le Corbusier was invited by the Punjab government to be architectural adviser for its new capital. (Punjab had been sliced in half when it gained independence and Pakistan's section included the city of Lahore.) The Frenchman was impressed by the grand scale of Lutyens's New Delhi and by the abstract shapes of the Jantar Mantar (see pp. 89–90). He incorporated these ideas into his uncompromising designs for Chandigarh (see pp. 118–119), where he employed his modular system and *brises-soleil* (sun breakers), using mainly raw concrete.

This break with the vernacular was welcomed; it underlined the new India's ambition and idealism. Le Corbusier also picked up commissions from progressive patrons in Ahmedabad, capital of Gujarat state, where he

built Shodhan House, Manorama Sarabhai's houses, and the Mill Owners Association building, all in the 1950s.

A posse of young Indian architects absorbed his tenets, and anonymous concrete buildings sprang up all over India. Two exceptional architects, Balkrishna V. Doshi and Charles Correa, both have early buildings in Ahmedabad, including Doshi's Tagore Hall and Correa's Sabarmati Ashram.

Meanwhile, the successor to Habib Rahman—who built the New Secretariat in Calcutta in 1954—was J. M. Benjamin, designer of Delhi's High Court and Parliament House Annexe. Architects returning from abroad included Shiv Nath Prasad, who designed Delhi's landmark Akbar Hotel, and Vanu Bhuta who created the elegant Gandhi Memorial. These and others, known as the First Moderns, were exposed to contemporary ideas but also aware of continuing craft skills in the labor force—they used decoration, textured surfaces, and kept the traditional courtyards and shaded spaces.

Today's Architecture

Today's architects benefit from recent economic explosion, a free market, a sophisticated building industry, and—importantly—the confidence to be inspired by both India's rich past as well as global contemporary ideas. The best buildings exhibit a richness of expression that respects and develops India's architectural legacy. Much of the best is private housing, but there are some public buildings to seek out.

In Delhi, the Gurgaon area features Aniket Bhagwat's Devi Art Foundation, boldly designed with brick and Corton steel that will rust, as well as Rajiv Agarwal's Time Tower, Time Centre, Galaxy Hotel, and Nair House. Other notables include Agarwal's Euro School and the Vedic Village resort in Kolkata; Kamal Malik's Cancer Centre in Jaipur; and a string of dynamic buildings in Mumbai and Pune.

India is also experiencing a strong building conservation movement, with many notable

Le Corbusier's designs proved very influential to Indian architects.

architects helping revive historic treasures. Humayun's Tomb in Delhi, the Champaner Fort outside Vadodara, the Chow Mohalla Palace in Hyderabad, and the University Convocation Hall in Mumbai have all been expertly restored.

EXPERIENCE: Historic Walking Tour

Taking a walking tour is a good way to learn about local styles, and your guides are often either architects or architectural historians. At the same time, you explore a city's lesser known areas.

Several thousand interesting buildings lurk in Delhi's sprawling mass. **Delhi Heritage Walks** (tel 921/253-4868, delhiheritagewalks.com) runs a monthly calendar of morning and afternoon walks through such areas as Chandni Chowk in Old Delhi, Lodi Gardens in New Delhi, and Hauz Khas to the south; they can also tailor the walks to your tastes. In Mumbai,

Bombay Heritage Walks (tel 022/2369-0992, bombayheritagewalks.com) reveal the layers of the financial capital, from the Gothic glories of the university to the Kala Ghoda art district.

In Ahmedabad's old city, locals leading the morning **Heritage Walk** (tel 098/2403-2866, gujarattourism.com) show you pol (district) gateways, pigeon houses, havelis, and temples. In Kolkata, the enthusiasm of the **Calcutta Walks** (tel 983/0184-030, calcuttawalks.com) staff is infectious, be it for tours of colonial highlights or a customized walk.

EXPERIENCE: Soaking Up Contemporary Indian Art

Contemporary India has burst out of a stiflingly rich artistic heritage to find its own voice, and now its artists are some of the most dynamic presences in the international art world.

Delhi's 2008 India Art Summit, focusing on modern and contemporary art, showcased more than 200 artists in 35 galleries.

Trailblazers such as Raja Ravi Varma, Shantiniketan artists, and Amrita Shergill paved the way for the founders of Indian modernism—M. F. Husain, F. N. Souza, S. H. Raza, and others who, in the mid-20th century, reinterpreted traditions such as folk and primitive art while looking West to movements like American abstraction.

India's next generation of artists blossomed and gained global attention. Today, Subodh Gupta, Atul Dodiya, Justin Ponmany, Aditya Pande, and others fetch high prices at auction. To learn more about contemporary Indian art, visit *saffronart.com*.

Art aficionados should visit the **Devi Art Foundation** *(Sirpur House, Sector 44, Plot 39, Gurgaon, deviart foundation.org, closed Mon.)*, run by the Poddar family. The foundation displays Indian contemporary art and installations, and hosts informative and interesting shows on Indian craft tradition.

Delhi

In Delhi, the **National Gallery of Modern Art** (see p. 85) tells the story of 20th-century Indian art movements (and has satellites in Mumbai and Bangalore), while the **Delhi Art Gallery** *(11 Hauz Khas Village,*

011/4600-5300) consistently exhibits stunning collections of contemporary Indian art. Several galleries, including Peter Nagy's **Nature Morte Gallery** *(A-1 Defence Colony, New Delhi)*, the **Vadehra Art Gallery** *(D-40, Okhla Phase 1, New Delhi)*, and the newer **Gallery Espace** *(16 Community Centre, New Friends Colony, New Delhi)*, are well worth visiting.

Mumbai

Mumbai has a lively gallery scene, especially in Kala Ghoda, the art district at the tip of the island: Check out **Bodhi Art** *(Plot no. 14, Elphinston Estate, Malet Bunder Rd., Near Orange Gate, Wadibunder)*; **Jehangir Art Gallery** *(161 M. G. Rd.)*; **Pundole Art Gallery** *(369 Dadabhai Naoroji Rd., Fort)* and **Chemould** *(Queens Mansion, Talwatkar Marg, Fort)* galleries to the north; **Mirchandani & Steinruecke** *(2 Sunny House, 16/18 Mereweather Rd., Colaba)*, tucked behind the Taj Mahal Hotel; and plenty others along Colaba Causeway. Well north of Kala Ghoda, another dozen galleries lie between Chowpatty Beach and Worli Sea Face.

Others

Bangalore, Chennai, and Kolkata also have lively contemporary art scenes.

More Places to Visit in Delhi

Agrasen Ki Baoli

This step well is thought to have been built during the Tughlaq sultanate and has a tiny mosque at the top of the steps. ✉ N on Kasturba Gandhi Marg, turn right on Hailey Rd., then first lane on left.

Ashoka's Rock Edict

In 1966 another set of Ashoka's rock edicts (see p. 26) was discovered, this time on a rock in southeast Delhi, proving that a trading center or crossroads had existed in this area as early as Mauryan times. ✉ Off Shaheed Captain Gaur Marg, Srinavaspuri

Baba Kharak Singh Marg

This radial road at Connaught Place is lined with the high-quality, fixed-price, good-value official stores of each Indian state, selling state specialties. An excellent introduction to India's geographic-specific crafts. ✉ Connaught Pl. 🕐 Closed Sun.

Baha'i Temple

The nine soaring white marble petals of this lotus-shaped temple make this a landmark in the south Delhi suburbs. An average of 12,000 visitors each day join guided tours of the spectacular central hall. See *bahai.in*. ✉ Kalkaji District Park, Nehru Pl. 🕐 Closed Mon. & for services

Chanakyapuri

Chanakyapuri is the diplomatic area of the city, where foreign nations were given plots of land at the time of independence. This affluent neighborhood in New Delhi soon became a showcase for each nation's contemporary architecture and established itself in the 1950s. Drive down its main avenue, **Shanti Path,** to guess which style belongs to which country. Pakistan's building is the one with the distinctive blue dome; Edward D. Stone designed the U.S. Embassy.

Christian Cathedrals

Both the Anglican and Roman Catholic cathedrals in New Delhi are stunning landmarks, built to the winning designs of British architect H. A. N. Medd. The Anglican **Church of the Redemption** (1927–1935) is a dignified Palladio-inspired design on Church Road. The Roman Catholic **Church of the Sacred Heart** (1930–1934) is a bold, Italianate design on Bangla Sahib Road.

Connaught Place

T. R. Russell's great amphitheater of stuccoed colonnades was named after George V's uncle. It remains the hub of Delhi's regular stores, modest hotels, and offices, even if the classy south Delhi colonies (as residential

INSIDER TIP:

If you have an hour to kill, visit the Jaipur Polo Grounds and watch the horses being trained. But beware: The ever present monkeys might try to share your food; they can be aggressive.

—DONOVAN WEBSTER
National Geographic Traveler
magazine writer

areas of the city are known) each have their own upscale commercial centers. If the combination of the eight radial roads running into the three concentric ones (see map p. 65) confuses you, just look for Jan Path, which will lead you back to Raj Path. 🅰 65 B5

Jantar Mantar

Maharaja Jai Singh II of Jaipur was a noted astronomer. He built the first of his five outsize observatories here in 1724, although his principal one was in Jaipur (see pp. 129–130). These huge, pink stone, abstract-looking instruments were a gift from the Maharaja to the Mughal emperor Muhammad Shah, for whom he revised both the Muslim calendar and astronomical tables. ✉ Sansad Marg, Connaught Pl.

Lakshmi Narayan Mandir

Built by the prominent Birla merchant family, this ostentatious, tiered marble temple is appropriately dedicated to Lakshmi, goddess of wealth. ✉ Mandir Marg, W of Connaught Pl.

National Philatelic Museum

This collection of rare stamps, first-day covers, and other treats is not easy to find: Go to the main post office on Sansad Marg and ask the head postmaster, who will happily direct you. Commemorative stamps are on sale at the main post office, too. ✉ Sansad Marg, Connaught Pl. ☎ 011/371-0154 🕐 Closed Sat.–Sun.

National Rail Museum

The well-preserved great engines and royal coaches—about 30 engines and 20 railcars—found at this museum bring to life the great days of subcontinental railroad travel in India. Those on display outside include the Maharaja of Baroda's gilt parlor car (1886) and the Maharaja of Mysore's teak car with ivory and gold trim. Inside, you will find a model of India's first-ever train, the steam engine that chugged from Bombay to Thana on April 16, 1853, sent off with a 21-gun salute; there are also models of other famous engines and displays of old tickets ✉ S end of Chanakyapuri 🕐 Closed Mon.

St. Martin's Church

Looming over the cantonment area, this was the British garrison church. Completed in 1930, it is an extraordinary feat of German Expressionism in British New Delhi, a huge monolith with a high, square tower, built of three million bricks. *stmartinschurchdelhi.com* ✉ Church Rd., Delhi Cantonment

India's Ubiquitous Sacred Cows

In India, cows demand right of way in narrow backstreets, block busy crossroads while chewing their cud, and even wander along highways. Delhi alone has some 40,000 cows. Hindus believe the cow is sacred, the living symbol of Mother Earth.

For India's earliest people the cow was respected as essential, providing nutritious milk and its by-products butter and cheese, as well as dung for fuel and manure; it also helped till the fields and pull carts. For the Ayran migrants who introduced fire sacrifice ritual, cow's butter was essential for worshipping their fire-god, Agni: They kept the sacred fire on the altar alive by feeding it melted butter.

As animal sacrifice waned and Brahmans ate less meat, thanks to the influence of Jain and Buddhist vegetarians, the cow's significance as Gaumata (cow the mother) and Aditi (mother of the gods) strengthened. Meanwhile, the cow's sanctity was enhanced by its close association with two gods: Shiva acquired as his vehicle the bull called Nandi, while the popularity of Vishnu's incarnation as Krishna the cowherd grew. In later centuries, Vedic references to the cow were emphasized and the cow symbolized solidarity against Muslim invaders of the 12th to 16th centuries. Today's politicians win votes by pledging to protect the cow.

Mahatma Gandhi summed up the cow's importance neatly: "If someone were to ask me what the most important outward manifestation of Hinduism was, I would suggest that it was the idea of cow protection."

The famous Taj Mahal and a wealth of medieval forts and Buddhist stupas, Hindu carvings and Sikh temples, and flora and fauna

Around Delhi

Carved gateway at Sanchi

Around Delhi

Slipping out of Delhi for a few days can bring great rewards. Tempting as it may be to head west to better known Rajasthan, it is worth considering the riches lying in wait for you to the north and south of India's capital.

This map shows how you can follow the Yamuna River as it flows south from Delhi through ancient Mathura to the royal Mughal buildings of Agra. Both cities are just inside Uttar Pradesh, a large state stretching up to the lower Himalayan mountains and eastward far beyond its capital, Lucknow. The contrasting attractions of Fatehpur Sikri, a deserted royal city, and Keoladeo Ghana National Park, a wondrous bird sanctuary, are nearby.

To the south is Madhya Pradesh, India's second biggest state; it covers much of central India and has several notable wildlife parks—Panna, Bandhavgarh, and Kanha. Dramatic forests and rocky outcrops provide attractive settings for the forts of Gwalior, Datia, and Orchha and, east of them, the isolated temples of Khajuraho. The capital of Madhya Pradesh is Bhopal, an excellent base for visiting Sanchi and other sites in the area before continuing to Indore and Mandu.

If the weather is hot, a trip north from Delhi might be more comfortable. The Grand Trunk Road runs through Haryana, a small state that accommodates Delhi's overflow (notably Gurgaon district) and has the fastest growing economy of all the states in India. It shares its capital, Le Corbusier's specially built Chandigarh, with neighboring Punjab, whose western border meets Pakistan. The unspoiled towns of Patiala and Amritsar stand on either side of Punjab's lush landscape of almost continuous wheat fields.

North of Chandigarh, the cool beauty of the lower Himalayan mountains inspired the British to create their summer capital, Shimla (Simla), here; the government would spend up to six months out of the year. A trip northeast from Delhi can lead to other cool retreats, such as the hill stations Mussoorie and Nainital, or you could join Hindu pilgrims at Hardwar and Rishikesh, ending with a visit to lovely Corbett National Park.

Transportation is easy by car, train, and plane. The *Shatabdi Express* trains, running from Delhi through Agra, Gwalior, and Jhansi to Bhopal, make travel to and around this region particularly easy, as does the train up to Chandigarh. There are some particularly delightful hotels in the unspoiled provincial towns. ■

NOT TO BE MISSED:

Agra's Taj Mahal at sunrise 98–101

Seeing *pietra dura* (stone inlay) craftsmen at work 101

Exploring the ghost city of Fatehpur Sikri 102–103

Sunrise bird-watching at Keoladeo Ghana National Park 104–105

Taking the Delhi–Agra *Shatabdi Express* train 106

Climbing to the top of Govind Mandir Palace 109

The prehistoric paintings at Bhimbetka 113

Bicycling around Mandu 115

Visiting Kanha National Park 116

Helping put the Guru Granth Sahib away at Amritsar's Golden Temple 120–121

Area of map detail

New Delhi

Agra & Around

Sikander Lodi moved the capital from Delhi to Agra. But the Mughal emperors transformed it into the dazzling, fairy-tale court whose fame reached Europe, and one, Shah Jahan, built the Taj Mahal here. Today the empty buildings need plenty of imagination to bring them to life; looking at some jewel-like Indian miniature paintings of Mughal court scenes can help.

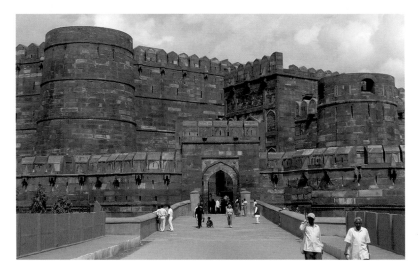

With massive sandstone double walls, Agra Fort was well designed to withstand long sieges.

Agra

 93 C4

Visitor Information

✉ Government of India Tourist Office, 1 The Mall

☎ 056/2222-6368, 056/2222-6378

incredibleindia.org

✉ State Tourist Office, 64 Taj Rd.

☎ 056/2222-6431

up-tourism.com

Agra Fort

After Babur's brief rule, during which he held a great celebratory feast at Agra, Humayun took the capital back to Delhi. But when Akbar (r. 1556–1605) built his fort between 1565 and 1573, Agra burst into life. When his grandson Shah Jahan returned to Delhi in 1648, the fort was left to plunderers.

Grand Fortifications: Cross the moat to reach the first great gateway of Akbar's magnificent double-walled fort. Qasim Khan designed it, using the glowing red sandstone that distinguishes many great Mughal buildings.

With soaring fortifications and the Yamuna River's waters lapping its walls, the treasury was safe and the army, court, and citizens could withstand long sieges. Note the battlemented parapets with ramparts and loopholed merlons. Today's Indian Army still occupies much of the fort. Next comes **Amar Singh Gate,** built at right angles in order to deflect elephant charges.

Akbar & Jahangir's
Buildings: At the top of the ramp, a **stone bath** stands in the gardens on the right, possibly a wedding present from Jahangir (r. 1605–1627) to Nur Jahan in

1611. It is said that the rose petals used to scent her bathwater inspired her to develop attar, a type of pungent perfume still sold in Indian bazaars; jasmine is one of the lighter ones to try.

It is believed that Jahangir added the long, marble-inlaid facade of the building behind. Through the archway you find a fascinating suite of **Akbar's rooms.** Built by local craftsmen, they are not remotely Islamic. Instead, the stocky proportions, pillar-and-beam structure, and densely carved decoration give them the look of pure Hindu buildings, constructed in stone instead of wood. Look for the central courtyard's square arches, broad decorative brackets, and the Hindu motif of parrots in the carving.

From the courtyard ahead, Akbar watched his elephant fights, a sport only royals were permitted to take part in. In 1605 Akbar staged a fight between the elephants of his son Salim and his grandson Khusrau, to see whose would win and thus who would succeed. Salim's elephant won. Later, Jahangir lived in these and other, similar, rooms commissioning paintings and enriching the simple walls with gilt-painted stucco. You can also enjoy your first tantalizing view of the Taj Mahal from here.

Shah Jahan's Marble Additions:

Moving on, the next rooms are a striking contrast. Sandstone is exchanged for white marble, stockiness for elegance. Shah Jahan (r. 1627–1658) built them, living here with his beloved wife, Mumtaz Mahal, when not on campaign. After her death and his subsequent move to Delhi, the emperor was deposed by his third son, Aurangzeb, in 1658 and kept prisoner here, tended by his daughter Jahanara until he died in 1666. Shah Jahan's buildings are thus suffused in romance and sadness. **Khas Mahal** is his suite of private rooms, and **Mussaman Burj** is the exquisite mini-palace inlaid with *pietra dura,* built for Mumtaz. Upstairs, **Diwan-i-Khas** ("public audience hall," 1628) is his most elegant building of all. In front of it stand two thrones; the black one was made for Jahangir when, a rebelling prince, he prematurely announced himself emperor in Allahabad in 1603. Underneath here was the treasury; the royal *hamams* (baths) were opposite,

Agra Fort

✉ Rakabgan

☎ 056/2296-0457

💲 $$$$$ (One-day, cost-saving combined entry ticket to Agra's main sites can be bought here and at the Taj Mahal.) $$$$ (Taj Mahal only)

Shah Jahan & Architecture

Shah Jahan indulged his passion for architecture and brought Mughal designs to their height. In Udaipur, as a young prince, he built a suite of rooms on Jagmandir Island in Lake Pichola. At Agra, he added exquisite inlaid white marble spaces in the fort. Then, once the Taj Mahal was under way, he laid out a new city in Delhi, Shahjahanabad, now known as Old Delhi and still thriving today.

**Tomb of Itimad-
ud-Daulah**
- E bank of
  Yamuna River,
  2 miles (4 km)
  upstream of
  Taj Mahal
- $$

Sikandra
- 93 C4
- 5 miles (8 km) N
  of Agra, off NH2
- $, free Fri.

and the lawn was laid out with a formal pattern of water channels, fountains and flowerbeds.

Walk around the cloisters to find the tiny **Nagina Masjid** ("gem mosque") and then, on the right, steep steps down to the **Diwan-i-Am.** Built by Shah Jahan to replace an earlier wooden version, it has elegant arches in front

INSIDER TIP:

Plan your visit to Vrindavan and the other nearby Braj villages to coincide with a big Hindu festival.

—LOUISE NICHOLSON
National Geographic author

of a richly decorated raised throne alcove, where the emperor gave his daily audience. Just imagine the citizens of Agra pouring in through the gate on the right to attend a royal *durbar,* a morning of pomp, ceremony, and entertainment.

After the Mughals

Once the Mughals had moved to Delhi, Agra was occupied successively by the Jats, Marathas, and, from 1803 onward, the British. The British cantonment area still has its wide avenues, elegant bungalows, and carefully sited public buildings. Try exploring Mall or Taj Roads, and look for the **Central Post Office** at Sadar Bazar. Also, nearby stand handsome **St. George's** cantonment church (1826) and the **Havelock Memorial Church** (1873). In this

area, you can see the supreme Agra local craft, pietra dura (marble inlaid with semiprecious stones). The **Subhash Emporium** (also called the Marble Emporium; *Gwalior Rd., tel 056/2222-5828, marbleemporium .com*) has some excellent pieces. To sample some local dishes, try *petha* (pumpkin candy), *dalmoth* (fried lentils), and various other Mughal-inspired favorites.

North of old Agra city, go past **St. John's Church,** the Roman Catholic cathedral with its landmark tower, and Sir Samuel Swinton Jacob's fine St. John's College, to find the **Roman Catholic cemetery.** This is one of India's earliest Christian cemeteries. Christians who died in Lahore and Ajmer were brought here for burial. Its impressive monuments include the tomb of John Mildenhall (1614), envoy of Elizabeth I, and a miniature copy of the Taj Mahal built for the Dutchman General Hessing (1803), who was in charge of Agra Fort for the Marathas when the British took it.

Across the Yamuna River

Tiled with polychrome mosaics, the stately, casketlike **tomb of Itimad-ud-Daulah** (see p. 39) was built by his daughter Nur Jahan, Jahangir's empress, in 1622–1628. Find delicate decorations inside, and outside enjoy serene gardens and river views. There are remains of **Ram Bagh** to the north, a Mughal garden that was probably the work of Babur and later Nur Jehan. To the south, the waterside tomb of **Chini-ka-Rauza** (1635) lies behind the market gardens. Farther south, the recently rediscovered and renovated **Mahtab Bagh** ("moonlit garden") completed the original Taj Mahal complex and now provides some glorious views of the Taj.

Around Agra

At **Sikandra,** northwest of Agra, visit Akbar's great garden mausoleum. He began it in 1602, but after his death in 1605 Jahangir aggrandized it and swapped modest sandstone for marble; **Akbar's mausoleum** is on the roof. Akbar's huge entrance gateway is impressive; look for Jahangir's floral painted vaults. *(Beware of black-faced monkeys: They are quite tame, but they expect handouts and might snatch your belongings.)* East of the complex is Jahangir's fine Kanch Mahal. On the drive up here, look for various tombs and the *kos minars* (milestones) that guided Mughal travelers.

The ancient city of **Mathura** stands on the Yamuna 39 miles (62 km) northwest of Agra, at the center of the holy land of Braj, and in Hindu mythology was the birthplace of Krishna. As such, Mathura is one of the Hindus' Seven Sacred Cities. Its waterfront is lined with bathing ghats and temples. See especially **Dwarkadhish Temple** (1814), built by Seth Gokuldas Parikh of Gwalior; river trips leave from Vishram Ghat. The town's **Archaeological Museum** has a superb collection that reflects Mathura's place as a trading center under the Sunga,

Kushana, and Gupta dynasties. It houses ravishing Buddhist and Jain stone sculptures, which often use the distinctive Mathura speckled red sandstone. The collection also includes sculptures made in Gandhara but found locally.

Vrindavan, the most important of a group of Braj villages sacred to Hindus and especially devotees of Krishna, lies about 6 miles (10 km) north of Mathura. Here, Krishna flirted with the milkmaids; at Mahaban, his foster father, Nanda, tended the young god; at Gokul, Krishna was raised in secrecy; at Barsana, his consort Radha was born; and Goverdhan is the hill Krishna lifted to protect the female cowherds from the god Indra's storms. ∎

Akbar's Mausoleum
☎ 056/2264-1230
 $$

Mathura
🅼 93 C4
✉ 39 miles (62 km) N of Agra on NH2

Archaeological Museum
✉ Dampier Park, Mathura
🕐 Closed Fri.

Vrindavan
🅼 93 C4
✉ 42 miles (68 km) N of Agra off NH2

Shah Jahan gave Agra this landmark mosque in 1648.

Taj Mahal

Mumtaz Mahal (Chosen One of the Palace), wife of Shah Jahan, died in June 1631 after bearing their 14th child. She had been the emperor's wife, companion, adviser, and support for 17 years. Channeling his despair into the creation of her mausoleum, Shah Jahan called a council of top architects and craftsmen: He chose Ustad Isa Khan Effendi, a Persian from Shiraz, as master builder, his pupil Ustad Ahmed for the detailed work, and Ismail Khan for the dome.

The Yamuna River reflects Shah Jahan's masterpiece, the world-famous Taj Mahal.

Taj Mahal
🅰 93 C4
✉ Tajganj
🕐 Closed Fri.
💲 $$$$

tajmahal.gov.in

Enter through any of the three gates to the complex and you leave chaos for order. The great gate prepares you further for the serenity within, with its inlaid Koran passage known as Al-Fajr (daybreak), which ends: "O Soul that art at rest. Return to the Lord, at peace with Him and He at peace with you. So enter as one of His servants. And enter into His garden."

You then do just that, emerging into a *char bagh* (four gardens), which is how paradise is described in the Koran: a lush, well-planted, walled garden divided symmetrically by water channels. Pause to take it all in.

Mumtaz Mahal's garden tomb takes to ultimate refinement the Mughal garden tomb built for Humayun (see p. 71). At Taj Mahal, the proportions are more satisfying; luxurious marble is used instead of sandstone, and the whole platform and mausoleum building is pushed from the center of the garden to the end, to benefit from the river light and from being silhouetted against the sky. The dome shape is more elegant and, as close inspection will reveal, the inlay work is finer.

But this memorial is more than a symbol of paradise to reward the faithful. It also symbolizes the royal pleasure garden and a lush oasis in the dry desert heat. To this, Shah Jahan added another, political

INSIDER TIP:

Security restricts evening visits to two days before and two days after the full moon. Reservations are required [asi.nic.in].

—ADITI SENSHARMA
National Geographic contributor

image: The Taj Mahal symbolizes the might of Islam embodied in the all-powerful Mughal rulers.

It took 22 years to build the Taj. Craftsmen and laborers came from Baghdad, Delhi, Samarkand, Turkey, and elsewhere in Asia. The marble was from Makrana,

Best Taj Views

The Taj Mahal is always impressive, but if you plan your visit, you'll get much more out of the experience. Arriving at the Taj, pause to enjoy the great gateway and view through it to the mausoleum; on the other side of the gateway, pause again before going down into the gardens to the left, ending at the mosque; up on the platform, walk around the mausoleum and finally go inside. Some say the best time to visit is late afternoon, when the softening light sets the stone aglow; others say sunrise, when the light is totally different and fewer people ensure tranquility. Finally, be sure to visit Mehtab Bagh, the rediscovered pleasure gardens across the Yamuna, which were part of the original Taj plan.

near Jaipur; the precious and semiprecious stones from various places—jasper from the Punjab, jade from China, lapis lazuli from Afghanistan, agates from Yemen.

As you wander through the gardens, you see the white marble of the Taj through the contrasting dark green trees; you see it too reflected in the long fountain pool. At the front of the platform, railings mark the spot where Mumtaz's body was buried while the Taj Mahal was being built. A **mosque** stands to the left of the Taj. On the platform, verses from the Koran, panels of low-relief carving, and inlaid designs cover the exterior. Inside, cenotaphs for Mumtaz (central) and Shah Jahan lie surrounded by an intricate trellis screen (their real tombs lie in the now closed vault below).

The time of day that you first visit the Taj is important. The hard light of midday flattens it, whereas to enter the precincts mid-afternoon and slowly explore the gateway views and the lush gardens, ending at the platform as the sun ripens, is a near-perfect experience. You may find yourself inspired to return at sunrise to enjoy the magical and soft morning light.

Marble Inlay

Mogul patrons lifted the craft of *pietra dura* (hard stone) inlay decoration to new heights. The results are even more impressive if you know a little about this difficult, precise skill and see it being practiced.

Materials are supplied to the *ateliers* of Muslim craftsmen by Hindu merchants. The hard, nonporous white marble comes

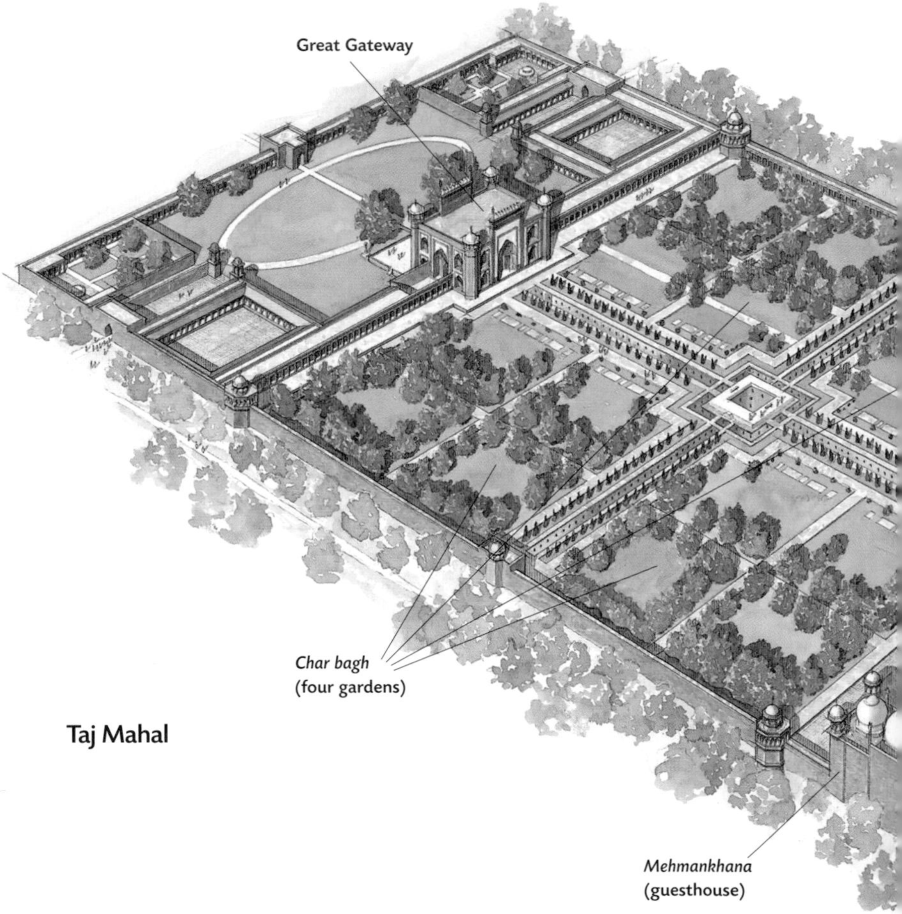

Great Gateway

Char bagh
(four gardens)

Taj Mahal

Mehmankhana
(guesthouse)

from Makrana, near Jaipur; coral
and stones including turquoise,
carnelian, and lapis lazuli come
from all over the world. Once the
design is agreed upon, a master
craftsman draws it on the marble.
The stones are selected, cut, and
chiseled, then the beds for each
pattern gouged out. Each design
is then fitted, fine-tuned, and
stuck. Finally the whole surface is
polished with fine emery.

Today, more than 5,000 pietra
dura craftsmen are working in
family-run ateliers in the Agra back
lanes. To watch some more easily,
visit **Subhash Emporium** (see
p. 96) on Gwalior Road. ∎

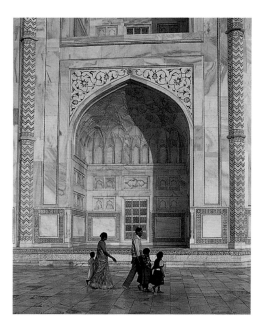

At the Taj Mahal, a family visits Mumtaz's memorial.

NOTE: Ticket prices
and security restric-
tions vary, and the
Taj Mahal may close
if government guests
are visiting. Currently,
no bags are permitted
and video cameras are
permitted no closer
than just inside the
great gate, after which
they must be put in
a locker. Because of
the thorough security
check, it is advisable
to carry only a camera
and a small amount of
cash when you visit.

Masjid
(mosque)

Main tomb

Yamuna River

Fatehpur Sikri

Fatehpur Sikri is a perfect ghost city. This group of mysterious buildings is all that remains of the city conceived and built by Akbar as his ideal capital. Bursting into life in 1571, it was an instant success; just 14 years later it was virtually abandoned when Akbar was called to defend the northwest frontier of his empire. His court followed him there; he never returned.

Why did Akbar choose this spot? In 1568 the powerful 26-year-old emperor had consolidated his empire but, despite many marriage alliances, had no heir. After his annual pilgrimage to the Chishti tomb at Ajmer, on the way back to Agra he stopped here to visit a living Chishti saint, Shaikh Salim, who predicted that Akbar would soon have three sons. The next year, Akbar's Amber wife, Jodha Bai, gave birth to a boy, who was named Salim after the saint. The following year Murad

Shaikh Salim Chishti's tomb, with exquisite marble *jali* work, stands in the Jami Masjid's huge courtyard.

Fatehpur Sikri

🅰 93 C4

✉ 25 miles (40 km) W of Agra on Jaipur Rd. in Uttar Pradesh

☎ 056/2222-6368, 056/2226-378

💲 $$

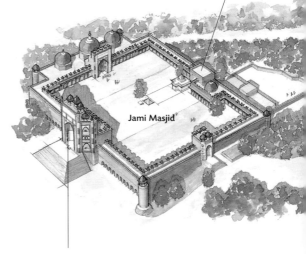

Shaikh Salim's tomb

Jami Masjid

Buland Darwaza

was born, and in 1572 Daniyal fulfilled the prediction.

After just two sons had been born, Akbar began to build a new city where the saint lived. He called it Fatehpur Sikri (City of Victory) and envisaged it as the cultural, commercial, and administrative center of his empire; most of his army and treasury stayed at Agra.

A good way to start visiting the buildings is to imagine the bazaars lining the road from inside the gateway up to the ticket office. Remember: There are no contemporary texts or plans, so each building's possible function is guesswork. Start by exploring the **Abdair Khana,** probably the royal workshops. Then see the so-called **Diwan-i-Am** ("audience hall"), whose built-in throne is decorated

INSIDER TIP:

To avoid heat and crowds, go early or in the late afternoon; take drinks and snacks.

—LOUISE NICHOLSON
National Geographic author

with *jali* work, and, behind here, the exquisite palace rooms, treasuries, and discussion halls. Beyond them, several palaces of what was probably the imperial harem have surviving painted decoration. Out through the back gate, you must run the gauntlet of peddlers to reach the **Jami Masjid** and see the saint's tomb, the prayer hall, and the soaring **Buland Darwaza** (Gate of Magnificence) that celebrates Akbar's conquest of Gujarat (1573). ◼

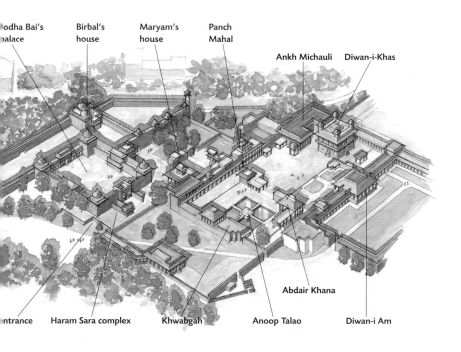

Jodha Bai's palace · Birbal's house · Maryam's house · Panch Mahal · Ankh Michauli · Diwan-i-Khas · Abdair Khana · Entrance · Haram Sara complex · Khwabgah · Anoop Talao · Diwan-i Am

Keoladeo Ghana National Park

A few hours spent in the silence and wondrous nature of this park (also known as Bharatpur Bird Sanctuary) quickly restores one's soul after the whirlwind of Agra sightseeing.

On an early-morning cruise, a local ornithologist identifies each bird's morning song.

Keoladeo Ghana National Park

- 93 B4
- 33 miles (53 km) W of Agra, 10 miles (16 km) NW of Fatehpur Sikri, in Rajasthan
- Guided tours: 056/4422-2777
- $
- No cars; visit by boat, on foot, on rented bicycle, or by cycle rickshaw

bharatpur.nic.in

The variety of habitats and climates, and the traditional respect for birds in India, have made the country especially rich in birdlife. More than 1,200 of the world's 8,650 species of birds are found here, with 2,000 subspecies among them. This makes India's checklist twice the size of those of North America and Europe. Moreover, the dramatic shapes and colors of many species make bird-watching easy and rewarding for the amateur. For once, patience is not essential, since the birds are everywhere. All you need are sharp eyes, a pair of binoculars, and a good reference book–Bikram Grewal's *A Photographic Guide to the Birds of India & Nepal* (Chelsea Green Pub. Co., 1998) has plenty of helpful photographs. Using this, you will soon find that you are identifying plenty of birds on your own.

The Sanctuary

Keoladeo Ghana National Park takes its official name from the local temple dedicated to Keoladeo (Shiva). Established in 1956, it became a national park in 1981 and is today one of the world's most important sanctuaries for migratory birds and herons. Although just inside Rajasthan, it is only an hour's drive from Agra and is best visited from there.

The Maharaja of Bharatpur developed the 11 square miles (29 sq km) of freshwater swamp during the British period as the focus for his grand duck shoots. Viceroy Lord Curzon attended the first one in 1902; Viceroy Lord Linlithgow was there in 1938 when 4,273 birds were shot, the biggest "bag" ever.

Resident Species

With the guns now silenced, energetic and enlightened conservation has brought results. There are sometimes more than 375 species of birds to be seen here in winter, when migrating birds arrive from all over Russia, Central Asia, and other parts of the world, to join the 120 or so resident species. When the monsoon begins, so does the nestbuilding. Some 10,000 nests are constructed in the heronries of acacia trees by big birds such as painted and openbill storks, white ibises, spoonbills, and purple herons. Sleek black cormorants, dazzling white egrets, and the common and pond herons play their parts, too. Other species of waterfowl arrive from August to October. Late arrivals to the park include rosy pelicans and flamingos, and, during December and January only, the rare Siberian crane.

By the beginning of March, those chicks who have eluded the vultures and other birds of prey and have become strong and fat begin to depart, bound for their summer homes.

As the land dries, terrestrial birds begin to breed, so even in April there is a rich assortment of birds to spot during a three-hour morning walk. At this time the park's animals—spotted deer, sambar, blackbuck (small antelopes), mongoose, and others—can also be seen. So can large numbers of rock pythons, especially near the temple and main entrance.

INSIDER TIP:

Birdwatchers should not miss this park, near Bharatpur. Even during dry season, spotting 50 species in 3 hours is not unusual.

—KEN ROSE
National Geographic grantee

Still, the best time to visit the park is at dawn from September to February. Take a rowboat (and a local ornithologist) out on the lake. As the mist lifts at sunrise, morning birdsong and flapping wings bring the islands of kadam trees alive. Metallic blue kingfishers eye breakfast from low branches, eagles glide through still air, and large painted and black-neck storks stand up to stretch in precarious treetop nests. As the sun rises and the mist clears, the cacophony of sound rises to a climax: a magical experience. ∎

NOTE: The park is best visited at sunrise or sunset. Check in advance that the monsoon was good; if it wasn't, many migrating birds will not have come.

Trains

Ever since the first steam train puffed out of Bombay's Victoria Terminus station to a 21-gun salute on April 16, 1853, the Indian railways have had their own character. For many British arrivals at Bombay port, their first experience of India was a three-day train ride to their final destination. Soot blackened the travelers' clothes, there were unaccountable stops between stations, and locals sold their wares at every possible opportunity.

That first train carried just 400 people along 21 miles (34 km) of track in 75 minutes. Railroads were soon built by the British to carry valuable trading goods to India's ports, and by the Indian princes to amuse themselves in their princely states: The Gwalior train still runs. Since then, India's railroad system has played a vital role in its economic, industrial, and social development.

Today India is one of the few countries in the world that is expanding its railroad system. The figures are impressive. A fleet of almost 7,500 engines, 37,800 coaches, and 300,000 wagons uses the 67,108 miles (108,000 km) of railroad track, which is punctuated by 7,068 stations. The longest route is Guwahati–Trivandrum, which carries passengers 2,469 miles (3,974 km) from the mountainous northeast to the steamy south. Each year, freight trains carry in excess of a million tons of goods; each day more than 7,500 passenger trains carry 11 million passengers (plus more riding ticketless on the roof). So all-pervading is the railroad that mobile eye hospitals reach isolated rural areas by train, not road.

The Indian railroad employs more than 1.54 million people, making it one of the country's largest employers. At large junctions, such as at Hubli in Karnataka, the workers live in neatly laid-out model towns, each with its own houses, stores, churches (many railroad families are Christian), cricket ground, schools, and other public buildings. In India, one can be a railroad man from birth to death.

Largely gone now are the steam engines, except for tourist enjoyment, and the delightful complexities of broad, meter, and narrow gauge are being simplified into broad gauge only. But some trains retain their romantic names—*Himalayan Queen, Pink City Express,* and *Grand Trunk Express.*

Grand new projects are at hand. The fast, reliable *Shatabdi Express* train was introduced in the 1980s; its first route was Delhi to Bhopal. The Delhi–Agra stretch takes just over two hours compared to a driving time of four. As India's labyrinth of tracks is simplified and modernized, these trains connect most major cities. The great feat, however, has been the construction of the Konkan Railroad, which runs from Mumbai southward down the west coast to Mangalore (see p. 202). Next on the agenda is a line along Gujarat's long coast.

EXPERIENCE:
Riding the Rails

Today, a short train journey on a real train—as opposed to a tourist train—is an important element in a visit to India, allowing you to experience firsthand the dizzying balance between the apparent chaos of the Indian railroad station and the laboriously meticulous requirements of the ticket-selling staff. The process of buying a ticket, reserving a seat, understanding the departures board, and then finding the train and your seat demands plenty of time and possibly some new skills. For reservations visit *irctc.co.in* or *the luxurytrains.com* (see Travelwise p. 338).

Steam trains are now very rare in India. This one, carrying freight only, awaits a signal outside Agra.

Gwalior, Datia, & Orchha

This triangle of elegant architectural sites set in a wooded landscape south of Agra is easy to enjoy, provided clambering up and down stone steps is not a problem.

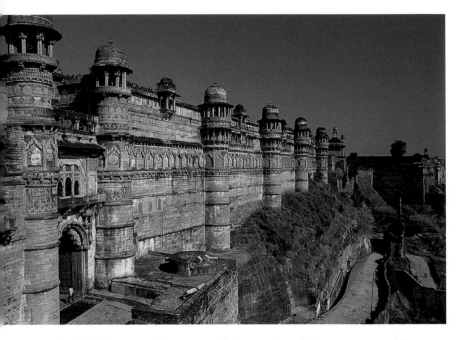

Gwalior's palace rooms and great outer walls impressed even the fort-weary emperor Akbar.

Gwalior, Madhya Pradesh

 93 C3

Visitor Information

✉ Gwalior Tourist Office, Railway Station, Gwalior

☎ 075/1404-0777

🕐 Open 11 a.m.– 5 p.m. Mon.– Sat. Closed Sun. & 2nd & 3rd Sat. of every month

mptourism.com

Gwalior

Once the capital of the prestigious princely state of the same name, whose ruler had the title the Scindia, this large town is still dominated by its imposing fort built on top of a huge natural sandstone bluff.

The city's history starts at **Gwalior Fort** ($), reached through a series of fortified gateways. Turn right at the top and you pass two ornate **Saas Bahu temples** (tenth century), possibly built by the Kachwaha Rajputs, who founded the fort. **Man Mandir** (1486–1517), built by the Tomar ruler

Man Singh, is the centerpiece and one of India's finest early Hindu forts. Note the two courtyards ringed by suites of rooms, the bold decoration, the variety of roofs, and the glazed tiles on the exterior.

The Tomar Rajputs had seized the fort from Delhi's Tughluq sultan in 1398 and held it until 1516. After the Tomars, the fort passed successively to the Mughals, Marathas, and Jats; it was the scene of fierce fighting in 1858 between the British, led by Sir Hugh Rose, and the freedom fighters led by the Rani of Jhansi (see sidebar opposite). In 1886, it was ceded to the Scindia. This brief history helps explain the other monuments here—four more **palaces** lie beyond Man Mandir, another Hindu temple, some British remains, a Sikh temple, and the **Archaeological Museum's** (*closed Fri., $*) sculptures found in the area. On the way down, look for the Jain statues (7th to 15th centuries, defaced by Babur) cut into the rock. In the city see the **Jami Masjid** (1661) and the grand **tombs of Muhammad Ghaus** (late 16th century)—a Muslim saint who helped Babur win the fort—and **Tansen** (early 17th century), Akbar's court musician, in whose honor a national **music festival** (*Nov.–Dec.*) is held here annually.

For a flavor of the heights of extravagance reached by India's self-indulgent princes allied with the British, visit the colossal 1874 **Jai Vilas** (*$*), designed by Lieut. Col. Sir Michael Filose and now partly a museum. The palace has two Belgian chandeliers, each weighing 3.5 tons and measuring 41 feet (12.5 m) in height.

Datia & Orchha

On the road south from Gwalior to Datia it's worth stopping at **Sonagiri,** a Jain pilgrimage center for the Digambar sect (see p. 60). Take a look at the mirror temple and the white shrines leading up to the hilltop temple.

At Datia, a street crosses a causeway and leads through the walled village to the surprising sight of soaring **Govind Mandir Palace** (1620). Inside, dark stairways and labyrinthine corridors

rise level by level to reveal a design of such symmetrical clarity and stone carving of such precision and beauty as to make this one of the finest Rajput palaces.

Both this and the grandest of Orchha's palaces were built by Bir Singh Deo of Bundelkund, who sealed his future with Emperor Jahangir by assassinating Emperor Akbar's court historian, Abul Fazl, who disapproved of Jahangir's (then Prince Salim) behavior.

Orchha is a medieval palace city. Its island fort is composed of the **Raj Mahal,** with bright murals of Hindu myths, and the later **Jahangir Mahal** (Bir Singh Deo's addition for Jahangir's state visit). **Sheesh Mahal** stands between them, now a government-run hotel. Other treats include **Rai Praveen Mahal palace, Lakshmi Narayan** hilltop temple with its murals, and walks beside the Betwa River to see the royal *chhatris* (tombs). ∎

Datia, Madhya Pradesh

🅰 93 C3

✉ 39 miles (63 km) S of Gwalior

Orchha, Madhya Pradesh

🅰 93 C3

✉ 10 miles (16 km) S of Datia

A Legendary Woman

In 1858, the Rani of Jhansi, wife of the Raja of Jhansi, held Gwalior Fort against the British and Sir Hugh Rose with the help of her personal bodyguard until her husband sided with the British in the Mutiny. When the fort finally fell, she joined the main rebel force at Gwalior, rode into battle dressed as a man, with her baby strapped to her back, and was killed while defending Gwalior.

Khajuraho

Forested isolation protected Khajuraho's cluster of resplendent Hindu temples from Muslim destruction. Created between the 10th and the 12th centuries by the rulers of the Chandella dynasty, a Rajput clan who resisted Muslim invasion, they were then lost until 1819. Their rediscovery is a remarkable story.

A voluptuous Lakshmi nestles against her partner, Vishnu, adorning one of Khajuraho's temples.

**Khajuraho,
Madhya Pradesh**

[M] 93 C3

Visitor Information

[✉] Tourist
Interpretation
& Facilitation
Center,
Madhya Pradesh
Tourism,
Near Circuit
House, Khajurao

[☎] Tel: 076/8627-
4051
Fax: 076/8627-
2330

[🕑] Closed Sun. &
2nd & 3rd Sat.
of every month

**Email: khajurao@
mptourism.com**

In 1819 a British military surveyor spotted the temples in the dense jungle. His report map was unclear: Did the labels read "mines" or "ruins"? Twenty years later, Capt. T. S. Burt, who was traveling in the area, heard rumor of the temples and sought them out. He reported: "I found seven Hindoo temples, most beautifully and exquisitely carved as to workmanship, but the sculptor had at times allowed his subject to grow a little warmer than there was any absolute necessity for his doing."

The eroticism of the sculptures attracts visitors, but new research reveals that Khajuraho was once known as Shivpuri (City of Shiva), and the sculptures decorating the temples recount and celebrate the marriage of Shiva, god of creative and destructive energy, to Parvati. Thus, they portray the consummation of marriage and, at the same time, the highest spiritual experience achievable. According to Hindu theory, lovemaking demands that all the senses be given fully to achieve total physical and mental union.

The structure of each temple lends weight to this theory of marriage, consummation, and procreation. The *jangha* (body) of the temple, between the base and spire, is the celestial realm. Thus, the copulating couples are mostly the divine Shiva and Parvati, and the nymphs are expressing surprise that the god is attending the wedding party. Every Hindu temple mirrors the creation of life: The sanctum, or *garbha griha* (womb), is where Shiva's *lingum* (phallus), representing potential creativity, is kept.

Khajuraho's 25 temples may have been part of a nonmonastic center of learning and religion. The most spectacular are in the Western Group, walkable from nearby hotels and the museum. To go farther afield, either use a cycle rickshaw or rent a bicycle.

Western Group

The added serenity of sunrise and sunset intensifies the surreal experience of seeing these temples. Pass Varaha Temple, with its massive sandstone boar, to reach **Lakshamana Temple** (ca 950), the oldest of this group, whose riotous carvings of processions, domestic scenes, musicians, and dancers are full of vitality and movement. Next, visit the **Kandariya Mahadeva Temple** (1025–1050), possibly the finest of all the temples in its architecture, its rising silhouette, and its sublime and fluid carving. An elaborate wedding garland at the entrance symbolizes the marriage gate; niches along the outside of the sanctum have carvings of the Sapta Matrikas (Seven Mothers) responsible for dressing the bridegroom, Shiva. Finally, pass the three temples of Mahadeva, Devi Jagdamba, and Chitragupta

to find **Vishwanath Temple,** built in 1002 by Dhangadeva (r. 950–1002). Shiva's Nandi bull vehicle sits outside, while up on the jangha of the temple the sculptures of amorous couples, sensuous nymphs, and idealized women are especially delicate.

Elsewhere on the Site

The simple, old **Matangeshwara Temple** stands just outside this complex and is still in daily use. Near it, random Khajuraho artifacts are kept in the **Archaeological Museum,** including a frieze showing how

INSIDER TIP:

At a weeklong festival in late February/early March, classical dancers perform at sunset against the illuminated Chitragupta and Vishwanath Temples.

—STEPHANIE ROBICHAUX
National Geographic contributor

the sandstone for the temples was dug from the Ken River, 20 miles (32 km) away, transported to this area, then cut and carved. The soft river stone then hardened; hence its crispness today. The eastern and southern groups are less spectacular, but nevertheless rewarding. In the first, the early **Parsvanatha Temple** is especially fine; in the second, the isolated **Duladeo Temple** (12th century) shows the Chandellas' decline. ■

Archaeological Museum

✉ Near entrance to Western Group of temples

🕐 Closed Fri.

💲 $ (museum only)
$$ (includes temples)

Bhopal & Around

As the capital of Madhya Pradesh state, Bhopal benefits from some impressive public buildings. By keeping its rampant modern expansion separate, it remains a delightful provincial town, only now bursting out of its preindependence mix of palaces, mosques, gardens, and lakes.

Bhopal, Madhya Pradesh

🗺 93 B2

Visitor Information

✉ State Tourist Office, Palash Residency, near 45 Bungalow, T. T. Nagar, New Market

☎ 075/5276-6750, 075/5255-3006

mptourism.com

The Hindu ruler Raja Bhoj (1018–1085), a scholar of the Paramara dynasty, founded Bhopal in the 11th century. He sited the city on a crescent-shape ridge and created artificial lakes. But Bhopal's present character took shape only from the end of the 17th century. Dost Muhammed Khan, an opportunistic ex-general of the Mughal emperor Aurangzeb's army, took the then deserted city and laid out a fresh one. Through consistent loyalty to the British, his descendants, including three city-improving *begums* (female Muslim rulers), became major Indian princes and princesses ruling over a happy mix of Hindu and Muslim cultures, a mix that continues today.

Tragically, Bhopal's most recent fame came on December 3, 1984, when a lethal cloud of toxic chemicals escaped from a tank at the Union Carbide factory, resulting in death or chronic illness for thousands of people. The factory is closed, and the site is a wasteland, but the effects continue to haunt the locals.

Visitors can stay in Noor-Us-Sabah, a delightful converted palace (see Travelwise p. 347). The **Taj-ul-Masjid** (Crown of All Mosques), built by Shah Jahan Begum (r. 1868–1901), is a good place to begin sightseeing. The spaciousness of this and **Imam Square,** once the royal heart of Bhopal, contrasts with the smaller mosques and narrow streets of the **Old City,** where ladies wrapped in burkas bargain for silver, silks (local Bilaspur and Chandheri examples are stunning), and jewelry.

Bhopal's museum collections are very impressive. Do not miss

Boys come to the courtyard of the Taj-ul-Masjid for a drink of water or a surreptitious game of cricket.

the stone sculptures in the **Birla Mandir Museum** (next to Birla Mandir, overlooking Lower Lake, closed Mon., $) and in the **Indira Gandhi Rashtriya Manav Sanghralaya** (National Museum of Mankind), the tribal homes complete with murals and furnishings. Bhopal's impressive contemporary buildings include Charles Correa's 1982 multi-arts complex, **Bharat Bhavan** (Lake Drive Rd., closed a.m. & Mon.), always alive with exhibitions and performances, and his boldly majestic and colorful **State Assembly** (1999).

Around Bhopal

Beyond the industrial suburbs south of Bhopal, a dirt road leads to **Bhimbetka** rocks. These are part of a 5-mile-long (8 km) ridge, where layers of pink, caramel, and cream sandstone have been weathered into fantastical shapes. Under some outcrops early humans left several hundred paintings, which were only rediscovered as recently as the 1950s. Most are line drawings in red or white. They show elephants, antelope, and wild boar, as well as people fishing, fighting, shooting arrows, dancing, and playing the drums. The paintings offer a glimpse of an ancient world and probably span the paleolithic to the neolithic periods. Beautiful and vulnerable, they as yet have no protection.

Best visited with Bhimbetka, **Bhojpur** is where Bhopal's founder dammed the Betwa River to make a reservoir, began his colossal Shiva Temple, and built

Udayeshvara Temple

True temple lovers will want to make the effort to reach the Udayeshvara Temple (1080), set in the center of the small village of Udayapur. Its ambitious scale, rhythmic proportions, and rich sculpture proclaim its royal patronage, confirmed in an inscription. Its quality, style, dedication to Shiva, and an image of Parvati behind the _lingum_ in the sanctum suggest a close relationship with Khajuraho's temples (see pp. 110–111).

the nearby Jain shrine with its stone image of Mahavira.

To see the beginnings of monumental Hindu sculpture, seek out the remarkable fifth-century rock-cut Gupta caves at **Udaigiri.** Climb up the steep steps in the rock face just before Udaigiri village; then stroll among the caves, ending at the best, **Cave no. 5.** Inside, the 13-foot-high (4 m) composition shows Varaha, Vishnu's boar incarnation, rescuing the earth goddess Bhudevi, possibly an allegory of the unification of northern India by Gupta ruler Chandragupta II.

Nearby at **Besnagar,** you will find a remarkable survivor of the ages: the **Column of Heliodorus,** a stone pillar erected in 113 b.c. and dedicated to Krishna's father by Heliodorus, a Greek envoy from Taxila, capital of Gandhara. ∎

Rashtriya Manav Sanghralaya
- ✉ Shamla Hills, overlooking Upper Lake
- ☎ 075/5252-6531
- 🕐 Closed Mon.

Bhimbetka
- 🅰 93 C2
- ✉ 27 miles (43 km) SE of Bhopal

Visitor Information
- ✉ Highway Treat
- ☎ 074/8028-1558
- **Email: bhimbetka@ mptourism.com**

Bhojpur
- 🅰 93 C2
- ✉ 10 miles (16 km) SE of Bhopal

Udaigiri Caves
- 🅰 93 C2
- ✉ 6 miles (10 km) N of Sanchi

Besnagar
- 🅰 93 C2
- ✉ 4 miles (6 km) N of Sanchi

Udayapur
- 🅰 93 C2
- ✉ 82 miles (132 km) NE of Bhopal via Sanchi

Sanchi

Sanchi, whose great stupa, with its four soaring gateways embellished with intricate carvings, constitutes one of India's oldest surviving stone buildings and is certainly its finest surviving Buddhist monument.

Sanchi, Madhya Pradesh

🗺 93 C2

Archaeological Museum

✉ Sanchi

☎ 074/8226-6611

🕐 Closed Fri.

💲 $

Monuments spanning the third century b.c. to the seventh century a.d. crowd the hill rising above the plain: stupas, monastic buildings, elaborate railings, columns, and temples. Yet, despite the size and importance of the site, there may well be so few visitors that you can imagine how General Taylor might have felt when he rediscovered it, completely overgrown, having trekked the 37 miles (60 km) out from Bhopal, in 1819.

Although Sanchi has no known link with Buddha, there are relics here of two of his disciples and of later teachers. Inscriptions indicate that merchants from nearby Vidisha were donors.

The relatively complete preservation of **Stupa 1** (third to first century b.c. and fifth century a.d.), including railings and gateway sculpture, makes it the most important piece of architecture and narrative art of the Shunga era. The stupa itself is 120 feet (36 m) in diameter and encases an earlier one. The surrounding stone balustrade and gateways imitate wood in their structure, but their fully developed motifs (flowers, animals, birds, etc.) and sophisticated iconography narrating the life of Buddha and the *Jataka* tales (stories of his former lives) may be derived from ivory carving. Buddha is never shown in human form (out of respect). ∎

EXPERIENCE: Focusing Your Lens on India

Many photography tours and workshops address the needs of the photography enthusiast—the one willing to catch the early morning light, sit for long periods to get the perfect river scene, spend hours in a bangle market, and wait patiently in the cold for elephants to cross a river

Some tours go to just one destination; others might visit a colorful fair such as Sonpur or Pushkar; still others head to the ultimate light-filled destination, Varanasi—also called Benares or Kashi, city of light. Led by professional photographers who get you to the right place at the right time, they also advise on what lenses to pack and what other equipment might be useful. They have already researched the best times to be where, and know when a street will be empty or a temple full with worshippers. Their tips are invaluable, for getting both the classic and offbeat shots.

All too often, photo trips focus on Rajasthan; try to find one that also explores the other parts of India's visually extraordinary land. Consider **Photo Safari India** (*photosafariindia.com*), which does group tours focusing on wildlife, Rajasthan color, and the Himalaya; it can also create individual tailor-made tours. **National Geographic Expeditions** (*national geographicexpeditions.com*) also offers photo trips in India.

Mandu

The isolated remains of the once grand capital of the central Indian kingdom of Malwa make Mandu one of India's most magical forts to visit, especially during monsoon lushness. More than 70 Muslim and Hindu monuments built between the 11th and 16th centuries stand amid farming villages on an extensive fortified hilltop, with the Vindhya Mountains as a backdrop.

Rani Roopmati, after whom these pavilions at Rewakunk, to the south of the main site, are named, was the consort of Mandu's 16th-century ruler, Baz Bahadur.

The powerful Paramar ruler Raja Bhoj (see p. 112) fortified the hilltop, but in 1305 it fell to the Khilji sultans of Delhi. A later Afghan governor of Malwa declared independence from Delhi and moved the capital from Dhar—41 miles (66 km) west of Mandu, with two mosques, Bhojshala and Lat Masjid, that anticipate Mandu's triumphs—to Mandu. His son, Hoshang Shah, gave Mandu some of its finest buildings (Jama Masjid and his own tomb). Having won the city back in 1436, the Khiljis added more buildings, distinguished for their elegant simplicity, mixing Gujarat and Delhi styles. The Mughals later restored some buildings and in 1617 Jahangir spent his birthday here.

Wandering the palaces, tombs, mosques, and tanks needs time. Here are a few highlights. Beside the modern fort entrance is Hoshang Shah's **Delhi Gate.** The village buildings surround the magnificent pink sandstone **Jama Masjid** and Hoshang Shah's white marble **tomb** (ca 1440), the earliest of its kind on the subcontinent. **Jahaz Mahal** (Ship Palace) is beautiful at sunset. ■

Mandu, Madhya Pradesh

A 93 B2

Visitor Information

✉ Malwa Resort

☎ 072/9226-3253
&

✉ Malwa Retreat, email: mretreatm@ mptourism.com

☎ 072/9226-3221

Wildlife Parks of Madhya Pradesh

The wildlife sanctuaries deep in central India are exceptional for their wild terrain and abundant animal life and birdlife, so they are worth the effort needed to get there. Furthermore, accommodations are increasingly comfortable and staffed with experienced naturalists.

Bandhavgarh National Park

The attractive combination of trekking by elephant and the likelihood of spotting a tiger reward you for making the journey. For those devoted to elephants, there is the added bonus of visiting their compound to learn how they are reared and trained.

The park was established in 1968. Its 169 square miles (437 sq km) of rugged and hilly landscape stretch across the heart of the Vidhya Mountains and currently harbor the highest density tiger population of any Indian park; next best are Kanha, Satpura, and Ranthambhor (see p. 134). Also look for langurs, sloth bears, wild boars, gaur (wild ox), and porcupines. There are several kinds of deer and antelope—*chital* (spotted deer), *nilgai* (blue bull antelope), sambar, and *chowsingha* (four-horned antelope)—amid the *sal* trees of the valleys and mixed foliage of the upper areas. *(Nearest airports Varanasi and Khajuraho, mptourism.com, closed July–mid-Oct., stay at Tala)*

Kanha National Park

One of India's largest and best parks, Kanha covers more than 770 square miles (2,000 sq km) of fauna-rich land in the Banjar Valley. Rudyard Kipling's *The Jungle Book* (1894), made into a movie by Walt Disney, is set in this area and depicts the truly idyllic jungle life that you can still experience.

The park was established in 1955 as the start of a successful project to save the almost extinct hard-ground *barasingha* (Indian swamp deer). As you travel through the beautiful landscape, you may spot the now flourishing barasingha, and chital deer, langur monkey, gaur, nilgai, wild boar, mouse deer, sambhar, bee-eaters, black ibises, golden orioles, serpent eagles, and even the elusive leopard. *(Nearest airports Nagpur and Jabalpur, mptourism.com, closed July–Oct.)*

Panna National Park

Conveniently close to Khajuraho, this wilderness of valleys and gorges bordering the Ken River is glorious when monsoon rains have given it lushness and copious waterfalls. You may see nilgai, sloth bear, sambhar, and *chinkara* (Indian gazelle) in the teak forest, and the rare wolf gharial and mugger crocodiles in the Ken.

But the 210-square-mile (543 sq km) park is best known for its big cats. There is a good chance that patience will be rewarded with sightings of a leopard or a panther. A good place to wait for one is near the beautiful lake fed by Pandava Falls. *(Nearest airport Khajuraho,*

Visitor Tips

Accommodations tend to include all meals, guides, jeep rides, and, if an option, elephant safaris; reservations are required. Prices range hugely nowadays, reflecting the quality of each element. To experience a park's habitat properly, allocate three days.

Beware of temperature extremes: It's chilly at dawn and dusk in winter (with occasional frosts) but blisteringly hot after February. All parks offer good animal sightings, especially in the heat and dust between March and June. Take your own binoculars and field guides.

Riding an elephant through Bandhavgarh's wild landscape, a group of children looks for tigers.

mptourism.com, closed July–Oct., best time to visit Oct.–April, stay at Madla)

Satpura National Park

Just three hours' drive from Bhopal, this 650 square mile (1,700 sq km) park covers central India's highest mountains, providing a wide range of flora and fauna. There are especially good chances of sighting tiger, giant gaur, and chowsingha on walks or from boats, canoes, and hides. *(Nearest airport Bhopal, closed July–mid-Oct., best time to visit Nov.–June)*

Madhav National Park

This small park of deciduous plains forest was once the summer capital of the Scindias of Gwalior (see pp. 108–109); their grand mausoleums were built in white marble for recent Gwalior royals. In the park, ornithologists can enjoy plenty of birdlife, including sightings of demoiselle cranes. Animals to see include sambhar, chital, sloth bears, nilgai, and chinkara. *(Nearest airport Gwalior, mptourism.com, open year-round, best time to visit Nov.–May)*

Chandigarh

The flat, fertile, and prosperous land stretching from Delhi to the Indus was once all the Punjab. At independence, half was lost to Pakistan and since then further areas have formed two more Indian states: Haryana and Himachal Pradesh. The Green Revolution of the 1960s transformed the area into the breadbasket of India. A quarter of India's wheat and a third of its milk and dairy foods are produced here. Today, Haryana and Punjab share their capital, Chandigarh.

Chandigarh

🅰 93 B5

Visitor Information

✉ Tourist Office, Interstate Bus Terminus, Sector 17

☎ 017/2270-3839

chandigarhtourism .gov.in

In Chandigarh, the Rock Garden's sculptures provide a whimsical contrast to Le Corbusier's dramatic architecture.

Chandigarh was independent India's first planned city. It was conceived by Le Corbusier (see pp. 86–87), with grid boulevards divided into blocks ("sectors"). Begun in 1952, it was completed ten years later. Today, the initial dramatic effect of the city's grand civic buildings has been softened by extensive planting.

Le Corbusier envisaged his ideal city as a living organism, with the **Capitol Complex** *(guided tours, apply in advance via chandigarh tourism.gov.in or call Department of Tourism, tel 017/2274-0420)* as its "head" and the green spaces as its "lungs." The capital is one of Le Corbusier's most innovative designs. Set against the Siwalik Hills, his monumental buildings for the High Court, Legislative Assembly, and Secretariat over- look the 1,300-foot-wide (400 m) square. Down the main avenue, Jan Marg, is the **Government Museum and Art Gallery** *(Sector 10C, Capitol Complex, tel 017/2247- 2010, closed Mon., $, chdmuseum .gov.in)*, whose collection reflects the long, rich history and culture of the area, from Gandhara Bud- dhas to Sikh paintings.

On the city outskirts, behind the High Court, is the upbeat, witty artwork, the **Rock Garden** *(open Apr.–Sept.: 9 a.m. to 7 p.m.; Oct.–March.: 9 a.m. to 6 p.m., $).* This is retired road inspector Nek Chand's life work: The garden is composed of a succession of open-air rooms, each one deco- rated with colorful mosaics or surreal sculptures of animal and human figures.

Grand Trunk Road

If you drive out of Delhi, you will be following the route of one of the world's great ancient roads. It stretches 1,200 miles (2,000 km) across the subcontinent, from mountainous Peshawar on the Pakistan–Afghanistan border to Kolkata on the Bay of Bengal. In the Punjab, you see Muslim and Sikh tombs beside it; on the Delhi–Agra route you see milestones; on the stretch east of Varanasi, you can pause to visit Sher Shah Suri's isolated, ravishing tomb.

Trade has traveled along this route since at least the fourth century B.C., when it was called the Uttar Path

(High Way). The Mauryan emperor Ashoka gave it paving stones, watchtowers, and some of his edict pillars (see p. 26); portions survive beside the current road. Sher Shah Suri carried out major maintenance work, built *serais* (medieval motels)—one survives at Sirhind, near Chandigarh—and employed spies at them to report rumor and discontent. The Mughals added wells; the British added asphalt and gave it its present name.

Today, India's National Highway 1 (NH1) is nicknamed "G. T. Road." Trucks, cars, bullock carts, bicycles, and cows share this great road.

INSIDER TIP:

Ask for a ride on the back of a motorcycle, if you are feeling bold. This is a great way to see the quieter scenic areas and to reach places within a city more quickly.

—HARISH VASUDEVAN
National Geographic Books

Around Chandigarh

As you head north into the Siwalik Hills along the road to the hill station Shimla, visit **Pinjore's** walled **Yadavindra Gardens** (*haryanatourism.gov.in*). The Mughal emperor Aurangzeb's brother, Fidai Khan, reorganized the ancient gardens, giving them three pleasure palaces and broad terraced lawns; they're good for picnics. From **Kalka**, 2 miles (4 km) farther on, the

Himalayan Queen and other trains leave for Shimla, a 5.5-hour journey. Quaint **Nalagarh** is nearer—37 miles (60 km) from Chandigarh—and quieter, with good walking opportunities and the ruined **Ramgarh Fort.**

Southwest of Chandigarh lies **Patiala,** where tourists are hardly ever seen. In this charming, unspoiled city, once the capital of the Sikh state Patiala, do not miss the multistory **Motibagh Palace** (*may be closed to public*) with its many painted rooms, nor the busy street markets.

Farther up the Grand Trunk Road toward Amritsar, **Sirhind** has a cluster of Mughal and Sikh monuments you might visit. Then, bypass Ludhiana's wool factories and Jalandhar's bicycle industry to arrive at **Kapurthala,** a Paris-influenced model town and home to the **Jalaukhana Palace,** built in the 1890s by the French-educated ruler, Jagatjit Singh Ahluwalia. ∎

Visitor Information

Punjab Tourist Office, Directorate of Tourism, Additional Deluxe Building, Sector 17

017/2270-2955

punjabtourism.gov.in

Pinjore

93 B5

13 miles (21 km) NE of Chandigarh on Kalka Rd.

Patiala

93 B5

42 miles (68 km) SW of Chandigarh

Sirhind

93 B5

30 miles (48 km) NW of Ambala

Kapurthala

93 B6

113 miles (180 km) W of Chandigargh

Amritsar

The old, walled core of Punjab's largest city is a network of bustling bazaars surrounding the beautiful Golden Temple and Jallianwalla Bagh. These, the gems of Amritsar, are filled with an intense calm and peacefulness, despite their political associations.

Pilgrims cross Guru's Bridge to the Harmandir Sahib to hear the reading of the Guru Granth Sahib.

Amritsar, Punjab
🅰 93 A6
Visitor Information
✉ State Tourist Office, Amritsar International Hotel, City Center
☎ 018/3255-5991, 018/3255-9992, 018/3254-0058
punjabtourism.gov.in

Amritsar is the Sikhs' holy city. Every Sikh is required to visit at least once. The fourth Guru, Ram Das, founded the trading town in 1577 and enlarged the Amrit Sarovar ("pool of nectar," hence Amritsar) to commemorate a crippled person being cured while bathing in the waters there. His son, Arjan Dev, built the first temple (1589–1601) in the lake: the Harmandir Sahib (Golden Temple).

After multiple Afghan attacks and persecutions in the 18th century, Ranjit Singh led the Sikhs to victory in the Punjab and in 1830 gave 220 pounds (100 kg) of gold to gild the restored temple.

In the 20th century, Sikhs saw their dream for Khalistan, an independent Sikh state based on the whole of Ranjit Singh's kingdom, shattered. Nehru made promises; Indira Gandhi offered a reduced version, then withdrew her offer. As a result of the ensuing conflicts, the Golden Temple was fortified, the Indian Army made an assault on it in June 1984, and Mrs. Gandhi was assassinated in the same year. Rajiv Gandhi drew up the Punjab Accord in July 1985, but the problem remains unresolved.

Visiting the Temple

Start by enjoying your first view of the shimmering **Amrit**

Sarovar, where the Harmandir Sahib temple appears to float. Then take a slow clockwise walk, around the tank, following pilgrims as they pause at small shrines devoted to the founding gurus. Along this route, called the Parikrama, are four booths where devotees take turns to maintain a continuous reading of the Guru Granth Sahib, the Sikhs' sacred book. On the east side, up to 6,000 pilgrims a day eat in the Guru-ka-langar ("communal dining room") to remind themselves that all are equal.

The climax of your visit is on the west side. Here is the Akal Takht, the temple's second most sacred structure. Built by Guru Hargobind to house the religious and political governing body of the Sikhs, it has been immaculately rebuilt since the Indian Army destroyed it during the violent conflicts of 1984.

Before visiting it, worshippers collect their prasad (offering) and go along Guru's Bridge to the highly decorated Harmandir Sahib, which houses a huge copy of the Guru Granth Sahib. You can enter through one of its four open doors (symbolizing welcome to all four Hindu castes) to witness the readings, chanting, and music. The book is set on a throne by day, but each evening it is paraded to the Akal Takht to the sound of singing and the loud beating of drums.

Whenever you visit Amritsar, expect to encounter thousands of pilgrims. ■

INSIDER TIP:

All are welcome at the Harmandir, but shoes must be removed and feet washed; no socks can be worn, heads must be covered, and tobacco and alcohol must be left outside the complex (there are lockers available).

—LOUISE NICHOLSON
National Geographic author

Jallianwalla Bagh Massacre

On April 13, 1919, without warning, Gen. R. E. H. Dyer and his 150 troops fired continuously for 15 minutes on some 20,000 unarmed people gathered peacefully in a square hemmed in by buildings. The official death toll was 400, with 1,200 injuries. It was one of the worst atrocities perpetrated by the British in India.

The cause was the Rowlatt Act, which empowered the British to imprison without trial any Indian suspected of sedition. A series of one-day strikes in Amritsar escalated into looting, and Mahatma Gandhi called a mass demonstration for April 13 at Jallianwalla Bagh. No speech or aggressive action had been made when General Dyer ordered his troops to fire.

Today, the square is an extremely evocative memorial park, reached through one of the original narrow alleys. A small gallery houses firsthand accounts of the massacre, contemporary photographs, newspaper reports, and poet Rabindranath Tagore's moving letter, returning his British honors.

Delhi's Hill Stations

If the searing heat of the plains is unbearable, the cooling comfort of the lower Himalayan mountains and their quaint British-founded hill stations are near at hand. The climate and flowers are best in spring and fall.

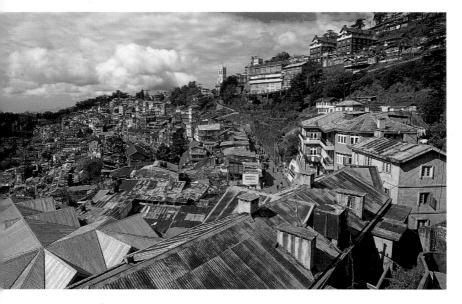

Shimla clings precariously to the mountainside.

Shimla, Himachal Pradesh

 93 B5

Visitor Information Offices

✉ Railway station

✉ Near Victory Tunnel

☎ 017/7265-4589

✉ Bypass road

☎ 017-7283-2498

himachaltourism .gov.in

NOTE: For information on places in Uttarakhand state, visit *uttarakhand.com*, *uttaranchaltourism.in*, or *hill-stations-india.com*.

Shimla

The capital of modern India's mountainous Himachal Pradesh sustains its position as queen of India's hill stations. Set at an elevation of 7,260 feet (2,213 m) in the pine-forested Siwalik Hills, Shimla (Simla) was the summer capital of the British administration from 1864 to 1939. Each year, the huge machine of bureaucrats and papers, together with servants, coolies, packhorses, women, and children, made the long journey up here from Calcutta (and later Delhi) until the Kalka to Shimla Railway opened in

1903. From here, for more than half the year, amid the plays, games, dancing, hunting, and gossip, the British governed approximately one-fifth of the world's population.

Shimla's modern mix of mountains, imperial British buildings, Indian town, and wealthy Indian visitors makes it unlike anywhere else in India. To get the most out of it, be prepared to walk, as the center is restricted to pedestrians.

On **The Ridge,** in the town center beside Christ Church (which has fine stained-glass windows), there are splendid views over the surrounding hills.

Walk along **The Mall** (the main street), past British buildings whose designs range from seaside flippancy to stoic Scottish baronial, past the refurbished Cecil Hotel, to find **Viceregal Lodge** (Observatory Rd., partially open to public, $).

Haridwar & Rishikesh

As one of the Seven Sacred Cities, Haridwar is a busy Hindu pilgrimage center. Here the sacred Ganga River leaves the rugged mountains for the flat plains, and Har-ki-Pauri ghat marks the exact spot. All day long the faithful visit the ghats, bridges, and islands; each evening, hundreds gather for the **Ganga Arati ceremony** at dusk, when lights are floated down the river to the sound of gongs and music.

Rishikesh lies within sight, up the mountains of Garhwal. The Beatles put it on the hippie trail with their famous visit to the Maharishi in February 1968. Today, ashrams of all kinds abound, continuing and expanding the spot's ancient tradition as a Hindu pilgrimage stop. Travelers who are seriously interested in yoga should reserve in advance at the **Sivananda Ashram** (The Divine Life Society, Shivananda Nagar, tel 013/5243-0040 or 013/5243-1190, fax 013/6431-196, sivanandaonline .org). If you're seeking peace and tranquility, visit in winter and spring when the temples are shut and pilgrims fewer. Those wishing to follow the Ganga to its source can journey on to Gangotri (see p. 320) from here.

Nainital

Set in the Kumaun Hills at 6,358 feet (1,938 m), this town overlooking a large, natural lake has sustained its popularity since a sugar merchant, Mr. Barron, discovered its joys in 1841. Find action along **The Mall,** which runs

Mussoorie

At an elevation of 6,561 feet (2,000 m) and only 172 miles (277 km) from Delhi, this hill station makes for a good quick break. Discovered by the British in 1823, its popularity is sustained by its spectacular views of the Himalaya and the Dehra Dun Valley.

Childers Lodge, situated above Landour, has the most exquisite views of all, while a walk out to Tchenchen Choling *gompa* (monastery) and its gardens is highly rewarding. If you would like to try a more ambitious trek, you can spend four days exploring the Harki Dun Valley.

the length of the lake from Mallital, the colonial area, to Tallital. Try boating on the lake, visiting a Tibetan market, climbing the ropeway to **Snow View,** and walking longer trails to **Naina Peak** and **China Peak** for more views. From Nainital you can visit Corbett National Park (see p. 124), with charming hotels along the route. ∎

Haridwar, Uttarakhand
93 C5
Visitor Information
✉ Tourist Office, Haridwar
☎ 013/3422-7370
✉ Tourist Information Centre, Railway Station
☎ 013/3422-7817
gmvnl.com

Rishikesh, Uttarakhand
93 C5
Visitor Information
✉ Tourist Information Centre, GMVN Ltd., Shail Vihar, Haridwar By Pass Road
☎ 013/5243-1793
gmvnl.com

Nainital, Uttarakhand
93 C5
Visitor Information
✉ Tourist Office, The Mall
☎ 059/4223-5337
✉ Tourist Information Centre, Kathgodam
☎ 059/4626-6638
uttarakhandtourism .gov.in

Mussoorie, Uttarakhand
93 C5
Visitor Information
✉ District Tourism Development Office, GMVN Ltd., Library Road
☎ 013/5263-1281
gmvnl.com

Corbett National Park

Established in 1936 by Jim Corbett (1875–1955), India's first wildlife sanctuary now preserves a rare expanse of sub-Himalayan wilderness. The dramatic scenery of the 201 square miles (521 sq km) of Kumaun hills, valleys, and rivers makes it particularly beautiful, and especially lush after the monsoon months (Nov.–Jan.), even if much of the core area of 127 square miles (330 sq km) is off-limits to visitors.

Rhesus monkeys are often seen in Corbett National Park.

Corbett National Park, Uttarakhand

🅰 93 C5
✉ Ramnagar
🕐 Closed mid-June–mid-Nov.
💲 $$$$
✈ Nearest airport Pantnagar

corbettnationalpark.in

Jim Corbett, a hunter turned conservationist and author, was born in Nainital and knew the area intimately. Repeatedly called to save locals by killing man-eating tigers and leopards, Corbett was already concerned about threats to India's wildlife by the 1940s, when he began to champion the conservation awareness of Indians. It was appropriate, then, that in 1973 this park was the first Project Tiger reserve. Ironically, the project's success here has led to overpopulation, as each tiger needs 31 square miles (80 sq km), and there are now regular reports of man-eating incidents.

The park's good infrastructure and naturalists mean there is a fair chance of sighting the elusive tiger. Look in the rivers for snout-nosed gharial crocodiles, large mugger crocodiles, and river tortoises. On land, you may see wild boar, sambar, Himalayan black bear, delicate *chital*, hog deer, porcupine, and trees full of playful rhesus and common langur monkeys.

For ornithologists this park is a paradise, since it attracts an abundance of both plains and hill birds. An hour in a *machan* (watchtower) will be richly rewarded—perhaps with sightings of black-necked stork, honey buzzard, crested serpent eagle, gray hornbill, scarlet minivet, and many different waterfowl, pigeons, parakeets, and kingfishers.

It is best to visit November to March; after this it gets hotter, but elephant sightings increase. ■

INSIDER TIP:

Stay outside the park at Ramnagar, on the Kosi River; the upscale hotels can arrange two- or three-night stays inside the park, providing their own staff and food.

—LOUISE NICHOLSON
National Geographic author

A parched land of vivid colors, soaring forts, and fairy-tale palaces that fulfills a visitor's most exotic dreams

Rajasthan & Gujarat

A village woman carries her water supply home.

Rajasthan & Gujarat

These two dry and dusty states extend across the Great Indian Desert to Pakistan and the Arabian Sea, separated from the rest of India by the Aravalli, Vindhya, and Satpura mountain ranges. Their location has brought wealth through trade—more so in Gujarat because it lay on the route to Mecca used by northern India's Muslim rulers. Each state has forward-looking governments, with dramatic modernization paralleling tradition.

Rajasthan is India's most popular area for visitors. It lies on the doorstep of Delhi and Agra; its former royals were quick to turn their palaces into hotels, and it offers classic romantic India, easily enjoyed without coping with much of India's complex history.

Most of the feuding Rajput rulers turned to lives of pure pleasure once they accepted British protection. A journey through Rajasthan gives you an idea of that life: visiting forts, shopping in colorful markets, riding painted elephants, spotting wildlife, and staying in one former palace after another.

But there are contrasts. The former states within Rajasthan have stoically held on to their individual characters and traditions. Jaipur, conceived as a commercial hub for the Jaipur princely state, is now the chaotic capital of all Rajasthan. Udaipur is distinguished for its lakes, beauty, and proudly defiant Mewar rulers, who poured their energy and vision into creating the most idyllic Rajput city. In the west, Marwar's Jodhpur continues to feel like a royal frontier desert city. The arrival of a camel train is no surprise here.

Gujarat is very different from Rajasthan. Its coastal trading and agricultural production were so lucrative that Emperor Akbar built the Buland Darwaza at Fatehpur Sikri when he finally conquered it. Today the many little pre-independence kingdoms have metamorphosed into India's second wealthiest state—and one of the country's most enlightened. As an indicator, the literacy rate is 79 percent, compared with Rajasthan's 66 percent. Ahmedabad, its capital, offers a mix of grand Islamic buildings, fine museums, and strong Gandhi associations: Gujarat was his home state. From Ahmedabad, you can journey to see Harappan sites, Jain monuments, Hindu temples, art deco palaces, and rare wildlife. Hotels are often simple, visitors few, and the rewards great. ■

NOT TO BE MISSED:

Making your own block print at Anokhi Museum **129**

Riding a painted elephant up to Amer Fort **130**

Staying in a maharaja's former palace or fort **132–133**

Cocktails at the art deco Umaid Bhawan Palace **139**

Singing *bhopas* (balladeers) **143**

Watching a puppet show **143**

Calico Museum of Textiles **145**

Hiking up the sacred hill of Palitana **150**

Kachchh village weaving **153**

0 ____ 200 kilometers
0 ____ 100 miles

6 ▷

Ganganagar
Hanumangarh
Suratgarh

PAKISTAN

Nohar

AROUND DELHI
P. 91

Sardarshahr

Churu
Mahansar
Jhunjhunun
Fatehpur
Shekhawati
Nawalgarh
Alwar
Dig

GAJNER WILDLIFE
SANCTUARY

Bikaner
Deshnoke
Thar
Kishangarh
Ramgarh
Didwana
Sikar

SARISKA
NATIONAL
PARK
Bharatpur

Desert

15
11
11

Phalodi
Nagaur
Makrana
Samode
Amer
Jaipur

KEOLADEO
GHANA
NAT. PARK
Dhaulpur

Jaisalmer
Pokaran
RAJASTHAN
Osian
*Sambhar
Salt Lake*
Sambhar
Dausa
11

Lodurva
M SAND DUNES
ESERT NAT. PARK)
Shergarh
Saraswati
Mandor
Pushkar
Ajmer

Chambal

12
RANTHAMBHOR
NATIONAL PARK

Shiv
Jodhpur
Raipur
Beawar
Kekri
Tonk
Sawai
Madhopur

15
Balotra
Pali
14

nabao
Barmer
Luni
Sukri
Devli
Bundi

Chauhtan
Jalor
Kumbhalgarh
Ranakpur
Nathdwara
Bhilwara
Kota
Baran

Sirohi
Haldighati
Chittaurgarh
Atru
Jhalawar

Sanchor
**Mount
ABU**
Pindwara
Eklingji
Shilpgram
Bahas
Nimbahera

12

15
Abu Road
Kumbharia
Udaipur
Ahar

14
Palanpur
*Rajsamand
Lake*

Radhanpur
Siddhapur
Taranga
Dungarpur
Gangdhar

15
Patan
(Anahilvada)
Mahesana
Banswara

*Little
Rann*
Modhera
Himatnagar

E
F

GUJARAT
Gandhinagar
Sabarmati
Mahi

Halvad
Dhrangadhra
✈ **AHMEDABAD**
Dahod

Morbi
Sarkhej
Nadiad
Godhra

Wankaner
Surendranagar
Anand
Champaner

8A
Lothal
Vadodara

Rajkot
VELAVADAR BLACK
BUCK SANCTUARY
Dabhoi

Peninsula
Botad
AROUND DELHI
P. 91

ashtra
Bhavnagar
Bharuch

Amreli
Palitana

unagadh
Alang
Surat
Bardoli
*MUMBAI AND
MAHARASHTRA*
p. 155

SASAN GIR
NATIONAL
PARK
Mahuva
Navsari
Ahwa

nnath
Diu
(Daman & Diu)
Valsad
Daman

Gulf of Khambhat
**DAMAN
& DIU** ◉ Daman

C
D

Area of map detail

★ New
Delhi

Rajasthan

This land created the image of the maharaja hunting, fighting, dallying with his princesses, and dripping in pearls, emeralds, and diamonds. Whether you palace hop from one fairy-tale historic hotel to the next, or indulge in India's most luxurious contemporary leisure hotels, be sure to spend time in the bazaars to find brightly colored textiles, folk art, and costume jewelry.

Maharaja Pratap Singh built the Hawa Mahal in Jaipur in 1799 as a grandstand for the palace women.

Amer

📍 127 E4

Amer

A visit to Amer's medieval fort and then the nearby walled town of Jaipur, each in turn the capital of the powerful Kachwaha clan, makes a good introduction to Rajasthan.

Of the 36 proud and warring Rajput clans, all *kshatriya* caste Hindus, the Kachwaha of Amer became one of the greatest. They won Amer Fort in the 12th century when waves of Muslim invaders controlled nearby Delhi. It lay on the route to the Muslim Chishti shrine at Ajmer. Thus began a story of alliance and mutual benefit. Alliances were strongest with the Mughals in 1562. The Amer princess who sealed this alliance gave birth to Salim, later Emperor Jahangir (see p. 26).

The results were wealth, prestige, and the **Amer Fort** and palace complex. Viewed from the road across Maota Lake, the left-hand section was built by Man Singh (r. 1589–1614), who led Akbar's troops to repeated victories, while the right section, which emulates Mughal buildings at Agra and Fatehpur Sikri (see pp. 94–96, 102–103), was built by Jai Singh I (r. 1621–1667), who fought for three Mughal emperors.

The least tiring way to reach the palace is by car. Once there, don't miss the **Kali Mata Temple,** with Jai Singh's elaborately decorated suites (with good rooftop views) and the warren of Man Singh's simpler rooms.

On the way down to the main road, find **Anokhi Museum of Hand Printing** (Kheri Gate, tel 014/1253-0226, closed Mon. & May 1–June 15, anokhi.com), where the local craft's fascinating story is set out in an immaculately restored haveli (mansion).

Jaipur

Fourth in succession after Jai Singh I, the precocious, 11-year-old Jai Singh II (r. 1699–1743) came to the Kachwaha throne and was awarded the title Sawai (One-and-a-Quarter) to put him above his fellow Rajputs. In 1727, having shone on the battlefield, he indulged his love of science and the arts and began to lay out a model palace-city, Jaipur, employing a Bengali called Vidyadhar Bhattacharya as his architect.

Your visit could start with **City Palace** and its collections of fabrics, decorated weapons, paintings, and carpets; the One-and-a-Quarter flag flies above. Nearby stands Jai Singh's **Jantar Mantar** ("instrument for calculation"), an intriguing set of outsize

Jaipur

127 E4

Visitor Information

India Tourist Office, Paryatan Bhawan, Khasa Kothi Hotel Campus, Mirza Ismail Rd.

014/1237-2200

incredibleindia.org
jaipur.org.uk

State Tourist Office, Platform No. 1, Railway Station

014/1231-5714

rajasthantourism .gov.in

City Palace

Closed religious festival days

$$ (ticket also valid for Jaigarh Fort)

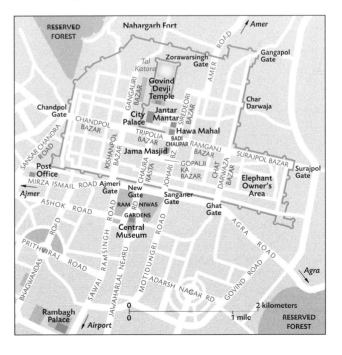

EXPERIENCE: Riding an Elephant in Rajasthan

If you've ever dreamed of riding a painted elephant—toenails as well in many cases—then the ride up to Amer Fort outside Jaipur is your wish come true, with your gentle giant mount swaying from side to side. Be sure to visit the elephants' waiting area, too, where they munch on sugarcane. To arrange a ride, simply go to the elephant steps at the bottom of the hill and a mahout will help you. Elephants are on hand daily in the mornings; there is no pre-booking.

You do need to reserve a spot if you wish to play elephant polo on the playing field near the Rambagh Palace Hotel (*Bhawani Singh Rd., tel 014/1221-1919, tajhotels.com*). Elephant polo is like horse polo in slow motion. You can usually watch matches for free. Finally, if you are partying in Jaipur or Udaipur, have your travel agent arrange a Royal Welcome to your hotel, which includes dancers, drummers, and a full parade of painted elephants—with rides for the partygoers.

astronomical instruments, mostly designed to calculate time more precisely. Of the five sets he built, this is the biggest.

Outside the palace complex Jaipur's markets are a riot of color. Find bangles, shoes, puppets, and attar (perfume) at Badi Chaupar, in front of the landmark **Hawa Mahal** (Palace of the Winds), cotton cloth and jewelry along **Johari Bazar,** gems and jewels particularly down two lanes of it, Gopalji Ka Bazar, and Haldion Ka Rasta.

If the fervent worship in the Kali Mata temple at Amer (see p. 129) interested you, so will **Govind Devji Temple** (*Jaleb Chowk, govinddevji.net*). Jai Singh brought the image of Krishna from Govinda; it is worshipped especially fervently at the 6 p.m. and 8 p.m. *pujas*.

South of the walled city, at the **Central Museum** (*Ram Niwas Bagh, $, discounted on Mon., alberthallmuseum.com*) a delightful collection of puppets, costumes, models, and Jaipur brasswork

fills Sir Samuel Swinton Jacob's Albert Hall, begun in 1876 in the spacious lung of Ram Niwas Gardens. The Durbar Hall (*often closed*) contains superb carpets.

Farther south again is the **Rambagh Palace** (*Bhawani Singh Rd., tel 014/1221-1919, tajhotels .com*), built by Maharaja Ram Singh II as a hunting lodge, which Madho Singh II transformed into a royal playground with extensive English gardens. It is now a hotel (see Travelwise p. 353), but the public can enjoy the gardens, the Lalique fountains, and the Polo Bar of the lodge.

Jaipur's Outskirts: As you head east from Jaipur on the road toward Agra, 4 miles (6 km) on the walled garden **Vidyadhar ka Bagh,** on the right, remembers Jaipur's architect, Vidyadhar Bhattacharya. On the left, **Sisodia Rani ka Bagh** ($) is the country palace built for Jai Singh II's Udaipur queen; there are lively murals and lush gardens. Behind it, troops of langur monkeys are fed daily at 4 p.m. at the **Hanuman Temple.**

On the left, along the Jaipur–Amer road at Gaitor, doors lead to the **Royal Cenotaphs.** Madho Singh II's is the largest tomb; Jai Singh's, at the back, has columns carved with mythological scenes supporting a marble dome.

INSIDER TIP:

While in Pushkar, wake up early for sunrise *puja* [prayers], to see worshippers taking dips in the holy lake and making offerings to Hindu gods.

—DANIELLE WILLIAMS
National Geographic contributor

Around Jaipur

The Rajasthan countryside around Jaipur has some intriguing, atmospheric places.

Jaipur has a ring of protective forts, the most imposing of which is **Nahargarh** *(5 miles/9 km NW of Jaipur, $),* reached either from the Amer road or by a brisk hike from the city's Nahargarh Fort Road. Sunset is marvelous, when Jaipur's city noises float up through the softening light.

An ideal detour after Amer, the spectacularly sited **Jaigarh** *(Amer Rd., $)* is where Man Singh and his successors stored their treasure. It was expanded by Jai Singh II in 1726, and you can see the great cannon, armory, gun foundry, and palace complex. In times of danger, Amer's royals retreated here.

Moving farther afield, the following sights are listed clockwise around Jaipur from the west. At **Ajmer** *(112 miles/135 km from Jaipur)* find the **Dargah Sharif** ("holy shrine") of the Sufi saint Khwajah Muin-ud-din Chishti, who came to India in 1192 and died here; this is still a popular pilgrimage center, with regular *qawwali* singing. See also Akbar's fort-palace, the finely carved Arhai-din-ka-Jhonpra mosque (1193), and Shah Jahan's marble pavilions. In contrast, the quiet Hindu town of **Pushkar's** draw is its sacred lake and its annual Cattle Fair (see Travelwise p. 385.)

The rugged area of northeast Rajasthan known as **Shekhawati** *(continued on p. 134)*

Jaipur Literature Festival

A creative initiative of the Jaipur Virasat Foundation, which helps Rajasthan's craftspeople and musicians practice their traditional skills, the Jaipur Literature Festival debuted in 2005 and has since exploded onto the global literary stage. Each January, more than a hundred authors gather for a five-day extravaganza of talks, debates, and evening musical programs held at the pretty, city-center Diggi Palace. The festival's events are free and open to the public. For more information, see *Jaipur literaturefestival.org.*

India's Palace Hotels

India is awash with palaces. There are thousands of them, huge and unnecessary in today's democratic India. Yet they are the core of every old city and dominate villages; they overlook lakes, perch on hills, and are found down the most unlikely mud lanes.

Ahilya Fort, which contains the 18th-century palace of Queen Ahilya Bai, is now a beautiful hotel.

Before independence, these were great households, often giving employment to several hundred people. They were places of patronage for painters, writers, musicians, and weavers. After 1947, the former rulers and nobles were obliged to give up some of their land, wealth, and properties. With them went the communities they headed. The grandest palaces and forts became landmarks open to the public, while others remained the ancestral homes of nobles, who found their upkeep increasingly difficult to finance. Hundreds more simply fell empty and silent, waiting quietly for their moment to come alive again.

Now, as visitors prefer palaces to high-rises to stay in, these buildings have their chance, encouraged by government tax breaks. All over India, they are being dusted down and opened up as hotels. Some are sensational, others less so; but all have a special charm that adds to a visit to India. The local staff, proud of their area, often ensure that guests have an especially memorable stay.

EXPERIENCE: Staying at a Jaipur Guesthouse

The 18th-century planned city of Jaipur is peppered with vestiges of that era, notably the residences of the feudal aristocrats, where they stayed while in town to attend palace functions. Today, some of their descendants run these homes as family-run informal homestays, providing guests with an intimate glimpse into Indian life and a wealth of local knowledge. Guests are treated to home-cooked meals and old-fashioned spacious rooms, not to mention cheaper rates. Among Jaipur's many guesthouses, **Loharu House** (12 rooms; *Civil Lines*) and **Barwara Kothi** (7 rooms; *Jacob Rd., Civil Lines*) both lie in a leafy, residential neighborhood, whereas the good value **Dera Rawatsar** (15 rooms; *Vijay Path*) is in the city's center. For more information, visit *hotelsjaipur.com*.

Palace Potential

It was the Maharaja of Jaipur who first saw the potential of renting palace rooms to visitors. He opened the Rambagh Palace Hotel in Jaipur on December 8, 1957; tragically, while other hotels are being lovingly restored, its art deco suites have recently been ripped out. In 1961, Maharana Bhagwat Singh of Udaipur also recognized the end of an era and began to transform Jag Niwas Palace into the Lake Palace Hotel. His energetic son, Arvind Singh, has continued his work with an attention to quality that is rare. Having restored his own palaces to create the Udaipur hotel cluster of Shiv Niwas, Fateh Prakash, and Dovecote, he now has a palace-hotel network stretching to Jodhpur, Jaisalmer, and Bikaner.

Heritage hotels, as they are known, are not restricted to Rajasthan. They extend from the Himalayan mountains down to Tamil Nadu. Nalagarh Fort nestles in the Himalayan foothills near Chandigarh. In the west, there is Nilambagh Palace at Bhavnagar in Gujarat, Orchard Palace at Gondal in Saurashtra, and Hingolgadh Castle at Jasden. Central India has Jhira Bagh Palace and Ahilya Fort, both convenient for Mandu; Bhanwar Vilas Palace at Karauli; and Kawardha Palace—convenient for Kanha National Park. Down in the south, Mysore's Lalitha Mahal Palace Hotel is a gloriously extravagant Victorian palace hotel; and there are many more.

Such is the success of heritage hotels that enterprising Indians with flair have started to buy old properties and imbue them with their own, more democratic taste. The team of designer Aman Nath and businessman Francis Wacziarg took on the challenge of restoring Neemrana Fort with some friends, then went solo to bring other forts, Raj bungalows, and even a French colonial house in Puducherry, to life. Lekha Poddar has taken the chaotic pile of Devi Garh Fort outside Udaipur, stripped it back to its origins and, with immaculate taste, created an uncompromisingly contemporary world-class hotel. For details of these, and more suggestions, see sidebar opposite and the hotels section of this guide on pp. 342–376.

Famous for its school of miniature painting, Rajasthan's family-run Deogarh Mahal Hotel has finely decorated rooms.

Alwar
🗺 127 E5

Bharatpur
🗺 127 F4
✉ 34 miles (55 km) W of Agra

Dig
🗺 127 E5
✉ 61 miles (98 km) NW of Agra on NH. 2
💲 $

Ranthambhor National Park
🗺 127 E4
✉ 112 miles (180 km) SE of Jaipur
🕐 Closed July–Sept.
💲 $$

rajasthantourism
.gov.in

is dotted with more than 360 villages. During the 19th and 20th centuries, Marwari families, such as the Birlas, Poddars, and Goenkas, made their money in commerce and then lavishly decorated their homes with lively frescoes inside and out. A trip to see these might include Fatehpur, Mahansar, Jhunjhunun, and Nawalgarh.

At **Samode** (*26 miles/42 km NE of Jaipur, samode.com*), descendants of Jai Singh II's finance minister have energetically restored his isolated **Samode Palace,** whose rooms are covered with murals. Nearby, they have also brought the walled royal garden alive again, complete with working fountains.

Sariska National Park (*64 miles/103 km NE of Jaipur, $*) is a Project Tiger reserve off the Delhi–Jaipur highway, sprawling over 300 square miles (800 sq km); dawn and dusk jeep rides

may give sightings of a tiger but will certainly include good birds. **Alwar,** once capital of Alwar state, is dominated by **Vinay Vilas** (1840), the atmospheric city palace with a top-floor museum; see also the royal *chhatri* and Mughal tomb of Fateh Jung.

In the center of **Bharatpur,** the Jat kings' Lohargarh retains its decayed splendor. Part is now a museum. However, the Bharatpur maharaja's evocative summer palace at nearby **Dig** (ca 1750) survives intact: Wander its gardens, complete with marble swing, and explore the magnificent apartments, some decorated with marble booty from Agra Fort (see pp. 94–96).

Another Project Tiger reserve is **Ranthambhor National Park,** 154 square miles (399 sq km) of deciduous forest rambling over the Aravalli and Vindhya Hills and around Ranthambhor's great fort. It provides the ideal habitat for tigers and is very popular, so it's essential to reserve accommodations in the area well in advance.

Udaipur

Udaipur is Rajasthan's most congenial and romantic city, with its gentle light, shimmering lakes, compact center, bustling prosperity, and several sensitively restored palaces. A far cry from the commercial rush and pollution of Jaipur, Udaipur is perfect for a day or two of relaxation.

Choose from a cluster of palace hotels and nobles' havelis to stay in; whichever you pick, you can visit the others for meals and drinks.

EXPERIENCE:
Take a Spin in a Vintage Motor Car

Enjoy a chauffeur-driven ride in one of the 20 lovingly maintained cars collected by the last three maharajas of Mewar, still housed in the Royal Garage underneath Udaipur's City Palace. Now a museum, the circular art deco courtyard has separate stalls for each car, including four Rolls Royces, a 1930 Ford A, and a 1946 MG-TC convertible. The 1934 Rolls Royce 20H.P. was converted into a pickup for the maharaja to transport his cricket team to and from the grounds. A pair of 1938 Cadillacs are still used. To book a ride, contact the **Royal Garage** (*Garden Hotel, Udaipur, e-mail: museums@eternalmewar.in*).

Start exploring the city by taking the evening boat ride from the main jetty around **Lake Pichola,** dug when Udai Singh fled Mughal danger at Chittaurgarh in 1567 and made this the capital of his state, Mewar. Udai Singh was head of the top Rajput clan, the Sisodias, who according to legend were descended directly from the sun via the god Rama. He and his successors built the huge and very Hindu City Palace. The boat chugs past the **Taj Lake Palace Hotel** (1754; see Travelwise p. 357), built by Maharana Jagat Singh as a summer retreat, then stops at **Jag Mandir,** the island where Jahangir's son, the future Shah Jahan, sought refuge when he was a rebellious prince; his exquisite little **palace** (1622) anticipates his later buildings.

On land, there is much to see. The fleet of gleaming royal cars is kept beside the **Garden Hotel,** opposite **Gulab Bagh** ("rose garden"). At the **City Palace** (closed for religious festivals), with its jharokas (projecting balconies), maze of rooms, and wall decorations of inlaid glass, clamber up and down the narrow stairways of the **Mardana** ("men's section"), then see the recently restored **Zenana** ("women's section"). There is barely a touch of Mughal influence here. Finally, visit the restored Durbar Hall and its Crystal Gallery in **Fateh Prakash Palace** (tel 029/4252-8016) where a fine collection of British crystal is on display, including items from water basins to spitoons.

In the town, the main street

The colored glass on this City Palace peacock contrasts with the simple surrounding lanes and traditional houses.

leads downhill to the lively bazaars, passing Jagdish Temple and tiny shops selling cottons, wooden toys, and silver jewelry.

Fateh Sagar is an artificial lake. It was constructed in 1678 and Maharana Fateh Singh added the embankment (1889). The pretty shore road leads to well-kept **Saheliyon-ki-Bari** (Garden of Ladies); the island garden is **Nehru Park.**

Around Udaipur

If you can tear yourself away from the relaxing charm of Udaipur, there is a wide variety of outings, long and short, to suit all interests that will take you across Rajasthan's rugged Aravalli Mountains.

Udaipur
⚑ 127 D3
Visitor Information
✉ Udaipur Tourist Office, Surajpole
☎ 029/4411-535
rajasthantourism .gov.in

Fateh Memorial
✉ Fateh Memorial, Surajpole
☎ 029/4241-1535
Visitor Information
✉ Tourist Information Counter, Railway Station
☎ 029/4241-2984

Shilpgram

 127 D3

✉ 5 miles (8 km)
   W of Udaipur

$ $

shilpgram.in

Mount Abu

🗺 127 C3

✉ 116 miles
   (185 km) NW
   of Udaipur

To the west of Udaipur you can visit the model crafts village of **Shilpgram,** founded to preserve western India's traditional architecture, music, and crafts. The houses include a carved wooden Gujarat building; you may see weavers, musicians, potters, and other craftsmen at work.

A short distance southwest of Udaipur (9 miles/15 km) a hike up the hill to the abandoned **Monsoon Palace** (1880), now used by the local radio station, is rewarded with magical sunset and sunrise views.

North of Udaipur:

A number of sites are within easy reach of one another. The rocky outcrops of **Mount Abu** provide Rajasthan's only cool retreat from the searing summer heat. Enjoy the walks, views, lakes, and the two sets of temples: the Jains' five finely carved marble Dilwara temples and the Hindus' temples at **Achalgarh** and **Guru Shikar.** See also the nearby **Adhar Devi Temple,** which lies at the top of an extremely long flight of steps; the views from the top are magnificent.

Also north of Udaipur, the spectacular 15th-century ghost fort-town of **Kumbhalgarh** rises from rugged countryside, the finest of 32 forts built by Maharana Kumbha. Inside the massive ramparts are Jain temples, cenotaphs, and the citadel, which can be climbed. Near the entrance, Aodhi Hotel provides sustenance.

At **Ranakpur,** one of India's finest Jain temples lies hidden in a wooded valley—hence its survival (see sidebar opposite). Named for the ruler Rana Kumbha, the settlement was undertaken by the Jain merchant Dharna Sah, a minister at Udaipur's court, and his architect, Depa. The main temple (1439) is dedicated to Adinath, an enlightened Jain teacher, and built entirely of white marble, almost every surface of which is carved. Wander the 29 interconnecting halls and courtyards around the central sanctuary; two more

A fabric weaver at work in Shilpgram village

EXPERIENCE: Savor Ranakpur's Quiet Magic

Ranakpur is one of the five most important pilgrimage sites for Jains, and Jain pilgrims are almost always present. Walking in their footsteps, visitors can experience the quiet magic of Ranakpur.

First, travel through the rugged Aravalli hills into the lush valley, symbolically retreating from the hurly-burly of the city. Like the pilgrims, leave your shoes and all leather items outside the gleaming, unadorned exterior. Mount the steps to enter the exuberantly decorated interior; pause to absorb its richness before making your way clockwise around the central shrine to explore the 29 halls. Notice how a gentle light comes through the clerestories of the multilevel domes to illuminate sculptures of Jain saviors on the outer walls, and dancers, musicians, and floral patterns on the columns. As the calm envelops you, pause at one or two of the 86 little temples cut into the walls, and sit on a step to enjoy the geometric ceiling patterns.

Then, having paid your respects at the central shrine, join pilgrims at the refectory for a totally hygienic and strictly vegetarian meal of rice and vegetables.

small temples nestle among the nearby trees. For a final Jain temple visit, see Varkana's well-preserved **Parshwanath Temple** (15th century).

Beside the lake at rural **Nagda** *(14 miles/22 km N of Udaipur)*, the exquisite, intricately carved tenth-century **Sasbahu temples** demonstrate the scale of Hindu achievement in northern India and its destruction by invaders. At **Eklingji** village you can witness *puja* (worship) at two temples: Lakulisha (972) and Ekalinga (15th century), whose elaborately screened Shiva image is highly revered by all Sisodias; major pujas take place throughout the day on Mondays, the special day for Shiva.

Rajsamand Lake was created by Maharana Faj Singh to help prevent drought. The pavilions (1660), carved with Krishna scenes, commemorate his marriage to a Kishangarh princess to save her from Mughal clutches. Enjoy the views from **Digambara Jain Temple.**

Shri Nathji Temple at **Nath-dwara** is a pilgrimage center for devotees of Krishna, whose image is from Mathura; there is an elaborate puja here at sunset. The *pitchwais* (cloth paintings) on sale have decorative value only. At nearby **Haldighati,** Udaipur's hero, Maharana Pratap Singh, denied the Mughals (led by the Jaipur ruler) their victory in 1576.

East of Udaipur: Two miles (3 km) from Udaipur, **Ahar** *(closed Fri., $)* is the site of Mewar, the ancient capital. The Sisodias' royal cremation ground has elegant cenotaphs, especially that dedicated to Rana Amer Singh I (1621).

Farther east, **Chittaurgarh** *(75 miles/120 km, $)*, Rajasthan's most spectacular fort-city, was founded by Bappa Rawal in A.D. 728 on a wide, natural ridge rising from the plains. Three bloody sieges by Ala-ud-din Khilji of Delhi in 1303, Bahadur Shah *(continued on p. 140)*

Kumbhalgarh
- 127 D3
- ✉ 40 miles (65 km) N of Udaipur

Ranakpur
- ✉ 56 miles (90 km) N of Udaipur; 16 miles (25 km) SW of Kumbhalgarh

Eklingji
- 127 D3
- ✉ 14 miles (23 km) NE of Udaipur

Rajsamand Lake
- 127 D3
- ✉ 40 miles (65 km) NE of Udaipur

Nathdwara
- 127 D3

Haldighati
- 127 D3

Chittaurgarh
- 127 D3
- ✉ 75 miles (120 km) NE of Udaipur
- $ $

(continued on p. 140)

A Walk Around Jodhpur

Rising up from the dusty desert, the great sandstone walls of Jodhpur city enclose a maze of bazaars and lanes crowded with people and camels that huddle around the base of a magnificent fort built on a soaring bluff. In 1549, Rao Jodha made this the capital of his powerful, ever warring Rathore clan's Marwar (Land of Death) state. Today, expanded Jodhpur is Rajasthan's second largest city, after Jaipur.

Mehrangarh Fort glows in the sunlight.

To explore its ancient core, begin by taking a rickshaw up to the old city. Through **Nagauri Gate ❶**, one of seven in the 6-mile-long (10 km) city wall, a steep, zigzag path leads to the fort entrance. On the way, **Jaswant Thada ❷**, the royal cremation ground, is on the right; the white marble memorial (1899) is to Jaswant Singh II. As you pass through the sixth massive defense gateway, **Loha Pol ❸**, notice the handprints of royal wives who committed *sati* (self-immolation on their husband's funeral pyre). **Mehrangarh Fort ❹** (*$$, including audio-guide, mehrangarh.org*) combines serious defense

NOT TO BE MISSED:

Mehrangarh Fort • markets around the Clock Tower • Umaid Bhawan Palace

with refined courtly elegance. Beyond Suraj Pol is the palace area, now the Mehrangarh Museum. From the interconnecting courtyards you can enjoy fairy-tale views of the sandstone walls, whose windows are carved into such delicate *jali* (lattice) work that they look like lace.

Inside, an organized route takes you through **Moti Mahal** (Pearl Palace, 1581–1595) and **Phool Mahal** (Flower Palace, 1730–1750, decorated 1873–1895), both of which have exquisite painted ceilings and walls, with dancing girls, deities, and proud Jodhpur rulers. **Moti Vilas** (1638–1678) houses the marble coronation seat on which all rulers except Jodha have been (and continue to be) crowned. This and the adjacent Zenana ("women's quarters") court have especially fine *jali* work. In **Sheesh Mahal** (1707–1724) and **Rang Mahal,** see how inlay and mirrors are used in the decoration. The swords and shields in **Sileh Khana** (the armory) are more works of art than war implements. Finally, the sumptuous interior of **Takhat Vilas** (1843–1873) has jolly dancing-girl murals. Do not miss the splendid silk Mughal tent, booty from a raid on Delhi, nor the terrace with its ancient cannon and magnificent views.

To walk down into the city, take the path beside the painted building at the U-bend above the fort shops. At the bottom, wind

INSIDER TIP:

To discover Rajasthan, where camels outnumber *tuk-tuks* and high-rises are replaced with sandstone fortresses, choose local guides for freedom from timetables. Establish prices up front.

—TALA KATNER
National Geographic contributor

your way through narrow alleys to the central Sardar Bazar and its landmark **Clock Tower** ❺—this is not a large area, and you will not get lost—to see street barbers, water pot sellers, and **Tulahti Mahal** (1638–1681), a palace turned into a women's hospital.

A wide road leads to **Sojati Gate** ❻, where good locally made *bandhani* (tie-dye) cotton is sold. From here, take a rickshaw through the New City, pausing to enjoy the Victorian bric-a-brac in the **museum** ❼

in Umaid Gardens and the crazy Anglo-Rajput style of the **Judicial Court** (1893–1896). *(Agree on a price with your rickshaw driver in advance, pay on completion, and add a tip if appropriate; he waits while you make visits.)*

To end, sweep up the hill to the 347-room **Umaid Bhawan Palace** ❽ (1929–1944). Designed by H. V. Lanchester, it combines beaux arts with art deco, Western lifestyles with strict *purdah*, and tempers high European 1930s style with Rajput royal taste. It is now divided into private palace, public museum, and deluxe hotel. The massive bronze front doors lead to a grand hall with sweeping marble stairway, circular basement swimming pool, and grand pillared hotel terrace, ideal for refreshment. The **museum** section includes the Durbar Hall, miniature paintings, armor, and fine clocks.

⚏	See also area map pp. 126–127
▶	Nagauri Gate
⟷	About 4 miles (6 km)
⏱	3–4 hours
▶	Umaid Bhawan Palace

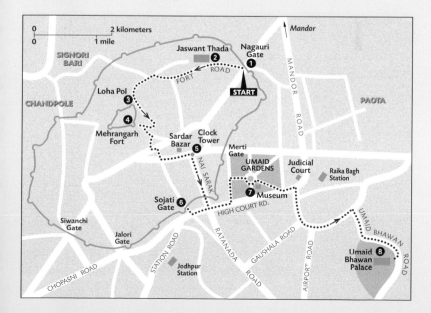

Bundi

127 E4

Kota

127 E3

Jodhpur

127 D4

Visitor Information

India Tourist Office, Hotel Ghoomar, High Court Rd.

029/1254-5083

jodhpur.nic.in

Mandor

127 D4

of Gujarat in 1535, and Akbar in 1567, when the capital was moved to Udaipur—caused thousands of soldiers' deaths and women's *johar* (ritual mass suicide), but they have only added to its Rajput romance. Inside the massive gateways, see the Palace of Rana Kumbha (1433–1468), the towers of Fame (12th century) and Victory (1457–1468), good temples, lakes, *sati* stones, and other buildings.

Until recently, **Bundi** seemed frozen in time. Visitors to the hilltop Taragarh Fort (1342), City Palace (begun 1580), Chatar Mahal palace (1660), and Raniji-ki-Baori step well (1699) in the bazaar, all built by the Hara Chauhan Rajputs, can view the main street's restored havelis, some now housing restaurants and crafts stores.

The thriving industrial town of **Kota,** on the banks of the Chambal River, has a charming old quarter. **City Palace** (begun 1625) has remarkable murals and inlay work, and houses the **Maharao Madho Singh Museum** *(closed Fri.),* which has a superb collection of deadly looking weapons and royal artifacts. The weaving village of **Kaithoon** and the temples of Jhalrapatan and Baroli are nearby.

Beyond Jodhpur

Across the dry and dusty Thar Desert—which can be crossed by car, train, jeep, or camel safari— lie isolated Rajasthani towns whose buildings reflect past wealth accumulated by virtue of being on one of the world's great east–west trading routes.

Five miles (8 km) north of Jodhpur is **Mandor,** where the Parihar Rajputs ruled Marwar from the sixth century until the Rathores toppled them in 1381. The fort is gone, but Rathore royal

Rajput cenotaphs with Jaisalmer Fort in the background

cenotaphs stand in lush **Mandor Gardens;** one is dedicated to Maharaja Ajit Singh (1724), who also built the pleasure palace.

Rajasthan's largest group of early Jain and Brahmanical temples (8th–11th centuries) stands on the outskirts of **Osian.** Most temples stand on a platform, have a curved tower, and are very finely carved.

The **Karni Mata Temple** at **Deshnoke** may not be a first choice for sightseeing: It swarms with holy rats. Devotees believe departing souls can evade the wrath of Yama, god of death, by reincarnation as a rat. The temple is dedicated to Bikaner's patron goddess, an incarnation of Durga.

Some 145 miles (231 km) north of Jodhpur, reached across arid scrub and sand, **Bikaner** is less picturesque than Jodhpur and Jaisalmer but just as interesting; it also has fewer visitors and a choice of palaces. Founded in 1488 by Bhika, sixth son of Rao Jodha of Jodhpur, it quickly benefited from the lucrative trade route. **Junagarh Fort** (1588–1593), built by Raja Rai Singh, one of Akbar's generals, protects beautiful, treasure-filled palaces: Chandra Mahal has Bhika's bed; exotic Anup Mahal the Coronation Hall is enriched with ornamental lacquer work. Inside the Old City's pink sandstone wall, wander the lanes to find the piazza lined with merchants' houses and, in the southeast corner, two Jain temples with colored murals. Don't miss the fine stone carvings at the **Ganga Golden Jubilee Museum**

(closed Fri.), or Sir Samuel Swinton Jacob's Anglo-Rajput **Lallgarh Palace** *(lallgarhpalace.com),* begun in 1881 and now a hotel (see Travelwise p. 352).

Just west of Bikaner, overlooking the artificial lake of Devi Kund

INSIDER TIP:

Head to the Sam Sand Dunes in Jaisalmer just before sunset to catch a dinner and dance show. Local food, Gypsy dancing, and trancelike music are perfect under the desert stars.

—SARAH WHITE
National Geographic grantee

Sagar, stand the magnificent marble and sandstone royal **cenotaphs.** Farther out, a royal hunting ground is now preserved and protected as the **Gajner Wildlife Sanctuary.** Here you can see *nilgai,* black buck, antelope, wild boar, *chinkara,* gazelles, and in winter, important migratory birds such as the Siberian grouse.

Eighty-four miles (135 km) northeast of Jodhpur, **Nagaur** offers grand mosques and painted palaces that reflect its Muslim and Hindu rulers. The town is the site of a businesslike **Cattle Fair** *(Jan.–Feb.),* when thousands arrive to trade cattle, camels, and Nagaur's famously stout bullocks, with time off for dancing and racing.

Osian
 127 D4
40 miles (64 km) N of Jodhpur

Deshnoke
127 D5
125 miles (199 km) N of Jodhpur

Bikaner
127 D5
145 miles (231 km) N of Jodhpur
bikanertourism.com

Gajner Wildlife Sanctuary
127 D5
164 miles (263 km) N of Jodhpur

Nagaur
 127 D4
84 miles (135 km) NE of Jodhpur
nagaur.nic.in

Barmer
 127 C4

✉ 145 miles
(232 km) W
of Jodhpur

Pokaran
▲ 127 C4

✉ 116 miles
(185 km) NW
of Jodhpur

Jaisalmer
▲ 127 C4

✉ 184 miles
(295 km) NW
of Jodhpur

Some 145 miles (232 km) west of Jodhpur, lying on the route to Jaisalmer, is **Barmer's** quiet crafts center. It leaps into life as thousands of Rajasthanis arrive for the annual **Mallinath Fair** (*held in Tilwara Mar.–Apr.*), the largest cattle fair in Rajasthan and, so far, less commercialized than Pushkar's Cattle Fair (see Travelwise p. 385).

At **Pokaran**, a modest version of Jaisalmer (see below) with

A tassel-wearing camel at Jaisalmer's Desert Festival

Sam Sand Dunes
▲ 127 B4

✉ 209 miles
(325 km) NW
of Jodhpur

fewer visitors, you can explore the ornate, red-sandstone fort and its splendid havelis.

The fortified desert city of **Jaisalmer** is built of fragile, golden sandstone, often exquisitely

carved. It has stood isolated in the Thar Desert since its founding by Rawal Jaisal, a Bhatti Rajput, in 1156. Despite its turbulent history, this defiant city thrived thanks to the lucrative trade routes that brought travelers and merchandise to India from worlds beyond: Persia, Arabia, Egypt, Africa, and Europe.

More recently, when Western tourists discovered its beauty, it was threatened, first with unsympathetic new buildings, then with a detrimental increased water consumption. Valiant work to save the city is currently being done by the British-based charity, Jaipur in Jeopardy. You can witness their efforts as you visit the fortifications, fort-palace, and several of the grand havelis. The colorful **Desert Festival** (*Jan.–Feb.*) is aimed at tourists.

A camel safari and sleeping under the desert stars around a campfire can be magical. Safaris last from one to four days and usually head out from Jaisalmer toward the **Sam Sand Dunes** (pronounced "Sum"), Amar Sagar lake, and Lodurva's Jain temples or the magnificent royal cenotaphs at Bada Bagh; enthusiasts can ride to Bikaner or Jodhpur. Remember to bring high-SPF sunscreen for days and warm woolens for nights.

On a village jeep safari you can learn about desert wildlife and the local Bishnoi tribe: See the tribes thatched huts, learn about their herbal remedies, and appreciate their crafts (often on sale). Trips can be arranged by your hotel. ■

Crafts & Traditions of Rajasthan

Every town in Rajasthan has its markets, brimful with life, especially toward the end of the day when the heat is less oppressive. Walking through them is a treat, particularly to see all the different crafts on sale. Peek behind the shops and you see a silversmith or a painter; cast your eyes up and you see yards of tie-dye drying on the rooftops. People throng the stalls, and as night falls, itinerant puppeteers set up their shows.

Tourism has helped revive several almost lost traditions. In Jaipur the art of block-printing on cotton, whose heyday was the 18th century, thrives once more. Recipes for natural dyes have been rediscovered, blocks of teak are being carved with new and traditional designs, and printers can barely keep up with demand. Another revival is Jaipur pottery, a soft-paste pottery decorated with azure blue flowers and patterns.

Both Jaipur and Bikaner have the best *meenakari* work, the art of enameling that used to depend upon court patronage. These delicate patterns of birds and flowers in ruby red, deep green, and peacock blue often remain hidden on the reverse of gem-studded jewelry.

Jodhpur is known for its *bandhani,* the ancient Indian technique of tie-dyeing fabrics found throughout Rajasthan and Gujarat. Each community has its own designs. The merchant supplies the fabric to a family, usually Muslim. The father draws the pattern on the fabric using tiny dots. The women and children bind the cloth tightly, following the pattern, dye the fabric, then remove the strings. The process may be repeated with a darker color to build up the pattern. Jodhpur is also a center for wooden lacquerwork, especially bangles and boxes.

Helped by some dynamic Delhi patrons, miniature painting is reaching new peaks. Rajasthan's many painting schools declined in the 19th century, but artists are now practicing this very disciplined art using both traditional iconography and innovative designs.

Another joy of Rajasthan is the quantity of traditional entertainment still in evidence:

The rich red tones of a densely and laboriously crafted cotton patchwork fabric from Jaisalmer

Songs and stories are often so simple that mime is sufficient to explain them. In a land where evening entertainment is minimal, hotels often employ talented families of entertainers to put on a show for their guests. *Bhopas* (balladeers), originally from Marwar, have a visual aid, a *phad* (scroll painting); while the father sings the story, the mother holds a lantern and they dance. Folk dances often relate to Holi, Gangaur, and other Rajasthan festivals: the *gingad* is accompanied by the big *chang* drum, the *teratali* is more like ritual acrobatics than dancing, and the *ghoomar-gair* is Rajasthan's version of the age-old stick dance. But the puppet show is always the favorite. *Kathputli,* as it is known, is performed by itinerant families. Drawing back the embroidered curtain known as the Taj Mahal, they back up the antics of their beautifully carved, painted, and costumed puppets with music, song, and high-pitched yelps.

Gujarat

In Gujarat, Ahmedabad's glories—handsome sultanate buildings, Le Corbusier's landmarks, art museums, great markets—are little touched by tourism, and the rest of this fascinating state is barely visited. The rewards for simple accommodations are Palitana's exquisite hilltop Jain pilgrimage temples, coastal art deco palaces, and villages each with their own textile tradition.

Ahmedabad

This dynamic city is the capital of Gujarat, a modern state with a very ancient history. It comprises three distinct geographical regions: hilly peninsula Saurashtra, barren Kachchh with its Rann (desert), and the central, fairly flat portion. As the country's prime producer of cotton and groundnut oil, and its second greatest producer of tobacco, Gujarat is India's wealthiest state. A visit to Ahmedabad's formidable and distinctive Islamic monuments, with their remarkably fine *jali* work, and to its many good museums, makes a perfect springboard for exploring this rarely visited state.

The Old City: The city's ancient citadel, **Bhadra,** is a good place to start. When Ahmad Shah became Sultan of Gujarat in 1411, he moved the capital here from Patan (see p. 147) and built this solid, red stone citadel. It is closed to the public, but it is often possible to climb the staircase inside the main gate to enjoy good views from the roof. Trade flourished, boosted by east–west trade to the ports, and the building of mosques followed. In this area, you can see Alif Shah's green-and-white mosque in front of the citadel and Ahmad Shah's small, private mosque by Victoria Gardens, whose intricate *mihrabs* contrast with Sanskrit inscriptions on stones from an earlier Hindu temple.

Stay in this area to visit **Sidi Sayyid's Mosque** (1573), built shortly after the Mughal emperor Akbar finally absorbed Gujarat into his vast empire in 1572 to

Thousands of exquisite kites fly at Ahmedabad's festival.

benefit from its wealth and its location on the hajj (pilgrimage) route to Mecca. The mosque is isolated on a traffic island, but it is worth risking the traffic to enjoy its ten magnificent jali (carved latticework) screens, especially those wooden **Swaminarayan Temple,** and surrounding traditional **Gujarat** *havelis.*

Other Ahmedabad Sights

After 1630, Gujarat's run of famines, Marathas, and Muslims

2001 Earthquake & Rebuilding

At 8:46 a.m. on January 26, 2001, western India experienced an earthquake that measured a magnitude of 7.7. Its epicenter was near Bhuj, a town in the Kachchh region of Gujarat. Shock waves reached as far as Chennai and Nepal. Bhuj and more than 300 villages nearby were wiped out, and the whole state was affected. More than 20,000 people died, and many more were left homeless. In all, 1,016 villages and eight cities suffered substantial damage, much now repaired thanks to a huge international effort. In Ahmedabad, 179 buildings were affected but many of the old wooden *havelis* survived. This fact has made locals appreciate their stability and their beauty afresh; now many are being restored.

---

in the western wall (these can be seen from outside; the mosque is closed to women). Observe how local Hindu and Jain craftsmen were allowed to carve heroes and animals from Hindu mythology.

Walk along Mahatma Gandhi Road to find more sites dating back to Ahmad Shah. First is his monumental **Teen Darwaja** ("triple gateway") in Khas Bazar. Next is his magnificent **Jama Masjid** (completed 1424); go up the great steps to see the courtyard, prayer hall (elaborate carving), and Zenana jali screens. Finally, his family **mausoleum** (1442; *closed to women*) and that of his wives stand in Manek Chowk among the streets of jewelers, dyers, and merchants. See the Hindu styles and the fine inlay decoration.

To finish, take three short detours to Rani Sipri's very Hindu **mosque** (1514), the carved turned the city's fortunes. In 1817, under British influence, modern machinery made Ahmedabad the industrial powerhouse of the East. Mahatma Gandhi's arrival (see pp. 148–149) further boosted its textile production and political power. Thus, Ahmedabad's most important museum is the **Calico Museum of Textiles** (*Shahibagh Rd., closed Wed., a.m. tours only, reservations req., calicomuseum .com*), where guides explain a dazzling variety and quality of weaving, embroidery, mirrorwork, tie-dye, printing, and skillful ikat weave, all collected by the Sarabhai textile magnates.

For other specialist interests, visit the **Shreyas Folk Art Museum** (*near Shreyas Railway Crossing, closed Mon., $*), displaying Gujarati crafts; the **Tribal Museum** (*Gujarat Vidyapith,*

Ahmedabad

⚑ 126 C2

Visitor Information

✉ Gujarat Tourist Information, H. K. House, Ashram Rd., S of Gandhi Bridge, Ahmedabad

☎ 079/2657-8044, 079/2657-8046, 079/2658-9172

gujarattourism.com

NOTE: The tourist information center in Ahmedabad services all of Gujarat. Get all Gujarat tourist information before you leave Ahmedabad. There are excellent morning and afternoon tours of Ahmedabad offered by the State Tourism Corp ($$). For reservations, tel 079/2658-9172 or 079/2657-6434.

Gandhinagar

127 D2

14 miles (23 km) N of Ahmedabad

Modhera
127 C3

66 miles (105 km) NW of Ahmedabad

Ashram Rd., closed Sun.), about the various peoples of Gujarat; the **Kite Museum** (closed Mon.); and the **N. C. Mehta Gallery** (Indology Institute, Radhakrishnan Rd., tel 079/2630-2463, closed Mon.), with its collection of top-quality Indian miniature paintings. Just outside town, **Vishalla** (Sarkhej Rd., Vasana, tel 079/2660-2422) combines traditional huts, craftsmen, a splendid museum of Gujarati metalware, and a restaurant. Le Corbusier enthusiasts can see several of his buildings here (see pp. 86–87).

Ahmedabad played a vital role in India's freedom movement (see p. 148). You can visit the Charles Correa–designed **Gandhi Smarak** (Sabarmati Ashram, Ashram Rd., tel 079/2755-7277, gandhiashram .org.in, $) in Mahatma's Sabarmati Ashram, where Gandhi lived from

1917 to 1930; an excellent exhibition tells the freedom story. To complete the picture, the **Sardar Patel Memorial Museum** (near Shahibagh Rd., closed Sun.) remembers the politician and freedom fighter who was deputy to Jawaharlal Nehru.

For a final taste of Ahmedabad's past glory, visit three multi-layered, galleried, and elaborately carved step wells called *vavs*. In town is **Dada Harini Vav** (1435), and nearby is **Mata Bhavani Vav** (11th century); on Ajmer Road to Gandhinagar is the best of all, **Adalaj Vav** (1498), 11 miles (17 km) north of Ahmedabad.

A 30-minute drive beyond here is **Auto World Vintage Car Museum** (Dastan Estate, Sardar Patel Ring Rd., tel 079/2282-0699), Pranlal Bhogilal's fine collection of more than one hundred antique cars.

North of Ahmedabad

Rural Gujarat north of Ahmedabad has a variety of quality sites that reward intrepid travelers.

Gandhinagar, founded in 1965 and named after the Mahatma, was India's second planned town and, like Chandigarh (see p. 118), was designed by Le Corbusier, assisted by B. V. Doshi. Greenery has considerably softened the impact of this *"cité idéale."* The most important site, however, is the lavish Akshardhan, the wealthy Swaminarayan sect's temple complex, built in 1993 to honor its founder, Sreeji Swami.

Continuing farther, to the northwest of Ahmedabad, visit the Surya Temple at **Modhera,**

Nano, the World's Cheapest Car

Developed by Tata Motors, this revolutionary car is being produced at Sanand, outside Ahmedabad. The tiny, light-bodied, four-seat car costs around $2,000, a price accessible to India's ever growing middle class. Dubbed "the people's car" by company chairman Ratan Tata, it gets 50 miles to the gallon (5 km/L), using a rear-wheel drive and a 35-horse power engine that can push speeds to 60 miles an hour (96 kph). The deluxe models come with air-conditioning.

begun in 1027 by Bhimdev I. The temple was an early achievement of the rich Solanki rulers (11th–13th centuries) and, despite its dilapidation after Mahmud of Ghazni's attack (see p. 33), remains one of Gujarat's great Hindu temples. It was financed by public subscription and built by voluntary labor, and its monumental conception is matched

founded in 1796, watch the ikat weave being created in one of its finest forms, the *patola* silk sari; see also carved havelis, domes, and Jain temples.

Nearby **Siddhapur** is a time-capsule trading town with grand early 20th-century merchants' houses. At **Taranga** there is a well-preserved Jain temple (1166), dedicated to Ajitanatha, the second

Anahilvada
🏛 127 C3
✉ 106 miles (169 km) N of Ahmedabad

Patan
🏛 127 C3
✉ 106 miles (169 km) N of Ahmedabad

Siddhapur
🏛 127 C3
✉ 100 miles (160 km) N of Ahmedabad

Taranga
🏛 127 C3
✉ 84 miles (135 km) NW of Ahmedabad

Kumbharia
🏛 127 D3
✉ 118 miles (189 km) N of Ahmedabad

A weaver creates the soft pattern of ikat-weave silk.

Saurashtra
🏛 126 B2 & 127 C2

Visitor Information
✉ See Gujarat Tourist Information

by rich ornamentation. From the huge tank with its double flights of steps, two *mandapas* (halls) lead to the sanctuary; here, note especially the carvings of Agni (south) and Surya (north). Enjoy these in the glow of sunset.

Farther north you will come to **Anahilvada,** the Solanki capital sacked repeatedly by Muslim marauders, then abandoned for Ahmedabad. Among the remains of the fortifications, temples, and tank is the Solanki queen Udaimati's exquisite Ran-ki-vav (ca 1080), Gujarat's finest step well. In the Sadvi Wada area of the bustling adjoining city of **Patan,**

Tirthankara, and built by the Solanki ruler Kumarapala. Farther north, by the border with Rajasthan, join Jain pilgrims for the hill climb to **Kumbharia's** five Solanki period Jain temples (1062–1231), which rival Mount Abu's (see p. 136); each is built of marble and stands in its own court.

Saurashtra
This rural area of Gujarat fills the Kathiawar Peninsula bordered by the Gulfs of Kachchh and Khambhat and the Arabian Sea. The ancient ports, forts, and temples recall occupants

(continued on p. 150)

Mahatma Gandhi

One of the most influential men of the 20th century, Mohandas Karamchand Gandhi (1869–1948) was born in Porbandar in western Gujarat, where his father and grandfather were *diwans* of the princely state. Trained as a lawyer in London, he worked in South Africa, where his passive resistance against the government's color and race prejudice prompted Bengali poet Rabindranath Tagore to give him the title Mahatma (Great Soul).

Returning home in 1915, Gandhi joined India's struggle for freedom and founded the Sabarmati Ashram in Ahmedabad (see p. 146). Two years later he moved in.

Gandhi began a nonviolent moral protest against oppression, known to Indians as *satyagraha* (literally "grasping truth"), and to the British as civil disobedience. It meant peacefully defying laws and willingly taking punishment. Then, appalled by the atrocities at Amritsar generated by his peaceful, national, one-day strike in 1919 (see p. 121), he waged his Non-Cooperation Movement of 1920–1922.

Gandhi's aim was to use *ahimsa* (nonviolence) and *satya* (truth) to achieve a united, independent India. When he spun cotton and wove the thread into cloth, it symbolized his vision of an autonomous, self-reliant India free of foreign domination. When he rejected European clothes for the homespun cotton *dhoti* and shawl in 1921, his popularity soared with most Indians. Believing in the equality of all, he tried to give the untouchables dignity by renaming them *harijans* (children of God).

Gandhi had a strong, charismatic character matched by an austere code of living and huge ambitions for India. He campaigned relentlessly, fighting for *swadeshi,* the rejection of the imported cotton that had devastated India's weavers. He also supported the Congress Party president, Jawaharlal Nehru, when, on January 26, 1930, the resolution demanding complete independence was adopted.

That same year Gandhi launched a second civil disobedience campaign, given focus by the mass appeal of his Salt March, protesting against the British monopoly of salt production. On March 12, it left Ahmedabad amid Gandhi's rousing speeches for *swaraj* (freedom); a month later the protesters reached coastal Dandi, where they began to collect water and boil it to make illegal salt, thus expressing their objections to a system that touched every Indian household.

Salt was made illegally, saltworks were raided, government servants resigned, and on May 5 Gandhi was imprisoned. In January 1931, he and the British viceroy, Lord Irwin, signed a pact that led eventually to the Government of India Act of 1935.

During World War II, Gandhi introduced the "Quit India" slogan and worked to keep an undivided, free India. When Jinnah's call for "Direct Action" in 1946 provoked riots in

The Symbolic National Flag

India's horizontal orange-white-green tricolor has deep meaning for its citizens. The top stripe is saffron, or Kesari, representing courage and sacrifice. The white middle stripe represents peace and truth; in the center of it is the wheel, or Ashoka Chakra, which signifies the eternal wheel of law. The bottom stripe is a rich dark green for faith and chivalry. The flag was adopted on July 22, 1947, in anticipation of independence, which would come less than a month later, on August 15.

India's last viceroy, Lord Mountbatten, and his wife Edwina flank Gandhi at the Viceroy's House, in 1947.

Kolkata, Gandhi fasted until the violence had stopped. He again fasted for peace when, at partition, an estimated five million Hindus and Sikhs came into India, while the same number of Muslims left for Pakistan amid terrible bloodshed. On January 30, 1948, a Hindu extremist angered by Gandhi's tolerance toward Muslims assassinated him in Delhi. Ironically, this dreadful act had the effect of finally quelling the violence.

Climb the hill at Palitana for beautiful views like this one.

Sarkhej
🏛 127 C2
✉ 5 miles (8 km)
SW of Ahmedabad

Lothal
🏛 127 C2
✉ 66 miles (105 km)
S of Ahmedabad
💲 $

**Velavadar Black
Buck Sanctuary**
🏛 127 C2
✉ 113 miles (181 km)
S of Ahmedabad

Bhavnagar
🏛 127 C2
✉ 129 miles
(204 km) S of
Ahmedabad

Palitana
🏛 127 C2

Diu
🏛 127 C1

Somnath Temple
🏛 126 B1

of all faiths stretching back to the Harappans (see p. 26). In 1807 the fragmented land of 220 petty states, many ruled by Rajputs, came under British supremacy. The sights listed below are most rewardingly visited with a car and driver.

Southern Saurashtra: On the road down toward Lothal, you come first to **Sarkhej,** the site of the tomb of Ahmad Shah's spiritual leader, Sheikh Ahmed Khattu (1445). At **Nal Sarovar Bird Sanctuary** *(40 miles/60 km SW of Ahmedabad)* you can see migrant waterbirds *(Nov.–Feb.),* and at **Dholka** *(28 miles/44 km S of Ahmedabad)* there are three monumental medieval mosques and a beautiful wooden haveli temple to visit. The remarkable and evocative remains of **Lothal,** an excavated Harappan port, include the dock and the town's bazaars. The site

museum has jewelry, weights, and compasses.

At **Velavadar Black Buck Sanctuary,** it's best to pay a guide to learn more about the elegant Indian antelope (or black buck), traditionally protected by the Bishnoi tribe.

Founded in 1723 by Maharaja Bhavsinghji, the old city of **Bhavnagar,** a cotton-exporting port, has vibrant bazaars for silver, gold, cloth, and *bandhani* (tie-dyed fabrics). Exhibits at the Gandhi Smriti Museum range from Harappan terra-cottas to the story of Gandhi's life. From here you can visit **Palitana,** joining Jain pilgrims to climb their sacred hill of Shatrunjaya, dedicated to the saint Adinath; 900 little temples make its summit India's largest temple city.

The 8-mile-long (13 km) island of **Diu** was Portuguese until 1962. This is where to relax, enjoy the beaches and cafés, and rent a bicycle to see the old town and fort. Avoid holiday seasons, when Gujaratis flock here to enjoy unrestricted alcohol.

Sadly, there is more myth than reality at **Somnath Temple.** The early versions are part of Hindu mythology; the later ones were successively destroyed by marauding Muslims. Today's temple (1950) was built by Sardar Patel, keeping to the plan of the Solanki temple at Modhera (see p. 147).

The last of the southern sites is **Sasan Gir National Park,** the final Indian refuge of the Asiatic lion, which roamed northern India's forests until the 1880s.

About 300 lions (the number is rising) live in 100 square miles (260 sq km), together with panthers and the local Maldhari cattle breeders. It is best to visit from November to mid-June—the later the better for seeing lions.

Western Saurashtra: From **Junagadh,** the ancient capital of Gujarat, Jain pilgrims climb their sacred Mount Girnar. Junagadh's old citadel, Uparkot, once a Maurya and Gupta stronghold, is reached through openings in solid rock—three gateways and massive walls; features inside include several

The fine stone was exported to Bombay and Karachi, and the city's rulers added two waterfront palaces: **Daria Rajmahal** *(54 miles/95 km from Diu Airport, closed university holidays)* and **Anut Nivas Khambala** (1927, museum in the Rajput Room; *15 miles/25 km E of Porbandar).* Gandhi's simple, unfurnished house, the **Kirti Mandir** *(closed sunset–sunrise),* is where he lived until his family moved to Rajkot (see p. 152). The neighboring temple, Kirti Mandir (1950), was constructed to commemorate him.

Devotees of Krishna believe he fled Mathura to make **Dwarka**

Sasan Gir National Park
- 🗺 127 C1
- ☎ 028/7728-5541
- 🕑 Closed July–Oct.
- 💲 $$$$$

Junagadh
- 🗺 126 B2

Porbandar
- 🗺 126 B2
- **Visitor Information**
- ✉ Tourist Information Bureau, Collector Office, Ground Floor
- ☎ 028/6224-5475

General Elections in the World's Largest Democracy

Indians take their democracy seriously. General elections to the Lok Sabha, parliament's lower house, take place every five years or when the government calls one. With an electorate of 714 million, more than the United States and European Union combined, the voting takes almost a month. The numbers are astounding: 543 constituencies, 828,804 polling stations (one polling station in Gir, rural Gujarat, has just one voter, the local priest), 1,368,430 electronic voting machines, and an overall turnout of 60 percent. Then, thanks to a finely tuned and efficient system, the results are announced after three days.

---

third- to fourth-century caves with richly carved columns, and two 11th-century vavs (step wells). In town, the Junagadh rulers' mausoleums are some of Gujarat's finest. Out of town, on the way to Mount Girnar's 12th-century temples, a building encloses a boulder inscribed with Ashoka's edicts (see p. 26).

Porbandar, now renowned as the birthplace of Gandhi, is a port with ancient trading links to Africa and Arabia. Under British protection the port prospered.

his capital. Pilgrims flock here for the Hindu **festivals of Shivratri** *(Feb.–March)* and **Janmashtami** *(Aug.–Sept.),* the latter of which celebrates Krishna's birthday.

Maharaja Ranjit Singh, who played cricket for England with W. G. Grace, gave **Jamnagar** city its first boost into modernity. Head for the old city built beside Ranmal Lake and protected by **Lakhota** *($$)* and **Bhujia forts.** Inside the walls is Chandni Bazar, with its ancient havelis and decorated Jain temples dedicated

Dwarka
- 🗺 126 B2

Jamnagar
- 🗺 126 B2

Rajkot
⚠ 127 C2

Visitor Information

✉ Tourism
Corporation of
Gujarat Limited,
Bhavnagar
House,
Jawahar Rd.

☎ 028/1223-4507

gujarattourism.com

Wankaner
⚠ 127 C2

Morbi
⚠ 127 C2

**Dubargadh
Waghaji**
✉ Morbi
🕐 Courtyards only

New Palace
✉ New Palace,
Morbi
🕐 Write to request
a visit

Halvad
⚠ 127 C2

Dhrangadhra
⚠ 127 C2

to Adinath and Shantinath; there are glorious murals inside. See also **Ratan Bai Mosque,** with its inlaid doors, Ranjit Singh's sweeping Willingdon Crescent at Chelmsford Market, and enjoy the excellent local bandhani work.

Central Saurashtra: The teeming industrial city of **Rajkot,** once the British headquarters of the Western States, is where Gandhi's family moved from Porbandar in 1881. Their new home was the modest **Kaba Gandhi no Delo** (open 9–12 p.m., 3–5 p.m., closed Sun.), which can be found off Ghitake Road in the old city, among traditional wooden

INSIDER TIP:

During December's full moon in Kachchh, the Rann Utsav festival pays tribute to the region's culture and nature with folk music and dance.

—STEPHANIE ROBICHAUX
National Geographic contributor

Gujarati houses with carved shutters and stained glass. In the **Watson Museum** (closed Sun., $), there is a variety of Harappan, medieval, and Rajput treasures, plus a splendid statue of Queen-Empress Victoria (1899) by Alfred Gilbert, creator of London's bronze statue "Eros." Other colonial buildings include Alfred High School (1875)

and Rajkumar College (1870), designed to be Gujarat's equivalent of Eton.

Wankaner was the capital of the former state, where Gandhi's father was once *diwan* (chief minister) to the maharaja. Under British protection, Maharaja Amarshinghi (r. 1881–1948) transformed the city into a model of self-reforming enterprise and helped the state engineer design his own palace, Ranjit Vilas (1907–1914). This landmark building combines Victorian Gothic, Italianate, and Mughal styles. Inside is a marble double spiral staircase. You can stay in the palace's outer buildings.

In this area of Saurashtra, keep a look out for *pallias,* tombstones commemorating bravery. Various images are used to describe the manner of death: A carved hand records a *sati* (self-immolation by a widow on her husband's funeral pyre); a mounted bard with spear indicates a poet who committed suicide because his master defaulted on a loan for which the poet was surety.

Dominating access to the Gujarat peninsula, tiny **Morbi** state was threatened until Thakur Sabhi Waghaji (r. 1897–1948) gave it stability and modernization, with a streetcar line and railroad. He was also the man responsible for two palaces: **Dubargadh Waghaji** (1880), in Venetian Gothic style, and **New Palace** (1931–1944), a stunning art deco building with an immaculate interior. **Halvad** has a lakeside palace and plenty of pallias, while **Dhrangadhra** is home to herds of wild asses that also live in the Rann of Kachchh.

Kachchh

The salt flats of this wild, arid, and isolated area dotted with villages are the world's largest breeding area for flamingos, and a refuge for the prancing Asiatic wild asses. In the north, the marshy Great and Little Ranns of Kachchh (Kutch) flood palace, and the grand, elaborately carved palaces of the great merchants including that of Ram Singh's with its later Dutch facade.

For the adventurous traveler, the rewards of visiting Kachchh's **villages** will compensate for basic accommodations. Taking a guide with you from the area capital

FESTIVAL:
Bhuj (Jan.–Feb.) is a five-day celebration of traditional music, dance, and crafts held in Kachchh.

In Kachchh, famous for its textiles, women wear stunning colors daily.

in a good monsoon, making Kachchh an island. Although once part of various empires, the area has remained highly individual in its traditions and crafts and highly independent in its maritime trading with Africa, the Gulf, and the Indian coast.

The wealth of Kachchh's second city, **Mandvi,** mostly came from its role as the port used by Mughals for their vast annual hajj expeditions to Mecca—more than 800 ships went in 1819, and the great dhows are still built here today. You can also see Vijay Vilas Bhuj, where you need a day or two to enjoy the town, you might include **Mundra,** near the Jain temples of Bhadreswar, **Bhujodi,** with its weavers, or **Anjar,** with its bright embroideries. Along the way you can see various tribal communities, each with their distinctive dress: the pastoral Rabari, known for their embroidery, the Bharvad, who came from Mathura, the nomadic Ahir cattle breeders, and the Charans, whose women are often worshipped for their traditional association with the goddess Parvati.

Kachchh

126 B3

Visitor Information

✉ Tourist Information Bureau, Office of District Information Centre, First Floor, Exhibition Hall, Opp: Bahumali Bhavan, Bhuj

☎ 028/3222-4910

gujarattourism.com

NOTE: Check carefully on permit requirements for the Kachchh areas on your itinerary.

Vadodara

⚑ 127 D2

Visitor Information

✉ Tourism
Corporation
of Gujarat
Ltd., Narmada
Bhavan, C- block,
Indira Avenue

☎ 026/5242-7489,
026/5243-1297

🕐 Closed Sun.

gujarattourism.com

Champaner

⚑ 127 D2

Daman

⚑ 127 D1

✉ 131 miles
(208 km) N of
Mumbai

Vadodara & Area

This little-visited strip of land, so significant when the British established their first trading station at Surat in 1614, has several interesting sights.

Driving from Ahmedabad, stop at painstakingly conserved **Champaner,** outside Vadodara. After Muhammad Begada took the Chauhan Rajput stronghold in 1484, he spent 23 years building it up as his capital, then abandoned it. Here you'll find historic walls, gateways, mosques, and tombs, and fine views of Pavagadh hill.

Dusty Vadodara (Baroda) is an ever expanding industrial town,

INSIDER TIP:

For the best cycling trips, head to Rajasthan and south India during winter, the lower Himalaya in spring and fall, and Ladakh in summer. Avoid the always congested Ganga Valley!

—BILL WEIR
National Geographic author

redeemed by the old havelis and bazaars in its old town and by the well-maintained parks, lakes, and public buildings added by Baroda state's enlightened and extravagant rulers known as Gaekwads ("protectors of cows"). Worth a visit is Gaekwad Maharaja Sayajirao III's palace, **Lakshmi Vilas** *(Nehru Rd., closed Sun., $; to visit the palace, you must request a permit from the Maharaja's secretary at*

the palace office, or call 026/5242-6372). This is reputedly the most expensive building constructed by a private individual in the 19th century. Designed by Maj. Charles Mant and completed by Robert Fellowes Chisholm in 1890, this mix of Indian styles also has London stained glass, Venetian mosaics, and a garden designed by experts from London's Kew Gardens. More practically, this Gaekwad built roads, railways, and hospitals, outlawed child marriage, and made school compulsory. On the grounds, the **Maharaja Fateh Singh Museum** *(closed Sun., $)* houses a large collection of the influential early 20th-century Indian artist Raja Ravi Varma and much European art. See, too, Pratap Vilas (ca 1910), Makarpura Palace, the Kalabahavan Technical Institute (1922), the Vadodara Museum and Art Gallery's sculptures and miniature paintings, and the university's sculptures from Vadaval and Buddhist monuments from Devnimori. Do not miss Naulakhi Baoli or the royal mausoleum of Kirti Mandir.

Drive past Bharuch (Broach) and Surat, once vital trading towns, to relaxed, quiet **Daman,** but avoid public holidays, when it is besieged by locals for its freely available alcohol. Daman was ruled by the Portuguese from 1531 until 1961, and south of the Damanganga River, in **Moti Daman,** you will find grand walls, Portuguese mansions, and some of the best preserved churches in Asia. Nani Daman, on the north bank, has hotels, markets, and docks. ∎

A spectacular combination of business and Bollywood, Buddhist caves and Hindu temples, historic forts and dramatic landscapes

Mumbai & Maharashtra

Bollywood dreams and dramas loom large in Mumbai.

Mumbai & Maharashtra

Maharashtra sweeps from the Arabian Sea across the paddy fields and coconut groves of the Konkan, up across the rugged Western Ghats (Sahyadri Hills), and into the heart of peninsular India.

This expansive state, India's third largest in size and population, nevertheless has a unity. Its Marathi-speaking people share a common history, enriched by cultures to the north and south. After a period when Maharashtra was part of the Mauryan Empire (321–185 B.C.), successive Hindu dynasties held power for a thousand years until 1294, when the Yadavas yielded to the first of a string of Muslim rulers. The great port city of Bombay, now renamed Mumbai, rose toward the end of the 17th century, just when the warrior hero Shivaji was consolidating the Maratha people of the area into a powerful nation. Despite defeat by the British in 1817, Shivaji's

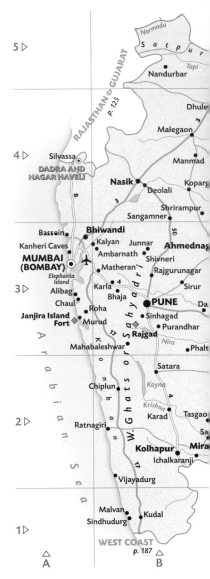

NOT TO BE MISSED:

inspiration lives on; notice the plethora of statues of modern Maharashtra's founding father in downtown areas.

Visitors often rush through Mumbai and on to other areas of India. This is a shame. Mumbai is not just about trading: Its treasures include remarkable early Buddhist cave sculptures, a deserted Portuguese fort more atmospheric than anything to be found at Old

AROUND DELHI
p. 91

Tapi

Range
Bhusawal Akot •Achalpur 6 Katol **Gondia**
alner Bhandara 6
Jalgaon •**Amravati** **NAGPUR**
dhora 6 **Akola** 6 Sevagram
•Khamgaon• Murtajapur Wardha
alisgaon Buldana• S a h y a d r i p a r v a t R a n g e •Yavatmal •Hinganghat
Ajanta Chikhli •Warora
ora **Caves**
ves •Khuldabad Washim EASTERN INDIA *p. 287*
•**Aurangabad** •Pusad Wani• Garhchiroli
latabad **Jalna** Hingoli •**Chandrapur**
H A R A S H T R A Pengana Satmala Range

Paithan Godavari **Parbhani** T H E   D E C C A N
Bid •Nanded *p. 219*
•Parli
Balaghat Range Sironcha
Manjra 16
Sina **Latur** Udgir △ △
arenda• E F
•Barsi △
•Osmanabad D
Naldurg 9 0   200 kilometers
dharpur 9 **Solapur** 0   100 miles
•Sangola THE DECCAN *p. 219*

△
C

Area of map detail

★
**New
Delhi**

in Mumbai have intrigued you, there are more caves to visit at Karla, Bhaja, and Bedsa, cut into the rock of the Western Ghats. But if you seek Raj charm in the cool hills, take a short train ride up to Matheran, Mahabaleshwar, or Pune, British hill stations now much loved by local Maharashtrans, set in the heart of what was once Shivaji's Maratha confederacy. For a more adventurous trip, the new Konkan railroad (see p. 202) and the hovercraft crossing Mumbai's harbor make an adventure southward easy; you can go on down to Goa, and extend your journey into a coastal trip right down to Kochi (see pp. 206–207).

Along the way, notice the rich soil. Seventy percent of Maharashtrans work in agriculture, producing India's largest crops of highly prized Alphonso mangoes, seedless grapes, Cavendish bananas, soft-seeded pomegranates, sugar, cashew nuts, and cotton. A convoy of bullock carts bringing in the cotton harvest at sunset is a memorable sight. ■

Goa, and a group of world-class, well-preserved high Victorian Gothic public buildings.

Away from the seething life of the city, whose humidity climbs sharply between April and October, the most important trip inland is to the cave temples of Ellora and Ajanta, whose paintings and sculptures are often said to be some of the greatest achievements in world art. If these and the other Buddhist sites

Mumbai

Mumbai—formerly Bombay, until its name was officially changed in 1995, to honor the goddess worshipped by early inhabitants here—is home to more than ten million people. It houses the headquarters of almost all of India's major banks, financial institutions, and insurance companies. It has India's largest stock exchange, port, and movie industry. It even has Manhattan-style high-rises, offshore oil fields, and is home to Bollywood, India's thriving film industry.

Completed in 1887, Mumbai's Victoria Terminus is India's grandest train station.

Mumbai

☒ 156 A3

Visitor Information

☎ India Tourist Office, Reservations: 1800-2299-30 Head Office: 022/2204-4040

✉ State Tourist Office, Gateway of India

☎ 022/2284-1877

maharashtratourism .gov.in mumbai.org.uk

For a city that began as seven boggy, malarial islands, Mumbai has done well. The islands were part of the dowry of Portuguese Princess Catherine of Braganza when she married the English king Charles II in 1662. In 1668 the British government leased them to the East India Company for £10 a year. The company, which had received its trading charter from Queen Elizabeth I in 1600, could make its own laws and collect all revenue of just under £3,000 per annum (the equivalent of about £300,000 or $470,000 today). Yet the climate was so unhealthy that of the 800 British living there in 1692, 700 died in that year.

However, Bombay was soon the focus of India's west coast trade. Gerald Aungier, known as the "father of Bombay," was governor from 1672–1675: He established the Courts of Justice and founded the company militia that became the East India Company Army. Most importantly, he actively encouraged Parsees from Gujarat, Banias (Hindu traders) fleeing Portuguese oppression in Goa, Arab traders, and others to settle in the city, so that by 1700 its population reached 120,000.

After the company lost its trade monopoly in 1813, the British presence increased. Trade boomed with China in cotton and opium, exchanged for the increasingly popular drink of tea. Fortunes were made. David Sassoon, whose Sephardic Jewish family eventually spread to Europe and America, arrived in 1833 and built up an international trading empire overseen by his eight sons, one of whom was knighted Sir Albert Sassoon of Kensington Gore in 1872.

opened the following year. Sir Bartle Frere, governor 1862–1867, gave Bombay its spacious streets and great Victorian buildings, and he began the land reclamation that continues today. During this time the American Civil War closed the Confederacy ports in America, and Bombay traders quickly profited from this by supplying extra cotton to Britain.

When the Suez Canal opened in 1869, Bombay on the west coast became as important as Calcutta on the east. Today, this truly cosmopolitan city has moved with the times and held its position. Neither the devastation of the July 2005 flood, caused by record rainfall and in which 1,000 people died, nor the November 2008

NOTE: Tourist offices and some hotels in Mumbai stock the useful fortnightly listings magazine, *What's On.*

Bollywood—the Mumbai Film Industry

Mumbai's answer to Hollywood is the capital of the all-singing, all-dancing, all-shocking-color, not-much-plot Hindi movie. Huge advertising billboards all over India lure millions into movie theaters every week to enjoy a slick, sophisticated, and perfectly timed mix of heroism, romance, and fighting on wildly extravagant sets, even when the story line is more contemporary and tackles India's social problems. Audiences may jeer at the villain, cheer the hero, and sing along.

Production is complex. Often, money is raised to fund just part of a movie then there is a pause while more financing is sought. Actors may be working concurrently on several movies. The essential music backing may be mimed by the beautiful star but sung by a favorite voice. To immerse yourself in India's foremost popular culture, go to a local movie theater. No one will mind if you do not watch all three hours of Bollywood-produced escapist entertainment.

Meanwhile, steamers brought out boatloads of single British women, known as the "fishing fleet," to supply the empire's men with wives. Bombay's railroad opened in 1853 (reaching the cotton-growing Deccan ten years later); the telegraph arrived in 1865, and the first cotton mill

terrorist attacks that killed 173 people has dampened the tremendous Mumbai spirit. It is India's most modern and international city, with the inevitable inequalities. Mumbai's rich are India's most ostentatiously rich; Mumbai's Dharavi area is India's largest and worst slum.

Colaba & the Maidan

This area is Mumbai's grandest, redolent of a vast British Empire, with its public buildings the proud legacy of fortunes made from trade with East and West and of men steeped in the Victorian belief in civic pride and duty. The architects mingled Eastern and Western ideas to create some of the finest Indo-Saracenic monuments in all of India.

The place to start is **Gateway of India** (1927). From the opening of the Suez Canal until the age of airplanes, this end of the Mumbai peninsula is where the ships arrived and passengers stepped ashore into India. George Wittet looked to Gujarat, specifically Ahmedabad (see pp. 144–145), for his honey-colored triumphal arch (1927) adorned with intricate carving,

which commemorates the visit of George V and Queen Mary to India in 1911.

On February 28, 1948, after independence, the last British soldier left from here. Today, gaily painted fishing boats and ferries bob in the Arabian Sea, the old ferries ready to take visitors to Elephanta (see p. 167), the newer

INSIDER TIP:

Join Mumbaiites taking an evening stroll along the "Queen's Necklace"—Marine Drive—and watch the sun sink into the Arabian Sea, turning the entire horizon pink.

—NATASHA SCRIPTURE
National Geographic contributor

Cricket, the Indian Obsession

Cricket is played everywhere in India—in parks, in wheat fields, in front of temples, inside mosques—and commands front page attention in the newspapers. You will be welcomed to join an informal game; to watch a more formal one, your hotel will know what matches are taking place and can usually obtain tickets.

The British brought cricket to India, founding a cricket club first at Kolkata (1792) and then at Srirangapatnam (1799), after they crushed their longtime enemy, Tipu Sultan. So-called first-class cricket took off in the late 19th century with the Bombay Quadragular (1892), the Europeans versus Parsees matches (1892–1893), and the first English team playing an All India selection (1893).

C. K. Nayudu's performance in a 1926 match led India to start dreaming big. At India's first test win in 1952, against England at Madras (today's Chennai), 20 years after their first Test Match, the player Pankaj Roy said the "victory against those who had been our master till five years ago had special significance." India's first overseas test victory, in 1968 against New Zealand, has been followed by many more, including the 1983 World Cup.

Today, Twenty20 cricket, a shortened game distained by many purists, attracts big money and controversy. For a spirited conversation, mention Kapil Dev, Sachin Tendulkar, Sunil Gavasker, or Mahendra Singh Dhoni, four of India's greatest players, then sit back and listen to the stories.

hovercraft heading for Mandve (see p. 183).

The red-domed **Taj Mahal Palace** (1903) is a hotel that stands beside the Gateway of India, overlooking the harbor. Built by Jamshtji Nusserwanji Tata (1839–1904) and equipped with its own Turkish baths, it is still an institution among today's Mumbai rich. Tata, a Parsee trading tycoon, expanded his cotton empire to include mills, hydroelectric plants, a shipping line, and this famous landmark designed by Sir Charles Chambers. The lanes behind the hotel lead to **Colaba Causeway,** a quality shopping area always buzzing with action. Damaged by blasts in the terrorist attack of 2008, the Taj Mahal Palace has since been renovated.

George Wittet, again influenced by medieval Gujarati architecture, designed the **Chhatrapati Shivaji Maharaj Vastu Sangrahalaya,** formerly the Prince of Wales Museum (1905–1937), too. It commemorates globe-trotting George V's first visit to India in 1905, when he was Prince of Wales (heir to the throne). Statues of him and of his father, Edward VII, stand in the mature gardens. Inside, beneath the tiled concrete dome, the wide-ranging collection offers something for everyone. Choose from delicate Indian miniature paintings, embroidered Kashmir shawls, or Indian silver, glass, brass, and jade; there are also arms and armor, and top-quality Indian sculpture dating from the Harappan period to 18th-century Christian ivory carvings from Goa.

Mumbai's Maidan is an informal cricket ground.

But it is the extravaganza of high Victorian Gothic buildings strung along **Mayo Road** (K.B. Patil Marg), facing the open grass of the Maidan, that take the prize. Many were built of hard, beige Porbandar stone, and most were enriched with skillful, lively, even ebullient, local carving, inspired by Britain's arts and crafts movement. John Lockwood Kipling, Rudyard's father, who was an avid supporter of crafts and ran Mumbai's art school encouraged this unlikely source of inspiration.

Captain Wilkins's **Old Secretariat** (1874) is really a Venetian Gothic palace. It is 470 feet (143 m) long, with a central arched gable carrying the great staircase window and a soaring 170-foot-high (52 m) tower. Here, the Porbandar stone is enriched with blue and red basalt.

Sir George Gilbert Scott's buildings take a different

(continued on p. 164)

Chhatrapati Shivaji Maharaj Vastu Sangrahalaya

✉ 159–161 M. G. Rd.

☎ 022/2284-4484, 022/2284 4519

🕐 Closed Mon.

💲 $$

themuseummumbai .com

Old Secretariat

✉ Karamveer Bhaurao Patil Marg, Fort

🕐 Closed Sat.–Sun.

A Drive Around Colonial Mumbai

The best days to look at Mumbai's remarkable legacy of classy colonial building are Saturday and Sunday, when there is less traffic and plenty of action on Chowpatty Beach. Tell your driver which places you would like to visit, and he will find the most logical way to reach each building. He will wait while you make visits to these British colonial sites.

The **Gateway of India** ➊ (1927), built to commemorate the visit to India of George V and Queen Mary in 1911, overlooks the harbor at Apollo Bunder. Standing in front of it, you have a great view of the **Taj Mahal Palace hotel** (see p. 161), one of the great hotels of the East, built by the Parsee industrialist J. N. Tata; it was the site of an infamous terrorist attack in November 2008. To the right, a statue of Mumbai's hero, Shivaji (1961), stands in front of the former Yacht Club (1898) with its half-timbered gables.

Drive past the Yacht Club to Wellington Circle (1865). On your left, Phillips Antiques (closed Sun.) is a delightful antiques curiosity shop; on your right, the Indo-Gothic Council

NOT TO BE MISSED:

Gateway of India • University Convocation Hall and Library • St. Thomas Cathedral • Victoria Terminus • Chowpatty Beach

Hall is the earliest of several Mumbai buildings designed by British architect F. W. Stevens (1870–1876). The domed **Chhatrapati Shivaji Maharaj Vastu Sangrahalaya** ➋ (see p. 161) is straight ahead, set in lush gardens. Beautiful and evocative **Keneseth Eliyahoo Synagogue** (see p. 167) is behind Rhythm House.

Next, stop to admire what is possibly the world's finest group of high Victorian Gothic public buildings, strung out along **Mayo Road** (K. B. Patil Marg), opposite the open maidan. Their towering confidence and romantic skylines reflect the progressive age in which they were built. The first is Captain Wilkins's **Secretariat** (see p. 161); next is Sir George Gilbert Scott's **University Convocation Hall** ➌ (see p. 164) with its spiral staircases, and his **University Library** and **Rajabai Clock Tower.** The group ends with Colonel Fuller's **High Court,** Wilkins's **Public Works Office,** and on Veer Nariman Road, James Trubshawe's General Post Office. There's also a good view of F. W. Stevens's Byzantine-style **Churchgate Station,** where trains leave for Kanheri Caves and Bassein (see pp. 168–169).

Farther down Veer Nariman Road, you come to the brightly painted **Flora Fountain** ➍ (1869), which gives its name to this area. There are charming period buildings. On the left, the domed one housed the publisher

India's Vibrant Stock Markets

Asia's oldest stock exchange was established in 1875 in downtown Mumbai, where the financial hub of the 1870s economic boom was Dalal Street, the "Wall Street" of India. Today, India has 22 stock exchanges across the country. A closed economy from independence until the 1990s, India's stock exchanges are now global players. Foreign companies may hold a majority stake in their Indian affiliates, foreign individuals may own 100 percent of a holding. Leading foreign companies are committed to India's growth. For instance, Goldman Sachs sends employees for training at India's highly respected institutes of technology (IIT) and management (IIM), and gives back by building libraries.

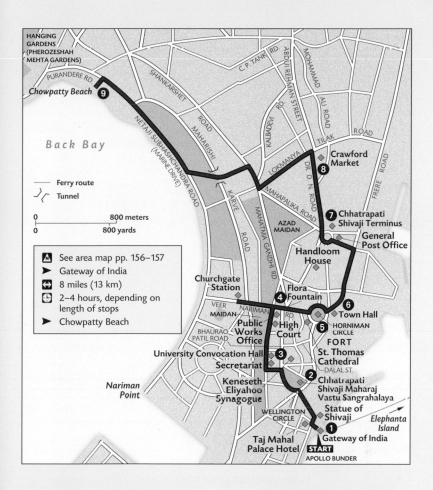

Macmillan, and on the right, Handloom House was built as the mansion of the Parsee Sir Jamsetjee Jeejeebhoy. Mahatma Gandhi Road has more period buildings.

Behind **Horniman Circle** ➎ (1860), with the Venetian palazzo of Elphinstone Buildings on the left, lies the old **Fort area** (see p. 166). Here are two fascinating colonial buildings: **St. Thomas Cathedral** (begun 1672) and Col. Thomas Cowper's **Town Hall** ➏ (1820–1823), possibly the finest classical building in India, now the Asiatic Library.

From here, take Frere Road past old fort bastions and the Bijapur-inspired **General Post Office** (1909) to stop and explore

Stevens's vast **Chhatrapati Shivaji Terminus** ➐ (still sometimes referred to by its original name of Victoria Terminus; 1878–1887; see pp. 164–165), India's finest Gothic building. Stevens's colossal, domed Municipal Buildings (1893) stand opposite; the gable statue represents Urbs Prima in Indis (first city in India). Cruise along Mahapalika and Carnac Roads past Victorian schools, hospitals, and colleges. Stop at **Crawford Market** ➑ (1865–1871; see p. 165), where mangoes and chilies are sold in a French medieval-style building. Then head for Marine Drive to stroll along **Chowpatty Beach** ➒, on the Arabian Sea, with its food stalls, street entertainers, and sand sculptors.

University

- M. G. Rd., Fort

High Court

- Bhaurao Patil Marg (entrance on Eldon Rd., off M. G. Rd.)

General Post Office

- P. D'Mello Rd., Fort
- 022/2264-4944, 022/2262-0693, 022/2262-6591
- Closed Sat.–Sun.

maharashtrapost .gov.in

Churchgate Station

- Maharshi Karve Rd.
- $

Chhatrapati Shivaji (Victoria) Terminus

- Dr. D. Naoroji Rd., Nagar Chowk
- $

inspiration. They were designed in England, built under the eye of construction engineer Col. James Fuller, and financed by the Parsee benefactor Sir Cowasjee Jehangir Readymoney (his statue is in the gardens). The **University Convocation Hall** (1874) dresses up the 15th-century French decorated style for the tropics and adds some Victorian pomp. It even has a staircase modeled on the Château de Blois. The **University Library** and **Rajabai Tower** (1869–1878), next door, combine 14th-century French and Italian Gothic, adding delicate carving and stained-glass windows. The tower, based on Giotto's campanile in Florence, is decorated with figures representing the castes of western India. The clock used

INSIDER TIP:

For an unforgettable Indian experience, go see a Bollywood film. Set aside at least three hours and be sure to visit the theater's chai stand at intermission.

—SARAH WHITE
National Geographic grantee

to cheer British residents with its chimes of "Home Sweet Home" and "God Save the Queen."

Fuller designed the huge **High Court** (1871–1879), with its steep, red tiles and skyline figures of Justice and Mercy (and beautiful Minton floor tiles inside). You now jump to the Venetian

Gothic of Captain Wilkins's **Public Works Office** (1869–1872), then to the Italianate **General Post Office** (1909), and end with the romantic oriental domes and polychrome stones of F. W. Stevens's Byzantine **Churchgate Station** (1894–1896).

Chhatrapati Shivaji (Victoria) Terminus

The British laid the first Indian train lines in Mumbai to help move goods to and from their trade capital. On April 16, 1853, the first train steamed off (see p. 106). Its station was built later and is, with the Gateway of India, modern Mumbai's best known landmark and India's finest Victorian Gothic building. It is now officially called the Chhatrapati Shivaji Terminus.

F. W. Stevens, a government architect, was commissioned in 1876 to build a new terminus for the Great Indian Peninsula Railway, the largest building project in India at that time. Stevens looked to George Gilbert Scott's St. Pancras Station in London for inspiration. What he achieved was a grander and more richly decorated, cathedral-like monument to the British Empire's progress, symbolized by the railroad. Built in just nine years, 1878–1887, it cost the then vast sum of £250,000 (about £15 million or $20 million in today's money).

If you stand at the great entrance, the effect is overwhelming. The huge facade has projecting wings crowned with a colossal, somewhat un-Gothic dome, on which a statue of Progress

EXPERIENCE: Peruse Mumbai's Markets

Mumbai is a rich trading city, great for shopping, either in the comfort of upscale hotel shops or—much more fun—on street after street of stores and stalls. **Colaba Causeway,** behind the Taj Mahal Palace hotel, is the place for global fashion, but you may want to be more adventurous.

A good place to start is **Crawford Market,** where Lockwood Kipling's frieze and fountain are the setting for piles of exotic fruit, spices, and vegetables, and a crowded wholesale wing. Stay in the area and take a wander through the streets north of Carnac Road, whose backbone is **Abdul Rehman Street.** Stores of one type tend to cluster together. Cloth can be found on **Mangaldas Lane,** jewelry in the **Zaveri Bazar** on Memon Street, near Mumbadevi Temple (dedicated to the titular goddess of Mumbai), and copper and brass on **Baiduni Chowk.**

Farther afield, **Mutton Road** has stores full of old (and fake) curiosities (see also **Bhuleshwar Market,** p. 170).

perches proudly. Thomas Earp made this, as well as the helpfully labeled stone medallions of imperial worthies on the facade (see if you can find Sir Bartle Frere, governor of the city from 1862 to 1867), and the gorgeous symbolic imperial lion and Indian tiger on top of the gate piers. The whole building is a riot of various colored stones, decorative ironwork, marbles, inlaid tiles, and exuberant sculpture. Most of this ironwork and decorative sculpture was crafted by the Indian students of the Bombay School of Art.

Inside the reservations hall in the left-hand wing, built with pointed arches like a church nave, you can enjoy more glorious high Victorian decoration. The ceilings have gold stars on an azure background, the dado has glazed tiles with rich leaf designs, and the windows are of stained glass or ornamental iron grillwork to reduce the sun's glare. The fixtures are of local woods, the railings are of brass, the floor is tiled, and the stonework is carved with leaves, animals, and birds.

When the building opened, Indians and British alike were amazed. Even today, VT, as it is fondly known locally, adds glamour to a train ride. Furthermore, the Mumbai municipality has honored this colonial building with a new name, albeit rarely used, that links it to the Maratha hero: Chhatrapati Shivaji Terminus (CST). For a truly great Indian train journey, try taking the 24-hour ride on the Punjab Mail from here to Agra, or ride the new Konkan Railway line down to Goa (see pp. 190–191).

Following the success of VT, Stevens received commissions to build Mumbai's ebullient **municipal buildings** (1888–1893) opposite the station. Combining Venetian Gothic with Indo-Saracenic styles and dressing them for the city climate, he managed to express imperial and civic pride at the zenith of the empire. Inventive, romantic, and resourceful, Stevens's final great Mumbai building was **Churchgate Station.** Here, to give a Byzantine character, he used

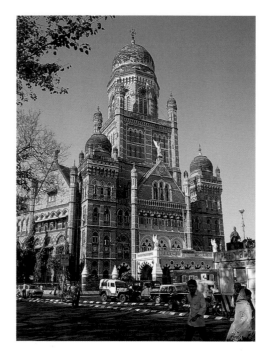

F. W. Stevens's municipal buildings embody Victorian and imperial pride.

Town Hall
✉ Horniman Circle
🕐 Closed Sat.–Sun.

St. Thomas Cathedral
✉ Veer Nariman Rd., Kala Ghoda

the local red stone from Bassein (see p. 169) to contrast with the white and blue stones. The statue over the entrance, personifying Engineering, is holding symbols of progress—a locomotive and a wheel—in her hands.

Fort

The fort area in south Mumbai is where European Mumbai began. Here today's crowded commercial streets were once a large walled fort facing Mumbai Harbor. The Portuguese struck a deal with Bahadur Shah of Gujarat to trade at Bombay and nearby Bassein (Vasai; see p. 169). When the Mumbai islands passed to the British

and were leased to the East India Company, the British built great defensive walls and gates. Although these were mostly destroyed in 1862, you can trace their path along Mahatma Gandhi and Dr. Dadabhai Naoroji Roads. As you walk around, look up at the old facades, some of them dating from the 18th century.

Begin at the **Town Hall** (1833) at Horniman Circle, right by the docks, which were begun in 1860 by the Wadia family of Bombay. Here, the great East Indiamen ships were built of teak, which lasted five times as long as English oak. Col. Thomas Cowper's Town Hall, built overlooking a common, is India's finest neoclassical building. Mostly paid for by the East India Company, it reflects the confidence of the rising British Empire. The windows, with their wooden shutters and curving sunshades, are original. Go up the broad steps and past the fluted Doric columns shipped here from England to find a fine set of marble statues of Bombay governors in the lobby and stairwell, three of them by Sir Francis Chantrey. Today, the building houses various learned societies, including the Asiatic Society of Bombay.

On the far side of Horniman Circle, Gerald Aungier began the **St. Thomas Cathedral** in 1672. Its fascinating and beautiful funerary monuments rival those in St. Mary's, Chennai (see p. 258). They include several by John Bacon: to Governor John Duncan, to Katharine Kirkpatrick, whose sons helped establish British supremacy in Central India, and to Maj. Eldred Pottinger.

Down Apollo Street, past several surviving old buildings, you find the simple neoclassical **St. Andrew's Kirk** (1819) on Marine Street. Nearby, behind Rhythm House, stands the 1884 **Keneseth Eliyahoo Synagogue.** Funded by David Sassoon, this is the best of Mumbai's several once grand, but now forlorn, synagogues. The fine upstairs prayer hall is still in use.

Elephanta Island

Visiting one of India's most important early Hindu cave temples is a delight, thanks to the boat ride needed to reach it and the energy of the local branch of the conservation body INTACH (see p. 72) responsible for the cave temple.

The Portuguese renamed the island, originally called Gharapuri, after the carved elephant they found there (now in Mumbai's Dr. Bhau Daji Lad Museum; see p. 170). Climb up the steps past the souvenir stalls manned by people from the island's villages to find a helpful exhibition in the restored custodian's cottage.

The **cave temple** dedicated to Shiva is just beyond. It was possibly the Kalachuri rulers who cut it out of a projecting chunk of the high basalt cliff in the sixth century, possibly with royal patronage. Enter the central opening into a simple, dark hall, whose columns have cushion-shaped capitals.

One spectacular, colossal stone carving of triple-headed Shiva in the center of the back wall dominates several images showing the god's different aspects. Only just emerging out of the rock, it subtly combines ideas of male-female and husband-wife; the right head is softly feminine, the left side fiercely masculine. The panels on either side show an androgynous Shiva and his consort Parvati on the left, and Shiva helping the descent of the Ganga on the right.

Continue to the right, past the *lingum* sanctuary with its huge guardian figures, to find first the panel of Shiva's marriage with Parvati and then Shiva spearing Andhaka. Across the courtyard, the panels show Shiva as the Yogi and as Nataraja (Lord of the Dance).

Teeming Slums

As the film *Slumdog Millionaire* (2008) made clear, every city has its dark side, and Indian cities have particularly horrifying ones, yet tempered with great spirit. India's worst slum is Dharavi, in Mumbai. Despite atrocious conditions, optimism abounds; incongruously, so does wealth. Small-scale industries from baking to potting have an annual turnover of $665 million. If you are mentally strong, **Reality Tours and Travel** (*realitytoursandtravel.com*) runs tours of the slums, with some of the ticket price going to local charities. Note: No photography is permitted.

Keneseth Eliyahoo Synagogue

✉ 55 Dr. V. B. Gandhi Rd., Kala Ghoda

☎ 022/2283-1502

Elephanta Island

◣ 156 A3

🕐 Closed Mon.

💲 $

NOTE: Ferries to Elephanta Island leave from the Gateway of India regularly from about 9 a.m. until about 2:30 p.m.; the journey takes one hour. The caves close at 5 p.m. Check on the time of the last boat back; if seas are choppy, change your plans. Those not wishing to climb the steps up to the temple can take a train to the site, or be carried in a thronelike chair.

Kanheri Caves

🅰 156 A3

✉ Train to Borivali Station, then taxi or rickshaw to Sanjay Gandhi National Park. Caves are 3 miles (5 km) from the north entrance.

☎ 022/2204-4482

🕐 Open 7 days: 7:30 a.m.– 5:30 p.m.

💲 $

Ahead you find another Yogi and Nataraja flanking the entrance, then two compositions of Shiva and Parvati on Mount Kailasha playing dice.

Kanheri Caves & Bassein

Kanheri Caves and Bassein's ruined fort each make thoroughly rewarding days out of the teeming city and into two very rural settings going north up the coast. Avoid the long and outcrop overlook the Arabian Sea. For almost a thousand years, starting with the Satavahanas of the first century, this was an important Buddhist community that lay on trade routes connecting Nasik, Paithan, Ujjain, Aurangabad, and other cities to seaports such as nearby Sopara. As such, it benefited from donations from merchants, goldsmiths, and blacksmiths, as inscriptions

Kanheri Caves, on the edge of Mumbai, bring tranquility and relief from the city's hubbub.

tiresome drive through Mumbai's suburbs and, instead, take the local train. From Churchgate Station you slice up through the central Mumbai peninsula; the stations are mapped out above the doors of each railway car. Then take a taxi or rickshaw to the site.

Kanheri Caves: At Kanheri, more than a hundred Buddhist monuments cut out of a granite

reveal. It may also have been where traveling Buddhist monks stayed during the monsoon, when numbers seem to have swelled to several thousand. It was a sophisticated monastic community and may have included a university. The caves were used for study, for meditation, and as homes, and they reveal both Hinayana and Mahayana Buddhist occupation (see p. 59).

Caves nos. 2 and **3** are the most impressive: No. 2 is a *vihara* with two stupas; no. 3 (fifth to sixth century) is a *chaitya* with carvings of Buddha and bejeweled couples. Other fine caves abound, some with water cisterns, others with Buddha carvings (Cave no. 67) and ovens for cooking. **Cave no. 11** may have been an assembly hall; **no. 14** contains a carving of the 11-headed Padmapani Avalokiteshvara. At the top of the hill, **Caves nos. 84–87** seem to have been part of a burial ground.

There is a small café on the steep forested hill. The caves are popular with locals on weekends.

Bassein (Vasai): Spend a great day at the most romantic and substantial Portuguese fort ruins in India, with massive walls and gateways, and soaring 16th- and 17th-century church and convent ruins, all completely overgrown. Now rarely visited, this large city—only Christians lived within its walls, while thousands of other people lived outside—was Portuguese from 1534 until the Marathas took it in 1739; it was visited four times by St. Francis Xavier (see sidebar p. 191). By 1818, when it became part of the British Bombay presidency, it was abandoned; today, fishermen untangle nets in the old citadel.

The sea gate, complete with its iron doors, is set into massive walls, and the bastions have cannon openings. Inside it, follow the path straight ahead to find the soaring triple-stage tower (1601) of the **Matriz of St. Joseph,**

Bassein's cathedral. Next, the **Citadel** on the right retains its stone gate, carved with the Portuguese coat of arms; a warren of rooms lies underground. A five-minute walk farther along the path are the **Church of St. Anthony** (1548), founded by St. Francis Xavier on his third visit, with a grand facade and, to the side, an atmospheric cloister. The climax is the **Church of St. Paul,** a Franciscan foundation whose grand columned portal leads to a vast nave, chancel, a gallery that you can climb up for good views, and a cloister; Portuguese tombstones are set into the floor.

To reach **Bassein Fort,** take the train from Churchgate to Vasai Station, then take a 20-minute auto-rickshaw journey to the sea entrance. Ask driver to wait, or agree on a time to meet at the other gate. ∎

Bassein

🔺 156 A3

✉ 38 miles (61 km) N of Mumbai. Carry bottled water.

💲 $

EXPERIENCE:

An Adventurous Day Trip Out of Mumbai

From the Gateway to India, take a fast boat to **Mandwa,** then a bus to **Alibag** *(boat ticket, purchased at kiosk next to Gateway of India, $, includes bus ride; tel 022/2284-5678, alibagtourism.com for schedule);* total travel time is about two hours. At Alibag (see p. 183), engage a taxi and travel down the coast to **Murud,** where you can hire a local to sail you out to **Janjira island fort** (see p. 184); with both the taxi driver and boatman, agree on a time to be picked up for the return journey, and hold payment until it is complete. On your return to Alibag, do the same to visit **Kolaba Fort** (if it is low tide, you can walk out).

More Places to Visit in Mumbai

Bhuleshwar Market

This market is found along the streets to the south of C. P. Tank Road, toward Mumbadevi temple. Locals crowd the wonderful vegetable market on Kumbhar Tukda. There are also stores supplying Hindi movie costumes, others supplying idols to temples. Phool Galli (Flower Lane) is where temple and wedding flower arrangements are made.

Byculla

During the racing season *(Nov.–April)*, this area north of Mumbai's center provides entertainment at **Mahalaxmi Race Course** *(tel 022/2307-1401)*. Established in 1878, it stimulated India's horse-breeding industry, which is still strong. During the season, stylish old men, flashy movie stars, and locals of all kinds come to watch the racing on most Wednesdays and weekends. Nearby, among Mumbai's 19th-century cotton mills, stands the walled **Magen David Synagogue** (1861; *Sir J. J. Rd., Byculla, tel 022/2300-6675*). Near it, **Dr. Bhau Daji Lad Mumbai City Museum** (*Dr. Ambedkar Rd., tel 022/2373-1234, bdlmuseum.org, $*) is a meticulously restored high Victoria 1870s building. Its display cases house local crafts and Mumbai history. The Elephanta sculpture (see p. 167) is in the garden; David Sassoon gave the clock tower (1865). The zoo is located next door.

Kala Ghoda

This lively arts district in downtown historic Mumbai centers around Jehangir Art Gallery, Max Muller Bhawan, and Bodhi Art Gallery. These main galleries know what is on in the area. The **Kala Ghoda Arts Festival** is usually a ten-day celebration, held in late January or early February.

Kondivita

To see more temples, take the train from Churchgate Station to Andheri. Here, 18 cave temples (the Mahakali Caves) surround a hillock. **Cave no. 9** (second century) imitates a thatched hut and **Cave no. 13** (fifth to sixth century) was once a monastery, with cells and beds cut out of the rock.

Marine Drive & Chowpatty Beach

Chowpatty Beach and the stretch of beach at the north end of Netaji Subhash Chandra Road are Mumbai's lungs, a refuge from the punishing humidity of the city. Mumbai's citizens promenade in the mornings and evenings, and children play cricket all day. Chowpatty Beach is the city's entertainment center, best visited late in the afternoon. You can buy Mumbai *chaat* (snacks) from the stalls and wander among the sand sculptors, musicians, astrologers, and other entertainers. The beach is the focus of Mumbai's popular Ganpati Festival (see sidebar below).

Ganpati Festival

Ganesh, the elephant-headed, sweet-toothed god of prosperity and good fortune, is loved by Mumbai's Hindu businessmen, who celebrate his September birthday with gusto. Huge, gaudy, pink-painted clay images of Ganesh, each with a morsel of last year's figure added to this year's clay mixture, are set up in factories, houses, and on street corners for ten days, decorated with garlands, flickering lights, and even working mini-fountains. On the day of the full moon, they are paraded through the streets to Chowpatty Beach amid music, dancing, and throwing of pink powder. Finally, they are immersed in the sea and bob on the waves until the images dissolve.

Maharashtra

Despite its huge size, Maharashtra's principal sites conveniently fall into geographic groups, each with a city base offering good accommodations. To reach them, the most indulgent form of transport is to be driven; this way you can see the landscape, the farms, and the village life and markets. Alternatively, take a train—especially recommended for Matheran—or fly.

Karla's Cave no. 8 has cut columns with boldly carved capitals, mock roof beams, and a giant stupa.

Aurangabad, where corporate majors have their industrial sites, has magnificent cave sculptures, and a 50,000-year-old meteorite crater. From here you can visit Daulatabad, Ellora, and, farther away, Ajanta.

Pune is the place to stay if you want to put on your hiking shoes and sun hat to explore the rugged Western Ghats with their spectacular forts associated with Shivaji (see pp. 178–179). From Mahabaleshwar, you can take trips through rural switchback roads with breathtaking views of Shivaji's hill and coastal forts. To see the early Buddhist cave

temples of Karla, Bhaja, and Bedsa, stay at the modest hill station of Lonavala.

The stretch between Mumbai and Goa is best visited in a progressive line. Until recently, Maharashtra's coast was among the least developed in India. With the new Konkan railroad and Mumbai–Mandve sea connections, this area is opening up. Accommodations are modest, except for the lovely, characterful hotel at Chiplun, with its lush terraced gardens, but the island fort of Janjira and the two coastal forts of Vijayadurg and Sindhudurg are well worth any discomfort.

Maharashtra

See pp. 156–157

Visitor Information

✉ State Tourist Office, Holiday Resort Hotel, Station Rd., Aurangabad

☎ 024/0234-3169

maharashtratourism .gov.in

✉ India Tourist Office, Krishna Villas, Station Rd., Aurangabad

☎ 024/0236-4999

🕒 Closed Sun.

incredibleindia.org

Aurangabad

157 C4

NOTE: Flights connect Aurangabad with Mumbai, Delhi, and Udaipur.

Aurangabad & Around

To visit the sculptured and painted caves of Aurangabad, Ellora, and Ajanta is to see several wonders of the world. If your visit to India includes Mumbai, it is well worth flying to Aurangabad for two or three nights, making it your base for Ellora and Ajanta.

Despite its newfound business wealth, Aurangabad retains much of its Muslim past, and you can sometimes glimpse an earlier period when the city flourished at the crossroads of ancient trade

A large teaching Buddha lurks in Ellora's Cave no. 10.

routes. Malik Ambar, a former Abyssinian minister for the Ahmednagar rulers, founded the city on the Khan River in 1610. He boosted trade enough for the Mughal emperor Shah Jahan to pillage it in 1621 and capture it in 1633. His son, Prince Aurangzeb, headquartered here when he was governor of the Deccan (1652–1658). He changed the city's name and built new walls. Later, as emperor, he moved

the Mughal court here in 1682, making Aurangabad the imperial city until his death in 1707. It then languished as a provincial town in the vast Hyderabad kingdom.

To see a little of the town, visit the bazaar area of Malik Amber's city, where streets converge on Gulmandi Square. Among the stores and mosques is the **Shah Ganj Masjid** (ca 1720); **Purwar Museum** *(closed Sun. & university holidays, $),* housed in a fine old *haveli;* and **Mughal tombs** such as Hazrat Qadar Auliya's, near Jaffa Gate. Out on the plain to the north of the city, the **Bibi-ka-Maqbara** (1679) mimics the Taj Mahal. It was built by Aurangzeb's son, Azam Shah, as the tomb for his mother, Begum Rabia Durrani.

Aurangabad's glories are its **Buddhist caves** *($),* built into the rock of the hills to the north and best visited in the afternoon. The groups are close together and date from the Vakataka and Kalachuri periods of the fifth and sixth centuries. The on-site guide lights up the sculptures, but take a flashlight.

Three caves are especially wonderful. In the west group, **Cave no. 3** (fifth century) has fine columns, capitals, and beams and, inside the sanctuary, a composition of devotees kneeling in front of a preaching Buddha. In the east group, **Cave no. 6** (sixth century) has a similar tableau plus traces of a painted ceiling. **Cave no. 7** (sixth century) has bold statues, including Panchika (potbellied guardian of the Earth's treasures) with his consort Hariti, plus Buddhas, goddesses, dwarfs, dancers, and musicians.

Daulatabad: Maharashtra's most spectacular fort surrounds, sits on, and is cut into the huge Balakot rock northwest of Aurangabad, on the road to Ellora. It began as Deogiri (Hill of the Gods), capital of the Yadavas, who lost it to the Khilji sultans of Delhi in 1294. Renamed Daulatabad (Abode of Prosperity), it was the Tughlaq capital from 1327 to 1347, the year the Bahmani governors declared independence. They later moved their capital to Gulbarga. Today's fort is a product of all these periods.

One set of massive fortifications leads into **Ambarkot,** the outer fort; the battlements, bastions, guardrooms, and moat of the next set lead into **Kataka,** the inner fort. Through the huge gateways, a street leads between ruined buildings, including the **Jama Masjid** (1318) on the left and a ruined **Mughal palace** on the right. Across from the Bahmani palace ruins, another imposing gate leads into **Balakot,** the citadel, where a succession of chambers, tunnels, blind alleys, and dark corners lead to the very top.

Khuldabad: Aurangzeb, last of the six great Mughal emperors, was a religious man. He chose a simple burial in a village where Sufi teachers lived, and he rebuilt the village's walls and gates. If you go into the **Dargah of Hazrat Kwaja Syed Zainuddin** (died 1334), you will find Aurangzeb's tomb in a corner, surrounded by a marble screen added in 1921.

Ellora Caves

Rock-cut architecture in the Western Ghats reached its glorious last phase here at Ellora, with large-scale figure sculpture, complex compositions, and a wide range of iconographic schemes. In contrast to Ajanta, where aggressive peddlers and substandard guides try hard to get between you and the art, here you can wander the long,

INSIDER TIP:

To visit the Aurangabad, Ellora, and Ajanta caves, you will need a minimum of two full days, preferably more; the day trip to Ajanta from Aurangabad is long.

—LOUISE NICHOLSON
National Geographic author

west-facing basalt escarpment, quietly soaking up the spirit of this place that has been sacred to Buddhists, Jains, and Hindus for many centuries.

Visiting the Caves: The caves span the sixth to the ninth centuries and divide into three groups: **Caves nos. 1–12,** at the southern end, are Buddhist; **Caves nos. 13–29,** in the middle, are Hindu, and **Caves nos. 30–34** are Jain. It is best to begin at the southern end, but be selective in your visits to avoid confusion. Try to reach **Cave no. 16** in the midafternoon to see it at its best.

Daulatabad
- 157 C4
- $

Khuldabad
- 157 C4

Ellora Caves
- 157 C4
- 18 miles (29 km) NW of Aurangabad
- Closed Tues.
- $$

The Hindu **Caves nos. 21, 28,** and **29,** of the sixth-century Kalachuri era, predate the Buddhist **Caves nos. 10–12,** which were built by the Early Chalukyas of the seventh and eighth centuries. The Hindu **Caves nos. 15** and **16,** Ellora's pinnacle of achievement, were created under the Rashtrakutas of the late eighth century to tenth century, as were the Jain **Caves nos. 30–34.**

Buddhist Caves: Of the dozen Buddhist caves, the first nine are variations on a standard monastic form: columned veranda, central hall, cells to the sides, and a Buddha shrine at the rear. This is seen clearly in **Cave no. 2,** whose guardian figures flank the entrance. **Cave no. 10,** a very fine *chaitya* (worship) hall, is named Vishvakarma after the mythical architect of the gods. It can be found at the end of a courtyard, the two stories set on a basement carved with animals; steps on the left lead up to the richly sculptured gallery. **Cave no. 12** (Tin Thal) has three stories. The top floor (found up steps to the right) is a simple hall with colossal enthroned Buddhas on the side walls, plus rows of meditating and ground-touching Buddhas flanking the sanctum, inside which are seated goddesses.

Hindu Caves: The Hindu group is even more impressive. **Cave no. 15,** named Dashavatara, is a Buddhist monastery later modified for Hindus and partly funded by the Rashtrakuta king Dantigurga (*r.* ca 730–755). Steps lead up to a *mandapa* (pillared hall) profusely sculptured with Shiva and Vishnu images. Clockwise, they begin with Shiva killing the demon and end with Vishnu as the man-lion Narasimha.

Cave no. 16, the Kailasha temple, is the spectacular centerpiece of Ellora: a monolithic temple to Shiva entirely sculpted out of the solid rock. In technique, decorative scheme, and quality of sculpture, it is unsurpassed. The Rashtrakuta king Krishna I (*r.* 756–773) began the work; his successors continued the royal patronage. If you walk up the cliff on the right, you have a bird's-eye

At Ajanta, locals help illuminate the breathtaking carvings and paintings in the rock-cut caves.

view of the whole complex: entrance, Nandi pavilion, temple with pyramid-shaped tower, and surrounding courtyard with shrines. Then go down for a closer look. Guardians, the Ganga, and the Yamuna flank the entrance, setting the tone for bold, vibrant sculpture inside. Amid the profusion of decoration, note especially the temple's elephants gathering lotuses on the lower story, the compositions from the *Ramayana* and *Mahabharata* on both sides of the steps, and a great Shiva composition in the center of the south side. And do not miss the small hall in the southeast corner, with its almost three-dimensional figures lounging on a seat.

Finally, there are two late sixth-century Hindu caves, earlier than the others. **No. 21** has remarkably sensuous sculpture: See the female bracket figures on the veranda, the loving couples on the balcony wall, and the river gods Ganga and Yamuna. **Cave no. 29** has a layout and large Shiva wall panels that may be influenced by the cave at Elephanta (see p. 167).

Jain Caves: It is a pleasant walk to the Jain group. The finest is **Cave no. 32,** called Indra Sabha. Make your way through the little courtyard, pausing to enjoy the delicate carving of Jina figures; then go upstairs to find exuberantly carved columns and large figures of Ambika (mother goddess) with a child, and Indra.

Ajanta Caves

The miraculously preserved paintings and sculptures that decorate 30 caves cut into the basalt rock of a beautiful crescent-shaped gorge provide the most extensive example of early Buddhist artistic traditions in India. They are also the sources for iconography and styles found in later Central Asian and Far Eastern Buddhist art.

The caves date mostly from two periods: the second and first centuries B.C., then the late fifth century A.D., when the Vakataka

INSIDER TIP:

Take a walk through small villages around the caves. Children love to practice their English, and you will have an opportunity to meet the elders and shop merchants.

—SUSAN COHEN
National Geographic contributor

rulers, especially Harisena (r. 460–478), were energetic patrons. These caves contain the most impressive sculptures, ranging from votive images to narrative tableaus with many interesting figures and elaborate decorative motifs.

These later caves also have India's only extensive series of Buddhist paintings of such virtuosity, quality, and wide range of subjects. They depict Buddha's life and the stories from the *Jataka* tales (former lives of Buddha). These are retold in huge, densely filled compositions depicting contemporary fifth-century city,

Ajanta Caves
- 157 C4
- 64 miles (102 km) N of Aurangabad
- 9 a.m.–5:30 p.m. Closed Mon.
- $$

ajantacaves.com

NOTE: Currently, the Ajanta Caves are closed on Mondays; these closings might increase. Take water and easily portable food such as bananas and cookies, because there is no good restaurant. Weekends are very busy.

This fresco in Ajanta's Cave no. 1 recounts a *Jataka* tale on the left and shows a compassionate Padmapani on the right.

court, and forest life. Tempera was used to achieve the sinuous lines and harmonious, soft colors. The rock was primed, then given a layer of white lime, on which the outline was sketched with red cinnabar. The artists then used lapis lazuli for blue, glauconite for green, soot for black, ocher for yellow, and kaolin chalk for white, thickening it with glue. Finally, the murals were polished with a smooth stone.

Abandoned in the seventh century and rediscovered in 1819, most caves are in fine condition. So, as with Ellora, selection is essential because you need time to drink in the detail. Here are eight to start you off: All except nos. 9 and 10 date from the late fifth century. They can be visited in any order, to avoid the crowds.

Cave no. 1 is one of the finest and deserves time. Elaborate sculpture includes flying couples on the column brackets and the great Buddha in the sanctum, preaching the first sermon at Sarnath, his wheel, deer, and monks

on the pedestal. The murals are some of Ajanta's best. Two Bodhisattvas flank the sanctum: Padmapani (left) and Avalokiteshvara (right). *Jataka* tales fill the walls, while to the right of the outer doorway some foreigners with caps and beards offer gifts to a figure who is possibly Harisena, the Vakataka king and patron of the cave.

The sculpture of **Cave no. 2** is more profuse than that in cave no. 1; see the fat *yakshas* (demigods) and attendants in the left shrine on the rear walls. In the right shrine, there are paintings of processions of female devotees, a very richly painted ceiling, and *Jataka* and life-of-Buddha stories on the walls.

Now for two early caves, nos. 9 and 10. **No. 9** (first century B.C.) is an elegant chaitya hall with plain octagonal columns and a curved vault; the stupa on its high drum is the devotional focus. Of the two layers of paintings on the walls, that underneath is contemporary with the building. **Cave no. 10** (second century B.C.) is similar but even earlier, with clearer layers of painting; on the left wall, a royal figure worships at a bodhi tree.

One of Ajanta's finest monasteries is **Cave no. 16,** with an inscription dating from Harisena's reign. Its ceiling is carved to imitate wood and there is an image of Buddha teaching. A mural shows the conversion of Nanda, Buddha's cousin. **Cave no. 17** is similar, but the decoration of the shrine's doorway is particularly elaborate. Of the murals here, several are outstanding, including the seated Buddhas over the doorway, the wheel of life on the left of the veranda, and the *Jataka* tales on the inside walls.

Cave no. 19 is an almost perfect chaitya hall with restrained yet elaborate carving. Before entering, see the couple on the left wall; inside, the votive stupa, unusually, has a Buddha image on the front. Finally, wonderful sculpture occupies **Cave no. 26.** The large chaitya hall has a splendid Parinirvana: A 23-foot-long (7 m) Buddha reclines on a couch, his eyes closed in peaceful sleep, his disciples mourning him below.

Pune

High in the Western Ghats, on the edge of the Deccan Plateau, thriving Pune is Maharashtra's second city and offers striking contrasts: an old city, the spacious British-built new one, and a controversial ashram, more resort than religious school.

It was not Shivaji but the later Peshwas who, from 1750, made Pune a center of Maratha power. The British took over in 1818, after the battle of Khadki (Kirkee). To see the best of Old Pune, find the remains of **Shaniwar Wada Fort** and then wander the crowded lanes of traditional houses and many brightly painted Hindu temples to reach busy **Mahatma Phule Market** (1886), opposite Bel Bagh Temple. A few streets farther south, at **Raja Dinkar Kelkar Museum** *(1378 Natu Baug, Shukrawar Peth, closed Jan. 26 & Aug. 15, $, rajakelkar museum.com)*, there is a vast collection of everyday arts and crafts amassed by the poet Kelkar (1896–1990) from all over India, displayed on three floors of his beautiful Peshwa-period mansion.

After 1818, the British, calling the city Poona, built southern India's largest cantonment and attracted commerce, Parsees, and Jewish people from Mumbai. From 1820 Pune was the summer retreat of the Mumbai presidency. Today the Indian Army keeps the white colonial houses and their

INSIDER TIP:

If you wish to jog or want to join locals for some exercise, check out the Pune Race Course. Built and used for horse racing, it is open early mornings and evenings to all.

—STEPHANIE ROBICHAUX
National Geographic contributor

gardens spick-and-span. Along the broad, tree-shaded roads are the 1870 **Vidhan Bhavan** *(closed Sat.–Sun.),* the former Council Hall, on Maneckji Mehta Road and **St. Paul's Church** (1863) nearby. David Sassoon funded the 1863 **Ohel David Synagogue** *(9 Dr. Ambedkar Rd., tel 020/2613-2048),* where he is buried; Sir Jacob Sassoon funded the **Sassoon Hospital,** built in the English Gothic style in 1867.

Pune is best known, however, for Bhagwan Rajneesh, or Osho

(continued on p. 180)

Pune

🗺 156 B3

Visitor Information

✉ State Tourist Office, I Block, Central Building

☎ 020/2612-6867, 020/2612-8169

🕐 Closed Sun.

maharashtratourism .gov.in

Shivaji, the Maratha Hero

This extraordinarily able and charismatic leader founded a Maratha polity that gave his people an identity, inspired later generations, and affected Indian history. It is a story worth telling.

Shivaji (1627–1680) was born into war-torn and famine-struck Maharashtra. In 1647, aged 20, Shivaji began subverting local Bijapur authority. He stormed or tricked his way into forts of the *deshmuks* (landed nobles) to carve out an independent and Hindu Maratha zone around Pune, agitating the two powerful Muslim forces that dominated the area, Bijapur and Mughal.

Inspiring and dazzling his people, Shivaji used guerrilla tactics to annoy both enemies. Among his many exploits, in 1659 he killed Bijapur's top general at Pratapgarh Fort and then grabbed Panhala Fort and a tract of the Konkan coast between Mumbai and Goa, where he formed a navy. When Aurangzeb sent Mumtaz Mahal's brother, Shaista Khan, to deal with him in 1660, Shivaji lost many forts and his hometown, Pune, but recovered

and promptly sacked Surat in 1664. Mughal pride was wounded. The next year Aurangzeb sent Jai Singh I of Jaipur with 15,000 men. At Purandhar, Shivaji agreed to give up 20 forts, and the next year arrived at Agra to pay obeisance to Aurangzeb. Unexpectedly put under house arrest, he promptly escaped to become the ultimate all-Indian hero.

In 1674 the rebel Shivaji underwent a succession of Brahmanical rituals, acquired the ancestry essential to Hindu kingship, and made himself king of the Marathas. Back on his campaigns, he took Vellore and Gingee Forts near Madras, before dying of dysentery in 1680.

The next year, his son Shambhaji gave refuge to Aurangzeb's rebel son, Akbar. This, together with the fear that the Marathas and Rajputs might ally against the Mughal throne, plus the desire to convert peninsular India to Islam, made Emperor Aurangzeb decide to move his entire court and administration—some 180,000 people—down to Aurangabad in 1682. Before his death in 1707, he had killed Shambhaji, besieged his brother-successor Ramjan at Gingee Fort for eight years, and taken and almost immediately lost countless Maratha forts.

Peshwa Rule

It was at this time that the Maratha chiefs, inspired by Shivaji, began to strike out independently. Maratha raiders reached Malwa in central India and sacked the cities of Hyderabad and Masulipatnam to control almost the whole peninsula. Then, in 1714, Shambhaji's son made Kanhoji Angria, admiral of the Maratha fleet on the west coast, his *peshwa* (prime minister). Soon the peshwas, not the royals, were ruling the Marathas from Pune.

The scene was set for the Maratha state to become the Maratha confederacy. As

Shivaji's hero image lives on in a modern idealized statue.

Shivaji was for centuries, and still is, the main subject in the age-old art of miniature painting.

the Mughal empire devolved into provincial governments, the Marathas concentrated on revenue over territory. Out of this opportunism emerged the great Maratha families of the 1800s and 1900s: Baroda's Gaekwads, Gwalior's Scindias, the Holkars of Indore, the Bhonsles of Nagpur, and the Kolhapur Tarabais.

Simultaneously, the romantic story of Shivaji inspired Bal Gangadhar Tilak and other nationalists to shake off the British yoke. Conceived in Pune, the first conference of the Indian National Congress was held in Mumbai in 1885. It was to be instrumental in the eventual winning of India's independence.

EXPERIENCE: Explore Matheran, a Natural Retreat

While some British hill stations can disappoint, Matheran has been careful to preserve its traditions of escaping the steamy Mumbai heat and humidity into fresh pure air, unspoiled greenery, and slow-paced colonial-style relaxation. This effort has been endorsed by the Ministry of Environment and Forest, which has declared Matheran an eco-sensitive region.

By banning cars in town—and thus eliminating their polluting smoke and horns—Matheran retains its charming demeanor. People can stroll in peace and quiet to some of the 28 viewpoints, or take a hand-pulled rickshaw.

The surrounding hills provide numerous options for exploring. The word Matheran means "mother forest" or "jungle on top," and you may spot orchids and medicinal herbs in the forested **Sahyadri Hills**—Matheran produces delicious honey. The trekking is excellent—often walking on shaded earth pathways of red laterite—and especially rewarding after the monsoon, when the waterfalls are cascading. Or you may rent a horse from one of the many outlets along the main street from the railway station. Be sure to have a well-fitting hat and consider taking someone with you who not only knows the good routes but also some information on the area's bountiful trees and flowers.

To top off your visit, stay in one of the grand mansions built by the British, Parsees, and Bohras, such as the lovingly restored, well-run **The Verandah in the Forest** (neemranahotels.com).

Osho Commune International

- ✉ 17 Koregaon Park
- ☎ 020/6601-9999
- ⏱ Tours 10:30 a.m. & 2:30 p.m.
- 💲 $

osho.com

Ambarnath

- 🅰 156 B3

(1931–1990), founder of the **Osho Commune International.** To the amazement of locals, thousands of foreign hippies flocked here to join the ashram he founded in 1974. Far from promoting the traditional Hindu ashram aims of nonmaterialism, peacefulness, and meditation, its bywords were sexual liberation, partying, and heady materialism—at least for the ashram. When the experiment of creating a utopian city called Rajneeshpuram in Oregon, U.S., failed, the Bhagwan returned to Pune, where he died. His ashram was likened to a spiritual Disneyland by the *Wall Street Journal,* and it claims more visitors than the Taj Mahal.

The Western Ghats

A heady cocktail of rock-cut caves, forts, and hill stations excites interest in the rugged Sahyadri ranges of Maharashtra's Western Ghats that climb steeply from the Konkan coast up to the Deccan Plateau. The whole region is historically linked with the rise of the Marathas, led by their hero, Shivaji (see pp. 178–179). Stay in Pune and make a series of one-day trips.

Ambarnath: This place is a short detour from Kalyan. Ambarnath Temple (ca 1060) has a curved tower and, inside, graceful female figures in recesses. Together with the temple at less accessible Sinnar, this is the best surviving monument of the Yadava period, which immediately preceded the Muslim arrival in the south.

Matheran: People flock to Matheran on weekends to enjoy the fresh air, 2,460 feet (750 m) above sea level, at the closest hill station to Mumbai. A delightful way to arrive is by train, first on the *Pune Express* from Mumbai to Neral, then on the narrow-gauge train up the hill. Even if you go by car, it must be parked 3 miles (5 km) from the center, where cars are banned in order to preserve Matheran's historical and ecological heritage.

Matheran was popularized by a certain Hugh Malet, who built the first European house here in 1851; Lord Elphinstone, governor of Mumbai, had a road built to his lodge in 1858, sealing its place in fashionable Mumbai society. This is a place to take walks for sensational views down to the plains from **Panorama Point** and **Duke's Nose.** For sunsets, try **Porcupine Point.** Walk to **Louise Point** for views across the plateau to the ruined hill forts of Prebal and Vishlagarh. It is best visited after the monsoon, for lush vegetation and waterfalls.

**Bhaja, Rajgurunagar, &
Around:** Visitors who like early Buddhist rock-cut temples can take in these on the Mumbai–Pune road, near the hill resort of **Lonavala,** which has plenty of restaurants. Avoid weekends, when crowds disturb the peace.

To visit the temples chronologically, begin at **Bhaja,** where 20 caves date from the early Satavahana period of the second century B.C. **Cave no. 12,** possibly the earliest apsidal rock-cut chaitya hall in the western Deccan, once had a teak beam roof; **Cave no. 19** has exceptionally early figural compositions showing, possibly, Surya (left) and Indra (right). At Bedsa, about 6 miles (10 km) away, the chaitya hall of **Cave no. 7** has a richly carved exterior.

Four miles (6 km) north of Bhaja, **Karla's** caves and cisterns surround the largest and most completely preserved early Buddhist chaitya hall in the area, known as **Cave no. 8.** Constucted during the short-lived Kshatrapa rule of the first century, a monolithic column topped with a capital of four lions stands in front of the doors, decorated with the six pairs of donors (the Buddha images were added later); the side walls have splendid elephant sculptures. Inside, see the magnificently

Matheran
156 B3

Bhaja
156 B3

Karla
156 B3

You must walk, take a rickshaw, or rent a horse to get about Matheran and explore the narrow ridge and its viewpoints.

Sunset at Porcupine Point, Matheran, a popular retreat from the summer heat of Mumbai

Rajgurunagar
🔺 156 B3

Junnar
🔺 156 B3

Purandhar
🔺 156 B3

carved columns and stupa.

If you are traveling on to Nasik (see p. 186), pause at **Rajgurunagar** (Khed) to see the mosque and tomb of Dilawar Khan (1613), who headquartered here when he commanded the Ahmednagar forces against the Mughals. Farther along the road, a detour left reaches **Junnar,** renowned as the birthplace of Shivaji, which has various 15th- and 16th-century fortifications, mosques, and tombs. Ancient Junnar's position on a trade route to the Gujarat coast brought patronage for a flourishing Buddhist center during the Satavahana and Kshatrapa periods (second century B.C.–third century A.D.). About 50 simple Buddhist caves are cut into **Shivneri Hill,** 11 more on **Tuljabai Hill,** 26 on **Lenyadri Hill,** and 50 on **Manmodi Hill.** There is very little decoration, but walking around the hills to seek them out is peaceful and satisfying.

A trio of offbeat places, Purandhar, Sasvad, and Jejuri, are accessible on a day trip south from

Pune. First, head for the great **fort of Purandhar,** perched 4,839 feet (1,475 m) above sea level. You have to walk the final 1,148 feet (350 m) up to the entrance—imagine taking this fort by force as Shivaji did in 1670 and Aurangzeb in 1705. Through the gate, pass the bold Bahmani walls (15th century) and continue up three levels to the ruined buildings; from here there are good views of Wazirgad, the fortified hill to the east.

The pretty town of **Saswad** has several of the *peshwas'* fortified palaces, some with partly surviving carved wooden structures. **Sangameshvara** and **Changla Vateshvara Temples,** west of the town, are hybrids of Mughal and Hindu architecture with tortoises carved on the hall floors.

Jejuri is a popular pilgrimage center for Maharashtran merchants and farmers who follow the Khandoba cult, and it is especially lively during the April and December fairs. Find the temple through the town and up steps where peddlers sell brass masks of Khandoba. At the top of the steps, four lamp columns stand near a huge brass tortoise.

It's easy to visit the fort at **Sinhagad,** rising 2,296 feet (700 m) above the surrounding plain and once known as Kondhana: The road from Pune almost reaches it. The wonder is to see the walls of the three-pronged fort rising sheer from the steep cliffs, reinforced with ramparts and towers. Follow the steep path up through three gates. Although little still remains inside, you can imagine Muhammad Tughlaq of Delhi trying to besiege it in 1340 and Malik Ahmad of Golconda taking it in 1486. Shivaji took it in 1647, when he changed its name to Sinhagad (Lion Fort), after which Marathas and Mughals vied for it.

It is worth the journey and the two-hour climb from Vajeghar, where the road ends, to see **Rajgad.** This spectacular fort rises sheer from its three-pronged hill and, once inside, you'll have views of Sinhagad, Torna, and Purandhar. Ruined stores, granaries, and halls fill the northern spur. Climb farther to reach Bala Kila ("inner fort"), 4,320 feet (1,317 m) above sea level, and find Shivaji's palace remains. Having taken Torna Fort in 1646, Shivaji used its treasure to buy arms for Rajgad (King's Fort) and make it his seat of government until 1672, when he moved west to Raigad Fort. It was from there that he left to campaign on the Konkan coast in 1666.

Mumbai to Goa

This isolated and unspoiled area of coastal Maharashtra has become much more accessible due to new railroads and faster sea transportation. Hovercrafts and catamarans regularly leave the Gateway of India for **Mandve;** your ticket includes the bus ride on to Alibag, where there are taxi stands. If you are traveling by private car, the driver will meet you at Mandve. Alternatively, make use of the Konkan Railway (see p. 202).

Alibag was the headquarters of Shivaji's Maratha fleet from 1662 on. Later, the Angres, who mixed trading with piracy, used it as a base from which to annoy European shipping until the British took it in 1840. You can visit the

INSIDER TIP:

On the trains in India, the first- and second-class air-conditioned compartments are the most comfortable, with clean cars and closed, tinted windows. Traveling in the general or "sleeper" cars can be risky, especially if you have valuables.

—AMIT KAPIL
National Geographic author

island **Kolaba Fort** (1820) at low tide or see it as you walk along the beach. The main road goes straight through dusty **Chaul,** reducing the pleasure of seeking out the remains of churches that were once part of a major Konkan port governed by the Bahmanis of Gulbarga, then the Portuguese.

Janjira
 156 A3

Vijayadurg
156 B2

Malvan
156 B1

India's most spectacular island fort, **Janjira** is reached by rowboat from Murud town. It is famed as being the only fort on India's west coast to remain unconquered despite attempts over three centuries. As you roam the massive fortifications, guardrooms, cannon, and the four-story *durbar* (audience) hall, imagine its proud history. The Sidis, Abyssinian admirals in the service of the Adil Shahis of Bijapur, built it in 1511 but by 1618 had asserted their independence. Mixing piracy with providing armed escorts for pilgrims on *hajj* to Mecca, they never lost to Shivaji or the British. Today's former royals live in the hilltop palace; the creekside road south from Murud passes by their tombs. Because Janjira is isolated, visit it after a night or so at

Chiplun, a thriving town on the Vashishti River.

Almost as magnificent as Janjira, the fort of **Vijayadurg** sits at the mouth of the Vaghotan Creek. The Adil Shahis of Bijapur built it but Shivaji took it, renamed it Vijayadurg (Victory Fort), and refortified it. This was his base for attacking Janjira, and the Angres later used it as a piracy base. Explore the three concentric sets of fortifications, the residences, the barracks, and the granary. Continue to **Malvan.** It's worth the somewhat basic accommodations to enjoy this charming town, its cafés, and cashew nut production. Take a boat out to the island **Sindhudurg Fort** to walk along some of the 2 miles (3 km) of fortifications built by Shivaji when he made this his coastal headquarters around 1665. ∎

If you miss the low tide walk from Alibag to Kolaba Fort, you can sometimes take a ferry there to explore its 17 wall towers, teak doors, stables, and storerooms.

More Places to Visit in Maharashtra

These places are for the enthusiastic traveler, especially those keen on India's history. Here you will encounter few fellow tourists and stay in simple, modest accommodations. A quality driver and guide (or specialist book) is recommended.

Ahmednagar

Founded in 1494 by Ahmad Nizam Shah, who broke away from the Bahmanis of Bidar (see p. 239), this was the capital of the powerful Nizam Shahi rulers. Wars with Bijapur and Golconda ended when all three states, plus Bidar, formed a Muslim alliance to overthrow the Hindu kingdom of Vijayanagar in 1565 (see pp. 234–236). Later, Ahmednagar lost out to the Mughals in 1636, after which it belonged to Hyderabad, the Marathas, and, from 1808, the British. It was in the splendid **Ahmednagar Fort** (1563), with its moat and 22 bastions, that Jawaharlal Nehru wrote most of his book *The Discovery of India* while an imprisoned freedom fighter. See also the exquisitely decorated **Damri Mosque** (1568), the **Jami Masjid**, and the **Mecca Mosque** in the heart of the city; the **Kotla** (1537), which was a Shia college of education; and **Ahmad's Tomb** (1509) in Bagh Rauza gardens. Out of town, the **Dargah of Alamgir** (1707) marks the spot where the Mughal emperor Aurangzeb collapsed and died (see p. 173). Nearby stand two garden palaces: **Farah Bagh** and **Hayat Behisht Bagh.** 🄼 156 B3 ✉ 72 miles (116 km) NE of Pune, 68 miles (110 km) SW of Aurangabad, 90 miles (145 km) S of Nasik

Kolhapur

This busy commercial city in southern Maharashtra traces its history back to the Satavahana period, when it traded with the Mediterranean. More recently, it was the capital of the breakaway Maratha maharajas of Kolhapur, who commissioned fine Indo-Saracenic buildings by Maj. Charles Mant, better known for his Chennai buildings (see pp. 256–259). In the Old City, find **Rajwada** (Old Palace) and the popular **Mahalakshmi Temple.** Then visit Mant's splendid and influential buildings. There is the **Town Hall Museum** (1872–1876; *closed Mon.*), built as the Town Hall, and **Chhatrapati Pramila Raja Hospital** (1881–1884). His masterpiece is **New Palace** (1884; *closed Mon.*),

INSIDER TIP:

If someone tells you that you are a "squeezer of limes" in Hindi, don't be flattered. The idiom means you're a self-invited guest or an idler.

—JAG BHALLA
Author of National Geographic's
I'm Not Hanging Noodles on Your Ears

where former royals still live. The basalt-and-sandstone building has neo-Mughal cusped arches and a *durbar* hall with stained glass illustrating the life of Shivaji. The royal paraphernalia ranges from a silver elephant saddle to a veritable zoo of stuffed animals; one maharaja was an expert taxidermist. Take a look inside the **Shalini Palace** (1931–1934), now a hotel overlooking Rankala Lake and furnished with fine Belgian glass. Don't miss the chance to buy Kolhapur leather sandals, to see *kushti* (wrestling) training near the Rajwada, to visit the spectacularl **Panhala Fort,** which guarded trade routes to the coast. This is a good base for visits to Vijayadurg and Sindhudurg (see opposite), and is on the road to Bijapur (see pp. 237–238) and Belgaum. 🄼 156 B2 **Visitor Information** ✉ 254-B Udyog Bhavah, Assembly Rd. ☎ 023/1265-2935

Buying fruit from local markets can be a fine form of entertainment.

Mahabaleshwar

This is where the sacred Krishna River springs, making it a pilgrimage site for the faithful. The British, after making a treaty with the local ruler in 1829, exploited this lush, wooded site in the Sahyadri Hills as a hill station. Still popular for its views, streams, and fresh air, this is a good base for visiting **Pratapgarh** (1656), where Shivaji (see pp. 178–179) murdered the Bijapur commander, and **Raigad,** which he captured in 1636 and made his capital in 1672. He and his son were crowned here. Trips can be made to the island forts of Janjira (see p. 184) and Suvarnadurg, by Harnai, from here. There are more Shivaji sites at Pune (see p. 177). ⚑ 156 B3 ✉ 74 miles (120 km) SW of Pune

Nasik

The sacred Godavari River, flowing through this ancient holy city, attracts a continuous stream of pilgrims, swelling to vast numbers every 12 years for the **Kumbh Mela**

festival (next in 2015; see p. 303). Hindus believe Rama spent part of his exile here, with Sita and Lakshmana. Visit the riverside temples, including **Rameshwaram** (18th century), leaving time to visit three sites out of town. **Pandu Lena** has rock-cut Buddhist caves (second century B.C.–third century A.D.); nos. 3, 10, and 18 are especially interesting. Within the dramatic cliffs of Trimbak lies the source of the Godavari River, much visited during two annual fairs (Oct.–Nov. & Feb.–March). At Sinnar, on the road to Pune, **Gondeshvara Temple** (11th century) was built by the Yadava rulers and is one of Maharashtra's best preserved temples. ⚑ 156 B4 **Visitor Information** ✉ 81 miles (130 km) NE of Mumbai, 130 miles (209 km) N of Pune ✉ Paryatan Bhavan, Govt. Guesthouse Premises ☎ 025/3257-0059

Paithan

Archaeologists and weaving enthusiasts will enjoy Paithan. The thriving settlement founded by the Satavahana ruler Shalivahana as his capital in A.D. 78 is being unearthed at Nag Ghat. And local weavers create the distinctive Paithan designs in fine silk and cotton. ⚑ 157 C3 ✉ 32 miles (51 km) S of Aurangabad

Solapur, Naldurg, & Parenda

In southeast Maharashtra, on the road to Bijapur and Gulbarga, **Solapur**'s strategic importance has made it the focus of many battles. Its impressive **fort** with sloping walls was built by the 14th-century Bahmanis, with inner additions by the Adil Shahis of Bijapur. **Naldurg,** 28 miles (45 km) to the east, has a magnificent fort (16th century) built by the Adil Shahis on a bluff above the Bori River. If your route is to or from Ahmednagar, it is worth detouring to **Parenda** to see one of Maharashtra's most perfect early military forts, built around 1500 for the Bidar sultans. ⚑ 157 C2–C3

A strip of palm-fringed beaches, fishing villages, forts, and ports with a history and culture distinct from the rest of peninsular India

West Coast: Goa & Kerala

Fresh red chilies are sorted for quality and size.

West Coast: Goa & Kerala

A narrow band of lush, verdant land runs down the west coast of India's peninsula, sandwiched between the Western Ghat mountains and the Arabian Sea. From northern Goa to southern Kerala the visitor can relax on the beaches or take advantage of a variety of water sports. There is here something for everyone, in this mixture of east and west with its easygoing ambience.

The lush Goan landscape is complemented by the rich colors of the traditional clothing worn by its inhabitants.

July and August, so hundreds of little rivers flow down to the coast. They run from the steep Sahyadri Hills to the Konkan coast of Goa and the Kanara coast of Karnataka. They flow from the even higher Cardamom Hills to the Malabar Coast of Kerala, slowed down by such quantities of inland lagoons and rivers that land and water become inseparable.

Today these busy rivers continue to carry the local merchants' traditional sources of wealth (pepper, cardamom, other spices, and quantities of rice) to the ports. They also carry tea from the Nilgiri Hills, coffee from Karnataka's plantations, and lucrative rubber and turmeric.

The map shows how mountains and sea have played their part in India's west coast story. The mountains have been a barrier crossed more often by traders than by empire builders, the seas a tool to bring trading wealth and introduce new cultures, peoples, and religions. Arabs, Romans, and, later, Europeans arrived, bringing Judaism, Islam, and various forms of Christianity. Coastal people have tended to look outward across the water, rather than inward to the great empires of the Deccan and Tamil Nadu, and their coast is littered with ancient forts and modern ports—Panaji, Mangalore, Kannur (Cannanore), Kozhikode (Calicut), Kochi (Cochin), and others—all centers for shipbuilding.

None of India's great rivers empties here, but India's great southwest monsoon hits Kerala in July and soaks the Western Ghats in

NOT TO BE MISSED:

Once so dependent on the sea, the coast now has the Konkan Railway. Opened in 1998, it stretches from Mumbai to Kochi and is already hauling the more isolated, undeveloped parts of the coast into the modern world. Goa and Kerala have been quick to respond with some charming upscale hotels. Visitors can comfortably explore a beautiful area of mostly unspoiled India, while enjoying palm-fringed beaches and outstanding local cuisines. A week in this region makes a relaxing and striking contrast to touring India's great monuments. ■

Goa

Goa, a tiny state of 1,429 square miles (3,702 sq km) located along India's southwest coast, was created only in 1987; its language of Konkani given official status in 1988. With its recent boom in tourism imports and mineral exports, as well as energetic building of holiday homes for Indians living in the rest of the country, the coast and roads immediately behind it are mostly no longer quiet.

Panaji's hilltop Our Lady of the Immaculate Conception, a dazzling, whitewashed Catholic church

Old Goa

🗺 189 B5

goa-travel-tourism .com

goacentral.com

Old Goa & Panaji

Panaji is the slow-paced, friendly capital of Goa. Explore Panaji after visiting Old Goa, the former capital, reached by road or by passenger boat up the Mandovi River.

Old Goa: A few surviving churches and monasteries, with baroque high altars and encroaching palm trees, evoke Goa's most recent great city, for this ancient river port was used by the Ashoka,

Satavahana, and Chalukya empires. The Kadambas (11th–12th centuries) made it their capital on two nearby sites, attracting Khilji, then Tughlaq forces from far away Delhi. Later, Goa was wrested from the Bahmanis by the all-powerful Vijayanagars, won back (when the port capital was moved to this site), but in 1489 lost for good to the Adil Shahis of Bijapur.

Meanwhile, Portuguese explorer Bartolomeu Dias

rounded the Cape of Good Hope in 1488. A decade later Vasco da Gama rounded the cape and sailed across the Indian Ocean to Calicut, and in 1503 Alfonso de Albuquerque built Fort Cochin. In 1510, Albuquerque sailed up the Mandovi and took Goa on November 25, establishing it as the capital of a fast-growing Portuguese maritime empire.

Goa was an entrepôt for trade up and down the coast, in and out of India, and from the Arabian Gulf across to Malacca. The Portuguese levied taxes on everything—cargoes of indigo, cotton, cinnamon, mace, nutmeg, Chinese silk, porcelain, and the very valuable pepper. For a century Goa was known as Goa *dourada* ("golden Goa"). It was an international city of churches, convents, palaces, mansions, docks, and markets, swarming with activity. It was a center for Roman Catholicism, for the Portuguese trading zeal was matched with a missionary zeal. Missionaries arrived early in Goa, closely followed by the Jesuits and their Counter-Reformation (1540) and Inquisition (1560).

But the Portuguese Empire faded. The reasons were many: loss of trade after the fall of Vijayanagar, the proselytizing zeal against Hindus, the taxation of Muslims on hajj (pilgrimage) to Mecca, plagues of cholera, deceitful Portuguese business practices, and the arrival of Dutch and English traders in 1595 and 1600. Goa sank into isolation that the removal of its capital from unhealthy Old Goa to Panaji in 1843 did little to alleviate. Portugal clung to her colony until December 19, 1961, when Nehru's Indian forces liberated the city.

To enjoy Old Goa town, wander through the baroque colonial churches with their ebullient decoration, twisted columns, flying angels, and lashings of gilt. The major churches (see p. 192) are the **Basilica of Bom Jesus** (1594–1605), the **Cathedral of St. Catherine** (1562–1619), and the **Convent and Church of St. Francis of Assisi** (1521 and 1661), which also has the town's museum.

(continued on p. 194)

Old Goa Churches

$ $ for each

FESTIVALS: Carnival, week preceding Lent: festivities throughout Goa. **Holy Week, Easter,** and **Christmas,** dates vary: grand processions, various churches; contact local tourist offices for information.

St. Francis Xavier

Goencho Saib (Lord of Goa) is the affectionate Konkani title all Goans, regardless of faith, give to their local saint. Born in Spain in 1506, Francisco Xavier y Jassu met Ignatius Loyola in Paris, took a vow to convert infidels, and joined the Society of Jesus. The Portuguese king Dom Joao III sent Xavier to Portugal's new colony, Goa. He arrived in May 1542 and made Goa his base for five voyages to the Far East. After his death on Sancian Island in 1552, his body was returned to Goa in 1553 and carried in triumph from the riverside. He was canonized in 1662. The saint's festival is held on the anniversary of his death, December 3.

A Drive Through Old Goa, Ponda, & Margao

This gentle day excursion takes in Portuguese monuments and mansions, and some of Ponda's most distinctive temples.

The road to **Old Goa** ➊ rises over a hill to give you a first glimpse of the overgrown city with St. Augustine's soaring tower. In the center stands a group of big churches. In the **Basilica of Bom Jesus** (1594–1605), built by the Jesuits next to their home, the Professed House (1589 and 1633), is St. Francis Xavier's elaborate mausoleum, given by the Duke of Tuscany, Cosimo III. Inside the casket, a light shines continuously on St. Francis's body. Across the square stand the grand **Cathedral of St. Catherine** (1562–1619), built for the Dominicans, and the beautiful **Convent and Church of**

NOT TO BE MISSED:

Basilica of Bom Jesus, Old Goa
• Church & Monastery of St. Augustine, Old Goa • Sri Mangesh Temple, Priol • Largo de Igreja, Margao
• Covered market, Margao

St. Francis of Assisi (1521), housing Goa's best museum with a collection of sculptures and portraits of Portuguese governors.

Take a walk west of the cathedral to see the **Church of St. Cajetan** (1655–1700), whose dome was modeled on that of St. Peter's in Rome. Continue through the **Viceroy's Arch**, built by Francisco da Gama (viceroy 1597–1600), to the silent docks, where more than a thousand ships were loaded each year. From here either walk or drive up Holy Hill to the **Church and Monastery of St. Augustine** (1602), its pink laterite stone lit by morning sun. The 152-foot-high (46 m) church tower, eight chapels, 100 or so carved granite tombstones, and monastic buildings testify to a substantial community. A path across the road leads to the **Church of Our Lady of the Rosary** (1544–1549), which overlooks the Mandovi River; here St. Francis preached at evening Mass.

Leaving Old Goa, the **temples of Ponda** (see pp. 196–197) are a total contrast. Instead of riverside colonial style, you now have secret temple buildings in secluded valleys. Driving southward, the road twists and climbs into hills where spreading cashew trees and jackfruit trees grow. Here are three contrasting temples to visit. **Sri Mangesh Temple** ➋ (see p. 196),

The Basilica of Bom Jesus is a focal point for Goa's substantial Catholic population.

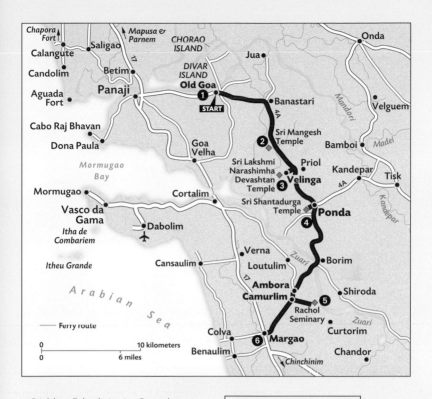

at Priol, has all the distinctive Goan elements and is Goa's richest temple. Up the steps, find the large courtyard with a *tulsi* (basil) planter, a lamp tower, and an elephant on wheels in front of the lemon yellow and white-domed temple; inside, look for the tiles and Belgian glass. **Sri Lakshmi Narashimha Devashtan Temple ❸**, dedicated to Vishnu and Lakshmi in the gods' abode, stands in an appropriately idyllic woodland setting at Velinga and is probably Goa's most beautiful temple. Finally, **Sri Shantadurga Temple ❹**, near Queula, is Goa's most popular temple, especially crowded with people buying flowers before the main *puja* at 1 p.m., held in a *mandapa* (hall) of baroque splendor.

From here, the road goes through Borim before crossing the Zuari River. A detour left after Camurlim village leads through lanes to **Rachol Seminary ❺** (see p. 200), with its great entrance hall, chapel, and museum.

	See also area map p. 189
►	Old Goa
↔	20 miles (30 km)
⏱	5–6 hours
►	Margao

Margao ❻ (see pp. 194–195) is southern Goa's main town. Bustling yet rural, it has two good areas to visit. As you drive in along the one-way street, you can see some of the town's grand old houses. Stop at **Largo de Igreja** (Church Square), the old central square, to see a cluster of old houses that overlook the gleaming white **Church of the Holy Spirit** (1564, rebuilt 1675), with its baroque and rococo interior. Then visit the **covered market,** where locals buy spices, vegetables, household goods, and, outside, fresh fish. In the Margao outskirts of Borda, reached by taking Agostinho Lourenço Street from Largo de Igreja, find the huge palace of **Sat Burnzam Ghor.**

Panaji

🅰 189 B5

Visitor Information

✉ State Tourist
Office, Trionara
Apartments,
Dr. Alvares Costa
Rd.

☎ 083/2242-4001,
083/2242-4002

goa-tourism.com

✉ India Tourist
Office,
Communidade
Bldg., Church Sq.

☎ 083/2222-3412

incredibleindia.org

Margao

🅰 189 A5

Visitor Information

✉ Margao Tourist
Office, Tourist
Hostel

☎ 083/2271-5204

Panaji: Still with a definite Portuguese air, Panaji sits at the mouth of the Mandovi River. It only became the capital of Goa when the port at Old Goa town silted up. It is worth paying a visit to the 1619 hilltop parish church, **Our Lady of the Immaculate Conception** (*$*), built in Portuguese baroque style with twin towers; then walk through the old Latin Quarter of Fontainhas to see old buildings, such as the **Casa de Modea** (Mint) and **Idalcao Palace** (Secretariat). The riverside area west of here is home to the colorful municipal market and Charles Correa's splendid **Kala Academy** (1973–1983; *$*), decorated with Mario Miranda's monochrome murals.

Margao's well-kept, traditional colonial streets make the town a pleasure to visit.

Margao & Around

Goa's second largest town is a good place to feel the influence of 450 years of Portuguese rule, partly because there are few tourists, partly because it forms part of the heartland of the Old Conquests (the rest of Goa was conquered in the 18th century).

As you approach Margao from the surrounding countryside, you notice the whitewashed baroque facades of colonial Catholic churches standing beside the paddy fields and rivers. Women often wear pretty dresses with puffed sleeves, rather than saris. Widows dress in European black, not Hindu white, and sit crocheting on the deep *balcaos* (porches) of their houses. These are painted blue, red-umber, and yellow, with the large windows outlined in white. The cuisine is a mixture of Portuguese and Indian traditions, and wine is readily available. Soccer, not cricket, is the favorite sport. Even the Portuguese siesta is maintained: Everything closes from 2 p.m. to 4 p.m.

When the city of Old Goa declined, the Old Conquests were barely affected. Here, the Portuguese-speaking Christian Goans ran the government and trade, and in due course they formed the local aristocracy in Margao and the villages. Prosperity here peaked in the 18th and 19th centuries, when the great houses were built.

For a breathtaking view over Margao and the Arabian Sea, go up to **Mount Church.** Down in the town, the markets are the hub for trading the fish and farming produce of southern Goa. Behind the big red-and-white Municipal Building you can find the fisherwomen, their saris tucked up, crouching beside baskets of shrimp, pearl spot, Indian salmon,

Coconut Palm

This versatile tree plays an essential role in Goan life. Seaside clumps help protect villagers from the sun, wind, and monsoon storms. Inland, more than half of Goa's agricultural land is devoted to coconut and cashew production, something the Jesuits encouraged: Tended, watered, and fertilized, an acre (0.4 ha) of coconut palms will produce 7,000 nuts a year against 1,000 in the wild. The juice of green (unripe) coconuts is a refreshing drink. Ripe nuts have their fibers twisted into ropes, fishing nets, and rigging, or woven into coir matting. Shells become fuel or eating bowls. Coconut milk and the kernel are used in cooking; dried and pressed, they produce valuable coconut oil. The timber is used for building, its fronds for thatched roofs, fish traps, mats, and baskets. Sap is tapped to make *jaggery* (raw sugar) or to distill into the alcoholic drink *feni*, which can also be made from the bitter cashew fruits.

and other catches of the morning. Nearby, you can buy fruit from the great piles of bananas, pineapples, *chikoos,* jackfruits, and, starting in March, mangoes. Inside the old **covered market** you'll find dried mangoes, flowers, fresh Goan bread, tobacco leaves, and sacks full of turmeric, garlic, Goan red chilies, and the dried tamarind that gives a bitter richness to local dishes. The box-shaped stores stocking wines, jewelry, and hardware form the walls of the market.

To see a good cluster of old houses, go to the old **Market Square** district and brave the thundering traffic to walk along the two one-way streets that lead in and out of town and run along both sides of **Largo de Igreja** (Church Square). These grand town houses with their painted walls, iron balconies, and carved balustrades surround the tall, dazzlingly white **Church of the Holy Spirit** (1564, rebuilt 1675), one of Goa's finest late baroque churches. If it is open, venture inside to enjoy the finely coffered ceiling, grand gilt pulpit, rococo

altar, and the various baroque transept altarpieces.

To see more fine houses, go along Agostinho Lourenco Street behind the church and toward Curtorim. About half a mile (1 km) along stands the huge palace of **Sat Burnzam Ghor,** built around 1790 by Inacio Silva and now lived in by his descendants. As well as a string of grand salons, it has one of Goa's earliest private chapels.

Follow a lovely circular route around the villages of this area, **Salcete,** to see more. Begin at the old Portuguese administrative center, **Loutolim,** found by turning north from Carmurlim on the Margao–Ponda road. The clutch of fine old buildings includes **Casa de Miranda** (contact tourist office to arrange visit; archgoa.org), still lived in by the Miranda family. Built early in the 18th century, it has a chapel, bedrooms, salon, and deep internal veranda on the first floor, and a banqueting room and library upstairs. Two other fine Loutolim houses are **Roque Caetan Miranda House** (1815), a typical Goan country house, and

Sat Burnzam Ghor

✉ Borda

🕒 Visits by written or telephone appt.

Menezes-Braganza Mansion

✉ Chandor

☎ 083/2278-4201

🕐 Usually open 9 a.m.–5 p.m.

💲 $

Palacio do Deao

✉ Opposite Holy Cross Church, Quepem

☎ 098/2248-0342

🕐 By appt. only

💲 $

palaciododeao.com

Ponda

🗺 189 B5

Salvador **Costa House** with its spectacular chapel *(arrange visits to both houses through tourist office)*.

Continue to **Chandor,** through undulating land with old houses scattered around and flashy new ones built with money newly earned in the Middle East. You may wish to pause at **Rachol**

INSIDER TIP:

Quench your thirst with the sweet juice of a freshly sliced coconut from one of the many streetside coconut *wallahs* [vendors].

—NATASHA SCRIPTURE
National Geographic contributor

Seminary (see p. 200) or to see Curtorim's splendid church facade. Chandor is dominated by the vast, ornate **Menezes-Braganza Mansion** whose second-floor rooms are furnished with gilt mirrors, four-poster beds, and quantities of elegantly carved chairs. Do not miss the ballroom, with its blue-and white-painted zinc ceiling, Italian chandeliers, Belgian mirrors, and portrait of the mansion's builder, Anton Francesco Santana Pereira. For more villages to visit, see **Chinchinim** (see p. 200). A short drive on to Quepem, **Palacio do Deao** is an immaculate house with 2 acres (0.8 ha) of lush gardens and a restaurant.

Ponda's Temples

When Portuguese missionary zeal sparked the publication of

an edict to destroy Hindu temples in 1540, some Hindu priests fled with the temple deity to the forested hills around Ponda, outside the Portuguese territories. Thus, while more than 550 temples were destroyed, many Hindus continued to worship in secret. Today, about 50 of Goa's temples have deities who are, in effect, long-term refugees, still situated close to, but outside, Ponda.

Hinduism flourished freely again under more benign Portuguese rule at the end of the 18th century. Despite the number of churches you see across the state, Goa is today 60 percent Hindu. Furthermore, Christians sometimes join Hindus to pay their respects to an ancient deity worshipped by their Hindu ancestors.

Goa's temples have a unique style. The laterite walls are usually plastered and painted, and there are often domed central roofs, red-tiled side roofs, and tall *deepastambhas* (lamp towers). Inside, you may find Greek-inspired columns and grand chandeliers.

The pick of Ponda's temples is probably **Sri Mangesh Temple** *(tel 083/2234-3338)* at Priol, whose Shiva *lingum* was brought here for safety from Cortalim and hidden until the 18th century, when the temple was built. The seven-story deepastambha, elaborate doorway, and Belgian glass testify to the temple's wealth and status. **Sri Mahalasa Temple** lies between here and Ponda, in Mardol village. Do not miss the tall, brass pillar topped by Garuda and set on a turtle's back, signs that the temple is dedicated to Vishnu. At Velinga, **Sri Lakshmi Narashimha Devashtan Temple** is especially beautiful in its peaceful wooded setting and is dedicated to Vishnu and his consort Lakshmi. The gleaming image of Narasimha, Vishnu's fourth avatar (earthly form), was brought here for safety from Sancoale in the 1560s. The key features are the original entrance and the tank around the back.

Goa's Beaches

Fishermen going out to sea, dolphins playing in the frothy waves, and infinite stretches of sand beneath a canopy of blue sky await you on Goa's beaches. Have breakfast in a beachside café, go for a swim, and then retreat to the shade to read until lunch—grilled giant shrimp are popular. After a siesta, enjoy swimming and strolling along part of the 66 miles (106 km) of beach until the spectacular sunset over the sea.

Goa's dark sand is clean and fine. Some beaches are very long: The *uba dando* ("straight rod") is the great 12-mile (21 km) stretch in southern Goa from Velsao to Mobor. Each beach is named after the fishing village nestling in the coconut palms behind it, so the uba dando has several names. Each beach has its own character, from isolated Agonda to sociable and popular Calangute, or the almost private coves like Vainguinim. Different beaches attract different crowds: Sinquerim Beach is next to two upscale hotels, Anjuna is a hippie hangout,

and Indians arrive in busloads at Calangute and Colva.

It is easy to beach hop: Simply walk to the next beach, rent a bicycle or motorcycle, or take a taxi. Where you need to cross a river, your only problem is waiting for the ferry to arrive; in Goa, there is always time to wait.

Goa takes an active interest in ecology. New buildings must be 660 feet (200 m) back from the high-tide line. Sand dunes and their salt-tolerant vegetation are encouraged and litter cleared regularly. These laws particularly affect the owners of beach cafés, temporary structures where you

Goa's Beaches
▲ 189 A5 & B5

EXPERIENCE: Goa's Beaches by Motorbike

Beach hopping in Goa is much easier if you rent a scooter or motorbike. Your hotel can direct you to the nearest reliable supplier. Prices start around $10 a day; some suppliers also have bike chauffeurs. To abide by Indian law, you need to be 21 and have driven for two years; you pay a deposit and possibly leave your passport (or photocopy). Ask to see the owner's insurance, and test all the bikes available, especially the brakes. Do buy a map; don't bike at night. Check *classic-bike-india.com*, based in Candolim.

---

can have a drink. Try local *feni* (see sidebar p. 195) or its lighter equivalent, *urrack;* do nothing much and watch the waves to a soundtrack of old Motown and Beatles hits. Licenses are given and taken away seemingly arbitrarily, but there should always be some friendly cafés waiting to serve you.

Goa's beach etiquette is simple: Nudity is unacceptable, drugs are illegal, the sea should be checked locally for undertow, and peddlers need fierce bargaining or a polite "no, thank you." To help you find the right beach, here are the best of them, from north to south.

Quiet Northern Goa Beaches:

To reach these peaceful spots, take the ferry from Siolim across the Chapora River into Pernem district, little influenced by the Portuguese. Isolated **Querim Beach** is best reached by a pleasant walk from Arambol (Harmal) Beach past a mixture of palms, fishing boats, Hindu-owned cafés, a handful of hippies, and a good local bakery. Turn left from the Chapora Ferry and follow the riverbank.

Morjim Beach (Morji) tends to be very quiet unless a busload of Indians arrives, and there is good bird-watching.

Busier Northern Goa Beaches:

Six miles (10 km) of beach stretch from Baga down to Sinquerim along the coast of Bardez district. This is where the action is, with beach parties, a choice of restaurants, bars, and nightlife. Behind the beaches, old Portuguese houses and churches stand among paddy fields. **Anjuna Beach** is a social center for hippies and beach parties, with safe swimming, cafés, and the Wednesday afternoon market with vendors from Rajasthan, Gujarat, and Karnataka; nearby Mapusa's Friday market (see p. 200) is inland. Pretty, crescent-shaped **Baga**

After a night at sea, fishermen unload their catch on the beach at Colva.

EXPERIENCE: Family Fun & Water Sports in Goa

Goa is known for its water sports, especially on the central Goa beaches—Calangute, Dona Paula, Cavelossim, Candolim, Bogmalo, and Sinquerim—where there is also some degree of patrolling and safety. At **Fort Aguada Beach Resort** (*Sinquerim, Bardez, tel 083/2664-5858*), young children are given supplies of glitter and colored powders to decorate their sand castle creations. Older children can enjoy good waterskiing and sailing at the Enterprise class, and the whole family can take a motorboat ride or go parasailing.

Watersports Goa (*Bogmalo Beach Park Plaza Resort, tel 022/6628-8000, watersportscenter.com*) has instructors for just about every water sport, from windsurfing (the gentle morning breeze is best) to scuba diving. Divers should bring their PADI certificates and do a refresher course before making a dive to see plenty of corals and fish around wrecks of Portuguese galleons. The underwater life in Goa is similar to that of the Maldives, although the water can be murky. People have had good dives near Grand Island, at Suzy's Wreck, Bounty Bay, and other spots.

Beach has good accommodations, tempting restaurants, and a lively social life, which is also true of neighboring **Calangute Beach. Candolim Beach** is next, with its charming inns and cafés. Finally, **Sinquerim Beach,** lined with palm trees, runs right down to Fort Aguada, where you will find upscale hotels, cafés, water sports, and the inevitable peddlers.

Beaches Near Panaji: These are small beaches, where the sand has a silver tint because of the iron content. Some of the beaches are private, and thus free of peddlers. **Dona Paula Beach** is reserved for guests of the hotels overlooking it; **Vainguinim Beach** is reached through Cidade de Goa Hotel, whose garden encircles it.

Long Southern Goa Beaches: Uba dando's 12-mile (19 km) stretch is, so far, quieter than the main northern Goa beaches. Its sand is cleaner, and its sea is usually calm. Margao, Ponda, Panaji, and Old Goa are fairly accessible, but avoid Bogmalo, right on the airport flight path. Beaches run from Velsao to lively **Colva,** with its fishermen, beach cafés, village market, and restaurants. Peaceful **Sernabatim, Benaulim,** and **Varca** beaches are little-used by patrons of the nearby upscale hotels. **Cavelossim** fronts the pretty village of Carmona, and **Mobor** is home to a super-chic hotel. You then come to Betul village and the Sal River.

Quiet Southern Goa Beaches: To enjoy nearly empty beaches with their wilder scenery, go for the day and take a picnic. **Agonda Beach** is usually particularly quiet, whereas **Palolem's** beauty is threatened by development. South of here are **Rajbag** and **Galgibaga.** ∎

More Places to Visit in Goa

Calizz Museum

The Calizz is a beautifully conceived museum of half a dozen old buildings immaculately preserved, and containing family collections of photographs, kitchen implements, walking sticks, and more. The focus is a trio of houses belonging to Shri Laxmikant Prabhakar Kudchadkar, with fine hardwood doors, stucco window moldings, and distinctive Goan floor tiles. *calizz.com*
✉ Bammon Vaddo, Candolim, Bardez (N of Panaji) ☎ 093/2673-3292

Chapora Fort

This fort was a refuge for locals when Shivaji's son Shambhaji swept down here in 1739. The Portuguese treaty won them back this district, Bardez, in exchange for the Marathas having Bassein (see p. 169). Hike up the hill to see the laterite battlements and bastions (1617) and to enjoy views down over Chapora estuary, past mango and cashew orchards. ✉ N of Panaji

Colva, Benaulim, & Chinchinim

These three Salcete district villages, are all situated west of Margao. Colva has a high baroque church, **Our Lady of Mercy** (1630, rebuilt 18th century), and nice old houses. Nearby Benaulim has the baroque **Church of St. John the Baptist** and more charming houses such as **Vincent Correia Fonsecos** (now apartments). Finally, twisting lanes lead through paddy fields and cashew orchards to Chinchinim. In the pretty square, Dr. Alvaro Loyola Furtado's **mansion** stands next to the peppermint green church. ✉ W of Margao

Fort Aguada

Goa's strongest fort, built in 1612, defends Aguada Bay and the mouth of the Mandovi River. Built using the latest Italian engineering theories of low, broad walls, wide moats, and cylindrical turrets, it surrounded Sinquerim and Candolim villages and had 79 cannon. Reach it through Betin, Verim, or Nerul fishing villages. The fort archway leads to the church, lighthouse, and citadel which has views across the Mandovi to Cabo promontory and the governor of Goa's mansion. ✉ N of Panaji

Mapusa Market

Every Friday the main square of Mapusa is a hive of activity. Locals buy their fruit, fish, and household goods such as tiffin cans (lunch boxes); visitors look for Goan terracotta pottery and crafts from other states. Stores sell cashews and Mumbai-made accessories. ✉ N of Panaji

Rachol Seminary

Rachol Seminary is one of four seminaries devoted to training the priests for Goa's many churches. Founded in 1574, the fortlike building has a chapel with an ornately gilded altar and impressive relics, pulpit, and murals. The small **Museum of Christian Art,** which opened in 1994, has exquisite pieces, including a gilded St. Ursula figure, processional flags, and the Loutolim priest's palanquin. ✉ 4 miles (7 km) E of Margao

Sea & River Cruises

Locals often run informal sunset boat rides up Goa's many rivers, where you can spot birds such as sandpipers, terns, ospreys, and sea eagles. Trips also go out on the sea to look for schools of humpbacked dolphins. ✉ S of Panaji

Spice Plantations

There are two spice gardens at Khandepar near Ponda, both well run for visitors: **Savoi Verem Spice Garden** (tel 083/2234-0272) and **Garden of Eden** (tel 976/6329-632) See tiny chilies; nutmeg fruits that must be pried open for the lacelike mace around the nut; fragrant cinnamon bark; cloves drying in the sun; vines of black pepper (once known as black gold); and much more. ☒ E of Panaji

Tambdi Surla Temple

A day trip inland from Panaji takes you to Goa's best building: a beautiful temple hidden in a clearing in the thick forested hills. Built of basalt stone, the decoration is crisp and deep, the roofs powerfully primitive. It is a rare survivor from the Kadamba empire, which ruled Goa in the 11th and 12th centuries, ran the west coast's major port, and was India's finest maritime power. Turn left at Molem crossroads, then right to Surla. Then take the next right turn; follow this road to its end, then walk a short distance through the trees. From the main road it is about 11 miles (17 km) ☒ E of Ponda

More Northern Goa Temples

Some of the best temples in northern Goa include **Mauli Temple** at Sarmalem, near Pernem, with graffito decoration, and **Sri**

Bhagavati Temple at Parcem. Eastward into Bicholim district, **Sri Saptakoteshwar Temple** at Naroa had a refugee deity brought here from Diva Island by Shivaji in 1668. ☒ N of Panaji

More Southern Goa Temples

Near Ponda, two temples stand in lush valleys near Bandora. **Sri Nagesh Temple** was founded here and has friezes of scenes from the great Hindu epics. At nearby Queula, **Sri Shantadurga Temple** (1738) was partly funded by Shivaji's grandson Shambhaji. At 1 p.m., you can witness the main *puja* of the day, with men standing on the right and women on the left beneath a gilded ceiling. Mirrors outside spotlight the deity for the benefit of the overflow. Down in the south of Salcete district, there are two hilltop temples, founded in the fifth century or earlier, with splendid views. **Sri Chandranath** has its *lingum* carved out of the hill, while **Sri Chandreshwar Bhutnath Temple,** dedicated to Shiva as Lord of the Moon, has a similarly carved Nandi bull. ☒ S of Panaji

---

EXPERIENCE: Boating & Birding in Goa

Hundreds of little rivers dribble, gurgle, and glide down the Deccan Plateau westward through Goa to the Arabian Sea. Visitors can explore them on a simple boat, enjoying good bird-watching, seeing local life, spotting colorful butterflies, and possibly eating a home-cooked lunch at a local farm and learning how the farm operates—the farmers mostly grow their own vegetables and spices. Fishing can be arranged, too; simply ask.

There are organized cruises up the **Cumbarjua River** and canal, the boat sailing between the mangroves with their tangled roots; you may even spot local crocodiles. Trips to **Grand Island** off the coast are often accompanied by frolicking dolphins and seabirds.

Serious bird-watchers will want to visit **Dr. Salim Ali Bird Sanctuary** on Chorao island in the Mandovi River, reached by ferry from Ribander; once there, you use a canoe. **Beira Mar, Baga Fields,** the **Chapora River estuary, Lake Maem,** and **Candolim Marsh** are good spots, too. Take binoculars and a field guide.

For a simple pleasure, ask in a riverside village if someone can give you a boat ride one evening—you might see a fish eagle struggling with its wriggling prey; black-headed ibises nibbling in fields; a tree full of suspended bats; locals gathering mollusks; and, suddenly, the grand white facade of a Portuguese baroque church rising above the coconut palms. Remember to tip your boatman.

The Konkan Railway

While other countries abandon their trains, India wisely promotes this low-pollution form of transportation and even builds entirely new lines. The Konkan Railway *(konkanrailway .com)* is the country's most recent triumph, an engineering feat that runs 472 miles (760 km) through three states—Maharashtra, Goa, and Karnataka—from Mumbai (Bombay) down the coast to Mangalore. There it links up to an older railroad line to Kochi (Cochin).

Initiated in 1984, begun in 1990, and opened in 1997, Konkan was the largest railroad project of the 20th century. Billed as "A Dream Come True," it provides a north–south transportation infrastructure that will boost the economy and increase employment of a poor area where the monsoon regularly destroys roads and makes port connections by inland waterways and sea unnavigable.

INSIDER TIP:

When booking a train, if your ticket is "wait list," or WL, make alternative arrangements as well. The WL doesn't always clear, and you may find yourself without transportation.

—TALA KATNER
National Geographic contributor

Along the route, trains cross 143 major bridges, of which the longest is a mile (1.6 km), and 1,670 minor ones. They pass through 75 tunnels, the longest one more than 4 miles (6 km). They cross India's highest viaduct, 211 feet (64 m) high, roll over 85,630 tons (87,000 tonnes) of rails and 1.2 million railroad ties, and stop at up to 59 stations.

The railway has changed the lives of coastal people. They are less isolated; traveling distances and times have been reduced—a train journey from Goa to Mumbai is cut from 20 to 10 hours—and the fare is cheaper.

But ecologists and environmentalists, albeit pleased at the prospect of less pollution from trucks, are anxious. They fear the area's rich mineral resources—iron ore, bauxite, chromite, manganese, and silica sand—and its dense forests will be ravaged. Iron ore is already a major Goa industry. Maharashtra has the last tract of untouched coastal forest in India. They also worry about increased population, urbanization, and industrialization, and the consequent pollution of the coast's fragile ecosystem.

Thermal plants, an oil refinery, and copper-smelting complexes are already planned, and train passengers are expected to reach 21.5 million each year by 2015.

For the visitor, the Konkan Railway opens up travel along the coast south of Mumbai. The grueling drive out of Mumbai can be avoided by boarding a southbound train from Victoria Terminus. Roha makes a good stop for visiting Janjira, and Chiplun for staying in a quaint hotel while exploring the Vashishti River and valley. Farther south, Sawantwadi is the station for seeing the forts at Malvan and Vijayadurg. In Goa, there are stations at Pernem, Old Goa, Margao, and Canacona. The scenic route continues down coastal Karnataka with stops that include Karwar, Kundapura, and Mangalore (see p. 204). Here the Konkan Railway links into the older Southern Railway, built to serve British trading needs, and continues down to Kochi, stopping at such towns as Kozhikode (Calicut) and Thrissur (Trichur).

The current schedule enables you to hop on a train in Mumbai at 4:40 p.m., enjoy a good night's sleep, meals on board, a day's window sightseeing, and arrive at Kochi at 9 p.m the next day. This is a fast train: You do not stop at every station.

The Konkan Railway line crosses many rivers, including the wide Zuari near Cortalim, where fishing families continue to mend their nets using traditional methods.

Coastal Karnataka

The coastal strip of Goa's neighboring state Karnataka is called Kanara. Its landscapes are among the most scenic in India. Laterite cliffs alternate with almost empty beaches and mangrove-lined river estuaries. Tourists are rare; facilities are simple.

Coastal Karnataka

🗺 189 B4

Visitor Information

✉ State Tourist Office, Dept. of Tourism, #49, 2nd Floor, Khanija Bhavan, Race Course Rd., Bangalore

☎ 080/2235-2828

Email: info@karn atakatourism.org

Traveling south from Goa, you pass through **Gokarna** first— an ancient pilgrimage center focused on its **Sri Mahabaleshwar** and **Sri Maha Ganpati temples.** Pilgrims shave their heads, take a holy dip in the sea, and then visit the temples to perform their *puja* (worship) and *darshan* (ritual viewing of the deity); the splendid *rath* (temple chariot) is still used for Shivratri, Shiva's festival *(Feb.).*

A string of perfect beaches follows, some the home of Goa's long-stay beach bums. A detour inland from Bhatkal leads to **Jog Falls** *(avoid Nov.–Jan. monsoon*

INSIDER TIP:

Be aware of Bandh days. Bandhs are protests that last from morning to evening. Businesses close, and traffic stops with little or no warning.

—HARISH VASUDEVAN
National Geographic Books

season). The falls are India's highest and set amid breathtaking hill scenery; hikers can follow the path down to the water, but should take a guide to avoid getting lost.

At Barkur, turn inland to **Mekkekattu** for a fantastic sight: about 170 new, bright red *bhuta* (spirit) images in the Nandikeshvara Temple complex.

Farther down the coast you come to **Udupi** (Udipi), famed as the birthplace of delicious *masala dosas,* the thin rice pancakes stuffed with vegetables and first made in the town's brahman hotels. Having sampled one or two in a café at the Hotel Sharada International *(tel 082/0252-1968)* or Kediyoor, go to the square to join pilgrims visiting the amazing wooden Krishna temple, with its copper-clad sloping roofs, founded by the Hindu saint Madhva (1238–1317). It is well worth coinciding your visit here with the spectacular biennial temple festival held in January.

Finally, you reach cosmopolitan **Mangalore,** a great port since the sixth century, later owned by the Vijayanagaras, Portuguese, Tipu Sultan, and the British. From here, pepper, ginger, and other spices were traded with the Middle East. Today, its exports are coffee, cocoa, cashew nuts, and granite. Sadly, scant remains of its past—the **Manjunatha Temple** (tenth century) with its fine bronzes, and **St. Aloysius College Chapel** (1885), with its Italian frescoes and murals, are probably the best. ∎

Kerala

Kerala is distinct from the rest of India. Trade winds made this corner of India the natural landfall for early sailors from East Africa, who introduced international trade and religions. This distinct and enriched culture enjoys the first monsoon showers, ensuring a bountiful land.

Traditional fishing villages dot India's coastline; here, Keralites haul their boat up onto the beach.

Kochi & Ernakulam

Spread out over several islands where Vembanad Lake meets the Arabian Sea, Kochi's main center is historic Fort Cochin and Mattancherry; its twin city, dynamic, expanding Ernakulam, lies across the water to the east.

St. Thomas the Apostle is said to have come to the isthmus of Kochi in about A.D. 50 and created a Christian community called the Moplars. Jewish people came, too, then Syrian Christians, Chinese, and Persian travelers, and, in 1502, Vasco da Gama. He established a Portuguese factory to process spices for export. The next year, Albuquerque arrived with friars to begin the fort and church.

The English set up their spice factory in 1635 only to lose it in 1663 to the Dutch, who converted the Catholic church to a Protestant chapel and the cathedral into a warehouse. When the Netherlands fell to the French in 1795, the British were quick to grab Kochi and its lucrative and strategic port.

Gentle trading continues. You can still see spice go-downs (warehouses) in the Mattancherry area of Kochi, but its character is preserved thanks to the growth of Ernakulam on the mainland. Little fishing boats still bring their catch to the harbor at sunset, though Kochi's real wealth is its *(continued on p. 208)*

Kerala

🏚 189 C2

Visitor Information

✉ Kerala Tourist Office, Shanmugham Rd., Ernakulam

☎ 048/4235-1015

keralatourism.org

Kochi & Ernakulam

🏚 189 C2

Visitor Information

✉ India Tourist Office, Willingdon Island, near Taj Malabar Hotel

☎ 048/4266-8352

✉ Tourist Centre, Fort Kochi

☎ 048/4221-6567

incredibleindia.org

(continued on p. 208)

A Walk Around Kochi

The best days for this walk are Sunday through Thursday, as the Dutch Palace is closed on Fridays and the Paradesi Synagogue is closed on Fridays and Saturdays. Reach Kochi (Cochin) by ferry from Ernakulam and Willingdon Island, rather than by car; or negotiate for a private boat. At Kochi, if walking is too tiring, hire a rickshaw or rent a bicycle.

Pulleys and weights lower and raise the teak frames of these huge Chinese fishing nets.

The walk begins at **Mattancherry Jetty ❶**, where the shoreline has beautiful old tiled buildings with pastel-colored walls, many still used as go-downs (warehouses). Go to the main road and into the Mattancherry for **Dutch Palace ❷** (1557; *closed Fri.*), in fact built by the Portuguese for the Kochi Raja, Veera Keralavaram (r. 1537–1561), to help win a better trading deal; the Dutch merely renovated it in 1663. Inside, there are court dresses, paintings, and palanquins in the Coronation Room and India's most spectacular 16th- to 18th-century frescoes in the other rooms. Upstairs, a rich palette coats the walls with illustrations from the *Ramayana*; downstairs, the later paintings show Shiva and Mohini, and Krishna holding Mount Govardan and playing with the *gopies* (milkmaids).

Turn right on leaving the palace to stroll through an area called Jew Town, past stores

NOT TO BE MISSED:

Dutch Palace • Paradesi Synagogue • St. Francis Church • Chinese fishing nets

selling packaged spices. Turn right at the end, by the **Indian Pepper & Spice Trade Building**, and peek inside. You will find Synagogue Lane, and at the end is the **Paradesi Synagogue ❸** (*open Sun.–Thurs. 10 a.m.–noon & 2–5 p.m.; hours may vary*). Founded in 1568, then destroyed by the Portuguese, the synagogue was rebuilt in 1664 under Dutch approval and given its prized floor of Cantonese willow-pattern tiles in the mid-18th century by Ezekial Rahabi, who also gave the clock tower. As a result of emigration to Israel, the local Jewish community is so reduced that services are not always possible.

The rabbi depends upon Jewish visitors to make up the numbers, but he is often there to show them special copper plates. These record the grant of privileges to White Jews (see p. 62), made by King Ravi Varman (962–1020) to the Jewish merchant Joseph Rabban.

To walk to **Fort Cochin,** go back through Jew Town and along Calvathy (Bazaar) Road; then turn left on Tower Road to pass some old houses and lush walled gardens. Take a left on K.B. Jacob Road, and on the third block on your right is the **Kerala Kathakali Centre** ❹ for Kathakali performances (see p. 208). Backtracking on K. B. Jacob Road, and taking the first left will bring you to toward a parody of an English village: a lawn for cricket, surrounded by British merchants' houses and **St. Francis Church** ❺ (1546). The Portuguese Franciscan friars built the plain, massive structure to replace the earlier wooden one. Inside, the memorial on the far right is to Vasco da Gama (viceroy 1524), who died here on Christmas Day 1524; his body was later moved to Lisbon. There are also fine tombstones of Portuguese, Dutch, and British

traders. On Sundays, the congregation overflows and the church is cooled by *punkas,* the manual air-conditioning system.

Turn right out of the church and walk past some very handsome colonial traders' houses to the tip of Fort Cochin, finding a handful more on the right, shaded by giant rain trees. At the water's edge, the cantilevered **Chinese fishing nets** ❺ were introduced to Kerala by traders from the court of Kublai Khan. Kerala's distinct temple architecture, conical fishermen's hats, paper, and porcelain also evolved thanks to Chinese trading. A complicated system of pulleys and weights lowers and raises each of these huge teak frames.

Farther on, off Calvathy Road, is **Fort Cochin Jetty** ❼, where you can find boats back to Willingdon Island and Ernakulam, or sunset boat rides in the harbor.

▲	See also area map p. 189
▶	Mattancherry Jetty
⬌	2 miles (3 km)
⏲	2–3 hours
▶	Fort Cochin Jetty

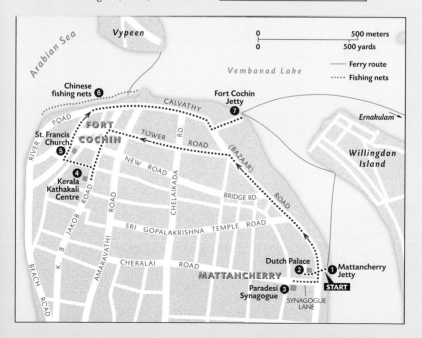

Kathakali Dance

The highly sophisticated and dramatic dance-drama Kathakali is one of Kerala's distinctive cultural traditions. Derived from a form of yoga, its name means "story-play" and the ritual of the performance begins with the application of elaborate makeup and costumes, whose colors are symbolic. The dance itself is a stylized religious pantomime recounting stories from the great epics and can last from dusk through the night. Shortened shows are designed for the tourist; they are of high quality, clearly explained, and give a good idea of the full-length performance.

For the real thing, though, ask if there's a performance happening in a temple, which you can attend for a few hours, or even leave and return later at the next stage. You can join local families to parade in the elephants, watch the makeup process, enjoy riotous drumming and piping, and then watch in the temple courtyard as each scene unfolds.

Vembanad Lake

189 C2

commercial port, which handles much of the state's phenomenal production of rubber, coconuts, tapioca, bananas, ginger, coir (coconut fiber), and cashews.

Ernakulam is a fast-growing, affluent city where flashy jewelry, silk, and other luxury boutiques thrive thanks to the wealth generated by spice-growers, rubber barons, and the many Keralites who work hard stints for high wages in the Middle East.

The Backwaters

The greatest pleasure in Kerala is to boat slowly through the shimmering backwaters, where you'll see kingfishers diving for prey, boats delivering their goods, boys splashing in the water, and women preparing meals in the shade of coconut palms.

Kerala's coastal region is more water than land in places. There are 44 rivers and their tributaries that meander their way to the Arabian Sea. Rivers, estuaries, deltas, and man-made canals interlink to create a vast, ancient, and labyrinthine water transportation system still used to carry spices, rubber, and rice. The longest canal stretches 228 miles (367 km) from the capital, Thiruvananthapuram (see pp. 211, 213), up to Tirur.

Backwater Culture: The bigger backwaters lie between Kochi (Cochin) and Kollam (Quilon), where **Vembanad Lake** spreads over 77 square miles (200 sq km). Known as Kuttanadu, this area is where life is spent on narrow slivers of land of dense tropical vegetation beside the water. Families live in brightly painted houses that appear to float on the water. Tiny grocery stores somehow squeeze on, too, as do tightly planted orchards of jackfruit trees, coconut palms, and mango trees, and each homestead's chickens, ducks, and cows. Everything from the morning newspaper to the sari chest is transported by boat.

Locals may skim through the canals using a thick paddle at a furious speed. Or they may punt their narrow dugout boats along with a tall pole, which they plunge into the water, push hard, and then slip out just before it disappears. On bigger boats, carrying coir, copra (dried coconut flesh), and piles of coconuts or cashew nuts, locals have small palmyra palm leaf huts as their onboard homes. Lazy boatmen tag on to motor ferries; others put up sails; still others carve the prow.

Coir and fishing are the main industries; you may see fishermen diving for freshwater

INSIDER TIP:

The heavy rains that fall during Kerala's monsoon season [late June–early Aug.] add to the beautiful scenery and are perfect for sleeping and lazing.

—HARISH VASUDEVAN
National Geographic Books

mussels or simply dangling a rod and line. Farmers must harvest any paddy growing before the monsoon, when the whole area is flooded—not surprisingly, since the water level of the canals is often higher than the fields on either side. When the monsoon ends in August or September, Keralites celebrate the **Onam festival,** believing it to mark the return of the benign, mythical King Mahabali from his exile in the underworld. Great boat pageants and races are held, which used to be between rival princes. The best are the snake boat races held near Alappuzha (Alleppey). Having slicked down their great *chundan vallam* (racing boats) with special oil to make them glide faster, a hundred oarsmen each hurtle through the water to great roars from the crowds. For the benefit of visitors, this and Thrissur's Puram festival (see p. 218) are now repeated in mid-January each year.

The Kerala backwaters enclose a world where bountiful nature and simple village life are in harmony.

NOTE: Entry to most of Kerala's temples is barred to non-Hindus.

Environmental Issues: The big threat to Kuttanad—apart from population growth and land reclamation—is African moss, a fast-growing water weed. The velvety leaf with its thick cushion of intertwining fibrous roots was introduced about 30 years ago and has already had a drastic effect on the ecosystem: The water can no longer be used for drinking or washing; fish and aquatic life have reduced in numbers because no sunlight reaches them; and boats cannot navigate rivulets and canals throttled by the vegetation.

Visiting the Backwaters: To see the backwaters, you can rent a converted country rice boat called a *kettuvallam*, modeled on the type that used to transport goods down to Kochi. It comes complete with crew, so you can opt out of "real life" to spend a few days being pampered in this watery paradise. If this is too exotic, rent a private boat and driver for the day from Alappuzha or Kottayam (the waterscape from Kochi is dull for the first two hours); you can be dropped off at one of two upscale waterside hotels at Kumarakom, overlooking Vembanad Lake. Or simply join locals on a public ferry from one town to another.

INSIDER TIP:

Along Kerala's coast, be sure to try the wide variety of seafood and fish, with *karimeen* [pearl spot fish] and traditional fish curry at the top of the list.

—HARISH VASUDEVAN
National Geographic Books

Kalarippayattu, Kerala's Martial Arts

One of the world's oldest martial arts traditions, possibly influenced by Japan, Kalarippayattu is a rigorous system of self-discipline and self-defense. *Kalari* means "training place," *payatt* means "practice" or "exercise." Experiencing an hour-long fast-moving demonstration in a mud-floored training hall is a truly breathtaking spectacle.

This ancient art is believed to have evolved in the second millennium B.C. It was an integral part of warring medieval Kerala's sociopolitical life, when systematic training was essential and the Kalari became a formal institution. Massage is key: Before practicing, the whole body is massaged in preparation, to cure problems and help its suppleness. The system has various styles, from the body-twisting and leaps of Maithari and the stick wielding Kolthari to the spectacular Ankathari exercise using a very long flexible sword. Practitioners of Kalarippayattu usually also practice yoga and follow the ayurvedic system, saying that together these can help us make a better, wiser, hardworking world.

You can see Kalarippayattu performed at various places in Kerala, but one of the best is E. N. S. Kalari *(enskalari.org.in)* in Nettoor, an area on the fringes of Kochi. Crash courses of one or two weeks or a month are available for interested parties, but committed training takes years.

Thiruvananthapuram

Kerala's seaside capital rambles over seven hills. Unlike other state capitals, it is laid-back and easygoing, with leafy parks and traditional red-tiled houses lining the wide, quiet streets.

When India won freedom in 1947, the princely states of Travancore and Cochin and British-administered Malabar were amalgamated to form Kerala, whose official language is Malayalam. Since then, the state has enjoyed a radical reputation. In 1957 it was the first in the world to democratically elect a communist government. Reforms led to a fairer distribution of wealth, much improved education and health care, but little industrial development. Today, its birthrate is India's lowest, its health is among the best, and its literacy rate is an impressive 93.9 percent, the highest in India.

Thiruvananthapuram, called Trivandrum when it was the capital of Travancore state, took its new name to honor the god Vishnu. It means "holy city of Anantha," and Anantha is the coiled snake on which Vishnu rests in the cosmic ocean. It is in this form, called Padmanabha, that the royal family of Travancore worshipped their principal deity. When Raja Marthanda Varma (r. 1729–1758) moved the capital here in 1750, he dedicated the whole state of Travancore to her and built the temple his descendants still control, the **Shri Padmanabhaswamy Temple,** which stands in the historic heart of the city. Although

Visitors to Kerala can watch a demonstration of Kalarippayattu, rigorous martial arts training.

non-Hindus cannot go inside, you'll find the surrounding area of interest. Walk around the temple, and at the front see the faithful bathing in the tank or buying souvenirs and *puja* offerings. Here, too, you may see students practicing the special Kerala martial arts exercise, Kalarippayattu, in the early morning.

The Travancore rajas moved into nearby **Kuthiramalika Palace** (*Chalai Bazaar Rd., closed Mon., $*) when they left Padmanabhapuram (see pp. 213–214). They still live here, visiting their great temple early each morning, but have opened some rooms to the public. The polished floors, delicately carved wooden screens, and royal crystal are superb treasures; see especially the fine murals and columns carved as rampant horses.

Thiruvananthapuram

🗺 189 C1

Visitor Information

✉ Tourist Information Centre, International Airport Counter

☎ 047/1250-2298

✉ Domestic Airport Counter

☎ 047/1250-1085

incredibleindia.org

✉ State Tourism Office, Park View

☎ 047/1232-1132

keralatourism.org

India's Spice Box

Spices have been a source of great wealth to India, and they are essential to every Indian meal—and have been for centuries, even if the *masala* (blend) varies from region to region. Spices give each dish its distinctive flavor and character. The meat, fish, or vegetables are added after the spices have cooked a little.

From early times, Greeks, Romans, Arabs, and Chinese have paid highly for powerful spices to perfume themselves, improve room odors, help preserve food, act as medicines, and disguise the pungent smells of rancid meat. Southern India was the chief source, and prices could compare with gold.

INSIDER TIP:

There is a fantastic spice store in Karol Bagh in New Delhi. It is called Roopak [roopaksince 1958.com]. I buy my spices from there when I am in India.

—MONICA BHIDE
National Geographic contributor

In the 15th century the urge to break the Arab and Venetian stranglehold on the spice trade led to Christopher Columbus's arrival in America, while looking for a westerly route to India, and Vasco da Gama's discovery of the sea route around Africa. From then on, the Portuguese, Dutch, French, and British began to trade directly with India.

Pepper, once known as black gold, is the king of spices, and Kerala produces 95 percent of India's pepper crop. All over Kerala you can see the pepper vines growing up trees shading other crops, and peppercorns drying in the sun. Most pepper is grown alongside cashew, coffee, coconut, areca nut, tapioca, banana, and rice crops on homesteads lying between the high mountains and the coast.

In fact, most of India's spices are grown in the south of the country on small plantations.

More than 60 percent of India's **cardamom** is grown on the high Kerala hills, alongside tea, coffee, and rubber, and in mountain forests. The seeds sprout from the base of a big, broad-leafed bush and are picked by women who dry them and keep a few for use as aphrodisiacs. **Ginger** is part of the same plant family, and about 70 percent of the world's requirement is grown here; it is used in food and as a digestive medicine. *Haldi* **(turmeric),** another rhizome, is mostly grown in neighboring Andhra Pradesh. As well as being used in cooking, it is used in medicine as an antiseptic and rubbed onto babies' and women's skin to soften and lighten it. Thanks to such attractive properties, the domestic market consumes 98 percent of the 350,000 tons (371,350 metric tonnes) that are produced in India every year.

Buying these and other spices in the local markets is a lot of fun—depending on the spice, they may be sold whole or already ground up. Did you know that **nutmeg** is a fruit, from which we get mace? The kernel of the fruit is the nutmeg that we use in cooking; the strands of mace are wrapped around it. **Cinnamon** is the inner bark of the lateral shoots of pruned cinnamon trees, and it is sold in tightly curled quills. **Chilies** come in all sizes: The big ones are eaten as vegetables or are crushed to make mild paprika; the small ones have the "fire" in them.

Cashew nuts, most often ground and used in the gentle sauces of Mughal dishes, grow in a most interesting way. Just one pair of nuts grows outside each large, yellow, bitter fruit. When harvested, the nuts must then be laboriously shelled and skinned by hand, then sorted according to size—the reason for their high cost.

Beyond the old quarter, at the far end of M. G. Road, lie the **Public Gardens,** 64 acres (26 ha) of lawns and trees and the home to the **Arts & Crafts (Napier) Museum** *(closed Mon., $)*. Inside R. F. Chisholm's brightly colored 1880 brick building with stained-glass windows, there are fine Chola bronzes and Kerala wood carvings, masks and puppets, gold jewelry, musical instruments, and various royal memorabilia. The **Shri Chitra Art Gallery** *(closed Mon., $)* is also in the gardens, as well as the **Natural History Museum** *(closed Mon., $)*, whose models of the Kerala *taravad* (manor house) and traditional *nalekettu* (four-sided courtyard) house show you what to look out for while driving through the countryside.

Padmanabhapuram Palace:

Although this palace is in Tamil Nadu state, it makes sense to visit the Travancore rulers' former capital from Thiruvananthapuram. The splendid palace, one of southern India's finest royal buildings, dates from 1550, although Raja Matanda Varma (1729–1758) remodeled much of it. The teak rooms with their deep, overhanging roofs are arranged around four courtyards and enriched with elaborate carving, rosewood furniture displaying a strong Chinese trading influence, and spectacular murals, superior even to those in Mattancherry's Dutch Palace (see p. 206). Furnishings range from mica windowpanes to granite milk coolers.

During your tour with the obligatory and informative guide, note the delicate perforated screens, foliated brackets, and *dhatura*-flower pendants. The many rooms include a carved open hall, where the king addressed his people. The upstairs council chamber has an ingenious air-conditioning system using herbs soaked in water, broad-seated chairs for ministers to sit on cross-legged, and a floor gleaming with polish achieved by mixing burned coconut, sticky sugarcane extract, egg white, lime, charcoal, and sand. The tower's top room is reserved for the god, complete with bed and murals. There is also the **Ekandamandapam** (Lonely Place), the oldest section reserved for rituals for the goddess Durga.

Padmanabha-puram Palace

▲ 189 C1

✉ 39 miles (64 km) SE of Thiruvananthapuram in Thuckalay

🕐 Closed Mon. Best to avoid weekends

💲 $

FESTIVALS: Arat festivals, March–April, Oct.–Nov.: activities and street processions during two ten-day festivals

In marketplaces around Kerala and across India, sackfuls of precious and fragrant seeds and pods await cooks.

Kovalam

189 C1

Varkala

189 C2

33 miles
(53 km) N of
Thiruvanantha-
puram, 12 miles
(19 km) S of
Kollam

It has a stone-columned dance hall and includes the bedroom of the raja, whose bed was made from medicinal woods. The whole ensemble brings to life the very special Travancore royal house, where succession was matriarchal through the eldest sister's eldest son; the ruler did not marry, to prevent his love being diverted from his state to his children.

The empty beaches punctuated with cliffs or fishing villages make wonderful places for refreshing and peaceful walks and a quiet swim. The two areas where beach life has developed are Kovalam and, to a lesser degree, Varkala; both are reached from Thiruvananthapuram.

To seek out the best of **Kovalam**, go to quiet **Samudra**

Visitors are guaranteed to find peace and natural beauty on the idyllic Lakshadweep Islands.

Kerala's Beaches & Lakshadweep Islands

If it is time to chill out, you have several choices. Very little of the long, sandy shoreline of the Malabar coast, stretching 342 miles (550 km) from Goa down to Kanya Kumari, is developed by Western standards. Unlike Goa (see pp. 190–201), Kerala has few beachside hotels or cafés, and locals may well be upset by scanty swimsuits. For a complete escape, head for Bangaram Island.

Beach, watch the fishing boats on **Hawah Beach,** discover restaurants on **Lighthouse Beach** (with a nice afternoon walk down to Vizhinjam village), and find peace on **Pozhikkara Beach.**

Varkala is quite different from Kovalam, though it may well change. This pilgrimage center draws Hindus to the **Janardhana Swamy Temple** overlooking the sea, where they pay respect to their ancestors; after 5 p.m. non-Hindus may enter. A lane next to it leads down to the beach, which so far retains its charm.

You can enjoy its white sands and promontory walks. There are also natural springs, the local town's market, and, if you like, you can take an elephant ride into the nearby forest.

Lakshadweep Islands:

Coming here is still a total escape because foreign tourism is tightly controlled. To conserve the islands' culture, only Bangaram Island is open to non-Indians. Visitor numbers are limited, prices are high, and there is nothing much to do except relax. A snorkel and mask are essentials.

As you fly in from Kochi, look down on the 36 coral islands lying in the azure Arabian Sea between 137 miles (220 km) and 273 miles (439 km) off the Kerala coast. They are India's smallest Union Territory. Just 52,000 people live here on the ten habitable islands, with Kavaratti the capital and Agatti the airport. Most inhabitants are

INSIDER TIP:

If you want to visit the Lakshadweep Islands, you will have to fly from Kochi, or alternatively book a cruise through a travel agent.

—LOUISE NICHOLSON
National Geographic author

Sunni Muslims, speak Malayalam, and live by fishing and coconut cultivation. Other crops here include jackfruit, banana, and wild almond.

Bangaram Island, with a resort that is currently closed, is reached by a two-hour boat ride from Agatti, 5 miles (8 km) away: Watch the boatman carefully avoiding the coral in the shallow sea. This beautiful teardrop-shaped island is surrounded by white sands and guaranteed warm calm water—about 79°F (26°C), perfect for spending hours watching the exotic underwater world. ∎

Lakshadweep Islands
🄰 189 A2 & A3
lakshadweeptourism
.nic.in

Ayurvedic Medicine

The ancient medicinal philosophy called *ayurved* has been practiced in India for at least 5,000 years, especially in Kerala. Ayurved considers that disease reveals a body that is totally out of balance. Thus the imbalance, not the disease, is treated. First, you must accept that the body is controlled by three forces: *pitta* (the sun's force over digestion and metabolism); *kapha* (the moon's cooling force over the body's organs); and *vata* (the wind's effect on movement and the nervous system). Diagnosis is by considering physical complaints, emotions, family background, and daily habits. Treatment may involve herbal preparations and yoga exercises. Ayurvedic doctors and pharmacies throughout India often have training in both Western and ayurvedic systems, and can help tackle long-term problems such as migraines and asthma. To find out more, visit one of the many ayurvedic centers, such as C. V. N. Kalari Sangam *(near Shri Padmanabhaswamy Temple)* in Thiruvananthapuram or Kalari Kovilakom in the Kerala hills, the most serious of the Casino hotel group's ayurvedic facilities *(cghearth.com)*.

More Places to Visit in Kerala

As Kerala is so long and thin, the suggestions below are arranged in two sections, each with a good central base.

Kozhikode & Northern Kerala

Bekal: Here you will find northern Kerala's best preserved coastal **fort:** Grand ramparts, walls, and bastions (17th century) were built by Shivappa Nayaka of Nagar and later taken by Haider Ali in 1763. 189 B3 ✉ 49 miles (79 km) N of Kannur, 37 miles (60 km) S of Mangalore

Kannur: Kannur (Cannanore) was the capital of the powerful Ali Rajas, Kerala's only Muslim royal dynasty. They used the massive triangular Fort St. Angelo, built by the Portuguese (1505) in their 1770s alliance with Tipu Sultan against the British. 189 B3 ✉ 14 miles (23 km) N of Thalassery, 57 miles (92 km) N of Kozhikode

Kozhikode: Kozhikode (Calicut) is a thriving, modern town trading in spices, timber, coffee, and tea. It is the former capital of the Samutiri rulers, better known as the Zamorins. They had close ties with Arab Muslim traders, who equipped their army and were threatened by the Portuguese, then the English, French, and Danes. See the **Tali Temple** and mosques with multi-tiered tile roofs: **Mithqalpalli** (16th century), **Jama Masjid,** and **Mucchandipalli** (both 15th century). 189 B3

Taliparamba: Two of Kerala's finest temples are here, both founded in the ninth century but mostly rebuilt in the 16th and 17th centuries: **Rajarajeshvara Temple,** in town, and **Krishna Temple,** which stands in a pretty grove 1 mile (1.6 km) to the south and has beautiful friezes recounting the Krishna story. 189 B3 ✉ 14 miles (23 km) N of Kannur

Thalassery: Attractive coastal Thalassery (Tellicherry) is where the British set up a factory in 1683. See their impressive **fort** (1708) and overgrown **cemetery,** the Mappila traders' traditional **warehouses** and **homes,** and the Kerala-style **Odathilpalli Mosque** (17th–18th century). 189 B3 ✉ 34 miles (55 km) N of Kozhikode

Around Kochi & Ernakulam

Alappuzha: This pretty, affluent town, with enough bridges to make it an Indian Venice, owes its character to vigorous development by the Travancore rulers after they took it over in 1762. Merchants flocked to Alappuzha (Alleppey) to use the new warehouses, and a shipbuilding industry blossomed, boosting trade with Bombay and Calcutta. 189 C2 ✉ 35 miles (56 km) S of Kochi, 52 miles (84 km) N of Kollam

Angamali: Angamali has unusual 17th- and 18th-century Christian monuments: baroque **St. George's, St. Mary's,** with its nave murals showing the Last Judgment

Mahouts ride atop gold-caparisoned elephants at the Puram and Elephant festivals.

and Christ telling St. Thomas to go to India, and, at Kanjoor village, another **St. Mary's,** whose murals curiously include the defeat of Tipu Sultan (see p. 223). Ⓐ 189 C2 ✉ 20 miles (32 km) N of Ernakulam

Cheruthuruthi: This town is home to the **Kerala Kalamandalam,** the state's finest academy for classic Keralas Kathakali and other performing arts, such as Kutiyattam (an archaic kind of Kathakali). The academy was founded in 1930 by the Malayali poet Vallathol, and visitors are permitted to watch the fascinating training sessions and performances in the beautiful theater. Ⓐ 189 C2 ✉ 18 miles (29 km) N of Thrissur ☎ 049/262-2418

Guruvayur: At Kerala's most popular pilgrimage town, you can join pilgrims to enter the **Krishan Temple** (but not the sanctuary), then drive 2 miles (3 km) east to see the temple's elephants in the compound of the mansion at **Punnathoor Kotta.** Ⓐ 189 C2 ✉ 18 miles (29 km) N of Thrissur

Kayankulam: Kayankulam's **Krishna-puram Palace** is less ornate than Padmanabhapuram (see pp. 213–214) but just as interesting. It was probably built by Ramayya Dalawa, who was governor of northern Travancore under Rama Varma (1758–1798); one room off the small interior courts has a beautiful mural of Vishnu riding on Garuda. Ⓐ 189 C2 ✉ 30 miles (48 km) S of Alappuzha 🕒 Palace closed Mon.

Kodungallur: There's little to see, but Kodungallur (Cranganore) is historically very important. It was from here that Arabs and Romans imported spices to Alexandria and Oman, and that early Jews, Christians, and Muslims arrived to make their first settlements in India. Christians claim St. Thomas arrived at Pallipuram, near here; Muslims claim that Malik bin Dinar, an Arab

missionary, founded the Cheraman Mosque here in 630. Ⓐ 189 C2 ✉ 32 miles (51 km) N of Ernakulam

Kollam: A lively town between the sea and Ashtamudi Lake, Kollam (Quilon) was already a port of call for seventh-century Chinese merchants. Traces of its Portuguese, Dutch, Travancore, and British administrators can be found around the town, attesting to Kerala's cosmopolitan history. **Ganapati Temple** stands opposite **Old Tobacco Godown,** while the baroque **cathedral** is a reminder that Kollam is probably the oldest Catholic diocese in southern India, established in 1328. Also of interest is a **Syrian Church** (1519) with unusual 18th-century murals, the **Valiakada Arikade mosque,** and the **Travelers Bungalow,** built as the British Residency. Ⓐ 189 C2 ✉ 53 miles (85 km) S of Alappuzha, 44 miles (71 km) N of Thiruvananthapuram

Kottayam: This affluent, charming town lies on the Minachil River, which connects

---

Kerala's Compassionate Living Saint, Amma

Known worldwide for her humanitarian services, Amma was born in 1953 in a fishing village near Kollam. By the age of five she was composing devotional songs and displaying a special compassion. "An unbroken stream of love flows from me towards all beings in the cosmos," she later said. "That is my inborn nature." With the power of a warm embrace, she has blessed and consoled more than 25 million people—simple spiritual healing on a massive scale. You can visit the headquarters of her ashram, Amritapuri, located at her village (about two hours' drive from Kochi); non-Indians need to register at *amritapuri.org.*

with Vembanad Lake. Most of Kerala's hill produce arrives here before continuing to Kochi and Alappuzha, often by boat. You can stroll around for a few hours, catch water buses, watch life, and maybe visit the **Syrian Church** in Puthenangadi area. Kottayam is the headquarters of Kerala's Orthodox Syrian and Roman Catholic communities. ⚊ 189 C2 ✉ 45 miles (72 km) S of Ernakulam

Munnar: A spectacular drive along a country road follows the ridge of the hills, with panoramic views of rolling tea gardens on either side. British tea, coffee, and cardamom planters created this mini–hill station at 5,000 feet (1,524 m), centered on the **High Range Club** and **Protestant Church** (1910), which appear unchanged since their establishment. While here, go to **Lockhart Gap** for breathtaking views over the Anaimali Hills; serious hikers can tackle **Anamudi,** southern India's highest peak at 8,838 feet (2,694 m). From here you can visit Periyar, or continue through the hills to Kodaikanal (see p. 278). ⚊ 189 C2 ✉ 139 miles (224 km) E of Ernakulam

Periyar National Park: After a beautiful drive up through the Cardamom Hills, you have 270 square miles (700 sq km) of hilltop deciduous woodland and a huge artificial lake to explore. Established in 1934, this is one of the best sanctuaries for watching wild elephants, especially at either sunrise and sunset. The sanctuary also provides visitors with excellent forest walks and bird-watching for traveling nature lovers. ⚊ 189 C2 ✉ 74 miles (119 km) E of Kottayam, 99 miles (159 km) W of Madurai in Tamil Nadu

Syrian–Christian Churches: A rich and rewarding day trip inland from Kochi visits three churches; all of them welcome visitors to join their services where singing is lusty and rituals mix Hindu and Christian traditions. The **Forane Church of the Holy Ghost** at Muttuchira has a granite courtyard cross and

a terrific carved and gilded altarpiece. At nearby Kaduthuruthi the baroque **St. Mary's** was rebuilt after the Synod of Diamper in 1599, reuniting the Syrio-Malabar and Roman churches. See its very elaborate gilded altar (18th century) and the brass flagpole and granite cross in the courtyard. Continue to Palai, seat of a bishop of the Syrian Catholic church. The old **Cathedral of St. Thomas** (1002) is one of Kerala's grandest churches, with magnificent gilded altars. ⚊ 189 C2

Thiruvalla, Kaviyur, & Chengannur: Although only Hindus can enter these three grand and elaborate temples, non-Hindus can glimpse them from outside. First, Thiruvalla's **Vallabha Temple** is one of Kerala's largest temple complexes, while its simple St. Thomas Church shows distinctive Kerala Christian rituals. North of Kaviyur (and its fine Mahadeva temple) is a Chera period **cave temple** (eighth to ninth century), with fully rounded figures including a proud chieftain. Chengannur's **Narashimha Temple** also has exceptionally beautiful woodwork. Much of Kerala's renowned brass is made at nearby **Mannar;** ask at any shop to visit a big atelier. ⚊ 189 C2 **Thiruvalla** ✉ 17 miles (27 km) S of Kottayam

Thrissur: Thrissur (Trichur) is famous for its magnificent **Puram festival** (April–May), when richly decorated elephants parade through the crowded streets, accompanied by music and fireworks. Their final destination is the huge **Vadakkunnatha Temple** (16th–17th century) with its walled courtyards, tiered roofs, dancing hall, and several shrines. Thrissur was the Kochi rulers' second city, and the museum complex reflects its rich history. There are superb bronzes in the **Art Museum** and other interesting artifacts in the **Archaeological Museum** (closed Mon.) and **State museums.** ⚊ 189 C2 ✉ 43 miles (69 km) N of Ernakulam

Where Hindu and Muslim kingdoms rose and fell, leaving grand
monuments strewn across the dramatic, still rural landscape

The Deccan

Piles of brightly colored, finely ground
dyes in a Mysore market

The Deccan

Traveling through the Deccan, which comprises most of Karnataka and Andhra Pradesh states, can be demanding, but the region's magnificent monuments and stunning landscapes make it one of the most rewarding areas of India to visit. You encounter a succession of utterly different, wondrous sights.

There are two focal points: Bangalore and Hyderabad, the capitals of Kannada-speaking Karnataka and Telegu-speaking Andhra Pradesh states. Bangalore, once an elegant British town now a powerful state capital, is India's Silicon Valley. Hyderabad, thick with the remnants of its royal Muslim Qutb Shahi and Nizam rulers, has followed Bangalore's lead and exploded into the global economy.

Outside these great cities lies a challenging, rural landscape. The great Godavari, Krishna, and Kaveri Rivers and their tributaries, which all empty into the Bay of Bengal, feed the rich soil of the Deccan Plateau, where agriculture accounts for 70 percent of both states' employment. On your travels you will see fields of rice, ground nuts, chilies, cotton, and sugarcane, plus Andhra Pradesh's tobacco and Karnataka's mulberry bushes for its silk industry. One village will be sleepy, the next in the midst of a festival; a single goatherd and his flock will block a road; an empty field will transform into a livestock fair where cattle have been daubed with pink polka dots.

In the west, you can visit British hill stations nestling in the lush Nilgiri Hills and view the protected forests and wildlife of three adjoining national parks. If you feel a lack of romance, you have the palaces of Mysore. To the north, forgotten empires have left some of India's finest temples, from the earliest efforts at Aihole, which imitated wooden structures, to the final glories of Vijayanagar.

North and eastward again, the rulers of the great Bahmani kingdom, Vijayanagar's rivals, built citadels at Gulbarga and Bidar. Then they broke up into rival sultanates, decking their cities with romantic, bulbous-domed mosques and tombs, while facing the inevitable onslaught of Mughal expansion from the north. Finally, there are rarely visited sites along Andhra Pradesh's beautiful 621 miles (999 km) of coast near Tirupati and around Vishakhapatnam port and the Godavari and Krishna Deltas.

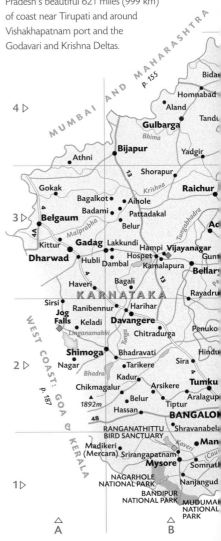

Amid all this, heroes abound. You can follow the stories of Vikramaditya, the eighth-century ruler of the Chalukyas, and Krishnadeveraya, who later ruled the Vijayanagar kingdom. You can also see evidence of the enlightened 18th-century expansionism of Haider Ali and his son, Tipu Sultan, which resulted in their clashes with the British. ■

Area of map detail

New Delhi

NOT TO BE MISSED:

Cocktails at Amba Vilas
Palace **227–228**

Watching elephants in Nagarhole
National Park **230–231**

The morning sun illuminating
Badami's cave sculptures **232–233**

Bicycling around Vijayanagar's
stone monuments **234**

Whispering in Gol Gumbaz gallery
before the crowds come **240**

Shopping for Karnataka silk **242**

Staying on a coffee plantation in
Kodagu (Coorg) **243**

Buying pearls in Hyderabad **249**

Karnataka

Karnataka's dramatic landscape of barren hills, bountiful paddy fields, and leafy coffee plantations serves as the backdrop for stunning monuments of great Hindu and Muslim dynasties,
whose struggles for power survive in local tales. Dynasties rose and fell from the 7th to the
18th centuries, landmark events were the defeat, in 1565, of the last great Hindu empire,
Vijayanagar, and the death of the enlightened hero Tipu Sultan in 1799.

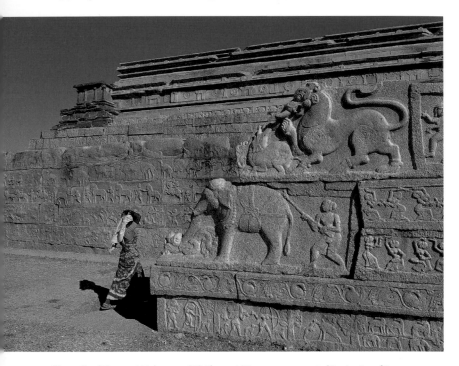

The walls of the great Mahanavami Platform at Vijayanagar are coated in vivacious friezes.

Karnataka's capital is the dynamic city of Bangalore, where you may hear just as much English spoken as the official state language, Kannada. As India's foremost center for IT (see sidebar opposite), office buildings, luxurious hotels, and quality shops make a stark contrast with Mysore, just three hours' drive away. This slow-paced historical city is dominated by grand and fanciful palaces.

Either city makes an ideal stop between visiting the national parks of Nagarhole, Bandipur, and Mudumalai.

But less than 30 percent of the state's population lives in the cities. As you cross countryside irrigated by the great river systems of the Kaveri and the Krishna, you cross the high Deccan Plateau that gives Karnataka its name: It is Kannada for "lofty land."

Bangalore

Once known for its fresh air, trees, and parks, which brought relief to visitors from the hot upper plains, Bangalore, capital of Karnataka state, is now a thundering, commercial city whose climate is no longer so benign. Bangalore's new name, Bengalum, is little used so far.

The city was founded by Kempe Gowda, a lord of the Vijayanaga empire, who built a mud fort here in 1537. The Wodeyars of Mysore took the city in 1687. Haider Ali (r. 1761–1782) took Bangalore in 1758 and three years later usurped the Wodeyar throne. Keeping Mysore and nearby Srirangapatnam as

men, with its superb light cavalry, Telugu marksmen, and herds of huge, white Deccan cattle. The army was used to win ports on the Kerala coast, aiming to crush the *peshwas* of Pune and the Nizams of Hyderabad and to establish trade with Arabia and Persia. Far from being the despot painted by the British, Tipu was imitating their mercantile and expansionist ideology, which is why Arthur Wellesley (later Duke of Wellington) needed to defeat him.

After Tipu's death (see p. 243) in 1799, Bangalore became a flourishing British garrison town and continued to be important up to independence. The British cantonment had everything a

Bangalore

🗺 220 B2

Visitor Information

✉ India Tourist Office, KFC Bldg., 48 Church St.

☎ 080/2558-5417

incredibleindia.org

✉ State Tourist Office, No. 49, 2nd fl., West Entrance, Khanija Bhawan, Race-course Rd.

☎ 080/2235-2828, toll-free: 800-425-1414

karnatakatourism .org

karnataka.com/ tourism/bangalore

Information Technology

Bangalore is India's information technology (IT) capital and the world's third most important IT city. It is also India's software capital, with exports growing at 46 percent a year. IT has made Bangalore a more international city than even Mumbai. Soaring glass skyscrapers indicate a sensational new affluence. Indian IT brains no longer head to the United States: They set up their own companies in India. Bangalore is the headquarters of TCS, Wipro, and Infosys.

Many multinationals today find they need offices in Bangalore. Meanwhile, their Indian counterparts buy and expand Western IT companies and stock their offices with Indian-made, not American, equipment, proven comparable to the products of the best U.S. brands. Hyderabad, with an enlightened state government, is following Bangalore's lead; it has developed "Cyberabad" for its IT and outsourcing companies, including the Madhapur and Kondapur campuses.

---

his base, he made Bangalore a crossroads for east–west southern trading and for exporting cotton and other crops from this rich agricultural area. He and his son, Tipu Sultan (r. 1782–1799), whose palace remains are well worth visiting, could thus raise huge taxes. These funded the famous Mysore army of 60,000

homesick servant of the empire could wish for: horse racing, tennis courts, a pretty park, Victorian Gothic bungalows with herbaceous bordered gardens, the obligatory statue of the Queen-Empress Victoria, and grand clubs for cards, croquet, snooker (a game similar to billiards), and lavish parties.

(continued on p. 226)

NOTE: Bangalore's new airport is 22 miles (35 km) north of the city, whereas the industrial park Electronics City, the Silicon Valley of Bangalore, is to the south. Traffic is usually heavy, so business-people should plan their time carefully.

A Drive Around Old Colonial Bangalore

Hire a driver for a morning or afternoon to explore British life in Bangalore and to glimpse the town's past as southern India's elegant, relaxed garden city. It is best to go on Saturday or Sunday, when there is less traffic.

Start by going to the **High Court ❶** (Attara Kacheri), a classical, arcaded stone building, painted Pompeian red and originally built in 1868 as the public offices. A statue of Bangalore's commissioner from 1834 to 1861, Sir Mark Cubbon, stands in front. The jacaranda trees to the left add a cloud of contrasting mauve when they blossom in springtime.

Across a ceremonial road that is often the scene of farmers' union protests, the imposing polished granite **Vidhana Soudha** (1956) (see pp. 226–227) stands as the symbol of the fulfillment of the Kannada-speaking peoples' long ambition—to unite in one state. K. Hanu-manthaiah, chief minister when the building was completed, said this "people's palace" would "reflect the power and dignity of the people." Certainly, it is India's largest civic structure. Its design takes inspiration from Karnataka's tem-ple architecture: See the projecting balconies, the curving eaves, and the temple-like, curving towers that are added to the huge wings.

Now drive through **Cubbon Park,** almost 300 acres (121 ha) laid out by Cubbon in 1864. You may wish to get out for a stroll near the **Seshadri Iyer Memorial Hall ❷** (1913), built to house the public library and named to honor a prime minister of Mysore state. Leave the park at the southern corner and go up R. R. M. Roy Road to glimpse the timeless, stucco **Bangalore Club ❸** *(members only),* with some nice old houses nearby. Return along Kasturba Gandhi Road to find three public buildings on the left. The middle one is the **Government Museum ❹** (1876), whose sculpture gallery, hero stones, and Mysore school miniature paintings are worth a look.

NOT TO BE MISSED:

Vidhana Soudha • Cubbon Park
• Russell Market

At the far end of Kasturba Gandhi Road, an incongruous trio of **statues ❺** stands at the main gate of Cubbon Park: a memorial statue of Queen Victoria (1906), and statues of Edward VII and Mahatma Gandhi.

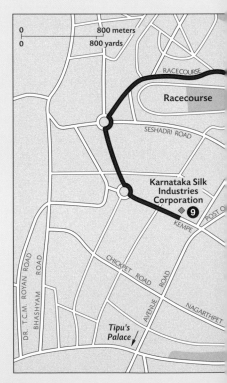

Turn right along Mahatma Gandhi Road to see the neoclassical, domed **St. Mark's Cathedral** (1812) on the right. Then turn left to find the Victorian Gothic **St. Andrew's Church** ❻ on Cubbon Road (1867). Drive past the church facade and down to **Russell Market** ❼, built so that British *memsahibs* could shop in safety after a scandal concerning a moneylender and an abortion.

From here, drive up across Infantry Road and turn right back on Cubbon Road again to pass the palatial, whitewashed **Raj Bhavan** ❽ (1831), built as the British Residency, and go down Racecourse Road to the end. Turn left, and you will find **Kempe Gowda Road,** an excellent place for fixed-price silk stores such as **Karnataka Silk Industries Corporation** ❾ (KSIC; *ksicsilk.com*). Helpful assistants advise on the lengths needed for your requirements and the suitability of the various silk weaves—crêpe

INSIDER TIP:

To instill some calm into a hectic Bangalore day, why not stop by a few street vendors to put jasmine in your hair, eat a green coconut, and drink *badam* [almond] milk, which is flavored with saffron.

—SARAH WHITE
National Geographic grantee

de chine, georgette, chiffon, soft and spun silk, stonewashed and raw silk.

If you are feeling inspired by this drive, and are energetic enough, you can continue on to see Tipu's Palace and Lalbagh Botanical Gardens (see p. 226).

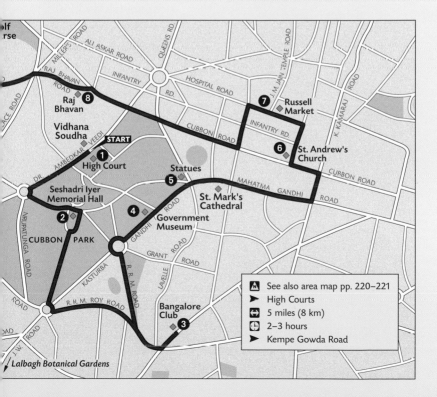

These British buildings and the city's two green spaces—**Cubbon Park** *(M. G. Rd.)* and the **Race Course** *(Racecourse Rd., tel 080/2226-2391)*—give Bangalore its spaciousness and lingering elegance today. It may have high-rises, new affluence, a population of almost eight million, and top-quality stores, but you can easily imagine colonial times, not long ago, when servants in white livery and gloves served cucumber sandwiches and chili-cheese toast to *memsahibs* wearing flower-printed dresses. Try driving through Cubbon Park or visiting the High Court or one of the many churches. Do visit **Lalbagh Botanical Gardens** *(080/2657-1925)*, the 240-acre (97 ha) expanse founded by Haider Ali in 1760 and still the site for extravagant British-style flower shows. And do not miss the **National Gallery of Modern Art**

(Manikyavelu Mansion, Palace Rd., closed Mon., $, tel 080/2234-2338, ngmaindia.gov.in), where shows on loan from its parent museum in Delhi fill some 20 rooms of a whitewashed Raj-style mansion.

It is significant that the Karnataka government chose to site its huge neo-Dravadian-style granite **Vidhana Soudha** (Secretariat and State Legislature) right in the

INSIDER TIP:

Be sure to read the local newspapers. Many list current food festivals, religious celebrations, museum openings, and, of course, great new shopping places.

—MONICA BHIDE
National Geographic contributor

Completed in 1912, Amba Vilas Palace is a fantastic representation of the Indo-Saracenic style.

Dussehra (Dassera)

Mysore celebrates with pageantry this ten-day festival *(Sept.–Oct.)* of the triumph of good over evil that harks back to the annual extravaganza at Vijayanagar. It is symbolized in the goddess Chamundeswari's (Durga's) triumph over the demon buffalo Mahishasura, rather than the northern India version, of Rama's triumph over Ravana. Vijayadashami marks the finale: Caparisoned elephants, horses, and cavalry, plus some movie-starlike deities, parade to the Banni Mantap, and dramatic fireworks end it all. A cultural festival runs in parallel to honor Saraswati, goddess of the arts, offering the special Carnatic music and dance of Karnataka in the palace's Durbar Hall and grounds—and some *yakshagana* dance-drama. The Mysore royals would hold their Mysore Week at this time. Events included horse races at the racetrack and an extravagant outing to witness the *khedda* (elephant roundup) in the forest at Nagarhole (see pp. 230–231).

British area, opposite the Law Courts. Winston Churchill, who always opposed India's desired independence, would doubtless have taken this as flattery. He came to live here in 1937 as a young soldier and wrote happy letters home describing his huge bungalow with its 2 acres (1 ha) of gardens, rose beds, and deep verandas wreathed in purple bougainvillea. He and two of his friends kept about 30 horses and devoted themselves to the serious purpose of life: polo.

Mysore

The Wodeyars, originally governors of southern Karnataka under the Vijayanaga emperors, rose to be rulers of Mysore and to determine its delightful character, preserved today partly because the city does not have an airport. The former royal family still lives in a corner of the vast, city-center Amba Vilas Palace, the place to begin exploring the city.

Extravagant, fantastical **Amba Vilas Palace** (1897–1912), also known as the Maharaja's Palace, was designed by Henry Irwin and outstrips most Rajasthan palaces. It takes most of a morning just to follow the route around it and to see the outbuildings. The Wodeyars built a fort here in 1524 while governors, but they moved away when they became rulers. Tipu later razed Mysore, intending to rebuild it; when the British reinstated the young Krishnaraja III as a puppet Wodeyar ruler in 1801, Mysore still needed rebuilding.

After a fire in 1897, Irwin was awarded the commission to rebuild. He created an Indo-Saracenic palace that manages to be simultaneously imperial, traditional, and progressive. On your way through, details to look for include the maharajas' *howdah* (seat used to ride elephants), encrusted with 24-carat gold, and the eight enormous bronze tigers by Robert William Colton. In the octagonal wedding hall, see the long friezes recording the 1930 Dussehra procession, the cast-iron pillars shipped out from Glasgow, and the Belgian stained-glass

Mysore

🗺 220 B1

Visitor Information

✉ State Tourist Office, Yatri Niwas, J. L. B. Rd.

☎ 082/1242-3492

karnatakatourism .org

mysore.org.uk

Amba Vilas Palace

✉ Entry on S side only; shoes and cameras must be deposited before entering; socks permitted

peacocks. In the Durbar Hall are whole avenues of carved pillars, huge inlaid doors, walls coated in arabesques, and a Mughal-style floor. Before leaving the compound, explore the rooms of the older palace, now a museum, and some of the old temples. The palace is illuminated by tiny lights on Sundays and festivals in the evening between 7 and 9 p.m.

INSIDER TIP:

If you travel from Mysore to Wayanad, known for its coffee and tea plantations, the route goes through the Mysore Forest, where, if driving at dusk, there is a good chance of seeing wild elephants.

—HARISH VASUDEVAN
National Geographic Books

Nearby, part of **Jaganmohan Palace** (1900) was transformed into a museum of musical instruments and miniature paintings in 1915 by Krishnaraja IV, who followed tradition in his enlightened and progressive policies, in his energetic building program for his model state, and in his loyalty to the British. You will find the **Sri Chamarajendra Art Gallery** (*closed Wed.*) at the back of the building, where Lord Curzon attended Krishnaraja IV's coronation; do not miss the murals of royal pastimes.

Near Amba Vilas are the **City Corporation Offices** and the **Public Offices.** Up Siyaji Rao Road are hospitals, schools, and the grand **Government House.** On Kalidasa Road, the **Manasagangotri Folklore Museum** (*Jayalakshmi Vilas Mansion, closed Sat. p.m.–Sun.*) has wonderful wooden *bhuta* figures from Mekkekattu (see p. 204). **Dvaraja Market** has sacks of flowers, pyramids of spices, neat arrangements of polished fruits and vegetables, and piles of fresh herbs.

Chamundi Hill makes a pleasant afternoon trip. Drive to the top to see the **temple** (12th century) dedicated to Mysore's titular deity, Chamundeshwari (Durga), which is made of solid gold; then walk down steps past the huge **Nandi bull** (1659) carved out of black granite. End the day with a visit to **Lalitha Mahal Palace Hotel** (*Siddharth Nagar Rd.*), built in 1931 for the foreign meat-eating guests of the strictly vegetarian maharaja. It has a wonderful double staircase, a period bar, and dining in the former ballroom.

Nagarhole, Bandipur, & Mudumalai National Parks

Even though Mudumalai is in Tamil Nadu, these three parks are treated together, since they border each other. Their wildlife, notably the herds of Karnataka elephants, roams freely among them. Furthermore, they are now collectively referred to as the Nilgiri

EXPERIENCE: Practicing Yoga

The word "yoga" is from the Sanskrit *yuj* meaning "yoke" or "unite," implying the aim to unite with God; it has little to do with the gyms or diets it is associated with in the West. The discipline of yoga is holistic, encompassing a person's whole body inside and out and the relation of that person to the world. Meditation and practice are essential for success.

Yoga is especially useful for people who carry responsibility—think of the creator-destroyer Shiva, sometimes shown eyes closed as the cosmic dancer, or sitting cross-legged to receive the Ganga. A quick lesson by the hotel pool to master the sun salutation is a good start, but not enough. You can get a good introduction to yoga in India by dedicated application for several days (Indian teachers prefer several weeks) at an ashram, retreat, or hotel spa, depending on your comfort zone.

There is a yoga path to suit everyone and it can be as simple as you wish—in the *Bhagavad Gita,* Krishna defines it succinctly: "Yoga is skill in action." Although one can broadly classify the options as a mixture of the emotional, intellectual, active, and meditative, each balancing and strengthening the others, theorists describe the yoga discipline as a series of eight progressive steps.

The Progressive Steps

Yama and **Niyama** purify the heart and promote ethical discipline; the first rejects evil, the second seeks purity. The next three steps are preliminary to yoga: **Asanas** (yogic postures that steady the mind for concentration and discipline the body), **Pranayama** (breathing exercises to improve the lungs, heart, and nervous system), and **Pratyahra** (to promote looking inward). The last three are collectively called Raja Yoga. **Dharana** concentrates on one object (it can just be a light in your mind). **Dhyana,** or meditation, is the flow of thoughts and ideas toward this object. This leads to **Samadhi,** when the subject and object become one, at first consciously, then superconsciously as a liberated soul. Some *sadhus* (holy men) in Himalayan retreats slow down their heartbeats. (Do not confuse these genuine holy men with those sitting on the ghats at Varanasi, waiting for donations.)

A good place to start looking for the appropriate yoga center for you is *yoga-centers-directory.net.*

Many yogis enjoy practicing outdoors, uniting mind and nature.

Nagarhole National Park

 220 B1

✉ 60 miles (96.5 km) SW of Mysore

💲 $ (game viewing extra)

Biosphere Reserve and constitute India's most extensive tract of continuous protected forest. To protect the wildlife, access is limited and visits are usually only permitted at certain hours each day.

All three parks are relatively easy to reach from Bangalore, Mysore, or Ooty. Roads are good, and the scenery around Ooty is spectacular. The parks also fit well into a southern India itinerary, so be sure to reserve accommodations. As usual, prices tend to include all meals, guides, jeep rides, and elephant and boat rides where available. The best time to visit is from October to May, staying at least three nights to get the full benefit. It takes time to learn how to spot the animals and identify the birds.

(In June the heat is punishing; in postmonsoon September the groundcover is too thick to see game.)

In addition to elephants, you may come across gaur (Indian bison), sambar, several other species of deer, crocodiles, and a rich selection of birds; lucky and patient visitors may see a tiger or leopard. The great variety of birdlife is another bonus.

Nagarhole National Park: Centered on the Kabini River and the lake created by damming it, this is one of the best parks in India for seeing and learning about animals and birds in a variety of settings. Accommodations, including in the maharaja of Mysore's hunting lodge and viceroy's buildings, add further charm, as does the team of expert naturalists and the almost certain chance of seeing wild elephants.

The 110 square miles (284 sq km) of mixed deciduous trees, swamps, streams, and soaring bamboo clumps are home to hundreds of elephants. This is where the maharaja's annual *khedda* (elephant roundup) was held, and where the movie *Sabhu the Elephant Boy* was made—movies of both events are shown in the evenings. To watch a group of elephants for an hour or so at sunset simply moving through the riverside grasses, the baby elephants frolicking under the watchful eye of their nanny carers, is a truly memorable experience.

The drier it is, the better your animal sightings along the river

---

EXPERIENCE: Working in a National Park

Requiring no pre-arrival training, working in one of India's national parks is an ideal way to start learning about the various complexities of nature conservation. Stays can range from two weeks to a full season, usually October to June. The easiest way to find a placement is to apply directly to a lodge where visitors stay or to one of India's parks (*ispsquash.com/Link_Wildlife .htm* links to most Indian wildlife websites), offering your skills and enthusiasm. You might find yourself helping run the lodge, preparing nature information for guests, or assisting naturalists. When applying to a park, consider how isolated you want to be: Kanha, Nagarhole, and Ranthambore have plenty of visitors; Kaziranga and Manas have fewer.

In an elephant herd, the young are looked after by their mothers and by special "nanny" elephants.

banks will be. On an evening boat ride you may see fat crocodiles lounging on the banks, while many elephants, bison, and deer arrive to populate this Indian Garden of Eden.

On arrival, plan your itinerary with your naturalist. This might include jeep drives, a sunrise expedition on the lake in coracles (small boats made of buffalo hide), observing a water hole from a *machan* (blind), and cruising up the Kabini at sunset. At the elephant camp you can see the elephants being bathed and you can feed them their breakfast of lentils and rice hay. Each day includes a siesta period and ends with a simple dinner around a campfire beside the lake.

Bandipur National Park:
Created in the 1930s by the maharaja of Mysore, then expanded in the 1940s to join the Nagarhole and Muduma-lai land, this park covers 340 square miles (880 sq km) of dry, deciduous forest south of the Kabini River.

You may sight elephants anywhere in the forest. Bird-watching is good here, too, and you can enjoy fine views from Rolling Rocks, over the deep and craggy Mysore Ditch, or from Gopalswamy Betta, a high ridge overlooking Mysore Plateau.

Mudumalai National Park, Tamil Nadu: This tract of 150 square miles (400 sq km) of forest nestles under and into the Nilgiri Hills and attracts a variety of wildlife. You may see giant squirrels, and bonnet and common langur monkeys, as well as the usual gaur, sambar, and other deer. The birdlife includes

Bandipur National Park

⚠ 220 B1

✉ 50 miles (80 km) S of Mysore

$ $ (game viewing extra)

Mudumalai National Park, Tamil Nadu

⚠ 220 B1

$ $ (game viewing extra)

NOTE: More information on Nagarhole, Bandipur, and Mudum-alai National Parks can be found at *india-wildlife.com* and *indianwildlife.com*.

Badami

222 B3

Medieval Sculpture Gallery closed Fri.

$

species of the plains and hills attracted by springtime fruit trees. There are also delightful accommodations and the Kargudi elephant camp to visit.

Badami, Pattadakal, & Aihole

Three clusters of exquisite caves and temples, isolated in the dry but beautiful Malprabha River Valley of rural Karnataka, rival

Aihole, the Chalukyas rose from the fourth century to rule most of Karnataka, as well as parts of Andhra Pradesh and Maharashtra, until the Rashtrakutas overthrew them in 757. Pattadakal was the Chalukyas' religious center and coronation city.

Badami: Pulakeshin I (r. 543–566) moved the capital to Badami, doubtless attracted by

Badami's soaring cliffs and lake make a dramatic yet peaceful setting for Bhutanatha Temple.

those at Mahabalipuram in Tamil Nadu (see pp. 260–261). Together they form the foundation of the glorious achievements that followed in medieval cities throughout the subcontinent. They are worth every effort to reach them across the open Deccan plains from Vijayanagar, Bijapur, or Hubli.

Early Chalukya rulers were responsible for these masterpieces. From their first base at

the soaring, protective bluffs surrounding a beautiful lake. Later, Pulakeshin II (r. 610–642) left from here to defeat Harsha of Kanauj, the most powerful king of northern India, and to push the Chalukya boundaries south when he came into conflict with the Pallavas of Kanchipuram. After repeated Chalukya raids on Kanchipuram in 612 and after, the Pallavas retaliated and took Badami in 654. Pulakeshin lost his life, but his successor Vikramaditya I expelled the Pallavas, and his son Vinayaditya (r. 696–733) enjoyed a long and peaceful reign. Pallava troubles returned under Vikramaditya II (r. 733–744), whose son lost out to the Rashtrakutas.

To enjoy Badami's treasures in their best light, you need to see some in the morning and the rest in the evening. In the morning, see the cave temples cut into the southern cliffs. The morning sun illuminates both the sculptures and the pinks and purples of the sandstone. Created in the sixth century, their bold and rounded sculptures have a stunning robustness, while the column, capital, and ceiling decoration is a delicate mix of figures, foliage, jewels, and garlands. Find images of Harihare (left) and Shiva with Nandi (right) in **Cave no. 1,** with a magnificent 18-armed dancing Shiva nearby. **Cave no. 2** has images of Vishnu as Varaha (left) and Trivikrama (right), while **Cave no. 3,** inscribed with the date 578, is even richer and has traces of painting; see especially Vishnu on the coiled serpent and the Narasimha composition. **Cave no. 4** is Jain, adorned with restrained images of Tirthankaras.

In the evening, you can take a pony and trap through the narrow lanes of Badami village and then walk along the lakeside to enjoy the sunset from **Bhutanatha Temple** (7th and 11th centuries). To explore farther, see the two lakeside temples in town and, up the path behind it, three clifftop temples and gorgeous views.

Mahakuta, a village not far from here, has a group of four temples built in the years between Badami's and Pattadakal's.

Pattadakal: Outside the village, set in manicured lawns beside the Malprabha River, these now isolated eighth-century temples mix various styles to achieve the climax of Early Chalukya building.

Unless you are a truly passionate temple aficionado, be selective in your choices here. Go across the lawns, past the earlier and simpler temples, to see the two largest and most developed, dedicated to **Virupaksha** and **Mallikarjuna,** two forms of Shiva.

INSIDER TIP:

Getting to the Badami cave temples is rather demanding for the average traveler; be prepared for a bumpy, 20-mile [35 km] ride from Bagalkot.

—STEPHANIE ROBICHAUX
National Geographic contributor

Built by the queen in about 745 to commemorate Vikramaditya II's victory over the Pallavas, they are decorated with large sculptures full of a vitality that is almost contagious. See especially the panels flanking the east porch of Virupaksha; inside, there are the sensuous courting couples and delicate narrative friezes on the columns.

Pattadakal
222 B3
$$

Aihole
⚑ 222 B3

Aihole Archaeological Museum
🕐 Closed Fri.
☎ 083/5128-4551
💲 $

Vijayanagar
⚑ 220 B3

Aihole: The many Hindu and Jain monuments here, both rock-cut caves and temples, span the periods of the Early Chalukyas, the Rashtrakutas, and the Late Chalukyas (10th–13th centuries), who ruled northern Karnataka from Basavakalyan and built splendid temples at Ittagi (see p. 238) and Dambal. Their patrons were kings and merchants, since the town

---

EXPERIENCE:
Bicycling Through Vijayanagar's Ruins

Renting a push-bike or moped in Hampi village or Kamalapura makes it easier for you to explore the farthest reaches of Vijayanagar's expanse. Compare the various rental shops for pricing and bike condition—for instance, although Vijayanagar is not too hilly, it is useful to have working brakes! Moped users can fill up with gas at Kamalapura. The system is fairly informal, but you will need to deposit some sort of identification; do not leave your passport. Before you set off, stock up on bottled water, bananas, and snacks, plus a map of the site; be sure to return by sunset.

---

was then an important trading center. Together they display the bold experiments of this period. The best way to enjoy them is to make your base the little government rest house, whose staff can prepare food if asked on your arrival.

Vijayanagar

Considered by many to equal Petra in Jordan with its impressive buildings amid large rocks beside the mighty Tungabhadra River, Vijayanagar's ruins were forgotten until a team of archaeologists started work here in the 1960s. Yet the powerful Hindu rulers of this once huge metropolis controlled all of southern India and provided the unifying power to keep the Muslim threat at bay until 1565. Today, royal, religious, and civic buildings dot the former city, sharing space with banana groves, paddy fields, and villages.

Vijayanagar's rulers rose in parallel, and in rivalry, with the Muslim Bahmanis based at Gulbarga and Bidar. They established their base at Vijayanagar (City of Victory) in 1336, after seizing the waning Hoysala territories in southern Karnataka, then swiftly regained most lands lost to the Delhi sultans. Thus they achieved the allegiance of the newly liberated rulers of the whole region, down to the tip of Tamil Nadu, apart from most of the Malabar coast.

The consequent vast amounts of tribute and taxes were used by Bukka I (r. 1356–1377) and Devaraya II (r. 1423–1446), then by Krishnadevaraya (r. 1510–1529) and his brother-in-law, Achyutadevaraya (r. 1529–1542), to create their truly international and cosmopolitan imperial capital. Its size, trading wealth, grand buildings, and grandiose rulers were compared to Rome by its visitors.

But on Achyutadevaraya's death the commander of the imperial forces, Ramaraya, took control and kept the rightful successor in prison. It was

Ramaraya's high-handedness with the sultans who had emerged from the Bahmani breakup that led to war. In January 1565, at Talikota near Aihole (see opposite), the combined forces of Bijapur, Bidar, Golconda, and Ahmednagar crushed the Vijayanagar army and then spent a reputed four years sacking the city of its vast wealth, burning the wooden buildings to melt off the gold decoration. Many stone buildings survived, however, and a visit to see the remains of Vijayanagar is still highly recommended. There are two main areas: The sacred and the royal, with extras for those with time.

A very good place to start is **Hampi village** (*7 miles/11 km NE from Hospet, $, karnataka.com/tourism*). Here you can visit **Virupaksha Temple** (13th–17th century;

$), the only temple in the area still in use; its resident elephant helps with the *pujas*. Hemakuta Hill rises above it, a huge slope of granite that provides fine views up the river and has small temples and shrines. Through the great rocks there are two monolithic Ganeshas and Krishnadevaraya's 1513 **Krishna Temple** (*Hemakuta Hill*), built to celebrate a military campaign in Orissa. Just beyond, a lane on the right leads through a banana grove to a huge monolithic Narasimha.

A second walk from Hampi goes up the main street of stores and cafés, then left along a path that passes the riverside Kodandarama Temple, where busloads of pilgrims come to worship Rama. Indeed, this is epic country: Farther along the path, after a detour

Hospet
🅰 220 B3
Visitor Information
✉ State Tourist Office, Old Fire Station Building

✉ Tourist Information Office, Hampi
☎ 083/9424-1339

A view over Hampi village and the tall *gopura* (gateway) of its Virupaksha Temple

Hot pink temple flowers for sale at merchants' booths in Bidar

down a wide bazaar to see the 16th-century **Achyutaraya Temple** *(foot of Matanga Hill),* you pass what is believed to be the cave where Sugriva hid Sita's jewel. The riverside path continues from here to Krishnadevaraya's 16th-century **Vitthala Temple** *($)* and surrounding city bazaars. Roaming the complex, you will find the piers carved into rearing animals and riders, the great stone chariot, and a basement frieze of Portuguese horse traders, who made rich profits from the Vijayanagas.

A third walk starts at the Royal Enclosure. First, see the private **Lotus Mahal** *(Zenana Enclosure, $)* and the amazing elephant stables. Return around the palace walls and go along the road to the **Ramachandra Temple** (15th century). Its outer wall is covered with an incredible relief showing the Mahanavami festival procession; there are more reliefs of Rama stories inside. Beyond the temple lies the area for royal public performance. You can find the platform for the hall of justice, the step-well, and the magnificent **Mahanavami Platform,** entirely covered with friezes of royal hunting, partying, and marching; the platform is thought to be the place where the king sat to watch the Mahanavami festivities.

Finally, for a special atmospheric outing, choose either sunrise or sunset to climb Matanga Hill: There are a lot of big steps, but the trip is worth the effort.

Southern Sultanates

Although small today, each of the old sultanate cities of Bijapur, Gulbarga, Bidar, and Golconda was once a great medieval fort city, powerful enough to hold back the invading Mughal armies. Each has left monuments, whose romantic designs and silhouettes are a rich amalgam reflecting the peoples who migrated there, initially to Gulbarga. Due to a lack of much recorded history, we know little about these sultanates. However, we have a number of their artifacts, especially some stunning miniature paintings, whose vivid colors and lyrical lines confirm strong cultural links with Safavid Iran, with the addition of the sensuality found in local southern Indian sculpture.

Bijapur: As you wander the streets of this laid-back provincial town, where a pony and trap is still a regular form of transportation, it is only the evidence of the immensely grand buildings and monuments at every turn that convinces you Bijapur was once great. This was the prosperous capital of the Adil Shahi dynasty (1490–1686),

Bijapur
🅰 220 B4
**karnatakatourism
.org**

INSIDER TIP:

If you want to visit Vijayanagar from Bangalore, Hyderabad, or Goa, avoid the long and bumpy drives by taking a pleasant, albeit long, train ride to nearby Hospet.

—LOUISE NICHOLSON
National Geographic author

Sufism, the Mystical Thread of Islam

Sufism can be seen as the inner, mystical dimension of Islam. Adherents of the Sufi path seek love and knowledge through direct personal experience of God. Sufi poets such as Rumi, the best-selling poet in the United States today, express this well. In India, many Muslims and non-Muslims follow the Sufi path, and saints' *dargahs* (shrines) are lively places with plenty of visitors and often musicians and singers performing *qawwalis*, light devotional songs.

An aesthetic movement born as a reaction to the worldliness, decadence, and military emphasis of the Umayyad Caliphate (661–750), Sufism soon formed individual orders that arrived in North India with the waves of Islamic invasions through the mountains. The Chhishti order, for instance, arrived from Afghanistan in 1192 and gained prominence

at the Delhi Sultanate courts and then under Mughal patronage, with important pilgrimage centers at Nizamuddin (Delhi), Ajmer, and Fatehpur Sikri.

When the Delhi sultan Mohammed Tughluq expanded into South India in 1327, Chhishti saints went, too. Later, at the sophisticated sultanate courts of Gulbarga, Bidar, Golconda, Ahmednagar, and Bijapur, Sufi saints of various orders often wielded considerable power and were, effectively, ministers of state. In and around these cities can be found large, regal, and elaborately decorated tombs created for top Sufi saints, as well as dargahs. Be careful to cover your head, arms, and legs and to show great respect; if you have some Sufi poetry with you, it is nice to read it at these spots—there is rarely any spoken English, nor anything for sale in English.

Gulbarga

 220 B4

established by Yusuf Adil Khan (r. 1490–1510). Its rulers tempered their extravagant patronage with an acute aesthetic sense. But protracted and expensive wars and then decline under Mughal rule finally extinguished Bijapur's power.

Gulbarga: Though a busy city today, a few key monuments

to consolidate his gains. But when he returned to Delhi in 1334, the Muslim governors of Madurai and Daulatabad proclaimed their independence, and the Hindu Vijayanagar rulers began to liberate their fellow chieftains.

The governors of Daulatabad rose to become the powerful Bahmanis, moving to Gulbarga in 1347, then departing for Bidar

Muhammad Adil Shah II built his own mausoleum, the Gol Gumbaz, in Bijapur.

remain to testify to the sultanate story starting here, 103 miles (165 km) northeast of Bijapur. It is a story worth telling, because the history of this part of India, where north meets south, can be confusing.

A succession of incursions into southern India by the Delhi sultans began in 1296 and finally brought the Yadava, Kakatiya, Hoysala, and Pandya dynasties to a close. Muhammad Tughlaq even moved his capital down to Daulatabad (see p. 173) in 1327

in 1424. Their vast territories included Maharashtra, northern Karnataka, and Andhra Pradesh. Gulbarga became a metropolis attracting other Muslims—Persians, Arabs, Turks, and Abyssinians—and its buildings reflect this in their Persian forms and decoration.

Mosques and palaces filled the great circular **citadel,** whose 52-foot-thick (16 m) crenellated walls and 15 watchtowers now surround just one beautiful mosque (1367). Outside the walls the Bahmanis built their tombs and those of saints who boosted their image; the lively **dargah of Hazrat Gesu Nawaz** (died 1422), with its Persian painted neighbor, attracts many pilgrims but is open only to men. Early royal tombs lie in the fields west of the fort: massive cubic chambers with domes. Find later tombs at Haft Gunbad, near the dargah.

Gulbarga's fate was to achieve independence and lose out to, first, the Adil Shahis of Bijapur, then the Mughals.

Bidar: After moving its capital here in 1424, the Bahmani kingdom reached its zenith under Ahmad I (r. 1422–1436), Muhammed Bahmani III (r. 1463–1482), and Bahmani's able prime minister, Mahmud Gawan. At its height, the Bahmani kingdom stretched from the Arabian Sea to the Bay of Bengal. Internal rivalries, however, soon broke up the kingdom and five sultanate states emerged. Qasim Barid (r. 1488–1504) took control of a much reduced Bidar, and his successors mixed patronage with decline. Three other sultanates—Golconda, Bijapur, and Ahmednagar in Maharashtra—had Shia Muslim rulers, which contributed to their antagonism to the Sunni Mughals.

Today, a visit to Bidar transports you to those distant times, more so than a visit to Gulbarga. The **fort,** whose massive walls and seven gateways are Baridi work, overlooks the plains. Inside are substantial remains of the royal

INSIDER TIP:

When taking photographs, look for repeating patterns, such as one arch after another. For added drama, include shadows. These will add depth and perspective.

—SUSAN COHEN
National Geographic contributor

Bidar
⚠ 220 B4

palaces, including tiled and inlaid walls, the Solah Khamb Mosque (1327), and the throne room. In the walled city, see the **Shihabuddin Ahmad Is Takht-i-Kirmani gateway** and the huge **Madrasa** ("place of learning") founded by Mahmud Gawan in 1472 for Shia studies. Its minaret and front arcade have bold calligraphic motifs and, in places, still retain their richly colored tiles. ∎

EXPERIENCE: Traveling the Hospet–Hubli Road

Traveling the Hospet–Hubli road (93 miles/150 km; 3.5 hr.) allows you to experience some rural villages and lovely temples. **Itagi,** for one, makes a wonderful picnic spot. On the way to Itagi from Hospet, visit the ninth- and tenth-century temples at **Kukkunur,** where you can enjoy the highly decorated Mahadeva Temple (1112). Closer to Hubli, the walkable village of **Lakkundi** has Late Chalukya temples of gray-green schist, all richly carved. Finally, the 12th-century **Dodda Basappa Temple** at Dambal is one of the most beautifully carved Late Chalukya temples.

Open-air Ride Through Bijapur

Bijapur's great black mosques, walls, and tombs look most impressive in the early morning or late afternoon, and what better way to travel to them than by auto rickshaw? Women should cover their arms and legs and take a head shawl. Agree on a price before you set out. Ask your driver to wait when you want to get down, and pay him at the end with a suitable addition for waiting time.

Outside Bijapur's city walls, the early morning sun illuminates the tomb of Ibrahim Rauza.

During your ride, imagine an exotic court of energetic patronage, funded by Vijayanaga booty. It found expression in buildings, miniature painting, music, and religious Sufi learning and science. Only after the final Mughal onslaught and victory by Aurangzeb in 1686 did the decline set in.

Start at the landmark **Gol Gumbaz ❶** (1655), the majestically simple tomb of Muhammad II, with a huge, hemispherical dome on a cube-shaped base; the interior is almost austere in its simplicity. Hop back on your rickshaw and go straight ahead from the Gol Gumbaz gateway; then turn right on Jama Masjid Road. Here, you will find a **trio of monuments ❷**: the incomplete but nevertheless monumental **Jama Masjid** (1576), **Yusuf's Old Jama Masjid** (1513),

NOT TO BE MISSED:

Gol Gumbaz • Asar Mahal
• Walking the walls • Ibrahim Rauza

and, down a side street, the tiny **Ali Sahib Pir Masjid,** with fine plaster decoration.

Now go toward the citadel and past its entrance to find **Asar Mahal ❸**, built as a hall of justice but later converted into a reliquary to hold two hairs of the Prophet. Its civic origins give us a good idea of the character of Bijapur's palace buildings. Perhaps, like this building, they had slender timber columns, inlaid wooden panels, and murals of courtly scenes or floral patterns, and they overlooked formal gardens.

Go into the **citadel** ❹, protected by thick inner walls, to find **Karimuddin's Mosque** (1310), begun when the Delhi sultans were in residence and built with stones from destroyed temples. Gangan Mahal, Ali I's audience hall, is easy to identify: Its great triple arch faces the open area where the people sat.

Outside the west wall of the citadel is the small and finely decorated **Malika Jahan Masjid** ❺, possibly specially built for women. Nearby, **Jod Gumbaz** ❻ is a pair of tombs with elegant facades and slightly bulbous domes containing the remains of Khan Muhammad, commander of the Adil Shahi troops, and Abdul Razzaq, his spiritual advisor. The large, square tank with stepped sides and arcades is **Taj Bauri** ❼, where the entrance steps descend to a big arched gateway.

Now go out of the city by the Mecca Gate, turn right, and go in at the next one, Atke Gate. Here, you can climb the wall to see the Malik-i-Maidan, Bijapur's famous gun, which sits on the **Sharza Bastion** ❽. This is a good moment to look at Bijapur's magnificent **walls** (1565), built by Yusuf Adil Khan. They are 32 feet (10 m) high, reinforced by 96 round

bastions, and equipped with guardrooms and a parapet. You can walk along the broad path on top of them around much of the city.

Your ride ends with a visit to the best of all the sights in Bijapur, the Adil Shahi buildings: **Ibrahim Rauza** ❾ (1628). This is a tomb and mosque built by Ibrahim II for his queen, Taj Sultana, but later converted into a mausoleum for himself and his family, too. You enter through a single gateway and go through a formal garden to reach both buildings, which stand on a plinth. Take time to look carefully at the exterior of the tomb: It rises up in layers, crowned by a bulbous dome that sits on a ring of petals. Now go into the veranda to look closely at its outer walls, doorways, and windows, and enjoy the precision-cut geometric and calligraphic designs. Some are cut through as screens, others are cut in shallow relief.

⛰	See also area map pp. 220–221
►	Gol Gumbaz
⟷	About 2 miles (3 km)
⏱	2 hours
►	Ibrahim Rauza

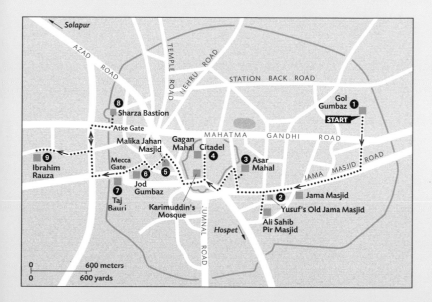

More Places to Visit in Karnataka

Arsikere & Aralaguppe

For more 13th-century Hoysala temple elegance and richness, visit the towns of Arsikere and Aralaguppe. A second Aralaguppe temple, **Kalleshvara** (ninth century), has a beautiful ceiling panel. ⚠ 220 B2 **Arsikere** ✉ 27 miles (44 km) NE of Hassan

Bagali, Kuruvatti, & Harihar

Bagali and Kuruvatti are villages with Chalukya temples. Bagali's 10th-century **Kalleshvara** has surprisingly provocative sculptures. Kuruvatti's 11th-century **Chalukya** has masterpiece bracket figures on the east doorway. Harihar town has a splendid Hoysala temple, **Harihareshvara** (1224). ⚠ 220 B3 **Bagali** ✉ 34 miles (55 km) SW of Hospet

Belur & Halebid

The great Hoysala ruler Vishnuvardhana (r. 1108–1142) built the **Channekashava Temple** at his capital, Belur, to celebrate his defeat of the Cholas in 1116. The dense, fluent carving riots over the squat yet refined building; note the high plinth, star-shaped plan, lathe-turned pillars, and polished surfaces.

At nearby Halebid, visit the incomplete double **Hoysalesvara Temple,** designed and begun by Kedaroja for the Hoysala ruler Narasimha I (r. 1141–1182). Up on the platform you can follow the bands of decoration with their lively carving and precision, showing rows of elephants, stories from the epics, baroque scrollwork, and scenes from courtly life. Above them, the great sculptures include Shiva dancing with the flayed skin of the elephant demon and Brahma seated on a goose. The sumptuously bejeweled temple-guardian figures are especially fine, as is the fat Ganesh figure. To visit longer at the Hoysala temples, you can stay in Hassan. ⚠ 220 B3 **Belur** ✉ 23 miles (38 km) NW of Hassan; **Halebid** ✉ 20 miles (32 km) N of Hassan

Chitradurga Fort

The midpoint on the Bangalore–Hospet road is a good place to stretch your legs. Go through several great gates to find two **Hoysala temples** and various tanks, palace

---

Silk, the State Industry

Karnataka produces 65 percent of India's raw silk, and the government closely controls the industry. Japanese male moths are mated with local Mysore females, who are carefully checked for disease. Once hatched, the pupa are sold to the mulberry-bush owner or to farmers, who rear them to cocoon stage.

This is when you can see woven mats propped up in the morning sun outside small farms. The worms on them eat mulberry leaves continuously for 26 to 28 days, during which they molt four times and grow to be 4 to 6 inches (10 to 15 cm) long. They then turn from white to yellow and for about four days furiously spin their cocoons with a viscous solution; each one of these will be unraveled to about 4,000 feet (1,200 m) of silk yarn. The cocoons are then sold for boiling, reeling, dyeing, and weaving. You will be made very welcome at most roadside silk-production units, where the managers are usually happy to explain the precise workings of each of the processes to you.

Recently, due to globalization and the fashion for man-made textiles, India's silk industry, both machine made and hand-loom, is suffering. But Karnataka silk is still high quality; to buy some of the best at fair and fixed prices, go to one of the stores listed at *ksicsilk.com*.

buildings, and lamp columns   🔺 220 B2
✉ 124 miles (200 km) NW of Bangalore

Kodagu (Coorg)

This beautiful area mixes rugged mountains with cardamom jungle, paddies, and orderly coffee plantations established by the British. The tall and graceful people, known as Kodavas or Coorgis, have maintained their distinct culture, including heavy jewelry, very rich saris, ancestor worship, and cuisine. Driving through the area, pause at **Madikeri** (Mercara) with its fort-palace, and **Talakaveri,** where the Kaveri River springs from the wooded slopes of Brahmagiri Hill.   🔺 220 B1 **Madikeri** ✉ 60 miles (96 km) W of Mysore

Malnad

This wild, forested region offers a combination of waterfalls (see Jog Falls p. 204), craggy peaks, and monuments created by 16th- and 17th-century Nayaka rulers. Having done well under the Vijayanagas, they became independent, with capitals at Keladi, then Ikkeri. Your base can be **Shimoga**, whose restored **Shivappa Nayaka Palace** overlooking the Tunga River is worth visiting. One outing is to **Keladi** and **Ikkeri's temples,** another to **Nagar, Devaganga's** tanks and pavilions, and **Kavaledurga's** citadel. Go north to **Balligave** and **Banavasi's** Hoysala and Late Chalukya temples, or south to **Amritpur's** outstanding Hoysala temple (1196).   🔺 220 A2 **Shimoga** ✉ 97 miles (156 km) N of Hassan, 120 miles (193 km) SW of Hospet

Ranganathittu Bird Sanctuary

An early morning or evening visit to this bird sanctuary near Srirangapatnam is magical. Take a boat out on the lake with an ornithologist for some peaceful bird-watching, looking out for electric blue kingfishers to great gangling herons, spoonbills, and openbill storks; there are also crocodiles in the water.   🔺 220 B1 ✉ 12 miles (19 km) N of Mysore

Shravanabelagola

Southern India's most sacred Jain site is believed to have been where the Mauryan emperor Chandragupta died in about 300 B.C. If you are physically fit, the reward of walking up Indragiri Hill is to see the 58-foot-high calm, monolithic figure of Gomateshvara (981) that has been carved out of the rock; or, visit the priest's house with its painted walls.

It is worth arranging a visit to **Nritgram dance village** *(tel 080/8466-312),* founded by dancer Protima Bedi, to learn about different forms of Indian dance and see dancing.   🔺 220 B2 ✉ 56 miles (90 km) N of Mysore

Somnathpur

Even if you think you have seen enough temples, you will delight in this little gem found down country lanes, a 90-minute drive out of Mysore. Built in 1268, the **Keshava Vishnu Temple** is the last and most complete of the three great Hoysala temples (see Belur & Halebid opposite). Try asking the guardian if you may go up onto the walls to enjoy fabulous views of the star-shaped plan and the densely carved roofs that top each of the shrines.   🔺 220 B1 ✉ 21 miles (75 km) E of Mysore

Srirangapatnam (Seringapatam)

The island fortress on the Kaveri River is synonymous with Tipu Sultan (see p. 223), killed here in 1799 when General Harris stormed the citadel, confirming British supremacy in southern India. Get a flavor of the fort's great ramparts and visit the possible site of the breach and the place where Tipu fell. Then find the pretty, Mughal-influenced **Daria Daulat Bagh** (1784), Tipu's pleasure resort, where there are delicate murals and drawings of his sons. A small formal garden surrounds the cenotaphs of Tipu and his father, Haider Ali, who are buried together underneath them.   🔺 220 B1 ✉ 9 miles (14 km) N of Mysore

Fabrics of India

Until you first visit India, your experience of Indian fabrics might be limited to pictures of old woolen Kashmir shawls with richly patterned borders. The best date from the 15th to mid-19th centuries, woven with fleece from Central Asia. Sophisticated Mughals and other rulers prized them for their intricate designs and precision craftsmanship: Each shawl required a dozen specialists, from pattern drawers to dyers, and took months to make.

Traditional dress continues to be popular among Indian women, especially for weddings.

Introduced into European high fashion in the 1770s, the Kashmir shawl became an essential chic fashion accessory, especially in France. A century later, however, the Jacquard looms of Lyons and Paisley made the shawls so inexpensively that they lost their appeal.

Today's Western fashion for so-called pashmina shawls (from the Persian word *pashm*, meaning "wool") is a pale imitation of past glories and India's present weaving skills. That the variety and quality of India's weaving is unequaled is quickly evident if you simply keep your eyes open as you travel around India.

The incredible colors, patterns, and weaves are infinite. These remarkable fabrics may be woven in many kinds of cotton, silk, and wool. For instance, cotton may be fine muslin, hand-spun and handwoven *khadi* made famous by Mahatma Gandhi, or mill-spun but handwoven "handloom" cotton. Indians tend to drape rather than cut and tailor their fabrics, wearing them as shawls, saris, or *lunghis* (or *dhotis*, a cloth worn by a man). Depending on where you travel, you may also see local people in finely woven or intricately embroidered jackets, skirts, tight shirts, hats, and even shoes.

Weaving has been serious business in India since at least the period of the Indus Valley Civilization, from which spindles and pieces of cotton cloth wrapped around a silver vase survive. In the 1630s, the British established their first major foothold in India at Madras expressly to buy cotton from the nearby weavers. Today, textiles are a major part of the economy. India has about three million cotton handloom weavers. Sericulture (silk farming) and silk weaving, first introduced by Buddhist monks from China, is a government-controlled industry in Karnataka state (see sidebar p. 242). Master weavers are revered and receive national awards, and fine silks dress temple deities. A bride-to-be is the focus of serious family outings to choose her wedding saris; one may be a shopping trip to Varanasi to buy a luxurious Barnasi brocade encrusted with silver and gold threads, another a more modest outing to Jaipur's cotton market.

The best way to buy local weaves is to visit the village and town markets. If you are in a weaving area, maybe traveling through the villages of Tamil Nadu, weavers will welcome you into their homes, where great wooden looms dominate the living space.

Hot-toned, hand-dyed silk saris set out to dry

To see the range and quality of traditional Indian fabrics, visit Delhi's National Crafts Museum (see p. 73) and the fixed-price, high-quality, government-run stores of Baba Kharak Singh Marg at Connaught Place; in Ahmedabad, visit the Calico Museum (see p. 145).

EXPERIENCE: Tying Your Own Sari

Indian women drape their ravishing fabrics, rather than cut and tailor them. The saris are woven specifically for this. Typically, one end is fancy, the other plain. The wearer drapes the fancy *pallu* over the shoulder, showing it off; the plain end of the sari fabric is cut off to make into the tight-fitting bodice, the *choli*. The long piece of fabric in between has a border decoration on one side only—this hangs at the floor.

To wear a sari, first put on either a choli or a tight-fitting top, plus a tight-waisted petticoat or a belt.

With the fabric flowing to the left, tuck the end of the undecorated long edge into the petticoat so that the decorated edge touches the ground.

Holding the sari, turn a full circle clockwise, tucking in the sari all around.

Using the first and fourth fingers of one hand, fold five to seven pleats, each about 5 inches (11 cm) wide. Tuck this block into the petticoat (or belt), slightly to the left of your belly button. These pleats are key to the sari's gracefulness.

Circle clockwise again, holding the spare fabric and not tucking it in.

Gather or pleat the remaining fabric and drape the pallu over the left shoulder. Let some of the material fall to cover most of the left arm.

Andhra Pradesh

Andhra Pradesh has much to offer, though visitors are few. Hyderabad is littered with dilapidated palaces, the backdrop to a modern, dynamic city that today looks to Bangalore's IT success as its inspiration. Its infrastructure is being rebuilt at a furious speed, adding overpasses, new airport terminals, a high-tech city, and entertainment parks; a film city is up and running.

Hyderabad's Char Minar, a ceremonial gateway, has been a focal point since the late 16th century.

If you are feeling adventurous, leave the capital and venture into the rugged countryside, where you will be well rewarded with evocative, offbeat sites. Not far from Hyderabad lie the remains of Nagarjunakonda and Warangal, whose ramparts and fort you might have to yourself.

At Tirupati, in southeastern Andhra Pradesh, you can join the seething masses of Hindu pilgrims in their daily *pujas* to Lord Venkateswara in what is believed to be the world's richest temple. Around Vishakapatnam is a rich landscape made up of the Kailasha Hills, Orissan temples, and Buddhist and Dutch ruins.

Golconda & Hyderabad

Golconda Fort is one of India's most spectacular forts. Great crenellated walls with round bastions run 3 miles (5 km) around the bottom of a rocky bluff in a forbidding, boulder-strewn landscape. Inside, substantial remains

INSIDER TIP:

Hyderabad's Birla Science Centre contains a "Dinosaurium," showcasing, among other things, sauropod eggs and a mounted sauropod skeleton.

—JEFF WILSON
National Geographic grantee

cover the hill, with the royal Durbar Hall at the top. Adjacent Hyderabad developed as a result of Golconda's expansion.

Golconda: Already in the 12th century, Golconda was a wealthy fort city. Later, it was an important outpost of the Bahmani kingdom, whose Turkish governor, Quli Qutb al-Mulk (r. 1494–1543), broke free to establish his own kingdom and Qutb Shahi line of sultans. An outstanding military leader, he consolidated his gains over rival rulers, including those of Vijayanagar and Orissa, putting Golconda on a level footing with Bijapur.

The **royal necropolis** (*closed Fri., $*), near the fort, reflects the magnificence of these rulers. Seven **tombs** stand in a formal garden. Each has an onion dome perched on a cube-shaped mausoleum, surrounded by a richly ornamented arcade, with additional corner minarets. In early morning or sunset light, the whole ensemble is hauntingly romantic.

The reign of Ibrahim Qutb Shah (r. 1550–1580) marked

Golconda's peak. Under his successor, Muhammad Quli Qutb Shah (r. 1580–1612), plans were made for expansion, and in 1591 the city of Hyderabad was laid out beside the Musi River.

Hyderabad: Comparative peace followed. Mughals and Marathas watched for opportunities to pounce on Hyderabad's wealth and its stocks of diamonds; in 1687 the Mughals conquered the city. Later, Mughal emperor Muhammad Shah's representative in Aurangabad, Nizam ul Mulk, declared independence and took the

---

The GQ Bonanza

The Golden Quadrilateral, known as the GQ, is a massive, government-financed, highway-building project to link Delhi, Mumbai, Kolkata, and Chennai. It aims to provide smooth, quick transportation, help farmers, and stimulate economic growth. With the completion of the 3,632-mile (5,846 km) multilane highway, the project has been expanded. Inspired, some states are undertaking their own projects—with varying success. While Hyderabad has built a world-class airport–city highway, Bangalore is sending bulldozers into historic cities such as Bidar and Gulbarga to destroy buildings in the name of essential street widening.

Golconda & Hyderabad

🅰 221 C4

Visitor Information

✉ Andhra Pradesh Tourism Bureau, Tourism House, Himayatnagar, Hyderabad

☎ 040/2326-2151

aptdc.in
incredibleindia.org

✉ Tourism Department, Secretariat, Hyderabad

☎ 040/2345-0444

B.M. Birla Science Centre

✉ Opposite Birla Mandir, Adarshnagar, Hyderabad

☎ 040/2323-5081

💲 $

birlasciencecentre.org

title Asaf Jah I (r. 1724–1748). Hyderabad, India's largest state (82,000 sq miles/212,400 sq km), recovered to withstand British, French, and Maratha threats. It accepted the idea of independent India only in 1956.

Today Hyderabad is India's sixth largest city—a chaotic, ever-expanding urban sprawl that takes little care of its heritage. Encompassing Old and New Hyderabad plus Secunderabad, a station for British troops founded in 1853 after the British alliance, and now the high-tech Cyberabad, it is not an easy city to grasp.

Set the mood with a visit to the **Salar Jung Museum** (Sardar Patel Rd., tel 040/2457-2558, closed Fri. & public holidays, $, salarjungmuseum.in), a vast and random collection made by the Nizam's prime minister, Salar Jung (1899–1949). Then find the landmark pink **High Court** (1916), designed by Vincent Esch, whose

carved Agra sandstone has lapis lazuli–glazed domes and gilded finials. Esch's boys' school is next door. Along Mahboob Shahi Road there is a rare survivor of Quli Qutb Shah's original buildings, the 1596 **Badshahi Ashurkhana** (may be closed to public), the royal house of mourning, with beautiful enamel tile mosaics (1611). The Nizam's prime ministers lived in the **Diwan Deorhi** (Sardar Patel Rd., may be closed to visitors) across the road, while the last Nizam's clothes-filled wardrobes are in **Purani Haveli,** together with his 1937 silver jubilee gifts. Old Hyderabad's focus, the **Char Minar** ("four towers," 1591), was once the ceremonial gateway to the palace, now constantly threatened by developers.

In this area you can find bidri workers, bangle makers, and pearl stores (see sidebar opposite). The 1598 **Mecca Masjid** (Sardar Patel Rd.) is one of India's largest

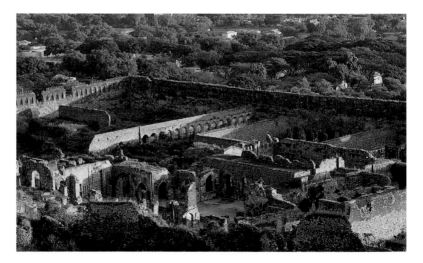

Golconda Fort's many surviving buildings give a vivid idea of medieval fort life.

Pearls & Bidri Work

The fabulously rich Nizams of Hyderabad loved pearls, which they wore, rubbed on their bodies, and even ate ground up. Hyderabad is still India's pearl market. In little workshops around Char Minar, pearls grown in Japan are sorted, pierced, sorted again, and either sold or re-exported. In the shops on nearby Pertheghatty Road, the pearls are sorted by color, size, and quality. Clients select their pearl type and the required number is counted out, priced by weight, and strung on silk; the family jeweler will add the gemstones and a fancy clasp. In the same area, the special Muslim craft of *bidriware* can be seen in the little alleys. This is the technique of decorating metalwork with a very fine silver or brass inlay of arabesque, floral, geometric, or calligraphic patterns.

Mangatrai *(Punjagutta Cross Rd., mangatrai.com)* is a reliable dealer of pearls and lovely ready-made pieces; it also has a museum of dazzling jewelry upstairs.

---

mosques; **Chowmahalla** *(Khilwat, tel 040/2452-2032, closed Fri., $, chowmahalla.com)* is a well-restored 1860s palace. Farther afield, seek out **Falaknuma Palace** *(now a hotel)* and the **State Archaeological Museum** *(Public Gardens),* which reflect Karnataka's rich history. Fans of Indian film should not pass up a visit to **Ramoji Film City** *(ramojifilmcity.com).*

Eastern & Southern Andhra Pradesh

Traveling from Hyderabad through the barren landscape to the northeast is quite a tough trip, but on the way you can explore the glories of the Kakatiya rulers of the 13th and 14th centuries, whose territories nudged the Gangas of Orissa to the north and the Cholas of Tamil Nadu to the south. Use a car and driver.

Eastern Andhra Pradesh: In the northeast is the Kakatiyas' second capital, **Warangal,** laid out by Ganapatideva (r. 1199–1262) and his daughter, Queen Rudrama Devi (r. 1262–1289); see the two rings of outer earthen walls, the monumental gateways, the massive granite inner fort walls, and the temple portals. Two miles (3 km) away, the fine gray-green basalt **Thousand-Pillared Temple** (1163) stands at Hanamakonda, the first Kakatiya capital. The enthusiastic can continue 42 miles (68 km) to **Palampet** for the superb Ramappa Temple (1213) and the nearby shrines of **Ghanpur;** clever Kakatiya engineers created both lakes.

Travel southeast from Hyderabad to reach Vijayapuri in time to catch the morning boat *(usually 9:30 a.m.)* to an island in the Krishna River, to see tantalizing limestone sculptures that testify to **Nagarjunakonda's** former glory. In the third and fourth centuries the Ikshvakus, Andhra's most powerful rulers, made this their capital and patronized fine Buddhist and secular buildings that extended over more than 8 square miles (20 sq km). Their monuments were rediscovered

Falaknuma Palace

✉ Falaknuma

Warangal

🗺 221 C4

Nagarjunakonda

🗺 221 C3

by archaeologists in the 1950s, but in 1960 the Nagarjuna Sagar Dam opened and almost the whole area was flooded; the island you visit was once the summit of Nagarjuna Hill. Visitors can see the fort remains, the reconstructed stadium and monastery, the third-century *maha chaitya* (great stupa) and other stupas, and the amazing sculptures on display in the **museum** (*closed Fri.*).

If you follow the Krishna River to its lush delta, you will come to **Vijayawada,** an isolated and fascinating spot best reached by train or air, because it is a long road journey. It has been an important commercial center since at least the fifth century. In town, the

INSIDER TIP:

Shop around before committing to anything. Prices can vary widely. Learn the art of bargaining, but never get worked up over a couple of dollars.

—TALA KATNER
National Geographic contributor

Victoria Jubilee Museum (*Bundra Rd., closed Fri.*) has impressive local Buddhist finds. Set off to see **Kondapalli's** fort and **Undavalli's** rock-cut sanctuaries. Farther away, southward through tobacco, cotton, and paddy fields, **Guntur's Boudhasree Archaeological Museum** (*closed Fri.*) has more local Buddhist finds. Continue to **Amaravati,** once known as Maha

Chaitya (Great Stupa), the site of India's largest stupa (third century B.C.–fourth century A.D.). The majority of its sculptures are now shared between Chennai Government Museum (see p. 259) and London's British Museum, but it is still worth going to this haunting site beside the Krishna River; its museum displays recent finds.

The verdant Godavari River Delta is a historically prosperous area dotted with fields of rice and sugar, with immensely beautiful scenery and fascinating places to visit. Stay in **Rajahmundry** and make an outing to see the temples of **Bikkavolu, Drakasharama,** and, best of all, **Samalkot,** an 11th-century temple and the area's largest East Chalukya monument. Alternatively, cross the Godavari to visit **Guntupalle's** Buddhist relics in a wooded ravine. And do not leave without taking the boat trip up the Godavari to visit **Godavari Gorge** in the wooded hills of the Eastern Ghats.

Vishakhapatnam, a huge port founded by the English in 1689, faces onto a fine broad bay that opens into the Bay of Bengal. As India's principal port, naval base, and industrial center on the east coast, it has good hotels. In the nearby forested Kailasha Hills, you can find **Simhachalam's** hilltop Varaha Narasimha Temple (1268) at the end of a winding road; the patron of this pure Orissa temple was commander of the armies of the Eastern Ganga kings of Orissa (see p. 296). Inside the granite temple enclosure are carved lions, friezes and garlands, royal princes, gods, and life-size prancing horses.

Meanwhile, hilly **Sankaram** is known for its Buddhist remains while coastal **Bheemunipatnam,** a major Dutch settlement, has sandy beaches, a Dutch fort, houses, and grand tombs. Farther up the coast, **Ramatirtham** and **Salihundram** have more Buddhist remains, and remote **Mukhalingam,** the early dramatically sited on a granite outcrop right beside the highway; east of here, Tadpatri's two major **Vijayanagar temples,** one in town and the other overlooking the Penner River, have ornate sculpture and even some surviving ceiling paintings.

Back on the highway and

This monolith, a mile (1.6 km) east of Lepakshi, shows Shiva's mount decked in garlands and bells.

capital of the Eastern Gangas, has good temples, including the ninth-century **Madhukeshvara,** with a curved tower and sculptures.

Southwestern Andhra Pradesh: Many fine but isolated monuments lie in this rarely visited region. If you are traveling through it on National Highway 7, which runs from Hyderabad to Bangalore, you may wish to stop and see one or two. For a closer look, stay overnight at **Anantapur.** You can take a walk up to **Gooty Fort,**

beyond Anantapur, the fort at **Penukonda** is where, after 1565, the defeated Vijayanaga rulers fled to before moving to Chandragiri. Be sure to see the Hoysala-period **Parshvanatha Temple** and the **Rama** and **Sita Temples,** whose facades are carved with the *Ramayana* and Krishna legends.

Farther south, **Lepakshi** lies 7 miles (11 km) west of the highway. Here, past the huge Nandi monolith, you find the **Veerabhadra Temple** (16th century), built by two brothers who were Vijayanagar governors of Penukonda. Its sculpture is glorious, and its ceiling frescoes the best surviving from the period: Note the costumes, faces, rich colors, and the donor brothers worshipping Shiva and Parvati (east side).

At **Alampur,** Andhra Pradesh's earliest large group of Hindu temples has been saved from the Srisailam Dam, a huge hydroelectric project on the Krishna River,

INSIDER TIP:

There are some great street-food stalls in tourist areas. Visit the most popular ones; avoid those off the beaten path.

—MONICA BHIDE
National Geographic contributor

which stretches east from here to Srisailam, 53 miles (85 km) away. Built by the Early Chalukyas of Badami in the seventh and eighth centuries, the temples overlooked the Tungabhadra River; now they are protected from the water by a barrage, and other threatened temples have been dismantled and re-erected here. Restrained and simple, each has enriching sculpture, especially **Svarga Brahma Temple** (689). If you are driving from Hyderabad, you could pause at Srisailam, where **Mallikarjuna Temple** (14th century), with its wonderful and unusual wall reliefs, overlooks a deep gorge in the Krishna River.

Puttaparthi is a remote, quiet village in the arid rocky hills of southwest Andhra Pradesh. It has leaped to fame because it is the birthplace, and the home from July to March, of one of India's best-known living saints, Sri Sathya Sai Baba. Thousands of disciples visit him each year, staying in the new **Prasanthi Nilayam Ashram,** which is like a model village. Born in 1926, the saint is credited with possessing supernatural abilities. He claims that his miracles are to shock materialists, while his message is really universal love: His image is seen all over India. At the ashram he gives *darshan* twice daily, which anyone may attend.

Southeastern Andhra Pradesh: With Tirupati, one of India's most important pilgrimage cities, as its main attraction, this area is best visited from Chennai (see pp. 256–257). Traveling here from Hyderabad is best done over several days, stopping at other sites.

If you arrive at **Tirupati,** from the rural peace of Andhra Pradesh, be prepared: Busloads of pilgrims arrive from Chennai for day visits. They make their way up switchback roads to worship at the **Venkateshvara Temple** (tenth century and later), on Tirumala Hill in the Seshachalam Hills. As the temple is open to non-Hindus, you have the chance to closely observe many aspects of Hinduism, from the preparatory, cleansing head shave on arrival to the almost intoxicating spiritual ecstasy of the chanting faithful at the sanctum. ■

A lush land fed by two monsoon seasons and peppered with ancient stone temples that soar above the viridian fields of paddy

Tamil Nadu

Bullocks sport brightly painted horns for the Pongal festival.

Tamil Nadu

The state of Tamil Nadu pulsates with energy and vitality. Most of its monuments are busy places, so you can experience the vigor and purity of the great Dravidian culture in huge temple complexes thronged with people. You can visit the British-built High Court of Chennai (Madras), busy with lawyers.

Tamil Nadu presents strong contrasts. Madurai's sprawling temple feels like a medieval temple town; hilltop Ooty is still reminiscent of its British hill station origins; Thanjavur retains some of its regal Chola majesty.

Furthermore, Tamil Nadu is comparatively compact. The relatively short drive from place to place through the clean, quaint villages is pure pleasure. You can easily drive from the British Victorian elegance of Chennai to a simple bronze-casting atelier, from the formal excitement of the Bharata Natyam dance to the bells and smells of Hindu worship aided by the temple's resident elephant. Undoubtedly, Tamil Nadu makes the gentlest introduction to India.

Look at the map, and it is clear why this is so. Tamil Nadu almost fills the southern tip of India. On the east, the Bay of Bengal's surf laps the sandy beaches of the Coromandel coast, which has for centuries brought international trade and cultural exchange with west and east. On the west, the steep and rugged Western Ghats are the barrier between Tamil Nadu and Kerala and Karnataka. British hill stations nestle in the northern Nilgiri Hills. South of here, the Anaimalai (Elephant) Hills are a mixture of dense forest and velvet-smooth tea gardens. South again, more tea gardens and the hill station of Kodaikanal sit in the Palani Hills. Thus, as you can see, all the rivers flow eastward, including the great Kaveri (Cauvery), southern India's most sacred river.

Pallava, Chola, and then Pandya empires fueled the distinct and very sophisticated Tamil culture beginning in the seventh century.

With little interference from the Mughals or the British, their monuments and culture survive today in this affluent, culturally rich, traditional, yet dynamic and modern state.

Tamil Nadu's capital, Madras, was renamed Chennai in 1996. Its economy mixes the historically important rice, sugarcane, and cotton production with fast-growing export business and industrial activity that is one of India's highest; and it leads the country in reviving traditional water conservation methods. As you might expect, literacy is high, and the state language of Tamil is often supplemented with skills in English rather than Hindi. ∎

NOT TO BE MISSED:

Area of map detail

New
Delhi

5 ▷

THE DECCAN p.219

Pulicat

CHENNAI
(MADRAS)

Tiruttani
Ambattur
Avadi

Vrinchipuram
Arcot
Sriperumbudur

Vellore
Kanchipuram

Ambur
Chengalpattu

Krishnagiri
Vaniyambadi
VEDANTHANGAL BIRD
SANCTUARY
Mahabalipuram
Tirukkalukkundram

Tiruppattur

Tiruvannamalai
Gingee
Tindivanam

Dharmapuri
Vettavalam
Panamalai
Auroville

4 ▷

THE DECCAN p.219

Villupuram
PUDUCHERRY
Puducherry
(Pondicherry)

Yercaud

Bay of
Bengal

Salem
Cuddalore

Attur
Neyveli

Coromandel Coast

2636m
Doda-Betta

hagamandalam
(Ooty)
Coonoor
Nilgiri
Hills
Mettuppalaiyam
Bhavani
Tiruchengodu

Chidambaram
Gangaikonda Cholapuram

Erode
Namakkal
Jayamkondacholapuram
Kilaiyur
Tharangambadi
Karaikal

Punjai
Perambalur
Kumbakonam
PUDUCHERRY

Tiruppur
Karur
Srirangam
Tiruvaiyaru
Darasuram
Thiruvarur
Nagapattinam

3 ▷

Coimbatore
Tiruchchirappalli
(Trichy)
Thanjavur
Velanganni

Pollachi
Palani
Kodumbalur
Kiranur
POINT CALIMERE
WILDLIFE
SANCTUARY
Vedaranniyam

Anaimalai
Hills
Palani
Hills
Dindigul
Narthamalai
Pudukkottai
Point
Calimere

Kodaikanal
TAMIL NADU
Alagarkoil
Chettinad
Karaikkudi

Teni
49
Madurai
Devakottai

Thirupparankundram
Sivaganga
Palk Strait

2 ▷

Srivilliputtur
Virudunagar
49
Ramanathapuram
SRI
LANKA
(CEYLON)

Sivakasi
Kilakkarai
Rameswaram

Rajapalaiyam
Dhanushkodi

Kalugumalai

Tenkasi
Tuticorin
Gulf of
Mannar

Tirunelveli
Palayankottai
Krishnapuram

Papanasam
Alvar
Tirunagari
Kayalpattinam
Tiruchchendur

1 ▷

Padmanabhapuram
Manapadu

Nagercoil
47

Suchindram
Kanniyakumari

Cape
Comorin

| 0 | 100 kilometers |
| 0 | 50 miles |

A
B
C
D

WEST COAST: GOA & KERALA p.187

Kuveri (Cauvery)

Nanganji

Vaigai

Tambraparni

Pennaiyar

Chennai

Tamil Nadu's sprawling coastal capital is tucked up in the northern corner of the state, just south of its huge port. With a population of around six million, Chennai is India's fourth largest city, but its seaside position and relative spaciousness make its center pleasant to explore.

A view of Chennai (Madras), with its busy streets and eclectic buildings

Chennai (Madras)
255 D5

Visitor Information

✉ India Tourist Office, 154 Anna Salai

☎ 044/2846-1459, 044/2846-0285

🕐 Closed Sat. p.m.– Sun.

incredibleindia.org

✉ State Tourist Office, 2 Wallajah Rd.

☎ 044/2536-8358

tamilnadutourism.org
tamilnaduonline.in

There is certainly plenty to see while strolling around the very fine streets or taking advantage of the busy beach. Chennai (Madras) is also the place to prepare for your inland temple tours by watching a performance of Bharata Natyam (see sidebar opposite) and visiting the small but exceptional museum collections. So Chennai deserves at least a long day's visit, possibly two.

Founded on the Cooum and Adyar Rivers in 1639 by the British merchant Francis Day, the city's site was chosen for its cheap local cotton. Despite having no port and ferocious surf, which meant much cargo was lost as it was landed in small boats, Madras grew fast. By 1644 the East India Company was building its fort and had a workforce of around 400 weavers working in the surrounding villages. This textile trade continues to be vital to Chennai today, as important as its leather and auto industries. In 1688 King James II granted a municipal charter, India's first, to a city that by then had about 300,000 inhabitants. (The population of London, Europe's largest city by far, was 575,000.) Soon there were twin towns on the site: the Europeans' Fort St. George and the Indians' Chennaipatnam, or Black Town (which was renamed Georgetown in honor of the King-Emperor George V's visit in 1911).

By 1740, British trade in India was so substantial that it represented 10 percent of all Britain's revenue and made a major contribution to London's Georgian wealth and affluence. Much of this trade passed through Madras, which remained the nerve center of British influence in India until the move to Calcutta in 1772 (see p. 290). The city's established merchants built their famous stuccoed houses outside the

general, Robert Clive, crushed them at the Battle of Arcot in 1751, consolidating Britain's supremacy in southern India; Britain's position in Bengal was confirmed at Plassey in 1757 (see p. 43). Even when the British focus moved to Calcutta, Madras remained an important city. To give the capital of the Madras presidency a promenade worthy of its status, Governor Grant Duff (1881–1886) laid out the splendid 3-mile-long (5 km) **Marina,** which runs right along the waterfront. Soon this classical city was adorned with a string of spectacular waterfront Indo-Saracenic buildings, several designed by Robert Fellowes Chisholm and Henry Irwin. Today the Marina is one of the

NOTE: Strong currents make it unwise to swim at Chennai.

Bharata Natyam

Bharata Natyam is probably India's oldest classical dance, created in the Tamil Nadu temples as a form of worship and now enjoying a vigorous revival. A woman performs the solo dance that begins with *alarippu,* symbolizing the body unfolding to offer itself to the gods. *Nritta* (pure dance) follows, when the dancer uses formalized face, hand, body, and dance expressions to expound on a poem sung by the *nattuvanar* (conductor), accompanied by musicians. The bodily rhythm is all-important, emphasized when the dancer replies to the music by stamping her feet to ring the bells of her ankle bracelets. A dancer's initiation performance should be for the gods in one of the great temples such as Chidambaram (see p. 265). Regular performances are held at Chennai's many *sabbas,* arts societies, and venues, and there are more than 500 dance and classical music performances during the Chennai Festival *(Dec.–Jan.);* tourist offices carry details.

walls of the fort and ensured that their departed loved ones were remembered in style in the fort's St. Mary's Church.

Madras was a relaxed, elegant, gleaming garden city cooled by sea breezes. The French occupied it in 1746–1749, but the young

most beautiful promenades to be found in any city, and is much loved by Chennai's residents, who come down here in the cool of the evening for a stroll, small talk, a snack of freshly barbecued fish, or a cooling frolic in the waves. ∎

A Drive Around Chennai

This drive around Chennai's current system of one-way streets gives you a good introduction to the city. Enjoy a walk on the splendid Marina Beach before you start—and maybe another after you finish.

Start with a visit to the historic **San Thome Cathedral ❶** (1547, 1896; *santhomechurch .com*), where St. Thomas the Apostle's relics are kept. It is believed that he came to India from Palestine in A.D. 52 and was killed in A.D. 78. Around 1100 the saint's remains were moved inland and a new church was built, possibly by the Persian Christian community. It stands in Mylapore, once the Tamil port, where the Portuguese made a settlement in 1522. Nearby **Kapaleeshwarar Temple** is lively with festivals, singing, and busy bazaars.

Enthusiasts can detour to the southwest to see **St. Thomas's Mount,** believed to be where the saint was stoned to death. The **Old Cantonment** is nearby, with lots of old flat-topped Madras villas; return via the racetrack and **Raj Bhawan** (1817), the former Government House built for Sir Thomas Munro.

The drive follows the Marina, renamed **Kamaraj Road,** for a group of Victorian buildings that are as impressive as Mumbai's. Moving up the drive, pause to see the circular former **Vivekananda House ❷** (1842), once the Ice House, where the Tudor Ice Company used to store blocks of ice imported from America; the Lutyens-style **University Examination Hall;** and **Presidency College.** The Presidency College's older part was designed in 1865 by Robert F. Chisholm, who mixed French and Italian Renaissance styles and various local details.

Next come the **Public Water Works** (1870), **Chepauk Palace** (1768) built for the anglophile Nawab of the Carnatic, with Chisholm's later tower (1870), and Chisholm's **University Senate House** (1873). This time he went for the Gothic-Saracenic style, with polychrome stones and arcades. A Golden Jubilee statue of Queen-Empress Victoria (1887) stands outside. Both she and Chantry's bronze equestrian statue of Sir

NOT TO BE MISSED:

Strolling up Marina Beach • St. Mary's Church • Government Museum Complex

Thomas Munro (1839), seen on the right after crossing the Cooum River, have survived India's postindependence cleansing of Raj memories.

Continue north to **Fort St. George ❸**, begun in 1644. Drive or walk through the fort to find **St. Mary's Church ❹** (1678–1680), the spiritual heart of old Chennai and the East's oldest surviving Anglican church. Look for the original, intricately carved teak gallery balustrade and the black Pallavaram granite font where Job Charnock, who would later found Calcutta, had his daughters baptized. A stunning collection of funerary monuments includes several by John Flaxman and John Bacon. Elihu Yale (governor 1687–1692) married here and was later a benefactor to Yale University.

Now for a contrast: the spectacular Indo-Saracenic warren of the **High Court ❺** (1888–1892), whose design by J. W. Brassington was revised by Irwin and J. H. Stephens. Up the stairs by the statue of Sri T. Muthasamy Iyer, the first Indian judge, the public courts have beautiful stained glass and tiles. Finally, drive past the Gothic arcades of **Chennai Central Station ❻** (1868–1872) to find, on the right, **St. Andrew's Kirk ❼** (1818–1821), considered India's most accomplished neoclassical church; the circular interior has its original louvered doors and cane pews.

The **Connemara Hotel ❽** (*vivantabytaj.com*) has an excellent lunch buffet of local dishes. You can get dance performance information from the tourist office on nearby Anna Salai.

The **Government Museum Complex ❾** (*Pantheon Rd., tel 044/2819-3238, closed Fri, $$,*

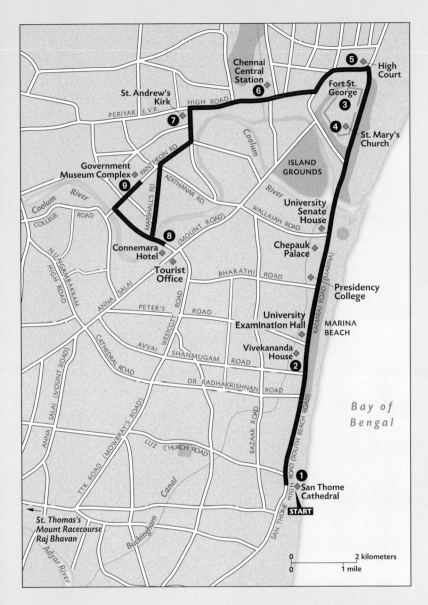

chennaimuseum.org), also called The Pantheon, is exceptional and deserves a whole afternoon. Founded in 1851, it has three main sections: stone carvings, including the Amaravati sculptures upstairs; bronzes, many from Chola temples; and musical instruments, photographs, and Chettinad carvings.

See also area map p. 255
San Thome Cathedral
About 4 miles (6 km)
Allow a full day, with lunch as indicated
Government Museum Complex

Mahabalipuram

Great caves, rocks and boulders, carved stones and friezes, and monolithic temples testify to the former importance of Mahabalipuram (Mamallapuram), port city of the Pallavas, the first great dynasty of southern India, whose royal capital was at Kanchipuram (see pp. 264–265).

The eighth-century Shore Temple has three shrines, one dedicated to Vishnu and two to Shiva.

Mahabalipuram
 255 D4

Visitor Information

✉ Tourist Office,
N end of village

🕐 Closed Sat.–Sun.

✉ Kovalam Rd.
☎ 044/2744-2232
💲 $$: Monuments

tamilnadutourism.org

mahabalipuram.co.in

NOTE: There is a huge amount to see here, mostly of very high quality. Start early, and take a break at a café or hotel.

Rising from local rulers to wealthy emperors, the Pallava dynasts believed in divine right and, in Hindu tradition, traced their ancestry back to Brahma. They called their empire Dravidia and extended it over present-day Tamil Nadu and into the Deccan. The Pallavas created much of the blueprint by which Tamil Nadu would live for centuries and promoted the village and temple culture known as Dravidian. Rice was the main crop and bartering unit, but coconuts, mangoes, plantains, cotton, and gingelly (sesame) were also grown. Each village built its own brick-lined tank as its essential water reservoir; many are still in use today.

Taxes were levied on everyone and everything; only weavers to the royal court were exempt.

Mahabalipuram's survivors are Tamil Nadu's earliest monuments. Mostly dating from the seventh and early eighth centuries, they seem to show a relentless thirst for experimentation, and much of the temple carving is sublime.

It was under the politically powerful Mahendravarman I (r. 600–630), a dramatist and poet who converted from Jainism to Shaivism, that some of the earliest rock-cut temples were chiseled. He was succeeded by Mamalla (r. 630–668) and later by Rajasimha (r. 700–728).

Start at the so-called **Tiger Cave,** about a mile (1.6 km) north of the village. A huge boulder has been carved to create a small portico surrounded by fierce masklike *yali* heads and two elephants. Along a path, find another early temple, a tiny living shrine roofed in coconut leaf. The row of upright stones, placed in the sand to face the sunrise, has its origins in pre-Hindu nature worship.

In the village, climb up the hill behind the center to find **Varaha Cave Temple.** Colossal, bold, and vigorous sculptures fill the interior: Varaha lifting up Bhudevi (left), Trivikrama (right), and Lakshmi and Durga on the rear wall.

In the village center, **Arjuna's Penance** is a remarkable piece of top-quality relief carving; of great complexity, it coats some 50 feet (15 m) of a rock face. Using delicate modeling and carefully observed detail, mixing naturalism with stylization, the craftsmen have enriched their story. Today, we interpret it as either the penance of Arjuna (standing on one leg) or the sage Bhagiratha persuading Shiva to receive the Ganga River in his matted locks. Next to this, find the **Krishna Mandapa;** its back wall has a gentle and bucolic scene of Krishna protecting the *gopies* by lifting Mount Goverdhana as an umbrella.

Now climb the steps up to **Mahishamardini Temple,** whose veranda sculptures are yet more masterpieces: Vishnu sleeping on the serpent (left) and Durga killing the buffalo-headed demon (right).

Beyond the village, standing alone in a sandy enclosure, the **Pancha Rathas** are five huge boulders carved to become temples. Their names mean little, but their variety of shapes and their carvings reveal an intensely creative period. See especially the tallest and most elaborate *rath* (chariot), whose sculptures already have a recognizable iconography; the south side shows Shiva with the royal patron, Mamalla.

Early in the eighth century, later than all these different caves and monoliths, **Shore Temple** was built. Together with Kailasanatha Temple at Kanchipuram, this is the first significant structural temple in Tamil Nadu; it provides the blueprint for the Dravidian temple (see pp. 262–263). ■

How to Buy a Stone Carving

In Mahabalipuram, hundreds of stone carvers at the foot of Mahishamardini Temple use traditional hammers and chisels to create Shivas, Parvatis, and Ganeshas for Hindu temples around the world, and the occasional contemporary piece. Buying a ready-made piece is fairly straightforward. Agree on a price that includes packing and overseas shipping, with full insurance. Then take photographs of it, measure it, and scratch your name on it. Take the workshop master's full contact information, so you can keep in touch.

Tamil Nadu's Dravidian Temples

Tamil Nadu's temples were built by the villagers to be their religious, social, cultural, and political focus—a position many still hold today. Funded by the king or a local man of means, they kept thousands of people employed for life, and still do. Temples remain the bedrock of Tamil Nadu communities.

The temple is often still the focus of daily life, which goes on all around a Kanchipuram temple.

The temple itself follows a basic format. One principal *gopura* (gateway) through the wall leads into a courtyard and so to the porch, *mandapa* (hall), and main shrine; the mandapas and shrine have increasingly lofty *vimanhas* (roofs). The elements are in line, so the worshipper progresses from the open spaces and their ebullient, symbolic sculpture to the increasingly dark, mysterious, simple, and womblike sanctum.

Many temples were founded by the Pallavas and Cholas, then enlarged by the Vijayanagar rulers and Pandyas. They sometimes added subsidiary shrines for the consort or family of the principal deity; thus a temple to Shiva could be given shrines for his consort,

Parvati, and his sons, Ganesh and Kartikeya. They might add extra mandapas for dance or special festivals, and around the central core they might build rooms for administration, facilities for cooking, sleeping rooms for the ever growing numbers of temple inmates, and libraries for study. Storage rooms were also needed for the festival chariots and for the coconuts, sugar, flowers, and spices sold in the temple to the faithful as offerings during their *puja* (worship). You can see this arrangement in many temples.

Walled Cities

As the temples got bigger, extra and taller walls were built to increase the space for these buildings and to protect the increasingly large treasuries from attack by greedy Muslim armies. Temples at Tiruchchirappalli and Madurai have several concentric walls and still function as complete cities. These later walls, whose tops were frequently decorated with Nandi bulls (Shiva's vehicle), have gopuras with higher and higher pyramid-shaped roofs covered with carvings of all the deities of the Hindu pantheon. This was because the untouchables, the lowest caste, were not permitted to enter the temples, and they therefore worshipped by looking up at the gopuras. It was for their benefit, as well as for that of the old and infirm that, at the many festivals, the temple deity was hauled around the village on an elaborately carved wooden *rath* (chariot).

Artistic Centers

Locals used their temples for much more than just simple worship. Their devotions became increasingly passionate, stimulating the great devotional poetry and music, the Bharata Natyam dance (see p. 257), and the legendary silk weaving to clothe the deities. Locals went to Sanskrit school in the temple; later they traded, held meetings, and celebrated there, too. Today, a Hindu may well do a special puja before making a journey or opening a store, or after landing a good job. In the past the income of whole villages was given to a temple—the inscriptions running around the temple

Signs on the Forehead

Indians believe in the supreme psychic power of the spot centered between the eyebrows. The sixth chakra (force center) of the body is located here. It is also where the eye of wisdom is supposed to be—Shiva's third eye is here—and devout yogis aim to open this third eye by meditation, to achieve unity between the conscious and unconscious minds.

All rites and ceremonies for Hindus begin with a vermilion *tilak* (mark) placed on this spot and then a few grains of rice stuck on while it is wet; the same is done to welcome and bid farewell to friends and guests. If you are welcomed with a tilak, it is polite to accept it with respect.

Each morning, a traditional Indian woman puts a colored mark on this spot, symbolizing her quest to open her third eye. The marks are usually made with *kumkum*, a red powder mixing the cleansing turmeric, alum, iodine, and camphor. Alternatively, it is a sandalwood paste blended with musk, which has a cooling effect and is often used in temples and after meditation. Devout Indian men, on the other hand, mark this spot to denote the deity they worship. A worshipper of Shiva has two or three horizontal lines on the forehead, that of Vishnu vertical lines; some men add a red dot to signify that they believe their deity to be the supreme being. The marks are white, red, yellow, or black, using ashes from sacrificial fires, cow dung, turmeric, sandalwood, lime, and glue-like binding rice water.

EXPERIENCE: The Art of Bronze Casting

The Cholas of the 9th to 12th centuries used their creative genius to push the art of lost-wax bronze casting to its peak of grace and harmony. See some of the world's finest in Chennai's **Government Museum Complex** *(Pantheon Rd., tel 044/2819-3238, chennaimuseum .org, closed Fri.)* and Thanjavur's **Nayak Durbar Hall Art Museum** *(Palace Compound).* The craft lives on today to supply temples, so you can easily visit one of the several bronze ateliers in and around Thanjavur, Kumbakonam, and Swamimalai to watch the process. Ask your hotel or guide to take you.

platforms are often a record of such donations. Nowadays, wealthy Hindus may pay for special pujas, maintenance work, or meals for the poor. The wealthy industrial Birla family has even completely funded several entirely new temples.

A Temple Odyssey

This tour from Chennai (Madras) to Thanjavur visits a handful of the many glorious temples, some now empty, others functioning just as they have done for centuries.

Kanchipuram: The only one of the Seven Sacred Cities dedicated to both Shiva and Vishnu, Kanchipuram was enriched by the Pallava rulers (see p. 260), who made it their capital. Chola, Vijayanagar, and Nayaka rulers further embellished it. Today this busy town, 35 miles (72 km) southeast of Chennai, has 50 or so functioning temples whose rituals gave birth to one of southern India's most important silk-weaving centers.

The buildings span a thousand years of creative and devotional output. Begin with the simple sandstone, eighth-century

Kailasanatha Temple *(0.5 mile/1 km W of city center),* the finest of the Pallava ruler Rajasimha's buildings, dedicated to Shiva as lord of Kailasha, his mountain home; you can see a variety of Shiva images. Late eighth-century **Vaikuntha Perumal Temple** stands to the east, near the train station. Built by Nandivarma II, the temple has one mandapa that leads to three shrines dedicated to Vishnu as the boar and lion; the rear wall sculptures illustrate Pallava historic events.

The later **Ekambareshvar Temple** (mostly 16th and 17th century), dedicated to Shiva as lord of the mango tree, is the city's largest temple *(N of city center).* Built in 1509 by the Vijayanaga emperor Krishnadeveraya, it has a soaring gopura (192 feet/58 m high), which leads toward an equally huge mandapa and corridor. The 12th-century **Varadaraja Temple** *(1.5 miles/3 km SE of city)* has a Vijayanagar addition, whose columns are elaborately carved with Vaishnava iconography and rearing horses. To see a little domestic history, visit **Kanchi Kudil** *(53A S. V. N. Dillai St., tel 044/2722-7680),* a traditional home.

INSIDER TIP:

If you familiarize yourself with the main stories of Hindu gods Shiva and Vishnu, you can have fun identifying them in temple sculptures.

—LOUISE NICHOLSON
National Geographic author

Kanchipuram to Chidambaram:

As soon as you leave Kanchipuram, you'll quickly find yourself on country roads. On the way to Mahabalipuram, **Uthiramerur** has two fine late Pallava temples built by Dantivarman (r. 796–817). If you want to see more Pallava monuments, spend a very quiet but long rural day inland; otherwise drive right down to Puducherry (see p. 266).

The rarely visited early cave temple at **Mandagappattu,** near Gingee, has an inscription that refers to Mahendravarman I (*r.* 580–630). Continue to the huge **Arunachaleshvara Temple** (16th–17th century) at **Tiruvannamalai** (major festival; *Nov.–Dec.*), where Shiva is worshipped as Lord of the Eastern Mountain. Finish with the hilltop temple (early eighth century) at **Panamalai,** 19 miles (30 km) east.

Chidambaram to Thanjavur:
Chidambaram's **Nataraja Temple** (12th–13th century) is like a fair every day. Nataraja is Shiva as the cosmic dancer, the Cholas' favorite form of Shiva. Try to arrive in time to witness the busy and elaborate main morning puja, usually around 9:30 a.m.; temple management and pilgrims' gifts make this one of India's richest temples. Then explore the warren of halls and corridors, mostly built in the late Chola period; do not miss the carvings of Bharata Natyam dance positions on the inside walls of the main gates.

The ride to evocatively named **Gangaikonda Cholapuram** goes inland through villages where ropemaking is a thriving cottage industry; pause to see how it is done. Then, seemingly in the middle of nowhere, you arrive at the windowless wall surrounding **Brihadishvara Temple.** Built by Rajendra I (*r.* 1012–1044) in his new capital, it celebrated his victory in eastern India up by the Ganga River and was intended to surpass the Thanjavur temple of his predecessor, Rajajraja I. Only a few village names (meaning "watchman's area," "firework makers," etc.) and some brick debris give clues to the extent of Rajendra's city. But the temple is testament enough. It is superb: Its glory is its monumental simplicity and its sculpture. Large panels on the outside of the shrine, mostly of Shiva, include one magnificent composition of Shiva garlanding Chandesha.

It is a short drive to **Kumbakonam,** a busy and ancient religious center between the banks of the Kaveri and its tributary, Arasala. Here you will find bronze-workers, traditional gold and jewelry dealers, and, of course, plenty of temples.

The ritual core of the city is **Mahamakam Tank,** the focus of the festival held here every 12 years (the next one is in 2016). The finest temple, however, is found just outside the city, across the Arasala at **Darasuram,** where the Airavateshvara Temple (mid-12th century) built by Rajaraja II (*r.* 1146–1172) is probably the finest late Chola building; the compact structure is coated in fine sculpture. From here the lanes twist through paddy fields and villages to Thanjavur (see pp. 267–269).

Detail of the *gopura* of Kailasanatha Temple, Kanchipuram, which is dedicated to Shiva

Puducherry

The French bought land from the sultan of Bijapur in 1672, and two years later, François Martin set up a trading post, Pondicherry (today's Puducherry). Although it was lost to the Dutch once and to the English several times, the Marquis de Dupleix restored its prestige, and Jean Law laid out the town (1756–1777) that still survives. The French only ceded their territories to India in 1954. Today, about 14,000 French nationals live here, in one of India's union territories.

Puducherry
- 255 C4

Visitor Information
- ✉ 40 Goubert Ave.
- ☎ 011/3233 9197
- **tourism.pondi cherry.gov.in**

Pondicherry Museum
- 🕒 Closed Mon.

The old core offers hints of French colonial times. In the main square, **Dupleix's statue** (1870) stands near the gleaming white **Raj Niwas,** a fine French colonial house (1752) built as his palace. (There is a brief but splendidly formal ceremony here each sunset.) Across the square, modest **Pondicherry Museum** occupies the French former Government Library.

On the waterfront, eight pillars from Gingee and a statue of Mahatma Gandhi stand at the entrance to the pier. South of here is a statue of Joan of Arc, the **Église de Notre Dame des Anges** (1855), and, in the cemetery opposite, the tomb of Dupleix's enterprising follower, Charles, Marquis de Bussy (1785).

Two French cultural institutions, in beautiful buildings, offer small exhibits: **L'École Française d'Extrème-Orient** (16-19 rue Dumas, closed Sat.–Sun., efeo.fr) and **L'Institut Français** (11 St. Louis, closed Sat.–Sun., ifpindia.org).

North of the pier, visit the reception center of the **Sri Aurobindo Headquarters** (rue de la Marine). Sri Aurobindo Ghosh (1872–1950), a Bengali educated at Cambridge, and his disciple, a Parisian known as The Mother (1878–1973), established this ashram. In 1968, she founded the nearby futuristic city of Auroville (see p. 284), designed by French architect Roger Anger. The handmade **paper factory** (tel 041/3233-4763) around the corner can sometimes be visited.

Finally, see if the home of 18th-century diarist Ananda Ranga Pillai (69 rue Rangapillai), a protégé of Dupleix, is open; it mixes Indian and French colonial styles. ∎

Church of the Sacred Heart of Jesus, on South Boulevard

Thanjavur & Trichy

Life in moderate-size, moderately paced Thanjavur still centers on the monumental royal Brihadishvara Temple (ca 1010) built by Rajaraja I (r. 985–1014), who donated the gilded pot finial on top of the 217-foot-high (66 m) tower. While nearby the small town of Tiruchchirappalli, better known as Trichy, lies beside the sacred Kaveri River. Between and around them are peaceful drives and charming hill towns.

Two bullock carts trundle through the unusually quiet courtyard of the great Brihadishvara Temple.

Thanjavur

Here, in the morning, locals hurry in through the sun-drenched gates of Brihadishvara Temple to pray before work. In the evenings they come in the hundreds as the last rays of sun are glowing on the tower and enliven the whole compound with their prayer, chattering, music, and religious readings.

Rajaraja I's capital, Thanjavur was built up under previous Chola rulers, chieftains in the area for centuries. One leader conquered Thanjavur in the ninth century and quickly claimed descent from the sun. Expansion of land and power followed under Rajaraja I and his son Rajendra I (r. 1012–1044). Campaigns in Kerala, the Maldives, Sri Lanka (Ceylon), and right up to Orissa brought most of the Indian peninsula under Chola control until the Hoysalas of Halebid and the Pandyas of Madurai expanded in the 12th century.

Chola trading in cottons, silks, spices, drugs, jewels, ivory, sandalwood, and camphor was lucrative,

Thanjavur
⬛ 255 C3

Visitor Information

✉ Hotel Tamil Nadu Complex

☎ 043/6223-0984

tamilnadutourism .org

while at home agriculture was made more efficient. Caste differences became stronger. The poor were encouraged to win spiritual and social respect by giving their skills and time to the temple, the wealthy to acquire prestige by donating whole villages to the temples. Church and state became intertwined: The god-king cult was promoted through image worship of past rulers and temple buildings, and the raja-guru (king's priest) became the king's chief spiritual and temporal adviser.

The thoroughly royal **Brihadishvara Temple** epitomizes this increasingly controlled and centralized state. The biggest especially the Shiva images on the outside of the sanctum. Inscriptions run all around the platform, documenting the construction of the temple and the names of the donors. Inside, join the faithful to see the colossal *lingum*. There are Chola period paintings here, too, including one of a royal visit to Chidambaram (west wall) and another of Shiva riding in a chariot drawn by Brahma (north wall); many others were overpainted by the Nayakas. The compound has a delicate 17th-century subsidiary temple dedicated to Subramanya, one of Shiva's sons, and a treasury, museum, and library.

In the royal palace compound is the **Nayak Durbar Hall Art**

Cholas & Shiva Nataraja

Hindu temple sculpture is the most sublime achievement of Indian art, reaching one of several peaks under Chola patronage. Shiva is a favorite deity. He represents dynamic energy, both creative—hence his symbol of the *lingum*—and destructive, which suited the powerful warring temple patrons. His developed personality was at once outrageous, amoral, and wild, yet ascetic and that of the perfect family man.

The Chola rulers especially worshiped Shiva Nataraja—Lord of the Dance—and dedicated entire temples to this form (e.g., at Chidambaram; see p. 265). In the classic iconography, Shiva dances in a wild, ecstatic frenzy or in a withdrawn yogic state, eyes downcast or closed, within a ring of flames. He carries the fire of destruction and the double drum, whose beat summons up creation, and calms and protects the worshipper. Shiva's hair contains the Ganga River goddess; below him, the demon Apasmara, personifying ignorance, looks up in hope. In all, Shiva symbolizes both endings and beginnings.

and richest Chola temple was conceived as a temple-fort and dedicated to Shiva as the Great Lord. The gateway leads into a large, rectangular court, where a Nandi bull lies in a high pavilion in front of the steep steps up to the temple. Rich sculpture decorates the porch and exterior; see **Museum,** a world-class collection of Chola bronzes found in the area, exhibited with beautiful simplicity in open rooms around the palace courtyard, together with equally fine stone carving. Several show Shiva as Nataraja (see sidebar above); the best were found at Thiruvelvikudi and Jambuvanodai.

Others show him as the archer, with his consort Parvati, or with their son Skanda. The masterpiece of all these sculptures is Shiva with Parvati, one arm outstretched.

Tiruchchirappalli

Today, Tiruchchirappalli (aka Trichy) is a vibrant temple city dedicated to Ranganatha—Vishnu when he is reclining on the serpent Ananta. Pilgrims swell the resident population daily, especially at festival time. It is a timeless yet thriving world. The first, huge gateway, with writhing sculptures painted bright yellows, greens, and pinks, was completed only in 1968. As you move forward, past stores selling everything from temple offerings and souvenirs to chilies and light bulbs, the sacred mystery of the temple increases.

Here, at Srirangam, one of southern India's largest and most complete sacred complexes, **Sri Ranganathaswamy,** was built. Founded by the Cholas, it received patronage from both the Pandya and Hoysala rulers, was sacked twice by 14th-century Muslim armies from Delhi, then expanded unabated during the 16th and 17th centuries.

The temple itself begins at the fourth wall, where you leave your shoes. Here you see the **Ranga-nayaki Temple** and the richly carved thousand-pillared **Kalyan Mandapa.** Even more spectacular carving has transformed the pillars of the **Sheshagiriraya Mandapa** into rearing horses carrying hunters armed with spears, a typical Vijayanagar double symbol of

good triumphing over evil—that is, of brave Hinduism protecting the temple against Muslim invaders. In contrast, the Nayaka-period **Venugopala shrine** on the south side is delicately carved with maidens leaning against trees.

At the fourth wall, ask to climb onto the roof to enjoy the splendid view right across all the walls

Rooftop view of the *gopuras* protecting the gold-roofed inner sanctum and treasury of Sri Ranganathaswamy Temple

to the gold-encrusted sanctum; the *gopuras* diminish toward the center. Inside the third courtyard, continue to the **Garuda Man-adapa,** a hall carved with maidens and donors that surrounds the shrine to Vishnu's man-eagle vehicle. Only Hindus can continue to the inner sanctum to see the image of reclining Vishnu.

As well as its stupendous temple, the town has a Chola-period earthen dam, the **Grand Anicut;** the great rock with temples including the **Lower Cave Temple** (Pandya, eighth century) and **Upper Cave Temple** (Pallava, 580–630); and the **Church of St. John** (1816) in the cantonment.

Tiruchchirappalli (Trichy)

 255 C3

Visitor Information

✉ Tourist Office, Williams Rd.

☎ 043/1246-0136

tamilnadutourism .org

Rural Routes from Trichy

The drives from Trichy to Thanjavur and to Madurai are not long. If you have time and a good driver, a detour from either one takes you right into peaceful, sometimes dramatic country with magical sites. Take water and snacks.

Trichy to Thanjavur: From Trichy, take the road southeast to Kiranur. Along this 34-mile (55 km) route you can stop to look at a group of hundreds of dilapidated, abandoned *ayyanars* on the right. These are heraldic terra-cotta figures of equestrian deities, sometimes with horses and elephants, often brightly colored, found on village outskirts throughout Tamil Nadu. Their functions are to protect the village from calamities such as plague, make barren land fertile, bring good harvests, and protect night watchmen. A priest regularly performs *pujas* at each group. On special occasions, such as the time of sowing seeds, new ayyanars are added and special pujas performed.

At Kiranur, turn right for the village of **Narthamalai.** Once there, leave your car at the far end of the village and walk for about 15 minutes up the granite hill to find a cluster of early Chola temples. One is cut into the granite and has 12 identical high-relief Vishnu figures carved into the back wall. The freestanding temple has guardian figures flanking the door, and fading murals.

It is about an hour's drive from Nartamalai to **Mallaiya-dipatti.** Here you find superb late Pallava caves (ninth century), one carved with a huge Vishnu reclining on the Cosmic Ocean, another carved with the nine gods. From here continue to the

Like many southern Indian temples, Trichy's has a resident elephant to help with *pujas* and festivals.

main Trichy–Thanjavur road, and turn right. Soon you will see on the left a memorial—two standing stones and a crossbar—to a death in childbirth, which travelers use to rest their load. A little farther along, on the right, a group of ayyanars stands beneath a banyan tree across a small field. The road continues to Thanjavur.

Trichy to Madurai: Leave Trichy on the country road to Madurai (88 miles/140 km), not the main one, toward Kodumbalur. You will pass brightly colored ayyanars, whose creators have kept them up to date by giving them wristwatches. At Kodumbalur, the isolated double **Muvakoil Temple** (ninth century) built by the Cholas is all that remains of the original nine shrines. Their sculptures are glorious; it's worth coming here just to see the Shiva Nataraja on the east side of the south shrine.

Continue to **Sittanavasal** to find a Jain cave temple (ninth century) cut into a long granite outcrop. Inside the hall, find images of Parshvanatha (right), Mahavira (left) on the sides, and more Jinas in the rear walls. Delicate paintings survive, too: dancing maidens and royal figures on the columns, a lotus pond in full blossom on the hall ceiling, a design with knotted patterns on the shrine ceiling. A rocky overhang on top of the hill has a natural cavern with polished beds for Jain monks and an inscription that dates from the second to first century B.C. **Pudukkottai** is the next stop: Its Tondaiman rajas supported the

---

Vishnu: Clarifying the Confusion

All over India you will encounter the god Vishnu, preserver of the universe, but you may not always recognize him. According to the mythologies, he assumed the appropriate form to deal with each world-threatening demon, thus the confusion. Vishnu has been Matsya the fish, Kurma the turtle, Varaha the boar, Narasimha the man-lion, Vamana the dwarf, Parashurama (Rama with an axe), Rama as hero of the *Ramayana* epic, Krishna, and Buddha—and he will come again as Kalki to save mankind. Seen in a temple or a painting, any one of these figures is probably Vishnu, telling a heroic story.

British against Tipu Sultan and the French; thus they received titles and security and left a well-built city. In the old area, Tirugorakarna, find the **Gokarneshvara Temple** (begun in the seventh century), with its 18th-century *Ramayana* paintings and rock-cut Pallava inner chamber, whose carvings include a fine set of Matrikas (mother goddesses). Near the temple entrance, **Government Museum** (*closed Fri.*) displays quality local finds.

You can now go direct to Madurai or make four final stops. First is at the village of **Avudaiyarkoil,** where the broad temple passageway has supports carved with Tondaiman royals, their ministers, and, at the end, Shiva in his fierce aspects. Farther into the temple, find a shrine dedicated to the local saint, Manikkavachakar.

A road leads cross-country to **Karaikkudi** in the heart of the Chettinad communities, where merchants made their money in the 19th and 20th centuries in trade and finance with Madras, Burma, and Malaya. Their mansions have some of the finest wood carving in Tamil Nadu but display a masonry facade to orderly streets in small settlements. See them here and in **Devakottai** to the south and **Chettinad** village to the north from where it is approximately 59 miles (95 km) to Madurai (see pp. 279–280).

Tamil Nadu's Hill Stations

Although the early British adventurers adopted Indian ways and dress, and had Indian wives, by the 19th century an altogether more powerful and bureaucratic British presence seemed determined to remain as British as possible. Rather than adapting to the hot and humid climate and self-preserving ways of Indians, they wore too many clothes, ate and drank in quantities suited to northern Europe, and dreamed of green hills, gentle rain, and rose gardens.

As a result, they fell ill and many died of typhoid, cholera, and malaria. Soldiers stationed in the hill forts, however, did not. So sanitariums were built in the hills for ailing servants of the empire. Once it had been proved that the

Kolams: **Daily Meditation with Rice**

As you drive through the rural areas of South India, especially in the days before a major Hindu festival, you may see women squatting outside their modest homes making sophisticated geometric patterns on the ground by dribbling a fine, even stream of dried rice powder from their fists, moving in swift curls and sweeps. They are creating the *kolam* for the day as a form of meditation. Soon, it will be lost in the day's movement; tomorrow, they will create another and the pattern will be different.

First the ground is washed to symbolically purify it, sometimes adding a little cow dung, which has antiseptic properties; its dark color also increases the visual impact of the white kolam. The rice kolam has several functions: It is a sign

of welcome, especially to the goddess Lakshmi who brings prosperity; traditionalists believe it provides food for ants, birds, and small creators, thus respecting the coexistence of man and nature.

Most communities have master kolam creators who are called on to make the elaborate multicolored kolams for festivals and weddings, which can cover a street. Tamil Nadu ladies seem to push the art's boundaries, creating huge complex patterns without lifting their hand or getting up from start to finish. The women are usually very happy to demonstrate their art and let visitors have a go. Having placed the guiding grid of dots on the ground, they will start creating their pattern, mesmerizing onlookers. Then, it is your turn; it is not as easy as it looks.

An elaborate *kolam,* a ritual pattern created using colored rice flour

hills were healthier, enterprising officers set off to discover suitable sites. British hill stations were born.

Shimla, then called Simla, was the first, dating from 1819 (see pp. 122–123). During the next 30 years more than 80 hill stations were established at elevations of between 4,035 feet (1,230 m) and 8,071 feet (2,460 m), and vast resources were spent on constructing mountain roads and railroads to reach them. Built on open hilltops with no fortifications, they represented a British confidence in themselves, their power, and their home culture.

The hill stations were cocktails of ideal British countryside, town activities, and beach town resorts. Highly social, elitist, and yet trapped in an isolated dream far from home, the British in the hill stations lived life to the fullest. The theater, clubs, churches, sports, flower shows, and promenades along the Mall ensured a continuous whirl of activity and a fair number of romantic flings.

But underneath there was homesickness, too. Lady Betty Balfour wrote from Ooty in 1877 of "such beautiful English rain, such delicious English mud. Imagine Hertfordshire lanes, Devonshire downs, Westmoreland lakes, Scotch trout streams and Lusitanian views." She and her compatriots loved the colder climate, tolerated the leaking houses and discomforts, and built British-style houses with names like Rose Bank and Glenthorn.

But India was never far away. For all the attempts to create a drop of pure "home," every British hill station had a certain Indianness about it. Today, it is the reverse: Every Indian hill station retains a certain Englishness about it.

Coimbatore

255 A3

Visitor Information

State Tourist Office, Hotel Tamil Nadu Complex, Dr. Nachiappa Rd.

042/2230-3176

coimbatore.com
tamilnadutourism.org

Coonoor

255 A3

coonoor.com

Up to Coonoor: Leaving the hot, lush, and sparkling paddy fields of the Tamil Nadu plains, roads twist and turn up gentle slopes into the fresh air and forests of the Western Ghats. These are truly spectacular drives, so it is worth allowing time to stop and enjoy panoramic views, do some bird-watching, and visit tea or coffee gardens. From north to south, the Ghats run more than 1,000 miles (1,609 km), reaching their height in the Nilgiris

to the Nilgiris. Its industrial wealth soared after hydroelectric power was harnessed from the Pykara Falls in the 1930s, boosting cotton manufacture. The town has no tourist attractions, but if you stay overnight, take a morning stroll in the **Botanical Gardens,** established around 1900.

From Coimbatore drive north to Mettuppalaiyam, where the steep ascent begins, bringing hair-pin bends, wonderful views, and a canopy of dark foliage. Northwest of Mettuppalaiyam is **Coonoor,**

As Ooty's popularity has grown since independence, its eclectic mix of colonial buildings has been joined by modern Indian housing, stores, and billboards.

(Blue Mountains) at Ooty, which stands at the foot of the 8,615-foot-high (2,626 m) Doda-Betta Peak.

Affluent **Coimbatore** (also now called Kovai) is strategically placed near Palghat, the broadest pass through the hills. Coimbatore serves as a gateway

which stands at 6,096 feet (1,858 m). It is at the head of the Hulikal Ravine in the Doda Betta Range and is less wet and cool than "The Queen" (see opposite). Huge tree ferns, impressive rhododendrons, and roses all flourish in **Sim's Park** (Upper Coonoor), where the prestigious

Coonoor Fruit and Vegetable Show is held annually.

This is a marvelous area for hiking: Visit **Lady Canning's Seat** (2 miles/3 km); **Lamb's Rock** (3.5 miles/6 km), with dramatic views; **Dolphin's Nose** (7.5 miles/12 km), with views of Katherine Falls and the Coonoor Stream; and **Law's Falls** (3 miles/5 km), named after the man who constructed the Coonoor Ghat Road. You can also hike the 2 miles (3 km) up to **The Droog** (Pakkasuram Kottai) for exhilarating views of the plains.

Udhagamandalam: At 7,349 feet (2,240 m), Udhagamandalam (Ootacamund, or Ooty) is the highest Nilgiri hill station and is surrounded by rolling, grassy slopes, natural woodland, and imported eucalyptus and conifer trees.

The original inhabitants here were four tribes, including the Todas, a tribe who tended herds of sacred buffalo. Today, their few surviving members have, sadly, been turned into something of a tourist curiosity. Following the death of Tipu Sultan in 1799, the East India Company annexed the Nilgiris and their tribes. In 1818 two assistants of John Sullivan, Collector of Coimbature, saw the possibilities of the area; in 1823, Sullivan built his Stone House. Word spread, the British arrived, and Sullivan planted English vegetables and trees. He enlarged the lake and introduced fast-growing eucalyptus trees from Australia.

By 1861 Ooty, as it was known, was the summer capital of the Madras Presidency and "The Queen of Hill Stations." The governor and his staff, servants, and all their families arrived, soon followed by other Europeans and anglophile Indian princes. According to their means and position, they came on foot or on horseback, were carried in palanquins, or, later, took the train; the

INSIDER TIP:

Because southern India is close to the Equator, its summers are hot and humid; the best time to visit is during the cooler winter months.

—DR. SHOURASENI SEN ROY
National Geographic grantee

first passengers arrived in Ooty in 1908. Nowadays the train can be taken from Mettuppalaiyam or, for a longer journey, from Coonoor.

To visit some of British Ooty, start with a walk through the orchids, trees, ferns, and medical plants of the glorious hillside **Udhagamandalam Botanical Gardens,** founded in 1848 by the Marquess of Tweeddale with the help of Mr. MacIvor from Kew Gardens in London. Above the gardens lies the 1877 **Raj Bhawan** *(Garden Rd., closed to public),* built for the Duke of Buckingham when he was governor of Chennai. Ooty's biggest events, the annual flower and dog shows, are held here.

(continued on p. 278)

Udhagamandalam (Ooty)

⚑ 255 A3

Visitor Information

✉ Udhagamandalam Tourist Office, Wenlock Rd.

☎ 042/3244-3977

tamilnadutourism
.org

Udhagamandalam Botanical Gardens

✉ Garden Rd.

Women & Marriage

It may be surprising to learn that for some years India's more privileged women have formed a greater percentage of leading company directors, surgeons, movie directors, and members of parliament than they do in most Western countries. This results from a form of backroom emancipation, reinforced by the extended family support system where grandparents and other relatives keep house and care for a working woman's children.

The exotic bangles and gaily colored saris only emphasize the fate of thousands of women who work as laborers for very low wages in terrible conditions of filth, dust, and heat.

But life for the vast majority of Indian women is different, full of inequality and deprivation. Even in India's more emancipated urban areas, tradition remains strong.

This starts at birth—even before birth. The use of illegal prebirth sex-testing in such wealthy states as the Punjab has been linked to the high numbers of private (and illegal) abortions by women carrying healthy female fetuses. After birth, more unwanted baby girls than boys have traditionally found their way onto the doorsteps of India's children's homes. During childhood, girls are often kept back from school to help with the housework, or they drop out. Despite government programs

and energetic women's movements, all too often daughters' health, schooling, literacy, and training lag substantially behind their brothers'.

The only incentive parents have to educate a daughter is to improve her marriage prospects. In essence, most Indian parents consider a daughter a burden, who should be married off as soon and as well as possible to remove her as a mouth to be fed and as a responsibility. Unlike sons, who stay at home, a daughter goes to live with her husband's family. Marriage in India is usually more of a contract between two families than a love match. This is clear from the frank advertisements in the Sunday newspapers: Questions of caste, skin color, healthiness, job prospects, and social standing are paramount.

Most marriages are still arranged, even if more enlightened parents give the couple the right of veto. A teenage village girl may be married to a man she has never met; she moves to his village or town, keeps his mother's house clean, does manual labor in the fields, and bears and raises his children. She has no property rights; divorce is rare; and there is no social security for divorcées or widows. A middle-class woman's lot is not much better, and if she fails to live up to expectations, primarily to produce a healthy son, she may suffer. One of the worst atrocities in India today, despite being outlawed, is "bride-burning"—that is, a "kitchen accident" in which a woman dies from burns caused by flaming "spilled" kerosene.

In almost all cases, marriage is sealed with negotiations over the dowry. To the traditional silks, saris, and jewels, the husband's family may now add demands for such luxuries as freezers, DVD players, or even a car. The wedding, paid for by the bride's family, is usually a spectacular string of processions and parties.

Brides wear a traditional red sari, gold jewelry, plenty of red bangles, and *mehndi* (henna).

Although apparently invisible, the women in a household wield considerable power in all decision-making, from investments and harvesting to who marries their daughters

Color & Meaning

India is a riot of color, but the kaleidoscope has order—indeed it functions to help create order. For Hindus—whose greatest philosophical fear is chaos—every color has a meaning and the proper use of color is believed to create an environment to keep people cheerful. This color coding helps you identify the bride at a wedding, the god in the yellow dress, etc.

Red is considered the most significant color, used for the most important events such as birth, marriage, and big festivals. A bride mostly wears red; a married woman puts red powder on her hair parting; she is wrapped in red cloth for her cremation. Red powder is thrown onto deities during *puja* (worship); a red dot is placed on a worshipper's forehead; deities who

triumph over evil are dressed in red. Saffron symbolizes purity and holiness; it is also the battle color of the Rajputs, as seen in miniature paintings. Green denotes peace and stability, while blue's meaning of bravery and determination makes it appropriate for the gods Rama and Krishna who protect humanity and destroy evil. Yellow is for knowledge, so Vishnu, Krishna, and Ganesh all wear it. White, being the mixture of all colors, represents each color's meaning. Saraswati, goddess of learning, wears a white dress sitting on her lotus. Conversely, a Hindu widow wears white for mourning. Thus, if you are dressed in white it is a good idea to add a splash of color, perhaps in the form of a belt or shawl.

Kodaikanal

⚠ 255 B3

Visitor Information

✉ Rest House Complex, Poet Thyagaraya Rd.

☎ 045/4224-1765

tamilnadutourism .org

kodaikanal.com

Yercaud

⚠ 255 B4

Snooty Ooty

French botanist M. Perottet introduced tea here; coffee had already been grown near Mysore since the 1820s. Visitors in the early years included the first governor-general of India, Lord William Cavendish Bentinck (1774–1839), and historian Thomas Babington Macaulay (1800–1859). Snooty Ooty, as the hill station was known, has changed radically and now feels more like a midscale Indian town transplanted to the hills.

Among the verdant lanes, you can get a feel of British Ooty by surveying the Ootacamund Club (founded 1843; *closed to non-members*) and the Ooty Gymkhana Gold Club on Wenlock Downs. Then go to **St. Stephen's Church** (1831), full of memorials to those who could not be saved by Ooty's fresh air, and to the **Taj Savoy Hotel** (*77 Sylks Rd., tel 042/3222-5500, $*), whose wood fires burn each night. Go down past the lake to see the racetrack, station, and beyond them, **St. Thomas's Church** (1870). Farther on down is the **Fernhill Palace** (1842), which once belonged to the ruler of Mysore and is now a hotel. In town, find Sullivan's **Stone House** near Charing Cross, the **Nilgiri Library** (1885), and the **District and Sessions Court** (1873).

There are good excursions and hikes, or you can make arrangements through your hotel for a guided horseback ride. Doda Betta Peak offers fine views, or go to Marlimund Lake, Tiger Hill, Kalhatti Falls, and Pykara Lake or Pykara Falls, 20 miles (32 km) west of Ooty. A scenic road leads to Avalanche, and from Mukerti Lake you can hike up Mukerti Peak.

Kodaikanal: Set in a natural bowl in the Palani Hills and surrounded by terraced hills, Kodaikanal has only recently lost its peaceful charm in favor of lucrative tourism. Known as "The Princess of Hill Stations," it was founded in 1844 by the American Madurai Mission, whose members moved up here from Madurai in a desperate search for renewed health.

If you can, avoid Kodaikanal's two monsoons and arrive here along picturesque **Laws Ghat Road** between January and March, when visitors are few. You can rent rowboats from the Boat Club and find good views over the plains along **Coaker's Walk**.

Yercaud: Across in the Eastern Ghats, the thickly forested Shevaroy Hills rise sharply. Here, at Yercaud, 4,920 feet (1,499 m) up, the first real hotel opened in 1971, offering a respite from the heat. Until then it had been a place for coffee estates since the 1820s and, more recently, for Catholic schools. Leaving the whitewashed, red-tiled houses of the town and its planters' club, there are pleasant walks through the wooded lanes around the coffee estates. ∎

Madurai

Pilgrims flock to Madurai's colorful and huge complex of the Meenakshi Sundareshvara Temple, dedicated to Shiva's consort, Parvati (Meenakshi), giving it a lively yet medieval atmosphere.

Built on the banks of the Vaigai River, Madurai was founded by the Pandyas, who made it their capital while they ruled south Tamil Nadu (7th–13th centuries). However, in 1323 Malik Kafur's Tughlaq forces from Delhi took Madurai and stayed until 1378, when the Vijayanagars liberated it. Their governors, known as Nayakas, slowly asserted their independence; Tirumala (r. 1623–1660) was an active builder throughout his kingdom. Resisting Mughals and Marathas, the Nayakas held on to their throne until the British established control in 1763.

Madurai's Temple

Madurai's temple is thus a testament to Nayaka royal and aristocratic patronage through the 17th and 18th centuries. Remodeling and redecoration continue to keep the ceilings, murals, and *gopura* colorful. Both mornings and evenings you'll find *pujas*, elephant processions, music, and singing in the various halls. The 12-day **Meenakshi Kalyanam festival** in April–May, to celebrate the coronation of Meenakshi and her marriage to Shiva, is spectacular.

While simply wandering through the corridors and halls will be rewarding, there are some special things worth seeing. Entering the **Ashta Shakti Mandapa**, notice how elegant and tall the gopuras are. Then find the lively dancing men flanking the corridor to the **Potramarai Kulam** (Golden Lily Tank), behind which you find superb carvings of the *Mahabharata* heroes in the

Madurai

255 B2

Visitor Information

Tourist Office,
1 W. Veli St.

045/2233-4757

maduraitourism.com

A riot of gaily painted, dancing and cavorting gods and goddesses decorate this *gopura* at Madurai's Meenakshi Temple.

Panch Pandava Mandapa. Just near here, in the gloom, you will find a beautiful and sensuous freestanding group of Shiva and Parvati. See also the **Kambattadi Mandapa** with its seated Nandi, the huge, corridor-like **Viravasantaraya Mandapa,** the **Temple Art Museum**'s carvings, and the **Pudu Mandapa** (full of fast-working local tailors), whose columns are sculptured into portraits of all the Nayaka kings up to Tirumala.

Madurai's temple is best seen by wandering the corridors and halls; only the inner sanctuaries of the shrines are off-limits to non-Hindus. All day, processions, worshippers, and visitors throng the temple. Climb the south gopura for a great overview and don't miss the carvings in the Temple Art Museum. ■

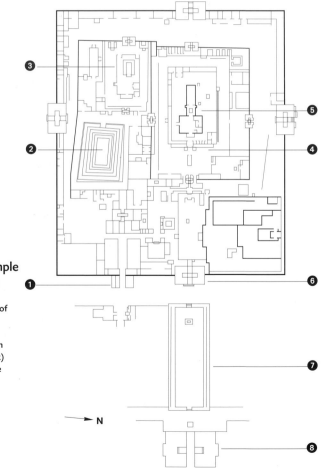

Madurai's Temple

1. **Entrance through the Ashta Shakti Mandapa (Porch of the Eight Goddesses)**
2. **Potramarai Kulam (Golden Lily Tank)**
3. **Meenakshi shrine**
4. **Kambattadi Mandapa**
5. **Sundareshvara (Shiva) shrine**
6. **Viravasantaraya Mandapa**
7. **Pudu Mandapa**
8. **South** *gopura*

N

Southern Tamil Nadu

What the south of Tamil Nadu lacks in architecturally stunning temples, it makes up for in coastal beauty, some fascinating offbeat sites, and the chance to visit Kanyakumari, where the waters of three seas mingle.

Sunrise at Kanniyakumari reveals fishing boats bobbing gently on the surf, waiting for their owners.

The far south of India has attracted devotion rather than war, inspiring temple-building rather than forts. **Rameswaram,** the 35-mile-long (56 km) peninsula jutting toward Sri Lanka, plays a vital role in the climax and finale of the Hindu epic *Ramayana.* The huge **Ramanatha Temple** (mostly 17th–18th century) marks the spot where Rama, having killed the demon Ravana, worshipped Shiva to purify himself. Today's pilgrims imitate this by bathing in the sea and then being doused with water from the 22 wells in the temple complex. Many also visit **Gandhamandana Hill** to see Rama's footprint, and **Dhanushkodi,** where Rama received submission from Ravana's brother.

On the way to the peninsula, you can stop at the village of **Ramanathapuram** to see the local Setupati rulers' palace, where the Ramalinga Vilasa rooms are

Rameswaram
🅰 255 C2
Visitor Information
✉ 14 Bus Terminus
☎ 045/7322-1371
tamilnadutourism .org

Padmanabhapuram Palace (16th–17th century) exemplifies traditional Kerala architecture.

Tirunelveli

🗺 255 B1

Visitor Information

✉ Collectorate Complex

☎ 046/2250-0104

tamilnadutourism .org

lavishly decorated with 18th-century paintings recounting the Hindu epics and Setupati royal life. Farther south on the Gulf of Mannar, huge maritime fossils have been found on the shores near Kilakkarai.

Set in the lush valley of the Tambraparni River, **Tirunelveli** makes a good base for visiting the tip of India. If arriving by car from Madurai, pause at Kalugumalai to see the monolithic **Pallava Temple** (eighth century) chiseled out of a granite outcrop and extensively decorated. In Tirunelveli itself, a major Nayaka city, the **Nellaiyappar Temple** (mostly 16th–17th century), dedicated to Shiva and Devi, has a riot of fine stone and wood carving; in the first enclosure find donor sculptures of the Tirunelveli chiefs.

The first stop on a tour southeast from Tirunelveli is the village of **Krishnapuram,** whose Venkatachala Temple, dedicated to Vishnu as Lord of the Venkata Hills, has glorious 17th- to 18th-century carvings and fine

figural piers in its Virappa Nayaka Mandapa. The Iron Age site of **Adichanallur,** beside the Tambrapani River, has fascinating ancient sepulchral urns. At the town of Alvar Tirunagari, the high-ranking Vishnu saint Nammalvar, born here in the ninth century, was the inspiration for the **Adinatha Temple** (mostly 16th–17th century) and its lively carvings. When you reach the coast, there are three places to visit overlooking the Gulf of Mannar: **Kayalpattinam,** with its mosques for locals descended from Arab traders; **Tiruchchendur's** pilgrimage temple; and **Manapadu,** whose Catholic associations go back to St. Francis Xavier's visit in 1542.

The tip of India is a rocky promontory overlooking the mingling waters of the Bay of Bengal, the Arabian Sea, and the Indian Ocean. The town of **Kanniyakumari** is named after Kumari, the Hindu goddess who protects the shores, and pilgrims come here to bathe near the temple. Two great

Indians have memorials here: Mahatma Gandhi, whose ashes were thrown into the ocean here; and Vivekananda, the Bengali philosopher who came here as a monk in 1892 and founded the Ramakrishna Vivekananda Missions. Headquartered in Kolkata, the missions still thrive today.

West of Kanniyakumari, you can stop at Suchindram to see the **Sthanumalaya Temple** (13th–18th century) beside the large tank. Dedicated to Vishnu and Shiva, grand and gaily painted *gopuras* and colonnades lead to the earlier shrines. Before Shiva's, see the splendidly carved corner columns of the small pavilion.

INSIDER TIP:

The best place and time to take a photo in Kanniyakumari is at the Gandhi Mandapam at sunset, when the memorial's warm colors glow in the light.

—CESARE NALDI
National Geographic contributor

Similarly, the pavilion housing the image of Vishnu's vehicle, Garuda, has columns carved with portraits of Nayaka donors and their queens. In the corridor inside the perimeter walls, **Alankara Mandapa** has carvings of royals, including Martanda Varma of Thiruvananthapuram (see pp. 211, 213). It is an easy drive northwest from Suchindram to the astonishing palace of the Travancore kings at **Padmanabhapuram.**

Another good route from Tirunelveli goes to Kollam (Quillon). Stop at **Tenkasi** to visit the capital of the Pandya in the 15th to 16th centuries. Their **Vishvanatha Temple** has very fine carvings; see Shiva with the wives of the sages on the gopura walls, and the huge carved piers of the hall in the first enclosure.

A different, more rural route west to Kollam goes through the village of **Tiruppudaimarudur.** Its **Narumbunatha Temple,** on the banks of the Tambraparni River, has unusually well-preserved sculptures and paintings. At **Papanasam,** up in the hills, you simply enjoy the beauty of the spot. ∎

Importance of Rice

If you are in southern India in early January, you may witness Pongal, the rice harvest festival. Farmers scrub their bullocks and paint their horns. On Pongal morning, each village home boils newly harvested rice amid a complicated ritual. When it boils over it is *pongal,* a sign indicating a rich harvest to follow.

Here, rice is more than a staple part of the diet and economy. It is a fundamental part of life. Before a child goes to school, there is a rice ceremony to Saraswati, goddess of learning. A bride tips a bowl of rice into her new home to symbolize fertility and prosperity; a mourning family offers rice balls at the *sradh* ceremony to help the spirit find peace. Throughout the state you can see *kolams,* intricate patterns of rice powder made by women to encourage prosperity and happiness and to ward off black ants from their houses.

More Places to Visit in Tamil Nadu

Alagarkoil

The **Algar Perumal Temple,** beside a forested hill, is dedicated to Vishnu as Kallalagar, Minakshi's brother; the temple is part of Madurai's great festival (see p. 279). Note the elegant donor figures with Nayaka queen, and the rare Pandya central shrine.
🗺 255 B2   ✉ 7 miles (12 km) N of Madurai

INSIDER TIP:

During Mandalapooja *[mid-Nov.–Dec.],* crowds of Hindu pilgrims fill the temples and markets of Kanniyakumari on their way to Sabarimala.

—CESARE NALDI
National Geographic contributor

Auroville

Inspired by The Mother (see p. 266), about 800 families live in this ideal coastal city founded in 1968. Houses with names such as Grace form an outward spiral, symbolizing continuous motion and the universality of faith; the Matrimandir (Meditation House; *tel 0143/2622-204*) is central. Stores in the city stock homemade goods. *auroville.org* 🗺 255 C4 ✉ 6 miles (10 km) N of Puducherry

Chengalpattu

Chengalpattu (Chilgleput) is famous for its fort, which was disputed by the French and English. At nearby **Vallam,** three fascinating Pallava cave temples date from the reign of Mahendravarman I (r. 580–630). 🗺 255 C5 ✉ 36 miles (58 km) W of Chennai

Chennai–Mahabalipuram Drive

There are two places to stop: **Cholamandel** coastal artists' community, with its permanent arts exhibition, and Muttukadu's

Dakshinachitra *(tel 044/2747-2603, $$, closed Tues., dakshinachitra.net),* to see old vernacular buildings. A building from each of four southern states is preserved, together with information on their respective ways of life. ✉ 13 miles (21 km) S of Chennai

Gingee

Tamil Nadu's most spectacular fortified site, Gingee was built by the Vijayanagas and contested by most subsequent armies in the south. Climb the steps to the citadel. 🗺 255 C4 ✉ 42 miles (68 km) NW of Puducherry

Kilaiyur & Tiruvaiyaru

Kilaiyur's finely finished twin temples, built in the ninth-century by local chieftains, make an interesting combination to visit in conjunction with nearby Tiruvaiyaru's temple, famous for its music festival. 🗺 255 C3 **Kilaiyur** ✉ 20 miles (33 km) N of Thanjavur

Panamalai

On the Villupuram–Vettavalam road, the eighth-century hilltop **Talagirishvara Temple,** dedicated to Shiva, is built of reddish granite and has a hemispherical roof, some nice sculpture, and traces of paintings. 🗺 255 C4 ✉ 46 miles (75 km) W of Puducherry

Point Calimere Wildlife Sanctuary

Saltwater tidal swamps are home to flamingos and other waterbirds, and you can also spot blackbuck, feral horses, and jackals. On a trip from Thanjavur, you can return via **Velanganni,** a Catholic pilgrimage center, and **Nagappattinam,** an ancient port and Buddhist center whose Karikop Cemetery has early Dutch tombs. 🗺 255 C3 ✉ 56 miles (90 km) SE of Thanjavur

Pulicat

Right on the border with Andhra Pradesh, Pulicat Lake attracts resident and migratory waterbirds such as pelicans and flamingos. The old tombstones in the Dutch cemetery are worth a look. 255 D5 ✉ 25 miles (40 km) N of Chennai

Pullamangai

The splendid **Brahmapurishvara Temple** (tenth century), dedicated to Shiva, sits quietly at the end of this rural village where in almost every house there lives a master silk weaver. Walk around the back to see the fine sculptures on the outside of the sanctuary. ✉ 6 miles (10 km) from Thanjavur

Srinivasanallur

There is fine sculpture on this early Chola temple (927) overlooking the Kaveri River and dedicated to Koranganatha, a form of Shiva. Westward, **Punaji** has a similarly good temple, while **Namakkal's** eighth-century Pandyan shrine, with vigorous and large sculptures, is hidden behind later additions. ✉ 28 miles (45 km) NW of Tiruchchirappalli

Sriperumbudur

Believed to be the birthplace of the Vaishnava saint Ramanuja, the 16th–17th-century temple has splendid *Ramayana* friezes. 255 C5 ✉ 25 miles (40 km) SW of Chennai

Srivilliputtur

The **Vatapatrashayi Temple** here, dedicated to Vishnu, has a 17th-century Nayaka period *gopura* 207 feet high (63 m) with an 11-stage tower. Said to be the tallest of all gopuras, it is Tamil Nadu's official emblem. 255 B2 ✉ 46 miles (74 km) SW of Madurai

Swamimalai

In the hamlet of Swamimalai (Tiruvalanjuli), the **Kapardishvara Temple,** dedicated to Shiva, has a Chola-period hall. In the village, craftsmen make religious bronzes using the lost wax method. ✉ 5 miles (8 km) W of Kumbakonam (255 C3)

Tharangambadi

From 1620 to 1807, Tharangambadi (Tranquebar) was the headquarters of the Dutch East India Company, and the European character survives intact today in the houses, churches, and fort with museum *(closed Fri.).* 255 C3 ✉ 39 miles (63 km) E of Kumbakonam

Srivilliputtur's Adal Temple, Vatapatrashayi Temple's twin, has brass-encased portraits of its patrons.

Thirupparankundram

The **Murugan Temple,** dedicated to Shiva's son Subramanya, began as a Pandya-period cave temple built in the sacred granite hill in 773. To reach it, go through the later additions of painted and sculptured halls. A major 14-day festival *(March–April)* is held here. ⛰ 255 B2 ✉ 4 miles (6 km) SW of Madurai

Thiruvarur

This important Chola temple is dedicated to Shiva as Tyagaraja, glorified by Tamil saints such as Appar and Sambandar in their hymns. Massive *gopuras* lead through to the shrine, whose Somaskanda form of Shiva (Shiva, his consort Parvati, and their son Skanda or Subramanya) was a favorite Chola image. ⛰ 255 C3 ✉ 33 miles (53 km) E of Thanjavur

Tiruchengodu

There are two Chola complexes to see here, much enlarged by the Nayakas and Wodeyars. Midtown **Kailasanatha** is crowded with stores and temple chariots; walk up to **Ardhanarishvara** for the best entrance, fine wood carving, and good views. ⛰ 255 B3 ✉ 31 miles (50 km) SW of Salem

Tirukkalukkundram

This ambitious temple built by the Nayakas of Gingee is dedicated to Shiva as Bhaktavatsaleshvara. Tirukkalukkundram's grand *gopura* has fine sculptures and paintings of royal visitors (west gopura). ⛰ 255 D4 ✉ 9 miles (14 km) W of Mahabalipuram

Tirumangalakkudi

The 18th-century paintings on the corridor ceiling in **Pramanatheshvara Temple,** dedicated to Shiva, make a trip across the Kaveri worthwhile. They depict local legends and the shrines along the river. ✉ 9 miles (15 km) NW of Kumbakonam (⛰ 255 C3)

Tiruttani

Follow a path up the hill to find a Pallava period shrine with fine images of Subramanya and, in the outer enclosure, a row of stone soldiers as his army. ⛰ 255 C5 ✉ 53 miles (86 km) NW of Chennai

Tiruvadaimarndur

There are two Chola shrines to Shiva here. First, see the grand and large corridors and halls of the **Mahalinga Perumal** temple complex (17th–18th century), with its Chola shrine, then Tribhuvanam's royal **Kampahareshvara Temple,** built by Kulottunga III (r. 1178–1218). ✉ 6 miles (10 km) NE of Kumbakonam (⛰ 255 C3)

Tiruvannamalai

Tiruvannamalai's **Arunachaleshvara Temple** is one of Tamil Nadu's grandest, dedicated to Shiva's fiery *lingum* (phallus). A crowded 14-day festival (Nov.–Dec.) here coincides with the cattle fair. North of here, **Tirumalai** has a 16th-century Jain complex. ⛰ 255 C4 ✉ 23 miles (37 km) W of Gingee

Vedanthangal Bird Sanctuary

A lake and marshy, low-lying ground attract ibises, gray pelicans, purple moorhens, nightherons, and other waterbirds (tel 044/2432-1471). ⛰ 255 C4 ✉ 25 miles (40 km) SW of Mahabalipuram

Vellore & Arcot

Vellore's fine **fort** has haunting associations with the Vijayanagaras, Marathas, Mughals, British, and Tipu Sultan, whose family was kept here after the fall of Srirangapatnam. A mile (1.6 km) northeast, find the *dargah* (tomb) of Tipu's mother and wife. ⛰ 255 C5

Vrinchipuram

Rising grandly above its modest village, the **Marghabandhu Temple** is dedicated to Shiva. It has a huge *gopura,* a columned hall, and twin marriage halls possibly inspired by Vellore's superb temple (see above). ⛰ 255 C5 ✉ 9 miles (14 km) W of Vellore

The Ganga's great, verdant delta, home to the Hindus' sacred
Varanasi city and monuments from the early Mauryas to the British

Eastern India

An intricately carved wheel at
Konark's Surya Temple

Eastern India

Although steeped in history, eastern India is little visited by foreigners. East of Delhi, India is mostly quiet and very accessible, with little of the aggressive tourism found to the west, in Rajasthan.

You can trace the path of the Ganga through three very different states: Uttar Pradesh, Bihar, and West Bengal. Uttar Pradesh has the highest population of any Indian state—more than 140 million; yet its literacy is just 69 percent, a telling yardstick. Its cities vary from the Mughals' Muslim Agra, the Hindus' sacred Varanasi, and Buddhist Sarnath, to Lucknow, now the state capital. Out in the fields, farmers produce more cereals than any other state and half of all India's sugarcane.

Neighboring Bihar is even more densely populated but less fortunate: Literacy is just 63 percent. However, it is India's richest state in minerals and is responsible for 42 percent of the country's production. Around the capital, Patna, you can follow the story of Buddhism at Bodh Gaya and Nalanda.

Kolkata (Calcutta) is West Bengal's capital and eastern India's commercial and cultural center. The state's recent history is one of reduction: It once stretched to Agra and included Bihar and Orissa, but it was divided in two in 1905, a move that fed the area's awakening patriotism. It was further divided at independence to form East Pakistan (now Bangladesh) and West Bengal. Kolkata has a state literacy rate touching 87 percent and still maintains Bengal's cultural tradition, while the farmers produce much of India's rice, jute, and, up in the hills, tea.

Between these three states and the Deccan Plateau to the south lie Madhya Pradesh, Tharkand, Chhatisgarh, and Orissa. A vast landscape of dry plains and forested hills, Madhya Pradesh is India's largest state; yet it is rarely visited by tourists. Orissa, bookended by the Eastern Ghats and the Bay of Bengal, is home to some of India's most interesting tribal communities. As in Bihar, you can visit vestiges of remarkable early empires in and around the capital, Bhubaneshwar.

The tropical Andaman and Nicobar Islands form India's most remote state, more than 600 miles (1,000 km) east of the mainland. Only a few islands are open to foreign visitors, but they offer fabulous beaches and pristine coral reefs. While Kolkata, Varanasi, and Lucknow may not be picturesque or easy to visit, they are rich in history and well worth the effort needed to explore them. ∎

NOT TO BE MISSED:

NEPAL

200 kilometers
100 miles

EASTERN
HIMALAYA
p. 328

...asti *Rapti*
Lauria
Nandangarh
Bettiah
Kushinagar
Motihari
Sitamarhi
Madhubani
Kishanganj

...aizabad
Basti
Gorakhpur 28
Lauriya Areraj
Muzaffarpur
Darbhanga
Araria
31

...tanpur
Azamgarh
Mau
Ballia
Siwan
Vaishali
Samastipur
Saharsa
Purnia
Raiganj

...apgarh
Ghazipur
Buxar
Chhapra
Hajipur
Khagaria
Katihar
Balurghat

...npur
Ara
Patna
Bihar Sharif
Munger
Pandua
Ingraj Bazar

Sarnarth
30
Bhagalpur
Jahangira
Gaur

Varanasi
Chunar
Dehri
Rajgir
Nalanda
Nawada
Rajmahal
Murshidabad

Mirzapur
Sasaram
Aurangabad
Gaya
Godda
Baharampur

...hi
Robertsganj
Bodh
Gaya
Devghar
Dumka
Baharampur

...grauli
Govind Ballabh
Pant Sagar
Daltenganj
Hazaribag
Giridih
Shanti
Niketan
Plassey

MADHYA
...ADESH
Samri
JHARKHAND
Dhanbad
Siuri
Durgapur
Navadwip

Baikunthpur
Lohardaga
Asansol
Bankura
Kalna
Krishnanagar

Hazaribagh Range
Gumla
Ranchi
Purulia
Bishnupur
Chandannagar
Barddhaman
Chunchura

...tghora
Ambikapur
Jashpurnagar
Jamshedpur
Chaibasa
WEST
BENGAL
Barakpur
Serampore
Basirhat
Dum Dum

Korba
Raurkela
Medinipur
Haora
(Howrah)
KOLKATA
(CALCUTTA)

Bilaspur
Sundargarh
Jharsuguda
Kharagpur
Haldia
Sajnekhali

Raigarh
Hirakud
Kendujhargarh
Baripada
Kakdwip
SUNDERBANS
NAT. PARK

...HATTISGARH
Bargarh
Sambalpur
SIMILIPAL
NATIONAL
PARK
Baleshwar
Sunderbans
Mouths of the Ganga

...pur
Mahasamund
Balangir
Dhenkanal
Bhadrakh
Ratnagiri
Palmyras Point

Bindra
Nawagarh
Ranipur Jharial
Phulabani
Kendrapara

Bhubaneshwar
Udaiayiri
Paradwip
Pipli

Chilka
Lake
Puri
Konark

Bhawanipatna
Aska

ORISSA

ndagaon
Rayagada
Chhatrapur
Brahmapur

Jagdalpur
Jeypore
Gopalpur-on-sea

Koraput
Parlakimidi

THE DECCAN

Eastern Ghats

Bay of Bengal

BANGLADESH

Area of map detail

New
Delhi

Coco Channel

North
Andaman
Cape Price
Narcondam

Interview
Port Cornwallis
Mayabaner

Middle
Andaman
Barren

Baratang
Ritchie's
Archipelago
ANDAMAN
ISLANDS

South
Andaman

North
Sentinel
Port Blair
Rutland
Cinque

South
Sentinel
Little
Andaman

Duncan Passage

ANDAMAN
AND
NICOBAR
ISLANDS

Ten Degree Channel

Car Nicobar

Tillanchang
Dwip

Tarasa Dwip
Camorta
Nancowry

Katchall

NICOBAR
ISLANDS
Sombrero Channel
Little Nicobar

Great
Nicobar

100 kilometers
50 miles
Indira Point

Kolkata

There is a strength and spirit in Kolkata (Calcutta) that, despite all it has suffered, makes it one of the world's great cities. It is not an exceptionally pretty city, but Kolkata allows you to touch the pulse of Bengal's culture, past and present, and see, through the decay, the grandeur of a colonial city—one that is fast catching up with the rest of India's business renaissance.

Former colonial grandeur is the backdrop to contemporary Kolkata life on Bentinck Street.

Kolkata

🗺 289 D3

Visitor Information

✉ India Tourist Office, 4 Shakespeare Sarani

☎ 033/2282-1475

incredibleindia.org

✉ State Tourist Office, 3/2 BBD Bagh (East)

☎ 033/4401-2659, 033/4401-2660

westbengaltourism .gov.in

calcuttaweb.com

Bengalis consider themselves, with some justification, the intelligentsia of India. The Bengali Renaissance of the 19th century witnessed a flowering of talent, led by Raja Ram Mohan Roy (1774–1833), which created a new intellectual elite whose legacy continues today.

Kolkata is relatively new. In 1690 Job Charnock, a maverick agent for the British East India Company, leased three swampy villages from Mughal Emperor Aurangzeb. Trading began, and six years later the company built Fort

William, but times were uncertain. When Nawab Siraj-ud-Daula of Murshidabad took the city and incarcerated British soldiers in a dark room later dubbed the "Black Hole of Calcutta," Robert Clive arrived from Madras and crushed him at the Battle of Plassey in 1757. Seven years later, Sir Hector Munro led the British triumph at the Battle of Buxar, wresting most of Bihar from the Nawabs of Bengal, who had recently won it from the weakening Mughals.

The fortunes of the British—and the city—took off. In

1772 Kolkata (Calcutta) usurped Chennai (Madras) as the British headquarters in India and appointed its first governor of British India, Warren Hastings. Kolkata's rich hinterland became the main source of the company's vast wealth (which, after 1858, went to the British government). Dazzling white stuccoed mansions with a lifestyle to go with them made Kolkata the greatest colonial city of the Orient.

Kolkata's position held until 1931, when New Delhi was inaugurated as the new capital, and kept its commercial prowess until independence, when colonial companies were obliged to become Indian. Since independence, the city's population has swelled first with Hindu immigrants from newly created Muslim East Pakistan, then with refugees from the Indo-Pakistan war of 1965 and the Pakistan-Bangladesh war of 1972, prompting the start of high-profile charity work. Today, Kolkata covers 40 square miles (104 sq km) and has a population of more than 13.2 million.

Begin your exploration of the city in the early morning, when you can best imagine the past elegance of this City of Palaces.

BBD Bagh & Around

Start early in the morning west of Assembly House, by the statue of Khudiram Bose, the first martyr for independent India, who was hanged in 1908 at the age of 19 for killing two British women with a bomb. In front of Walter Granville's very fine 1872 Gothic **High Court** *(closed Sat.–Sun.),* well worth exploring, stands a statue of the revolutionary Surya Sen (died 1930).

EXPERIENCE: Going to the Races

For a delightful afternoon in a British-founded city such as Kolkata, Mumbai, or Bangalore, head to the local track. Horse racing (the "sport of kings") is a legacy from the British, retaining much of its charm and tradition, including colonial courses with white picket fences, beds of blooming flowers, and, at some tracks, tea and cucumber sandwiches—and big pegs (measures) of whiskey.

Central Kolkata's **Royal Calcutta Turf Club** *(rctconline.com)* is especially pretty. Built in 1819, its grandstand offers great city views, while spreading banyans shade racegoers in the Members' Enclosure. India's first derby was held here in 1842. Today, after a few years in the doldrums, the club is rallying to its former glory.

More than 500 horses are kept on site. The high point of the season *(Nov.–late March)* is the Queen Elizabeth II Cup *(end of Jan.)*—the trophy is still signed and sent by the Queen. With India's growing wealth and horse racing losing its elitist stigma, the crowds are getting younger and the betting heavier; it's a great atmosphere.

Other colonial tracks are in **Mumbai** and **Bangalore** (which currently offers the richest purse)—both in the city center—as well as **Pune** and **Mysore.** Some upscale hotels can arrange tickets for the Members' Enclosure, which usually requires formal dress (jacket and tie for men). Visit *indiarace.com* for information on fixture dates and special races.

Writers' Buildings

☎ 033/2235-5601
⏱ Closed to public

John Garstin's **Town Hall** (*closed Sat.–Sun.*) is a handsome 1813 Tuscan-Doric building, remodeled in the 1990s. Beyond it, on your way around the back of Raj Bhavan's huge garden, find the statue of the political leader Subhas Chandra Bose's equally revolutionary brother, Sarat.

Raj Bhavan (Government House; *Red Rd., closed to public*) is the West Bengal governor's

the Black Hole of Calcutta (see p. 290). Clive Francis, who lived nearby, wrote: "Here I live, with a hundred servants, a country house, and spacious gardens, horses and carriages. . . . "

Down Government Place West, visit **St. John's Church** (1787), its design based on London's St. Martin-in-the-Fields. In the interior, memorials to Kolkata's British heroes include John

Durga Puja

Durga Puja is the most spectacular of Kolkata's many festivals, which fill the city's calendar. It falls in September and October, generates a near collapse of the city's offices, and brings families together for constant celebrations. The focus is Durga, Shiva's wife in her destructive form. Idolmakers living in the Kumatuli area work all year to create hundreds of Durga images, painting their straw and unbaked clay models gaudy colors to look like the latest film stars (to see them, visit Kumatuli; see p. 293). Offices, local

groups, or whole streets then create unashamedly glitzy temple-size *pandals* (temporary houses) for their goddess, who, fierce and furious with her ten arms, is shown either on or with her lion, slaying the demon Mahisasura, who has deviously taken the form of a buffalo to threaten the gods. For the ten days before Mahadashami, when the images are paraded down to the Hooghly and immersed in the water, you can join Kolkatans on their evening strolls to visit as many as possible of these spectacular creations.

residence. Beyond this take Old Court House Street past the Great Eastern Hotel to **BBD Bagh** (Dalhousie Square), renamed for Benoy, Badal, and Dinesh, three freedom fighters hanged by the British. BBD Bagh was the hub of company power. **Writers' Buildings** (1780, refurbished 1880) spanning the north side of the square, was built for company clerical staff and is still a bureaucratic hive. On the west side of BBD Bagh is Walter Granville's **GPO** (General Post Office, 1864–68), with its Corinthian columns standing over the site of

Bacon's to Maj. James Achilles Kirkpatrick; the altarpiece depicts famous Kolkata residents as Christ's Apostles; the churchyard has memorials to the Rohilla War (1794) and Job Charnock (ca 1695), who founded the city.

Haora Station & Bridge

To see this area, begin at the early morning **flower market** under Haora (Howrah) Bridge (1943), where gymnasts and wrestlers train at Armenian Ghat. Then drive over the bridge to see Halsey Ricardo's magnificent **Haora railroad**

INSIDER TIP:

One of the oldest and largest museums in Asia, Kolkata's beautiful, airy Indian Museum has extensive collections of art and natural science.

—JEFF WILSON
National Geographic grantee

station (1854–1928). From here, ferries cross the Hooghly to **Babu's Ghat** on the Maidan, or head upriver to **Kumatuli Ghat,** where craftsmen make inlaid woodwork and Durga Puja clay deities.

North Kolkata

North of BBD Bagh was where rich Kolkatans once lived, and some old families still do. Stroll the narrow alleys to find facades of crumbling mansions. Try **Barabazar** and its Armenian church (1724). North of M. G. Road, find the vast and decaying **Marble Palace** *(4 Muktaram Babu St., off Chittaranjan Ave., tel 033/2269-3310, closed Mon. & Thurs.),* begun in 1835 by Rajendra Mullick when he was 16 years old. It abounds with Belgian chandeliers, Venetian mirrors, and paintings by Rubens and others. Northeast of here, visit the restored house of Rabindranath Tagore, which is now the **Rabindra Bharati Museum,** and trace the story of the Tagores and the Bengal Renaissance. Finally, visit College Street in the university area,

where the **Asutosh Museum of Indian Art** has Bengali crafts and *kantha* embroidery.

South Kolkata

Alipore and Ballygunge, Kolkata's wealthy residential areas, developed around the Deputy Governor's House, now the **National Library.** Alipore's **Horticultural Gardens** *(tel 033/3262-5631, closed Mon., $)* are half a mile (1 km) south of here. At the **Kolkata Zoo** *(Jawahar Rd., 033/2579-1150, closed Thurs., $, kolkatazoo.in),* the snake, bird, and big cat collections are especially interesting.

Still farther south, **Kalighat,** the temple to Kali, patron goddess of Kolkata, is best reached via the Metro: The underground subway is Russian-designed, clean, and efficient. Zip down to Kalighat station, then walk five minutes to the city's most important temple. The East India Company servants used to give high-profile but controversial devotional offerings here. ■

Rabindra Bharati Museum
- ✉ 6 Dwarakanath Tagore Ln.
- ☎ 033/239-5241
- 🕐 Sound & Light Show, Mon. & Thurs.: Nov.–Jan. 7 p.m.–7:40 p.m.; Feb.–June 8 p.m.–8:40 p.m.
- 💲 $

museum.rbu.ac.in

Asutosh Museum of Indian Art
- ✉ Centenary Building, College St.
- 🕐 Closed Sun. & university holidays
- 💲 $

Indian Museum
- ✉ 27 Jawaharlal Nehru Rd.
- ☎ 033/2286-1702
- 🕐 Closed Mon. Tours: 10:30 a.m., 11:30 a.m., 2:15 p.m. & 3:15 p.m.
- 💲 $

indianmuseumkolkata .org

A stallholder finds his wares make a handy pillow.

A Drive Around Colonial Kolkata

After Clive's victory (see p. 290), the East India Company rebuilt the fort (1757–1770) and cleared thick jungle in front of it to create the defensive Maidan (open space) that is Kolkata's great lung today. This drive takes you past some of the colonial public buildings, churches, monuments, and houses built in Kolkata's heyday.

The Victoria Memorial Hall recalls Raj-era India

NOT TO BE MISSED:

South Park Street Cemetery
• St. Paul's Cathedral • Victoria Memorial Hall

Start at **Babu's Ghat ❶**, from where ferries go to Haora Station (see p. 293). Near the Ghat, **Eden Gardens ❷** contain Kolkata Stadium, where test cricket matches are held. Look across the Maidan to Jawaharlal Nehru and Chowringhee Roads: Enough buildings survive to help your imagination furnish them with 18th- and 19th-century grandeur.

Drive along Esplanade past Col. John Garstin's handsome, refurbished **Town Hall** (1813) and grandiose **Raj Bhavan ❸** (Government House, 1797–1803), begun by Viceroy Lord Curzon and designed by Capt. Charles Wyatt in imitation of Robert Adam's Kedleston Hall in Derbyshire, England.

At the corner with Jawaharlal Nehru Road, the **Shahid Minar ❹** (1828; formerly the Ochterlony Monument) is a tall column erected in honor of Sir David Ochterlony, the eccentric British hero of the Nepal War (1814–1816). Your drive down Chowringhee Road begins with the **Oberoi Grand Hotel**

(1911, much changed), which stoically holds on to its Raj character through every restoration. Down Lindsay Street bustling lanes are centered around **New Market ❺**; if you want to shop, a coolie will follow you around and carry your purchases on his head.

Proceed to the **Indian Museum ❻** (opened 1814), India's first national museum. It holds exceptional stone and metal sculptures rescued from eastern Indian sites. See the second-century B.C. sculptures from Vidisha, Sravasti, and Bharhut; the second-century A.D. panels from Mathura; India's finest collection of first- to third-century schist sculptures from Gandhara; and other treats from Khajuraho, Halebid, Konark, and Nalanda. Farther down Chowringhee Road, you pass the **Asiatic Society of Bengal,** founded by Sir William Jones in 1784, and the forerunner of such British learned societies.

Turn left on Park Street, then right into Middleton Row to find more buildings from Kolkata's past. The **Convent of Our Lady of Loreto** was once home to the great collector Sir Elijah Impey. Stop to take a stroll around **South Park Street Cemetery ❼** (*indian -cemeteries.org*), where pyramids, catafalques, pavilions, and obelisks, all saved from destruction, tell the amazing story of the city's growth and heyday. The cemetery guide, sold on site, is worth buying.

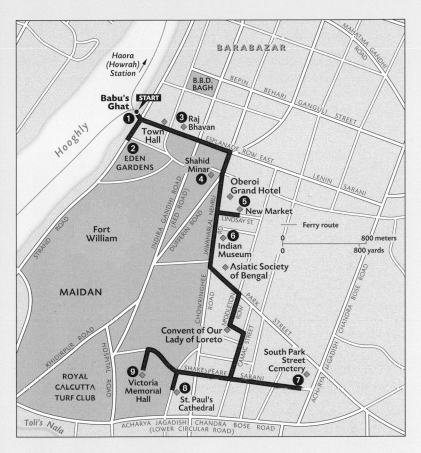

Back along Shakespeare Sarani **St. Paul's Cathedral** ❽ (1839), overlooking Chowringhee, is the British Empire's first Church of England cathedral. Treasures include Sir Edward Burne-Jones's west window (1880), Clayton and Bell's east window (1860s), and the pre-Raphaelite monument to Lord Mayo.

Finally, you reach the symbol of British imperialism in the east, the restored **Victoria Memorial Hall** ❾ (1921; *tel 033/2223-1891, closed Mon., victoriamemorial-cal.org*). Designed by Sir William Emerson and faced in Makrana marble from Jaipur state, it is topped off with a bronze figure of Victory. A statue of Lord Curzon stands at the south entrance. In front is Sir George Frampton's art nouveau statue of the Queen-Empress Victoria. Inside are quantities

of huge oil portraits of self-regarding servants of the empire, plus an excellent new gallery in the back, which explain Kolkata's history.

Farther west in the Maidan, you'll find the **Royal Calcutta Turf Club** (1820; *rctconline .com*), built as the home of a shipping magnate, now one of many traditional British clubs that have changed little apart from the nationality of their membership.

- 🗺 See also area map pp. 288–289
- ▶ Babu's Ghat
- 🔁 6 miles (10 km)
- 🕒 4–5 hours; leave early enough to reach the Indian Museum at 10 a.m., when it opens.
- ▶ Victoria Memorial Hall

Orissa

Bhubaneshwar, the state capital of Orissa (Odisha), has a long and glorious history. In the fourth century B.C. it was the capital of ancient Kalinga. Ashoka fought here in 260 B.C. before turning to Buddhism; he later placed a rock edict here. During the city's golden age of prosperity and religious fervor (7th–12th centuries), the Bhauma-Kara, Somavansi, and Ganga rulers built more than 7,000 temples around Bindu Sagar, as offerings to the gods and symbols of authority.

Two wonderfully realistic elephants stand in the compound of Konark's isolated Surya Temple.

Bhubaneshwar

📍 289 C2

Visitor Information

✉ India Tourist Office, B/21 B. J. B. Nagar

☎ 0674/243-2202

incredibleindia.org

✉ State Tourist Office, Paryatan Bhawan, Lewis Rd.

☎ 0674/243-1299

orissa.gov.in/tourism orissatourism.org

✉ State Tourist Office, Aruno-daya Market Bldg., Link Rd.

☎ 0671/231-2225

At three groups of temples on Bhubaneshwar's southern outskirts, you can trace the evolution of the distinctive Orissan style by visiting in order: **Parasumares-vara Mandir** (late 7th century), **Vaital Deul** (late 8th century), **Mukteshvara** (late 10th century), **Lingaraja** (late 11th century), and **Yameshvara** (late 13th century). The curved tower grows higher and more complex; the *mandapa* (hall) becomes larger with a pyramid roof; sculpture is increasingly fully modeled, more elaborate, and focused on the niches.

In Bhubaneshwar, the **Orissa State Museum** (*Lewis Rd., closed Mon., $, orissamuseum.nic.in*) has a collection of Orissa's archaeological finds, as well as ethnographic items and illustrated manuscripts. India's largest zoo is in **Nandank-anan Botanical Gardens** (*closed Mon., $, nandankanan.org*).

A day trip south to **Puri** winds through quaint villages with decorated houses, including **Pipli,** center of Orissa's colorful cotton appliqué-work. Puri is best known for its soaring **Jagannath Temple** (*closed to non-Hindus*); this is a true pilgrim town, especially during the annual **Rath Yatra festival** (*June–July*). You can also promenade along the waterfront.

Then drive up the coast to **Konark,** whose splendid **Surya Temple** (13th century), built by the Ganga king Narasimha (r. 1238–1264) marks the climax of all you saw at Bhubaneshwar: The temple is built as the sun god's chariot drawn by a team of horses.

Orissa's Early Monuments

Orissa's elaborate, rock-cut caves and substantial Buddhist remains testify to the wealth of the Kalinga empire of the fourth century and its mercantile strength, military power, and opulent lifestyle.

In two sandstone outcrops overlooking Bhubaneshwar are some remarkable caves left by a large Jain community that thrived here in the first century B.C. under the benevolent Chedi rulers. About 35 massive and austere caves, some natural and some dug out, provide our earliest evidence of the art found here in Orissa.

The dozen caves on the Khandagiri Hill are fairly simple. Those on the **Udayagiri Hill** include **Cave no. 1,** the largest and most elaborate. Two levels of cells surround a large courtyard. See the guardian figures, some in foreign dress (upper story, right wing), and the relief carvings over the doorways that show pious couples, musicians, dancers, and nature scenes. **Caves no. 3–5, 9,** and **10** are also interesting.

A long day trip north rewards with more caves at Lalitagiri, Udayagiri, and Ratnagiri, as well as stunning countryside. You first pass through Orissa's former capital, **Cuttack,** crammed onto a narrow

island on the Mahanadi River. In the old quarter's bazaars, find Orissa's distinctive filigree jewelry.

The caves are hidden amid lush farmland sprinkled with tiny villages. Each of these hill sites was an ideal place to found a Buddhist university during the great expansion of Buddhist teaching from the 5th to the 12th centuries. At that time the sea reached farther inland and the monks' patrons were often affluent merchants trading by sea. Some of these monasteries were training centers for Buddhist missionaries who were to spread the word eastward.

INSIDER TIP:

The beautiful temples south of Bhubaneshwar can be toured in about half a day; a cycle-rickshaw is handy, and its driver will know temples not in the guidebooks.

—BILL WEIR
National Geographic author

At **Lalitagiri,** the remains of platforms, shrines, mounds, and monastic buildings are still being excavated on Parabhadi and Landa Hills. At **Udayagiri,** archaeologists are finding more of these plus a colossal image of Buddha seated and panels of Bodhisattvas. **Ratnagiri,** once the center of Buddhism in Orissa, has a great hilltop stupa and two monasteries; one still has its courtyard, cells, and a Buddha figure. ∎

Udayagiri Hill Caves
- ✉ 4 miles (6 km) W of Bhubaneshwar
- 💲 $

Cuttack
- 🅼 289 C2
- ✉ 30 miles (48 km) N of Bhubaneshwar

Ratnagiri
- 🅼 289 D2
- ✉ 85 miles (135 km) NE of Bhubaneshwar
- 💲 $

NOTE: Both tourist information offices in Bhubaneshwar have information on Orissa's many festivals.

India's Tribal Communities

About 70 million of India's billion inhabitants live traditional tribal lives. Known collectively as Adivasis (original inhabitants) or by the government grouping of Scheduled Tribes, they trace their origins to pre-Aryan times. For many, their lifestyle has changed little over the centuries. Until recently, they had remained apart from the great empires and their developments, and had rarely met Hindu, Muslim, Western, or other cultures.

More than 500 named tribes, speaking more than 40 different languages and following ancient customs and religious rituals, still live on the periphery of society, with their distinctive lifestyles, although environmental pressure has forced the traditional hunters among them to change to cultivation. Most live in the thickly forested regions of India, such as southern Bihar, western Orissa, parts of Madhya Pradesh, the Andaman Islands, and the northeastern states.

Some tribes, such as the Jarawas of the Andamans, live at subsistence level, hunting and gathering in tiny communities of fewer than 500; others account for almost an entire population, such as the Mizos of Mizoram or the Nagas of Nagaland, who have adopted Christianity and Western lifestyles. India's tribal life has been under threat since the British period. The Todas of the Nilgiri Hills in Tamil Nadu had a rich culture, centered on their buffalo, which has been eroded by close encounters with the British and with Hindu Indians. The Bhils of southern Rajasthan, on the other hand, have for centuries been close allies with the rulers of Mewar, and this symbiotic relationship of mutual respect continues. The Abors and Apatamis of Arunachal Pradesh in northeast India, however, manage their own affairs.

The pull of modernity does cause friction. The more than three million Santhals of West Bengal and Bihar, who form the largest tribe of southern Asia, capture best this friction. Back in the 19th century, Hindu moneylenders dispossessed them of their land to the extent that they rebelled in 1855–1857; yet they wanted high-caste Hindu privileges. In the 20th century they were drawn into the emerging industrialization that arrived on their doorstep, and its attendant education and modernization opportunities: Tata Iron and Steel Company opened at Jamshedpur in Bihar in 1908.

Today, with improved communications and a ballooning population, ideas and people reach most of India's tribes. So does outside competition for land where the tribes have long lived; that these people are exposed to secular life and political awareness, and must make choices about them, is unavoidable but acceptable to them. That they are ruthlessly exploited, dispossessed, used as cheap labor, and left hungry is not. However, the Scheduled Tribes do have a voice in parliament: In each state, the number of constituencies reserved for them is in proportion to the state's total population.

Naga tribeswomen in traditional dress

Patna

This ancient city of great historical importance, founded in the fourth century B.C. as Pataliputra, was the center of the legendary Magadhan and Mauryan empires. From Patna, Chandragupta Maurya extended his rule to the Indus, and his grandson Ashoka pushed it even farther (see p. 26). Under the Guptas (4th century) and Sher Shah Suri (16th century), the city enjoyed revivals. However, this narrow city beside the Ganga has little to offer visitors today.

The few remains of Patna's one-time glory can be found in the superb collection of the **Patna Museum** (*patnamuseum.gov.in*). It includes a wooden Maurya wheel (third century B.C.) and pillar, both from Pataliputra's palace; beautiful sculptures, including a woman holding a *chauri* or fly whisk (third century B.C.), and a woman with a parrot (third–seventh century), which was once part of a door; and rooms full of gentle Buddhas and Bodhisattvas, Hindu carvings, and prints by the uncle-nephew team of Thomas and William Daniels, superb bronzes, and lively proto-Mauryan terracottas (2000 B.C.).

To see old Patna, avoid the worst of the city's traffic congestion by setting off very early and use the Old Bypass Road to reach **Harmandir Sahib,** one of the four holy temples for Sikhs (see pp. 60–61). It honors the tenth Guru, Guru Gobind Singh, who was born here. As in the temple at Amritsar (see pp. 120–121), there is an aura of peacefulness.

When the British lopped Bihar and Orissa off Bengal to make an independent administrative unit, Patna once again became a capital. New Patna, contemporary with New Delhi, was laid out as a

Elephants receive morning baths during Sonepur Fair.

modern imperial town, with wide avenues ending in vistas of grand buildings and a central axis, King George's Avenue. Drive or take a rickshaw and pass by **Raj Bhavan** (Government House), the **Secretariat** (1929) and **Council Chambers** (1920), and the **High Court** (1916).

West of Patna, 17 miles (29 km) along the road to Ara, lies **Munar** (Maner). In a clearing in the woods stands **Choti Dargah** (1616), the tomb of Shah Daulat, built by Ibrahim Khan. Its fine proportions, delicate *jali* (stone lattice) work, and surface ornament make it one of eastern India's finest Mughal monuments. ∎

Patna

- 289 C4

Visitor Information

- India Tourist Office, R-Block, Kranti Marg Institute of Engineering Bldg.
- 061/2657-0640

incredibleindia.org

- State Tourist Office, 9D Hutments, Main Secretariat
- 061/2222-4531

bstdc.bih.nic.in

Patna Museum

- Kotwali Thana Rd.
- 943/103-4172
- Closed Mon.
- $$

The Andaman & Nicobar Islands

In the Bay of Bengal, in the Andaman Sea, more than 300 tiny forested islands make up a far-flung Indian possession that is important predominantly for its strategic position. Difficult to reach—they are some 808 miles (1,300 km) from Kolkata—these islands offer a complete escape to superb beaches and wonderful underwater sightseeing on the coral reefs.

Pristine tropical beaches and crystal-clear waters await visitors to the Andaman Islands.

The Andaman & Nicobar Islands

🅰 289 (box inset)

Visitor Information

✉ India Tourist Office, VIP Rd., Jungli Ghat, Port Blair

☎ 031/9223-6348

incredibleindia.org

VISITING THE ISLANDS: You can visit some of the islands but not all. Consult the Tourist Office. Boats from Wandoor to Jolly Buoy and Red Skin Islands depart every half-hour from 8:30 a.m. onward. The last boat leaves at 10:30 a.m. (5 sailings daily except Mon.).

These islands form two groups: the Andamans in the north, where Port Blair is the capital on Middle Andaman Island, and the Nicobars (which you cannot visit) in the south. Geologically, they were once part of the landmass of Southeast Asia. About 300,000 people live on fewer than 40 of the islands.

In the past, the Portuguese, Dutch, British, and Japanese have controlled the islands. In 1956 the Indian government passed the Aboriginal Tribes Protection Act to help protect the island tribes' culture. However, this has not been wholly successful: Many Sri Lankan Tamils have migrated to

the islands, swelling the population sixfold in just 20 years, and much forest has been felled in favor of rubber plantations. Even the islands' most valuable possessions—their tribal people and unique ecology—are threatened by mismanagement. Tribal people now account for less than 10 percent of the population, and numbers continue to fall.

Tourism, on the other hand, is doing little damage. So far, just a few of the 260 islands, most with superb beaches and coral reefs, have been developed. This policy works well in the Maldive Islands, lying off the west coast of southern India.

Port Blair, where all the hotels currently are located, has several places to visit. The **Cellular Jail National Memorial** (*closed Mon., $*), once a British jail, is now a shrine to India's freedom fighters. The **Samudrika Marine Museum** (*tel 031/9223-2012, closed Mon., $*) provides a good introduction to the islands' geography, archaeology, and marine life. For more specialized information, visit the **Fisheries Museum & Aquarium** (*tel 031/9223-1848, closed Mon., $*) to discover more about the Andaman Sea, the

INSIDER TIP:

The best way to get to the Andaman Islands is to fly from Chennai or Kolkata. Travel by ship only if you have lots of time and are willing to spend three nights aboard.

—VARDHAN PATANKAR
National Geographic grantee

little **Anthropological Museum** (*Gandi Rd., tel 031/9223-2291 closed Thurs., $*) to learn about the indigenous but threatened tribes, and the **Mini Zoo and Forest Museum** to find out about the 200 or so animals exclusive to these islands. Out of town, you can visit **Mount Harriet National Park** (*day use only, $*) and climb its mountain; sometimes you can stay in the Forest Guest House. A trip to **Ross Island** is worthwhile to see the British

administrative buildings that are now very overgrown.

But the real joy of the islands lies in the surrounding water. Beautiful coral reefs and very clear water combine to offer some of the world's best snorkeling.

Beaches Near Port Blair

Corbyn's Cove is the nearest beach, 4 miles (7 km) south of Port Blair. **Snake Island** is surrounded by a coral reef; take a boat there rather than swim, since the current can be strong. At Wandoor, **Mahatma Gandhi National Marine Park** consists of 15 islands with mangrove creeks, tropical rain forest, and reefs supporting more than 50 types of coral. From Wandoor village, you can take a boat (*except Mon.*) 18 miles (29 km) southeast to **Jolly Buoy** and **Red Skin Islands** to explore the reefs. **Chiriya Tapu,** 19 miles (30 km) south of Port Blair, is a tiny fishing village with mangroves and beaches. From here you can sometimes arrange a boat to the Cinque Islands (see below).

Other Islands

Havelock Island, 33 miles (54 km) northeast of Port Blair, has perfect, white sandy beaches, clear turquoise water, and good snorkeling, plus dolphins, turtles, and large fish. **Long Island,** off Middle Andaman, is tiny, with one village and several perfect beaches. **North** and **South Cinque Islands,** some of the most beautiful of all, are part of Wandoor's national park (*day visits only*). ∎

Mini Zoo and Forest Museum

✉ Mahatma Gandhi Rd.

🕐 Museum closed Sun. Mini Zoo closed Mon.

💲 $

Mahatma Gandhi National Marine Park

✉ 19 miles (30 km) SW of Wandoor

☎ 031/9222-1549

💲 $

The Ganga River

The dominant force—physically and spiritually—of eastern India is the Ganga River. Its hundreds of tributaries trickle down the Himalayan slopes, link up into rivers, and create the life-giving Gangetic Plain and Delta.

During the Maha Kumbh Mela festival of 2001, more than two million Hindus gathered at Allahabad to witness the moon's eclipse.

In Uttar Pradesh, the Ganga flows past Kanpur, then continues to Allahabad, where it takes in the Yamuna River, which has already watered Delhi and Agra. On it flows through Varanasi and into Bihar state. Here, at the city of Patna, major tributaries swell its waters: the Ghaghara, the Son, and the Gandak. Soon the great river begins to split into hundreds of threads to become the vast delta whose blessings of nourishment and punishments of flooding are shared by West Bengal and Bangladesh.

The Sacred River

A Hindu's Ganga *yatra* (journey, pilgrimage) begins at the river's source, Gangotri, about 149 miles (240 km) from Rishikesh, then descends to Haridwar, Allahabad, and Varanasi. At each stop the river's water is revered. The Ganga's water is thought to be especially purifying since Hindus believe it to be the goddess Ganga flowing eternally from the summit of Mount Meru, the abode of the gods, down through Shiva's matted locks. To bathe in the waters is to cleanse oneself of the karma of previous and current lives and so be prepared for death and rebirth into a better life. Hindus from all over attend the mass ritual bathings that take place during Kumbh Mela, held every three years at Haridwar, Allahabad, Nasik, and Ujjain in turn.

Allahabad, also known as Prayag ("confluence") because the Yamuna and Ganga meet there, is especially sacred so the Kumbh Mela held here is known as Maha (Great) Kumbh Mela; the city also has an annual Magh Mela (Jan.–Feb.). At Chunar, upstream from Varanasi, the Ganga turns sharply north and then makes a great arc through the holy city. This, combined with the high west banks and the flat land on the east banks, creates an extraordinary, almost tangible bowl of light, especially at sunrise.

Historically, the Gangetic Plain was the core of Indian culture; settlements spread east from this region more than three millennia ago. The Ganga was a highway for east–west trade across the subcontinent, and it irrigated and fed the soil to produce rich farmland. Early cities such as Pataliputra (Patna) grew to be capitals of great empires. Later, the Mughals made Allahabad one of their capitals.

Devotees wash away their sins in the Ganga.

Today the rich alluvial plains formed by deposits from the Himalaya form one of the world's most densely populated regions. Deforestation of the Himalaya means additional silt is carried downriver and helps cause flooding; more than a third of Bangladesh is flooded annually. Ironically, this rich silt is essential to the nourishment of the rice crops being intensively farmed throughout the Ganga Basin.

EXPERIENCE: The Sights & Sounds of Sonepur Fair

India's largest livestock fair, held at the confluence of the Gandak and Ganga Rivers, lasts a full month and is a parade of nonstop color and amazing sights. It is so big that the local train station has India's longest platform, specially built to accommodate trains bringing farmers and their sheep, cows, goats, horses, and other wares for sale. The fair begins on Kartik Purnima, the night of the November full moon, which is the climax of the Chath Festival. After predawn *puja* at the tiny

Hari Hari temple, the faithful go down to the river. There you can rent a boat and be punted past saffron-saried women performing their pujas, to see mahouts scrubbing their elephants. Back on land, see the elephants, all painted up to look their best for sale, the animal trading, and the latest agricultural tools.

You can visit by making a day trip of it from Patna, or in some years the local tourist department arranges simple tents as accommodations (*bstdc.bih.nic.in*).

Varanasi

The Hindus' holiest city, Varanasi is perpetually overflowing with pilgrims. To visit it once in a lifetime is every Hindu's goal; to die here is to have the greatest chance of *moksha* (salvation, release). It is, therefore, not an easy city for a Western person to visit. But once you do, it may well become one of the most fascinating places of all your travels.

A Hindu pilgrim meditates as he witnesses the sunrise at Varanasi.

Walk down to the Ganga River for a boat ride (see pp. 306–307), either early in the morning or in the late afternoon when the sun's rays are enjoyable rather than punishing. Give this city some time; Varanasi is about watching a nonstop pilgrim city going about its business.

A city as old as Babylon, Varanasi is, for Hindus, quite simply Kashi (City of Divine Light), or Kashika (The Shining One), referring to the light of Shiva. Of the Hindus' Seven Sacred Cities, it is the most sacred. The others are Haridwar, Ujjain, Mathura, Ayodhya, Dwarka, and Kanchipuram. Each is dedicated to Shiva or Vishnu, except Kanchipuram, which is dedicated to both.

Thus, Varanasi's daily trade is pilgrims, India's most numerous and free-spending visitors. From the most humble upward, pilgrims often make their *yatras* (pilgrimages) by bus on an excursion, singing *bhajans* (religious songs) along the way. At their destination, the aim is to receive *darshan* (the meritorious glimpse of the god) and to bathe in the sacred waters. Emotional outpourings of religious fervor are common. Meanwhile, priests, gurus, peddlers, and con men of all kinds abound, often all too ready to relieve pilgrims, unused to the city and emotionally vulnerable, of their hard-earned money.

Varanasi was already thriving when Buddha came to Sarnath to deliver his first sermon (see p. 312), making it sacred to Buddhists, too. Later, Muslims periodically plundered the city; Shah Jahan forbade temple-rebuilding, and pious Aurangzeb converted one temple into a mosque. Early British arrivals wrote of being intoxicated by Varanasi's exoticism and mystery. Winding through the maze of narrow, filthy alleys swarming with cows and pilgrims, you feel something of this as you peek into temples, some simple, some flashy. Pilgrims flood in and out of them ceaselessly.

Cultural Center

Despite the city's squalor—for no other word will fit—the holiness of Varanasi has been the inspiration for some of the most sublime creations in Hindu culture. Classical music was nurtured in the temples, and today the city produces many of India's top musicians and stages important music festivals. Sanskrit and classical Hindu studies thrive in back rooms, on rooftops, and at the Banaras Hindu University, known as BHU. Here,

too, is the **Bharat Kala Bhavan** (*tel 054/2307-620, closed Sun., $*), with exquisite miniature paintings, whose religious message is heightened by the use of a rigid and highly symbolic iconography and intense colors.

Then there is the silk, originally woven to clothe the temple deities. Varanasi's weavers developed Baranasi brocade, a lusciously extravagant weave that includes threads of gold and silver. Much loved by the Mughals, it is still woven today. To see it, go to the daily **silk market,** found through an arch off Thatheri Bazar. In the late afternoon the weavers hurry through the maze of tiny alleys full of motorbikes, with their wooden boxes full of completed

INSIDER TIP:

For a good view of the Ganga Arati—the daily evening Hindu ritual worship of the river—hire a small boat and watch from the middle of the river.

—DR. SHOURASENI SEN ROY
National Geographic grantee

saris. They sell them to dealers sitting in cubicles on white cotton. Outside the silk market, find the **brass market** and continuous bazaars down to the water, where you can rent a boat and boatman for an evening cruise on the river, adding your tiny oil lamp made of leaves to the hundreds floating on the sacred water each evening. ∎

Varanasi

⓿ 288 B4

Visitor Information

✉ India Tourist Office, 15-B The Mall, Cantt

☎ 054/2250-1784

incredibleindia.org

✉ State Tourist Office, Tourist Bungalow, Parade Kothi

☎ 054/2220-6638, 054/2208-413

up-tourism.com
varanasicity.com
varanasi.nic.in

A Boat Ride on the Ganga at Varanasi

Take this boat ride in the early morning to see the sunrise and morning Hindu rituals, or go in the evening for pretty views of the ghats. Drive a hard bargain for your boat, and do not be persuaded into a short, hurried trip. Ask your boatman to point out the important sites.

As the sun rises, boatloads of pilgrims and visitors share the Ganga with bathing worshippers.

If you can do it, get up well before dawn, put on plenty of warm clothes, and go down to **Man Mandir Ghat ❶** in the dark. This is in front of the Maharaja of Jaipur's palace; beside it Jai Singh built one of his observatories (see pp. 131–132). Be on your boat as dawn creeps in, when you may hear the notes of the *shehna* reed instrument played by the musicians of the Shiva Temple to welcome the day. The dawn light is thin, liquid, and like no other light. It is easier to accept the various oil lamps and flowers pressed on you than to spoil the mood by entering into a bargaining session.

NOT TO BE MISSED:

Man Mandir Ghat • Asi Ghat
• Dasaswamedh Ghat
• Jalasai Ghat

First, go upstream (to your right) to **Asi Ghat ❷**, or as far as you can persuade your boatman to go. As the boat slides through the water, the city begins to wake, and pilgrims sleeping beneath the high walls of the maharajas' old riverside palaces rouse themselves.

By the time you turn around to go downstream, a pale sun rises, the light changes, and a steady stream of people flows down to the holy water. From the city's 80 or so ghats, each with its Shiva *lingum*, the faithful begin to bathe and do their *puja* (worship) to the new day. Each ghat has its own importance; ideally, a Hindu should worship at each one. Asi Ghat marks the confluence of the Asi and Ganga waters. Right next to it, **Tulsi Ghat ❸** commemorates the 17th-century poet Gosain Tulsi Das, who translated the *Ramayana* from Sanskrit into Hindi and later died here.

A little farther along, **Shivala (or Kali) Ghat ❹** is owned by the former royal family of Varanasi, whose fort across the river at Ramnagar is where the great Ram Lila festival is held annually. The ghat has a large Shiva lingum. Nearby **Hanuman Ghat ❺** attracts pilgrims who worship the monkey god, whereas **Dandi Ghat** is used by ascetics called Dandi Paths. **Harishchandra Ghat** is one of the city's two burning ghats; the other is Jalasai Ghat, which you see later.

Kedara Ghat ❻ has fine linga and a temple. Next you'll pass by **Mansarowar Ghat,** named after a lake in Tibet near the Gangotri, the Ganga's source. Moving downstream you pass by **Dasaswamedh Ghat ❼**, where brahmans are by now setting themselves up for the day's business, sitting cross-legged beneath their shabby umbrellas. Continue past your starting point of Man Mandir Ghat to **Jalasai Ghat ❽**, the famous burning ghat with a heap of lopsided temples (absolutely no photographs may be taken of this); the ghat is named after Vishnu when he is sleeping on the Cosmic Ocean. It adjoins **Manikarnika Ghat ❾**, the most sacred of all ghats, for here Mahadeo (Shiva) dug the tank to find Parvati's earring. As if to emphasize the Hindus' inequality in death, only the most privileged families are burned on the Charanpaduka slab marked with the imprint of Vishnu's feet. With the sun warming your back, the boatman will row you back upstream to Dasaswamedh Ghat.

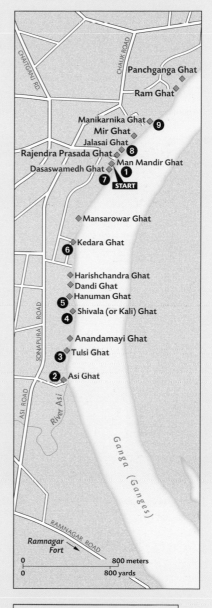

See also area map pp. 288–289
▶ Man Mandir Ghat
↔ 2–4 miles (3–6 km)
⊕ 1–2 hours
▶ Dasaswamedh Ghat

Lucknow & Kanpur

The capital of India's most populous state, Uttar Pradesh, Lucknow is spacious and calm, unencumbered by lots of industry and receiving relatively few visitors. Its key sites are in two groups: the faded, romantic Muslim buildings of the old city and the practical British buildings of the Residency, a silent and poignant reminder of a complete breakdown in the two countries' long relationship, a breakdown that also engulfed Kanpur, an important British garrison town.

Dhobi wallahs (washermen) use Lucknow's spacious Gomati River and its banks to do their washing.

Lucknow

The Old City: The city's Shia Muslim rulers, called the Nawabs of Avadh (Oudh, in Bihar), rose to power in the vacuum of 18th-century Mughal decline and made their final capital Lucknow. The ten lazy, debauched rulers set the tone for a distinctly self-indulgent yet highly sophisticated Muslim culture, especially under Asaf-ud-Daula (r. 1775–1797) and Saadat Ali Khan (r. 1798–1814). Today, the fruits of the Nawabs' extravagant patronage of buildings, artists, craftsmen, musicians, and Urdu poetry retain the atmosphere suitable for a decaying, decadent, and introverted court that ended in tragedy: The British deposed the last incompetent ruler, one of several actions that triggered the Rebellion of 1857.

The best of the Nawabs' buildings is the 1780s **Great Imambara** (House of the Imam; *closed during prayers*), one of the world's largest vaulted halls, entered through the Rumi Darwaza. Designed by Kifayat-ullah for Asaf-ud-Daula, its purpose is to be the focus of the Muharram festival. This is when Shia Muslims have a procession in memory of the martyrdom of Hussain and his two sons. Inside, see the *tazias,* ornate paper reproductions of the Shia Imam's shrine at Karbala in southern Iraq. Upstairs, there are good views of other buildings worth visiting: the **Jama Masjid,** the **Small Imambara** *(closed during prayers),* the **Tower** for watching the moon at Id, the **Clock Tower,** and various royal tombs and Muslim shrines.

Chowk, the old market area, is a mesmerizing maze of alleys perfumed with the spices of *paan* ingredients, a Lucknow specialty (see sidebar p. 311). On Chowpatia Street, near Akbari Gate, you can find the essentials of any Lucknow sophistication: gold leaf being beaten, *bidri* work (see sidebar p. 249), gold threadmakers, the practice of *chikankari* (embroidery), silk brocade, Koran bookstands, the scent of heavy attar (perfume), and delicious breads, kebabs, and

INSIDER TIP:

A well-preserved Turkish bath is but one of the attractions of the ancient city of Jaunpur, southeast of Lucknow. Its narrow streets require bicycle rickshaws.

—GOPI SUNDAR
National Geographic grantee

Lucknow
🗺 288 A5
Visitor Information
✉ State Tourist Office, Paryatan Bhawan C-13 Vipin Khand, Gomti Nagar
☎ 052/2230-7028, 052/2230-8916
up-tourism.com
lucknowcity.com

Jaunpur
🗺 289 B4

Rebellion of 1857

The 1857 Rebellion broke out in Meerut on May 10, when 47 battalions of the Bengal army mutinied against the British. The next day it reached Delhi (see p. 75) and quickly spread to Kanpur, then eventually Lucknow. The rebellion at Kanpur was particularly brutal: When the besieged British were evacuating on June 27, having been assured of safe passage, nearly all the men were massacred; the remaining men, women, and children were held hostage for two weeks before they were all killed.

At Lucknow, the rebellion gathered pace on June 30, 1857, when sepoys (Indian soldiers) poured over the Gomati River to join citizens already angry that their Nawab had been deposed. The British garrison, commanded by Sir Henry Lawrence, took refuge in the Residency. Fighting was aboveground and underneath in tunnels and mines. Gangrene, scurvy, cholera, and the general lack of hygiene took their toll on the British garrison. Gen. Sir Henry Havelock arrived with reinforcements after three months, retaking the fort on September 25 only to lose it immediately. On November 14 Sir Colin Campbell's relief troops began to attack Lucknow, succeeding in evacuating the British, whose numbers were greatly diminished by this time.

Lucknow Residency

☎ 052/2232-8220

💲 $

confections. To see taziamakers in action, go to the Hazaratganj area.

The Residency at Lucknow:

The Residency complex is the surreal, frozen reminder of the 1857 rebellion (see sidebar p. 309), which witnessed bloody scenes at Lucknow and Kanpur. This site, which marked a watershed in British and Indian history, has been left almost as it was at the end of the siege on November 17, 1857. Under the spreading banyan, neem, and bel fruit trees, you can visit the eerie remains of buildings where men, women, and children survived for five months, from the monsoon of July to the chilly days of November.

Through the Baillie Guard gateway, you will find the **Treasury** on the right, whose long central room was used as an arsenal in 1857. Next door, the grand and once sumptuous **Banqueting Hall** was the siege hospital. Dr. Fayrer's House, to the south, is a large, one-story building where women and children stayed; a tablet marks the spot where Sir Henry Lawrence died—there is a memorial cross to him on the lawn, and he is buried in the cemetery. **Begum Kothi** is where Mrs. Walters, a British woman who married the Nawab, once lived.

The elegant **Residency** building itself stands on the northeast side of the complex and was built by Nawab Saadat Ali Khan in 1800. The wives and children of high-ranking officers lived here in appalling and dank conditions in

The poignant remains of the Residency are well maintained, perhaps to remind Indians of their hard-won freedom, whose beginnings here are called by some the "First War of Independence."

Paan, the Indian digestive

This unique concoction forms the traditional finale to an Indian meal, to cleanse the palette and freshen the breath after all those spices and garlic. Freshly made by one of the hundreds of thousands of paan *wallahs* (vendors) sitting in cubicle-like shops or at little stalls or even just behind a tray on a stand, paan is in fact yet more spices—but special ones. The basic ingredients are slaked lime and the mildly addictive betel (also known as areca) nut, wrapped in a fresh green paan leaf. You pop it into your mouth and chew, swallowing the juices; when you have had enough, you usually spit out the paan. Although every paan wallah has his own recipe, and may tailor it to each of his local clients by adding a pinch of this or that from his dozens of little pots, there are two basic varieties: *mitha* (sweet) and *saadha* (unsweetened).

Paan is an integral part of Indian culture. The wealthy kept their paan in embossed silver paan boxes you now see in museums; princes had elaborate spittoons—as seen in Gwalior's massive palace, Udaipur's Crystal Gallery, and Jodhpur's fort. During Lucknow's sophisticated 18th-century culture, poems were written to paan. Today, if in Mumbai, take a stroll on Chowpatty Beach where the paan wallahs are famous for their elaborate paan, which you can enjoy to your palate's delight. However, just watching a paan wallah at work is pleasure enough for some.

the basements. The second floor is now a little **museum,** with a model of the Residency complex in 1857 and some block prints detailing the horrific scenes of the rebellion. On the wall is a poignant plaque to Susanna Palmer, killed by a cannonball on July 1, 1857. After this incident, residents moved to Dr. Fayrer's House. In the **cemetery** are simple graves of Lawrence and of Brig. Gen. J. S. Neill, whose frightful revenge on the Kanpur mutineers was not repeated at Lucknow; he was killed here on September 25, 1857. As for the British hero Gen. Sir Henry Havelock, who briefly retook the fort, he would die of dysentery a week after Sir Colin Campbell arrived.

Kanpur

Another significant site of this intriguing period of history, for India and Great Britain, is Kanpur (Cawnpore), a two-hour drive away. This, one of the most important British garrisons on the Ganga, was also besieged during the "mutiny." In the cantonment, Walter Granville's Lombardic-Gothic **All Souls Memorial Church** (1862–1875) has poignant tablets around the apse wall, and the adjoining **Memorial Garden** has eloquent angels and a screen commemorating the British women and children massacred and then dumped into the Bibighar well (see sidebar p. 309). In the nearby scrub find Gen. Sir Hugh Wheeler's entrenchment, where the siege took place. You can also visit nearby **Sati Chaura Ghat,** where British fleeing Fatehgarh down the Ganga River were massacred in their boats—a bleak, chilling spot. ∎

Kanpur
🅰 286 A4

up-tourism.com
kanpurcity.com

The Buddha Trail

Non-Buddhists rarely visit India's eight sites associated with Buddha; yet, these places are as fascinating as Hindu, Muslim, and Jain sites. So consider joining the groups of Buddhists that flock to these fascinating places. Bring good information on this area with you (and water and snacks); a good source is *buddhist-temples.com*.

Start the trail at **Sravasti,** near Lucknow, where the Buddha spent 24 rainy seasons: See where he stayed, plus monastic ruins and Jetavana Park. **Sankasya,** west of Lucknow, is where Buddha reputedly descended from heaven. **Lumbini,** just across the border in Nepal, is Buddha's birthplace, and at nearby **Kapilavastu** there is the palace of Buddha's father and a stupa. **Kushinagar** *(30 miles/50 km E of Gorakhpur)* is where Buddha died and attained Mahaparinirvana; see the stupa built after his cremation, monastic remains, and a large reclining Buddha made of stone.

INSIDER TIP:

An obvious but invaluable tip— dress appropriately, especially outside major cities. Women might invest in a simple *salwar kameez,* a common Indian dress. This small accommodation goes a very long way.

—TALA KATNER
National Geographic contributor

Or start the trail at **Sarnath,** near Varanasi in Uttar Pradesh, the leading Buddhist pilgrimage center. Here Buddha preached his first sermon, usually called Dharmachakra ("Setting in Motion the Wheel of Righteousness") (see p. 59); this was the basis of the religion's future development. Buddha also founded his *sangha* (monastic order) here. As you wander around the monasteries, the Dharmarajika Stupa (third century B.C.), and Main Shrine (mostly fifth century) notice the strong historical-religious atmosphere. Visit the excellent Sarnath Museum *(Ashoka Marg, closed Fri., $);* its Ashoka pillar capital is now the official symbol of India.

The G. T. Road

Now turn eastward into Bihar along the Grand Trunk, or G. T. Road, described by Kipling as "the backbone of all Hind . . ." with "such a river of life as nowhere else exists in the world." After 60 miles (97 km), detour to Sasaram to see Sher Shah Suri's five-story, midlake tomb (1540–1545), considered by some to be one of India's best buildings.

Leaving the G. T. Road, you enter a quiet, rural area. **Bodh Gaya** is where Buddha meditated, was tempted by the demon Mara, and finally received *bodhi* (enlightenment), making the place an important pilgrimage site. The bodhi tree that is believed to spring from the one he sat under stands at the back of a Buddhist temple; Buddhists sit here to meditate, chant, and read. The excellent Archaeological Museum *(closed Fri.)* displays fine sculptures and some modern temples built by Japanese, Vietnamese, and other Buddhist communities.

Country Lanes

Country lanes twist past medieval Gaya to **Rajgir.** Buddha and Mahavira, who spread Jainism, often visited the ancient Magadha kingdom, whose capital was here. Its rulers Bimbisara and Ajatashatru (ca 543–459 B.C.) converted to Buddhism, and the First Council was held here. You may need a guide to help find the localities associated with Buddha: **Venuvana bamboo grove,** the first Buddhist monastery; **Saptaparni Caves,** home of the First Council; and **Pippala stone house,** where the senior monk Mahakashyapa

The bodhi tree behind Mahabodhi Temple in Bodh Gaya is believed to have sprung from the tree under which Buddha attained enlightenment, making it an important pilgrimage site for Buddhists.

stayed. Take the walk up **Gridhrakuta Hill** (Vulture Peak) past two caves to the high terrace for a peaceful, restorative sunset.

Nearby, **Nalanda** was a huge monastery and university from the 5th to 12th centuries, and it was the seventh-century Pala rulers' principal seat of learning and place of art patronage.

Beneath the farmers' fields, nine brick Buddhist monasteries have been unearthed. Treasures in the Archaeological Museum ($) range from a naga deity to ancient rice grains.

Complete the trail at **Vaishali,** 20 miles (32 km) north of Patna, where Buddha preached his last sermon.

More Places to Visit in Eastern India

Barakar, Ghurisa, & Kabilaspur

This is a pleasant rural trip northwest from Kolkata into the Bengal countryside. Stop at Barakar for a ninth-century Orissan-style temple with miniature figures adorning its curved tower; at Ghurisa for a Bengali hut-style temple (1633) with terra-cotta panels, with some figures in European dress; and at Kabilaspur for a beautiful temple that lacks all decoration.

Barakpur

Formerly the summer residence of Calcutta's British governors-general, Barakpur (Barackpore), a model canton-ment on the east banks of the Hooghly, opposite Serampore (see opposite), retains its layout and spaciousness, and it is well maintained by the army. Drive around to the many original houses and bungalows, several of them part of the Ramkrishna Vivekananda Mission. Access is restricted to some parts, but try to see **Government House** (1813), the **Temple of Fame,**

Lady Canning's Grave, and **Semaphore Tower.** 🗺 289 D3 ✉ 15 miles (24 km) N of Kolkata

Bishnupur

An easy day trip by train, this sleepy village was once the capital of the cultured Malla rulers of Bengal. See their group of exquisite Bengali hut-style 17th- to 18th-century temples faced with beautiful terra-cotta story plaques, usually showing scenes from the *Ramayana*. See especially the **Shyam Rai Temple** (1643), **Keshta Raya Temple** (1655), and **Madana Mohana Temple** (1694). 🗺 289 D3 ✉ 93 miles (150 km) NW of Kolkata, most easily reached by train

Buxar

This Hindu pilgrimage site on the Ganga was the scene of Sir Hector Munro's decisive victory on October 23, 1764, when he used clever tactics to reverse near defeat against the forces of Shah Alam, Shuja-ud-Daula, and Mir Qasim, taking their entire camp

Two women sit outside their simple coastal home at Gopalpur-on-Sea.

and 160 guns. This built on Clive's victory at Plassey in 1757 (see below) and confirmed Britain's supremacy in Bengal. On the way here from Patna, pause at Ara, where 12 British and 50 Sikhs held the Little House of Ara from July 27 to August 3, 1857, against more than 2,000 sepoys and rebels. 🅰 288 B4 ✉ 73 miles (117 km) W of Patna, Bihar

Gaur & Around

A wonderful trip of several days from Kolkata takes you through rural Bengal to seek out the extensive, fine, and rarely visited Muslim capital of the Afghan rulers of Bengal during the 15th and 16th centuries. Later sacked by Sher Shah Sur (1537), Gaur became part of Akbar's Mughal empire in 1576. Find substantial ruins dotted among villages and farms covering some 20 square miles (52 sq km); there is a central group within huge embankments that includes a fort, mosques, tombs, a victory tower, and gateways. From here the intrepid can continue to **Malda** (Islamic buildings), **Pandua** (the Afghan capital before Gaur), **Bangarh** (archaeological site of an ancient city), **Rajmahal** (good Mughal city remains 4 miles/6 km west of the modern city), and **Sultanganj** (eighth-century carvings on granite rocks at Jahangira), ending at Patna. 🅰 289 D4 **Gaur** ✉ 200 miles (320 km) N of Kolkata

Gopalpur-on-Sea & Around

A delightful beach, small village, and a few cottages in Orissa state make this the best beachside escape from Kolkata. You can reach it by train to Brahmapur, where you may see silk weavers around the temple. North of here, **Chilka Lake** (chilika.com) is a large lagoon rich in migratory birds from December to February. 🅰 289 C1

Murshidabad & Around

The drive north through Bengal from Kolkata to Murshidabad passes **Plassey.**

Little remains here to mark Clive's victory beside the Bhagirathi River on June 23, 1757, against the Nawab Siraj-ud-Daula of Murshidabad. At **Baharampur,** the early British cantonment is interesting, with its grid-pattern streets interspersed with ditches and water tanks for defense. **Murshidabad** became the capital of Bengal in 1704 when Murshid Quli Khan moved his seat here from Dacca and Rajmahal. Later, the British moved the law (1772) and then the bureaucrats (1790) to Kolkata. Reminders of past

INSIDER TIP:

Patna Bird Sanctuary *[up-tour ism.com/weekend_agra1.htm]* in remote Uttar Pradesh is for the true birder. Wintering water-birds, flamingos, and breeding Sarus cranes are attractions.

—GOPI SUNDAR
National Geographic grantee

splendor include the **Palace of the Nawab, Imambara, Medina, mosques,** and **tombs.** North again, **Baranagar**'s 18th-century hutlike temples contain fabulous terra-cotta story plaques. From here you can link to the Gaur trip (see above). 🅰 289 D4 **Murshidabad** ✉ 122 miles (196 km) N of Kolkata

Serampore & North of Kolkata

Leave very early to avoid city traffic on this day trip from Kolkata, up the west bank of the Hooghly to visit sites evocative of intrepid European merchants and fine Bengali temples. First stop is Serampore, a Danish settlement (1755) where an English Baptist missionary set up Kolkata's first printing press (1799); see **Serampore College** (1821), **India Jute Mill,** and **St. Olave's Church** (1821). Continue to **Belur Math Temple** (1938), built by Swami Vivekananda, a disciple of Ramakrishna; a mile (1.6 km) or so beyond, Kolkata's popular **Dakshineshwar Temple** (1855) stands across the Bally Bridge. At **Chandannagar,** crumbling yet grand buildings testify to a successful French factory (1688). Beyond Hooghly and Bandel, both early European settlements, find first **Bansberia's** lovely terra-cotta-ornamented Bengali temples, then many more at **Kalna,** maintained by the former royal Burdwan family. ⊠ 289 D3 **Serampore** ⊠ 13 miles (21 km) N of Kolkata

Shanti Niketan & Around

This is a peaceful escape from the steamy city. Founded by Bengal's great writer and poet Rabindranath Tagore in 1921, as a settlement and center of study to promote Bengali culture, Shanti Niketan was the Bengali Renaissance's most ambitious and successful project. Tagore designed the **Uttarayan** complex of buildings, which includes a **museum** *(closed Wed.),* **gallery** *(closed Wed.),* and departments for art, music, and drama. ⊠ 289 D3 **Shanti Niketan** ⊠ 84 miles (135 km) N of Kolkata

Simhanatha & Ranipur Jharial

This is an adventurous trip through Orissa's countryside. Simhanatha's well-preserved temple (eighth century) stands on an island in the Mahanadi River. Continue into the hills to Ranipur Jharial, two villages whose rocky outcrop has more than 50 little temples. ⊠ 288 B2 **Ranipur Jharial** ⊠ 180 miles (290 km) W of Bhubaneshwar

Similipal National Park

The inhospitable, thickly wooded slopes of Orissa's Eastern Ghats have preserved this park, founded in 1957, from any form of taming—even today, the effort of reaching this very beautiful landscape, and the simplicity of accommodations, mean it has few visitors. However, the mixture of deciduous forest, streams, and open savanna provide the habitat for varied wildlife, from leopards and tigers to porcupines, elephants, and mugger crocodiles, plus more than 230 species of birds. Permits and reservations with exact dates are essential; otherwise, join an organized tour. ⊠ 289 C2 ⊠ Field Director Project Tiger, Baripada 757002, Mayurbhunj District, Orissa

Sunderbans National Park

Where the great Gangetic Delta meets the Bay of Bengal, water and land intermingle to form the world's largest mangrove ecoregion, 7,900 square miles (20,460 sq km)—the local word for "mangrove" is *sundari*. At the Sunderbans Tiger Reserve, encompassing a group of mangrove-covered islands, the Bengal tigers have adapted to the landscape; they both swim and eat fish. To visit, stay at Sajnekhali Tourist Lodge 75 miles (120 km) south of Kolkata; explore by boat and with a Project Tiger guide. Permits available from the West Bengal Tourist Office *(westbengal toursim.gov.in)* in Kolkata; the reserve is best visited November to March. ⊠ 289 D3

The Ganga Delta's Fragile Fertility

Spreading across West Bengal and Bangladesh, the world's largest delta is fed by the Ganga and Brahmaputra Rivers. One of the world's most fertile areas, it is also one most prone to flooding. Mostly deforested, it consists of alluvial swamps, lakes, and waterways. Jute, tea, and rice, and shrimp and salmon farming are mainstays. Its distinct flora and fauna include the well-known mangroves and Bengal tiger, but also herds of chital, the Irrawaddy and Ganges river dolphins, and birds such as the shalik, doel, and swamp francolin. The delta is at risk from rising sea levels and the exploitation of natural gas reserves.

The great Himalayan range—a landscape of lush, cool valleys; sparkling, clear rivers; forested hillsides; and spectacular mountains

The Himalaya

A woman from the western Himalaya Ladakh Valley

The Himalaya

The Himalaya, the world's highest mountains, are less than 130 million years old and still growing. When the ancient Indian plate of the peninsula, some three billion years old, moved under the Asian plate the dramatic crumpling and fissuring began, the Himalaya began to rise, and they continue to do so.

Remote villages, such as this one, dot the dramatic, bare landscape of the Lahaul and Spiti district.

The Himalaya are a formidable barrier, effectively isolating the Indian subcontinent from the rest of Asia. Varying in width from 93 miles (150 km) to 210 miles (400 km), and with 95 peaks reaching an elevation of more than 24,000 feet (7,500 m), they stretch 1,553 miles (2,500 km) from Pakistan's Pamirs to Assam's Brahmaputra River. Two large chunks of these mountain ranges are in India.

The mountains are made up of several ranges, where some of India's great rivers rise. In the west, the young Indus flows between the Karakoram Range in Pakistan and the Zanskar Range. Moving east, you find many beautiful lakes in the frontier Vale of Kashmir, the region's most famous valley, which suffers from Indo-Pakistan political tensions. Eastward, Himachal Pradesh's hills belong to the Siwalik Range—massively folded and faulted mountains

with longitudinal valleys known in the western part as "duns." Lowland orchards and cornfields rise through subtropical forests to steep, pine mountains and inhospitable ice fields, from which the Sutlej River hurtles down deep, craggy gorges. Eastward again into Uttarakhand, the young Yamuna River takes one path down through mighty gorges, while the Ganga River takes another. From Gangotri Glacier it foams and crashes down to Haridwar, where it becomes more sedate for the long journey through the Siwalik Hills, here called the Garhwal.

East of Nepal the mountains of the central Himalayan range receive the full deluge of the annual monsoon rains, and the postmonsoon waters of the Brahmaputra River thunder through Assam. This isolated region has wild rhododendrons and orchids, Kaziranga and Manas Wildlife Sanctuaries, tea plantations, and individual cultures and peoples.

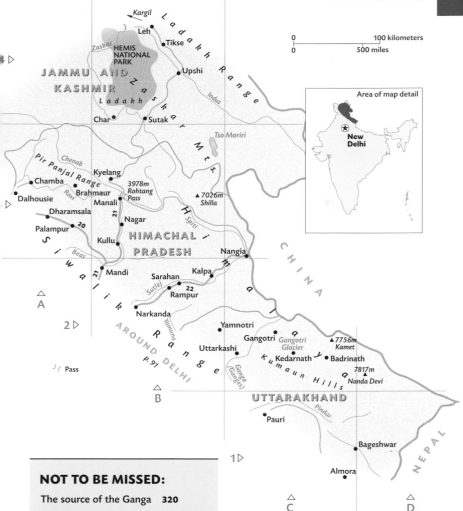

The Mughals loved Kashmir; later, the British discovered the vast, cool, and expansive beauty of all the Himalayan mountain scenery from lush lowlands to stunning high mountain passes. Today, the best way to experience it is to hike. This is nature in its most raw and awesome condition, with the occasional Buddhist monastery, Hindu shrine, and British hill station. Choose an area that appeals; then make reservations for the right trek for you: anything from gentle day walks to a challenging ten-day journey sleeping in tents. The more adventurous you are, and the less fussy about comfortable accommodations, the more rewarding your visit will be. ∎

Western Himalaya

As a contrast to the heady cocktail of monuments, history, heat, and city crowds, a hike in the foothills of the Himalaya invigorates you. The cool air, mountain scenery, culture, and lifestyle offer relaxation after touring the plains, and the lower slopes in Uttarakhand or Himachal Pradesh are easily accessible from Delhi. The more ambitious can press on north to Ladakh.

Uttarakhand

The Garhwal and Kumaun Hills that lie between Uttar Pradesh and Nepal and Tibet are known as the Uttarakhand, or Uttaranchal. From the fertile plains, or *terai*, they rise through summer mountain meadows called *bugyals* to a series of snowcapped mountains, including Nanda Devi (25,643 feet/7,816 m), the highest mountain completely in India. These hills have scenic variety as well as charming hotels (see Travelwise p. 376); the sacred Hindu pilgrimage center of Haridwar; the protected forests of Corbett National Park; and the gentle, still slightly Victorian British hill stations of Mussoorie and Nainital (for all of these sites see pp. 122–124).

Each of the deep river valleys has its own distinct culture, and the **Garhwal** and **Kumaun regions** have their own languages. Furthermore, although Hinduism dominates, a shrine may reveal elements of animism and Buddhism; it was through the Himalayan mountains that Buddhism was carried to China. Indeed, so distinct is Uttarakhand that it won autonomy from Uttar Pradesh and became a separate state in 2000.

The sources of the Yamuna and Ganga Rivers give the Garhwal special status and popularity. Here are the four *yatra* (pilgrimage) temples known as the Char Dham: **Badrinath, Kedarnath, Gangotri, and Yamnotri.** The hundreds of thousands of pilgrims who come here via Rishikesh from May to November each year have influenced the indigenous culture of this

The mountains north of Shimla offer spectacular views.

A Floral Treat in the Himalaya

The Himalaya boast more than 12,500 documented species and subspecies of flowering plants. In the 19th century, the British were entranced by the mountains' bounty: Botanists shipped countless specimens to the Royal Botanical Gardens at Kew and Edinburgh and to London's National History Museum, and artists recorded whole mountainsides purple with rhododendron blossoms. Today, deforestation threatens some species with extinction.

The Himalayan region has 15 bio-geographical domains, each distinctly different from the other, with altitude and local climate playing a part—those rhododendrons, for instance, vary in color according to both altitude and the direction the mountain slope faces.

Compare the following: In Valley of the Flowers National Park in the remote Garhwal Himalaya, the blooming of more than 300 species of wildflowers, including anemone, geranium, and the rare Himalayan blue poppy, begins after the snow melts and peaks in July and August. In Sikkim, meanwhile, a botanist's paradise of some 4,000 species of flora, the forests blaze color during the narrow window of late April to mid-May with tree-size blooming rhododendrons—and some of Sikkim's 600 varieties of orchid.

area. To experience purer Garhwal beauty, hike through the **Harki Dun Valley** or the **Tehri Garh-wal.** The temples and hill towns of the **Kumaun Hills** retain much of their original charm, but receive far fewer pilgrims and visitors.

Himachal Pradesh

The gateway to this small state of hills and mountains, sandwiched to the east and west by Tibet and Pakistan, is **Shimla** (see pp. 122–123). North of here are remote and distinct districts, lands crossed by the Gaddi and Gujjar, seminomadic shepherds. The area has seen Rajputs ruling Kangra, and Tibetans ruling Lahaul and Spiti; and since the 18th century control has passed from the Sikhs of the Punjab to the Gurkas of Nepal and finally to the British until independence.

After the lush valleys of the southern Sirmaur area, including delightful **Nalagar,** the landscape north of Shimla becomes more dramatic. Moving northeast past Narkanda you can follow the Sutlej River to find the wooden temple of **Sarahan** and, with a special Inner Line Permit, the **Kinnaur district**'s isolated and austere beauty up on the Tibetan Plateau. Ambitious treks lead through to Spiti and the Kullu Valley; simpler walks are along the Sutlej Valley.

North of Shimla, the road divides at Mandi. Keeping to the north, **Manali** is the increasingly developed base for exploring verdant Kullu Valley's terraces, forests, and apple orchards, and for whitewater rafting at Vashisht. But farther north, across the treacherous Rohtang Pass (13,051 feet/3,978 m), fewer people visit the bare mountains and snowfields of the Himalaya that encase Lahaul and Spiti Valleys. The 300-mile-long (500 km) **Manali–Leh Highway,**

Uttarakhand

🗺 319 C1 & C2

Visitor Information

✉ Uttarakhand Tourist Office, Pt. Deen Upadhyaya Paryatan Bhawan, Garhi Cantt, Dehradun

☎ 035/1255-9898

uttarakhand tourism.gov.in

uttaranchaltourism .in

euttaranchal.com

hill-stations-india .com

Himachal Pradesh

🗺 319 B3

Visitor Information

✉ Shimla Tourist Office, Railway Station

☎ 017/7265-3888

himachaltourism .gov.in

hill-stations-India .com

Dharamsala

319 A3

Visitor Information

Dharamsala Tourist Office, Main Bazaar

018/9222-4430

Visitor Information

Brahmour Mountaineering Institute; Kullu Tourist Office

019/0225-2175, 019/0225-2349

NOTE: Some of the hill areas are politically volatile, so it is wise to follow the State Department's advice (travel.state.gov /travel); currently, visits to Kashmir are discouraged, except to Ladakh. The Indian government requires foreign visitors to obtain special permits for some northeastern states. It is best to do your research, make your reservations, and obtain your permits before arriving in India.

one of the world's great drives, is open June through October. The mountain and valley views are incredible as it switchbacks through Keylong, Sarchu Serai, and the passes of Langlacha La (16,597 feet/5,059 m) and Tanglang La (17,480 feet/5,328 m).

Northwest of Mandi, the well-trodden trail leads through the heavily populated Kangra Valley toward the Dhauladhar mountains, where the Dalai Lama and his Tibetan exiles live at **Dharamsala.** From here, gentle treks lead through the tea-growing area of Palampur; more adventurous ones cross the mountains into the Chamba Valley toward the Pir Panjal Range.

Ladakh

High in the Zaskar and Ladakh mountain ranges and stretching up to the Karakoram, Ladakh ("land of high mountain passes") is a high-elevation desert crossed

by razor-sharp peaks. Here, the land is frozen for eight months a year and scorched for four, with rainfall the same as in the Sahara. Yaks, goats, and sheep are essential for their wool, milk, and butter, and to use as exchange for grain and fuel. Open to general visitors since 1974, the current unrest makes this the only area of Jammu and Kashmir state that it is advisable to visit.

This isolated and starkly beautiful spot is one of the large refuges of Mahayana Buddhism, Ladakh's principal religion, which historically has looked to Tibet for inspiration; the Dalai Lama is head of its most popular sect, the Gelug-pa (yellow hat). As you travel through the area, the thin mountain light sparkles on brightly colored prayer wheels, rooftop flags, and whitewashed chortens (stupas). Ladakh's medieval monasteries, perched on craggy cliffs and known locally as gompas, are still centers of learning

India's Ecology Crisis

Resource-rich India faces an ecology crisis. Rampant population growth is one reason; local politics, modernization, and unplanned development are others. Ancient forests and their ecosystems are falling to uncontrolled logging, mining, cultivation, and dams. An estimated 5,800 square miles (15,000 sq km) are lost each year. As a result, tribal groups are losing their means of survival, as are species of flora and fauna. And the land is overfarmed for cash crops—cotton, paper, rubber, jute, tobacco, and sugar—at the expense of food. Huge dam projects, such as the Tungabhadra and Narmada, have displaced more than 20 million people.

They have also affected fish breeding, wildlife, and animal migration; increased the dangers of waterborne diseases; and often silted up. Disadvantages have outstripped advantages.

Meanwhile, despite the green revolution making India self-sufficient in food, Western farming methods, fertilizers, and high-yield strains of crops have damaged the soil, demanded extra irrigation, and affected the environment and traditional by-products.

But there is hope: An energetic ecology movement is making its voice heard, and successful local projects may soon have state and national backing.

and worship, housing remarkable artifacts—brass Buddhas, walls painted with fierce divinities, *thangkas* (scroll paintings), and unusual musical instruments.

If you arrive via the Manali–Leh Highway, you go through the most concentrated area of these monasteries as you progress up the Indus Valley from Upshi to **Leh,** Ladakh's capital and once a staging post on the Silk Road. Having benefited from past trade and religious patronage, Leh is now buffeted by summer visitors. You can visit the old palace, **Namgyal Tsemo gompa,** and the old quarter. One-day trips

Trekking in the Himalaya requires a gentle pace.

INSIDER TIP:

In Ladakh, take a trip to the Nubra Valley and cross one of the world's highest drivable passes, the Khardung La at 18,000 feet [5,400 m] above sea level.

—LEWIS A. OWEN
National Geographic grantee

down the valley can take in pretty villages, **Shey**'s derelict palace, and the stunning **Tikse gompa,** returning via **Hemis gompa** and **Stok palace. Spitok** and **Phyang gompas** lie to the north, as do the 11th-century murals of **Alchi,** best seen during the breathtaking drive to **Kargil,** beyond which lies the beautiful Suru Valley and stunning but remote **Zaskar,** the goal for serious trekkers. The intrepid can

visit the stark Nubra Valley, opened to visitors in 1994.

Trekking Opportunities

Harki Dun Valley: This is an easy, four-day trek from **Mussoorie** through the beautiful **Harki Dun** (Valley of the Gods), a sparsely populated area of northwest Garhwal. The local people have their own customs and religious traditions; they live in alpine houses with carved wooden doors. You will stay in bungalows, except for the last night. On the first day, drive or take a bus via Netwar to Purola; the next day, continue by road to Sankri and trek to Taluka (6,233 feet/1,900 m). On Day 3, trek beside the Tons River to Osla (7,411 feet/2,259 m). On Day 4, go on to Harki Dun (11,679 feet/3,560 m), an excellent base for several days of trekking. From here, either return or, if physically fit and prepared, continue across the challenging Yamnotri Pass.

Manali
🗺 319 B3
Visitor Information
✉ Manali Tourist Office, The Mall
☎ 019/0225-2175

Ladakh
🗺 319 B4
Visitor Information
✉ Leh Tourist Office, Fort Rd., Bazaar
jktourism.org
Visitor Information
✉ Tourist Information, Airport
☎ 019/8225-3076
✉ Foreigners' Registration Office
☎ 019/8225-2200

Kargil
🗺 319 B4
Visitor Information
✉ Tourist Office, Hotel area, Kargil
☎ 019/8523-2721
✉ Foreigners' Registration Office
☎ 019/8523-2545

EXPERIENCE: Treks That Change Your Life

Walking in India's Himalaya, replete with pure air, exhilarating views, and fascinating flora, brings you closer to the essence of life than most vacations. You usually do not require any previous trekking or mountaineering experience; you just need to be reasonably fit and healthy, wear broken-in hiking boots, and be prepared to sleep out and eat simply. On a well-run trip, porters carry your possessions, pitch your tent, and cook your food. You just walk and enjoy. Companies running good trips include **Himalayan Safaris** (*himalayansafaris.com*) and **Trekking in Himalayas** (*trekkinginhimalayas.com*). October and November offer the clearest views of the high peaks.

Most areas have easy, moderate, and tough treks. You choose how long in distance and time (1–30 days) and distance covered each day (3–12 miles/5–19 km). Be sure to ask which is most suitable for you. It is wise to arrive a day or so early to acclimatize to the altitude at the trek starting point; many treks start at around 6,000 feet (1,830 m).

Garhwal has plenty of gentle treks; **Sikkim** offers ravishing flora; **Ladakh** provides true summertime adventures, especially the tough treks to the **Stok Kangri Climb** or to remote **Zaskar**. You can trek the **Kumaun valleys** year-round, but **Himachal** is too cold outside the summer months.

Pindari Glacier: This is an easy and varied five-day trek from **Bageshwar** into the heart of the forested Kumaun region; there are simple bungalows along the way. From the pilgrimage town of Bageshwar, drive or take the bus to Bharari and hike through the Sarayu Valley to Song; from here, walk to Loharkhet. Day 2 is a hard trek over the Dhakuri Pass (9,301 feet/2,835 m), with its spectacular views, and down to Dhakuri. Days 3 and 4 are gentler hikes along the Pindar Valley to Khati, and then beside the Pindar River and its great waterfalls to Dwali and on to Phurkia. Finally, you hike up to Zero Point (12,532 feet/ 3,820 m), the foot of the Pindari Glacier, and down again.

Kullu Valley: This is a five-day trek from Nagar to Jari, with **Manali** as your base, offering incredible alpine scenery and varied landscapes and flora, especially from mid-September to late October; this route requires some camping. From Nagar, hike through a beautiful forest and pastures, and camp above tree line or continue to the base of Chandrakani Pass (12,008 feet/3,660 m), which you hike over on Day 2 to reach Malana, whose people have distinctive houses and follow a strict cultural behavior (your guide will help you on this). You can stay two or three nights in a guesthouse and do day treks into the surrounding rugged country. Finally, take the steep descent into the Parvati Valley to Rashol and Jari.

Shimla to Leh: This is a 15-day combination of walking and driving/busing to the remote mountain reaches of **Kinnaur** and

Spiti. These spectacular drives are not for the faint-hearted. It is essential to allow extra days for acclimatizing to the elevation. In the first week, drive to Sarahan via Narkanda and Rampur; then trek to Sangla to see wooden Bhimkali Temple and the beautiful temples in the Baspa Valley. Continue to Kalpa via Chitkul, and hike over mountain terrain to the medieval villages of Kothi, Tehlangi, Pangi, Chini, and Peo; see Hubulankar Monastery at Chini. Drive on to Nako (12,008 feet/3,660 m) and visit Lotsabalhakhang Monastery.

In the second week, drive on to Tabo, where the frescoes of Chos Khor Monastery (A.D. 996) compare with those of Ajanta (see pp. 175–177). Continue through Pin, Ki, and Kibber to Rangrik and cross the Kumzum La pass (14,931 feet/4,551 m) to Chatru. Kyelang lies over the Rohtang Pass (13,057 feet/3,980 m), from where you drive over the Baralacha La pass (15,912 feet/4,850 m) to Sarchu, enjoying breathtaking mountain scenery. The Lachaalang La pass (16,617 feet/5,065 m) and Tanglang La pass lead to Leh.

Markha Valley: The classic Ladakh trek, this lasts eight to ten days, and goes from **Spiti** or **Stok,** near Leh, to **Hemis;** there are plenty of camps along the way. Best done mid-June to mid-October *(valley can be crowded July–Aug.),* the trek offers a variety of landscapes, some of it stunning, and mostly stays within **Hemis National Park.** The trek's first two days, through the Markha Valley, are gentle. From Spiti (10,498 feet/3,200 m), you proceed via Jingchan and Yurutse to Rumbak (12,467 feet/3,800 m), then on to Yurutse and Shingo (13,615 feet/4,150 m). The next stage is via a spectacular gorge to Skiu (11,154 feet/3,400 m) and Markha (12,139 feet/3,700 m), which offers glorious views of Mount Nimaling (20,997 feet/6,400 m). Continue on to Tahungste, the remote camp at Nimaling (15,485 feet/4,720 m), and through the Longaru La pass (16,732 feet/5,100 m) to Shang Sumdo camp (12,008 feet/3,660 m). End with a visit to Hemis monastery. ■

India: Noteworthy Geographic Facts

- The Himalaya is the world's youngest major mountain range (50 million years old).
- Highest peak: Kanchenjunga (28,210 ft/8,598 m)
- Longest rivers: Brahmaputra (1,800 miles/2,897 km) and the Ganga (1,559 miles/2,510 km)
- Length of border: land, 8,736 miles (14,103 km); coastline, 4,350 miles (7,000 km)
- Country area: 1,269,221 square miles (3,287,270 sq km)—the world's seventh largest country
- The monsoon can dump 39 inches (1,000 mm) of rain on Mumbai and nothing on Rajasthan.

Tea

When you drink a cup of tea, briefly ponder on the expertise required to produce the apparently simple dried tea leaf. The British introduced tea production into northeastern India in the 19th century, using tea seed imported from China. In 1841 Dr. Campbell raised his first tea bushes at his home in Darjeeling (Darjiling). Soon the government set up tea nurseries, whose bushes were planted in India's first commercial tea gardens in 1852.

Some workers hang their baskets high up their backs and toss the leaves over their shoulders.

By the 1870s there were 113 tea plantations, and tea had joined other cash crops such as cotton, sugar, jute, and coffee, which the British were producing in India for international trading.

While Darjeeling planters continued to grow Chinese tea, considered by tea connoisseurs to be the champagne of teas, British adventurers clearing plots of thickly forested land to lay out gardens in Assam discovered a more robust local bush. Land was parceled out on the almost uncharted maps in Kolkata, and many of the men with dreams died before their boats reached Guwahati.

Those who survived faced a tough and isolated life, whose highlight was the weekly gathering at the distant planters' clubs. It changed little until the 20th century when the telephone and television arrived. Still known as tea planters, the gardens' managers work a day that begins before sunrise and ends late. They must oversee their workforce, often comprised of whole villages transplanted from Bihar in central India. They build temples and schools for them, and provide child care and medical care. To the workers, the manager is *ma-bapu* (mother-father), the person to whom they bring disputes; who sits in judgment, punishes, and even presides over marriages. Meanwhile, the manager also oversees the job of producing the tea, from trimming the bushes to deciding when to pluck the precious shoots, from keeping rogue elephants from trampling through the gardens to keeping standards high enough to satisfy the frequent visits of the company tea taster.

During the season, women pluck the leaves in the morning, delivering their full baskets to the on-site factory; they do a second picking in the afternoon. At the factory the fresh leaves immediately undergo a succession of carefully monitored processes: They are withered, rolled to bruise them and bring the juices to the surface, and then left to ferment to develop the flavor. They are then dried and sifted into ever more precise grades.

The bigger the leaf, the better the flavor—so the whole and unbroken leaves of Darjeeling's Golden Flowery Orange Pekoe is the top grade, and Dust, literally the tea dust, is the cheapest. The tea is sent to auctions in great wooden chests, then on to the blenders. Almost every tea needs to be blended to produce the right balance of color, flavor, strength, and perfume, and each country has its own preferred blend.

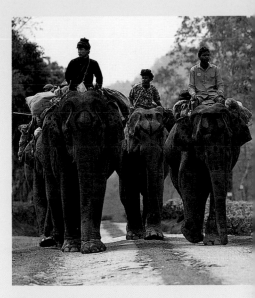

The manager of the tea garden (seated on left elephant) inspects the bushes.

Since independence, ownership of tea plantations has moved into Indian hands, although there is still a strong British interest. Assam's 750 tea gardens produce more than 55 percent of India's tea needs. India and China together produce half the world's tea. However, Kenya and Sri Lanka are rising competitors thanks to low labor costs, younger bushes, and state support.

EXPERIENCE: Bird-watching in the Himalaya

The Indian subcontinent boasts more than 1,200 species of birds. The lower Himalaya region is especially rich because it attracts both mountain-loving and plain-loving birds. So, if you are coming to the hills, pack your binoculars and a field guide to birds, such as *Birds of the Indian Subcontinent* (Helm Publishers, 2002) by Richard Grimmett and Carol Inskipp.

One of the pleasures of birding in the hills is that the vegetation changes with elevation; thus you spot new species as you trek. On the pine-covered ridges and in the temperate woodlands, you'll find the brown-fronted woodpecker, the blue-capped redstart, and the beautiful, big lammergeier (aka bearded vulture), which soars above the hills. Lower down, you see the Kalij pheasant, the Pallas's fish-eagle, the Himalayan flameback, and, perhaps, the rare tawny fish-owl. It's fun to keep a checklist, so carry a notebook.

To find dedicated tours for Himalayan birding, visit *indianbirdwatching.com*.

Eastern Himalaya

This entire Himalaya region shares mountains, wildlife, and flora, but the presence of Bangladesh divides it in two—only Indian citizens may take the train from West Bengal to Assam. Getting to the Eastern Himalaya is easiest by plane from Kolkata or Delhi. The necessary acquiring of permits and the long journey are richly rewarded.

West Bengal

🅜 328 A3 & B3

Visitor Information

✉ Tourist
Information
Centre,
New Car Park,
Laidena Rd.,
Darjiling

**westbengaltourism
.gov.in**

Darjiling

🅜 328 A3

Visitor Information

✉ Darjiling Tourist
Bureau,
1 Nehru Rd.,
Darjiling

☎ 035/4225-4050

darjeeling.gov.in

Sikkim

🅜 328 A4

Visitor Information

✉ Sikkim Tourist
Office,
Mahatma Gandhi
Rd., Gangtok

☎ 035/9222-3425,
035/9222-1634

sikkimipr.org

West Bengal
& Sikkim

The 56-mile (90 km) trip from Shiliguri up to Darjiling is spectacular. You can drive or make the nine-hour journey by the Darjiling Himalayan Railway, known as the Toy Train because of its resemblance to a toy train set, built in 1879–1881, and still pulled by steam engines. Alternatively, take a short run from Darjiling to Ghoom and back.

Darjiling (Darjeeling) (7,218 feet/2,200 m) makes up for its faded British style with its spectacular mountain views toward Kanchenjunga. Watching the sunrise from atop Tiger Hill and visiting the Ghoom monasteries and a tea garden are must-dos. In town, get a taste of Victorian Darjiling by walking along Chowrasta, then down the Mall to see the **Planters' Club,** founded in 1868. At the other end of town, the **Botanical Gardens'** paths lead to dilapidated but atmospheric greenhouses filled with ferns and orchids. Treks to see Everest leave from Darjiling.

Smaller **Kalimpong** (4,101 feet/1,250 m) is ideal for investigating mountain flora, especially orchids; you can visit commercial

INSIDER TIP:

Watch dawn on 8,600-foot [2,600 m] Tiger Hill [Darjiling], with its view of three of the tallest mountains on Earth: Kanchenjunga [the closest], Makalu, and snow-covered Everest.

—DONOVAN WEBSTER
National Geographic Traveler
magazine writer

orchid nurseries. Nearby Rachela Pass (10,341 feet/3,152 m) leads into **Sikkim,** India's smallest state, which combines deep valleys and soaring mountains. From the

CHINA

Anini

ARUNACHAL PRADESH

5108m

Dihang

Lohit

52

Along

Pasighat

Tezu

37

NAMDAPHA
NATIONAL
PARK

Daporijo

Selek

Tinsukia

7089m
Kangto

Ziro

Dibrugarh

38

Tawang

Seppa

Lakhimpur

37

Khonsa

Bomdila

52A

Sibsagar

Itanagar

KAZIRANGA
NATIONAL
PARK

Jorhat

Mon

Tezpur

Golaghat

MANAS
TIONAL PARK

Mangaldai

52

37

Mokokchung

MYANMAR

Barpeta

31

Nagaon

39

Wokha

Tuensang

Brahmaputra

ASSAM

Zunheboto

(BURMA)

GUWAHATI

Dispur

NAGALAND

alpara

37

Diphu

36

Dimapur

3826m

40

Kohima

William
Nagar

Shillong

Jowai

Khasi

44

Karong

39

Ukhrul

MEGHALAYA

Hills

Tamenglong

Cherrapunji

40

Haflong

53

Imphal

Karimganj

Silchar

Thoubal

Bishnupur

MANIPUR

39

Dharmanagar

Churachandpur

Chandel

44

TRIPURA

Aizawl

Agartala

MIZORAM

Udaipur

Mizo
Hills

54

Lunglei

BANGLADESH

Lawngtlai

E

F

0   100 kilometers
0   500 miles

Area of map detail

New
Delhi

C

D

Gangtok
 328 A4

Northeastern States
328–329

Visitor Information

India Tourist Office, B. K. Kakati Rd., Ulubari, Guwahati

assamtourism.org
shubhyatra.com
ignca.nic.in
incredibleindia.com

Visitor Information

Arunachal Pradesh Tourist Office, Naharlagun, Itanagar

arunachaltourism
.com
arunachalpradesh
.nic.in

capital, **Gangtok** (5,164 feet/1,574 m), trekkers through the Teesta and Rangit Valleys enjoy orchids, rhododendrons, magnolia blossoms, and other flora. Sikkim has almost 70 Buddhist monasteries, many with fine murals and images; try to see Phodang, Rumtek, Tashiding, and Pemayangtse.

Northeastern States

This entire region was Assam until the 1960s, when separatist movements led to the creation of six states: Arunachal Pradesh, Nagaland, Manipur, Mizoram, Tripura, and Meghalaya. These states surround the now reduced but fertile valley of **Assam** and rely heavily on its road, rail, and air transportation routes.

Guwahati, Assam's capital until the new one is built at Dispur, sits on the great 1,800-mile-long (2,900 km) Brahmaputra River, which sweeps through the state.

Assam is mostly peopled by Hindu Bengalis, mingled with the Ahoms and Bodos originally from Thailand and Tibet. Some 750 tea estates produce half of India's tea (see pp. 326–327), their clipped bushes giving way to rice fields and then forested mountainsides. Guwahati's Kali temples and tea auctions are interesting.

The spectacular national parks of **Kaziranga** and less developed **Manas,** both World Heritage sites, deserve every effort to reach them. Kaziranga, home to 1,200 rhinos, is 172 miles (215 km) from Guwahati; the park offices are in Kohara. Manas is a Project Tiger reserve; contact Assam Tourist Information *(Station Rd., Guwahati, tel 036/1254-7102 or 036/1254-2748, assamtourism.org)* for details.

An unspoiled wilderness of forested mountains, rushing

Sprawling Gangtok, capital of Sikkim, straddles a hill that was a major India–Tibet trade route.

INSIDER TIP:

In Wakro, the most distant village in Arunachal Pradesh, try to barter with a Naga tribesman for his bear-skin headpiece. It's a one-of-a-kind souvenir.

—DONOVAN WEBSTER
National Geographic Traveler
magazine writer

rivers, and few roads, the state of **Arunachal Pradesh**—"land of the dawn-lit mountains"—offers a tantalizing glimpse of how the Himalaya was when Europeans first explored it, not so long ago. From **Itanagar,** the capital, you can take treks through magical scenery rich in flora and fauna.

Nagaland, only recently fully charted, is a state of densely forested mountains inhabited by the fiercely independent Nagas. The British built the capital, Kohima, but for something more ethnic, visit nearby **Bara Basti.**

The mainly Hindu Meitheis live in **Manipur** state. Their distinct culture includes classical dance, martial arts, and, in September, the colorful Heikru Hitongba Boat race—all found in the capital, **Imphal** (2,575 feet/785 m).

Mizoram state is home to the peaceful, egalitarian, and mostly Christian Mizo people who live on forested and bamboo-covered hills sprinkled with churches and farms. Beautiful handicrafts can be found in and around **Aizawl,** the capital.

A diversity of people, including Bengalis, lives in **Tripura** state,

whose Manikya rulers traced their ancestry to Rajput *kshatriyas* (see p. 25). See the capital **Agartala's** Ujjayanta Palace (1901), **Udaipur's** Tripura Sundari Temple, associated with female power, and **Neermahal** water palace.

In **Meghalaya,** orchid forests benefit from the monsoon that makes this one of the world's wettest places. The lakeside capital, **Shillong** (16,102 feet/4,908 m), retains some of the character of its Scots tea-planter founders.

Trekking Opportunities

Maneybhanjan to Rimbik: This is a relatively easy six-day trek along the **Singalila Range** to appreciate spectacular views of four of the world's highest mountain peaks: Everest, Kanchenjunga, Makalu, and Lhotse (best October–November or February–May). Stay in trekking huts, but take warm bedding.

Day 1, drive or bus from Darjiling to Maneybhanjan; then hike to Meghma and on up to Tonglu (10,072 feet/3,070 m), or sleep at a lodge in Jaubari; reach Sandakphu (11,929 feet/3,636 m) the next day. On Days 3 and 4, enjoy spectacular views along the ridge, first hiking to stay overnight at Molley, then returning via Sandakphu to Phalut (11,811 feet/3,600 m). On Days 5 and 6, trek to Gorkhey and on to Rammam (8,398 feet/2,560 m) for the night, before ending at Rimbik.

Darjiling to Kalimpong: The weeklong journey from West Bengal into Sikkim is a tour, not a trek. You stay in hotels, mixing

Nagaland

🏛 329

Visitor Information

✉ Nagaland Tourist Office, Near Japfu Ashok Hotel, Kohima

✉ State Tourist Office, Opposite Indoor Stadium, Raj Bhavan Rd., Kohima

☎ 037/0224-3124

tourismnagaland .com

Manipur

🏛 329

Visitor Information

✉ Manipur Tourist Office, Jail Rd., Imphal

☎ 038/5221-131

manipur.nic.in /tourism.htm

Mizoram

🏛 329

Visitor Information

✉ Mizoram Tourist Office, State Tourist Office, Bungkawn, Aizawl

☎ 038/9233-3475
038/9233-5677

tourism.mizoram .gov.in

Tripura

🏛 329

Visitor Information

✉ Tripura Tourist Office, Ujjayanta Palace, Agartala

✉ Tourist Information Center, Agartala Airport

☎ 038/1234-2393
038/1230-0332

**tripuratourism.nic.in
westtripura.nic.in**

Meghalaya

⚠ 328–329

Visitor Information

✉ Meghalaya Tourist Office, Polo Rd., Shillong

☎ 036/4222-2731 036/4222-4933

megtourism.gov.in

drives with walks and visits to monasteries, nurseries, and a botanical garden; best October–November or February–March (orchids best in March).

First, spend a day in Darjiling (see p. 328), and visit the Himalayan Mountaineering Institute on Birch Hill. On Day 2, drive through the Teesta Valley to Gangtok (5,075 feet/ 1,547 m), where you can visit the Orchidarium, the Cottage Industries Institute, and the unique Research Institute of Tibetology the next day, or do a local trek. On Day 4, drive to Ramtek (5,085 feet/1,550 m) to visit its monastery, and then enjoy a day trek the next day. On Day 6, drive along the Teesta Valley to **Kalimpong** (4,101 feet/1,250 m), the region's floriculture center, for two nights; you can mix local treks with visits to nurseries, Tarpacholing Monastery, and the School of Tibetan Medicine at Brang Monastery.

Dzongri Trail: This is a nine-day, high-elevation, circular trek through Sikkim's lush forests from **Yoksum** to **Dzongri** and back, with wonderful views and, in May, rhododendrons in bloom. Do this trek in an organized group, so that everything is arranged for you. On Day 1, walk from Pelling to the official start, Yoksum. On Day 2, hike through the cloud forests to Tsokha (10,000 feet/3,000 m); spend Day 3 hiking in the area to acclimatize to the altitude. On Day 4, hike up through pines and rhododendrons to Dzongri (13,221 feet/4,030 m); then take another day to acclimatize. On Days 6 and 7, trek on to Thangsing (12,467 feet/ 3,800 m), then to Samiti Lake (13,320 feet/4,060 m); camp here or continue to Zemanthang. On Day 8, ascend to Gocha La (16,207 feet/4,940m) and return. On Day 10, descend directly to Tsokha. ■

EXPERIENCE: Heli-skiing in the Himalaya

For the experienced skier, heli-skiing in the Himalaya is an incredible experience. Be warned: You should do it with an experienced international company. Check out the company thoroughly to ensure all safety precautions are taken, such as for the delivery system, the quality of lodging, equipment, and communications. Always have an experienced guide with you. Then, get up on those mountains and enjoy.

Heli-skiing is fairly new to the Himalaya, so many routes and ridges are unknown. Also, with consistent snowfall and little wind on the high slopes you can enjoy consistent powder snow. From Manali the heli-skiing expeditions drop skiers onto peaks as high as 21,330 feet (6,500 m)—Chandrakhani Pass is recommended. So, too, are Rohtang Pass, Deo Tibba, and Hanuman Tibba. All these are in **Himachal Pradesh** state (himachal tourism.gov.in), but there is also heli-skiing at Gulmarg in **Jammu and Kashmir,** and at Auli and Pithoragarh (Kamaon) in **Uttarakhand.** It is wise to take your own boots and skis, as local quality can be unreliable. And, be sure to stop and enjoy the views, some of the most beautiful in the world.

Travelwise

A sari-clad woman balances on the back of a scooter.

TRAVELWISE

PLANNING YOUR TRIP

India's variety of history, crafts, monuments, wildlife, and activities can satisfy almost any interest. Spend time planning your itinerary. Remember that if you spend a few days in one place, you usually experience much more than if you bounce from place to place, constantly on the move. India is vast, and no one can see it all in one visit. If you enjoy your first experience there, you will go again.

When to Go

India has such a wide range of climates and attractions that you can enjoy a visit at any time of the year. India has three seasons: October to February is winter, with warm sunny days, but chilly nights in the north. April to June is summer, progressively hot and humid, except in the hills. July to September is the monsoon, which moves up across India from the south (see p. 51).

To visit the forts, temples, and palaces, as well as beaches, the best time to go is from September to March. High season is from October to February, when you'll need to reserve hotel rooms in advance to be sure of a place to stay. To see India's wildlife, visit between February and August, when it gets drier and hotter and the undergrowth is less lush; you are likely to spot more of the animals going to water holes. Bird-watchers can see an astounding variety of migrating birds in winter, especially from December to February.

The searing heat from April to July, which pushes most visitors up into the hills, breaks with the arrival of the monsoon, which can be a fantastic experience and has the advantage of being a time when India is almost tourist free. Up in the hills, trekkers will find the spring and summer months, from May to October, best. It is worth arranging your itinerary to coincide with one of India's many colorful festivals (see pp. 382–385), although you are likely to bump into delightful minor festivals and village fairs wherever and whenever you go.

Tourist Information

For information, maps, brochures, and help planning a trip, contact one of the Government of India Tourist Offices. For a full list, visit *incredibleindia.org*

In the United States
3550 Wilshire Blvd., Suite 204, Los Angeles, CA 90010, tel 213-380-8855, fax 213-380-6111, e-mail: indiatourismla@aol.com

1270 Avenue of the Americas, New York, NY 10020, tel 212-586-4901, fax 212-582-3274, e-mail: rd@itonyc.com

In Canada
60 Bloor St. (West), Ste. 1003, Toronto, Ontario, M4W 3B8, tel 416-962-3787, fax 416-962-6279, e-mail: indiatourism@bellnet.ca

In the U.K.
7 Cork St., London, W1S 3LH, tel 020-7437-3677, fax 020-7494-1048, e-mail: info@indiatourist office.org

General Information Websites

The amount of information on the Web can confuse, and sadly some is plain optimistic or unreliable in describing areas of India, comforts, travel details, sites to see, and weather. The following sites are reliable sources:

incredibleindia.org
india-tourism.com
journeymart.com
indiasite.com
asia-planet.net
webindia123.com
indianembassy.org
hcilondon.in

Special Interest Websites
Culture: asi.nic.in (Archaeological Survey of India)
worldheritagesite.org
unesco.org
intach.org (Indian National Trust for Art and Cultural Heritage)
shubhyatra.com (covers religious sites for all religions)
templenet.com
Crafts: ignca.nic.in (Indira Gandhi National Centre for the Arts; information on crafts throughout India, state by state)
Hill stations: hill-stations-india .com
Judaism in India: spiritualjourneys.net/judaism.htm
whc.unesco.org
Maps: mapsofindia.com
Trains: irctc.co.in
indianrail.gov.in
theluxurytrains.com
Trekking: trekkingindia.com
greatindianoutdoors.com
Wildlife: envfor.nic.in (Ministry of Environment and Forests)

State Websites
Of the many websites available for India's states and union territories, the most useful and reliable are:
Andaman & Nicobar Islands: and.nic.in
Andhra Pradesh: aptourism.in
Arunachal Pradesh: arunachalpradesh.nic.in
Assam: assamtourism.org
Bihar: bihartourism.gov.in

Chandigarh:
chandigarhtourism.gov.in
Chhatisgarh
chhattisgarhtourism.net
Delhi: delhitourism.gov.in
Goa: goatourism.gov.in
Gujarat: gujarattourism.com
Haryana: haryanatourism.gov.in
Himachal Pradesh:
himachaltourism.gov.in
Jammu & Kashmir: jktourism.org
Jharkhand: jharkhandtourism.in
Karnataka: karnatakaholidays.net
Kerala: kerala.gov.in
keralatourism.org
Lakshadweep Islands:
lakshadweeptourism.com
lakshadweeptourism.nic.in
Madhya Pradesh:
mptourism.com
Maharashtra:
maharashtratourism.gov.in
Manipur: tourismmanipur.nic.in,
manipur.nic.in/tourism.htm
Meghalaya: meghalayatourism
.org, megtourism.gov.in
Mizoram: tourism.mizoram.gov.in
Nagaland: tourismnagaland.com
Orissa: orissatourism.gov.in
Puducherry:
tourism.pondicherry.gov.in
Punjab: punjabtourism.gov.in
Rajasthan:
rajasthantourism.gov.in
Sikkim: sikkimtourism.gov.in
Tamil Nadu:
tamilnadutourism.org
Tripura: tripuratourism.nic.in
Uttaranchal:
uttarakhandtourism.gov.in
Uttar Pradesh: up-tourism.com
West Bengal:
westbengaltourism.gov.in

Travel Agents

To make your holiday in India go
smoothly, use a travel agent who
is experienced in advising on India
and booking vacations there. If
you wish to travel independently,
an agent should be able to work
within your budget and cater to
your required levels of adventure,
culture, and comfort. The agent

should recommend sights and
tours that suit your interests—
while one person's dream is to
visit temples galore, another's is
to palace hop in Rajasthan, walk
in the hills, or explore the fort
cities of Karnataka. An agent
will handle the whole booking,
using reliable agents in India, and
should save you time and remove
much of the worry. Once in India,
local agents will ensure that your
reservations for hotels, cars,
guides, and other facilities are
honored, and can amend itineraries and hotel choices if necessary.

Package Deals

However much you may prefer
to plan and make your own
arrangements, when going to
India it is definitely easier to take
a tour. That way, you benefit from
other people's experience and
hard work, and when in India you
can enjoy the sites while someone
else organizes hotel reservations
and transportation.

Nowadays, there is a tour to
suit most interests, budgets, and
preferred paces of travel. Many
clubs and museums run tours, too.
The price might include airfare,
transportation, hotels, some meals,
and a guide or lecturer. Your local
Indian tourist office can suggest
reliable travel agents. Since the
British have a particularly long and
close relationship with India, it is
well worth looking at tours departing from London, both for range
and good prices.

Tours vary from the simple to
the deluxe in content and in price.
Look at the brochures and websites
to get an idea of the range of trips—
and prices. Even if your starting
point is the United States, do not
discount using a British agent.
Finally, should you find yourself in
India wanting to explore the country, the agents suggested here all
have countrywide knowledge and
can create itineraries quickly.

U.S. Tour Companies
Abercrombie & Kent
1520 Kensington Rd., Ste. 212,
Oak Brook, IL 60523, tel 800-
554-7016, fax 630-954-3324,
abercrombiekent.com

Absolute Travel
15 Watts St., 5th Fl., New York,
NY 10013, tel 800-736-8187, fax
212-627-4090, absolutetravel
.com

**Academic Arrangements
Abroad**
1040 Avenue of the Americas,
New York, NY 10018, tel 800-
221-1944, fax 212-344-7493,
arrangementsabroad.com

Artisans of Leisure
18 East 16th St., Ste. 301, New
York, NY 10003, tel 800-214-
8144, artisansofleisure.com

Asia Transpacific Journeys
2995 Center Green Ct., Boulder,
CO 80301, tel 800-642-2742, fax
303-443-1078, asiatranspacific
.com

**Destinations & Adventures
International, Inc.**
8907 Wilshire Blvd., Ste. 203,
Beverly Hills, CA 90211, tel 800-
659-4599, daitravel.com

Geographic Expeditions
1008 General Kennedy Ave., P.O.
Box 29902, San Francisco, CA
94129, tel 888-570-7108, fax 415-
346-5535, geoex.com

Greaves Travel
121 W. Wacker Dr., Ste. 2500,
Chicago, IL 60603, tel 800-318-
7801, greavestvl.com

**International Ventures and
Travel Inc. (IVAT)**
224 W. 35th St., Ste. 1401, New
York, NY 10001, tel 212-947-
7075, fax 212-563-7048,
ivattravel.com

National Geographic Expeditions
1145 17th St., NW, Washington, DC 20036, tel 888-966-8687, nationalgeographicexpeditions.com

Overseas Adventure Travel
124 Mount Auburn St., Ste. 200 N, Cambridge, MA 02138, tel 800-955-1925 oattravel.com

Remote Lands, Inc.
845 3rd Ave., 6th Fl., New York, NY 10022, tel 646-415-8092, remotelands.com

Silk Route Escapes
East 81st St., New York, NY 10028, tel 646-657-0281, silkrouteescapes.com

Tauck World Discovery
10 Norden Pl., Norwalk, CT 06855, P.O. Box 5020, tel 800-788-7885, tauck.com

Travcoa
4340 Von Karman, Ste. 400, Newport Beach, CA 92660, tel 800-992-2003/866-591-0070, fax 949-476-2538, travcoa.com

U.K. Tour Companies
Ampersand Travel
20 Bristow Gardens, London W9 2JQ, tel 020-7819-9770, ampersandtravel.com

Audley Travel
New Mill, New Mill Ln., Witney, Oxfordshire OX29 9SX, tel 019-9383-8000, audleytravel.com

Cazenove & Lloyd
Imperial Studios, 3-11 Imperial Rd., London SW6 2AG, tel 020-7384-2332, fax 020-7384-2399, cazloyd.com

Greaves Travel
53 Welbeck St., London W1G

LXR, tel 020-7487-9111, greavestvl.com

Indian Explorations
Fraser House, Wadham Close, Southrop, Gloucestershire, GL7 3NR, tel 013-6785-0566 indianexplorations.com

Scott Dunn
Head Office: 116 Putney Bridge Road, London, SW15 2NQ tel 020-3432-7639
Also: Madgwick Lane, Westhampnett, Chichester, West Sussex, PO18 0FB, tel 020-8682-5000/5075, fax 01243-792-990, scottdunn.com

Trans Indus
75 St Mary's Road and the Old Fire Station, Ealing, London W5 5RH, tel 0844-879-3690, fax 020-8840-5327, transindus.co.uk

The Ultimate Travel Company
25-27 Vanston Pl., London SW6 1AZ, tel 020-3582-1337, fax 020-7381-0836, theultimatetravelcompany.co.uk

Indian Tour Companies
The following agents have good reputations for reliability and financial integrity. All cover the whole of India. All have a network of local agents.

IVAT India Pvt
tel 91-124-401-7848 ivatindia.com

Peirce & Leslie
tel 91-124-404-9361 peirceandleslie.com

Quo Vadis
tel 91-124-428-6943 quovadis.in

Travelscope
tel 0124-4999-499 fax 0124-4999-477 travelscopeindia.com

What to Take
The old rule applies: The less you take the better. India has changed hugely in the past decade. Today, if you forget something and you are not far off the beaten path, you can buy it. This includes batteries, books, maps, and other essentials. The major exceptions to this rule are high quality sunscreen, quality razor blades, and makeup. Adventurous travelers need to be better prepared, but even they can augment their own supplies with anything from film equipment to mountaineering gear in the main cities in India.

Clothes
Cottons are the most comfortable clothes, but you will need extra layers for chilly mornings and nights in the north. Hotel laundries are quick and efficient, so you do not need to take much. Shorts are acceptable, pants best for wildlife parks and trekking, a hat for sun protection, and swimsuits for pools and the sea—topless bathing is frowned upon. Shoes need to be comfortable for walking, yet easy to slip off when visiting religious buildings. On these occasions, some people like to slip on a pair of socks rather than go barefoot. Indian people are informal, so it is not necessary to dress up in the evenings.

Gadgets
Voltage is 220, occasionally 230. American appliances may require both a voltage transformer and plug adapter. It is worth taking a small, light antimosquito machine and an iPod with favorite music for long journeys. A flashlight is useful for unlit palaces and sculpted temples and caves. Arrange for your cellular phone to operate in India (see p. 339), and remember to pack the battery charger for the phone

and for your digital camera. You can also use public phones (see p. 339).

Medicines
You may feel happier taking your own selection of pills, potions, and lotions. However, hotel doctors and local drugstores are very good. The best way to remain healthy is to drink plenty of bottled water and to eat freshly cooked vegetarian versions of local dishes. Stomach-calming, nutritious bananas can often provide an effective and simple remedy to minor upsets caused by unfamiliar foods.

There are, however, certain essential precautions. For the latest information on vaccinations or inoculations and malaria prophylaxis you should contact your doctor or travel clinic. Owing to the numbers of migrant workers, no area of India is now free of malaria. You should keep a note of the name of your tablets, so that if you lose them, more can be bought in India. The same applies to most medicines, so carry a copy of your prescription from home.

Other Items
Other miscellaneous items that may be useful for your India trip are: sunscreen, rehydration tablets or powders (the local equivalent is Electrol), antiseptic cream, throat lozenges (the dust can irritate your throat), lip balm (the sun dries the skin), sterilized wet wipes, insect repellent, and soft toilet paper.

Special Interests
Take a pair of binoculars for looking at birds, wildlife, and architectural detail. A notebook is useful to list the order in which you see buildings. This makes identifying your photographs later much easier. Bartholomew's Map of India (not available in India) helps you keep your location in perspective; state maps give more details. Those interested in design and crafts should take swatches of fabrics or paints, to match colors when buying bargain-priced silks and cottons.

Insurance
Be sure to take out adequate insurance policies for health, possessions, and cancellations. If you have opted for a package deal, you may want to have more insurance than is included in the price—always check.

Entry Formalities
Passports & Visas
You will need a valid passport and a visa. The passport must be valid for at least six months past the intended date of departure. The visa, of which there are many types, ranging from tourist to business, must be obtained before arrival. A tourist visa costs around $110. These and special permits for visiting certain areas are available from the Indian embassy or consulate in your home country.

At least two copies of key passport pages and all visas should be carried separately from luggage at all times (or scanned and put on an accessible digital file).

Customs on Arrival
It is prohibited to import Indian currency. Items brought into India for personal use are exempt from duty. So are gifts up to the value of ₹8,000, one liter of wine, one liter of spirits, and 200 cigarettes or 50 cigars or 250g of tobacco. Commercial goods must be declared, as must currency over $10,000 or its equivalent. Drugs and narcotics, apart from prescription drugs supplied by your doctor, are strictly prohibited.

Customs on Departure
It is prohibited to export Indian currency. Several items are prohibited from export without an export license. These include gold jewelry valued above ₹6,000, animal skins and products made from them, art objects more than a hundred years old, and wild plants. To verify art objects, contact the Archaeological Survey of India, Janpath, New Delhi, tel 011/2301-9487 & 011/2301-0789.

Indian Embassies
For detailed information on any of the above, you should contact your nearest Indian embassy. These include:

In the United States
Embassy of India
2107 Massachusetts Ave., NW, Washington, DC 20008, tel 202-939-7000, fax 202-265-4351, indianembassy.org

Consulate General of India
3 E. 6th St., New York, NY 10021, tel 212-774-0600, fax 212-861-3788, indiacgny.org. There are also consulates in Chicago, Houston, and San Francisco.

In Canada
High Commission of India
10 Springfield Rd., Ottawa, ON KIM 1C9, tel 613-744-3751/3752, fax 613-744-0913, hciottawa.ca. There is also a consulate in Vancouver.

In the United Kingdom
Applications to:
18 Spring Street, London W2 3RA, tel 0800-567-7692/020-7148-6117/080-5617-1225, visahq.co.uk & hcilondon.in. There are also consulates in Birmingham, Edinburgh, and Belfast.

HOW TO GET TO INDIA

International Flights

Most national carriers fly to India. The main international airports are New Delhi, Mumbai, Kolkata, and Chennai; some airlines fly into Bangalore. Charter planes fly into Panaji (Goa) and Trivandrum (Thiruvananthapuram, Kerala). Consider flying into one city and home from another, an option offered by many large airlines at no extra cost. Consider, too, whether to fly across the Pacific into Kolkata (Calcutta) or Chennai (Madras), or across Europe into Delhi or Mumbai (Bombay). Shop for a good deal as prices vary and may be particularly cheap if you travel via Hong Kong or London. Make sure the price includes all airport taxes.

GETTING AROUND

On Arrival

If you are not being met at the airport, it is best to go to the official taxi desk (where rates are controlled) rather than accept a ride with one of the many unaffiliated drivers.

Traveling in Major Cities

India has many transportation options. Select the one most suitable for your journey or sightseeing. In Delhi, for instance, you might use a taxi for long journeys, the Metro or a motorized rickshaw for shorter ones, and a bicycle rickshaw for exploring Old Delhi. In Mumbai you can use a combination of taxis and auto rickshaws; in Kolkata you can choose between taxis, underground trains, river ferries, and, possibly, rickshaws. The adventurous might like to tackle the local buses.

Taxis may or may not have meters that work. So for these and for all rickshaw journeys, agree on a price with the driver before starting your journey, make stops where you wish, then pay at the end adding extra money for "waiting time." Your hotel concierge should give you a clear idea of the local rates, which vary considerably. However, you can also opt for radio cabs—now available in most metropolitan cities. Their meters always work, so there is no haggling about rates.

Traveling Around the Country

Traveling is part of your vacation in India. See if you can travel by air, car, coach, bus, and train; by camel, pony, and elephant; and by auto-rickshaw. Air travel is useful for big leaps across the country, but is best avoided for short trips such as Delhi–Agra, when the train is faster and easier.

India's roads are like no others. Your car, coach, or bus may share the path with a herd of goats, some bicyclists, and overloaded bullock carts carrying farm produce. What appears at first merely to be movement between one palace or temple city and another becomes a colorful and memorable experience.

Riding an animal, though, is quite different. Even the shortest journey on a camel may be too much, so ensure you have tested your endurance before you embark on a five-day camel ride through the desert. Ponies are easier, and often used on treks; and sitting on an elephant to spot exotic birds or, perhaps, a tiger, is special indeed.

You can hire a car (which comes with a driver; it is sheer madness to drive oneself in India, see opposite).

By Air

Three large domestic airlines plus a handful of small ones service India's extensive network of 120 domestic airports. Your travel agent will have the most up-to-date information, as schedules change in October and April. The major and budget airlines below offer reduced child and youth fares, as well as special discount fares for visitors—usually a 15- or 21-day ticket for unlimited travel at a flat rate, with certain restrictions. Check-in time for all domestic flights is two hours before departure.

Major Airlines
Indian Airlines: airindia.com
Jet Airways: jetairways.com

Budget Airlines
GoAir: goair.in
IndiGo: goindigo.in
Jet Konnect: jetkonnect.com
SpiceJet: spicejet.com
Some good deals might also be found on: makemytrip.com, kayak.co.in, cleartrip.com, expedia.co.in, & goibibo.com.

By Train

For many visitors to India, a train journey is essential. India's railroad network (see pp. 106–107) operates about 7,800 passenger services each day. Rail schedules are now available on the net at *indianrail.gov.in*. For both schedules and tickets, go to *irctc.co.in*

At the top end of the market, where tickets should always be reserved well in advance, you can choose between tourist trains such as the *Palace on Wheels* and regular passenger trains such as the Rajdhani and Shatabdi superfast trains.

Indian Railways offers Indrail passes valid from just half a day up to 90 days, at very good prices.

Superfast Regular Trains
The deluxe, air-conditioned *Rajdhani Express* trains connect large cities and have sleeping berths, while the *Shatabdi Express* trains connect cities less far apart, such as Delhi with Agra, Gwalior, and Bhopal. India's newest

railroad, the **Konkan Railway** (see pp. 202 203), runs down the west coast from Mumbai.

Tourist Trains

The advantages: You unpack once and avoid most road and air travel. The disadvantages usually include the cramped cabins with bad lighting, monotonous food, little contact with local life, and short controlled stops at interesting places that deserve more time.

Deccan Odyssey

Travels from Mumbai's VT station to Goa, hilltop forts, Pune, Ajanta and Ellora. deccan-odyssey-india .com

The Golden Chariot

Departs from Bangalore on Mondays to visit Kabini and Bandipur, Mysore, Hassan and Hospet, Badami, and Goa. goldenchariot.org

Indian Maharaja

Two itineraries: Delhi, Agra, Sawai-Madhopur, Udaipur, Ahmabad, Aurangabad, and Mumbai. theindianmaharaja.co.in

Maharajas' Express

Four seven- or eight-day itineraries aimed at the upscale corporate charter market, and run in partnership with travel agent Cox & Kings. royalindiantrains.com

Royal Rajasthan on Wheels

...plus Agra and Delhi. The Rajasthan part starts in Jaipur and heads to Sawai Madhopur, Chittorgarh, Udaipur, Jaisalmer, Jodhpur, Bharatpur. royal rajasthanonwheels.com

Palace on Wheels

Circles Rajasthan in eight days from Delhi, then on the same route of Royal Rajasthan (see above). palaceonwheels.net

Toy Trains

These short rides, mostly through glorious scenery, are well worth the time. With the demise of most steam trains, and India's commitment to making all of its train track broad gauge, the charming, British-built lines up to the hill stations are rare chances to evoke earlier times. Routes include the **Kalka–Shimla** journey, 43 miles (69 km); the *Shivalik Queen,* offering the same run but with private rooms aimed at honeymooners; the **Nilgiri Mountain Railway** to Ooty; the **Matheran Railway;** and the **Darjiling Hill Railway** with the narrowest gauge of all and uninterrupted views of the Himalayan mountains. The *Fairy Queen,* the world's oldest running locomotive, is now used for weekend trips from Delhi to Alwar and back.

By Car & Driver

To "drive" in India means to rent a car with a driver. Budget permitting, this is the most luxurious way to travel around India. It is often the easiest way to reach interesting sites. You are free to go where you wish, when you wish, and to stop whenever you see anything interesting.

A good driver knows your route, knows the best restroom stops and the best *dhabas* (roadside cafés), protects you from untrustworthy guides and tiresomely pestering peddlers, keeps the car stocked with bottled water and soft drinks, helps with minor practical shopping, and generally looks after your interests. Many travelers strike up strong friendships with their drivers, who should be well rewarded when you part (see Tipping, p. 341).

When you first have your car and driver, it is important that you feel confident about both: If not, be sure to talk to your local agent immediately and request a change.

Travel agents should arrange a car and driver, and include the cost as part of the price of the travel arrangements they make.

By Bus

There are several classes of Indian public bus. At the top end of the market, deluxe buses are the most comfortable and have air-conditioning.

By Water

Sometimes a boat journey is an integral part of sightseeing. Sunrise at Varanasi seen from a boat on the Ganga River is magical (see pp. 306–307), as is exploring the backwaters of Kerala by boat (see pp. 208–210); you can even stay on one. The best way to move from south to north Kolkata is to take the public ferries on the Hooghly. On the west coast, ferries leave Mumbai for Elephanta Island, while hydrofoils and hovercrafts cross the harbor to the Maharashtran coast.

PRACTICAL ADVICE

Communications

To bypass the hotel markup on telephone bills, either bring your own cell phone, or use the local pay phones that usually have yellow advertising boards marked "PCO-STD-ISD." Internet cafés abound. However, local pay phones are decreasing. If your cell phone will not work in India, it makes sense to buy or rent a handset and a local SIM card for the duration of your stay. This is very cost effective, and your hotel concierge can help with this.

Note that American cellular phones normally operate on the frequency 1900 mHz. The operating frequency in India is 900/1800 mHz; contact your network operator to check whether your phone will work on those frequencies.

The phone numbers for hotels and restaurants included later in this section include long-distance area codes. The first digit (the zero) of the area code should be omitted when dialing from outside the country. In other words, to dial these numbers from within India, simply dial the number listed; to dial from the United States, dial 011 then 91 (India's international code), then the number listed, omitting the first zero.

Conversions
Temperature is measured in degrees Celsius, distance in kilometers, liquids in liters, fabric in meters, gold in grams. However, as some of the world's greatest traders, Indians will be able to adapt any measurement, from shoes to silk, to facilitate your understanding.

Food & Drink
Eating and drinking are either perpetual worries or perpetual delights. If you worry, then make sure you always carry bottled water with you, and if you are unhappy about the food available away from your hotel, buy and eat a few bananas every day to keep up your strength.

If you find the aromas of cafés too tempting to pass by, then take basic precautions and you should come to no harm. Always eat freshly prepared local food in a popular café with a bustling trade (which means regular clients know it is reliable and food does not hang around). Stick to vegetables, *dhal*, rice, and bread unless absolutely sure of the storage systems and hygiene levels. Take bottled water, crackers, and fruit you can peel on a journey or while sightseeing.

Health
If you need to use local medical facilities, these are usually of a

high standard. In fact, India trains some of the world's finest doctors who are often knowledgeable in both Western medicine and complementary remedies. If you have any health problems, your hotel will have a doctor on call 24 hours a day. Drugstores are well staffed and well stocked, and hospitals in the big cities are of a high standard. Keep receipts for all medical help and drugs as they will be needed for insurance claims. Also keep copies of prescriptions to show your doctor at home.

Holidays
In addition to the many festivals (see pp. 382–385), most offices close for the following official public holidays:

Jan. 26: Republic Day
Aug. 15: Independence Day
Oct. 2: Mahatma Gandhi's birthday
Dec. 25: Christmas Day

Liquor Laws
Almost all hotels serve beer and spirits in their bars and restaurants. However, depending upon the political party in power, individual states may call for certain days of the month to be "dry." It is important to respect these rules and restrict liquor consumption to your hotel room on these occasions.

Media
More than 40,000 newspapers and periodicals are published in 100 languages and dialects in India each year. Many are in English, including the *Times of India*, the *Hindu*, the *Hindustan Times*, and the *Indian Express*, each with several local editions. One or two will be delivered to your hotel room, and foreign newspapers are usually on sale in hotel shops.

India Today is India's answer to *Time* or *Newsweek*.

While India's own television networks tell you much about its culture and values—and some are in English—most hotel rooms are also supplied with satellite TV channels including BBC and CNN.

Money Matters
Indian currency is the rupee. Bills come in denominations of ₹1,000, 500, 100, 50, 20, 10, 5, and 2. The rupee is divided into 100 paise. Small bills and coins are useful for tips. However, visitors will find that large sums are often quoted in U.S. dollars, from hotel rooms to upscale shopping. Major credit cards are accepted in hotels, hotel shops and restaurants, and in larger stores. It is best to carry U.S. dollar traveler's checks and to change them at your hotel, where the rate is usually favorable, as the long lines at banks move slowly. When changing money, ask for an encashment certificate so that you can change back any money that you have left over at the end of your trip—it is not permitted to take rupees out of India. Cities, towns, and even some villages have ATMs.

Opening Times & Entrance Fees
Sites in the care of the ASI (Archaeological Survey of India) usually open sunrise to sunset. Admission fees are minimal except for a handful of notable exceptions (e.g., Taj Mahal), for which the fees are regularly revised. Museums often have quirky opening hours that vary from week to week; check out opening times upon arrival.

Government offices are open Monday through Friday from 9:30 a.m. to 5 p.m., plus some Saturdays from 9:30 a.m. to 1 p.m. Stores are mostly open between 9:30 a.m. and 6 p.m., but those in hotels and at tourist sites are open whenever there is a chance of business. Bazaars keep longer hours.

Photography & the Law

It is strictly prohibited to take photographs in a number of places. These include airports, ports, docks, and train stations. It is also forbidden to take photographs of any bridge, law court, or government defense building. If in doubt, ask. Otherwise you may be asked to hand over your camera, or even be detained by the police.

Places of Worship

Most towns have active places of worship for Christians, Hindus, and Muslims; many have *gurudwaras* for Sikhs. The cities historically linked with Jewish people, such as Mumbai, Kolkata, Delhi, and Kochi, have synagogues.

Restrooms

Restrooms in hotels and upscale restaurants are modern and clean, although water restrictions may mean that the flush is replaced by a bucket and tap. When traveling it may often be more comfortable (and more hygienic) to stop at the roadside near some bushes than to use a modest public lavatory, so carry a roll of toilet paper and packs of antiseptic wipes.

Time Differences

India has one time zone. It is 5.5 hours ahead of GMT; this means that it is 10.5 hours ahead of U.S. Eastern Standard Time, and 13.5 hours ahead of U.S. Pacific Standard Time.

Tipping

Just as it is vital to tip those who deserve and need it, it is also useful to know when not to tip. In India, it is not obligatory to tip at meals, although it is usual to add about 10 percent. It is, however, important to tip all room service (₹50 per food, drink, or laundry delivery, shoeshine, errand, etc.) and hotels and airport porters (₹200 per bag). A good sightseeing guide deserves ₹1,000 tip per day, a good driver the same, more if he has driven a hard and long route. In both cases, give the tip at the end of the service, when you say goodbye; do not feel obliged to tip for bad service.

Be careful to note which tips are included in a package deal, checking with the local agent if necessary.

Travelers With Disabilities

In India, where respect for the infirm and elderly is considerable, travelers with disabilities should have few problems. Being in a wheelchair does not mean you will not be able to ride on an elephant. You should be sure to inform your travel agent of any specific requirements that you might have, and reconfirm these with your Indian agent upon arrival. Certainly Indian people are always willing to help, but travelers with disabilities may find that a lot of places are not wheelchair accessible.

Visitor Information

There are numerous Government of India Tourist Offices in India, mostly staffed by knowledgeable and helpful people. In addition, each state and union territory has its own web of tourist offices in its area, plus one in the capital, Delhi (see pp. 334–335).

EMERGENCIES
Embassies
U.S. Embassy
Shanti Path, Chanakyapuri, New Delhi 110021, tel 011/2419-8000, newdelhi.usembassy.gov. Branches in Kolkata, Mumbai, and Chennai

U.K. High Commission
Chanakyapuri, New Delhi 110021, tel 011/2419-2100, ukinindia.fco.gov.uk

Accidents

If you witness a crime, are involved in an automobile accident, have something stolen, or experience anything that might require police assistance, make a clear note of the event at the time and include any necessary sketches. Then try to go to the local police station with your travel agent, your hotel manager, or, if serious, a representative of your embassy or consulate who will help with the bureaucracy and paperwork. It is important to report a crime if you are intending to make a claim on your insurance.

Difficulties

If something goes wrong in your hotel, contact the duty manager. If something goes wrong while touring, your driver or guide will deal with it. For any other problems, contact your travel agent's local representative. However, should you suffer a significant robbery, you should go to the local police station with your travel company representative to report it.

If you mislay your passport—and this really does happen—you will obtain a replacement more quickly by having photocopies of the essential pages and of your visa; so take these with you. To replace your passport, contact your country's local mission; they should send someone with you to get the required documents from local Indian offices, which may be difficult to do alone.

Hotels & Restaurants

India's accommodations and restaurants began to experience a total revolution in the 1990s. The country's unprecedented economic boom and its increasing appeal as an exotic travel destination resulted in a great growth of hotels of all sizes and qualities across the country.

Demand outstrips supply, however, at all levels—luxury, first class, standard, and moderate—resulting in some horrendous hotel room price increases. High prices in some instances do not necessarily mean good hotels; due diligence should be exercised. If the heat goes out of India's economic and tourism upward spiral, prices may well drop. Until then, when traveling in the high season try to make hotel reservations well in advance and to have written confirmation of the rates.

Here is just a tiny selection of what is available. If you plan your own trip, rather than opting for a preplanned package deal, beware: Upscale hotels and their in-house facilities from telephones to bar prices are not cheap, plus there are hefty taxes. Use websites to find the best deals. Consider staying in one or two memorable hotels, then economize with modest ones when you are sightseeing most of the day.

Large hotels often have several restaurants, some highly popular with locals, so it is wise to reserve a table; they also have a coffee shop offering informal eating and longer opening hours. The advantages of eating in such hotels is the range of cuisines (Chinese is especially good, Western food is known as Continental), fresh fruits from papaya to pineapple, and drinks—a favorite thirst-quencher is a fresh lime juice with soda.

India has few stand-alone restaurants of note, although this is changing, particularly in cosmopolitan cities. Highly regarded restaurants and chefs tend to be associated with the good hotels. To keep their local clientele happy, hotels often renovate their restaurants and change both name and cuisine. Where there are local neighborhood restaurants, the current extended government crackdown on illegal buildings is forcing many to close down overnight. Thus, consult with your hotel duty manager for local restaurants. That said, small hotels and independent cafés and restaurants can produce fresher and more authentic local food, especially if asked—Indians love to talk about food. A roadside café known as a *dhabba* can be the best of all, especially for a "rice dhal" meal or a *thali* (a whole meal arrives on one platter) in the south, or a kebab with naan or *paratha* along the Grand Trunk Road in the north, washed down with hot, sweet, milky chai (tea) and some bottled carbonated drinks.

Suspicion and fear all too often lead visitors to stick to disappointing, format food. It's far better, and safer, to eat freshly cooked local food. Include plenty of rice or bread with your meal; stick to vegetable dishes unless you are sure of the freshness of fish or meat; have a daily bowl of yogurt; and drink lots and lots of bottled water.

Types of Accommodations

The burgeoning of hotels in India is accompanied by the radical and repeated improvement of facilities in older hotels—from in-room Wi-Fi connections to fusion food and elaborate spas. Some of these upgrades are not easy to understand precisely; some openings are delayed. For up-to-date information, consult the hotel websites and for specific needs (e.g., nonsmoking rooms, sophisticated business center), use the website contact information to e-mail or, better still, call the front desk. (Telephone numbers are constantly being upgraded, so check the websites for the latest on those, too.)

The hotels listed below include the number of rooms, to give an idea of a hotel's size. They also note if there is a swimming pool and a health club. If swimming laps is important to you, check the shape and size of the pool. "Health club" can have a broad interpretation in India, ranging from a small gym or a single masseuse to a full-blown international standard spa or ayurvedic center; again, if specific services are important to you, check directly with the hotel.

There are an increasing number of "eco-hotels" in India. Some have only outdoor shower facilities, others restrict alcohol or do not have TVs or telephones in the rooms. In remote areas, cell phone signals are unavailable, so if such facilities are important to you, check with the hotels when making reservations.

Deluxe Hotel Chains
Ashok Group: theashokgroup.com
Casino Group: casinogroupkerala.com
cghearth.com
HRH Group: hrhindia.com
Heritage Hotels: heritagehotelsofindia.com
welcomheritagehotels.com
Neemrana Hotels: neemranahotels.com
Oberoi Hotels and Resorts: oberoihotels.com
Palaces: tajhotels.com
Park Hotels: theparkhotels.com
Taj Hotels, Resorts, and Welcomgroup: welcomgroup.com

State-run Hotel Groups

Some of these are very useful, especially in rural areas or for more moderate accommodations. Some include heritage hotels and old British buildings. For more information, visit the state websites (see pp. 334–335).

International Hotel Chains

The international chains Best Western, Country Hospitality (Regent, Radisson, Country Inns, TGIF), Four Seasons, Hilton, Holiday Inn, Hyatt, Inter-Continental, Kempinski, Mandarin Oriental, Marriott, Meridien, Park Plaza, Quality Inns, Sheraton, Aman, and others all operate in India.

Heritage Hotels

From sprawling palaces to modest hunting lodges, from imposing forts to cozy family homes, the former royals and aristocrats of India have taken full advantage of tax benefits to transform their properties into hotels. Some have joined forces for their marketing. A few are part of the big hotel chains or run by businesspeople; most are run by descendants of their creators. The vast majority are in Rajasthan, but there are a growing number in Kerala, Gujarat, and the hill states, including some tea managers' homes. Although romantic and often very beautiful, their success in delivering a comfortable room, hot water, good food, and lively service to their guests varies. That said, the ones that are run well provide a remarkable and personal experience that no big hotel can match—and good local food, too. To find out more: Heritage Hotels Association, 9 Sardar Patel Marg, C Scheme, Jaipur 302001, Rajasthan, tel 014/1381-906, fax 014/1382-214, heritagehotelsofindia.com

See also:
gujaratindia.com
hill-stations-india.com
welcomheritagehotels.com
neemranahotels.com
hrhindia.com

Other Lodging

If you are looking for a very good budget hotel, Ginger Hotels (gingerhotels.com) is a good nationwide chain in this category. Owner-managed hotels can be especially charming. Individual states run some hotels, indicated below with their state initials in brackets after the title. Some modest, British-built Tourist Bungalows and Traveler Lodges in offbeat places are also run by the states. Kerala's boats once used to transport rice are now pretty houseboats. Delhi, Goa, Mumbai, Kolkata, Chennai, and a dozen Rajasthan cities including Jaipur run paying-guest programs where you stay with an Indian family; all reserved through the local tourist offices. India's Youth Hostels Association of India (yhaindia .org) runs an extensive network of very cheap and often centrally located youth hostels. The YMCA (ymcaindia.org) and YWCA (ywca india.org) also provide good value for central accommodations.

Wildlife Lodging

This type of accommodation has improved immeasurably in the past few years. Some of the best are suggested in the following pages. See also:
himalayanlodges.com
indianwildliferesorts.com

Standards & Prices

Local star ratings have little significance in India, and it would be misleading to imply that membership of an international hotel group means a hotel will equate to, say, a hotel in New York belonging to the same group, so such information is omitted. All hotels and most enclosed restaurants have air-conditioning of varying types. Nonsmoking rooms are becoming more widely available throughout India, and most restaurants are now nonsmoking. Most hotels will change foreign currency into rupees; most accept payment with a major credit card. Hotel rooms above a certain price are subject to extra luxury taxes. Often a town's best restaurants will be in its hotels.

Credit Cards

Most hotels accept major credit cards. However, it is possible that some small establishments in remote areas might not, so check before you book. Most restaurants in India's large cities now accept credit cards, but in smaller cities and towns you should check for the sign of your card on the door.

Organization of Listings

The hotels and restaurants on the following pages have been grouped according to chapter, first by price category, then alphabetically within those categories.

■ DELHI

In this sprawling city, location is important. As business areas expand into the suburbs the term "central" has less meaning. To find the best location for you, check on where you will be spending your days. For more modest hotel options, see "Other Lodging" above. Whatever your choice, the capital's hotels are often full, so reserve in advance.

Traditional North Indian cuisines include the rich Mughlai dishes of the Mughal rulers, with plenty of cream, butter, and nuts, and the simpler Northwest Frontier cuisine of the soldier invaders, which is based on meat cooked on a griddle. Punjabi food, the most familiar to Western visitors, includes plenty of ghee (clarified butter), meat cooked in a tandoor oven, and hot naan breads.

Hotels

CLARIDGES
$$$$$

12 AURANGZEB RD.
TEL 011/4133-5133
claridges.com
Three-story, 1950s landmark in Lutyens's New Delhi, beside the Diplomatic Enclave. Now renovated into a smart and contemporary but unpretentious and friendly hotel, with Chinese, Mediterranean, and outdoor *dhaba* restaurants.
🛏 162 🏊 🎽

HYATT REGENCY DELHI
$$$$$

BHIKAJI CAMA PLACE, RING RD.
TEL 011/2679-1234
delhi.regency.hyatt.com
Located in south Delhi, an upscale business hotel with all conveniences including tennis court and Olympus fitness center. Restaurants offer Italian, Asian, and Indian dishes, and there is a patisserie and pool lounge on site.
🛏 508 🏊 🎽

THE IMPERIAL
$$$$$

JANPATH
TEL 011/4150-1234
theimperialindia.com
A row of royal palms leads to this lavishly renovated 1930s hotel, part of Lutyens's original scheme for Delhi. It is the capital's only deluxe heritage hotel, and the owners' notable collection of Company School art decorates the walls. Outdoor terrace eating overlooking sprawling lawns; indoors, a rich mixture of bars and restaurants (good Indian food in **Daniells**).
🛏 274 🏊 🎽

ITC MAURYA
$$$$$

DIPLOMATIC ENCLAVE,
SARDAR PATEL MARG
TEL 011/2611-2233
itchotels.in
Sited in the Diplomatic Enclave of southwest Delhi, between the airport and the government and historic areas, this hotel has three levels of increasingly elite rooms plus the well-established **Bukhara** (Northwest Frontier cuisine) and **Dum Pukt** (Mughlai-Lucknowi cuisine) restaurants.
🛏 484 🏊 🎽

OBEROI
$$$$$

DR. ZAKIR HUSSAIN MARG
TEL 011/2436-3030
oberoihotels.com
The nearby golf course and historic sites coupled with the elegant renovated public rooms make this a repeat choice for travelers, both businesspeople and tourists. In addition to the world cuisines of the spacious **Threesixty°** bar-restaurant, there is a big traditional bar and individual Chinese, Italian, and Northwest Frontier restaurants. Exceptional spa and pools.
🛏 279 🏊 🎽

THE PARK
$$$$$

15 PARLIAMENT ST.
TEL 011/2374-3000
theparkhotels.com
India's only chain of contemporary city-center luxury boutique hotels has its Delhi property right in the heart of Lutyens's core. There is a 35-foot-long (11 m) bar designed by Conran, equally modern restaurants inside and poolside, and a good spa.
🛏 220 🏊 🎽

RADISSON BLU PLAZA
$$$$$

NATIONAL HWY. 8
TEL 011/2677-9191
radissonblu.com
Convenient airport hotel for overnight stops to catch a few hours of sleep. If you are delayed, there is a nice bar and good restaurants (Thai, Continental, and Italian) plus an indulgent spa.
🛏 256 🏊 🎽

SHANGRI-LA HOTEL
$$$$$

19 ASHOKA RD.,
CONNAUGHT PLACE
TEL 011/4119-1919
shangri-la.com
Inside Lutyens's New Delhi, yet totally contemporary. Rooms are not especially spacious, but the public areas are superb, from the bar and **Café Uno's** world cuisines at live cooking stations to the **19 Oriental Avenue** restaurant's Japanese, Thai, and Chinese cuisines and the luxurious garden space.
🛏 232 🏊 🎽

🏨 Hotel   🍴 Restaurant   🛏 No. of Guest Rooms   🏊 Swimming Pool   🎽 Health Club

SHERATON NEW DELHI
$$$$$

DISTRICT CENTRE, SAKET
TEL 011/4266-1122
itchotels.in
Formerly the ITC Welcom-
hotel. Located in south Delhi's
upscale residential Saket area,
convenient for the airports
and new business areas, this
business hotel has specialist
restaurants serving South
Indian and Pan-Asian cuisine,
and a notable gym.

220

TAJ MAHAL
$$$$$

1 MANSINGH RD.
TEL 011/2302-6162
tajhotels.com
Benefiting from a total renovation that included a good spa
and club floors, this hotel right
in Sir Edwin Lutyens's core
New Delhi suits businesspeople and tourists. Angolie Ela
Menon's work decorates the
hotel's fine choice of restaurants: **Wasabi by Morimoto,
House of Ming** (Chinese),
and **Rick's** (wok cuisine, plus a
martini bar).

269

TRIDENT GURGAON
$$$$

NEW DELHI NATIONAL CAPITAL
REGION, 443 UDYOG VIHAR,
PHASE V, GURGAON
TEL 011-245 0505
tridenthotels.com
Contemporary luxury, signature design, delicious food,
and a remarkable pool make
this more than a convenient
airport hotel at Gurgaon,
west of Delhi—it also attracts
people working in the nearby
cyberspace city of call centers
and shopping malls. Well
worth attending the buffet
breakfast—and delaying your
next flight.

136

MAIDENS HOTEL
$$$

7 SHAM NATH MARG
TEL 011/2397-5464
maidenshotel.com
Opened in 1903, this is
where Lutyens stayed while
his garden city was being
built. Sited north of New
Delhi, its advantages are its
spacious classic colonial-style
rooms, restaurant hung with
original Raj photographs, lush
gardens, and easy access to
Old and New Delhi's core
historic buildings.

54

VIVANTA BY
TAJ-AMBASSADOR
$$$

SUJAN SINGH PARK,
CORNWALLIS RD.
TEL 011/6626-1000
vivantabytaj.com
This small, relaxed, and
friendly hotel is in a residential
area built by one of New
Delhi's developers, on the
edge of Lutyens's core plan,
near Humayun's Tomb and
Lodhi Gardens. Lovely lawns.

88

AHUJA RESIDENCY
$$

193 GOLF LINKS
TEL 011/2461-1027
ahujaresidency.com
This guesthouse, located
in Delhi's affluent deluxe
Golf Links residential area, is
patronized by many regular
Delhi visitors, both diplomats
and tourists. Rooms and apart-
ments are well maintained,
and come with the advantage
of home cooking. Two more
houses are nearby.

54

Restaurants

CAFÉ UNO
$$

SHANGRI-LA HOTEL,
ASHOKA RD., NEW DELHI
TEL 011/4119-1919
This contemporary culinary
spectacle runs 24/7, with
indoor and outdoor seating.
A combination of buffets and
chefs at live cooking stations
provide Indian, Continental,
and Mediterranean dishes,
and the desserts are amazing.
Upstairs, there is a similar
setup for Asian cuisines.

SHALOM RESTAURANT
$$

N18, N BLOCK MARKET,
GREATER KAILASH PART I
TEL 011/4163-2280
Reserve a table to enjoy
dinner in this chic, upscale,
contemporary restaurant in
one of Delhi's wealthier inner
residential districts, where
sophisticated cocktails precede
such dishes as paella and
other India-Continental
fusion dishes.

THE CULINARE
$

CHANDAN MARKET, S BLOCK,
GREATER KAILASH PART II
TEL 011/2921-8050
A good lunch stop while
shopping in Greater Kailash I
and II districts of south Delhi
(FabIndia, etc.), this simple,
kitchen-style restaurant serves
some of the best Thai food
in town to Delhi's discerning
foodies, at very cheap prices.

E KARIM'S
$

JAMA MASJID, GALI KABABIAN,
OLD DELHI
TEL 011/2326-9880
karimhoteldelhi.com
If you want to get a feel for
what Old Delhi was once like,
seek out Karim's on the south
side of the Jama Masjid, where
a succession of little courtyards
and rooms have cooks
preparing *khameeri roti* bread,
shami kebabs, *badshahi, badam
pasanda* (lamb), and more.

SOMETHING SPECIAL

🍴 GREAT KABAB FACTORY

$

THE RADISSON HOTEL,
NEAR THE AIRPORTS
NATIONAL HIGHWAY-8
TEL 011/2677-9191

This is the best place to have your last meal in India before catching a night flight home. Open only for dinner, the set price menu offers customers vegetables, *daal*, pickles, Indian breads, and as many kebabs as you wish chosen from 150 different kinds that you can watch chefs prepare through a glass wall.

■ AROUND DELHI

The Delhi–Agra and Delhi–Jaipur roads have several well-run restaurants with good restrooms and, sometimes, gardens. Try the ones at Hodal and Kosi.

AGRA

🏨 AMARVILAS
🍴 $$$$$

TAJ EAST GATE RD.
TEL 056/2223-1515
oberoihotels.com

One of the Oberoi group's super-deluxe Vilas trio of hotels at Agra, Jaipur, and Udaipur. Every room of this hotel has views of the Taj Mahal, which is barely 650 yards (600 m) away, and some have terraces. Golf buggies or a ten-minute walk reaches the Taj, if guests can tear themselves away from the Mughal-inspired hotel, gardens and pool, good food, and indulgent spa.

ⓘ 112 🏊 🏋

🏨 TIKLI BOTTOM
🍴 $$$$$

HARYANA, OFF DELHI–JAIPUR HWY.
TEL 012/4276-6556
tiklibottom.com

An hour's drive west of Delhi,

Annie and Martin Howard have created a spacious and luxurious Lutyens-style mansion in the countryside, a tranquil spot to recover from too much work, city life, or sightseeing.

ⓘ 4 🏊

🏨 ITC MUGHAL
🍴 $$$$

FATEHABAD RD., TAJ GANJ
TEL 056/2402-1700
itchotels.in

Well-designed, low-rise, brick buildings inspired by Mughal architecture are set on 35 acres (14 ha) of gardens in increasingly built-up Agra. This welcome oasis provides peace, tennis courts, and spa facilities. Restaurants serve Indian, Asian, and speciality Northwest Frontier cuisines.

ⓘ 300 🏊 🏋

🏨 JAYPEE PALACE
🍴 $$$

FATEHABAD RD.
TEL 056/2233-0800
jaypeehotels.com

This large, low-rise, Mughal-inspired hotel set in 25 acres (10 ha) of gardens has its rooms arranged around a Mughal-style *char bagh* (four gardens) complete with dancing fountains. Restaurants include Avadh cuisine from Lucknow, South Indian cuisine, a poolside barbecue, and a grand buffet. Ayurvedic spa, gym, and plenty of games. Ideal for families and hungry young people.

ⓘ 350 🏊 🏋

🏨 MANSINGH PALACE
🍴 $$$

FATEHABAD RD.
TEL 056/2233-1771
mansinghhotels.com

Named after the Amber ruler who owned the land on which his ally Emperor Shah Jehan built the Taj, this no-frills but reliable hotel has a Taj view from some rooms.

ⓘ 100

🏨 TAJ GATEWAY
🍴 $$$

FATEHABAD RD., TAJ GANJ
TEL 056/2660-2000
thegatewayhotels.com

Formerly the Taj View hotel. The top-floor rooms really do have views of the Taj, albeit distant ones across the city. The pool and lawns are good respites after early Taj visits, as is the good Indian food and the shopping mall's bookstore. Puppets, games, and other amusements for families.

ⓘ 100 🏊 🏋

🏨 TRIDENT AGRA
🍴 $$$

TAJNAGARI SCHEME,
FATEHABAD RD.
TEL 056/2223-5000
tridenthotels.com

A good value choice, not least because the hotel is one of the nearest to the Taj and thus good for repeat visits. The rooms are arranged around a central pool and courtyard; gourmets may wish to visit other hotels for dinner.

ⓘ 138 🏊

🏨 HOWARD PARK PLAZA
🍴 $$

FATEHABAD RD.
TEL 056/2404-8600
OR 1800-103-1919
howardplazaagra.com

No-frills hotel well aimed at businesspeople; located a mile (1.6 km) from the Taj, so it is possible to walk down or take a rickshaw. The rooftop barbecues provide lunch with views of the Taj, and, if you are lucky, later moonlit views.

ⓘ 83 🏊

AMRITSAR

🏨 HYATT AMRITSAR
$$$

MBM FARMS, M. G. RD.
TEL 018/3287-1234
hyatt.com

Hyatt's tradition of quality contemporary design, high-end service, and excellent facilities in spacious surroundings continues here, including in the spa.

ⓘ 248 ⛴ 🏋

🏨 HOTEL RANJIT'S
🍴 SVAASA
$$
47-A, THE MALL
TEL 018/32566-618
OR 018/3329-8840
svaasa.com
This beautifully restored 18th-century Nanak Shahi *haveli* (courtyard house) on Mall Road is a heritage hotel. It doubles as a holistic spa resort, and follows the *vaatsu* texts for room directions. All rooms have balconies, and therapies include ayurveda *panchakarma* treatments.

ⓘ 13 🏋

🏨 MOHAN
🍴 INTERNATIONAL
$$
ALBERT RD.
TEL 018/3301-0100
mohaninternationalhotel.com
This simple hotel, well located for visiting the Golden Temple, provides clean rooms and wholesome food both indoors and at a poolside barbecue.

ⓘ 76 ⛴

BANDHAVGARH NATIONAL PARK

🏨 BANDHAVGARH
🍴 JUNGLE LODGE
$$$$$
VILLAGE TALA,
DISTRICT UMARIA
TEL 011/2685-3760
(DELHI OFFICE)
bandhavgarhjunglelodge.com
The 12 cottages and 8 rooms are set out like a village, with an organic vegetable garden and some solar water heating. Guests are encouraged to

learn about conservation and to study nature as well as listen to it at night. Plenty of quiet areas, plus games (badminton, chess, etc.) and wildlife videos.

ⓘ 20

🏨 MAHUA KOTHI
🍴 $$$$$
VILLAGE TALA,
DISTRICT UMARIA
TEL 022/6601-1825
(MUMBAI OFFICE)
tajhotels.com
Taj Hotels has joined up with the wildlife lodges company CC Africa to create a new experience in Bandhavgarh National Park. Occupants of the very beautiful, ethnic-gone-chic *kutiyas* (jungle village huts), each with private courtyard and bicycles, can enjoy all the usual game park activities, from bird-watching to jungle safari rides.

ⓘ 12

🏨 SAMODE SAFARI
🍴 LODGE
$$$$
MARDARI
TEL 014/1263-2407 OR
014/1263-2370 (JAIPUR OFFICE)
samode.com
This wildlife camp on the edge of Bandhavargh National Park focuses on ecology—reforestation, local communities, regeneration of overgrazed farmland, and organic farming. While staying in one of two cottages and two tented cottages, guests explore the park to learn as much about its trees as about how to read the pug marks of a tiger.

ⓘ 4

BHOPAL

🏨 JEHAN NUMA PALACE
🍴 $$$$
157 SHAMLA HILL
TEL 075/5266-1100
hoteljehanumapalace.com

This Bhopal palace was built in the 1880s by Nawab Sultan Jehan Begum's second son, Gen. Obaidullah Khan, who was commander-in-chief of the Bhopal state forces. This perhaps accounts for the British colonial style. Today, its rooms are spread through four wings surrounding a lush garden; suitable for families.

ⓘ 98 ⛴

🏨 NOOR-US-SABAH
🍴 PALACE
$$$
VIP RD., KOH-E-FIZA
TEL 075/5522-3333
noorussabahpalace.com
Built in the 1920s for Nawab Hamid Ulah Khan's daughter, this informal palace sits on a cliff overlooking Bhopal Lake. All rooms have lake views, while the lawns transform into a starlit dining room serving good food patronized by locals.

ⓘ 60 ⛴

CHANDIGARH

🏨 TAJ CHANDIGARH
🍴 $$$$
BLOCK NO. 9, SECTOR 17-A
TEL 017/2661-3000
tajhotels.com
All rooms in this newly built hotel in Le Corbusier's city have ergonomic furniture and contemporary amenities, as well as views of the city's Rose Garden and the Shivalik mountain range.

ⓘ 149 🏋

🏨 HOTEL MOUNTVIEW
🍴 $$$
SECTOR 10
TEL 017/2274-0544
citcochandighar.gov.in
A functional hotel well located for visiting Chandigarh's Rock Garden.

ⓘ 156 ⛴ 🏋

CORBETT NATIONAL PARK

🏨 INFINITY
🍴 RESORTS
$$$$
RAMNAGAR
TEL 012/4465-5800
infinityresorts.com
Set amid mango trees on the banks of the Kosi River in the Kumaon Hills, the circular lodge room is where guests chat, drink, eat, and compare sightings after visits into Corbett Park. Other activities include trekking, fishing, and enjoying the holistic cures.
🛈 24 🏊 💇

🏨 THE CORBETT HIDEWAY
$$$
VILLAGE GARIJA
TEL 011/4652-0000
(DELHI OFFICE)
corbetthideaway.com
This resort, tucked away in a mango grove, stretches over an area of 13 acres (5.2 ha). Activities offered include elephant and jeep safaris, bird-watching, and sustainable catch-and-release fishing. The resort offers guided nature walks along a riverbank and a poolside bar.
🛈 52 cottages 🏊

GWALIOR

🏨 USHA KIRAN PALACE
🍴 $$$$
JAYENDRAGANJ, LASHKAR, BESIDE JAI VILAS (CITY PALACE)
TEL 075/1244-4000
tajhotels.com
The former guesthouse of Gwalior state's ruler, called The Scindia, and its 9 acres (3.6 ha) of gardens have all been lavishly renovated. The billiards room is now the bar, the restaurant overlooks the courtyard.
🛈 40 💇

KANHA NATIONAL PARK

🏨 BANJAAR TOLA
🍴 $$$$$
MANJITOLA MUKKI
TEL 022/6601-1825
(MUMBAI OFFICE)
tajsafaris.com
One of several super-luxurious, Africa-style safari camps launched by the Taj group. It has riverside tented suites decorated with Chattisgarh tribal art; food is elaborate for the jungle setting.
🛈 18

🏨 KANHA JUNGLE
🍴 LODGE
$$$$
MUKKI
TEL 011/2685-3760
(DELHI OFFICE)
tiger-resorts.com
Another ecologically aware lodge, with organic farming, solar energy, and medicinal herbs. As well as visiting the park, there is on-site bird- and butterfly-watching and nightly astronomy.
🛈 20

🏨 SHERGARH
🍴 $$$$
TEL 090/9818-7346
shergarh.com
Guests get close to nature and live well at Shergarh, at the quiet southern end of the park, where the owners, deeply committed to the area, have dug ponds, planted trees, built beautiful individual tented rooms, and created an immaculately run, ecologically aware piece of paradise.
🛈 6

🏨 SINGINAWA LODGE
🍴 $$$$
TEL 076/3725-6806
singinawa.in

PRICES

HOTELS
An indication of the cost of a double room in the high season is given by **$** signs.

$$$$$	Over $280
$$$$	$160–$280
$$$	$100–$160
$$	$40–$100
$	Under $40

RESTAURANTS
An indication of the cost of a three-course meal without drinks is given by **$** signs.

$$$$$	Over $80
$$$$	$50–$80
$$$	$35–$50
$$	$20–$35
$	Under $20

Conservation award winners run this 55-acre (22 ha) estate, ensuring top-quality learning opportunities. The stone-and-slate cottages have the best of traditional and modern, such as open fires and also rain showers, a colonial-style library–living room, a spa, and also a free-form swimming pool. Particular efforts are made to ensure wheelchair friendliness.
🛈 12 🏊

KEOLADEO GHANA NATIONAL PARK

🏨 THE BAGH
🍴 $$$
BHARATPUR
TEL 056/4422-8333
thebagh.com
Several elegant buildings are set in a mature old garden, where resident naturalist Vishnu Singh helps guests get their eyes ready for visiting the bird sanctuary. Rooms are

---

individually decorated, the restaurant serves the distinctive local Braj cuisine, and guests can relax in the orchard or gym or while having a massage.

🏨 23 🏊 🍷

🏨 LAXMI VILAS PALACE
🍴 $$$

BHARATPUR
TEL 056/4423-1199
laxmivilas.com
An 1880s little rural palace of the Bharatpur rulers, transformed into a small hotel in 1994. Family photographs in quantity, charming period rooms, and a modern pool and spa combine to wonderfully complement the purpose of being there: spending time watching birds.

🏨 30 🏊

🏨 CHANDRA MAHAL
🍴 HAVELI
$$

VILLAGE—PEHARSAR, JAIPUR—
AGRA RD., TEHSIL NADBAI
TEL 056/4326-4336
heritagehotelsofindia.com
A delightful 19th-century noble's courtyard mansion set in an unspoiled village, this makes a perfect break between Jaipur and Agra's hurly-burly. Ideal for observing India's village life, and for reading or sketching. It deserves more than a mere lunch stop.

🏨 23 🏊 🍷

KHAJURAHO

🏨 GRAND TEMPLE VIEW
🍴 $$$$

TEL 076/8627-2111
thelalit.com
This hotel really does have views of the temples. The rooms are well appointed and the extensive spa with seven treatment rooms is a bonus.

🏨 47 🏊 🍷

🏨 RADISSON JASS HOTEL
🍴 $$$

TEL 076/8627-2777
OR 076/8627-2377
radisson.com
Sited near the Taj Chandela, this hotel is its twin, with equally satisfactory no-frills rooms and facilities for relaxing between temple visits.

🏨 90 🏊

🏨 TAJ CHANDELA
🍴 $$$

TEL 076/8627-2355
tajhotels.com
A low-rise, practical hotel with garden, pool, shopping mall, and friendly staff, five minutes' drive from the main reason for being here: the temples.

🏨 94 🏊 🍷

MAHESHWAR

🏨 AHILYA FORT
🍴 $$$$$

TEL 092/0390-5948
OR 011/4155-1575 (DELHI OFFICE)
ahilyafort.com
Built to be the capital of one of India's celebrated women rulers, Ahilya Bai Holkar. Her descendant Richard Holkar has spent two decades restoring it and creating its gardens. Guests pass their days enjoying the rhythm of the fort and its on-site temples, the good food, the local weaving, and taking boat rides out on the Narmada River.

🏨 12 🏊

MATHURA

🏨 THE RADHA ASHOK
🍴 $$

MASANI BYPASS RD.
TEL 056/5253-0396
Reliable modern hotel with clean rooms, simple facilities, set among lawns on the edge of town.

🏨 28 🏊

MUSSOORIE

🏨 JAYPEE RESIDENCY
🍴 MANOR
$$$$$

BARLOWGANJ
TEL 013/5263-1800
jaypeehotels.com
Enjoying superb views from its hilltop location, guests can follow their walks with the indoor heated swimming pool and Sansha Ayurvedic Health Spa, play a wide variety of games, and eat wholesome Indian and Continental food.

🏨 90 🏊

🏨 KASMANDA PALACE
🍴 $$$$$

THE MALL
TEL 013/5263-2424
kasmandapalace.com
The Kasmanda royal family has transformed its summer retreat—built in 1836 by Capt. Rennie Tailour of the Bengal Engineers, and subsequently a sanatorium and a school—into a comfortable hotel for relaxation, walks, picnics, and bird-watching.

🏨 24

🏨 NABHA PALACE
🍴 $$$$

BARLOWGANJ RD.
TEL 013/5263-1426
claridges.com
The renovated period rooms with modern comforts (down pillows, duvets) open onto Victorian wraparound verandas that overlook lush gardens and wooded valleys. Ideal for taking a trek and then curling up with a good book in the well-stocked library, or relaxing in the spa.

🏨 22

🏨 Hotel   🍴 Restaurant   🏨 No. of Guest Rooms   🏊 Swimming Pool   🍷 Health Club

PADMINI NIVAS

$$

LIBRARY, THE MALL
TEL 013/5263-1093
hotelpadmininivas.com
This is one of Mussoorie's oldest buildings; it was originally called Rushbrooke Estate and the Maharaja of Rajpipla gave it to his wife, Padmini. With fireplaces inside, a wide veranda, and deodar and oak trees in the garden, this is hill station life revived.

ⓘ 24

NAINITAL

PALACE BELVEDERE

$$

AWAGARH ESTATE, MALLITAL
TEL 059/4223-7434
welcomheritagehotels.com
This was once the Raja of Awagarh's summer retreat, built in 1897; royal family treasures still furnish the rooms. The hotel enjoys views down the hills over Naini Lake.

ⓘ 24

ORCHHA

AMAR MAHAL

$$

TEL 076/8025-2102
OR 076/8025-2202
amarmahal.com
A surprisingly grand hotel for such a small village, but the Bundelkund-inspired architecture and characterful rooms are appropriate for exploring Orchha's royal buildings.

ⓘ 24

RANTHAMBHOR NATIONAL PARK

AMAN-I-KHAS

$$$$$

RANTHAMBHOR
TEL 074/6225-2052
amanresorts.com
Staying at Aman-i-Khas ("special peace") is to

understand that camping can be very stylish. Here, the specially designed tents, their furnishings, their service, the spa, and the open fireplace all enhance the perfect rural location.

ⓘ 10 ♥

OBEROI VANYAVILAS

$$$$$

RANTHAMBHOR RD.,
SAWAI MADHOPUR
TEL 074/6222-3999
oberoihotels.com
Each super-luxurious, well-appointed tent has its own little garden; the dining room is a real room but guests can choose to have their meals where they wish. Great pool and spa.

ⓘ 25 ≋ ♥

SHERBAGH

$$$$$

SHERPUR-KHILJIPUR,
SAWAI MADHOPUR
TEL 011/4617-2700
(DELHI OFFICE)
sujanluxury.com
Founded by Jaisal Singh, who regularly camped here throughout his childhood, Sherbagh focuses on how tourism can make people aware of the delicate balance between humankind and nature. Comfortable tents, wholesome food, a spa, and a friendly atmosphere.

ⓘ 12 ≋

KHEM VILLAS

$$$$

TEL 074/6225-2099
khemvillas.com
In an estate the owner has restored to lush, bird-filled wilderness, each well-designed, whitewashed cottage has its plunge pool, outdoor shower, and private terrace. There are also tents and a block of rooms. The food, naturalists, and activities are all high quality; activities can include

enjoying the owner's land by the Chambal River.

ⓘ 17 plus tents, 4 rooms, & cottages

SAWAI MADHOPUR LODGE

$$$$

RANTHAMBHOR NATIONAL PARK RD., SAWAI MADHOPUR
TEL 074/6222-0541
vivantabytaj.com
The former royal hunting lodge, built in the 1930s, has been renovated and its period gardens spruced up; the heritage atmosphere is maintained with croquet, badminton, and table tennis, and the modern is embraced by the gym and spa.

ⓘ 36 ♥

RISHIKESH

ANANDA IN THE HIMALAYAS

$$$$$

THE PALACE ESTATE, DISTRICT TEHRI-GARHWAL ULTARANCHAH
TEL 013/7822-7500
anandaspa.com
Once the home of the Maharaja of Tehri-Garhwal, this magical location in the Himalaya overlooking the Ganga River is rated a worldwide top spa hotel. While the former palace forms the public area, the rooms are state of the art as is, of course, the spa. For activities there is eco-friendly golf, river rafting, and walking. Located 162 miles (260 km) north of Delhi and best reached by train or car.

ⓘ 75 ≋

GLASSHOUSE ON THE GANGES

$$$

23RD MILESTONE RISHIKESH–BADRINATH RD., VILLAGE GULAR-DOGI, UTTARANCHAL
TEL 011/4666-1666
(DELHI OFFICE)
neemranahotels.com

This remarkable hotel on the Ganga has its own orchard filled with birds and butterflies, a mineral spring, and a beach. Guests venture out to walk, river raft, and join pilgrims visiting local temples. Vegetarian food and beer, but not spirits, are served to respect the sacred location.

⬛ 6

🏨 HIMALAYAN
🍴 HIDEAWAY
$$$

NEAR BADRINATH
RESERVATIONS ADDRESS:
C-1, BASEMENT, COMMUNITY
CENTRE, SDA, NEW DELHI
TEL 011/2685-2602
hhindia.com

A lovely peaceful lodge set in the Sal forest above the Ganga, where the garden is being planted with specimens of the lower Himalaya. After kayaking or hiking, there is traditional massage and great views from each room's balcony.

⬛ 10

SATPURA NATIONAL PARK

🏨 FORSYTH'S LODGE
$$$$$

CHENNAI OFFICE
TEL 044/2826-3155
forsythlodge.com

Named for the British officer who wrote a classic account of these hills, this lodge, created by consummate naturalist and host Hashim Tyabji, is one of India's finest: 12 locally inspired mud cottages set in private forest land adjoining Satpura National Park's wildlife-filled mountains. The lodge recycles its waste, practices water harvesting, and works closely with local villagers to train them as naturalists to create a template for wildlife management in India. Full board.

⬛ 12 cottages

SHIMLA

🏨 CHAPSLEE
🍴 $$$$$

NEXT TO AUCKLAND HOUSE
SENIOR SCHOOL,
CENTRAL SHIMLA
TEL 017/7280-2542
chapslee.com

Descendants of the Raja of Kapurthala run his former Edwardian summer home, maintaining its Raj flavor in its furnishings, croquet lawn, card room, and warm hospitality. Well-located for walking through Shimla and its outlying hills. Restaurant offers traditional royal cuisine from the palaces of the Maharajas.

⬛ 5

🏨 OBEROI CECIL
🍴 $$$$$

CHAURA MAIDAN,
CENTRAL SHIMLA
TEL 017/7280-4848
oberoihotels.com

This is the first of the Oberoi Group's hotels, in a magnificent century-plus-old building on Chaura Maidan in central Shimla, now lavishly and beautifully restored. Glorious views from the rooms, elegant teas to enjoy in the public spaces, immaculate service.

⬛ 79 🏊 🎖

🏨 WILDFLOWER HALL
🍴 $$$$$

SHIMLA–KUFRI RD., 8 MILES
(13 KM) FROM SHIMLA,
NEAR CHARABRA
TEL 017/7264-8585
oberoihotels.com

At 8,300 feet (2,500 m) in the Dhauladhar and Garhwal mountains, every room of Lord Kitchener's rebuilt country house has spectacular views. There is quality food, an outdoor heated pool, and a good spa; and Shimla is just a 40-minute drive away.

⬛ 87 🏊 🎖

🏨 WOODVILLE PALACE
🍴 $$$

RAJ BHAWAN RD.,
CENTRAL SHIMLA
TEL 017/7262-3919
welcomheritagehotels.com

The Rana of Jubbal built this château-style, fashionable home in 1938. Its guest rooms, billiards room, Hollywood lounge, and hunting trophies inside, and plant-covered trellises and lush garden outside all evoke those times.

⬛ 30

⬛ RAJASTHAN & GUJARAT

This colorful area of India has numerous charming heritage hotels, with more opening each year. A stay in any of these hotels will enhance any vacation in India.

RAJASTHAN

AJMER & PUSHKAR

🏨 CHHATRASAGAR
🍴 $$$$$

NIMAJ
TEL 029/3923-0118
chhatrasagar.com

The immaculate and beautiful tents are pitched between a reservoir and an idyllic farm on the Udaipur–Jodhpur road; micromanagement ensures every detail is perfect from homemade breads at breakfast to hilltop cocktails at sunset.

⬛ 13

🏨 FORT SEENGH SAGAR
🍴 $$$$$

3 MILES (5 KM) FROM
DEOGARH MAHAL
TEL 099/2883-4777
OR 093/1442-0016
deogarhmahal.com

The Deogarh family has converted a tiny fort into a villa; ideal for two or three couples to rent and enjoy the peace, the lake, boating and walking, and a personal staff.

⬛ 4

🏨 Hotel   🍴 Restaurant   ⬛ No. of Guest Rooms   🏊 Swimming Pool   🎖 Health Club

🏨 DEOGARH MAHAL
🍴 $$$

DEOGARH
TEL 099/2883-4777
OR 093/1442-0016
deogarhmahal.com
Set within the triangle of
Udaipur, Ajmer, and Jodhpur,
on the Udaipur–Ajmer road,
the palace is found in a fairy-
tale walled town, once the seat
of senior Mewar feudatories.
Rooms spread through the
palace and its outbuildings
are Indian in style, some with
lovely period wall paintings.
🛏 50 🏊

BIKANER

🏨 LAXMI NIWAS PALACE
🍴 $$$$

LALLGARH COMPLEX
TEL 015/1252-1188
laxminiwaspalace.com
Set within Lallgarh Palace gardens, this Bikaner palace was
originally the guest wing of the
main palace. The renovated
rooms keep the traditional
spacious format of bedroom,
dressing room, and bathroom.
🛏 42

🏨 BHANWAR NIWAS
🍴 PALACE
$$$

BIKANER
bhanwarniwas.com
This extravagantly carved pink
sandstone palace-mansion
mingling Indian and Western
styles was built in 1927 by
the great Rampuria family of
Bikaner. Its interior is strikingly
lavish and opulent, its staff
attentive and thoughtful.
🛏 24

🏨 GAJNER PALACE
🍴 $$$

15-MIN. DRIVE FROM BIKANER
TEL 015/3427-5061
hrhhotels.com
Sensitively renovated to its
1890s Raj perfection, this
elaborate, pink-stone hunting

palace of the Bikaner rulers
overlooks a lake where grand
duck shoots used to entertain
Indian royalty and Raj dignitaries. Great for bird-watching,
boating, and billiards.
🛏 44

🏨 LALLGARH PALACE
🍴 $$$

LALLGARH COMPLEX
TEL 015/1254-0201
lallgarhpalace.com
Sir Swinton Jacobs designed
the vast pink-sandstone palace
for the charismatic Maharaja
Ganga Singhji. It has so much
public space that you might
get lost looking for the bar or
the billiards room, or roaming
through the splendid collection
of period photographs.
🛏 56 🏊

BUNDI

🏨 ISHWARI NIWAS
🍴 $$

I CIVIL LINES
TEL 074/7244-2414
ishwariniwas.com
Built at the turn of the 20th
century for the Diwan (prime
minister) of Bundi state, this
delightful, simple, family-run
haveli with Bundi-style wall
paintings has its rooms ranged
around a central courtyard.
🛏 24

DUNGARPUR

🏨 UDAI BILAS PALACE
🍴 $$$

DUNGARPUR, OFF UDAIPUR–
AHMEDABAD HWY.
TEL 029/6423-0808
udaibilaspalace.com
Sited in quiet Dungarpur, off
the highway, lakeside Udai
Bilas was built as a hunting
palace by descendants of the
Chittorgarh rulers. Enjoy the
infinity pool, the home cooking, and a visit to the family's
private ancient fort-palace.
🛏 23 🏊

JAIPUR

🏨 OBEROI RAJVILAS
🍴 $$$$$

GONER RD., 30-MIN. DRIVE
E OF JAIPUR
TEL 014/1268-0101
oberoihotels.com
A multi-award-winning luxury
resort set in a lush oasis estate.
Every part displays taste and
style and is immaculately managed, from the fortress-style
central building to the clusters
of rooms and the indulgent
pool and spa.
🛏 70 🏊 🏋

🏨 RAJ PALACE
🍴 $$$$$

JORAWER SINGH GATE,
AMER RD.
TEL 041/1263-4077
OR 041/1263-4078
rajpalace.com
One of Jaipur's most evoca-
tive places to stay, thanks to
the dedicated restoration by
Princess Jayendra Kumari who

since 1995 has brought the entire palace and its historic contents back to life. The "museum suites" are like fairy-tale Rajput film sets.

ⓘ 38 🏊

🏨 RAMBAGH PALACE
🍽 $$$$$

BHAWANI SINGH RD.
TEL 014/1221-1919
tajhotels.com
The last Maharaja of Jaipur lived here, on the southern side of his Pink City. In 1957 he turned his palace and its extensive terraces and gardens into a hotel. Run by the Taj group since 1972, the palace has recently been refurbished.

ⓘ 79 🏊 🎽

🏨 JAI MAHAL PALACE
🍽 $$$$

JACOB RD., CIVIL LINES
TEL 014/1222-3636
tajhotels.com
Located in the Civil Lines area, the 18th-century Jai Mahal has totally refurbished rooms, renovated Mughal formal gardens, and a more relaxed tempo than its sister hotel here, the Rambagh Palace (see above).

ⓘ 100 🏊 🎽

🏨 SAMODE HAVELI
🍽 $$$$

GANGAPOLE
TEL 014/1263-2407
samode.com
The spacious town mansion of the Samode courtiers, feudatories of the Jaipur rulers, has restored mural walls and a swimming pool and is right inside the Pink City; ideal for enjoying the bazaars. This and its sister hotel, Samode Palace, have been beautifully restored by family descendants.

ⓘ 39 🏊 🎽

🏨 SAMODE PALACE
🍽 $$$$

SAMODE VILLAGE
TEL 014/3240-014
samode.com
This sister hotel of the Samode Haveli (see above) is set in the village of Samode in the Aravalli Hills an hour's drive north of Jaipur. Guests stay either in the palace or in tents in the walled *bagh* (garden). All has been beautifully restored by family descendants.

ⓘ 43 🏊 🎽

🏨 TRIDENT JAIPUR
🍽 $$$$

AMER RD.
TEL 014/1267-0101
tridenthotels.com
Every room in this good value yet attractive hotel built in traditional Jaipur style on the Jaipur–Amer road has a balcony so guests can enjoy the view across Mansagar Lake. Its good location makes visiting both Amer and Jaipur easy.

ⓘ 134

🏨 BARWARA KOTHI
🍽 $$

5 JACOB RD., CIVIL LINES
TEL 014/1222-2796
barwarakothi.com
Built in the early 20th century, Barwara Kothi's whitewashed Lutyens-style building is in the quiet and convenient Civil Lines area. The Barwara family maintains an immaculate yet friendly home and gardens, so the atmosphere is more of a homestay than a hotel.

ⓘ 7

🍽 CINNAMON
$$

JAI MAHAL PALACE HOTEL,
CIVIL LINES
TEL 014/1222-3636
To sample carefully prepared and authentic Mughlai dishes, reserve a table amid the cusped arches of the congenial

restaurant in this sprawling, restored palace. For tender meat, consider *maas ka soyeta* (lamb with millet) with *papad ki subji* (spiced lentil wafers) and *hara mattar sisua* (green peas with ginger).

🍽 THE CAFÉ
$

2ND FLOOR, KK SQ.,
C-1 PRITHVIRAJ RD.,
C-SCHEME
TEL 014/1400-2744
Not only do you have the original Anokhi shop, which often has "test" designs for upcoming seasons, but the attached café serves delicious soft drinks and homemade sweet and savory pastries.

🍽 HANDI RESTAURANT
$

M. I. RD., OPPOSITE POST OFFICE
TEL 014/1236-4839
Well-located on a main shopping street; you should ignore the unpromising surroundings. Enjoy rich Mughal dishes, especially *kathi kabab* (mutton wrapped in thin bread) and meat dishes cooked in the signature *handi* (clay pot), which intensifies the fragrant spices.

SOMETHING SPECIAL

🍽 LMB
$

JOHARI BAZAR
TEL 014/1256-5844
The Jain beginnings of this Jaipur landmark explain its fastidious standards. Locals come to the ground floor café-shop to stock up on the creamiest cashew nuts and best sweetmeats in town, while enjoying delicious fruit juices and snacks. The simple restaurant downstairs serves an excellent Rajasthan *thali*, which includes *ker sangria* (capers and desert beans) and *bela Rajasthani* (*besan* dumplings in a yogurt gravy).

🏨 Hotel 🍽 Restaurant ⓘ No. of Guest Rooms 🏊 Swimming Pool 🎽 Health Club

🍴 MUSEUM CAFÉ
$

ANOKHI MUSEUM OF HAND
PRINTING, AMBER
TEL 014/1253-0226
Sitting in the forecourt to
enjoy homemade lemon and
ginger cookies with freshly
brewed chai (Indian tea) or a
soft drink complete the visit
to one of India's best-run and
most fascinating museums.

🍴 THE PALACE CAFÉ
$

CITY PALACE
TEL 014/1261-6449
The perfect spot to relax over
a *nimbu* soda (fresh lime juice
soda), a samosa snack, or a
full meal, following a cultural
visit to the extensive City
Palace. Tables are either in an
air-conditioned room or—
much nicer—outside in a
shady courtyard.

JAISALMER

🏨 THE SERAI
🍴 $$$$$

BHERWA, CHANDAN
TEL 011/4617-2700
(DELHI OFFICE)
sujanluxury.com
The ultimate desert luxury:
large, opulent tents, some with
their own walled garden and
pool, set in an estate of 100
desert acres (40.5 ha) outside
Jaisalmer. Forget simple desert
camps in favor of a spacious
bar and restaurant, an infinity
pool, and a modern spa by
Raison d'Etre.
ⓘ 21 🏊 ☤

🏨 FORT RAJWADA
🍴 $$$

JODHPUR–BARMER LINK RD.
TEL 029/9225-3733
fortrajwada.com
Opera set designer Stephani
Engeln helped restore and
convert this extensive palace
set in 6 acres (2 ha) on the
edge of Jaisalmer. Its grand
facade and public rooms

are in the full tradition of
Jaisalmer's lace-like stone
carving; its rooms are
more contemporary.
ⓘ 95 🏊 ☤

🏨 TAJ GATEWAY
🍴 $$$

JODHPUR–JAISALMER RD.
TEL 029/9225-1874
tajhotels.com
Formerly the Rawal-Kot Hotel.
Set on a slight rise, both the
rooms and dining room of this
purpose-built hotel have fine
views over Jaisalmer. To spend
a night beneath the stars, the
hotel has a tented camp out
on the dunes.
ⓘ 31 🏊

🏨 GORBANDH PALACE
🍴 $$

1 TOURIST COMPLEX, SAM RD.
TEL 029/9225-3801
hrhhotels.com
One of the royal retreats that
belong to the reliable HRH
chain of Rajput heritage hotels,
Gorbandh Palace blends
Jaisalmer's cultural heritage
with contemporary comforts,
and has a tented camp.
ⓘ 83 🏊

🏨 NACHANA HAVELI
🍴 $$

GOVERDHAN CHOWK
TEL 029/9225-1910 OR
029/9225-5565
nachanahaveli.com
The 17th-century *haveli* of
the Bhatia family, right in
Jaisalmer, is now run by two
young brothers and a sister
who keep the atmosphere
informal and home-like.
ⓘ 11

JODHPUR

🏨 UMAID BHAWAN
🍴 PALACE
$$$$$

TEL 029/1251-0101
tajhotels.com

One of the world's finest and
grandest art deco palaces is
now a hotel, with sumptu-
ously refitted bathrooms,
numerous public spaces with
original furnishings, grand
gardens, and great views
across the city to Jodhpur's
fairy-tale fort.
ⓘ 64 🏊 ☤

🏨 MANVAR DESERT CAMP
🍴 $$$$

KHIYANSARIA, NEAR DECHU
TEL 029/1251-1600
manvar.com
A two-hour smooth drive
north from Jodhpur, then
into Jeeps and off through
the dunes, perhaps pausing
to visit a *dhurrie* maker,
brings you to this beautiful
tented camp (solid attached
bathrooms). Arrive in time
for dune-top sunset cocktails
to live flute; campfires, great
dancing, and morning tea
brought to your tent. Perfect.
ⓘ 20 tents

🏨 TAJ HARI MAHAL
🍴 PALACE
$$$$

5 RESIDENCY RD.
TEL 029/1243-9700
vivantabytaj.com
This modern and very com-
fortable hotel on Jodhpur's
city fringes echoes the local
Mawar designs in its decoration and the central courtyard,
where the pool is located.
ⓘ 93 🏊 ☤

🏨 AJIT BHAWAN PALACE
🍴 $$$

TEL 029/1251-0410
ajitbhawan.com
One of India's early heritage
hotels, well-located Ajit Bhawan today feels less heritage
than ethnic contemporary.
It has a good pool and a spa;
some rooms have balconies
overlooking the garden.
ⓘ 81 🏊 ☤

KOTAH

🏨 UMED BHAWAN PALACE
🍴 $$$
PALACE RD.
TEL 074/4232-5262
welcomheritagehotels.com
This beautifully carved, grandly
spacious 1905 royal palace
has a strong Raj-Rajput flavor.
Keep in tune with this era by
playing croquet on the lawns.
🛏 32

🏨 BRIJRAJ BHAWAN
🍴 $$
TEL 2450-529
indianheritagehotels.com
This whitewashed, modest
heritage hotel stands on the
banks of the Chambal River.
Oil portraits of royals, their
hunting trophies, and their
regal furniture create an
evocative atmosphere.
🛏 7

🏨 PALKIYA HAVELI
🍴 $$
NEAR SURAJ POLE
TEL 074/4238-7497
palkiyahaveli.com
The flagship of five boutique
heritage hotels owned
by a branch of the Rajput
Kachhwaha clan, this one has
fairly small rooms but prettily
painted public spaces and a
relaxing courtyard.
🛏 7

KUMBHALGARH

🏨 AODHI HOTEL
🍴 $$
NEXT TO KUMBHALGARH FORT
TEL 029/5424-2341
hrhhotels.com
Blending ethnic with con-
temporary, this isolated hotel
located right in the Aravalli
hills has a pool, serves good
Rajasthani food, and each
room has a balcony. Perfect
for walking and relaxing.
🛏 26 🏊

MOUNT ABU

🏨 CAMA RAJPUTANA
🍴 CLUB RESORT
$$$$
ADHAR DEVI RD.
TEL 029/7423-8205
camahotelsindia.com
Built in the 1880s in the
traditional hill station style
of rooms spread through
lush English-style gardens
with panoramic views, this
renovated club is the place to
enjoy British sports, from table
tennis and snooker to cricket,
tennis, and swimming.
🛏 40 🏊 🛡

🏨 CONNAUGHT HOUSE
🍴 $$$
RAJENDRA MARG, MOUNT ABU
TEL 029/7423-8560
welcomheritagehotels.com
Built in the quaint style of
an English country cottage,
this quiet unpretentious
retreat was once the home
of the chief minister of Mewar
state, whose capital was
nearby Udaipur.
🛏 10

🏨 PALACE HOTEL
🍴 BIKANER HOUSE
$$
DELWARA RD.
TEL 029/7423-5121
palacehotelbikanerhouse.com
Built in 1893 so the grand
Maharaja of Bikaner could
escape the summer heat,
guests have suitably regal and
spacious rooms and gardens.
There is tennis and volleyball
and the hotel will also arrange
picnics and pony rides.
🛏 33

NAGAUR

🏨 ROYAL CAMPS
🍴 $$$$
NAGAUR FORT
TEL 029/1257-1991 (JODHPUR)
jodhanaheritage.com
The tented camp is inside
impressive and well-conserved
Nagaur Fort, and operates
October through March. Each
luxury tent has a bedroom,
bathroom, and balcony, and
evening campfires complete
the setting. This is a good stop
between Jodhpur and Bikaner.
🛏 Flexible number of tents

OSIAN

🏨 OSIAN CAMEL CAMP
🍴 $$$$
C/O INDIA SAFARI CLUB
HIGH COURT COLONY, JODHPUR
TEL 029/1243-7023
camelcamposian.com
This is a permanent luxurious camp 37 miles (60 km)
from Jodhpur, run by the
experienced Reggie Singh. In
addition to going on one-,
two-, or three-day camel
safaris, guests learn about the
surprisingly rich culture of the
Thar Desert and visit temples
and oasis villages.
🛏 51 🏊

RANAKPUR

🏨 FATEH BAGH PALACE
🍴 $$$
RANAKPUR RD.
TEL 029/3428-6186
hrhhotels.com
In 2002, Arvind Singh Mewar
of Udaipur transplanted and
then restored a crumbling
palace from Jodhpur to
Ranakpur—all 65,000 pieces
of it. This good stop on the
rural Udaipur–Jodhpur road
is right near India's most
exquisite Jain temples.
🛏 18 🏊 🛡

🏨 MAHARANI BAGH
🍴 ORCHARD RETREAT
$$$
NEAR RANAKPUR TEMPLES
TEL 029/3428-5151
welcomheritagehotels.com
Set in an orchard laid out
by the Maharani of Jodhpur

in the late 19th century, the modest cottage-style rooms are shaded by mature trees and the atmosphere is informal.

[i] 16 ⚊

SARISKA NATIONAL PARK, KESROLI, & DEEG

▦ AMANBAGH
⑪ $$$$$
AMANBAGH AJABGARH, ALWAR
TEL 014/6522-3333
amanresorts.com
Set in an ancient oasis deep in the countryside about an hour's drive northeast of Jaipur, guests enjoy absolute peace and sublime facilities (some rooms have their own pools), and can explore local villages, fort ruins, or enjoy a sunset picnic.

[i] 40 ⚊ ⛉

▦ NEEMRANA
⑪ FORT-PALACE
$$$$
NEEMRANA
TEL 014/9424-6007
neemranahotels.com
This flagship of the successful Neemrana group of heritage hotels, off the Delhi–Jaipur road, spreads its many rooms over ten levels. Both rooms and the good cuisine mix Indian and European inspirations, and its size and conference facilities make it a convivial experience.

[i] 50 ⚊ ⛉

▦ HILL FORT
⑪ $$
KESROLI
TEL 014/6828-9352
neemranahotels.com
This massive 14th-century fortified palace north of Alwar is set in still unspoiled countryside. With few facilities beyond its own architecture and situation, this is ideal for time off during the hectic

Delhi–Agra–Jaipur circuit.

[i] 21 ⚊

SHAHPURA

▦ SHAHPURA BAGH
⑪ $$$$
BETW. JAIPUR & UDAIPUR
TEL 014/8422-2013
shahpurabagh.com
This whitewashed hideaway and very stylish oasis between Jaipur and Udaipur is set on 30 acres (12 ha) of lakes and woodland. Local skills have been honed to totally renovate the spacious rooms that mingle contemporary with period. Good food; excellent bird-watching.

[i] 10 ⚊

SHEKHAWATI

▦ CASTLE MANDAWA
⑪ $$$
MANDAWA
TEL 014/1237-1194
(JAIPUR OFFICE)
mandawahotels.com
Built in 1775, the castle dominates Mandawa town. Despite the number of rooms, there is plenty of peace to be found in the public areas—the Durbar Hall, dining room, courtyard, and up on the terrace where dinner is served. The hotel also runs a desert resort.

[i] 80

▦ MANDAWA HAVELI
⑪ $$
SANSAR CHANDRA RD., MANDAWA
TEL 014/1237-1194
mandawahotels.com
Built in 1890 by a Mawari jeweler, the courtyard of this classic painted Shekhawati *haveli* is especially heavily decorated. The Marwari vegetarian *thali* on the rooftop is a memorable treat.

[i] 37 ⚊

PRICES

HOTELS
An indication of the cost of a double room in the high season is given by $ signs.

$$$$$	Over $280
$$$$	$160–$280
$$$	$100–$160
$$	$40–$100
$	Under $40

RESTAURANTS
An indication of the cost of a three-course meal without drinks is given by $ signs.

$$$$$	Over $80
$$$$	$50–$80
$$$	$35–$50
$$	$20–$35
$	Under $20

▦ PIRAMAL HAVELI
⑪ $$
BAGAR
TEL 011/4666-1666
OR 011/4358-7183
(DELHI OFFICE)
neemranahotels.com
This witty and incongruous 1920s Raj-colonial mansion is encapsulated in its elegant living room, which has cane furnishings, tiles on the walls, and ceiling paintings of flying angels. Good Mawari food.

[i] 8 ⚊

UDAIPUR

▦ DEVI GARH
⑪ $$$$$
DELWARA, 50-MIN. DRIVE N OF UDAIPUR
TEL 029/5328-9211
lebua.com/devi-garh
This accomplished renovation blends historic palace with uncompromising contemporary hotel. All the suites,

---

▦ Hotel   ⑪ Restaurant   [i] No. of Guest Rooms   ⚊ Swimming Pool   ⛉ Health Club restaurants, and bars enjoy rural views. The spa by L'Occitane offers luxurious, relaxing treatments.

[i] 39 🏊 📺

🏨 LEELA PALACE
🍴 $$$$$
LAKE PICHOLA
TEL 029/467-01234
theleela.com
This quiet and very luxurious retreat outside Udaipur, the Leela's group's sixth and newest addition to its India family, offers magnificent spaces plus stunning views of the lake and City Palace.

[i] 80 🏊 📺

🏨 OBEROI UDAIVILAS
🍴 $$$$$
HARIDASJI KI MAGRI
TEL 029/4243-3300
oberoihotels.com
"Extravagant palatial splendor" might sum up this astounding hotel built on the banks of Lake Pichola, with views across to the City Palace. Everything is luxurious, from the towering lobby to the inlaid furniture and superb spa.

[i] 86 🏊 📺

🏨 SHIV NIWAS PALACE
🍴 $$$$$
CITY PALACE
TEL 029/4252-8016
hrhindia.com
While some of the big palace hotels have lost their original flavor, this carefully maintained one retains its character thanks to being managed by the former royal family. Rooms are arranged around the large courtyard where guests enjoy drinks and meals beneath the trees or beside the pool.

[i] 36 🏊 📺

🏨 TAJ LAKE PALACE
🍴 $$$$$
LAKE PICHOLA
TEL 029/4252-8800

tajhotels.com
Perhaps India's most famous hotel location, and certainly one of its most romantic, the former royal summer palace was an early heritage hotel but has recently undergone a total renovation. Guests reach it by boat across Lake Pichola.

[i] 83 🏊 📺

🏨 FATEH PRAKASH PALACE
$$$$
CITY PALACE
TEL 029/4252-8008
hrhhotels.com
Spread over two parts of the City Palace, the suites and rooms are decorated with original paintings and furniture from the royal storeroom, all with sweeping views of Lake Pichola. Guests use all Shiv Niwas's facilities (see above).

[i] 66

🏨 TRIDENT UDAIPUR
🍴 $$$$
HARIDASJI KI MAGRI,
MULLA TALAI
TEL 029/4243-2200
tridenthotels.com
Set on a 43-acre (17 ha) estate beside Lake Pichola about ten minutes' drive from the city center, this is worth it for the peace and space.

[i] 143 🏊 📺

🏨 UDAI KOTHI
🍴 $$$
HANUMAN GHAT,
O/S CHANDPOLE
TEL 029/4243-2810
udaikothi.com
A purpose-built, immaculate, and gleaming haveli a short walk from the old city, its glories are the rooftop pool, pavilions, and restaurant that have panoramic views across Lake Pichola.

[i] 30 🏊 📺

🏨 DEVRA
🍴 $$
SISARMA-BUJRA RD., KALAROHI
TEL 029/4243-1049
devraudaipur.com
This colonial contemporary house up on the hill to the west of Lake Pichola enjoys superb views across Lake Pichola to Udaipur city. Verandas, rooftop, and public rooms take advantage of this stunning setting; much of the food is organically grown.

[i] 9 suites

🏨 JAGAT NIWAS
🍴 PALACE HOTEL
$$
23–25 LAL GHAT (BETW. CITY PALACE & JAGDISH TEMPLE)
TEL 029/4242-0133
OR 029/4242-2860
jagatniwaspalace.com
This charming Udaipur lakeside heritage haveli is run by family members. Both guests and visitors enjoy socializing at the rooftop restaurant with its panoramic views.

[i] 29

🏨 KANKARWA HAVELI
🍴 $$
26 LAL GHAT, NEAR JAGAT NIWAS (SEE ABOVE)
TEL 029/4241-1457
indianheritagehotels.com
Kankarwa haveli has been sensitively renovated and a restful tranquility is preserved by having no phones or TVs in the rooms. Delicious food prepared in the family kitchen is served at the rooftop restaurant.

[i] 16

GUJARAT

AHMEDABAD

Hotels

🏨 CAMA HOTEL
🍴 $$$

KHANPUR RD.
TEL 079-2560-1234
camahotelsindia.com
Located between the banks
of the Sabarmati River and the
old battlements, the restaurant
of this well-located 1960 hotel
is a good place to eat meat in
mostly vegetarian Ahmed-
abad. Be sure to visit the shops
at the back of the hotel, too.
(i) 40

🏨 FORTUNE LANDMARK
🍴 $$$
ASHRAM RD.
TEL 079/3988-4444
fortunehotels.in
This practical, city center hotel
aimed at businesspeople has
two restaurants: the **Orchid**
with multi-cuisine buffets and
the **Earthen Oven** serving à la
carte North Indian cuisine.
(i) 95

🏨 HOUSE OF MANGALDAS
🍴 GIRDHARDAS
$$$
OPPOSITE SIDI SAIYAD MOSQUE,
LAL DARWAJA
TEL 079/2550-6946
houseofmg.com
Renovated to blend historic
with contemporary, this merchant's mansion opposite Sidi
Saiyad mosque buzzes with
local life. Rooms have family
furnishings, and the rooftop
Agashiye restaurant (see
below) is superb. This hotel
is entirely vegetarian.
(i) 19 🏊

🏨 TAJ GATEWAY UMMED
🍴 $$$
INTERNATIONAL AIRPORT CIRCLE
TEL 079/6666-1234
tajhotels.com
A reliable hotel with good service, located near the airport
and about a 15-minute drive
from the city.
(i) 91 🏊

Restaurants
SOMETHING SPECIAL

🍴 AGASHIYE
$$
HOUSE OF MANGALDAS GIRD-
HARDAS, OPPOSITE SIDI SAIYAD
MOSQUE, LAL DARWAJA
TEL 079/2550-6946
The city's most congenial
place for lunch, when it is
not too hot, or dinner on any
evening. The rooftop has a
reception area, decorated with
sculptures, where inventive
mocktails (no alcohol) and
hors d'oeuvres are served; an
indoor restaurant; and open-air
tables. No decision-making
here: Servers bring a succession
of distinct vegetarian Gujarati
dishes served in a *kansa thali*
(round shallow dish).

🍴 VISHALA
$$
SARKHEJ RD.,
NEAR VASNA TOLNAKA
TEL 079/2643-0357
Designed as a Gujarati village,
with potters and weavers
working in mud huts and the
fine Vechaar Utensils Museum,
guests can enjoy all this and
local dance, music, and pup-
petry before and during a very
hefty Gujarati *thali* dinner.

🍴 GOPI RESTAURANT
$
ASHRAM RD., OPPOSITE TOWN
HALL, ELLIS BRIDGE
TEL 079/2657-6388
When you are exploring the
west side of the Sabarmati
River, this makes an excellent
lunch or dinner stop to enjoy
both regular Gujarati dishes
and the specialties of the
Kathiawadi Peninsula.

🍴 THE GREEN HOUSE
$
HOUSE OF MANGALDAS GIRD-
HARDAS, OPPOSITE SIDI SAIYAD

MOSQUE, LAL DARWAJA
TEL 079/2550-6946
The ground floor of the House
of Mangaldas (see above) is a
great meeting place for locals;
it buzzes from morning to
night. Some just have a fresh
juice, local ice cream, or cup
of tea; others watch the South
India *dosas* and *uttapams* being
made in the open kitchen.

🍴 VADILAL SODA
FOUNTAIN
$
THREE GATES, OPPOSITE KARANJ
POLICE STATION
TEL 079/2535-3032
Gujarat is famed for its fresh
and very creamy ice cream.
At this parlor, founded in
1926, try the almond or
pistachio flavors, or the
Indian mango *kulfi*.

■ MUMBAI &
MAHARASHTRA

MUMBAI
Choose a hotel where you will
spend most of your time, because
Mumbai has terrible traffic;
there's also a shortage of beds,
so reserve in advance. This style-
conscious and international city
has a wealth of restaurants
serving every cuisine of India
and many of the world's—consult
Time Out Mumbai to find the
latest hot spots.

MUMBAI–DOWNTOWN

🏨 GORDON HOUSE
🍴 $$$$$
5 BATTERY ST., APOLLO BUNDER
TEL 022/2289-4400
ghhotel.com
The Gordon House's contemporary rooms slipped into a
period building, fair room rates,
and location make it ideal for
exploring downtown Mumbai.
The upbeat restaurant, bar, and
nightclub attract a young crowd.
(i) 31

THE OBEROI
$$$$$
NARIMAN POINT
TEL 022/6632-5757
oberoihotels.com
Downtown Mumbai's most deluxe, contemporary hotel overlooks the Arabian Sea at Nariman Point. The historic and banking areas are right behind the hotel. Restaurants, bars, and shops are top-notch.
🛈 287 🏊 🏋

TAJ LAND'S END
$$$$$
BANDRA (WEST)
TEL 022/6668-1234
tajhotels.com
Very efficient deluxe business hotel overlooking the Arabian Sea, strategically located near the Bandra-Kurla, Andheri, and Worli business districts and 20 to 30 minutes from the downtown historic area. Gym, pool, jogging track; golf and tennis nearby.
🛈 493 🏊 🏋

TAJ MAHAL
PALACE & TOWERS
$$$$$
APOLLO BUNDER
TEL 022/6665-3366
tajhotels.com
Opened in 1903, the totally renovated "grand lady of Bombay" faces the harbor. Rooms are spread over the historic Palace Wing and in a newer tower; guests enjoy the internal courtyard with its big pool, loungers, and wicker chairs. The Colaba location is ideal for sightseeing and shopping.
🛈 560 🏊 🏋

TAJ PRESIDENT
$$$$$
90 CUFFE PARADE
TEL 022/6665-0808
vivantabytaj.com
Located downtown at Cuffe Parade near the historic district, this relaxed hotel—more practical than stylish—is used as much by locals as by visitors.
🛈 292 🏊 🏋

TAJ WELLINGTON
MEWS LUXURY
RESIDENCES
$$$$$
33 NATHALAL PEREKH MARG
TEL 022/6656-9494
tajhotels.com
An ideal place for a longer stay, these deluxe downtown apartments at Colaba range from studios to three-bedroom apartments to four-bedroom penthouses. Designed by John Portman and Sue Freeman, they have all amenities from home-theater systems to modular kitchens.
🛈 80 🏊 🏋

TRIDENT NARIMAN
POINT
$$$$$
NARIMAN POINT
TEL 022/2282-1854
tridenthotels.com
Formerly the Hilton Towers, this hotel boasts great views—especially from the high floors overlooking the Arabian Sea. The good lively atmosphere and excellent facilities, including tennis, attract a younger crowd than the Oberoi next door (see above).
🛈 575 🏊 🏋

MARINE PLAZA
$$$$
29 MARINE DR.
TEL 022/2285-1212
hotelmarineplaza.com
Overlooking the Arabian Sea at Nariman Point, this unpretentious boutique hotel is well located for both the tourist and business traveler, and the roof terrace is a major bonus.
🛈 68 🏊 🏋

MUMBAI–AIRPORT & BUSINESS DISTRICT

If you are passing through Mumbai airport and need overnight accommodations consider staying in this area to avoid drives of up to two hours or more through the city's 24/7 heavy traffic.

FOUR SEASONS MUMBAI
$$$$$
WORLI
TEL 022/2481-8000
fourseasons.com
Despite its relatively small footprint, this hotel is light-filled, airy, and contemporary, with particularly good public spaces, including—rare in Mumbai hotels—outdoor eating. Buzzy restaurants, excellent spa, and great views from the higher floors of the 33-story building.
🛈 202 🏊 🏋

GRAND HYATT
$$$$$
OFF WESTERN EXPRESS HWY., SANTA CRUZ (EAST)
TEL 022/6676-1234
mumbai.grand.hyatt.com
Mumbai's most stylish and spacious hotel, ideal for businesspeople and tourists alike, is notable for its owners' stunning contemporary Indian art collection on display in the open lobby and lower levels, where the bars and restaurants are superb. (See also Hyatt Regency hotel below).
🛈 547 rooms, 147 apartments
🏊 🏋

HYATT REGENCY
$$$$$
SAHAR AIRPORT RD.
TEL 022/6696-1234
mumbai.regency.hyatt.com
It is important not to confuse this hotel with the Grand Hyatt hotel (see above). The Hyatt Regency, located by

the international airport, is a deluxe, efficient business hotel with club rooms, tennis and squash courts, a spa, and good meeting areas.

(i) 401 🏊 📺

ITC GRAND CENTRAL
SHERATON
$$$$$
287 DR. AMBEDKAR RD., PAREL
TEL 022/2410-1010
itchotels.in
Located farther away from the airports (9 mi/15 km), this business hotel at Parel has colonial character and is more cosseting than the usual business hotel. It has five restaurants and a bar, including the exclusive rooftop **Point of View** with, as promised, great city and sea panoramas.

(i) 242 🏊 📺

ITC MARATHA
$$$$$
SAHAR
TEL 022/2830-3030
itchotels.in
This huge hotel sited between the two airports is essentially for businesspeople and provides four categories of increasingly well-serviced rooms. It has a total of six restaurants and copious conference facilities.

(i) 386 🏊 📺

LEELA KEMPINSKI
$$$$$
SAHAR
TEL 022/6691-1234
theleela.com
Equipped with probably India's most comfortable beds and best designed bathrooms, the Leela sits between the domestic and international airports and fully upholds its group's reputation, with four good restaurants and a spa.

(i) 400 🏊 📺

ORCHID HOTEL
$$$$
NEHRU RD., ADJACENT TO DOMESTIC AIRPORT
TEL 022/2616-4040
orchidhotel.com
Geared to serve guests arriving and departing from the airports, this eco-hotel near the domestic airport has practical rooms, and kind service for the weary. Its Maharashtran buffet is memorable.

(i) 372 🏊 📺

Restaurants—Mumbai

OLIVE
$$$
PALI HILL TOURIST HOTEL,
14 UNION PARK, BANDRA
TEL 022/2605-8228
OR 022/4340-8228
Requiring a reservation and a 30-minute drive from a downtown hotel, this continually popular Mediterranean bar and restaurant has indoor and outdoor tables, plenty of young celebrities, and good pastas and salads.

SOUK & MASALA KRAFT
$$$
TAJ MAHAL PALACE
& TOWERS, COLABA
TEL 022/6665-3366
The top-of-the-tower Souk presents a stunning Lebanese buffet at lunchtime, plus panoramic views, while a coveted dinner table at the bar in the old wing's Masala lets you watch one of three set menus of sublime contemporary Indian dishes being cooked before your eyes. Reserve at both.

SOMETHING SPECIAL

blueFROG
$$
D/2 MATHURADAS MILL COMPOUND, N. M. JOSHI MARG, LOWER PAREL
TEL 022/6158-6158

Mumbai's notorious cotton mills, now closed, are being conserved and revived. Among the projects, shops, bars and cafés, blueFROG has a great atmosphere. Food is fusion, cocktails creative, and the music live Tuesday to Sunday; the music featured changes nightly—jazz, blues, soul, or just about anything (*door charge after 9 p.m.*). Sunday brunch is especially good.

INDIGO
$$
MANDLIK RD., COLABA
TEL 022/6636-8999
foodindigo.com
Reserve a table to join Mumbai's most discerning and design-conscious in a sensitively restored and white-washed Mumbai mansion behind the Taj Mahal. Sip cocktails at the bar or linger over fresh Italian dishes; the risottos are always delicious.

⑪ MAHESH LUNCH HOME
$$
8B CAWASJI PATEL ST.
TEL 022/2287-0938
This offbeat, no frills, long-established downtown restaurant draws seafood lovers from all over town. They come for the Konkal coastal dishes of the Mangalore area, especially the black pomfret dishes and the amazing tandoor or curried crabs.

⑪ TRISHNA
$$
7 SAI BABA MARG, BY RHYTHM HOUSE, KALA GHODA
TEL 022/2270-3213
Found down a lane opposite the Wedgwood blue synagogue, this simple café-restaurant is a longtime favorite for many Mumbai celebrities. Quiet at lunchtime; crowded and boisterous at night. Be sure to try the signature butter garlic crab and the stuffed pomfret.

⑪ PARADISE RESTAURANT
$
SIND CHAMBERS,
COLABA CAUSEWAY
TEL 022/2283-2874
This long-established family restaurant, where locals have eaten since childhood, provides a rare chance to taste the Parsi community's very distinctive cuisine. Chicken *dhansak* is the classic dish.

Bars—Mumbai
Mumbai is India's most hip and Westernized city, so there are plenty of great bars. Consider this handful as a starter pack: **The Dome,** rooftop of the Inter-Continental Hotel *(Marine Dr., tel 022/3987-9999);* poolside at the **Taj Mahal Palace & Towers** (see p. 359); **Vie Deck and Lounge** on Juhu Beach *(102 Juhu Tara Rd., tel 022/2660-3003);* and all the bars at the **Grand Hyatt** (see p. 359).

MAHARASHTRA
AURANGABAD

⑯ TAJ RESIDENCY
⑪ $$$
8-N–12, CIDCO, RAUZA BAGH
TEL 024/0661-3737
tajhotels.com
The lush gardens, good pool, and kind staff, who will serve food outside if wished, make this a good base for visiting the astounding ancient sculptures and paintings of Ajanta, Ellora, and Aurangabad itself.

ⓘ 66 ⛱ ▥

■ WEST COAST: GOA & KERALA
The hotel selection assumes you will probably be relaxing in this region and will want to be on or very close to a beach or in a beautiful landscape.

GOA
There is a well-organized network of paying guest accommodations in traditional Goan homes; contact the Tourist Office. The following selection of hotels are almost all either right on the beach or just a few minutes' walk from it.

NORTH GOA

⑯ FORT AGUADA BEACH
⑪ RESORT & HERMITAGE
$$$$$
SINQUERIM
TEL 083/2664-5858
vivantabytaj.com
Built before the laws existed to keep buildings back from the fragile beachside ecology, the pool, restaurants, and rooms start right on the old Portuguese ramparts and sprawl back up the hill, ending with private villas. Guests can also use the facilities of Taj Holiday Village next door (see p. 362).

ⓘ 145 rooms plus 11 villas
⛱ ▥

⑯ NILAYA HERMITAGE
⑪ $$$$$
ARPORA
TEL 083/2226-9794
OR 083/2651-3692
nilaya.com
Owners Claudia Derain, Hari Ajwani, and architect Dean d'Cruz have indeed created a contemporary hilltop hermitage and made it a haven for the most discerning traveler. Guests enjoy riding hotel motorbikes to unspoiled nearby villages and the beach.

ⓘ 10 plus 4 luxury tents
⛱ ▥

⑯ POUSADA TAUMA
⑪ $$$$$
PORBA VADDO, CALANGUTE
TEL 083/2227-9061
OR 083/2227-9062
pousada-tauma.com
Set beside Calangute beach, the 12 suites built of Goa's red laterite stone stand in a lush garden. The emphasis is on ecology and ayurvedic treatments, and guests can consult with the doctors before taking single treatments or 7- or 14-day packages.

ⓘ 13 ⛱ ▥

⑯ VILLA AASHYANA
⑪ $$$$$
ESCRIVAO VADDO, CANDOLIM
TEL 083/2248-9225
aashyanalakhanpal.com
An immaculate contemporary Goa-inspired villa set in tranquil gardens that go down to Candolim Beach, the main house has five bedrooms while three cottages on the grounds each have two more. Guests can rent the villa, a cottage, or everything. Massage on call.

ⓘ 11 ⛱

⑯ FORT TIRACOL
⑪ $$$$
TIRACOL, PERNEM
TEL 023/6622-7631
OR 083/9038-3917

---

⑯ Hotel ⑪ Restaurant ⓘ No. of Guest Rooms ⛱ Swimming Pool ▥ Health Club

The fairy-tale fort at Tiracol, well up the coast from Panaji, has been transformed into a small boutique hotel. Guests must be prepared to climb a few stairs to enjoy the split-level rooms, superb views, the courtyard with its own church, and the local beaches.

🛈 7

🏨 PANCHAVATTI
🍴 $$$$

CORJUEM ISLAND, ALDONA
TEL 083/2248-4888
083/2248-4444
avanilaya.com

A quiet inland haven, this guesthouse sits on a hill out-side Mapusa, with expansive views over the gardens to the Mapusa River. Each room has its own balcony, and guests can enjoy yoga, ayurvedic treatments, good food, and lovely country walks.

🛈 4 🏊

🏨 SIOLIM HOUSE
🍴 $$$$

WADI, SIOLIM
TEL 083/2227-2138
siolimhouse.com

This quality boutique heritage hotel at Siolim, quite far north up the coast, is immaculately restored, spacious, well-run and sits in an unspoiled village and near equally unspoiled beaches such as Morjim and Ashwem. Good food; three of the rooms have air-conditioning.

🛈 7 🏊

🏨 TAJ HOLIDAY VILLAGE
🍴 $$$$

SINQUERIM, BARDEZ
TEL 083/2664-5858
vivantabytaj.com

This 25-year-old hotel benefits from a beachside setting, and its boardwalk restaurant is nice for beach-gazing. Rooms are situated throughout lush gardens. Guests can use the facilities of the adjoining Fort

Aguada hotel (see p. 361).

🛈 142 🏊 🏋

🏨 LAGUNA ANJUNA
🍴 $$$

SORANTTO VADO, ANJUNA
TEL 083/2227-4131
lagunaanjuna.com

Another Dean d'Cruz design, this time rustic-style cottages with spacious interiors by SOTOdecor of Switzerland, all arranged in tropical gardens around an old Portuguese mansion that is now the restaurant and bar. Ideal for families; near Anjuna Beach.

🛈 15 🏊

🏨 HOTEL BOUGAINVILLEA
🍴 GRANPA'S INN
$$

ANJUNA BEACH RD.
TEL 083/2227-3270
granpasinn.com

In a peaceful corner of hip Anjuna, this good-value and well-run homestay is in a sensitively converted old Goan house. Notably helpful family of resident owners. Simple fare is available, but most guests eat out.

🛈 14 🏊

🏨 PANJIM INN
🍴 $$

E-212 31ST JANUARY RD.,
FONTAINHAS
TEL 083/2222-6523
OR 083/2222-8136
panjiminn.com

Found in the lanes of Fon-tainhas, the old quarter of Panaji, Goa's capital, this grand old mansion has only 12 simple rooms (another 9 are in the quieter Casa Pousada, nearby). Panjim also has a friendly, informal restaurant that is the nicest place to eat in town.

🛈 24

SOUTH GOA

🏨 THE LEELA
🍴 $$$$$

MOBOR, CAVELOSSIM
TEL 083/2662-1234
OR 083/2287-1352
theleela.com

Set on a luxurious estate in Goa's deep south, guests can enjoy the on-site 12-hole golf course and the very quiet Mobor Beach. All rooms have essential gadgets such as DVD players; Leela Club rooms have butlers, Bose music systems, and private plunge pools.

🛈 206 🏊 🏋

🏨 PARK HYATT
🍴 $$$$$

AROSSIM BEACH, CANSAULIM
TEL 083/2272-1234
goa.park.hyatt.com

A convenient 15-minute drive south from the airport, this luxurious hotel sits on 45 acres (18 ha) beside Arossim beach at Cansaulim. On-site, it provides quality rooms and services for the whole family, from kids camp to serious spa; off-site, Panaji and Old Goa are nearby.

🛈 249 🏊 🏋

🏨 TAJ EXOTICA
🍴 $$$$$

BENAULIM
TEL 083/2668-3333
tajhotels.com

This hotel at Benaulim, with lots of sports and activities, is set on a large 50-acre (20 ha) plot that goes down to South Goa's great long beach. Good business and expansive meet-ing facilities make it a popular conference location.

🛈 140 plus 5 villas 🏊 🏋

Restaurants—Goa

In addition to the hotels and the delightful beach cafés, where a plate of freshly grilled shrimp makes a perfect light meal, Goa has a large number of informal,

---

friendly, family-run restaurants serving distinctive Goan dishes, such as Goan fish curry with rice (a spicy, tangy dish) and *rava* fried fish (fresh fish coated with a crispy fried batter made with semolina). Goa's restaurants tend to come and go with the seasons, so ask locally for recommendations; or simply walk outside your hotel and try the first one you like the look of—that way, you enter into Goa's informal lifestyle.

KERALA

South Indian cooking is distinct, lighter, and less rich than northern cuisines. Kerala's is especially good and uses plenty of coconut, mustard seed, and tamarind. Rice predominates over breads. Breakfasts may be *dosas* (think rice-flour crepes) or *idlis* (steamed rice cakes); main meals can be ordered with one word, *thali* (leaf), which brings a number of dishes served on a leaf or a circular platter—soup-like *sambaar,* vegetables, yogurt, dessert, with plenty of rice. On the coast, the fish dishes are delicious. Many Kerala hotels give cooking demonstrations.

NORTH & INTERIORS

🏠 AYESHA MANZIL
🍽 $$$$$
TELLICHERRY
TEL 049/0234-1590
keralahomestay.org.in
Email: ayishamanzil@
rediffmail.com
Built by a British cinnamon planter in 1862 and owned since 1900 by local spice traders, this beautifully furnished colonial hilltop guesthouse has great food and sea views. The local village and beaches are unspoiled. All meals are included and cooking classes offered. No alcohol (but beer can be obtained).
🛏 5 🌊

🏠 KALARI KOVILAKOM
🍽 $$$$
KOLLENGODE, PALAKKAD

TEL 049/2326-3921
OR 049/2326-3929
cghearth.com
A stunningly beautiful old palace of the Venganad rulers has been transformed into a retreat dedicated to serious ayurvedic treatments. Guests come for 7, 14, or 21 days, leaving behind their cell phones, wearing special clothes and shoes, and eating only vegetarian fare.
🛏 18

🏠 TRANQUIL
🍽 PLANTATION HIDEAWAY
$$$$
ASWATI PLANTATIONS LTD.,
KUPPAMUDI COFFEE ESTATE,
KOLAGAPARA P.O.
TEL 049/3622-0244
tranquilresort.com
Guests on this working coffee and vanilla plantation in the Wayanad Hills enjoy two treats: a swimming pool and a tree-house suite for the more adventurous. Activities include visiting the plantation, hiking, bird watching, and ayurvedic massages.
🛏 8 rooms plus 1 treehouse & 1 tree villa 🌊

🏠 VYTHIRI RESORT
🍽 $$$$
LAKKIDI P.O., WAYANAD
TEL 049/3625-5366
OR 048/4405-5250
FOR RESERVATIONS
vythiriresort.com
Inland from Calicut's steamy coast and 2,600 feet (792·m) above sea level, the rooms of this eco-aware hotel in the lush forests of the Wayanad district are tribal-style cottages and tree houses. Escorted day walks into the stunning scenery are a highlight; the spa offers ayurvedic packages.
🛏 28 🌊

🏠 COSTA MALABARI
🍽 $$$
NEAR ADIKADALAYI TEMPLE,

KANNUR
TEL 048/4237-1761
touristdesk.in
A six-hour ride north from Kochi (Cochin) or west from Mysore reaches a real hideaway guesthouse just south of Kannur (Cannanore). Set amid cashew and coconut groves, the home cooking is good and a five-minute walk brings you to empty idyllic beaches.
🛏 5

🏠 GATEWAY HOTEL
🍽 $$$
BEACH RD.,
CALICUT
TEL 049/5661-3000
thegatewayhotels.com
On the edge of the busy town, this hotel combines business facilities with therapy, and the ayurvedic spa offers 7- to 35-day packages.
🛏 74 🌊 🌂

🏠 KANDATH THARAVAD
🍽 $$$
THENKURUSSI
TEL 049/2228-4124
tharavad.info
Lying among the paddy fields two hours' drive northeast of Kochi (Cochin) airport, the beautiful 18th-century ancestral home of the Kandath family welcomes guests, with airy courtyards and verandas. Plenty to do, from visiting sights and trekking to learning to cook local dishes.
🛏 6

🏠 RAIN COUNTRY RESORT
🍽 $$$
LAKKIDI P.O., WAYANAD
TEL 049/5251-1997
OR 049/3632-9798
raincountryresort.com
Inland from Calicut and 1,300 feet (396 m) up in the cool, undulating hills of the little-explored Wayanad district, the beautiful Kerala-style one-, two-, and three-bedroom cottages are your eco-friendly

🏠 Hotel 🍽 Restaurant 🛏 No. of Guest Rooms 🌊 Swimming Pool 🌂 Health Club

base for enjoying a landscape of hills, waterfalls, lakes, and forest; good flora and birds.
🛈 18

KOCHI (COCHIN)

🏨 BRUNTON BOATYARD
🍴 $$$$$
FORT COCHIN
TEL 048/4399-0555
cghearth.com
Built on the site of a boatyard, this new building and its quality wood furnishings perfectly evoke Dutch and Portuguese colonial styles. Spacious public areas surround a lush courtyard, and all the rooms on the ground and upper floor have harbor views.
🛈 26 🏊 🏋

🏨 MALABAR HOUSE
🍴 $$$$
1/268–1/269 PARADE RD., FORT COCHIN
TEL 048/4221-6666
malabarhouse.com
This contemporary hotel in a converted colonial bungalow at Fort Cochin is much patronized by the world's social set. Others prefer to visit for dinner in the courtyard, noting the small public spaces, tiny pool, and lack of water views in this pretty port.
🛈 17 🏊 🏋

🏨 TAJ MALABAR
🍴 $$$$
WILLINGDON ISLAND
TEL 048/4664-3000
vivantabytaj.com
Located on Willingdon Island, which hovers between historic Cochin and its twin city, Ernakulam, little remains of the 1930s house at its core. Guests enjoy grand views from the upper floors of the high-rise tower and good open-air bayside barbecue.
🛈 96 🏊 🏋

🏨 TRIDENT COCHIN
🍴 $$$$
WILLINGDON ISLAND
TEL 048/4308-1000
tridenthotels.com
A practical hotel located on Willingdon Island. The rooms overlook the central courtyard and its pool or the lush gardens; nice poolside barbecue, good ayurvedic spa.
🛈 85 🏊 🏋

🏨 TRINITY HOUSE
$$$$
FORT COCHIN
TEL 048/4221-6666
malabarhouse.com
Three contemporary suites skillfully slotted into an old Dutch building at Fort Cochin by designer Soumitro Ghosh. Ideal for a family or group of friends. Guests use Malabar House facilities (see above).
🛈 3 🏊

🏨 CASINO HOTEL
🍴 $$$
WILLINGDON ISLAND
TEL 048/4301-1711
cghearth.com
This modest hotel is where the excellent, eco-friendly Casino Group of hotels began and is still headquartered. Well located on Willingdon Island, with restaurants worth visiting wherever you are staying.
🛈 67 🏊 🏋

SOUTH & INTERIORS

🏨 LAKE PALACE
🍴 $$$$$
THEKKADY
TEL 048/6922-3887
ktdc.com
A real hideaway in the Cardamom Hills, this renovated royal lodge sits on a peninsula jutting into Periya Lake. Lucky residents enjoy good early morning and sunset birdwatching and sometimes see elephant, wild boar, and deer.
🛈 6

PRICES

HOTELS
An indication of the cost of a double room in the high season is given by $ signs.

$$$$$	Over $280
$$$$	$160–$280
$$$	$100–$160
$$	$40–$100
$	Under $40

RESTAURANTS
An indication of the cost of a three-course meal without drinks is given by $ signs.

$$$$$	Over $80
$$$$	$50–$80
$$$	$35–$50
$$	$20–$35
$	Under $20

🏨 THE LEELA
🍴 $$$$$
KOVALAM BEACH
TEL 047/1305-1234
theleela.com
Rooms sprawl down from the clifftop lobby of Kerala's largest beach resort, near the capital, Thiruvananthapuram. Beach-view rooms have sundecks; pavilion rooms are at beach level; rooms in the discerning Leela Club have balconies. Facilities are deluxe.
🛈 181 🏊 🏋

🏨 NIRMAYA-SURYA
🍴 SAMUDRA
$$$$$
PULINKUDI
TEL 047/1226-7333
niraamaya.in
The name means "sun and sea." This long-established, deluxe, German-owned hotel near Vizhinjam has contemporary and historic cottages scattered over its 20-acre (8 ha) site, each with privacy

---

and good sea views. Natural rock swimming pool, reputed ayurvedic center.

🏨 31 🏊 🛎

🏨 TAJ GARDEN RETREAT
🍴 $$$$$

1/404 KUMARAKOM,
NEAR KOTTAYAM
TEL 048/1252-5711
vivantabytaj.com.com

These restored colonial houses in the backwaters near Kottyam were previously called Baker's Bungalow, the original structure on the property. The newly built rooms range from villas with private pools to cottages and rice boats.

🏨 33 🏊 🛎

🏨 TAJ GREEN COVE
🍴 $$$$$

G. V. RAJA VATTAPARA RD.,
KOVALAM
TEL 047/1661-3000
vivantabytaj.com

Overlooking the backwaters outside Thiruvananthapuram, the granite cottages with elephant grass roofs each have a balcony and overlook Kovalam Beach. Good meeting facilities mean visitors can mix business with pleasure.

🏨 59 🏊 🛎

🏨 COCONUT LAGOON
🍴 $$$$

KUMARAKOM
TEL 048/1301-1200
cghearth.com

A collection of beautiful old Kerala houses saved from demolition sets the tone of this backwater retreat overlooking Vembanad Lake, near Kottayam. Rooms have open-air bathrooms; waterside restaurant serves quality Kerala cuisines; good ayurvedic spa.

🏨 50 🏊 🛎

🏨 KUMARAKOM LAKE
🍴 RESORT
$$$$

KUMARAKOM NORTH POST,
NEAR KOTTAYAM
TEL 048/1252-4900
klresort.com

This smart hotel is composed of Kerala-inspired villas, some opening onto the 250-foot-long (76 m) meandering swimming pool, others with private courtyards and sunken baths. Guests enjoy the manicured gardens, infinity pool, seafood bar, and hotel rice boats.

🏨 52 🏊 🛎

🏨 MARARI BEACH
🍴 $$$$

MARARIKULAM
TEL 048/4286-3801
cghearth.com

Kerala-style thatched cottages, some with private pools, dot the coconut plantation that continues to its beach, bordered by fishing villages. Good seafood, yoga classes, ayurvedic center, and opportunities to visit local fishing villages. Kochi (Cochin) is 37 miles (60 km) away.

🏨 52 🏊 🛎

🏨 PARADISA
🍴 PLANTATION RETREAT
$$$$

MURINJAPUZHA P.O.
TEL 048/6921-0519
paradisaretreat.com

Set on the route up to the Cardamom Hills, on an organic coffee and spice plantation, each traditional Kerala wooden guesthouse has hand-picked furnishings, absolute privacy, and glorious views. Good food, yoga, and serious ayurvedic treatments.

🏨 11 🏊 🛎

🏨 SPICE COAST
🍴 CRUISES/RICE BOATS
$$$$

PUTHENANGADI
TEL 048/4266-8221
cghearth.com

The best way to visit

Kerala's extensive network of backwaters is to spend a night or two on a *kettuvallom*, a houseboat of jackfruit wood inspired by the local rice boats. Departing from Kottayam, each has a full staff; bedrooms have adjoining bathrooms.

🏨 1–2 (depending on boat size)

🏨 SPICE VILLAGE
🍴 $$$$

5-MIN. WALK FROM CENTRAL
THEKKADY
TEL 048/6922-2315
cghearth.com

Up in the Cardamom Hills, the spacious thatched cottages with verandas are scattered through a mature spice garden—the resident naturalist gives afternoon tours. Quality food and ayurvedic center and a commitment to ecology keep the tranquil ambience.

🏨 52 🏊 🛎

🏨 RAHEEM RESIDENCY
🍴 $$$

BEACH RD., ALLEPPEY
TEL 047/7223 0767
OR 047/7223-9767
raheemresidency.com

Its Irish-Indian owners have immaculately restored and furnished this 1860s colonial villa set on the fringes of delightful Alleppey town, making for a stay that mixes elegant comfort with local color. Rooftop restaurant, good ayurvedic spa, and a beach across the road.

🏨 10 🏊 🛎

🏨 WINDERMERE ESTATE
🍴 $$$

WINDERMERE HOUSE,
THRIKKAKARA
TEL 048/4242-5237
windermeremunnar.com

Munnar, Kerala's British hill station for tea and spice planters, retains its Raj feel, as do the unpretentious rooms on this working cardamom estate. Some have views over the lovely Chithirapuram Valley.

Activities are trekking, visiting the estate, and family dining.
ⓘ 15

KARNATAKA

🏨 SWASWARA
🍴 $$$$$

OM BEACH, DONIBHAIL, GO-KARNA, UTTAR KANNADA
TEL 083/8625-7132
swaswara.com
Lying four hours' drive south from Goa airport on a virgin stretch of the Konkan coast, the immaculate Konkan-inspired villas, gardens, and empty beach form a haven of repose. Quality ayurvedic treatments; no meat or spirits.
ⓘ 24 🏊 🦺

🏨 DEVBAGH BEACH
🍴 RESORT
$$$

KODIBAGH, UTTAR KANNADA DISTRICT
TEL 083/8222-1603
OR 080/2559-7944
FOR RESERVATIONS
junglelodges.com
Just inside Karnataka, across the border from Goa, this eco-friendly lodge's simple cottages and log hut rooms are built in a grove of trees. Guests can swim, snorkel, parasail, go hiking, bird-watch, or even stay in a houseboat.
ⓘ 12

■ THE DECCAN

BADAMI

🏨 BADAMI COURT
🍴 $$

17/3 STATION RD.
TEL 083/5722-0230
hotelsone.com
To see some of the best sites in India requires staying in simple accommodations. Badami Court is simple but can provide welcome smiles,

hot water, and, if asked, good homemade country food.
ⓘ 28 🏊

BANGALORE

Bangalore has developed an extensive restaurant, café, and bar network. Consult the almost exhaustive listings at *karna taka.com/burp*.

Hotels

🏨 HYATT
🍴 $$$$$

1/1 SWAMI VIVEKANANDA RD., ULSOOR
TEL 080/4936-1234
bangalore.hyatthotels.hyatt.com
Benefiting from great views across Ulsoor Lake, this contemporary hotel works well for tourists and business travelers. Rooms are spacious; dining options include Continental and Indian.
ⓘ 143 🏊

🏨 ITC WINDSOR MANOR
🍴 SHERATON & TOWERS
$$$$$

25 WINDSOR SQ., GOLF COURSE RD.
TEL 080/2226-9898
itcwelcomgroup.in
A large white stucco hotel evoking the Raj, sited near the golf course, its rooms and facilities designed to keep the fussiest person happy. Restaurants dedicated to Anglo-India, Raj, Northwest Frontier, and Lucknowi cuisines.
ⓘ 240 🏊 🦺

🏨 THE LEELA PALACE
🍴 $$$$$

23 HAL AIRPORT RD.
TEL 080/2521-1234
theleela.com
This palatial hotel with gold-leaf domes set in lush gardens is right by Bangalore's airports and is

convenient for city business. Asian and Indian restaurants.
ⓘ 357 🏊 🦺

🏨 THE OBEROI
🍴 BANGALORE
$$$$$

37–39 MAHATMA GANDHI RD.
TEL 080/2558-5858
oberoihotels.com
Set in an oasis of gardens and trees right in the city's heart on M. G. Road, this hotel is what the Oberoi group does best: efficient business facilities, professional service, understated luxury, and reliable quality food (Continental, Szechwan, and Thai cuisines).
ⓘ 160 🏊 🦺

🏨 THE PARK
🍴 $$$$$

14/7 MAHATMA GANDHI RD.
TEL 080/2559-4666
theparkhotels.com
Part of India's only group of inspired contemporary, city-center boutique hotels, this one designed by Conran and Partners of the U.K. lies off M. G. Road. Rooms and public areas have plenty of color, creating an upbeat ambience. Notable Italian restaurant, I-T.Alia (see p. 367).
ⓘ 109 🏊 🦺

🏨 TAJ RESIDENCY
🍴 $$$$$

41/3 MAHATMA GANDHI RD.
TEL 080/6660-4444
vivantabytaj.com
A good downtown location, with views of Ulsoor Lake, the rooms have ergonomically designed desk chairs by Herman Miller to keep businesspeople happy. Dining includes Chinese and Continental restaurants.
ⓘ 166 🏊 🦺

🏨 TAJ WEST END
🍴 $$$$$

25 RACE COURSE RD.

TEL 080/6660-5660
tajhotels.com
Located downtown beside the racecourse and golf course, this long-established hotel maintains its distinctive Bangalore style in its renovated form. Businesspeople like the club rooms; one restaurant is Vietnamese, another is a poolside barbecue.

[i] 118 [pool] [health]

VILLA POTTIPATI
$$$

142 8TH CROSS, 4TH MAIN RD., MALLESWARAM
TEL 080/4114-4725
OR 080/4091-4015
neemranahotels.com
This elegant villa in the Malleswaram area of central Bangalore is a rare case of conservation in this city addicted to the new. Sensitively renovated, beautifully furnished, and set in shaded gardens.

[i] 6 [pool]

I-T.ALIA
$$$

THE PARK HOTEL,
MAHATMA GANDHI RD.
TEL 080/2559-4666
The contemporary hotel's restaurant is avant-garde Italian, so reserve a table to enjoy flavorful salads, remarkable pizzas, fresh artichokes, and gorgonzola cheese, accompanied by Italian wines.

KARAVALLI
$$

TAJ GATEWAY HOTEL,
RESIDENCY RD.
TEL 080/6660-4545
Sit outside beneath a beautiful spreading rain tree or in a Mangalore-inspired interior and sample coastal Karnataka and Goan delicacies such as baby lobster, black pomfret, pearl spot, ladyfish, tiger shrimp, and other fish dishes—and a few meat dishes, too.

VINDU
$$

VAISHNAVI RESIDENCY,
KANAKAPURA RD.
TEL 080/4031-5555
Vindu focuses on the distinctive cuisine of Nellore on coastal Andhra Pradesh. Meats are marinated in masalas whose spices are sent down from Hyderabad, gravies have their *gongura* (a high-protein vegetable) sourced from the owners' farm.

SOMETHING SPECIAL
CAFÉ DARSHINI
$

In 1983, inspired by fast food chains abroad, Mr. Prabhankar started Café Darshini to bring high-quality, low-cost, hygienic South India dishes—crunchy *masala dosas*, soft *idlis*, and crispy *vadas*—to the Bangalore public. Today there are more than 5,000 Darshinis in the city of which the most popular are Upahara Darshini in Netkalappa Circle, Basavanagudi district, and Ganesh Darshini in Jayanagar, Palahara Darshini district. Outlets all over town.

MAVALLI TIFFIN ROOMS
$

14 LAL BAGH RD.
TEL 080/2223-0471
A traditional tiffin (light meal) room founded in 1924, last redecorated mid-century. This flagship of the local chain is always bustling with locals rushing in to gobble their *thali* meals, which are served by waiters walking from table to table spooning out the food from buckets.

BIJAPUR

HOTEL SHASHINAG
RESIDENCY
$

NH-13 SOLAPUR-CHITRADURGA BYPASS
TEL 083/5226-0344
OR 083/5226-0444
hotelshashinagresidency.com
Simple accommodations on the city fringes. City-facing rooms have views to the Gol Gumbaz; meals can be taken in the restaurant or the spacious garden.

[i] 27 [pool]

CHIKMAGALUR

The stunning natural beauty of this area, with its additional draw of fresh air on the higher slopes, now offers quality countryside escapes from the city or a pause during sightseeing and traveling. Each accommodation is, to a different degree, good for hiking, visiting coffee plantations, and seeing the Hoysala temples.

THE SERAI
$$$$$

MUGTHIHALLI, OUTSIDE CHIKMAGALUR
TEL 082/6222-1903
theserai.in
Set on the 10,000-acre (4,047 ha) Amalgamated Bean Coffee Trading Company plantation founded in 1870, the contemporary Serai keeps rooms close together yet each has its own pool and gazebo. Tranquility is enhanced by the rolling landscape—scenic walks and learning about coffee are your recreations.

[i] 20 [pool] [health]

FLAMEBACK LODGE
$$$$

MUDIGERE, OUTSIDE CHIKMAGALUR
TEL 082/6221-5170
OR 082/6321-5470
flameback.in
Set in untamed forested hills, each traditional room has its own living room and fireplace (as in colonial days) plus mini kitchen and Jacuzzi

(for today's independence and indulgence). Delicious food, panoramic views, and staff to show you around the waterfalls, streams, forest, and nature's bounty.

🛈 8 🏊 🏋

🏨 THE GATEWAY HOTEL
🍴 $$$
4 MILES (6.5 KM) OUTSIDE CHIKMAGALUR
TEL 082/6266-0660
thegatewayhotels.com
A mixture of rooms and cottages make up this very congenial, established rural hotel, especially convenient for visiting the Hoysala temples.

🛈 29 🏊 🏋

HOSPET

🏨 HAMPI'S BOULDERS
🍴 $$$
NARAYANPET
TEL 085/3926-5939
092/4264-1551
094/4803-4202
hampisboulders.com
Set among the dramatic boulders of Vijayanagar's landscape, the cottages are reached by coracle, crossing the Tungabhadra River. Guests at this tranquil oasis of bamboo, coconut, and mango enjoy good food, a pool, and well-appointed cottages.

🛈 13 🏊

🏨 KRISHNA PALACE
🍴 $$
TEL 083/9429-4300
krishnapalace.com
This newly built, sparkling, modest hotel in Hospet has spacious clean rooms and a big bar area. It's ideal if you seek value comfort after days exploring Vijayanagar's ruins.

🛈 72 🏊 🏋

🏨 MALLIGI HOTEL
🍴 $$
TEL 083/9422-8101

malligihotels.com
The Malligi, in Hospet town, is an institution that has grown along with the numbers of visitors coming to see Vijayanagar's magnificent ruins. Unpretentious, friendly, with simple rooms and home-cooked food, it now has a pool and caters to conferences.

🛈 100 🏊 🏋

HYDERABAD

The city's rich royal Muslim legacy—Abyssinian, Persian, and Mughal—lives on in its cuisine, especially the classic *biryani* (fragrant rice and meat steamed together) and other flavorful meat dishes, such as kebabs, *kheemas,* and *shorvas.*

Hotels

🏨 HYATT HYDERABAD
🍴 $$$$$
GACHI BOWLI
TEL 040/4848-1234
hyatt.com
Luxury of green space in the high-tech Gachi Bowli of glass-walled offices, just 25 minutes from the airport, well outside downtown Hyderabad. Superb restaurants, a spa covering 10,000 square feet (929 sq m), and—so you remember where you are—distant views of Golconda Fort.

🛈 166 🏊 🏋

🏨 ITC GRAND KAKITIYA
🍴 SHERATON & TOWERS
$$$$$
BEGUMPET
TEL 040/2340-0132
itchotels.in
This modern, light, and well-decorated hotel in the Begumpet district—convenient for sightseeing and business—has all the necessary facilities. The three restaurants are good, and the 24-hour coffee shop is superb, especially for *biryanis.*

🛈 188 🏊 🏋

🏨 TAJ KRISHNA
🍴 $$$$$
ROAD NO. 1, BANJARA HILLS
TEL 040/6666-2323
tajhotels.com
Hyderabad's oldest deluxe hotel is well-placed for sight-seeing, with great facilities and Taj Club rooms. The **Firdaus** (see p. 369) serves good Hyderabadi dishes.

🛈 261 🏊 🏋

🏨 TAJ BANJARA
🍴 $$$$
ROAD NO. 1, BANJARA HILLS
TEL 040/6666-9999
tajhotels.com
The smallest of the Taj Group's three hotels in Hyderabad, this hotel overlooks its own lake in the Banjara Hills. Guests and non-residents can enjoy the notable waterside buffet at both lunch and dinner.

🛈 122 🏊 🏋

TAJ DECCAN
$$$$
ROAD NO. I, BANJARA HILLS
TEL 040/6666-3939
tajhotels.com
Also in the Banjara Hills, set
in mature gardens. Friendly
service includes an upbeat bar
and restaurant.
151 🏊 🏋️

WESTIN HYDERABAD
MINDSPACE
$$$$
MADHAPUR
TEL 040/6767-6767
starwoodhotels.com
Hyderabad's newest super-
deluxe business hotel is
10 miles (16 km) from the
downtown area, in the
business area of Cyberabad's
technology park, Mindspace.
Located near a huge mall and
multiplex, the hotel has a
cathedral lobby, two bars, and
several restaurants.
427 🏊 🏋️

GREEN PARK
$$$
GREENLANDS, BEGUMPET
TEL 040/6651-5151
hotelgreenpark.com
This Hyderabad establishment
is in the Begumpet district so
it is well located for business
and pleasure. It has a bar and
restaurant that are popular
with locals.
146

ADITYA PARK INN
$$
ADITYA TRADE CENTRE,
AMEERPET
TEL 040/6678-8888
sarovarhotels.com
Located in Ameerpet, the
business district, this no-frills
business hotel is ideal for
those who want a location but
intend to be out and about
during the day.
88 🏋️

Restaurants

DAKSHIN & DUMPUKT
$$
ITC GRAND KAKITIYA SHERATON
& TOWERS, BEGUMPET
TEL 040/2340-0132
Choose between two
top-flight restaurants in this
hotel, conveniently located
for Hyderabad sightseeing.
Dakshin's southern dishes
include refreshing *vasantha neer*
(coconut water with honey
and lime) and the Iyer special
(a deluxe *thali*). Dumpukt
offers fine Hyderabadi and
Lucknowi *biryani* and kebabs.

FIRDAUS
$$
TAJ KRISHNA, RD. NO. 1,
BANJARA HILLS
TEL 040/6629-3306
Make a reservation here
for the lunch buffet or, even
better, a leisurely dinner
reminiscent of the days of
the Nizam's refined court.
Hyderabadi mutton *biryani*
(rice cooked with mutton)
and tomato *qoot* are
signature dishes.

SOMETHING SPECIAL

ABHIRUCHI
$
1-7-274 A, S. D. RD.,
SECUNDERABAD
TEL 040/2789 6565
Journey to a spot near Secunderabad's Parade Ground
to join locals eating the true
Andhra *thali*. For less than $5
you can savor a medley of
local recipes for vegetables
and meat. Be sure to try the
prawn *biryani* and curd-chili
(tiny chilies marinated in curd
and then fried).

MALGUDI
$
6-3-1 1192/2/1-16, 1ST FL., MY
HOME TYCOON, BEGUMPET
TEL 040/6663-2277

The same effort put into the
decor, which includes jeweled
doors, is put into the meticulously prepared southern
food. The menu lists dishes by
state—such as Malabar *parotha*.
Or you can simply order a
regional *thali*.

SOUTHERN SPICE
$
8-2-350/3/2, RD. NO. 3,
BANJARA HILLS
TEL 040/2335-3802
Well-located if you are staying
in a Banjara Hills hotel. Locals
like the way "southern" is
interpreted as Andhran and
recipes are absolutely authentic—try chicken Chettinad or
chaapa vepudu (fish fry) and
the essential side dish of *peru-
gannam* (spiced curd rice).

KODAGU (COORG)

ORANGE COUNTY
COORG
$$$$$
SIDDAPUR
TEL 080/1191-1000
orangecounty.in
An incredibly lush 300-acre
(121.5 ha) coffee and spice
plantation 2,600 feet (800 m)
above sea level offers a total
escape into the cool Dubare
forest and valleys west of
Mysore. Accommodations are
in Kodava-style cottages, many
with private pools; guests
enjoy the coracles on the
Cauvery, bird-watching, and
the ayurvedic spa.
29 🏊 🏋️

MYSORE

ROYAL ORCHID
METROPOLE
$$$$
5 JHANSI LAKSHMI BAI RD.
TEL 082/1425-5566
OR 082/1425-5555
royalorchidhotels.com
In another royal guesthouse

turned hotel, this time 1920s Raj-classical white stucco in the town center, the period decor and ambience is mixed with the quality service of this Royal Orchid hotel group. Good for an in-town restaurant, barbecue, bar, and tea.

[i] 30 ⊠ ⊻

LALITHA MAHAL PALACE
$$$
TEL 082/1252-6100
lalithamahalpalace.in
In this extravaganza of a palace, built in 1931 as the Maharaja's guesthouse overlooking his city palace on the plains below, guests enjoy spectacular public rooms, a sweeping double staircase, a billiards hall, extensive gardens—and a certain evocative shabbiness.

[i] 58 ⊠ ⊻

GITANJALI FARM
$$
P. B. NO. 6 SIDDARTANAGAR
TEL 082/1247-4646
gitanjalifarm.com
Located near the Lalitha Mahal Palace, this redbrick farmhouse and garden are home for the Kodava family who wish their guests to have the experiences they want—home cooking, going to market, massages, visiting weavers. They also run a countryside cottage.

[i] 4

NAGARHOLE & BANDIPUR

ORANGE COUNTY KABINI
$$$$$
BHEERAMBALLI VILLAGE
TEL 080/4191-1170 RESERVA-TIONS, 082/4191-1000 RESORT
orangecounty.in/kabini
-resorts
A great combination of luxury and tradition. The Karuba

tribe–inspired thatch-and-mud huts each have 2,400 square feet (223 sq m) of space, a living room, courtyard, plunge pool, and views of Kabini River; the cottages have Jacuzzis. Visitors can explore Nagarhole National Park, and enjoy Kuruba heritage perfor-mances and river outings.

[i] 8 huts, 37 cottages ⊠ ⊻

CICADA KABINI
$$$$
MANGALA VILLAGE
TEL 080/4115-2200
OR 099/4560-2305
Located adjacent to Bandipur National Park, which adjoins Nagarhole, the simple log huts and tents have great open views to the Nilgiri Hills. In addition to regular Jeep safa-ris, there are walks, bike rides, a big telescope for stargazing and nightly campfires.

[i] 20 ⊠ ⊻

KABINI RIVER LODGE
$$$$
KARAPURA
TEL 080/2559-7944
(BANGALORE OFFICE)
junglelodges.com
Held in deep affection by all its visitors, this lodge that began as a royal hunting lodge has rooms, cottages, and tents. Guests explore the jungle by Jeep, boat, or coracle, and meet up around the dining table and campfire to recount their sightings of the day.

[i] 25

■ TAMIL NADU

CHENNAI (MADRAS)

Madrasis enjoy dining out. Almost all the restaurants in the streets will be busy and hygienic and serve delicious fresh vegetar-ian food, and sometimes fish; they make delicious fresh fruit juices and milk shakes, and like to

drink frothy, sweet, milky coffee and tea. You can safely break out from dining in hotels in Chennai.

Hotels

HYATT REGENCY
$$$$$
365 ANNA SALAI (MOUNT RD.), TEYNAMPET
TEL 044/6100-1234
hyatt.com
This sleek contemporary hotel is a creation of Namita Saraf, using local Chennai artists. The five restaurants and bars and serious spa make it ideal for longer stays.

[i] 327 ⊠ ⊻

ITC GRAND CHOLA SHERATON
$$$$$
63 MOUNT RD., GUINDY
TEL 044/2220-0000
itchotels.in
Half of the rooms are duplexes, with a separate living area. The hotel is strong on business facilities, and the Welcomgroup's usual high standards in food are well maintained at the Italian, Northwest frontier, and Chinese restaurants.

[i] 600 ⊠ ⊻

THE PARK CHENNAI
$$$$$
601 ANNA SALAI
TEL 044/4267-6000
theparkhotels.com
This fine contemporary hotel starts with Hemi Bawa's lotus artwork at the entrance and ends with a rooftop pool. Extra luxury in the residence rooms; designer shop; upbeat bar and restaurants serving Indian, Italian, and Thai dishes.

[i] 214 ⊠ ⊻

TAJ CONNEMARA
$$$$$
BINNY RD.
TEL 044/6600-0000

[hotel] Hotel   [restaurant] Restaurant   [i] No. of Guest Rooms   ⊠ Swimming Pool   ⊻ Health Club

OR 044/6600-6600
vivantabytaj.com
The city's only heritage hotel, so far, whose colonial origins reveal themselves in the white stucco columns and the central courtyard, which has a pool. Low key, with an excellent buffet restaurant for in-town eating while sightseeing; also visit the bookshop, Giggles.
🏨 150 🏊

🏨 **TAJ COROMANDEL**
🍴 **$$$$$**
37 MAHATMA GANDHI RD., NUNGAMBAKKAM
TEL 044/6600-2827
tajhotels.com
Guests enjoy notable service in Chennai's leading hotel that keeps business and holiday travelers happy. Rooms cater to every need; it's worth considering the club and executive rooms. Exceptional food is guaranteed here, be it at the coffee shop or South India and Szechwan restaurants.
🏨 205 🏊 🎽

🏨 **TAJ MOUNT ROAD**
🍴 **$$$$$**
2 CLUBHOUSE RD.
TEL 044/6631-3131
tajhotels.com
The huge Taj hotel group's new contemporary and efficient hotel, set among old Madras villas, is well sited for business or sightseeing. Restaurants include one on the roof.
🏨 220 🏊 🎽

🏨 **TRIDENT CHENNAI**
🍴 **$$$$$**
1/24 G.S.T. RD.
TEL 044/2234-4747
tridenthotels.com
Sited near the airport, this pleasant and efficient hotel is useful for an overnight stay or pre-flight meal. It is also near Chennai's new business districts—Sriperumbudur,

Maramalai Nagar, and Guindy.
🏨 167 🏊 🎽

🏨 **AMBASSADOR**
🍴 **PALLAVA**
$$$
30 MONTIETH RD., EGMORE
TEL 044/2855-4476
ambassadorindia.com
This unpretentious central hotel offers spacious but simple heritage rooms, each with a separate living area. Ideal for economic business and family travel. There is also a squash court and snooker table.
🏨 100 🏊 🎽

🏨 **GRT GRAND**
🍴 **$$$**
120 SIR THYAGARAYA RD., T. NAGAR
TEL 044/2815-0500
grthotels.com
The good value, high-quality GRT group's well-located Chennai hotel focuses on what many travelers on a budget want: good service, unpretentious rooms and food, and a particularly good pool and spa.
🏨 133 🏊 🎽

🏨 **SAVERA HOTEL**
🍴 **$$**
146 DR. RADAKRISHNAN RD., SALAI
TEL 044/2811-4700
saverahotels.com
This large, economic, no-frills hotel works well for the budget traveler who is happy to exchange some comforts for a very central location.
🏨 230 🏊 🎽

Restaurants

🍴 **AMETHYST**
$
14 PADMAVATHI RD., GOPALAPURAM
TEL 044/2835-3581
A quiet, period enclave in the city center. Sit on the veranda of this sprawling old

mansion to enjoy Indian and Continental snacks and drinks overlooking the lush garden.

🍴 **ANNALAKSHMI**
$
18-3 RUKMANI LAKSHMIPATHY RD. (MARSHALL'S RD.), EGMORE
TEL 044/2852-5109
OR 044/4214-1210
Sublime home-cooked vegetarian dishes, especially the thali, served in a beautiful room. The food is prepared and served by "annalaksmees"—devotees of Swami Shanthanand Saraswathi who believe food is for both body and soul. Reservations recommended.

🍴 **DAKSHINACHITRA**
$
EAST COAST RD., MUTTUKADU
TEL 044/2747-2603
This fascinating museum collection of beautiful South Indian buildings saved from destruction also serves up home-cooked thali. An insider's tip: Chennai mothers come here to seduce the chef into cooking for their daughter's weddings.

🍴 **KAARAIKUDI**
$
84 DR. RADHAKRISHNAN SALAI, OPPOSITE A. V. M. RAJESHWARI KALYANA MANDAPAM
TEL 044/2811-1893
OR 044/2811-1128
The waiters in this elegant and atmospheric restaurant devoted to Chettinad cuisine dress the part in their panchakacham (dhoti tied and tucked with five folds). Signature dishes include the Chettiar special chicken pepper roast and the pigeon varuval (fry).

SOMETHING SPECIAL

🍴 SARAVANA BHAVAN

$

19 VADAPALANI ANDAVAR, KOIL ST., VADAPALANI
TEL 044/2481-6955
OR 044/2481-7866

Mr. P. Rajagopal, known as Annachi, opened the first Saravana Bhavan to serve quality South Indian vegetarian food in 1981. Today he serves some 350 different dishes at 20 restaurants in Chennai (find them by asking almost anyone) and around the world. Spotlessly clean and fast, smiling service adds to the joy of the crisp *dosas*, onion *uttapams*, superb *sambaar* sauces, and freshly squeezed juices.

COVELONG

🏨 FISHERMAN'S COVE

🍴 $$$$

COVELONG BEACH
TEL 044/6741-3333
vivantabytaj.com

Set in gardens that stretch down to the beach, rooms are in the main building or, much nicer, individual cottages and villas—the nicest ones are nearest the sea. A good rural base for Chennai and temple visits.

ℹ️ 88 🏊 🎽

KARAIKKUDI

🏨 THE BANGALA

🍴 $$$

KARAIKUDI
TEL 044/2493-4851
OR 045/6522-0221
thebangala.com

To explore the great mansions of the Chettinad district traders, stay at this heritage hotel. Its fresh and immaculate decoration and its delicious home-cooked Chettinad food is overseen by the owner, Meenakshi, who arranges

visits to the mansions.

ℹ️ 25

MADURAI

🏨 THE GATEWAY HOTEL

🍴 $$$

PASUMALAI, NO. 40 TPK RD.
TEL 045/2663-3000
thegatewayhotels.com

Guest cottages surround the former hilltop home of the manager of Coats Cotton, now the bar and billards room, while the 62-acre (25 ha) estate has mature trees, pool, spa, and great views over the city. Good food in the restaurant and barbecue.

ℹ️ 63 🏊 🎽

🏨 HERITAGE MADURAI

🍴 $$$

11 MELAKKAL MAIN RD.
TEL 045/2238-5455
heritagemadurai.com

An oasis in the city center, the Heritage Madurai offers Chettiar-inspired individual villa rooms set on a lush 18-acre (7 ha) estate that was formerly the Madurai Club. Excellent food.

ℹ️ 35 🏊

🏨 HOTEL SANGAM

🍴 $$

ALAGARKOIL RD.
TEL 045/2253-7531
sangamhotels.com

This well-located, good-value hotel has a welcome freshness—light, spacious, and colorful. It has an indoor restaurant and a congenial outdoor one, popular with locals.

ℹ️ 50 🏊

MAHABALIPURAM (MAMALLAPURAM)

🏨 RADISSON BLU RESORT

🍴 TEMPLE BAY

$$$$

KOVALAM RD.
TEL 044/2744-3636

radissonblu.com

A great location for visiting Mahabalipuram's extensive Pallava sculptures and other nearby treats. Lovely thatched seaside cottages and good food at the indoor and beachside restaurants. If not staying here, this is an ideal meal stop.

ℹ️ 72 🏊 🎽

PUDUCHERRY (PONDICHERRY)

🏨 HOTEL DE L'ORIENT

🍴 $$$

17 RUE ROMAIN ROLLAND
TEL 041/3234-3067
neemranahotels.com

Pondicherry's first heritage hotel is beautifully restored and furnished by the Neemrana group whose specialty is conservation. It is very intimate, with a delightful central courtyard evocative of the town's French colonial days; serves good Creole cuisine.

ℹ️ 10

🏨 Hotel   🍴 Restaurant   ℹ️ No. of Guest Rooms   🏊 Swimming Pool   🎽 Health Club

🏨 LE DUPLEIX
🍽 $$$
5 RUE DE LA CASERNE
TEL 041/3222-6001
sarovarhotels.com
One of several restored 18th-century buildings in Puducherry, this one has been transformed into a hotel that mixes historic with dramatic contemporary, for the most part with success. Rooms vary, so inspect closely on arrival. Good atmosphere, with bar and courtyard dining.
ⓘ 14

🏨 THE PROMENADE
🍽 $$$
23 GOUBERT AVE.
TEL 041/3222-7750
sarovarhotels.com
This freshly built contemporary boutique hotel stands on Beach Road—which has no beach but directly overlooks the Bay of Bengal. Good public spaces include its rooftop bar and restaurant. Same owner as Le Dupleix (above), so guests can use both hotels' facilities.
ⓘ 38

THANJAVUR

🏨 HOTEL PARISUTHAM
🍽 $$$$
G. A. CANAL RD.
TEL 043/6223-1844
hotelparisutham.com
This family-run hotel with simple rooms is just two minutes' drive or a pleasant walk from the great Chola temple. The large pool, spa, and outdoor eating make this a good relaxation package after temple visits.
ⓘ 52 🏊 🟥

🏨 HOTEL SANGAM
🍽 $$
TRICHY RD.
TEL 043/6223-9451
sangamhotels.com

Part of the reliable Sangam group, this spacious and bright hotel is within sight of the great Brahadeshwara Temple built by the Chola. Rooms are practical, and the pool and spa are a quality bonus.
ⓘ 54 🏊 🟥

TIRUCHCHIRAPPALLI (TRICHY)

🏨 HOTEL SANGAM
🍽 $$
COLLECTOR'S OFFICE RD.
TEL 043/1424-4555
OR 043/1241-4700
sangamhotels.com
Although a 20- to 30-minute drive from Srirangam, this hotel is very well run and serves good food. Its staff goes to great lengths to keep guests happy. For those staying more than one night, there are some good restaurants at the nearby bus stand.
ⓘ 90 🏊

UDAGAMANDALAM (OOTY)

🏨 SAVOY HOTEL
🍽 $$$$
77 SYLKS RD.
TEL 042/3222-5500
tajhotels.com
With its English cottage-style rooms, complete with fireplaces for chilly evenings, built in the 1830–1860s and set amid English flowerbeds, the Savoy encapsulates Udagamandalam. Plenty of original furnishings evoke the Raj.
ⓘ 40 🟥

🏨 SULLIVAN COURT
🍽 $$$
123 SELBOURNE RD.
TEL 042/3244-1415
fortunehotels.in
Named after John Sullivan, who founded Ooty in 1861, this modern hotel with conference facilities has sweeping

staircases, simple rooms, and scenic views. A reliable base for exploring Ooty and its ravishing surrounding countryside.
ⓘ 67 🏊 🟥

■ EASTERN INDIA

KOLKATA (CALCUTTA)

Bengali food is delicious—always fresh and delicately spiced; fish dishes are exceptionally good. Try *dahi maachh* (fish in a yogurt-based gravy) at the few Bengali restaurants in town—Peerless Inn *(next to Oberoi Grand),* Suruchi (see p. 375), or Kewpies Kitchen (see p. 374)—or ask your hotel restaurant if it will prepare it. Also, sweetmeat shops offer special delicacies, such as *rossogolla* and *rasmalai,* that have inspired sonnets.

Hotels

🏨 TAJ BENGAL
🍽 $$$$$
34B BELVEDERE RD., ALIPORE
TEL 033/2223-3939
tajhotels.com
A large hotel in leafy Alipore district of south Kolkata, it seems even larger thanks to the busy 11,000-square-foot (1,022 sq m) atrium and the several popular restaurants—French, barbecue, Bengali, Chinese, Italian, and more.
ⓘ 229 🏊 🟥

🏨 HYATT REGENCY
🍽 $$$$
JA-1 SECTOR III, SALT LAKE CITY
TEL 033/2335-1234
kolkata.regency.hyatt.com
This luxurious hotel is located at Salt Lake City, convenient for the airport and the new business areas. Guests enjoy Malaysian teak floors in their rooms, three stylish restaurants (all worth a detour for visitors), and a great spa.
ⓘ 233 🏊 🟥

🏨 ITC SONAR BANGLA
🍴 SHERATON & TOWERS
$$$$

1 J. B. S. HALDEN AVE.
TEL 033/2345-4545
itchotels.in
The super-luxurious Sonar
Bangla is located by Science
City in Kolkata's new business
area. Overlooking one of the
city's greenest areas, it has
a stylish pool, tennis courts,
golf putting greens, and five
elegant restaurants.

🛈 238 🏊 🍸

🏨 OBEROI GRAND
🍴 $$$$

15 JAWAHARLAL NEHRU RD.,
CHOWRINGHEE
TEL 033/2249-2323
oberoihotels.com
Located on Chowringhee
beside the Maidan, the grand
lady of Calcutta, opened in the
1890s, maintains its style and
is one of India's finest hotels
today. Guests enjoy beautifully
furnished and appointed
rooms, and colonial-style
public spaces, a bar, and tea.

🛈 119 🏊 🍸

🏨 THE PARK KOLKATA
🍴 $$$$

17 PARK ST.
TEL 033/2249-9000
theparkhotels.com
Well-located near the Maidan,
the city's traditional clubs, and
the buzzing shopping district,
the Park is a contemporary,
elegant, and lively hotel drawing plenty of locals to its bars,
restaurants, and club. Those
who ask can enjoy superb
Bengali dishes.

🛈 262 🏊 🍸

🏨 THE KENILWORTH
🍴 $$$

1 & 2 LITTLE RUSSEL ST.
TEL 033/2282-3939
kenilworthhotels.com
A Calcutta institution, the
Kenilworth opened in 1947

as a guesthouse but is now a
successful, well-run, and good
value hotel. Very well located
downtown, on Little Russell
Street near the Maidan. The
staff is friendly and helpful.

🛈 95

🏨 LYTTON HOTEL
🍴 $$$

14 & 14/1 SUDDER ST.
TEL 033/2249-1875
OR 033/3894-1900
lyttonhotelindia.com
This small, no-frills hotel is
usefully located on Sudder
Street off the north end of
Chowringhee and is ideal
for those who will spend
their days out sightseeing.
In addition to its own
restaurant, the Oberoi and
Peerless hotels are nearby.

🛈 80

🏨 FAIRLAWN HOTEL
🍴 $$

13/A SUDDER ST.
TEL 033/2252-1510
fairlawnhotel.com
Violet Smith continues her
family's long tradition of
running this heritage hotel.
Guests—often writers—chat in
the garden or upstairs lounge,
enjoy the simple period
rooms, and usually return
for a second visit.

🛈 20

Restaurants

🍴 SAFFRON
$$$

THE PARK KOLKATA, PARK ST.
TEL 033/2249-9000
Dishes from various Indian
cuisines are served in the
beautiful Saffron hotel dining
room. For local ones, try
Kolkata *bekti* and Bengali *dab
chingri* (prawn). And have
a pre-dinner cocktail at the
hotel's chic bar, **Roxy.**

🍴 AAHELI
$$

THE PEERLESS INN,
12 JAWAHARLAL. NEHRU RD.
TEL 033/2228-0301
Located in the hotel adjacent
to the landmark Oberoi
Grand, Aaheli takes Bengali
food as seriously as it is
possible to do so. Old recipes
are sought out and prepared
meticulously, then served as a
set menu *thali* with soft drinks
to accompany. Reservations
are required.

SOMETHING SPECIAL

🍴 KEWPIES KITCHEN
$$

2 ELGIN LN.
TEL 033/2486-1600
Reserve a table to experi-
ence a meal in this traditional
Calcutta home. You sit in the
dining room, decorated with
family furniture and pictures,
and enjoy real Bengali home-
cooked *thalis* following tradi-
tional recipes for vegetables,
fish, and meat. The food is
delicious and absolutely fresh.

🍴 TRINCA'S
$$

PARK ST.
TEL 033/2229-7825
Of the several good Park
Street restaurants, this one is
great for dining alfresco in the
early evening or enjoying a
beer, a simple meal, such as a
Thai platter, and the live bands.

🍴 FLURY'S
$

18 PARK ST.
TEL 033/4000-7453
Despite its makeover and
uneven food standards, this
old-established Swiss teahouse
remains a Calcutta institution.
Join locals who meet here for
a cup of tea or a milk shake
and tuck into vegetable pat-
ties, pineapple pudding, and
chocolate cake.

🍴 SURUCHI
$
89 ELLIOT RD., PARK CIRCUS
TEL 033/2229-1763
This difficult-to-find restaurant is well worth the effort for its delicious and totally authentic, freshly made Bengali lunch; try the fish curries with rice.

BHUBANESHWAR

🏨 MAYFAIR LAGOON
🍴 $$$$
8-B JAYDEV VIHAR
TEL 067/4666-0101
mayfairhotels.com
Spread over 10 acres (4 ha), nicely furnished cottages overlook a lagoon. Guests can play tennis and snooker. Its restaurants serve Chinese, Thai, Continental, and roadside *dhabar* food. It is near the Trident (see below), so guests can visit either one for meals.
🛏 64 🏊 🏋

🏨 TRIDENT
🍴 BHUBANESHWAR
$$$$
CB-1 NAYAPALLI
TEL 067/4230-1010
tridenthotels.com
A whitewashed, low rise, modern and reliable hotel that makes a well-located base for exploring Orissa's distinctive architecture and villages. Good food and pool for post-sightseeing relaxation.
🛏 62 🏊 🏋

BODH GAYA

🏨 LOTUS NIKKO
🍴 BODH GAYA
$$$
BODH GAYA
TEL 0631/220-0700
lotusnikkohotels.com
This is the flagship of Lotus Nikko hotels, located at Buddhist sites. Since many Far Eastern pilgrims come here, the restaurant serves both Chinese and Japanese food, and some of the rooms are Japanese style while others are traditional European.
🛏 60

LUCKNOW

Uttar Pradesh's state capital serves a rich and complex Avadh cuisine, including fine kebabs, *romali rotis* (handkerchief bread), and *dum pukht* (sealed and steam cooked meat and rice). Kebabs and breads from stalls in the old market are delicious.

🏨 TAJ RESIDENCY
🍴 $$$$
GOMTI NAGAR
TEL 052/2671-1000
vivantabytaj.com
A hotel fit for a nawab, with plenty of marble and set in 25 acres (10 ha) of gardens, yet the rooms are surprisingly simple. The **Oudhyana** restaurant's rich local Avadh cuisine is worth the wait.
🛏 110 🏊

PATNA

🏨 MAURYA-PATNA
🍴 $$$
SOUTH GANDHI MAIDAN
TEL 061/2220-3040
maurya.com
Patna's most upscale hotel—and Bihar state's only five-star hotel—is relatively simple and makes a good base for exploring this ancient city and its historic surroundings.
🛏 80 🏋

VARANASI

🏨 NADESAR PALACE
🍴 $$$$
NADESAR PALACE GROUNDS
TEL 054/2666-0002
tajhotels.com
Varanasi's first luxury boutique hotel was built by the British, then owned by a Maharaja. The spacious suites have some antique furniture, and the food is tailored to guests' spiritual requirements. The Taj Gateway hotel is also on the estate (see below).
🛏 10 🏊 🏋

🏨 TAJ GATEWAY
🍴 $$$$
NADESAR PALACE GROUNDS
TEL 054/2666-0001
thegatewayhotels.com
Formerly the Taj Ganges. Renovated rooms, friendly staff, and expansive gardens make this hotel a welcome retreat from the intensity of the city. Guests can snack poolside or while playing croquet, use the buffet restaurant, or, at night, eat quality Indian food in **Varuna** restaurant.
🛏 130 🏊

🏨 CLARKS VARANASI
🍴 $$$
THE MALL, CANTT
TEL 054/2250-1011
clarkshotels.com
Varanasi's oldest quality hotel has large colonial-style rooms with simple furnishings; some rooms have verandas overlooking the gardens.
🛏 125 🏊

🏨 GANGES VIEW
🍴 $$
ASSI GHAT
TEL 054/2231-3218
OR 054/2329-0289
hotelgangesview.com
Built in the 1920s by two devotees of Varanasi's music and literature, this modest accommodation overlooks the Ganga River. It continues to draw writers and musicians as guests; it hosts occasional concerts.
🛏 14 ⚙ No cards

■ THE HIMALAYA

These hotels are useful bases for trekking or exploring the region. Many are historic buildings in beautiful settings. For hotels in Mussoorie, Nainital, Rishikesh, and Shimla, see pp. 349–351.

DARJILING (DARJEELING)

⊞ GLENBURN TEA ESTATE
ⅰ $$$$

RESERVATIONS: KANAK BLDG, 41 CHOWRINGHEE RD., KOLKATA
TEL 033/2288-3581
glenburnteaestate.com
This third-generation-owned tea garden, an hour's drive outside Darjiling, was first planted in the 1860s. Guests can learn about tea growing, take hikes, bird-watch, and much more.

ⓘ 5

⊞ WINDAMERE HOTEL
ⅰ $$$$

OBSERVATORY HILL
TEL 035/4225-4041
windamerehotel.com
This heritage hotel that served English and Scottish tea planters is still a real time warp; some rooms lack TVs and phones. Guests enjoy the nostalgia that includes porridge for breakfast and, of course, Darjiling tea. The tariff includes all meals (breakfast, lunch, afternoon tea, and dinner)

ⓘ 46

⊞ CEDAR INN
ⅰ $$$

JALAPAHAR RD.
TEL 035/4225-4446
cedarinndarjeeling.com
Most rooms in this heritage hotel have great Himalayan views and their own fireplaces, useful when the mist comes down. Guests return from

hiking to enjoy the billiards, bar, health club, and panoramas seen from the garden.

ⓘ 22 ▼

KAZIRANGA NATIONAL PARK

⊞ DIPHLU RIVER LODGE
ⅰ $$$$

KAZIRANGA
TEL 036/1266-7871
OR 036/1266-7872
diphluriverlodge.com
Great views from the extensive grounds, straight across the river into Kaziranga National Park. Eight of the cottages are on stilts, for better views. Excellent service, food, and naturalists; outings include safaris, canoeing, and visiting local tea gardens. Tariff includes all meals.

ⓘ 12

⊞ WILD GRASS LODGE
ⅰ $$$$

KAZIRANGA
TEL 0377/6266-2085
oldassam.com
This is the ideal place to stay for visiting Kaziranga National Park. The colonial-style lodge is thoughtfully designed, the food imaginative, and the pickles homemade; guests enjoy knowledgeable naturalists and well-arranged park visits.

ⓘ 18 ≋

MANAS NATIONAL PARK

⊞ BANSBARI LODGE
ⅰ $$$

MANAS
TEL 036/1260-2223
OR 036/1260-2186
jungletravelsindia.com
This simple but excellent lodge set between wild jungle and tame tea gardens is the base

for exploring little-visited Manas National Park.

ⓘ 16

RIVERBOATS

⊞ ASSAM BENGAL
ⅰ NAVIGATION
$$$$

RESERVATIONS: 3RD FL., DIRANG ARCADE, GNB RD., CHANDMARI, GUWAHATI
TEL 036/1266-7871
OR 036/1266-7872
assambengalnavigation.com
This successful Indo-British joint venture offers a variety of short boat cruises on the Brahmaputra, Hugli, and Ganga Rivers. They vary from temples and rhinos or villages and wildlife parks, to early colonial settlements, the Ganga up to Sonapur near Patna, and the Sunderbans. Best combined with some land travel.

ⓘ 2 ships with 12 cabins each

UTTARAKHAND

⊞ SHAHEEN BAGH
$$$

DEHRADUN
TEL 011/4663-3333
(DELHI OFFICE)
shaheenbagh.in
The seven-bedroom, beautifully furnished colonial-style house with winter heating and summer air-conditioning sits in the forested hills. Wide verandas enjoy grand views to Mussoorie and the rich birdlife close by; complimentary daily yoga classes in fresh mountain air. You can visit Rishikesh or Mussoorie, hike, or go rafting.

ⓘ 7 ≋

⊞ Hotel   ⅰ Restaurant   ⓘ No. of Guest Rooms   ≋ Swimming Pool   ▼ Health Club

Shopping in India

Pack an extra duffle bag in the bottom of your suitcase. This is for your inevitable shopping. Indian craftsmanship of almost every kind can be remarkable for its quality and originality, and prices are often lower than in other countries.

If you see something you really want, buy it. If it is specifically local or particularly good, you may not see something similar again. If you have an idea of what you want to buy before you leave home, such as silk furnishing, dress fabrics, or a piece of jewelry to match an outfit, take color swatches with you as the Indian light can confuse the memory. Also, research equivalent prices in your own country to correctly identify bargains.

Shopping opportunities come in various forms: Fueled by India's economic boom, boutiques, department stores, and shopping malls are opening all over India every month, some showcasing India's very talented designers. The established state-run emporia, often in dowdy concrete buildings, should not be ignored: They stock high-quality crafts produced in that state and sell them at fixed prices. They have knowledgeable staff, accept credit cards, and will ship goods (after you fill out some forms). You do not bargain.

Beware: Do not be seduced by private shops that pose as state-run emporia, giving themselves almost the same title, slipping in words such as "authorized" and "emporium"; they often stock shoddy goods at high prices or nice crafts at outrageous prices.

The hotel shops are often extremely good and are even patronized by discerning locals. Park Hotels have excellent designer in-house shops. Their convenience and their long opening hours compensate for the slightly above average prices; bargaining is perfectly acceptable. Those selling fabric will usually offer a very fast tailoring

service, too; if you are returning to a city, then there is time to order a garment and have a fitting to ensure it is precisely correct.

The markets provide the most shopping fun, even if you only buy small items. A successful purchase demands your own judgment and your own sense of the right cost—remember, however hard you bargain, the trader will always sell for more than cost price.

There are two high-priced items that need special care: carpets and jewelry. Even in a reliable hotel shop, carpet buying should be undertaken with extreme caution. It is wise to research prices at home, bring along a note of them, and compare various local prices. Bargain hard, and, if making a purchase, sign the carpet on the back, measure it yourself, and take a picture of it. Also get a detailed receipt so that when it arrives home, usually after about three months, you can be sure it is the one you chose.

With few exceptions, stores in deluxe hotels are the safest places to purchase major jewelry. Town bazaars are good for modest buys. You can buy stones, either loose or set, including garnets, topazes, amethysts, and black stars, all mined in India. Pearls, sorted and pierced in Hyderabad, are also a good value. A reputable jeweler should always be prepared to give you a certificate of authenticity and be prepared to buy back a piece you later decide you do not want.

The variety of India's fabrics is infinite and impossible to resist. Whether it is a woolen shawl, Karnataka raw silk, or just some dazzlingly bright cotton from Jaipur's market, most people buy

something. Silk and cotton are sold in sari lengths (which vary slightly around the country) or by the meter.

To find out more about traditional master craftspeople, contact Paramparik Karigar *(Flat #5, 2nd Floor, 10 Kumaram, Abdul Gaffar Khan Rd., Worli Sea Face, Mumbai, tel 022/6581-1059, paramparikkarigar.com).*

Note: In Indian law, the sale of an item that is fully paid for by the buyer is deemed to be final. Shopkeepers are not obliged to accept returns. Thus, it is best to think carefully before making a purchase and, if necessary, to ask a shopkeeper to reserve an item pending finalizing a purchase.

For the latest designer and high-end outlets' locations and stocks, pick up some of India's many glossy magazines: *Verve* (India's answer to *Vogue* and *Vanity Fair*), *L'officiel-India*, *In Touch with Fashion*, and *Elle–India*. For interiors, seek out *Elle Décor–India, Inside Outside*, and *idi* (Indian Design & Interiors).

The following listings should serve as a springboard to help you get started. It is a mix of markets (called *bazaars* in India), government craft shops (known as emporia), and private stores.

■ DELHI

For markets, the most traditional are in Old Delhi (see pp. 66–67). Around Connaught Place find **Shankar Market** (fabrics, cheap tailors), **Janpath Market**, and various others.

Delhi is the best place to take advantage of the unglamorous but well-stocked and well-priced government-run emporia. **Central Cottage Industries Emporium** *(on Janpath, opposite the Imperial Hotel)* is a multistory department store that stocks goods from all over India, especially fabrics sold by the yard/meter. A ten-minute walk away on Baba Kharak Singh Marg are all the individual state emporia where you can focus on, say, Varanasi brocade at the Uttar Pradesh store called **Gangotri.**

Delhi claims to be India's fashion capital. Certainly, it has excellent concentrated shopping areas used by locals, the huge diplomatic corps, and visitors. The following are not too far from the center. Try **Khan Market** for books (Bahri and Sons), boutiques (Good Earth and Anokhi), and general goods (luggage, pharmacy), and nearby **Sunder Nagar** for antique arts, jewelry, and serious textiles at reliable **Bharany's** (*No. 14*). For designer clothes go to **Santushti** shopping complex (Anokhi, Noorjehan, Shyam Ahuja, etc.), and **Hauz Khas** (Ogaan, etc.). Visit **South Extension Part II** for FabIndia, Samsara, and Orra. Go to huge **Emporio** for India's favorite upscale designers (Satya Paul, Ritu Kumar, Ranna Gill, Tarun Tahiliani). Throughout the city, Indian-made leather clothes and goods are worth considering (such as **Khazana, Khan Market,** and **Central Cottage Industries Emporium**).

■ AROUND DELHI

Most towns are laid-back, with local shops and markets to enjoy. But Agra, with its heavy tourism and consequent aggressive shopkeepers, is different. Here, the obvious craft to buy is marble inlaid with semiprecious stones, made in ateliers all over the city. It is vital not to confuse this with the cheap, soft soapstone—which can also make a nice gift. For genuine marble-inlay work using genuine semiprecious stones, one of the most reliable stores is the

multi-award-winning **Subhash Emporium** *(18/1 Gwalior Rd.).* In addition to traditional designs, they also do the bold, Italian-style work and some contemporary pieces.

■ RAJASTHAN & GUJARAT

This area is a shopper's paradise for lovers of folk art and tribal textiles. Puppets, embroidered shoes, startingly bright cloth and jackets, and intricate embroidery are available at low prices as well as higher for knowledgeable collectors. (Beware: Heavy tourism means some shopkeepers charge high prices.)

In Jaipur, find fabrics, bangles, puppets, *bandhani* (tie-dyed) cloth, and other goods on and around **Johari Bazar, Badi Chopar,** and **Hawa Mahal;** find loose gems on **Gopalji ka Bazar.** Go to M.I. Road (**Gem Palace, Manglam, Amrapali, Meenu Tholia,** etc.). Seek out **Anokhi**'s headquarters and café and **Leela Bordia**'s Jaipur blue pottery, both in **C-Scheme.** Go to **Soma** for contemporary clothes and furnishings, **Hot Pink** in Narain Niwas hotel gardens for colorful high fashion, and **AKFD** opposite the Birla Auditorium for cutting-edge Indian design. Some of the best Kashmir shawls are sold at exquisite **Andraab's** (*38 Gupta Garden),* near Brahampuri police station, on the Jaipur–Amber road just outside Jaipur. At Amber, **Anokhi** block print has an excellent designer boutique. For big furniture buys, consult **La Voute Exports** in Sanganer. To commission very high standard stone carving, *dhurries,* brocade, and embroidery, contact Mitch Crites at **Saray Design** (*Delhi, tel 011/4174-8991, saraydesign.co.uk).*

In Jodhpur, Mehrangarh Fort has good boutiques, the multifloor **Maharani Textiles** in the old city has a huge stock, and the new **Rani Bagh mall** next to Ajit Bhawan

has contemporary fashion (Tulsi, Anokhi, Amrapali, Raghu Rathore, plus Jodhpur crafts).

Udaipur, with so many congenial little shops, has a few specials: in the City Palace square, beside the café, the former ruler's daughter runs **Aashka,** selling items inspired by the royal collection. A branch of **Anokhi** is next door. Two minutes' walk down the main street, on the right, is the warren of rooms that is **Ganesh,** stocking not just fun clothes and fabrics but also museum-quality pieces. **Royal Arts,** opposite Hathipole Gate has good fabrics and tailors who can whip up a fitted evening jacket overnight. If you visit Devigarh, do not miss their designer boutique—the same is true for **Deogarh**'s shop in the palace-hotel compound.

Ahmedabad, an ancient traders' city, is wonderful for shopping. Wander through the old town to find colorful *bandhani* and other cottons including the distinctive Vadodara block prints. The **National Institute for Design** has an excellent shop. For books, go to **Art Book Center** or **Crossword** in Freeway Mall (the notable designer fashion store **Bandhej** is in the basement). For quality antique Gujarat, Punjabi, and other textiles, go to **Honeycomb** in the Cama Hotel; they will also help with other dealers for textiles, wooden furniture, etc. If you go into rural Gujarat, buy good embroidery and weaving whenever you see it to support local communities and keep the art alive.

■ MUMBAI & MAHARASHTRA

Mumbai's ostentatious wealth is served by high-end stores with an alluring buzz. If you stay downtown in the Fort area, explore some of the very good shops at the Oberoi Hotel and the Taj Mahal (**Nalanda** bookstore, the **Indian Textile Co.,** Joy

Shoes, etc.). Colaba has shoe shops, **Tantra's** wacky T-shirts and plenty more, sidewalk stalls, and **Phillips,** the long-established antiques store at the end; just off Colaba is **Ahilaya,** by Indigo restaurant. Around the synagogue find **Ensemble** (lots of high-end designers) and **FabIndia** (light, cheap cottons). A five-minute walk from the Taj brings you first to **Tarun Tahiliani,** and then **The Courtyard** for a cluster of top designers, very wearable in the West (**Tulsi, Hot Pink, Rohit Bal,** etc). The keen go farther afield to **Kemps Corner, Raghuvanshi Mills Compound, 7 Best Road, Aza, Kimaya, Fuel,** and **Designer Studio.** To buy Parsee embroidery, call Parveez Aggarwal *(tel 022/4050-9200, mybeautiful embroideries.com)* and arrange a visit. For major jewelry, visit **Gazdar** in the Taj Mahal Hotel, **Tijori** in the Oberoi, or **Moksh, Satyani's, Divi, Lalchand, Rose** or **Jamini Ahluwalia, TBZ The Original, Maia,** or **Notandas;** bargain hard.

If you are visiting the caves of Ajanta and Ellora, note the revived fine weaving of nearby Paithan, stocked by shops in Aurangabad.

◼ GOA & KERALA

North Goa's seaside shopping reaches a peak of concentration behind Sinquerim, Candolim, and Calangute beaches, outposts of hot city designers such as **Malini Ramani**.

Kerala, new to mass tourism, is relatively quieter; most cities have more fresh spices and traditional cream-colored Kerala saris than anything else. Kochi is the exception, where **Jew Town's** spice warehouses are now either "antiques" stores (goods gleaned from all over India; shipping easily arranged) or stocked with run-of-the-mill Rajasthani or Kashmiri products. Exceptions are the bookstores

next to the synagogue, the local Catholic nuns' or fishermen's quality embroidery, and, up at the Fort area, some designer boutiques. In Ernakulam, you'll find silk shops, south Indian jewelry, and household stores.

◼ THE DECCAN

Hyderabad is rapidly modernizing; however, head to the old Char Minar area for the big bangle bazaar, brass pots, and pearls of all sizes, colors, and qualities. Andhra Pradesh state has some of India's finest weavers working in the villages—find local *ikats* in cotton and silk on Tilak Road.

Bangalore's IT and international workforce means high-end fashion shopping—**Evoluzione, Fflolio, Collage,** etc. And as silk is a state-run industry, this is the place to buy it at the best prices by the yard/meter and in quantity. Lots of large silk stores line M. G. Road and side roads. You can also find carved local sandalwood and rosewood and chunky Lambani jewelry.

◼ TAMIL NADU

Chennai is a sophisticated shopping city. **Spencers** is the great glitzy mall. **FabIndia** and various other stylish boutiques can be found all over the city, such as **Amethyst** *(next to Corporation Bank, Whites Rd., Royapettah),* which stocks high-end designers and has a garden café. The quality fabric stores have top Kanchipuram silk, Madrasi check, Chettinad weaves, and other Tamil specialities.

Down the coast, Dakshinachitra museum has a good shop, and Puducherry's phoenix-like rise includes several nice boutiques in heritage houses in the old French quarter, and more in the main town. The **Sri Aurobindo** paper-making factory has glorious stock, and outside town, **Auroville** has

extensive eco-friendly items.

In Mahaballipuram, you can commission a granite sculpture to be carved and shipped for your garden; in Thanjavur and Thiruchirapalli, bronze ateliers will make you a traditional Nataraja or Parvati and ship it. In Madurai, **Hajeemoosa** stocks all kinds of silk, saris, and linen in its rabbit warren shop opposite Meenakshi Temple's East Tower Gateway; beside it, **Pudu Mandapam** is a great carved temple hall where local tailors sew garments in a few hours. To see traditional South Indian jewelry, visit **Joy Alukkas** *(W. Masi St.).*

◼ EASTERN INDIA

As Kolkata's fortunes rise, so do its shopping options. In-house hotel shops are increasingly good; as are the small shops on Russell Street in the city center (**Ananda** has quality Bengali saris and *kurtas*). For something more dynamic, visit the multistory **Forum** on Lala Lajpat Rai Sarani *(Elgin Rd.)*—it has everything from **Aldo** to **Anokhi,** and several shops run by Indian designers. For very special dyes and weaves, visit **Kanishka** *(2/1 Hindustan Rd., Gariahat);* products are dyed locally. **Hughli's** has the finest reed weaving imaginable, while the **Weavers Studio** *(Anil Moitra Rd.)* has a huge selection.

Varanasi is synonymous with silk brocade, known as baranasi brocade. Take some time to learn what brocade is and what makes a good one. Then bargain very hard before you buy. Brass is a good buy here, too. For serious master weaving, go to Hasin Mohamed's **HM Textiles** on Dulli Gaddi.

◼ THE HIMALAYA

India's hills are for relaxing or hiking, not for shopping. Local woolen shawls and walking sticks are good buys.

Activities & Entertainment

Most people visit India to see its outstanding monuments, experience its fascinating lifestyle, stay in historic hotels, and shop for great crafts. Some visitors may like to spend at least part of their time there taking part in India's two most popular activities: trekking and visiting wildlife sanctuaries and national parks. But India can also offer you plenty of other activities and entertainment to add to your sightseeing. Why not a round of golf in the cool of the morning? Or a visit to a festival performance of dance-drama in the evening?

Performing Arts

Many artistic performances in India are connected more or less directly to its religions. Although there is plenty going on, it is not always easy to find. Town tourist offices can tell you what events are going on; some even have a printed list of one-off events and festivals (see also Festivals in India pp. 382–385)—a religious festival may draw top stars in classical music or dance. Tourist offices can book tickets, which are usually modestly priced and readily available; most Indian people do not like to book up their time in advance the way Western people do. The local English edition of national newspapers such as the *Times of India,* the *Hindustan Times,* the *Indian Express,* the *Asian Age,* or the *Hindu* also list the day's events. Delhi, Mumbai, Bangalore, Chennai, and Kolkata each have their own local events magazines, usually available free in hotels.

You may expect quality dance, dance-drama, and music to be performed in custom-built halls such as those in Delhi or the Bharat Bhawan in Bhopal. But many top performances are given outside, by or in temples, in ruins, at shrines, in forts, or beneath modest awnings—Delhi's major Ram Lila spectacle is performed on a temporary platform rigged up outside the Red Fort; Chennai's musicians sometimes perform in backstreet gardens. The one place top artists do not like to perform is hotels. Kathakali shows (see pp. 207, 208) are a special event in Kerala.

Sports & Recreation

Sports in India are serviced to a degree rare in the West. Hikers and trekkers have their equipment carried for them, horseback riders have their horses prepared for them, fishermen even have the bait put on the hook for them. In Goa you can enjoy most water sports, while in the lower Himalaya you can ski and river raft.

Golfing

Golfers are especially well served in India, the first country outside Britain to lay golf courses. The Royal Calcutta Golf Club was founded in 1829. At most clubs visitors are welcome and given temporary membership, and can rent equipment. Spectacularly beautiful courses include Shillong with its wooded dells, Delhi with its Mogul remains, and Gulmarg with a mountain backdrop.

Horseback Riding

Riders are increasingly well catered to in India, especially at Udaipur and other Rajasthan cities. There are imaginative and well-run expeditions, or you can simply arrange an individual ride when you arrive at your hotel. The adventurous could try a camel ride in a desert area such as Rajasthan. A good travel agent can set up a reliable trip.

Scuba Diving

Scuba diving is popular in the Andaman Islands and in Goa. Equipment can be rented from local dive centers, which also run courses from beginner to advanced.

Spectator Sports

Indians love to bet, and horse racing is a favorite source of inspiration. Much of the horse training in India is centered around Bangalore. Here and at Mumbai, Mysore, and Kolkata there are very pretty courses that make an afternoon at the races great fun. So, too, is a polo match. You are most likely to find the latter on a weekend at either Delhi or Jaipur polo grounds.

Cricket, however, is the national obsession. You do not have to understand very much about it; simply enjoy the gentle rhythm of the game. Two batsmen take turns defending one of the "wickets" (wooden frames of three uprights and two crosspieces) from the bowlers of the opposing side. The batsman's aim is to score runs, either by running between the wickets while the ball is out in the field, or by hitting the ball to the boundary (four runs) or over it (six runs). The bowler's aim is to knock down one of the wickets or to cause the batsman to hit the ball into the air where it can be caught by one of the fielding side—that batsman is then "out" and another takes his place. When ten men from one side are all out, the other side bats and the first side fields.

You will see kids putting bat to ball anywhere they can—inside a mosque, on a road, in a field of sugarcane, on a railway siding—even sharing valuable space with another team and having players field for two teams simultaneously.

Other spectator sports are soccer and also field hockey—at which Indians have been champions for decades.

Swimming

Many hotels have swimming pools, but these may be closed when there is a big local function using the adjoining terrace. If a pool is important to you, check its availability. Most hotels allow non-guests to use their pools, usually for a small fee.

There are long stretches of delightful beaches along India's coasts; Goa in particular is known for its beach resorts. Check carefully for a possible undertow and check that the lifeguard is on the beach when you swim. In areas with few tourists, be sure not to wear a scanty bikini or locals will be upset; put a T-shirt over your usual outfit, and do not go topless.

Tennis

Some hotels have tennis courts, although their conditions vary, and supply balls and rackets, but keen players should bring their own equipment. Other hotel facilities might include table tennis, badminton, and mini-golf. If the hotel does not have the sports facility you want, the management can usually arrange for you to use a local club.

Trekking

Trekking can mean a rugged 14-day high-altitude expedition in the Himalaya with a guide and porters or a day hike in the Nilgiri Hills guided by information from the local tourist office.

The toughness of the trek you choose and your own fitness determine the preparation you need to make; age is no barrier.

If you keep below 11,000 feet (3,360 m) you should need little preparation if you are reasonably fit. In the Himalaya a trek can be a gentle hike with porters and ponies, a climb with just a Sherpa (mountain guide), or a rigorous expedition into the high mountains. Confident and experienced trekkers can arrange a route and porters for themselves, but it is always wise to consult the local tourist office, which will have knowledge of local conditions. Alternatively let the tourist office arrange the trek for you. They should be able to provide an English-speaking leader who will hire porters, deal with problems, and may even be able to serve as a decent naturalist on your trek.

For most people it is best to go in a group, organized by a specialist trekking company. This will be more expensive, but such companies have experience of what suits most foreign visitors and have all the necessary backup should anything go wrong. There are plenty of such companies in India as well as in the United States and the United Kingdom.

Check your itinerary precisely and do not challenge yourself too much. Ensure you have all your inoculations; mountain air and water may feel healthy but they can carry diseases; and do take malaria prophylactics, even if you are above the transmission cutoff height of 6,500 feet (2,000 m) for most of your trip. As for packing, the less and the lighter the better. Use the expertise of a good mountaineering store to buy all your specialist items, from backpack to water bottle and boots. Once on your trek, a good Sherpa will ensure you pause to acclimatize as you climb, and will never push you too far. Remember that the Himalaya trekking season can be short and tip generously as your porter may only have a few earning months a year. Your company will advise what is appropriate.

Wildlife Sanctuaries & National Parks

A stay in one of India's many wildlife sanctuaries or national parks may be a highlight of your visit. It is a chance to relax, catch up on your diary, and learn from the usually well-informed guides something about the geography, wildlife, and nature of the extraordinary country you have come to visit. You may arrive thinking only of seeing a tiger, but a successful visit is much more than this.

Park accommodations can be good, although this is not always the case. A fixed price usually includes your room and washing facilities, your meals, early morning and afternoon tea, jeep, elephant and boat rides with naturalists as guides (you are not usually allowed to walk in the parks unescorted), and extra nature walks, wildlife films, or talks. Beware of temperature extremes: chilly at dawn and dusk in winter, blisteringly hot at noon in summer.

Best viewing is from March to June, the pre-monsoon period when the animals have less choice of water holes. Do not wear brightly colored clothing; wear a hat; take good binoculars and a camera; use a cushion or back pillow for rides in jeeps. Take great notice of your guide's safety instructions. Tipping on departure is important. Consult with the lodge manager for appropriate sums and distribution; tipping is sometimes distributed evenly for fairness.

Beware: Some parks now have so many visitors that numbers are restricted and some areas may be closed. This is especially likely in late December and may seriously affect game and bird viewing. Some of India's best park lodges are listed in the hotels section of this book.

Festivals in India

You will almost certainly bump into a festival in India. It may be a small village fete with the temple deity dressed up and enthroned in a field surrounded by drummers, pipers, a small fair, and some cows with brightly painted horns. It may be a wedding procession, with dancing through the town's backstreets to the accompaniment of a brass band. It may be an arts festival, such as the Bharata Natyam dance season in Chennai. Or it may be one of the great Hindu festivals, such as Durga Puja in Kolkata or Diwali in Rajasthan. Whatever it is, Indian people will welcome your joining them.

Fortunately, many of the most spectacular festivals are held during the cooler winter months when visitors tend to time their India trips. Here is a tiny selection of month-by-month suggestions for especially colorful festivals to look out for. The state where the festival is held (or, for nationwide festivals, the best place to witness each) is given after the name, if relevant; the specific date is given if there is one. Since many festival dates are determined by the lunar calendar, even some of the major festivals can vary their dates from year to year. Other festivals may be arranged with little warning, such as the elephant march in Kerala. You should check for major dates with the Government of India Tourist Office before you leave home, and then check at local tourist offices to see what is going on as you move around India. Also, beware that apart from such major festivals as Republic Day, when everything closes across the country, such things as closures of local forts or museums at festival times are often unpredictable, so be flexible.

January

Feast of the **Reis Magos** or Three Kings, Goa, January 6. Elaborate processions at Cansaulim, Chandor, and Reis Magos churches.

Elephant March, Kerala. More than one hundred caparisoned elephants parade from Trissur to Thiruvananthapuram over three days, during which snake boat races are held at Alappuzha. The spectacular fourth-day finale involves many otherwise hard-to-see regional Kerala dances and displays of Kalaripayattu (local martial arts).

Pongal, Tamil Nadu, mid-January. This event celebrates the rice harvest and is southern India's most important festival. It is at its most colorful in Tamil Nadu where four days of celebrations start with houses and bullocks being scrubbed and painted, and women drawing *kolams* (elaborate rice patterns) outside their doors. On Pongal, the first dish of newly harvested rice is boiled up with sugarcane and turmeric—according to tradition the more the boiling mixture froths and spills over the pot, the better the next harvest will be. The next day, the bullocks, with their long horns newly painted, are garlanded and raced through the villages by young men.

Delhi Rose Show, Delhi. An impressive show in mid-January with serious judges and proud winners, held against the backdrop of Safdarjang's grand tomb.

Kite Festival, northern India, mid-January. Flimsy, brightly colored paper kites are flown by people of all ages. Kite battles are staged from the rooftops, and for these the kite strings are coated with crushed glass and gum to turn them into lethal weapons for their handlers to use against their opponents' kites.

Lori, Punjab, mid-January. Music and dancing to celebrate the height of winter.

Republic Day, nationwide, January 26. India's principal national holiday celebrates the inauguration of the Republic of India and the adoption of its constitution in 1950. Celebrations are most dramatic in New Delhi, where the president's bodyguard leads a spectacular morning-long public parade of state floats, dancers, camels, elephants, and military equipment. Tickets are on sale at travel agencies, tourist offices, and hotel bell desks. All the events are televised nationwide. Each evening during the week, Rashtrapati Bhavan (see p. 84) is illuminated and, once the visiting foreign dignitaries have left Delhi, its spectacular Mughal Gardens are open to the public for about six weeks.

Folk Dance Festival, Delhi, last week of January. The capital's public halls are filled with performances of colorful and fascinating dances from all over India.

Beating the Retreat, Delhi, January 29. A brief but impressive ceremony held at sunset at the bottom of Raisina Hill. Massed bands parade, camels stand at attention on the ramparts, and the Last Post is sounded by a lone trumpet from one high pavilion as the North Star comes out. Fireworks then burst into the sky. This, like the Republic Day celebrations, is televised. A few tickets are on sale.

January–February

Teepam, Madurai. Known as the Floating Festival, this celebrates the birthday of the 17th-century ruler Thirumalai Nayak. Temple deities are dressed up in silk, garlands, and jewelry, and paraded to the city's large tank. Here, they are put on barges that are pulled through the water, accompanied by plenty of music and chanting.

Desert Festival, Jaisalmer. First held in 1979, this is a good chance to see some camel polo and races, and some traditional Rajasthani dance, music, and crafts.

Nagaur Fair, Nagaur, near Jodhpur. This is one of India's biggest livestock fairs and now augments its traditional trading with dance and entertainment for visitors.

Ulsavom, Ernakulam. The eight-day festival at Shiva Temple includes an elephant procession, dance, and music.

February

Tansen Music Festival, Delhi. There are, in fact, two festivals honoring this great musician who was part of the Mughal emperor Akbar's court; the other is held at his home city, Gwalior, in December. Tansen helped to develop and elaborate the stately *dhrupad* form of Hindustani classical vocal and instrumental music, as well as the particular *Gwalior gharana* form of singing. At both festivals, some of India's greatest musicians play for several days and nights.

Dhrupad Music Festival, Delhi and Varanasi. A chance to hear top musicians who have mastered northern India's demanding and complex classical music. Look out for other classical music and dance arts festivals in Delhi this month.

Delhi Flower Show, Delhi. Spectacular blooms of all colors and sizes, from marigolds to gladioli and chrysanthemums, are on show at Purana Qila. Around this time, the fiercely competitive gardens created on Delhi's many traffic circles are judged and signs are posted to indicate the proud winners.

February–March

Shivratri, nationwide. Devotees of Shiva spend the whole night worshipping their deity, and major Shiva temples are alive with *puja*, music, bell ringing, processions, and chanting. Good places to witness this include Chidambaram, Khajuraho (which holds a ten-day-long fair), Mandi, Ramaswaram, Udaipur (and Eklingji), and Varanasi.

Holi, Rajasthan and Mathura. Although this festival is to an extent celebrated across India, Rajasthan is the place to experience it. The festival marks the arrival of spring and the triumph of good over evil. Homes are cleaned, and bonfires sizzle with unwanted possessions. On Holi eve, the first dish of lentils is singed in the communal bonfire, then eaten ceremoniously at home. On the day of Holi itself, social rules are suspended until noon while men and women flirt, dance through the streets, and play holi by squirting colored water at one another and throwing handfuls of pink, red, and mauve powder. Children, elders, and visitors join in the state-wide party—but be sure to wear old clothes. At Mathura and its surrounding villages—associated with Krishna—the celebrations are equally intense and include plays acting out Krishna's life.

Carnival, Goa. For the four days before Lent, this informal, open-air fancy dress party focuses on a different city each day: Panaji, Margao, Mapusa, and Vasco. Everyone is welcome to join in the celebrations with the processions, dancing, bands, barbecues, and floats that fill city and village streets and continue as all-night beach parties.

March

Khajuraho Dance Festival, Khajuraho. Each evening for a week, top dancers perform India's classical dances such as Kathak in front of the illuminated Western Group of temples (see pp. 112–113).

March–April

Gangaur, Udaipur. Rajasthan's important spring festival, is celebrated about two weeks after Holi and best seen at Udaipur. Gauri (a name used for Shiva's wife, Parvati) is the goddess of abundance and fertility. Women pray in temples to painted images of her, asking for bliss and faithfulness in marriage. Then, dressed in yellow, they parade these images down to Lake Pichola to give them a ceremonial bath, singing all the way. The same festival is celebrated in Bengal and Orissa, where it is called Doljatra.

Mahavir Jayanti, Gujarat. Jains remember Mahavira, the 24th Tirthankara and founder of their religion, with special pilgrimages to sacred sites such as Palitana. Celebrations also occur at Ranakpur and Shravanabelagola.

Lent Procession, Goa. The Procession of All Saints of the Franciscan Third Order is held on the Monday after Palm Sunday at St. Andrew's Church, Velha. More than 20 figures of saints are paraded through the streets on decorated floats, a tradition begun in the 17th century.

Hindu New Year (Makar Sankranti), nationwide, April 14. An official public holiday, with local fairs.

April–May

Meenakshi Kalyanam, Madurai. The vast and warrenlike Meenakshi Temple is thronged with the faithful, who spend ten days celebrating the marriage of Meenakshi (a name for Parvati) to Shiva. It ends with a great procession of deities on a huge *rath*. More impressive and inclusive than the similar and better known Puri festival.

Baisakhi, northern India. This spring festival is celebrated with particular fervor in the hills, with dancing among the almond blossoms of the orchards and in the green wheat fields of the Punjab. There Sikhs also celebrate Guru Gobind Singh's forming of the faithful into Khalsa (the pure one) in 1689.

May–June
Buddha Purnima, Bodh Gaya. Celebrated on full-moon night at all sacred Buddhist sites, to remember Buddha's birth, enlightenment, and attainment of nirvana. This is a particularly intense experience at Bodh Gaya, where Buddha received enlightenment.

June–July
Hemis Tse Chu, Leh. Crowds of locals dressed in their traditional garments watch the two-day pageant that includes wonderful *chaam* dances performed with crashing cymbals and thundering drums, and lamas dressed in silk and ghoulish masks performing mime dance-dramas from Buddhist mythology. The festival ends with a symbolic triumph of Buddhism over ignorance. Every 12 years (next time 2016) the *gompa*'s prize *thanka* (painted scroll) is unwound and hung across the entire facade of the building.

July–August
Teej, Rajasthan. If you have suffered from the pre-monsoon heat and humidity of Rajasthan, you will empathize with locals who celebrate the onset of the monsoon with singing, dancing, and playing on garlanded swings. The women wear striped green veils. The moment also remembers the reunion of Shiva and Parvati, and at Jaipur caparisoned

elephants escort Parvati's image and crowds of faithful worshippers from her parents' symbolic home to her husband's.

August
Independence Day, nationwide. This is a public holiday across the country in remembrance of the midnight hour on August 14–15, 1947 when Viceroy Lord Mountbatten handed over power to Jawaharlal Nehru and independent India was born. In Delhi each year, the prime minister makes a televised speech from the ramparts of the Red Fort, and Rashtrapati Bhavan is illuminated.

August–September
Janmashtami, Vrindavan. Celebrations of Krishna's birthday are best seen in the villages associated with his mythical, flirtatious, and eventful youth, particularly in Vrindaban, just south of Mathura. Here, temple festivities include the lyrical *ras lila* dances which are performed in circles just as they appear in miniature paintings, where Krishna is pictured with his consort, Radha.

Onam, Kottayam. Kerala's harvest festival and new year are rolled into one for a celebration that lasts for a week leading up to full-moon day. Amid the feasting and dancing, its highlight is the series of snake boat races held on the backwaters, especially those at Kottayam. Fiercely competitive teams of up to a hundred members each row their long, narrow, dugout boats. The men sing and shout war cries while their fast paddling is kept in time by a man pounding a wooden pole.

September
Ganesh Chaturthi, Mumbai. The elephant-headed god of good fortune and prosperity is eminently suited to moneymaking Mumbai, where his festival brings the city to a standstill. More than

6,000 gaudily painted clay images are made annually, the large ones for factories that display them on top of trucks. Ten days of celebration begin with *pujas* performed to smaller images in homes and on street corners. On full-moon day, citizens parade their idols down to Chowpatty Beach, which is already adorned with multicolored Ganesh sand sculptures, amid much dancing, singing, and throwing of colored powder. Finally, the people give up the images to the water and then watch them bob out to sea and disintegrate.

September–October
Dussehra, nationwide. This is a celebration of good over evil, which takes place throughout India, but is particularly elaborate in certain cities. In the north, celebrations focus on Rama's defeat of the demon Ravana to save his wife Sita. In Delhi, classical and contemporary plays, dance, and music fill every hall; special nightly play cycles recount the *Ramayana;* and in Old Delhi there are processions and spectacular open-air *Ramayana* shows. In Varanasi, a month of nightly Ram Lila plays and music, each in a different venue, ends with a huge procession and continuous temple readings of the epic. In Kolkata, where the festival is called Durga Puja, celebrations take over the city for three weeks and focus on Durga, destroyer of evil: Here huge, brightly painted and tinsel-decorated images, made throughout the year, are set up in the streets, and Bengalis visit them on nightly promenades, enjoying plenty of dance, music, and theater until the final day when the images are taken through the decorated streets down to the Hooghly and immersed in the water. At

Mysore, this festival is called Dassera and focuses on Chamundeswari's triumph over the demon Mahishasura (see p. 227): Ten days of medieval pageantry and classical and folk dance and drama end with a sumptuous procession and fireworks.

October–November

Diwali, nationwide. This nationwide festival is best seen in the north of the country. About four weeks after Dussehra, Diwali celebrates the return of Rama with his rescued wife, Sita, to his capital city, Ayodhya. Tiny terracotta oil lamps symbolically light the way for the couple while also welcoming Lakshmi, goddess of wealth, to the new Hindu financial year (not to be confused with the Hindu New Year on April 14; see p. 383), ending with late night fireworks. This is a time for families to come together, for giving boxes of sweetmeats, and for going to cultural events.

November

Sonepur Fair, Patna. Held just outside the city on the banks of the Ganga, this centuries-old, month-long fair claims to be the world's largest agricultural fair. India's longest station platform allows for trainloads of livestock to be transported here. Starting on full-moon day, this is the place to see cows, horses, parrots, goats, and dozens of elephants traded. All kinds of seeds, plants, and equipment are also sold.

Guru Nanak Jayanti, Amritsar. The birthday of Guru Nanak, founder of the Sikh religion, is celebrated by Sikhs, especially at the Golden Temple in Amritsar.

Desert Festival, Bikaner. This Rajasthan city's desert festival is more modest and less crowded than that in Jaisalmer during February (see p. 383).

November–December

Pushkar Cattle Fair, Pushkar. This was once just a cattle fair, full of natural interest and charm. It is now almost drowned by tourists and caters overtly to their requisite shopping opportunities.

December

Tansen Music Festival, Gwalior. See February (p. 383).

December–January

Chennai Dance and Arts Festival, Chennai. Four weeks of nightly performances by the country's top classical musicians and dancers, often in deceptively informal settings of simple white awnings in backstreets. A superb opportunity if you are touring southern Indian temples, since the music and dance you see now was developed in the temples and originally only performed in them. Tickets can be bought at the tourist office on arrival in the city.

Kumbh Mela. This great religious cleansing festival is held every three years in one of four places consecutively: Allahabad, Nasik, Ujjain, and Haridwar—it is at Nasik in 2015. According to legend, each of these cities is located where a drop of nectar was spilled by Vishnu, thus allowing the devout to cross from this world into that of the gods. Literally millions of Hindu pilgrims and holy men gather for their holy bath, stimulating the arrival of fairs, stalls, and entertainers. Foreign visitors are beginning to take a keen interest in the Kumbh Mela, but facilities are rudimentary and hygiene not always good.

Mohini Alankaram, Tiruchchirappalli. The huge, rambling Sri Ranganathaswamy Temple fills with the faithful, temple elephants, and worship of all sorts for this festival. Two other festivals are also held here at around the same time:

Vaikunta Ekadasi and the Car Festival.

Muslim Festivals

Muslim festival dates change each year and are celebrated with feasts, fairs, fine literature, and revelry. The best places to witness them are the old Muslim centers such as Lucknow, Old Delhi, Hyderabad, and Ahmedabad. The principal ones are:

Id-ul-Fitr (also called **Ramzan-Id**). Celebrates the end of 30 days of fasting during Ramadan.

Id-ul-Zuha (also called **Bakr-Id**). Commemorates Abraham's attempted sacrifice of his son.

Muharram. Lasting for ten days, this commemorates the martyrdom of Muhammad's grandson, Imam Hussain, and is best seen at Lucknow where *tazias* (reproductions of Hussain's tomb) are paraded by mourning men, accompanied by drummers.

Glossary

English is the connecting language of India and used by the travel industry, hotel staff, shops, guides and, usually, drivers. You do not need a phrase book for Hindi, the predominant language of northern India, nor for the languages of other areas; even if you go off the beaten path you are likely to have a guide or driver who will translate. However, it is useful to know the meanings of some everyday words, some words to do with India's religions, and some unfamiliar uses of English words. Words related to food can be found at the front of the book on pp. 54–55.

A

adivasi tribal person

agarbati incense

ahimsa nonviolence

apsaras heavenly nymphs who seduce men and escort gods

arak liquor distilled from coconuts or rice

ashram spiritual retreat; center for yoga and meditation

auto-rickshaw two-seater scooter-powered taxi

avatar incarnation of a god, especially Vishnu

ayurveda ancient system of medicine

ayyanar large terra-cotta images of deities

B

baandhini tie-dye craft

baba term of respect for old man

bagh garden

baksheesh bribe to get service; tip to reward service; gift to beggar

Balarama brother of god Krishna

baoli (or *vav*) stepped water well, often elaborately decorated

banyan huge fig tree, often with drooping lateral roots

bazaar market, marketplace

beedi small, hand-rolled cigarette

betel leaf or nut that is an ingredient of paan

bhakti emotional religious devotion

bharata natyam classical dance of Tamil Nadu

bhavan house

Bhumi Earth goddess

bindi (bindu) fashion decoration on a woman's forehead

bodhi enlightenment; pipal tree, see p. 59

Bodhisattva Buddhist saint who shows others the way

Brahma Creator of the universe; head of the Trimurti (Hindu Trinity) of Brahma, Vishnu and Shiva; Saraswati is his consort/daughter; Hamsa, the goose, is his vehicle

brahman highest Hindu caste group, the teachers and priests, see p. 56

Buddha The Enlightened One, see pp. 59–60

burqa body-covering garment worn by orthodox Muslim women

C

caste broad Hindu social status at birth; see also p. 25

chaat savory snack

chai tea

chaitya Buddhist shrine

chappals sandals

char bagh garden divided into four symmetrical parts

charpoi string bed with wooden frame

chhatri tomb, mausoleum, cenotaph, domed pavilion

choli blouse worn with sari

chorten see *stupa*

chowk crossroads; courtyard

chowkidar watchman, caretaker

coolie porter, laborer

crore 10 million

curd yogurt, also called *dahi*

D

daal pulses, especially lentils

dargah Muslim saint's tomb

darshan for Hindus, the merit-winning glimpse of a deity

deepastambha lamp tower

deva god

devi goddess

dhabba roadside café

dharma religious and social duty (Hindu); Buddha's teachings (Bhuddist)

dhobi washerman

dhoti white cloth worn by men

dhurrie flat-weave rug

dikpalas guardians of the four directions, often sculptures at temple doorways

diwan chief minister

diwan-i-am public audience hall

diwan-i-khas private audience hall

dowry agreed marriage gifts from bride's family to groom's family

Dravidian culture of southern India, derived from Dravidadesh, the former name for Tamil Nadu

dupatta long, wide scarf or stole

durbar government meeting/hall

Durga malevolent aspect of the goddess Parvati

E

emporium shop, often large and selling local crafts

F

feni an alcoholic drink made in Goa by distilling coconut or cashew fruit

fresco a method of painting using colors ground in water, laid on the wall or ceiling while the plaster is still wet

G

gadi throne

gandharvas Indra's heavenly musicians

Ganesh elephant-headed god of learning and good fortune, son of Shiva and Parvati

garbha griha womb of a Hindu temple

garh fort (see also *kot, qila*)

Garuda eagle or mythical sunbird, vehicle of Vishnu

ghaghra skirt

ghat step; stepped mountains

ghazal Urdu song

ghee clarified butter

godown warehouse

gompa monastery

gopi young cowgirls who play with Krishna

gopura temple gateway with tapering tower

guru teacher, mentor

gurudwara Sikh place of worship

gymkhana social club with good sports facilities

H

hajj Muslim pilgrimage to Mecca

haldi turmeric

Hanuman the monkey god, Rama's ally in the *Ramayana*

Hanti Panchika's consort

harijans children of God, Gandhi's word for untouchables; see p. 25

haveli courtyard house (mansion)

Hinayana Lesser Vehicle, the Buddhist sect that spread to Sri Lanka, Burma, and Thailand

hookah cooling water pipe for smoking tobacco

howdah elaborate elephant saddle

I

imam Muslim teacher/leader

Indra god of rain and thunder

J

jali pierced screen

jangha body of a Hindu temple

jatakas tales about Buddha's life and teachings

-ji name suffix to show respect

jihad justified holy war for Muslims

jina Jain Tirthankara/saint

johar mass self-immolation by women after war defeat

K

kailasha mountain abode of the gods

Kali fearsome goddess of destruction, an aspect of Parvati

karma idea that deeds in previous existences determine one's status at rebirth

Kartikeya god of war, son of Shiva and Parvati, also known as Skanda or Subramanya

katcha no good, opposite of *pukka*

kathak classical dance of northern India

kathakali dance-drama of Kerala

khadi hand-spun and woven cotton

kolam a ritual pattern created using colored rice flour

kot fort (see also *garh, qila*)

Krishna blue-skinned human incarnation of Vishnu

kshatriya warrior caste, see p. 25

kumkum red mark on forehead worn by married women

kurta man's loose-fitting shirt

kushti wrestling

L

lakh 100,000

Lakshmi goddess of wealth and good fortune, consort of Vishnu

lingum Shiva's phallic emblem symbolizing energy

lunghi similar to *dhoti*, often colored

M

machan watchtower (hide) in a wildlife park

madrasa Islamic school, often in mosque

mahal palace

maharaja great king

maharani great queen

Mahatma great soul; epithet of Gandhi

Mahayana Great Vehicle, the Buddhist sect that spread to China, Japan, and Tibet

mahout elephant keeper/driver

maidan large open space

makara aquatic monster, often symbol of sea god or of the Ganga River

mala garland

mandala religious diagram

mandapa hall, porch

mandir temple

mantra sacred verse

marg road

masala mixture, as in spices for cooking

masala dosa rice pancake stuffed with vegetables

masjid mosque

mela festival

memsahib term of respect for Western woman

mendhi henna

mihrab prayer niche of a mosque, with *qibla* (indicator) for the direction of Mecca

mimbar mosque's pulpit

minaret the faithful are called to prayer from a mosque's minaret or tower

mithuna amorous couple, as in temple sculpture

moksha blissful release from rebirth

monsoon rainy season, see p. 51

mudra hand gestures in rituals, dance, and art (Hindu, Jain); teachings of Buddha (Buddhist)

muezzin man calling Muslims to prayer

muggu colored rice flour

mullah Muslim teacher/scholar

N

naga snake

nala mountain stream, gorge

namaste word of respectful greeting

natak dance

natya drama

nawab Muslim prince

nirvana blissful state when personal identity is extinguished

O

om symbol for the origin of all things

P

paan betel nut and sweet/sour condiments wrapped in a leaf and chewed as a digestive

padma lotus

paise 100th of a rupee

pajama man's baggy trousers

palanquin covered couch carried by servants (litter)

pallu decorated end of a sari or a head veil

Panchika guardian of the Earth's treasures (Buddhist)

parikrama ritual walk clockwise around a temple/shrine

Parsee Zoroastrian, see p. 62

Parvati goddess of peace and beauty, symbol of female energy, malevolent aspects include Devi, Kali, and Durga; consort of Shiva

pietra dura patterned stone inlay

pol gate

prasad food offered in a temple, blessed, then shared by devotees

puja worship

pukka correct

Puranas ancient myths and legends, see pp. 20–21

purdah the practice of women living separately from men and covering their heads with veils in public

Q

qawwali devotional songs of Muslim Sufis (see p. 61)

qila fort; other words for fort include *garh, kot*

R

ragamala series of music themes, poems, or art iconography related to a specific mood, each called a *raga* or *ragini*

raja ruler, king

Rajput kshatriya subcaste that dominated north and west India

Rama incarnation of the god Vishnu, hero of the *Ramayana*; brother of Bharata and Lakshmana; his wife is Sita

rangoli geometric pattern of rice powder

rath chariot for parading temple deities

S

sadhu Hindu holy man free from caste or family ties

sagar lake, ocean

sahib term of respect for a man

salwar kameez baggy trousers and long shirt worn by women

samadhi site of Hindu saint's death or burial

samsara the spirit's movement across the generations enduring a cycle of rebirths, whose liberation is *nirvana* or *moksha*

sangam academy

sangeet music

sannyasi homeless ascetic; final stage of a Hindu's life

sarai inn, originally on the trade routes

Saraswati goddess of knowledge, music, arts; daughter or consort of Brahma

sari length of fabric worn by women

Sat truth, the Sikh idea of God revealed through the gurus

sati a widow's honorable self-immolation, often on her husband's funeral pyre

satya truth

satyagraha grasping truth; Gandhi's campaign of nonviolent protest

scheduled castes official name for untouchables

sepoy Indian soldier in European service

serai medieval equivalent of a motel

Shaivite worshipper of Shiva

shakti life force

shastra Hindu treatise

Sherpas Nepalese people renowned as high-altitude mountaineers

Shesha (also known as Anant) serpent on whom Vishnu reclines on the Cosmic Ocean

shikar hunting

shikara tapering temple tower

Shiva (Siva) The Auspicious, third member of the Hindu Trinity, symbol of destructive and creative energy, manifested in Nataraj (Lord of the Dance), etc.; consort Parvati, sons Ganesh and Kartikeya; vehicle Nandi the bull; emblem the *lingum*

Sita wife of Rama

shri title of respect

shudra laborer caste, see p. 25

singh lion

stupa Buddhist funerary mound signifying Buddha's presence

Surya god of the sun; Arjuna, symbol of dawn, is his charioteer

swami title of holy man

swaraj self-rule, Gandhi's word for independence

T

tandoor clay oven

tank water reservoir, artificial lake

tazia multicolored tinsel, silver, or brass reproductions of Hussain's tomb, paraded at the Muslim festival of Muharram

tempera a method of painting on plaster or chalk with powder

colors mixed with the yolk or white of egg, often used on internal walls

thangka scroll painting

tilak red dot priest puts on the forehead during worship

Tirthankara ford makers, the 24 Jain saints and teachers

thali platter, usually used for vegetarian meals

tiffin light meal

tiffin can lunch box

tulsi basil

U

uba dando straight rod

untouchable lowest strata of Hindu society; see also *harijan* and p. 25

urs Muslim saint's festival

V

vahana deity's vehicle

Vaishnavite worshipper of Vishnu

vaishya merchant caste, see p. 25

vedas Hindus' sacred early texts

vihara Buddhist or Jain monastery

vimana principle temple or central shrine of a Hindu temple; tower above temple

Vishnu The Preserver, second member of the Hindu Trinity; symbol of preservation to maintain the balance of the universe; incarnations include Rama and Krishna; consort Lakshmi; vehicle Garuda

W

wallah fellow, e.g., *dhobi wallah*

wazir chief minister

Y

yatra pilgrimage

yoga psychophysical discipline involving the practice of meditation, exercise positions, and breathing control to achieve spiritual peace

yoni symbol of the female sexual organ, often depicted in a temple as a circular shape surrounding a central *lingum*

Z

zenana women's quarters

INDEX

ILLUSTRATIONS CREDITS

National Geographic
TRAVELER
India

Published by the National Geographic Society
John M. Fahey, *Chairman of the Board and Chief Executive Officer*
Declan Moore, *Executive Vice President; President, Publishing and Travel*
Melina Gerosa Bellows, *Executive Vice President; Chief Creative Officer, Books, Kids, and Family*
Lynn Cutter, *Executive Vice President, Travel*
Keith Bellows, *Senior Vice President and Editor in Chief, National Geographic Travel Media*

Prepared by the Book Division
Hector Sierra, *Senior Vice President and General Manager*
Janet Goldstein, *Senior Vice President and Editorial Director*
Jonathan Halling, *Design Director, Books and Children's Publishing*
Marianne R. Koszorus, *Design Director, Books*
Barbara A. Noe, *Senior Editor, National Geographic Travel Books*
R. Gary Colbert, *Production Director*
Jennifer A. Thornton, *Director of Managing Editorial*
Susan S. Blair, *Director of Photography*
Meredith C. Wilcox, *Director, Administration and Rights Clearance*

Staff for This Book
Justin Kavanagh, *Project Editor*
Ruth Ann Thompson, *Designer*
Carl Mehler, *Director of Maps*
Mike McNey & Mapping Specialists, *Map Production*
Marshall Kiker, *Associate Managing Editor*
Gary Colbert, *Production Manager*
Galen Young, *Rights Clearance Specialist*

Production Services
Phillip L. Schlosser, *Senior Vice President*
Chris Brown, *Vice President, NG Book Manufacturing*
George Bounelis, *Vice President, Production Services*
Nicole Elliott, *Manager*
Rachel Faulise, *Manager*
Robert L. Barr, *Manager*

The information in this book has been carefully checked and to the best of our knowledge is accurate. However, details are subject to change, and the National Geographic Society cannot be responsible for such changes, or for errors or omissions. Assessments of sites, hotels, and restaurants are based on the author's subjective opinions, which do not necessarily reflect the publisher's opinion.

The National Geographic Society is one of the world's largest nonprofit scientific and educational organizations. Founded in 1888 to "increase and diffuse geographic knowledge," the member-supported Society works to inspire people to care about the planet. Through its online community, members can get closer to explorers and photographers, connect with other members around the world, and help make a difference. National Geographic reflects the world through its magazines, television programs, films, music and radio, books, DVDs, maps, exhibitions, live events, school publishing programs, interactive media, and merchandise. *National Geographic* magazine, the Society's official journal, published in English and 38 local-language editions, is read by more than 60 million people each month. The National Geographic Channel reaches 440 million households in 171 countries in 38 languages. National Geographic Digital Media receives more than 25 million visitors a month. National Geographic has funded more than 10,000 scientific research, conservation, and exploration projects and supports an education program promoting geography literacy. For more information, visit www.nationalgeographic.com.

For more information, please call 1-800-NGS LINE (647-5463) or write to the following address:

National Geographic Society
1145 17th Street N.W.
Washington, D.C. 20036-4688 U.S.A.

For information about special discounts for bulk purchases, please contact National Geographic Books Special Sales: ngspecsales@ngs.org

For rights or permissions inquiries, please contact National Geographic Books Subsidiary Rights: ngbookrights@ngs.org

National Geographic Traveler: India
(Fourth Edition)
ISBN: 978-1-4262-1183-6

Printed in Hong Kong

13/THK/1